1995-96 EDITION

AME~~RICA'S~~

SECRET

Recreation Areas

❖

Your Recreation Guide to the
Bureau of Land Management's
Wild Lands of the West

by Michael Hodgson

ISBN 0-935701-61-3

51795 >

Foghorn Press
BOOKS BUILDING COMMUNITY™

9 780935 701616

Copyright © 1995 by Michael Hodgson

America's Secret Recreation Areas

Foghorn Press, Inc.
555 De Haro Street
The Boiler Room #220
San Francisco, CA 94107
(415) 241-9550

Foghorn Press titles are distributed to the book trade by Publishers Group West, Emeryville, California. To contact your local sales representative, call 1-800-788-3123.

To order individual books, please call Foghorn Press at 1-800-FOGHORN (364-4676).

Library of Congress Cataloging-in-Publication Data

Hodgson, Michael.

America's Secret Recreation Areas: your guide to the Bureau of Land Management's wild lands of the west/Michael Hodgson.
p. cm.

Includes bibliographical references and index.
ISBN 0-935701-61-3: $17.95
1. Recreation areas—West (U.S.)—Directories. 2. Wilderness areas—West (U.S.)—Recreational use—Directories. I. United States. Bureau of Land Management. II. Title.
GV191.42.W47H63   1995
790'.02578—dc20

92-21179
CIP

Printed in the United States of America

1995-96 EDITION

AMERICA'S

SECRET

Recreation

Areas

❖

*Your Recreation Guide to the
Bureau of Land Management's
Wild Lands of the West*

by Michael Hodgson

Foghorn
Press

BOOKS BUILDING COMMUNITY™

CREDITS

Managing Editor—*Ann-Marie Brown*
Associate Editors—*Howard Rabinowitz, Emily Miller*
Maps/Book Layout—*Michele Thomas*
Indexing—*Julianne Boyajian, Amy Smith*

cover photo of Sukakpak Mountain in Alaska by Edward Bovy

ACKNOWLEDGMENTS

There were literally hundreds of individuals without whom this book would not have been possible. I would like to take this opportunity to sincerely thank all who had a part in providing details and offering assistance to me. It is not possible to name everyone, so a collective thank-you will have to do. A special collective thank-you to all the dedicated recreation planners who took the time to review this text for accuracy and who provided information regarding specific recreation areas. BLM Recreation Specialists are a dedicated crew who rarely get the credit they deserve. I tip my hat to every one of you.

—*Michael Hodgson*

Disclaimer

Foghorn Press, Inc. and Michael Hodgson assume no responsibility for the safey of any users of this guidebook. You alone are responsible for determining your level of fitness and ability to wander into Bureau of Land Management lands. Foghorn Press, Michael Hodgson and the BLM are in no way responsible for personal injury, damage to property, or violation of law in connection with the use of this book. Before heading out to any area described in this book, we recommend that you first check with the administering BLM office for updated information regarding the region.

Foghorn Press, Inc. and Michael Hodgson are not responsible for erroneous information, if any, contained within this book, nor for changes made in roads, trails and other features by agencies private or public, nor for changes brought about by weather conditions or acts of God. Further, nothing in this book implies the right to use private property. Public lands may be completely surrounded by private land, which restricts access. Private inholdings may exist within the boundaries of public land. Any and all landowner restrictions must be respected—it's the law and common courtesy.

Advisory

A few words about roads: It's true, much of our nation is crisscrossed with fascinating roads that aren't on highway maps at all. You will need BLM surface maps or Forest Service maps to find them. In fact, the National Forest Service alone has more miles of road than all the paved state and federal highways. Add to them the BLM roads and an infinite number of ranch roads, mining roads and timber company roads, and our land begins to look rather like a tangled mess of twine that a cat has scattered all over the living room floor.

Although you will read on Forest Service and BLM maps and hear from officials terms such as "improved," "graded," "primitive," "jeep," "unimproved," and "graveled," treat all ratings with skepticism. While the road you wish to travel on may indeed have earned an "improved" rating several months ago, rains and other weather may have turned it into a rutted, soupy quagmire. When in doubt, check with the locals—they travel and hunt on the roads and will be able to give you accurate and up-to-date information. Many BLM roads are passable when dry in an ordinary automobile, although I never venture out without my four-wheel-drive no matter what the road conditions state. As a rule, don't drive in farther than you are willing to walk out. Always pack along extra food and water in the vehicle just in case.

Regarding directions: While I have tried to be as specific as possible about how to get to destinations, please don't rely completely on my written directions. You will need BLM or Forest Service maps to be sure. The maps in this book are for representation only and are not drawn exactly to scale, nor do they show every back road and trail.

It is wise and heartily recommended that before heading out, you call the BLM office with jurisdiction over the area you're going to and ask for specific and detailed instructions. These will guide you through local road names (which can change), road conditions (which are guaranteed to vary), and access points (which given the state of public/private easement conflicts are sure to vary in some instances).

One other word of advice: If you are somewhat confused as to which way to go and end up asking directions at the local gas station, find no comfort in the smiling assurance "Heck, you can't miss it!" Hearing those words means only one thing—ask someone else for directions!

I have done my level best to ensure accuracy within this book, but as time and weather changes, so do the facts. If you discover something that has changed, facts that need revising, comments that need clarifying or know of another area that should be listed, please write to me at Foghorn Press, 555 De Haro Street, Suite #220, San Francisco, CA 94107, and I will add your comments to the next edition. I am committed to making *America's Secret Recreation Areas* the most accurate, detailed, helpful and enjoyable outdoor book of its kind. Many thanks—

Michael Hodgson

Contents

INTRODUCTION

Although many people have heard of the Bureau of Land Management (BLM), most do not realize the vastness of the lands it administers for the American public. The BLM is in charge of what remains of the nation's once vast land holdings—the public domain. This immense public domain originally stretched from the Appalachian Mountains to the Pacific Ocean. Of the 1.8 billion acres of public land first acquired by the United States, two-thirds went to private individuals, industries and states. Much of the remaining land was set aside for national forests, wildlife refuges, national parks and monuments, as well as other public purposes. The BLM was left to manage 272 million acres—approximately one-eighth of the United States. Most of these lands are located in twelve Western states, including Alaska, although small parcels are scattered across the eastern United States.

Although the BLM's mandate is one of multiple-use management, including logging, rangeland and minerals leasing, an increasing amount of energy is being directed towards recreation management. This includes National Conservation Areas, National Recreation Areas, approximately 2,000 miles of the Wild and Scenic River system and approximately 1,700 miles of national trails. In addition, the BLM oversees nearly 85,000 miles of streams containing trout, salmon and other sport fish (enough streams to circle the Earth three and one-half times, to put it in perspective), more than four million acres of lakes and reservoirs, more than 470 developed recreation sites, and many other recreational areas. The entire BLM public recreation area is larger than the National Forest and National Park systems—combined.

Couple the BLM's recreational use mandate with the fact that the BLM protects the U.S. government's largest and most varied body of cultural resources, from campsites of the hemisphere's earliest human inhabitants to physical reminders of the historic settings of the old West, plus a vast wildlife and botanical resource, and you have a recipe for unlimited adventure.

Much of the land you will find under BLM jurisdiction is wild—very wild. Many areas are no place for the uninitiated, the tenderfoot or the unprepared. It is exactly this wildness and ruggedness that is the primary attraction. With few restrictions you can wander and camp where you will—almost like when the west was known as the Wild West. Whether by boat, foot, horse or mountain bike, traveling through BLM lands will take you through time and across tundra, coastline, alpine meadows, sand dunes, slickrock canyons, dry lakes, scenic rivers and even subterranean caves.

These lands exist for you, and I hope that with this book in hand, you will experience the joy of discovering an untapped gold mine of recreational opportunity. Let common sense and courtesy be your traveling companion as a world of adventure spreads open at your feet. There is plenty of elbow room out there, so grab your pack, paddle, saddle or rope, and maybe, just maybe, I'll see you in the backcountry.

HOW TO USE THIS BOOK

The book is divided into several parts: a how-to introductory chapter ("A User's Guide to the Lands of the BLM"), 12 state chapters, an index and two appendices. The state chapters are arranged in the following order:

1) Maps: State maps with complete listings of BLM trails, recreation areas, available activities and campgrounds. Each listing has a page number next to it to help you quickly find the corresponding description within the chapter. BLM lands and recreation areas are denoted by an alphabetical letter (placed in a square) on the map. BLM campgrounds are indicated by a number (placed in a circle) on the map.

2) State by Map Region: Each state is divided into two or more geographical sections, as shown on the state map. Every BLM listing includes the following information: site name, activities most appropriate in that site (wildlife observation, hiking, backpacking, fishing, horseback riding, camping, mountain biking, spelunking, canoeing, rafting, etc.), area description, directions, a listing of available maps by name and publisher (BLM, USGS, Trails Illustrated, etc.), and BLM address and phone number for the office directly responsible for administration of the site.

3) BLM Campgrounds: At the end of each state chapter are several pages of descriptions of BLM campgrounds in that state. Information is given for facilities, fees, contact name and number, directions to the site and when it's open.

4) State Information Overview: The final pages (or pages) of each state chapter, this listing gives all of the addresses and phone numbers for the various BLM offices throughout the state.

You can look for your ideal recreation site in several ways. If you are planning to travel in a certain area of a state, you can look in the State by Map Region section for that area of the state to see what sites are close by.

You can also look in the appendix under "Recreational Activities by State" on page 630 to see where on BLM land you can partake in your favorite outdoor recreation. Or just look up your favorite trail, recreation area or activity in the easy-to-use index beginning on page 597.

ORDERING MAPS

A good map, or series of maps, is worth its weight in gold. Here's how to get the maps you'll need:

USFS MAPS
There is no single location for ordering Forest Service maps. By contacting state USFS offices, however, you will be able to obtain maps pertaining to the various national forests in each state. Many USFS lands abut BLM lands, so USFS maps may provide you with useful road and trail access information for traveling on BLM lands.

USGS TOPOGRAPHIC MAPS
You can obtain a USGS map catalog and all topographic maps for the western U.S. by mail from:
> Western Distribution Branch
> U.S. Geologic Survey
> Box 25286, Federal Center, Building 41
> Denver, CO 80225

In addition, many sporting goods stores, map centers and outdoor outfitters carry select USGS topographic maps pertaining to their region.

PRIVATE SOURCES FOR MAPS
• Trails Illustrated, P.O. Box 3610, Evergreen, CO 80439; (800) 962-1643.
• Map Link, 25 East Mason Street, Santa Barbara, CA 93101; (805) 965-4402.

BLM MAPS
When ordering maps from the Bureau of Land Management, specify that you want the BLM surface management series with topographic relief. Map prices vary depending on map type and size, ranging from $3.50 to $5.00.
Order BLM maps by contacting each state's office. See the State Information Overview at the end of each chapter for the address and phone number of the main state office.

A User's Guide to the Lands of the BLM

Backcountry Safety & Other Wisdom

Weather

Just when you were counting on it being sunny, it rains or snows. But guess what—this is not a problem unless you make it one. Check your attitude. Rain, snow, hail and ice are all just another scene in a marvelous outdoor set. How you view the occasion is up to you. Some of my best times outdoors have been during a rainstorm and the moments just following, as the clouds break and the sunbeams come streaming through like so many warming fingers. Of course, I was properly prepared and you should be too if you are going to enjoy everything Mother Nature may toss at you. Sunscreen, a hat, extra warm clothing, and rain gear are all requisite items to carry with you for even a basic hike.

Winter Travel

Heading out in the winter is a wonderful time, but be warned—the backcountry is an unforgiving hostess for the unprepared and uninitiated. It is essential for anyone heading into the snowy wilderness to have at least a basic grasp of avalanche safety and to know the current avalanche conditions in the area you plan on exploring. Know how to dress properly to prevent overheating or freezing and how to identify and prevent frost nip and frost bite.

Hypothermia

Even in temperatures above freezing, hypothermia is possible. If it goes untreated, it can kill. Anyone exposed to wet, cool and windy conditions can suffer hypothermia. It is caused when the body starts losing heat faster than it is being produced, causing a decline in internal body temperature. A person who is shivering, slurring their speech, showing signs of clumsiness or awkwardness, and feeling drowsy may lapse into unconsciousness and could quite possibly die. If you suspect hypothermia (and the victim is always the last to recognize a problem), get the victim dry and warm immediately (pitch a tent, start a fire, make a warm drink). Remove all wet clothing, replacing wet clothes with dry ones. Put the victim in a sleeping bag and give them something warm to drink. Keep in mind that if the victim has lost too much body heat, they may not be able to sufficiently rewarm themselves without assistance, even in a sleeping bag. It this case, climbing in the bag with the victim is required, helping to heat both the bag and the victim with your body.

Don't Drink the Water

Well, okay, maybe that is a bit severe. Actually, don't drink the water anywhere without first treating it. Crystal clear rivers, streams and mountain lakes may give the impression of purity, but that is far from the truth. Water clarity is not an indication of the presence or absence of bacteria or parasites. Giardia may in fact be present in all wilderness water sources. The only safe solution is to filter, chemically treat or boil all water before drinking it.

Altitude

Many mountainous areas within BLM lands lie above 8,000 feet—an altitude which can cause difficulty for city dwellers who are acclimated to far lower levels. Unless you take the time to acclimate slowly to higher elevations, you risk experiencing various forms of altitude sickness—shortness of breath, headaches, nausea, fatigue, and swelling of the extremities. Should these symptoms occur, check your ascent and rest for a while, overnight if necessary. Once your body adjusts to the different levels of oxygen concentration, you can safely climb higher.

Although rare in elevations below 10,000 feet, a more serious and possibly fatal form of altitude sickness, High Altitude Pulmonary Edema (HAPE) or Cerebral Edema (HACE) can occur. This results in fluid accumulating in the lungs (pulmonary) or brain (cerebral) and can cause death if not treated. If you suspect HAPE or HACE, evacuate the victim to the nearest hospital.

If You Get Lost

Careful route finding and use of a map and compass should keep you on the right track, but in the event of misdirection, it is possible to feel lost—even if you aren't really. If this happens, stop! Realize that you aren't lost, you are right here. Instead, the trail or car is lost because that is what you are trying to find. Study the area and the map and use your compass and awareness to identify surrounding landmarks. If you can carefully retrace your route, do so until you recognize a familiar point. In an emergency, follow a drainage downstream, because drainages almost always lead you to a road, a town or a trail. Keep in mind, however, that if you choose to hike away from your last known point of reference, you may in fact be making it that much more difficult for rescuers to find you.

Carrying and knowing how to use a whistle and signal mirror may be of some help in an emergency situation. A series of three flashes or sharp blasts of the whistle are a universal signal that someone is in distress and can help to summon help—providing someone is watching or listening.

GENERAL TIPS

• Be careful with fires—woe be the tenderfoot who lets a fire get out of hand and burn down a forest.

• Keep a weather eye skyward. You don't want to be caught on a ridge during a lightening storm, in a canyon bottom during a rainstorm, or on a mountain top during a snow storm.

• Stay on trails unless you are an experienced hiker well versed in orienteering skills and map reading knowledge.

• Learn a few basic survival skills.

• Don't hike alone.

• Learn as much about the area you are going to be traveling in as possible.

• Keep your trips simple and uncomplicated and don't try to travel too far, too fast. Always travel according to the needs of the slowest and least strong member of your group.

• File a travel plan with someone you trust and then stick to the plan. That way, if you get into trouble and don't check in, your chances of help being sent are greatly increased.

• Don't play amateur naturalist and begin foraging for wild foods unless you can positively identify what you are gathering. Many wild food eaters have succumbed to poisonous mushrooms, berries and the like.

DESERT TRAVEL TIPS

• Avoid heading out in the summer. In most cases, spring and fall are the best seasons to visit.

• Know what the water conditions are and where you might be able to find water. Don't count on finding water, however, as a spring that is said to be running and of good quality may have dried up since the last field check. In general, carry one gallon of water per person per day.

• Keep a weather eye skyward. Thunderstorms in the distance may mean flash flooding in a canyon through which you had planned on hiking.

• Biting flies can be bothersome. Carry insect repellent.

• The sun is usually intense. Wear a hat with a visor and light, loose, long-sleeve shirts and long pants. Apply sunscreen to all skin that is exposed. Remember to reapply sunscreen periodically, especially to bare legs after a stream crossing.

FISHING SAFETY

Use caution when fishing on riverbanks. An unstable bank may decide to suddenly drop you into swirling waters below. Ditto the advice when wading, as swift currents and slippery rocks may send you tumbling through the water like just so much bait. Always wear a personal flotation device when fishing from a boat—or anywhere around deep water.

DRUG LAB WASTE

I hate to say it, especially in a book about discovering the joys of wild places, but it's true. An increasing number of drug-manufacturing yahoos have decided that public lands were intended for garbage disposal sites for their manufacturing waste. If you come across a site that has large five-gallon buckets, gallon plastic jugs, large garbage bags, and pieces of lab equipment (beakers, tubes, etc.) get the hell out of Dodge, as both the site and the chemicals are dangerous. Report the siting to the BLM or local law enforcement authorities.

LYME DISEASE

Lyme disease-carrying ticks may be found on public lands in some areas of the country. In the Western United States, the ixodes tick carries the disease and can be identified by its size (tiny) and its color (black and reddish brown). The best prevention for avoiding tick bites is to tuck your shirt into your pants and your pant legs into your socks. Wear light-colored clothing so ticks are easier to spot. Use a tick repellent on your clothing—a number of good repellents can be purchased at most sporting goods stores or specialty outdoor outfitters.

Perform tick checks at least once a day, being especially careful to inspect armpits, behind the ears, and in the navel and groin areas. Prompt removal of the tick lessens the chance of disease transmission. Authorities state that a tick must be attached to the skin for 12 to 24 hours before the disease is transmitted. Lyme disease symptoms include a rash or lesion, flu-like symptoms, headache, stiff neck, fever, muscle ache and general malaise. If you suspect you have lyme disease, see your doctor immediately. If it is left untreated, it can become quite severe.

Minimizing Impact

Environmental impact problems associated with overuse or individual carelessness are visible in any wilderness or park setting. All you have to do is look—and not very hard at times. Scattered campfire rings, eroding gullies and trails, toilet paper and human waste littering a meadow, girdled trees from improperly tethered horses, food scraps and trash dotting a campsite, graffiti carved on trail signs or trees, vandalized park facilities—sadly, the list goes on.

Land use and impact guidelines are established by land managers for the protection of the wilderness and to enhance each visitor's experience. Before any hiking, boating, mountain biking, camping trip, or other recreational activity, check with the local BLM office for minimum impact recommendations specific to the area you will be traveling in.

Listed below are some general minimum impact guidelines that are appropriate nearly 100% of the time. These "rules to recreate by," when coupled with a dose of common sense, will help to keep the wilderness we love pure and pristine.

Hiking/Backpacking

• Plan your wilderness trips to avoid major holiday rushes. Trailheads and campgrounds can become so packed with humanity that the water, air and noise impacts become severe. Travel only in small groups—four or less is ideal.

• When hiking on a trail, hike in a single file and in the center of the trail. Resist the urge to take a shortcut across a meadow or down a switchback. Doing so will only result in encouraging severe erosion and trail damage.

• Take your rest stops only in areas where your presence will not damage the vegetation. Be careful to replace all gear in your pack—the most common time to forget gear or inadvertently litter is during a rest break.

• The perfect campsite is never made—it is discovered. Trenching, cutting branches, leveling or removing vegetation are inappropriate camping techniques. Look for a level site that has naturally adequate drainage and is not in a sensitive area that will be irreparably damaged by your presence.

• Whenever possible, select campsites that have already been used. This will eliminate the creation or expansion of unnecessary camping areas. Always camp out of sight of others and the trail. Practice no-trace camping.

• Use a stove whenever possible. Campfires have romantic appeal, but they have extreme impacts on the environment. Beyond the obvious impacts, keep in mind that the dancing light all but destroys your night vision, obscuring the larger world outside the boundaries of the flame.

• Carry out all that you carry in—this includes fishing line, lures, spent cartridges and cigarette butts. Pick up litter as you find it (although sometimes this is difficult because of weight considerations).

• Never bury food scraps. They will get dug up and scattered. Burn or pack out all leftover food. Fish entrails must be burned or packed out. Left-over food around campsites is an attraction to animals and a danger to other campers if the attracted animal is a bear.

• Use established latrines when they are available. Otherwise, dig a hole six inches deep and at least 200 feet away from the nearest water. Toilet paper does not break down readily so it must be either packed out or burned. Use caution in areas of high fire-risk.

• All washing must be done at least 200 feet away from the nearest water source. Use hot water and a minimum amount of soap (avoid using soap if at all possible). Boiling water will serve to sterilize dishes and utensils. Soap residue can cause more harm than the odd speck of grease.

MOUNTAIN BIKING

The following rules of the trail are provided courtesy of the International Mountain Biking Association:

• Ride on open trails only. Please respect and abide by all trail closures, private property notices and fences, and all requirements for use permits and authorization. All designated wilderness areas are closed to mountain bikes.

• Leave no trace. Do not skid your tires or ride on ground that is rain-soaked and easily scarred. Stick to established trails.

• Control your bicycle. Save your "need for speed" for a race. Stay alert at all times. Speed and an out-of-control mountain biker lead to trouble and often injury to other trail users. Always expect that others may be just around a blind corner.

• Always yield the right-of-way. When encountering other trail users (hikers, equestrians or fellow bikers), a friendly greeting to announce your presence is considerate and appreciated. Slow to a walk or stop your bike, especially when encountering horses.

• Never spook animals. Leave ranch and farm gates as you find them. Disturbing livestock or wild animals can cause serious harm and is considered a major offense. Give plenty of room.

• Plan ahead. Know your equipment, know your ability, know the requirements of the area you are riding in, and then plan accordingly. Be self-sufficient at all times.

CLIMBING

• Reduce chalk use whenever possible. Climb when it is cooler, chalk up less frequently, use dirt as an alternative agent. There is a new product which looks promising, called X-factor, which dries the hands for a better grip but leaves no unsightly residue behind on the rocks.

• If you use tape on your hands, pack it out. Little bits of tape lying around the base of a climb are ugly.

• If a path exists to a climbing site, use it. Don't make your own! Breaking off branches and vegetation that may be in the way on a climb may seem innocent enough, but the practice is indefensible. Work carefully around vegetation or choose another route. It is never acceptable to alter the natural process or balance merely because something is in the way of your climb.

• Never modify the rock to create handholds or to improve a hold. If you can't climb the rock face as it exists, then it wasn't meant to be climbed by you.

MOTOR VEHICLES

Off-terrain vehicle use is encouraged and supported on many of the BLM's vast acreages of wild land. Some people use four-wheel-drive or off-road vehicles to obtain access to trailheads and remote river put-ins or other recreational sites. Others use off-road vehicles wholly as a toy for fun-hogging through dunes, across desert lands and through mountain byways. Whatever your use, off-road vehicles are only appropriate if used with responsibility and care for the land—in some cases, this means not using them, even if it is legal. Before you head out with your vehicle, think about your responsibility to the land and the next visitor and tread lightly.

• Obtain a travel map from the BLM office or U.S. Forest Service that shows legal routes and passages for vehicles and lists the specific rules and regulations for that area.

• Do not run over young trees, shrubs or delicate grasses—it will damage and kill them.

• Stay off wet, soft roads and trails that will be readily torn up by a vehicle's churning wheels—this is especially true during hunting season!

• Skirt the edges of meadows, steep hillsides and streambanks or lakeshores. These areas are very fragile and traveling on them will irreparably scar them.

• Stay on established routes and avoid the urge to venture out and pioneer your own path.

• Stay away from wild animals, especially those that are raising young or appear to be suffering from a food shortage (in winter months especially). Human contact can alarm animals and cause them to use vital energy reserves that may kill them.

• Obey all gate closures and regulatory signs. Vandalism is on the rise—there is no excuse!

• Stay out of all wilderness areas. They are closed to all vehicles for good reason.

• Stay off private lands unless you have first obtained the landowner's permission.

• Respect the rights of hikers, skiers, campers and others to enjoy their activities undisturbed by roaring engines and spinning tires.

RIVER RUNNING

A river corridor is a thin strip of land and water where use impacts become highly concentrated. For that reason, minimum impact techniques are of utmost importance to keep riverways looking pristine.

• All solid human waste must be carried out. The typical method is to make a river toilet using an ammo can, heavy duty plastic bags, a toilet seat, chlorine bleach and toilet paper. Although carrying out all human waste may seem unpleasant, it is far less unpleasant than mounds of human waste scattered all along the river bank.

• Pack out everything that you pack in.

• Place a large tarp under your eating area to catch food scraps, so beach areas do not become feeding grounds for rodents and massive communities of insects.

• Use a fire pan at all times for campfires and only use downed wood. Better yet, bring your own charcoal. Fire pans should always be elevated so heat from the pan does not scorch the soil. All ashes, once cooled and doused, must be carried out. A five-gallon slush bucket is the easiest method.

• Camp on beaches, sandbars or a non-vegetated site below the high water line. When the river floods, your passing will be washed away and the site will appear pristine to river runners who follow.

• Washing or bathing with soap must be done at least 200 feet away from the nearest water source.

• Waste water from cooking should be filtered through a fine-mesh screen to remove food solids and then poured directly into the river. Do not scatter waste water on the beach as it will attract flies and other animals.

Archaeological Sites

The single biggest problem for archaeological land managers and cultural resource persons is dealing with the unintentional damage caused by visitors. Even with extreme caution, impacts can and do occur. It is imperative that extreme caution and respect be used when visiting and traveling near archaeological and historical sites.

• Viewing a site from a distance and not entering it will reduce the impacts a site receives. Although there may only be one or two of you, there are literally thousands of the same "one or two" visiting a site each year, and that's a lot of traffic.

• Stop, look and think before entering a cultural site. Identify the midden area (trash pile) so you can avoid walking on it—middens contain important and fragile bits of archaeological information.

• Stay on a trail if it has been built through a site.

• Looking at artifacts is fine, picking them up and taking them is not! Leave all potsherds and other artifacts where they lie for others to enjoy.

• Camping is not allowed in or around ruins.

• Move nothing, including branches or rocks, when scrambling around a site. Avoid touching plaster walls. Climbing on the roofs and walls of a site can lead to an immediate collapse of a cultural site that has stood for hundreds of years.

• Enjoy rock art by viewing, sketching or photographing. Never chalk, trace or otherwise touch rock art as any kind of contact will cause the ancient figures to disintegrate.

• Never build fires in or around cultural sites.

• Finally, some cultural sites are places of ancestral importance to Native Americans and demand to be treated with the respect and reverence they deserve.

Watching Wildlife

You can harm wildlife unintentionally by getting too close! Most wild animals react with alarm when approached by humans on foot or by vehicle. A panic reaction is stressful and causes the animal to use energy and food reserves that are needed for other activities. Repeated disturbances can cause animals and birds to avoid an area—even if that area offers the best food and habitat. Learn animal behavior patterns that will warn you if you are getting too close. You will get your closest peeks at wildlife if you let them come to you. Never, ever use food to attract animals!

• Quality binoculars (7 x 35 magnification as a minimum) or a spotting scope will help you to observe wildlife from a safe distance. Use a telephoto lens (300mm) and tripod to get close-up photos.

• Rushing around is no way to watch wildlife! The more time that you take, the greater your chances for seeing wildlife that would otherwise be missed. Set up a base camp and spend a few days in a given area. Wild animals are most often spotted at or around dawn and dusk.

• Wear muted colors, sit quietly and leave pets at home. Refrain from using scented soaps or perfumes.

• Spend time at local museums of natural history to learn about the wildlife in the area you are visiting. Natural history museums and organizations typically have books, brochures, maps and displays that will be of assistance to you. Learn to recognize an animal by its tracks, droppings and sounds.

There are many field guides on the market today that are area-specific pertaining to birds, mammals, animal tracks, edible plants, wildflowers, trees, rocks and gems, and more. Most major bookstores should carry a selection that will prove helpful.

You are too close to a bird if it:
• seems skittish
• raises its head to watch you
• preens excessively, pecks at dirt or feet, or wipes its bill repeatedly
• gives alarm calls
• flushes repeatedly
• gives distraction displays, such as feigning a broken wing

You are too close to a mammal if it:
• raises its head high, ears pointed in your direction with raised hairs on the neck and shoulders

- exhibits signs of skittishness, such as jumping at sounds or movements
- lowers its head, ears back in preparation for a charge
- moves away
- displays aggressive or nervous behavior

MAP AND COMPASS

Staring in bewilderment at a splotch of ink on a map, trying to determine whether or not that splotch is the mountain you are looking at, is not the time to wish you had a better grasp of map and compass skills. Take the time to learn how to use a map and compass before heading out. One excellent way to become proficient with a map and compass is to join a local orienteering club. Check with your nearest outdoor or backpacking store for information about clubs. I also recommend the *Outward Bound Map & Compass Handbook* by Glenn Randall, published by Lyons and Burford, as an excellent source of practical and instructional reading.

WATERPROOFING A MAP

There is nothing fun about trying to navigate while clinging to a soggy map in a downpour. Right before your eyes, the route home turns into a greenish-brown papier-mache clump. When this happens, your only hope is that your memory of the route didn't wash out like the map did.

Making a see-through, waterproof cover for your maps is an easy way to prevent soggy map syndrome. All you need is a large, freezer-weight Zip-loc bag and a few sections of sturdy, waterproof tape like duct or packing tape.

Simply cut the tape into a strip long enough to completely adhere to one edge of the bag from top to bottom. Press one-half of the tape, lengthwise, onto the bag, leaving the other half of the tape hanging over the edge. Now flip the bag over, and fold the tape down on itself and the other side of the bag. Repeat each step two more times, once for the bottom and once for the remaining side. You now have a wonderful waterproof map container that is reinforced on three edges.

Several other ways to waterproof a map are:

- Cover it with clear contact paper (this makes the map waterproof but very stiff and there is no way to write on the map).

• Paint on a product called "Stormproof," available at most map and outdoor specialty stores. The clear chemical coating renders the map waterproof, flexible, and the map can still be written on.

• Apply a coating of "Thompson Water Seal" or other brick and masonry sealant. It will make a map water-repellent, but not waterproof.

FOLDING A MAP

Map folding is an acquired skill. With a blowing wind, a little rain and a sprinkling of fatigue, you can get an irresistible desire to jam or crumple your trail map into the nearest pocket and forget the idea of folding.

Believe it or not, there is a better way—a map-folding technique that results in a very easy-to-use accordion-style configuration that is taught to British Boy Scouts. My cousin from England can fold a map like this in his sleep.

This method allows you to look at any portion of the map without having to fully open it, which is ideal in windy or wet weather. Further, the accordion configuration collapses to pocket-size with ease. Once you've established the creases, any map will fold up and down almost without effort.

Step 1—Lay the map flat, printed side up. Fold it in half vertically, with the face inside the first fold to establish the first crease. Make this and every subsequent crease clean and sharp.

Step 2—Working with only the right half of the map, fold the right side in half towards the center, resulting in quarter-folds.

Step 3—Fold the outside quarter-fold back to the edge, producing an eighth-fold. Use this fold as a guide and fold the other quarter the same way. Trust me, it's easier than it sounds.

Step 4—Half the map should now have four accordion-style folds.

Step 5—Repeat steps 2 and 3 on the map's other half so that you end up with a full accordion of eight folds in a long ruler-like shape.

Step 6—Finally, fold the map in the shape of a Z so it's in thirds. Voila! Now you can look at any section without having to completely unfold the map and it snaps into place almost by itself.

Bears & Other Furry Nocturnal Visitors

Snuffle, snuffle, slurp…It's a nocturnal sound that when heard outside your tent flap means one of two things—either your camping partner has developed a case of the sniffles while secretly gorging on your personal stash of sweets, or *Ursus americanus* is rototilling his way through your pack in search of anything remotely edible.

Before going camping, you will want to know which animals may or may not frequent your campsite. From kangaroo rats to bears, animals are an inquisitive lot that like to take advantage of each and every opportunity for free food. A kangaroo rat gnawing through a pack to reach some nuts inside is not an immediate threat to nearby humans, but the damage to your pack could create real problems.

A bear, on the other hand, rummaging through camp because it smells food, is going to be very surprised when it encounters humans as well as chocolate or fish. The surprise and resulting screaming and growling can, and has, led to very unfortunate consequences. In a conflict between bears and unarmed humans, bears usually cause the most immediate damage. This is not to say that bears should automatically invoke panic among humans, but that they should be respected and proper precautions taken to protect them and us.

The first step to take to avoid unpleasant encounters is to learn to bearproof your camp. Hang all food well away from camp, leaving no food in packs, and never take food or clothing that smells of food into tents. In general, if you keep your camp clean, you should experience no serious bear problems.

A bear may still periodically wander through just because you are on his selected route for the evening. If a bear should approach your camp, yell, wave your arms, bang pots—do anything to alert the bear to your presence, which should encourage it to retreat. If it chooses not to retreat, *you* should—slowly and methodically with your eyes to the ground and making no outward appearance of being aggressive. Speak to the bear in calm but firm tones to help it recognize that you are human and not a threat. If the bear attacks, don't run! Ball up and protect your vitals and lie still.

When traveling through bear country, your best defense is good ears and alert senses. Some people have taken to wearing bells or clapping hands or whatnot to alert bears to their presence. In theory, this sounds good. If the bear knows you are there, you are less likely to surprise him and he will more likely move out of the way. On the other hand, aside from the fact that some areas of our wilderness are beginning to sound like a bad rendition of Jingle Bells, there is evidence to support the idea that bears are learning to identify bells and other human noises like clapping as meaning "dinner's on!" Not exactly the approach you want.

A better idea is to travel quietly and learn to anticipate bear country. Look for signs. Listen frequently for noises. Try to see a bear before it sees you. If you are traveling in bear country that is managed by a BLM office, each district has its own rules and guidelines for you to follow. Be sure to check in and find out what they are.

If there is no bear hazard and you choose not to hang your food, at the very least you should leave your pack pockets open. An eager rodent will gnaw through fabric to get to food, but if an invitation is left via an open zipper or flap, it will usually take the easy route. To ensure you receive no unwanted visitors in your tent, leave all food outside of your sleeping area.

Repelling Biting Nasties

It smells bad, it melts plastic, and don't even think of getting any on your nylon jacket. So why are millions of people liberally applying Deet-based (N, N-Diethyl-Meta Tolumide) insect repellents to their skin? Because they work, that's why. But, are standard levels of 100% Deet, previously considered essential to combat biting nasties, now considered potentially risky and basically overkill?

The answer is yes, with a qualification since the EPA has yet to offer any official position on new percentage recommendations and still maintains that Deet is safe for human use. Still, it is hard to ignore the fact that Deet is a chemical solvent and easily absorbed through the skin. Which leaves you wondering about its potential toxicity to the human body.

A number of holistic repellents, made increasingly popular with the fears regarding Deet, rely on Citronella (a chemical derived from a grass native to India) as well as a whole host of other herbs to keep insects from alighting.

Avon's *Skin So Soft*, not advertised as a repellent (to do that, they would have to register their product with the EPA), has achieved almost cult-like distinction as a repellent among outdoorsmen and women. In fact, some say that *Skin So Soft* accounts for nearly 20% of repellent sales in this country.

But, like holistic remedies, studies have shown that *Skin So Soft* can't hold a candle to the repelling effectiveness enjoyed by Deet. Chemically, Deet does three things: masks body odor, creates a smell that insects do not like, and offers a surface insects do not like to be on. Frankly, given the choice, I wouldn't want to stand on something that melts dashboards either.

So if the chemical Deet is so bad for you, why keep using it? Because the alternative of being "meat on the hoof" for a myriad of insects is not only unpleasant, in certain circumstances it may be more dangerous than the chemical itself. (Lyme disease, Rocky Mountain spotted fever, malaria, yellow fever and many more debilitating illnesses are all transmitted by insect bites.)

There is, however, a growing resistance to the use of Deet in heavy concentrations, especially by children and those individuals who require frequent applications over a prolonged period, such as backpackers on an extended journey.

And what of the ongoing debate regarding Deet toxicity or safety? It's not likely that any clear answers will be offered soon, but unless you are inclined to stay home, hide in the tent, or bury yourself in mud, Deet remains the best alternative to slap, duck and run. Just apply it as you would a drug—with common sense—and only in concentrations of 30% or less.

For those of you still inclined to stay away from Deet and go with an alternative repellent, I dug up an old backwoods recipe for "fly-dope," although it comes with no guarantee of success: Mix one-half ounce of citronella, one-quarter ounce of cedarwood oil, one ounce of heated Vaseline for softening, and one-quarter ounce of camphor spirits. Cool and use.

Barring using repellent, what else can you do? Your best bet is to wear light-colored, long-sleeved shirts and long pants tucked into your boots. A good hat and a bandana around your neck helps. For extra protection, spray insect repellent on your clothing, not on your skin. There is also a mosquito netting product that drapes over your head and seals around your neck, but I find that it feels a little claustrophobic.

If you do get bitten, calamine lotion or a mixture of baking soda and water will help to relieve the itching.

OUTDOORS WITH CHILDREN

Children and the wilderness go together like peanut butter and jelly. The wilderness becomes a natural teacher, educating your children about themselves and their world in an unhurried setting. Memories of a child gazing intently at a ladybug crawling on her finger, and the uncontrolled giggling of youngsters searching for crawfish in a stream, make camping with children so enjoyable for me. Given the opportunity, I think you will find the same happiness.

Camping with children is not without effort. Constant vigilance on an adult's part is necessary. Care must be taken to ensure the safety of children at all times. Additionally, care must be taken to teach children that the wilderness is fragile and must be protected.

The following is a brief summary to aid in planning your family's camping experience:

• Always maintain a high level of flexibility.

• Begin with backyard camping, progressing to organized campgrounds and then to a simple backpacking experience.

• When hiking, keep elevation gain and loss to a minimum. Five hundred feet is about right.

• Plan your routes well within the hiking abilities of all adults and children.

• Let the children dictate the hiking pace.

• Plan rest breaks frequently and before children get tired.

• Include favorite foods for snacks and mealtimes.

• When planning, packing and hiking, let your children help so they become part of the entire adventure.

• Be clear about safety procedures and rules with your children.

• Always purify water.

• Pick campsites that are away from dangerous obstacles and that will minimize your impact upon the environment.

• Don't relegate yourself to the role of distant observer. Get down and dirty with your children.

• Have your children drink plenty of water and eat plenty of snacks—keep your children well fueled.

• Allow for lots of time to explore, romp and splash along the way.

• Keep smiling and make the best of every situation. Be prepared for anything!

Amphibious Canyoneering

Standing waist-deep in water while staring up at a 1,000-pound log wedged in the narrow canyon walls above your head may not give you the impression of traveling through a fragile and irreplaceable environment. On the contrary, the rugged nature of and difficulty presented by traveling through remote riparian canyons in Utah, Arizona and other states presents a picture of a magnificent yet unforgiving and potentially violent offering. Still, these amphibious canyons demand the highest level of wilderness ethic. Once polluted or vandalized, their resources and beauty are irreplaceable.

Some of your travel through canyons of this nature will be in the form of raftpacking—floating your pack along the streambed and pulling or pushing it. The rest of the time will be spent hiking through wet and lush canyon floors, often wading knee-deep in water. Only travel in small groups. Any group larger than four is really too large and the resulting impacts will be severe.

Do not bring pets along. Although some will argue that properly controlled dogs have a place in the wilderness, canyoneering is not one of those places. The intensity of swimming, jumping, climbing and rough scrambling will not be a pleasure for either your canine friend or yourself.

Always stay in the streambed unless circumstances force you out. Bushwhacking along the lush edges of these canyon-bottom, riparian environments will cause permanent damage both to the delicate soil structure (cryptogamic soil for you naturalists) and the vegetation. Do not pick or even touch the flowers.

On occasion, traveling through certain sections of a canyon will require you to use climbing ropes, slings and anchors. It is not a reasonable practice to leave behind an anchor, rope or sling. If you cannot take your equipment with you, then do not use it. Find an alternate method or route.

It is a difficult process, but do your best to refrain from sending wastewater directly into the stream. It is virtually impossible to practice washing and urination 200 feet from many canyon bottom streams. At least attempt to provide as much filtration opportunity as possible by dumping wastewater in the soil, rocks and sandy environs away from the immediate stream edge. Periodic flash flooding will flush the canyons clean. Adequately filter all waste water through a bandana so that all food and particulate matter is removed before dumping it. Pack out all solid waste.

Boaters rules should apply regarding defecation. Create a miniature river-runner's toilet using a coffee can lined with multiple plastic bags. Add small amounts of chlorine bleach to prevent odor and gas production. Do not urinate in the bags. Squeeze out all air when packing, seal the bags, and then replace the coffee can lid to secure the contents.

Camp only on sand banks, gravel washes or rocky ledges. Never set up camp in vegetated areas. Campfires are not acceptable, even with significant amounts of driftwood littering the canyon. The resulting blackening of rocks and ash/charcoal production leaves behind permanent reminders of your visit. Stoves are the only environmentally sound way of cooking.

CAVING ON PUBLIC LAND

CAVE CONSERVATION

Leave no trace. Pack out what you brought in. The pristine and fragile cave environment is no place to leave spent carbide, graffiti, trash or human waste. Leave nothing but footprints on established or designated trails.

Avoid sensitive areas. Examine each cave and cave passage for delicate features and sensitive formations. Be careful not to touch formations. Stay on established trails to avoid trampling areas needlessly. Be cautious to protect irreplaceable archaeological or paleontological artifacts. Collecting specimens or removing any materials from caves is strictly prohibited.

Respect cave life. Some caves have insect and bat populations that are easily disturbed. In the precariously balanced cave environment, any disruption could conceivably lessen a creature's survivability. Polluting pools and waking bats are two unacceptable examples of disturbing cave biological features.

CAVE SAFETY

Consider individual fitness levels and caving experience. The recommended minimum group size is three people, the maximum is eight.

Be informed of cave-specific conditions including physical and legal access, cave map availability, temperature, dust conditions, the presence of water, vertical drops, radon levels, and rock fall hazards.

Include as a minimum three reliable light sources, a helmet, sturdy boots, vertical gear and the knowledge for its proper and safe use, a first aid kit, food, water, and a container for wastes.

Let others know your specific caving plans, secure appropriate use authorizations, and be informed as to weather conditions and the possibility of flash floods. In the event of an emergency, know where the nearest phone is and dial 911.

LAND ACCESS CONCERNS

Recently, the Department of the Interior acknowledged that public access to public lands is not satisfactory—the understatement of the year. A recent investigation by the General Accounting Office has revealed that access was inadequate to nearly 50.4 million acres of public land managed by the U.S. Forest Service and the Bureau of Land Management. According to both the U.S. Forest Service and the BLM, private landowners' unwillingness to grant public easement access across their land is on the increase—while the public's use of federal land is also on the rise.

Private landowners cite concerns pertaining to vandalism and possible liability—understandable to be sure. What isn't so forgivable is the fact that some landowners won't grant access because of a desire for exclusive personal use and gain—such as pay-to-hunt privileges. "Want to hunt on the public land? Well then, you have to pay to cross mine." One friend, an outdoors editor of a major city newspaper, even reports being threatened and run off the land by a pick-up load of cowboys—this while looking for a place to camp on public land in Wyoming. Reminiscent of the range wars in the late 1800s, don't you think?

Much of the problem stems from inadequate or removed signs—especially in Wyoming, where the mingled federal, state and private lands represent a confusing mosaic. How are you to know if a road is public or private if it is not properly signed? That's anyone's guess. Fortunately, unsigned roads are becoming less common due to diligent efforts by the BLM and other public agencies. You can be sure that most private land in states other than Wyoming will carry obvious signage—sometimes to visual excess. Wyoming has no such sign requirement, leaving you, the visitor, with the responsibility of knowing when and if you are crossing onto private property.

Want to know what is open and what is closed? Your best bet is to contact the local BLM office that holds jurisdiction over the region and they will be more than happy to fill you in on the pertinent details. The BLM also publishes maps that show private and public land ownership. If you cannot contact the BLM for some reason, then the following guide should keep you out of trouble with the law and in the good graces of private land owners:

Just because there is public land lying over the rise and surrounded by private land does not mean the landowner must grant access. Obtain permission before attempting to cross private lands. Plying the owner's good favor with a bottle of wine or other favorite treat is a trick many hunters and fishermen have used to gain access to private lands owned by farmers—amazing what a little show of respect and gratitude does for opening gates, isn't it? If an owner denies access for any reason, don't rant and rave. Anger won't open the gates for you or any future visitor. Click your heels and return the way you came.

If you feel you are on public land but are hassled by a landowner or a group of cowboys, as in my friend's case, your best bet is to pack up quietly and quickly and then head to the nearest BLM office to sort things out. Chances are, although it doesn't happen too frequently thank goodness, the problem lies with a rancher who has leased BLM land for years and has come to think of it as his own.

The last thing to remember is this: Most landowners who I have come in contact with (ranchers, farmers, homesteaders) are wonderful people who are only concerned about protecting their land and livestock—and who can blame them. If you convey the fact that you only want to enjoy the land they love, it is more than likely that access will be granted with a smile—and often with a secret tip to a secluded swimming hole or great fishing area too.

ADVENTURES IN THE PAST

Tucked in among the nearly 270 million acres of public lands the BLM administers across the U.S. lies a virtually unparalleled resource of cultural wealth—Indian ruins, historic ghost towns, cross-country wagon trails, old forts, and prehistoric sites (some more than 10,000 years old). Perhaps what is most remarkable is that many of these sites are accessible while enjoying a backcountry adventure by either foot, bicycle or boat. There is, however, a problem with the accessibility—vandalism! Many sites are being looted and damaged beyond repair. Sometimes even innocent visitors commit unintentional vandalism simply by treading where they shouldn't tread, touching what they shouldn't touch. If you see any signs of vandalism or suspicious activity, report it as soon as possible to the nearest BLM office. As for your own travels? Look, but don't touch. Revel in the history before you that stands as a silent testimony to another time, another place. Listen quietly to the lessons and messages that are there for all.

SITES AT A GLANCE

Many of these sites are referred to in the chapters that follow. Many are not since they do not lie within the identified wilderness or recreation sites which are the primary focus of this book. I have given the state in which the site lies and more specific information is available simply by contacting each state's district BLM office.

Historic Gold and Silver Mining Camps
Coldfoot Gold Camp, Alaska
Rochester Gold Camp, Nevada
South Pass City Historic Mining District, Wyoming
Spanish Gulch Mining District, Oregon
Alpine Loop National Back Country Byway, Colorado
Garnet Ghost Town, Montana

Ancient Rock Carvings and Figures
Three Rivers Petroglyph Site, New Mexico
Rochester Muddy Creek Petroglyph Site, Arizona
Little Black Mountain Petroglyph Site, Arizona
Hickison Summit Petroglyph Site, Nevada
Wees Bar Petroglyph Site, Birds of Prey Conservation Area, Idaho

Whoopup Canyon Petroglyph Site, Wyoming
Blythe Intaglios, California
Carrizo Plain Pictograph Site, California
Canon Pintado Historic District, Colorado

Ancient Caves

Hidden Cave and Grimes Point Sites, Nevada
Tangle Lakes Archaeological District, Alaska
Hogup Cave, Utah
Catlow Cave, Oregon

Frontier Trails

Flagstaff Hill and Keeney Pass Trail Sites, Oregon
Iditarod National Historic Trail, Alaska
Pony Express Trail, Utah and Nevada
Spanish Trail / Old Mormon Road, Nevada
Honeymoon Trail and Beale Wagon Road, Arizona
Central Pacific Railroad Grade, Utah
Emigrant Trails of Southern Idaho, Idaho
Oregon National Historic Trail, Wyoming
Bizz Johnson Logging Railroad Trail, California
Lewis and Clark Trail, Montana

Cabins and Homesteads

Ward Ranch Site, New Mexico
Black Pine Valley Homesteads, Idaho
Rogue River Ranch and Whiskey Creek Cabin, Oregon
Fort Benton to James Kipp Recreation Area Float Trip, Montana
Riddle Brothers Historic Ranch District, Oregon
John Jarvie of Brown's Park, Utah

Indian Pueblos

Anasazi Heritage Center Escalante Ruins Complex, Colorado
Grand Gulch Archaeological District, Utah
Chama Gateway Pueblos, New Mexico
Perry Mesa Pueblo Sites, Arizona
Lowry Ruins National Historic Landmark, Colorado

Military Sites
Fort Egbert National Historic Landmark, Alaska
Patton's Camps, California
Boots and Saddles Forts, New Mexico
Santa Cruz de Terrentate Spanish Presidio, Arizona
Cantonment Reno, Wyoming

Ancient Campsites
Red Rocks Recreation Site, Nevada
Mack Canyon Archaeological District, Oregon
Murray Springs Clovis Site, Arizona
Baker Femont Site, Nevada
Fossil Falls Area of Critical Environmental Concern, California
Lower Salmon River Sites, Idaho
Hanson Folsom Site, Wyoming
Shelter Cove, California
Henry Smith Buffalo Jump Site, Montana
Warner Wetlands Area, Oregon

ARCHAEOLOGICAL RESOURCES—THE LAW

When hiking through many areas of BLM land, it is common to stumble across archaeological sites and artifacts—pottery, dwellings, ruins, arrowheads, grinding stones, etc. These discoveries can inspire a sense of intrigue and excitement and afford us a unique peek into a past lived by former cultures very different from our own. However, the opportunity to enjoy these discoveries without also seeing some form of violation is becoming more and more difficult. Ruins are being destroyed by eager hikers clambering all over them, graffiti scars the walls of many pictograph and petroglyph sites, and wholesale removal and vandalizing of artifacts has and continues to occur by amateur and professional trophy hunters.

Two federal laws, the Antiquities Act of 1906 and the Archaeological Resources Protection Act of 1979, forbid the removal or destruction of archaeological resources on public lands. Stiff fines and imprisonment can result from failure to abide by the law. This includes pocketing an arrowhead—a simple enough act by itself, but the person pocketing the arrowhead now prevents anyone else from enjoying a similar discovery of that arrowhead.

Besides operating under a "look but don't take" creed, you can

---

help the authorities by reporting any and all signs of vandalism or theft you see occurring. In many instances, there are rewards offered for information that leads to an arrest and conviction.

ADVENTURER'S CHECKLIST

The following checklist will help you to plan your next adventure. Not all items listed will be needed on every trip. Pack only what you need and leave the rest at home; remember, you've got to carry what you pack.

PACKS
Backpack (external or internal frame)
Waterproof pack cover
Child carrier (if camping with a child under four who has difficulty
    walking long distances)
Day pack or fanny pack

SHELTER
Lightweight tent (including poles, stakes and guy lines)
Mosquito netting (for around your head when sleeping under the
    stars)
9-foot by 12-foot nylon tarp with grommets

SLEEPING
Sleeping bag (down or synthetic)
Sleeping pad
Pillow
Ground cloth

TEN-PLUS ESSENTIALS
Sunglasses
Water bottle (carry two quarts per person per day in the mountains
    when water is available; one gallon per person per day in desert
    environments)
Water purification
Nylon cord (50 feet)
Waterproof/windproof matches
Flashlight (extra bulb and batteries)

Fire starter
Pocket knife
Toilet paper
Topographic map
Compass
Emergency blanket
Whistle
Signal mirror
Emergency snacks

KITCHEN
Stove
Fuel/fuel bottle
Primer paste
Lighter or matches
Windscreen
Cook set
Frying pan
Water bag (collapsible)
Storage containers for food
Zip-loc bags (freezer variety)
Large spoon
Knife
Spatula
Can opener (GI folding variety)
Small whisk
Small grater
Pot grips
Knife, fork, spoon
Plate
Cup
Bowl
Cutting board (small nylon variety)
Ice chest
Scrub pads
Biodegradable soap
Paper towels
Aluminum foil
Spice kit

FIRST AID
Antibiotics
Antiseptics
Tylenol
Benadryl
Tincture of benzoin
Sterile gauze pads
Roller gauze
Nonadherent dressing
One-inch adhesive tape
Steri-strips
Ace wrap
Large compress
Moleskin
Second Skin
Tweezers
Bandage scissors
Irrigation syringe
Low-reading thermometer
SAM splint
Space blanket
Sawyer snakebite kit
Emergency report form
Pencil
Emergency phone numbers and money for a phone call

HYGIENE
Comb/brush
Toothbrush/toothpaste
Dental floss
Deodorant
Small towel
Shaving kit
Biodegradable skin and hair soap
Moisturizing lotion
Towlettes
Sunscreen (15 SPF or better)
Lip balm
Tampons

Clothing
First Layer:
>   Underwear
>   Long underwear (tops and bottoms)
>   Liner socks
>   Wool outer socks
>   T-shirt

Second Layer:
>   Wool shirt
>   Synchilla, Polartec or wool sweater
>   Shorts
>   Long pants

Protective Layer:
>   Wool, A16 Bomber, or Synchilla hat
>   Sun hat
>   Bunting, Polartec, or Synchilla jacket
>   Parka (synthetic fill or down)
>   Wool mittens
>   Rain suit (jacket and pants)
>   Gaiters
>   Windbreaker
>   Hiking boots
>   Camp shoes or sneakers

Miscellaneous Gear
Butane or candle lantern
Fishing gear and license
Trowel
Thermometer
Bandana
Note pad and pencil
Camera, film, lenses
Binoculars
Plastic trash bags

Fun and Games
Frisbee
Nerf ball
Hacky sack

Miniature games (backgammon, checkers, chess, etc.)
Harmonica
Kazoo
Paperback books
Coloring books
Star guide
Mini microscope
Magnifying glass
Small plastic collection containers
Aquarium net
Sketch pad
Pencils
Crayons
Colored felt-tip pens
Gold pan and mineral book

Mountain Biking
Cycling shorts
Cycling gloves
Cycling shoes
Helmet
Tire-patch kit
Spare parts
Mini tool kit
Panniers

Cross-Country Skiing
Skis (waxless for convenience, waxable for performance)
Boots
Bindings
Poles
Extra ski tip
Basic repair parts

Canoeing
Canoe
Paddles
Life jackets
Waterproof duffles

Waterproof containers for camera gear
Rope to secure duffles and contents in boat

INFANT NEEDS
Bottles and extra nipples
Rubber or plastic pants
Diapers
Sleep suits
Extra clothing
Warm snuggle suit
Rain suit
Baby food
Baby wipes
Baby powder or corn starch

C H A P T E R   T W O

ALASKA

(SEE MAP A)   (SEE MAP B)

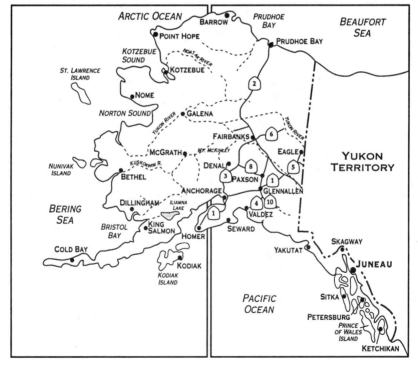

MAP A—ALASKA

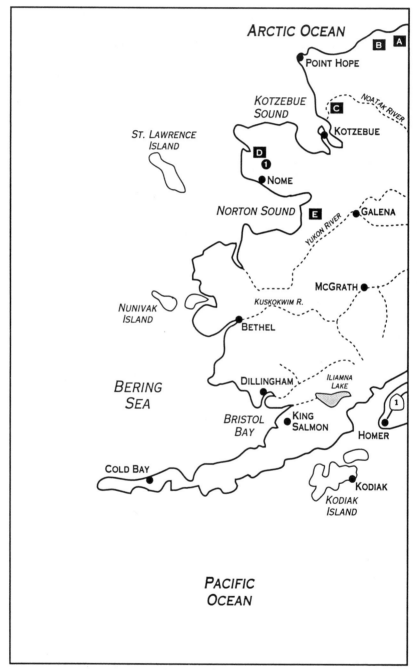

MAP REFERENCES

A. Teshekpuk Lake—p. 50
B. Kasegaluk Lagoon—50
C. Squirrel River—p. 51
D. Kigluaik Mountains—p. 52
E. Unalakleet River—p. 54

BLM CAMPGROUNDS

1. Salmon Lake Campground—p. 74

MAP B—ALASKA

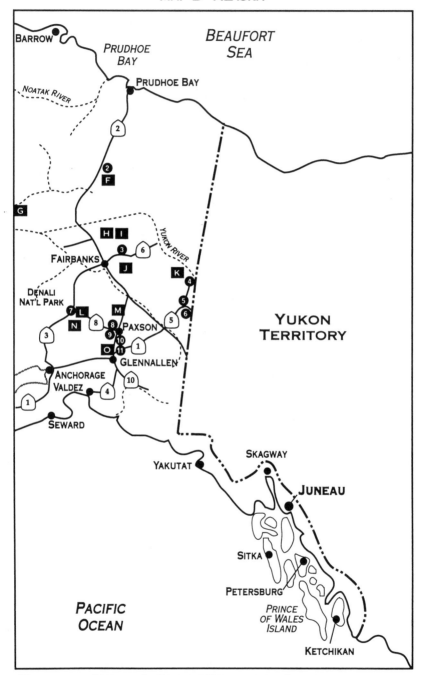

MAP REFERENCES

BLM CAMPGROUNDS

ALASKA—MAP A

TESHEKPUK LAKE

See letter A on map page 46

canoeing, wildlife observation, wildlife photography

Teshekpuk Lake lies just a few miles from the Arctic Ocean, tucked in among the wet tundra lowlands southeast of Barrow. The 22-mile-wide lake and its many smaller sister lakes are considered vital waterfowl and caribou habitats. Wildlife viewing and photographic opportunities are excellent. Migratory brants, greater white-fronted geese and Canada geese arrive in July and August. The lake system protects them from predators while they molt and regrow wing feathers. Plovers, sandpipers, phalaropes, dunlins, loons, old-squaws, jaegers, gulls and snowy owls nest in the lake region. Caribou, Arctic fox and lemming also may be seen. Access to the area is by charter plane from Barrow or Prudhoe Bay. No facilities exist at the lake, so expect wilderness camping only. Use restrictions are in effect during the summer months of July and August to minimize human impact on wildlife—check with the BLM for updated regulations.

Resources:

• *Alaska Atlas and Gazetteer*, published by DeLorme Mapping, P.O. Box 298, Freeport, ME 04032; (207) 865-4171.

For more information: Contact the BLM Arctic District Office, 1150 University Avenue, Fairbanks, AK 99709; (907) 474-2300.

KASEGALUK LAGOON

See letter B on map page 46

sea kayaking, wildlife observation

With shallow waters only three to six feet deep and protected from ocean waves, this is the largest barrier island-lagoon system in North America and offers fantastic ocean kayaking opportunities coupled with excellent wildlife viewing. Located along a 120-mile stretch of the Chukchi Sea coast, from south of Wainwright to just beyond Point Lay, Kasegaluk Lagoon is considered an important and extremely productive habitat by the Alaska Department of Fish and Game.

There are no facilities at the lagoon. Wilderness camping is the order of the day and visitors should be adequately prepared for high winds and cold, often biting weather year-round. The only access to the site is by chartered plane from Barrow or Kotzebue. Weather rules here, so it is critical that campers pack extra food in the event that a weather front socks in and flying is prevented.

Wildlife viewing is super all year long. Between July and September, hundreds of thousands of migrating eiders and thousands of terns, gulls, jaegers, loons, brants and more can be seen. Beluga whales frequent the area in June. Arctic fox, lemming, caribou, brown bear, seal and gray whale are seen frequently in the area at other times of the year.

Sod huts near the mouth of the Utokok River mark the remains of the abandoned Eskimo village of Tolegeak, a historic site. Wildlife in the area is protected by law and must not be harassed. Subsistence hunting is conducted in the area by local residents. At the north end of the lagoon is private land owned by the village of Wainwright—respect their privacy!

Resources:
• *Alaska Atlas and Gazetteer*, published by DeLorme Mapping, P.O. Box 298, Freeport, ME 04032; (207) 865-4171.

For more information: Contact the BLM Arctic District Office, 1150 University Avenue, Fairbanks, AK 99709; (907) 474-2300.

SQUIRREL RIVER

See letter C on map page 46

fishing, kayaking

Originating in the Baird Mountains and flowing southeast to the Kobuk River near Kiana, this 53-mile river float rewards paddlers with a sampling of the geography and scenery characteristic of classic northwest Alaska. All but the upper reaches of the river are rated Class I. The river is under consideration for designation as a National Wild and Scenic River. Arctic grayling, northern pike, northern chum and pink salmon may be fished on the river.

USGS topographic maps: Baird Mountains A-3, A-4, A-5, B-5; Selawik D-3

Resources:
• *Alaska Atlas and Gazetteer*, published by DeLorme Mapping, P.O.

Box 298, Freeport, ME 04032; (207) 865-4171.

For more information: Contact the BLM Kobuk District Office, 1150 University Avenue, Fairbanks, AK 99709; (907) 474-2330.

KIGLUAIK MOUNTAINS

See letter D on map page 46

backpacking, cross-country skiing, dog mushing, mountaineering, snowmobiling

This mountain range is inviting because of its ruggedness and awesome beauty. Visitors will find all kinds of superb recreational opportunities, from fishing, hiking, backpacking, mountaineering and backcountry skiing to snowmobiling, dog mushing and photographing wildlife. There is evidence of early gold seekers, who entered this region at the turn of the century, throughout the spectacular and changing panorama of mountain passes and glacial valleys.

Activity Highlight: Fishing

Sport fishing for Arctic grayling and Dolly Varden is excellent in Canyon Creek as well as in the Sinuk, Grand Central and Cobblestone rivers. Chum and pink salmon may also be caught from early July to mid-August.

Activity Highlight: Hiking

There are no established trails within the mountain range, and the lack of trails is the main attraction to the area—travel is spectacular, rugged and remote. All travel by foot requires more than basic backcountry skills. Navigational skills are at a premium. Drinking water must be purified. Bear precautions are a must—no food should be kept in or around sleeping areas.

While backpacking or mountaineering, you may encounter private lands or private structures. The local residents use much of this range to make their living and it is imperative that their privacy is respected. There are a large number of cultural resources that may be discovered within the mountain range, including old cabins. Artifacts are protected from removal, excavation or vandalism by law. Take only pictures and help preserve our heritage.

One point of outstanding interest and relatively easy accessibility is the Mosquito Pass area. Hike in from Windy Creek to the Cobblestone River through Mosquito Pass to view spectacular side canyons, steep and sharp peaks and cirque lakes—and don't forget your camera!

During the summer, it is possible to hike into the area by exiting the Nome-Taylor Highway near the confluence of Hudson Creek and Nome River.

Location: Fifty miles north of Nome on the Seward Peninsula, 100 miles south of the Arctic Circle. Anchorage has daily jet service to Nome. From Nome, you can rent a car and drive to either the west or east end of the range. The Kougarok Road provides perhaps the most central access, with the Salmon Lake Campground serving as an ideal starting point. If you would like to arrange drop-off or pick-up by air charter, there are numerous landing sites within the range. If you are visiting in the winter, and many Alaskans prefer this option, travel is easiest by taking a snow machine out of Nome, offering access to areas that are usually inaccessible during the rest of the year.

Camping: The BLM administers one campground, the Salmon Lake Campground, located at the eastern end of the Kigluaik Mountains on Salmon Lake, near milepost 40 on the Kougarok Road. The city of Nome also maintains a public emergency shelter in the Sinuk River area. All other camping is primitive and is allowed anywhere within the mountain range.

Season: You can visit this area all year. The "summer" season runs from mid-June to mid-August, but temperatures may vary from 20°F to 80°F. Wind and rain are common. Winter temperatures in the minus 10°F to minus 20°F range are commonplace. Avalanches can be a major hazard in the winter and early spring months—do not travel in this region unless you know how to read the country for avalanche dangers.

USGS topographic maps: Nome D-1, D-2, D-3; Teller A-1, A-2, A-3; Bendeleben A-6; Solomon A-6

Resources:
• *The Alaska Wilderness Milepost*, published by Alaska Northwest Books, 22026 20th Avenue Southeast, Bothell, WA 98021; (800) 331-3510.
• *Alaska Atlas and Gazetteer*, published by DeLorme Mapping, P.O. Box 298, Freeport, ME 04032; (207) 865-4171.

For more information: Contact the BLM Kobuk District Office, 1150 University Avenue, Fairbanks, AK 99709; (907) 474-2330; or the BLM Nome Field Office, P.O. Box 952, Nome, AK 99762; (907) 443-2177.

UNALAKLEET RIVER

See letter E on map page 46

canoeing, fishing, rafting, wildlife observation

With crystal clear waters free of waterfalls or rapids, this six-day, 76-mile journey is an ideal family float along a very scenic river. Ideal wildlife viewing opportunities exist at various places along the river, although at times the vegetation is so dense that it obscures views of the surrounding countryside. Fishing is excellent for chinook, coho, chum and pink salmon. Arctic grayling and Arctic char may also be fished here. The only drawback is the possibility of encountering power boats on the lower reaches of the river. The only way to reach the put-in at the confluence with Tenmile Creek is by air taxi. Take-out is at Unalakleet.

USGS topographic maps: Norton Sound A-1, A-2; Unalakleet D-2, D-3, D-4

Resources:
• *Alaska Atlas and Gazetteer*, published by DeLorme Mapping, P.O. Box 298, Freeport, ME 04032; (207) 865-4171.

For more information: Contact the BLM Anchorage District Office, 6881 Abbott Loop Road, Anchorage, AK 99507; (907) 267-1246.

ALASKA—MAP B

DALTON HIGHWAY

See letter F on map page 48

backpacking, car camping, hiking, mountain biking, wildlife observation

A trip along the James Dalton Highway provides easy and ready access to some of the most remote and spectacular land in Alaska. Although this highway was constructed as a means of delivering construction materials to the oil fields at Prudhoe Bay, it is being increasingly used as a way to see the Alaska interior and Arctic without having to pay for costly "bush" charter flights.

With no stoplights or stop signs for 417 miles, the Dalton Highway is the only ribbon of gravel that crosses the Arctic Circle. While the highway itself is owned by the state, the land surrounding it is administered by the BLM up to mile 301, just north of Toolik Lake—a 2.7-million-acre corridor of expansive fields of fireweed, spruce forests, unbridged rivers (all the road crossings have bridges), and unnamed mountain passes through which untold numbers of caribou, wolves and grizzly, and a small herd of musk-ox roam.

An excellent base of operations from which to explore the region is the town of Coldfoot, the northernmost stop for food, gas, vehicle repair, lodging, telephone and postal service on the highway. At mile 175 in Coldfoot is a tri-agency visitor center operated by the BLM, the National Park Service and the U.S. Fish and Wildlife Service. The center houses interpretive displays and serves as an unofficial registration point for backpackers trekking into the surrounding backcountry.

Activity Highlight: Backpacking

There are numerous trail and river adventures to be enjoyed in the Coldfoot area. One such adventure, a three- to four-day backpack, begins at mile 197 on the Dalton Highway. Head up Gold Creek along an old mining trail through the northern boreal forest. Bob Johnson Lake, 13 miles away, is your ultimate destination. Pack a fishing rod as there are grayling, lake trout, northern pike and whitefish to be had. Broad valleys, carved by ice-age glaciers and punctuated by tundra, marshes and lakes are typical of the terrain along the way. Waterproof boots are recommended as sections of the trail wind through wet marshlands. Take the time to explore massive Sukakpak Mountain (4,459 feet), which towers 2,400 feet above the surrounding land. Two obvious routes lead up the mountain. This unusual limestone/marble peak is one of the major landmarks along the Dalton and offers stunning vistas of the nearby Brooks Range, Dietrich Valley and down the Middle Fork of the Koyukuk. The rocks underfoot have been estimated to be approximately 380 million years old and were created in an intertidal marine environment. The mountain's base is cluttered with large aprons of rock rubble created by boulders breaking loose from the 2,000-foot vertical west face during extreme freezing and thawing.

Remember that all of this land is grizzly country. Maintain a clean camp, cook and store food at least one-quarter of a mile away from your sleeping area, and use bear precautions throughout your trip.

Special note: Services are minimal along the highway. Always carry in your vehicle supplies such as extra fuel, food, tires and a CB radio to contact truckers with in case of emergency. Despite its recreation potential, the Dalton Highway is still considered an industrial highway. Drive with your headlights on at all times for safety and do not park on the road or block the gates on pipeline maintenance roads. Truck traffic is heavy at times and truckers are usually reluctant to slow down for private vehicles unless there is an emergency—travel with caution.

Location: Paralleling the Trans-Alaskan Pipeline from Livengood, the James Dalton Highway runs from just north of Fairbanks to the Arctic Ocean. The town of Coldfoot lies 258 miles from Fairbanks. From Fairbanks, drive north on Highway 2 (the Elliott Highway), to the intersection with James Dalton Highway. Gas up in Fairbanks and again at Yukon Crossing, a commercial development 139 miles north of Fairbanks on the north side of the river. Food and lodging are available here, and the BLM operates a visitor contact station throughout the summer.

Permits: No permits are necessary up to mile 211. Beyond mile 211, a road-use permit from the Alaska Department of Transportation is required for travel on the highway. For information, call (907) 451-2200. Signs on both sides of the road indicate the turnaround point.

Resources:
• *Alaska Atlas and Gazetteer*, published by DeLorme Mapping, P.O. Box 298, Freeport, ME 04032; (207) 865-4171.

For more information: Contact the BLM Arctic District Office, 1150 University Avenue, Fairbanks, AK 99709; (907) 474-2301.

BEAVER CREEK NATIONAL WILD RIVER

See letter G on map page 48

canoeing, kayaking, rafting

Rated a Class I waterway, this clearwater stream is a National Wild and Scenic River, originating within the White Mountain National Recreation Area and flowing north through Yukon Flats National Wildlife Refuge before dumping into the Yukon River. The headwaters may be accessed by vehicle from milepost 57.3 on the Steese Highway via U.S. Creek Road to Nome. The distance from the headwaters to Victoria Creek is 127 miles, and usually takes 8 to 10 days to raft. Float planes are able to fly in and out of Victoria Creek. From here to the next possible take-out, 268 miles away at the Yukon River Bridge on the Dalton Highway, allow an additional 8 to 14 days. Fishing in Beaver Creek is excellent for grayling, burbot, whitefish and northern pike.

USGS topographic maps: Circle B-6, C-6, D-5, D-6; Livengood B-1, B-2, C-1, C-2, D-1

Resources:
• *Alaska Atlas and Gazetteer*, published by DeLorme Mapping, P.O. Box 298, Freeport, ME 04032; (207) 865-4171.

For more information: Contact the BLM Steese/White Mountain District, 1150 University Avenue, Fairbanks, AK 99709; (907) 474-2350; or the BLM Fairbanks Support Center, 1541 Gaffney Road, Fairbanks, AK 99703; (907) 356-2025.

WHITE MOUNTAINS NATIONAL RECREATION AREA

See letter H on map page 48

backpacking, cross-country skiing, fishing, gold panning, hiking, snowmobiling, snowshoeing, wilderness float boating

Located between the Elliott and Steese highways approximately 30 miles north of Fairbanks, this one-million-acre recreation area features nearly 200 miles of winter recreation trails appropriate for snowshoeing, cross-country skiing or snowmobiling, and approximately 50 miles of trails dedicated to summer recreation use. Significant sections of Beaver Creek, a National Wild and Scenic River, may be enjoyed within the area. Of special interest is the opportunity to participate in recreational gold panning within the Nome Creek Valley—a historic, as well as an active, placer gold-mining site. From milepost 57.3 on the Steese Highway, follow U.S. Creek Road north for approximately six miles to the Nome Creek gold-panning site. There is one stream crossing that is appropriate for most vehicles with high clearance, but keep a sharp lookout for submerged rocks which are just waiting to relieve unwary drivers of miscellaneous car parts.

Be warned that gold panning is limited to only the four-mile designated area. Panning out of bounds may mean illegally encroaching on surrounding established mine claims—which is not something you want to do if you wish to depart the area with all your fingers and toes in working order. Gold panning is limited to hand tools and basic equipment including gold pans, picks, shovels and rocker boxes. The BLM reports that there is construction scheduled for 1996 to create a new access road, recreation sites and trails in the area.

Activity Highlight: Backcountry cabins

There are 10 recreational cabins available for rent through the BLM and one additional shelter cabin, the Wickersham Creek Trail Shelter, for which no fee is charged and no reservations are necessary. These cabins are primarily for winter recreation use, although several are open and usable year-round. Reservations are accepted by the BLM up to 30 days in advance with complete payment. You cannot stay in the cabins without a reservation. The fee is currently listed as $20 per night and the stay is limited to three consecutive nights. (Check with the BLM for current fees as they may change at any time.) Phone reservations are accepted, but payment must be received by the BLM within 48 hours or the reservation will be cancelled. Of course, this precludes most people in the lower 48 from making a phone-in reservation. A receipt is issued and must be carried with you as proof of reservation.

Cabins come completely outfitted with wood stoves, a Coleman lantern, a white-gas cookstove (bring your own gas), an ax, a bow saw and an outhouse. Garbage must be carried out. Cut firewood is available. Always restock the firewood for the next visitor. Dead or downed wood is the only wood legally foraged for a fire.

For reservations: By mail or in person, contact the BLM Land Information Office, 1150 University Avenue, Fairbanks, AK 99709; (907) 474-2250.

Cabin facts:

• Borealis-LeFevre Cabin (near the junction with Wickersham and Big Bend trails): sleeps five, boat access, trail access, good fishing. Accessible off float trips.

• Colorado Creek Cabin (located at mile 14 on the Colorado Creek Trail): sleeps five, trail access.

• Cripple Creek Cabin (summer-use cabin, off mile 60 on the Steese Highway): sleeps three, trail access, fishing.

• Cache Mountain Cabin (located at the end of the Trail Creek Trail): sleeps six to eight, not accessible during hunting season.

• Moose Creek Cabin (located near the junction of the Moose Creek and Trail Creek trails): sleeps six, trail access.

• Windy Gap Cabin (located at mile 22 on Lower Fossil Creek Trail): sleeps four, trail access, fishing.

• Wolf Run (located at mile 1.5 on the Windy Creek Trail): sleeps four, trail access.

• Wickersham Creek Trail Shelter (located near the junction of the Wickersham Creek and Moose Creek trails): sleeps two, trail access, no reservations or fee, winter use only.

• Crowberry Cabin (located on the Trail Creek Trail): sleeps four, trail access.

• Caribou Bluff Cabin (located on a side trail off Fossil Gap near the junction with the Fossil Creek Trail and a three-mile hike from Beaver Creek): sleeps four, trail access.

• Lee's Cabin (located seven miles down the Trail Creek Trail): sleeps six to eight.

• Fred Blixt Cabin (located at mile 62.5 on the Elliott Highway): summer and winter access.

Big Bend Trail: cross-country skiing, dog mushing, snowmobiling and snowshoeing (winter use only)

Located in the White Mountains National Recreation Area, the Big Bend Trail is 15 miles in length and begins at mile 14.5 on the Colorado Creek Trail. The trail is moderately difficult and ends at mile 19.5 on the Wickersham Creek Trail. Because of several wet and very muddy sections in the lowlands during the summer months, winter is perhaps the best time to navigate this trail. From the Colorado Creek Trail junction, head past the Colorado Creek Cabin and through a large, open meadow for three miles. After a steep one-mile climb to the top of a ridge, follow the ridgeline in a southerly direction for three miles (the highest elevation is 2,675 feet). Descend approximately three miles to a bridge crossing over Beaver Creek. Five more miles of wandering over relatively level terrain through meadows and black spruce forests will put you at the junction with the Wickersham Creek Trail.

USGS topographic map: Livengood B-2

Colorado Creek Trail: cross-country skiing, dog mushing, snowmobiling and snowshoeing (winter use only)

This 23-mile trail is located in the White Mountains National Recreation Area and is moderately difficult. Wet and muddy conditions in the lowlands can hinder summer travel at times. Winter is the best season to traverse the trail, although use caution as blowing snow in some areas can make navigation difficult. The trail begins at milepost 57 on the Elliott Highway (making this a major access point for the entire trail system) and climbs easily for approximately 14 miles to the top of the ridge. In the last three miles, the elevation gain becomes more pronounced. Approximately one-half mile beyond the ridge, the trail splits. The left trail leads towards Beaver Creek, nine miles away, and the right trail heads one-half mile to Colorado Creek Cabin. Bear left towards Beaver Creek where the trail will take you through old burn and then through spruce forests and open meadows, some of which offer superb views of the White Mountains. Once you reach Beaver Creek, continue for one-half mile until you reach a sign designating the Windy Creek Trail.

USGS topographic maps: Livengood B-2, B-3, C-2, C-3

Fossil Creek Trail: cross-country skiing, dog mushing, snowmobiling and snowshoeing (winter use only)

Recommended only for winter use since the trail crosses two frozen lakes, this 23-mile route is moderately difficult. Beginning at Beaver Creek and mile 20 of the Wickersham Creek Trail, winter travelers are advised to watch for open water and water overflow during the first seven miles—both creeks are crossed during this section. From mile 13 on, the trail parallels Fossil Creek to the trail's termination at the junction of the Windy Gap Cabin and the Windy Creek Trail.

USGS topographic maps: Livengood B-1, B-2, C-1

Moose Creek Trail: cross-country skiing, dog mushing, snowmobiling and snowshoeing (winter use only)

The best time to hike this relatively flat, 10-mile trail is in the winter, as sections can get wet and muddy during the summer. Beginning at mile 11.2 on the Wickersham Creek Trail, the Moose Creek Trail winds its way through spruce forest and open burn and meadow areas before funneling into mile 10 of the Trail Creek Trail. Moose Creek Cabin is located just beyond the trail junction and at the eastern part of the meadow.

USGS topographic maps: Livengood A-2, B-2

Cache Mountain Loop Trail: cross-country skiing, dog mushing, snowmobiling and snowshoeing (winter use only)

The Cache Mountain Loop Trail is most suitable for winter travel, as sections can get wet and muddy during the summer. Beginning at Beaver Creek, mile 20 of the Wickersham Creek Trail, the route heads northeast for approximately three miles through open areas and spruce forest. At O'Brien Creek, the trail heads north and parallels the creek for the next nine miles. O'Brien Creek Cabin is located at approximately mile 6; a tiny trapper cabin located at mile 12 may be used in emergency situations. Several miles past the trapper cabin, the trail bears left and climbs, at times steeply, up a drainage to a high alpine meadow 3.5 miles away. The trail ends at the junction with the Upper Fossil Creek Trail and the Cache Mountain Divide.

USGS topographic maps: Livengood B-1, C-1

Ski Loop Trail: cross-country skiing, dog mushing, hiking and snowshoeing

Because of its accessibility from the Elliott Highway, this trail is an ideal day-hiking or cross-country skiing destination. Beginning at milepost 27.8 on the Elliott Highway, the easy five-mile loop follows 1.5 miles of the Wickersham Creek Trail and approximately two miles of the Summit Trail. Views of the Alaska Range can be enjoyed when the weather is clear.

USGS topographic map: Livengood A-3

Summit Trail: backpacking, cross-country skiing, dog mushing, hiking and snowshoeing

Beginning at milepost 27.8 on the Elliott Highway, this is the only trail besides the Pinnell Mountain National Recreation Trail that is designed for summer use within the White Mountains National Recreation Area. A boardwalk has been installed over many of the wet and boggy areas to make hiking easier and to minimize the environmental impact of foot traffic. From the highway, the trail takes seven miles, heading up and over Wickersham Dome. After two miles of fairly level trail through spruce forest, the hiker covers four miles of steep up and down. The last seven miles are downhill, heading back to the highway. The last two miles are on the Wickersham Creek Trail, following a crossing of Beaver Creek that can be hazardous during high water. Borealis-LeFevre Cabin may be found on the north side of the creek.

USGS topographic maps: Livengood A-3, B-2, B-3

Trail Creek Trail: cross-country skiing, dog mushing, hiking, snow-mobiling and snowshoeing

Best used during the winter months since sections can get wet and muddy during the summer, this 27-mile trail begins at mile 6 of the Wickersham Creek Trail and follows a forested ridge for four miles. After climbing steadily, the trail joins up with the Moose Creek Trail and Moose Creek Cabin at mile 10. At approximately mile 12, the trail reaches its highest point, 2,387 feet. The final 15 miles descend, at times steeply, to Beaver Creek and the O'Brien Creek Trail. Use caution when crossing Beaver Creek as ice here is notoriously thin and hazardous. During the summer, there is decent hiking or off-high-way-vehicle access to Lee's Cabin.

USGS topographic maps: Livengood A-2, B-1, B-2

Wickersham Creek Trail: cross-country skiing, dog mushing, snowmobiling and snowshoeing (off-highway vehicles and hiking are suitable on the first five miles to Lee's Cabin)

Much of this trail is recommended for winter use only. The route begins at milepost 27.8 on the Elliott Highway and serves as a main artery of sorts, connecting many trails within the region. The Wicker-sham Creek Trail meets the Trail Creek Trail at mile 6, Moose Creek Trail at mile 11 and O'Brien Creek at mile 20, and serves as an access point for both the Summit and Ski Loop trails. The Wickersham Creek Trail Shelter is found at mile 11.2. This small, two-person cabin is the only one in the BLM cabin system that requires no reservations.

USGS topographic maps: Livengood A-2, A-3, B-2

Windy Creek Trail: cross-country skiing, dog mushing, snowmobiling and snowshoeing (winter use only)

This 10-mile trail, beginning at Beaver Creek and mile 23 on the Colorado Creek Trail and ending at Fossil Creek, is recommended for winter use only due to very wet conditions during the summer months. At mile 1.5, the trail meets the Wolf Run Cabin. From here, it parallels Windy Creek five miles up the valley through black spruce and open meadows. After a steep, two-mile climb, the trail breaks through Windy Gap and crests on a plateau overlooking the Fossil Creek drainage. Views of the White Mountains, Limestone Gulch and Windy Arch are superb. From the plateau, descend rapidly for one mile to Windy Gap Cabin and Fossil Creek.

USGS topographic maps: Livengood C-1, C-2

Resources:

• *Alaska Atlas and Gazetteer*, published by DeLorme Mapping, P.O. Box 298, Freeport, ME 04032; (207) 865-4171.

• Obtain the "White Mountains National Recreation Area Winter Trails and Cabins" brochure from the BLM Steese/White Mountain District Office.

For more information: Contact the BLM Steese/White Mountain District Office, 1150 University Avenue, Fairbanks, AK 99709; (907) 474-2350.

PINNELL MOUNTAIN NATIONAL RECREATION TRAIL

See letter I on map page 48

backcountry skiing, backpacking, mountaineering, hiking

The Pinnell Mountain National Recreation Trail offers high alpine-style backpacking along its 27.3 miles. In the early 1970s, it became the first National Recreation Trail established in the state.

You hike through sweeping vistas of surrounding mountains and a profusion of summer wildflowers. Moss campion, alpine azalea, frigid shooting star, Arctic forget-me-not and Lapland cassiope are some of the more common varieties you'll see. Dominant woody plants include dwarf birch, alpine bearberry and blueberry. Wolves, grizzly bears and wolverines occasionally may be spotted from the trail by those who keep a sharp lookout. Small herds of caribou are also sometimes seen. In addition to a wide variety of migratory birds, the rock and willow ptarmigan, gyrfalcon and raven are year-round residents.

Amateur geologists will thrill to the fact that some of the oldest rocks in the state may be viewed along the trail—formations made of sediments deposited over a billion years ago and then compressed into rock 500 million years ago.

Activity Highlight: Hiking

The Pinnell Mountain National Recreation Trail follows a somewhat serpentine route along mountain ridges and through high passes mostly above 3,500-foot elevations. Vantage points along the trail offer excellent views of the surrounding landscape including the White Mountains, Tanana Hills and the distant Alaska Range.

The trail is clearly marked with rock cairns and mile markers.

Plan on three days to navigate the trail's entire length. Bad weather may occur at any time and force you to wait out a storm, so some flexibility in scheduling is advised. Also, be aware that low clouds and fog can obscure the trail, making hiking difficult or dangerous. The trail itself is very steep and rugged, crossing talus slopes and alpine tundra—backpackers must be physically prepared!

Location: Approximately 85 miles northeast of Fairbanks off the Steese Highway. From Fairbanks, drive northeast on the Steese Highway. The road is paved to mile 42; the remainder of the road is gravel. Trailheads are located at Twelvemile Summit (milepost 85.6) or Eagle Summit (milepost 107.1). Parking is available at both trailheads. Register at the trailhead before entering and leaving the trail.

Camping: Camping is possible anywhere along the trail. There are two permanent emergency shelters spaced eight miles apart, each approximately 10 miles from their respective trailhead. There is no wood along the entire trail, so bring a backpacking stove. Winds are sometimes fierce, making a windscreen necessary. Be careful with matches and any open flame as tundra burns very easily. Overnight accommodations may be found in Fairbanks or at several campgrounds located along the Steese Highway. Contact the Alaska Public Lands Information Center in Fairbanks for current campground information at (907) 451-7352.

Season: June through September is the best time to visit, although the trail is accessible year-round. Temperatures vary from 20°F to 80°F with snow possible at any time. Since the ridge is exposed, wind can become a problem. Winter temperatures of minus 60°F to minus 70°F are not unusual. Although it is south of the Arctic Circle, the high elevation creates super opportunities to view the midnight sun for two weeks in June, usually towards the later part of the month, making this an especially popular time with hikers. June is also the month when many of the wildflowers are at their peak.

USGS topographic maps: Circle B-3, B-4, C-3, C-4

Resources:
•*The Alaska Wilderness Milepost*, published by Alaska Northwest Books, 22026 20th Avenue Southeast, Bothell, WA 98021; (800) 331-3510.
•*Alaska Atlas and Gazetteer*, published by DeLorme Mapping, P.O. Box 298, Freeport, ME 04032; (207) 865-4171.

•The BLM offers a free brochure about the Pinnell Mountain National Recreation Trail.

For more information: Contact the BLM Steese/White Mountain District Office, 1150 University Avenue, Fairbanks, AK 99708-3844; (907) 474-2350.

BIRCH CREEK NATIONAL WILD AND SCENIC RIVER

See letter J on map page 48

canoeing, kayaking, rafting

This National Wild and Scenic River originates nearly 94 miles northeast of Fairbanks and flows predominantly east and north to the Yukon River, most of the way within the Steese National Conservation Area. The river meanders through low, rolling hills with occasional cliffs and outcroppings of bedrock. Remnants of mining and trapping cabins add flavor to the float. Much of the waterway is rated Class I or II, although there are several Class III rapids just above the confluence with Wolf Creek which may be portaged. Access to the river at both ends is via the Steese Highway, with the put-in located near milepost 94 (there is a dirt road and parking area). The take-out is located at milepost 147.1 (Steese Highway Bridge). The boatable section of the river is approximately 126 miles long and takes between 7 and 10 days to traverse. Fishing is for grayling, northern pike and whitefish. A word of caution—there are several actively mined areas along the river's tributaries. These are private claims and trespassing is illegal. Stay on the main river and you will have no cause for concern.

USGS topographic maps: Circle A-3, A-4, B-1, B-2, B-3, B-4, C-1

Resources:

• *Alaska Atlas and Gazetteer*, published by DeLorme Mapping, P.O. Box 298, Freeport, ME 04032; (207) 865-4171.

For more information: Contact the BLM Steese/White Mountain District Office, 1150 University Avenue, Fairbanks, AK 99709; (907) 474-2350; or the BLM Fairbanks Support Center, 1541 Gaffney Road, Fairbanks, AK 99703; (907) 356-2025.

FORTYMILE NATIONAL WILD AND SCENIC RIVER

See letter K on map page 48

canoeing, kayaking, rafting

Located in east central Alaska, this National Wild and Scenic River is fed by numerous streams and drainages as it flows east, dumping into the Yukon River in Canada. Its 392 miles of waterway, including the main river and its numerous forks, comprise the longest nationally-designated river of its kind in the United States. The fall foliage is absolutely outstanding. Rapids vary from Class II to Class V. The region is a historically significant gold mining area with remnants of cabins and mines from the turn of the century visible along the riverbanks. Float trips, lasting from one day to 10 days, are available.

Activity Highlight: Float trips

There are many options available to the river runner, including trips that offer anywhere from Class I to Class V water. In general, the further downstream you head, the more difficult the rapids become. All are easily scouted on foot and can be portaged, if necessary. The river and its various forks follow a wonderful, yet utterly confusing, serpentine route through rugged and mountainous countryside. No signs mark rapids or portages, so it is vital that you carry adequate maps and a good compass; you must track and verify your position on the river at all times. Should an accident occur on the river, a cross-country trek may be necessary, although it is not really practical due to the rugged terrain. Most likely, if an accident occurs, you will be left waiting to float out with another trip, hopefully one heading down the river not too far behind you. Carry sufficient supplies and maps of the surrounding terrain. Those running the river in canoes or kayaks are advised to wear wet suits as the water is very cold and hypothermia is a real threat. For those planning on floating the Fortymile River to the Yukon River, you will need to check in with Canadian customs upon arrival in the town of Clinton in the Yukon Territories. Phone (403) 667-6471 for further information from the Whitehorse Customs Office. After reentry into the U.S. on the Yukon River, check in with U.S. customs at Eagle.

Location: Off the Taylor Highway, northeast of Anchorage and adjacent to the Alaska/Canada border. If you are contemplating a trip on the Fortymile River, you have many starting and stopping point options. A longer trip might involve an air-taxi service from Tok to the Joseph Airstrip in the Middle Fork drainage, followed by a 7- to 10-day float out to Eagle, while a shorter trip could be an afternoon float from Mosquito Fork Bridge to the South Fork Bridge. Whatever your fancy, access is the key to success, which means that you should get the new BLM brochure entitled "The Fortymile River: Access Points and Float Times."

Camping: You can camp anywhere along the river, but stay clear of active mining operations! Bear precautions are a must—cook and store food well away from sleeping areas. All drinking water must be treated for Giardia.

Season: High water can be expected from late May to mid-June. Generally, flows drop to low levels by September. However, the river level can fluctuate dramatically at any time, due to sudden storms, even those occurring far up the valley. Be prepared for high waters during any month. July and August are the best months to float the river if you desire calmer waters and a safer but slower river trip.

USGS topographic maps: Joseph to Fortymile Bridge: Eagle A-2, B-1, B-2, B-3, B-4, B-5; South Fork Bridge to Fortymile Bridge: Eagle A-2, B-1, B-2; Fortymile Bridge to Eagle: Eagle C-1, C-2

Canadian maps: Fortymile 116C/7, Cassiar 116C/8, Shell Creek 116C/9, Mount Gladman 116C/10; Mosquito Fork Bridge to South Fork Bridge: Eagle A-2; West Fork Campground to South Fork Bridge: Eagle A-2, Tanacross D-2, D-3; Walker Fork Campground to Fortymile Bridge: Eagle A-2, B-1, B-2

Resources:
•BLM brochures: "The Fortymile River: Rapids," "The Fortymile River: Access Points and Float Times," "The Taylor Highway: Tetlin Junction to Boundary, Eagle to Fort Egbert."
•*Alaska Atlas and Gazetteer*, published by DeLorme Mapping, P.O. Box 298, Freeport, ME 04032; (207) 865-4171.

For more information: *General information:* Contact the BLM Steese/White Mountain District Office, 1150 University Avenue, Fairbanks, AK 99709; (907) 474-2350. *Specific information:* Contact the BLM Tok Field Office, P.O. Box 309, Tok, AK 99780; (907) 883-5121. *River information (summer only):* Contact the BLM Chicken Field Station, Mile 68.2, Taylor Highway, Chicken, AK 99732. There is no phone number; drive in for river flow information.

DENALI HIGHWAY

See letter L on map page 48

car camping/day hiking combination, fishing, mountain biking, wildlife observation

Once the primary travel route to Denali National Park, the Denali Highway is now bypassed by many visitors. It's too bad, because the scenery along this route is outstanding! Grab your mountain bike and head on out. Generally open for access from mid-May to October 1, the Denali Highway is only paved for the first 21 miles west of Paxson and the Richardson Highway. The remaining 112 miles to Cantwell and the George Parks Highway are gravel. Vehicles traveling this route must be sure that they are carrying necessary spare parts and tires. Extra water and provisions are advised. (Beginning in 1995, the state will begin paving this route, which pleases some people and disturbs others. Personally, I like the gravel and think that paving will ruin the wild feel of the route. Still, the decision has been made and plans are to pave from milepost 21 to 42 this summer. It is entirely possible that, at some point in the next two to three years, the entire route will be covered with asphalt.)

There are five inns or roadhouses along the route offering services (food, lodging and sometimes gas) as well as two BLM-administered campgrounds. Primitive camping is allowed anywhere along the highway on BLM land. The highway offers superb opportunities to view wildlife, including caribou, moose, black and grizzly bear, ptarmigan, trumpeter swan and more. Fishing is best for lake trout and grayling. Salmon may be found, but only in the Gulkana River near Paxson. Bring your canoe along to enjoy floating opportunities on the Tangle Lakes, Upper Nenana, Delta and Gulkana rivers.

Resources:
• *Alaska Atlas and Gazetteer*, published by DeLorme Mapping, P.O. Box 298, Freeport, ME 04032; (207) 865-4171.

For more information: Contact the BLM Glennallen District Office, P.O. Box 147, Glennallen, AK 99588; (907) 822-3217.

DELTA RIVER

See letter M on map page 48

canoeing, fishing, kayaking, rafting, wildlife observation

Flowing north out of Tangle Lakes, the Delta River, a National Wild and Scenic River, is a clear and silt-free waterway until its confluence with Eureka Creek. At the creek, the Delta River mixes with cold, silty glacial runoff and is filled with debris. The first 35 miles of the river, from Tangle Lake Campground to the Richardson Highway, are rated from Class I to II. From the highway to Black Rapids, a distance of 17 miles, the river is rated Class III. You cross one of the longest fault zones in the state of Alaska, the Denali Fault, during a mandatory portage located two miles after the last lake. Beware of rocks during the several miles following reentry to the river after the portage, as the river annually claims a number of canoes. It's a long trek out on foot. If you wish to boat this river, it is essential that you have prior whitewater experience.

If it is a river float you seek, then rafts are the perfect choice. For a little more excitement and involvement with the river, canoes and kayaks are recommended.

Fish in season for lake trout, Arctic grayling, whitefish and burbot. Wildlife viewing includes moose, brown and black bear, Dall sheep, caribou, beaver, muskrat, golden eagle, bald eagle and a multitude of waterfowl.

USGS topographic maps: Mount Hayes A-4, B-4, C-4

Resources:
Alaska Atlas and Gazetteer, published by DeLorme Mapping, P.O. Box 298, Freeport, ME 04032; (207) 865-4171.

For more information: Contact the BLM Glennallen District Office, P.O. Box 147, Glennallen, AK 99588; (907) 822-3217.

TANGLE LAKES ARCHAEOLOGICAL DISTRICT

See letter N on map page 48

camping, canoeing, fishing, hiking, historic sites, hunting, kayaking, mountain biking, off-highway-vehicle use, rafting, wildlife observation

Tangle Lakes has a rich archaeological history. Studies have documented more than 400 archaeological sites in the area, indicating that ancient peoples inhabited this area over 10,000 years ago. Damaging any artifacts or sites, or removing artifacts from sites, is prohibited by law. This subarctic region features a rich natural diversity as well, with visitors likely to spot grizzly bear, caribou, moose, wolf, coyote, ptarmigan and fox. At any time of the year, be prepared for all types of weather which can sweep in over the glaciers, lakes and tundra without warning. With low brush and relatively open terrain, Tangle Lakes is an area ideally suited for cross-country exploration. Cross-country travel should never be attempted without adequate navigational skills. There are at least eight side roads and trails in the immediate area that are suitable for mountain biking and hiking.

Activity Highlight: Hiking

There are several super hiking and backpacking trails in the area—inquire at the BLM office for details. The Maclaren River Road Trail begins and ends at milepost 43.5 on the Denali Highway. The trail is in good condition and runs approximately 12 miles each way from the highway to the Maclaren Glacier and back. There is a potentially deep ford of the West Fork of the Maclaren River at the four-mile mark. The river is a glacial stream that can force a very cold, waist-deep crossing, depending on the time of year. After the crossing, the trail continues for five miles before petering out through one-half mile of willow thicket. Watch out for grizzlies! Following the willow thicket, the trail returns to a good condition for the remaining three miles to the glacier. Return the way you came.

Activity Highlight: Mountain biking

There are several ideal mountain bike trails in the area—inquire at the BLM office for details. The Landmark Gap Trail North begins and ends at milepost 24.6 on the Denali Highway. The trail is rocky and there are a couple of deep mud holes. The route follows a two-mile-long path that will take you to Landmark Gap Lake. Please bike on the trail at all times. The surrounding hills—should you wish to get off your bike and explore—are excellent places from which you may be able to spot moose, caribou, grizzly, wolf and ptarmigan.

Location: Approximately 21 miles west of Paxson, between mileposts 17 and 38 along the Denali Highway. From Anchorage, take Highway 1 to Wasilla, then take Highway 3 North towards Fairbanks. Turn right onto Highway 8 (the Denali Highway). For an alternate route, you can take Highway 1 from Anchorage to Highway 45. Head north toward Fairbanks and after approximately 71 miles turn left onto

Highway 8 (the Denali Highway).

Camping: There is one BLM campground, Tangle Lake Campground, and one BLM wayside, Tangle River Wayside, in the area. Both have water and toilet facilities. There is no camping fee, but stays are limited to 14 days. Both of these areas make an excellent base of operations from which to enjoy a rich mountain biking or hiking experience. Wood is scarce along the river, so bring in your own or use a backpacking stove.

Season: Mid-May to mid-September is the best time to visit. All roads and trails in the area are open to off-highway-vehicle travel, but visitors should find relative solitude and little traffic, except during hunting season, which begins in mid-August. All off-highway-vehicle travel must stay on designated roads and trails within the Tangle Lakes Archaeological District. Expect the summer weather to be cool, moist and often overcast. Once October arrives, snow and bitter cold make this an unattractive area to casual visitors.

Permits: No permits are necessary, unless you are a commercial outfit.

USGS topographic maps: Mount Hayes A-4, A-5

Resources:
• *Alaska's Parklands, The Complete Guide,* by Nancy Lange Simmerman, published by The Mountaineers, Seattle, WA; (800) 553-4453.
• *The Alaska Wilderness Milepost,* Alaska Northwest Books, 22026 20th Avenue Southeast, Bothell, WA 98021; (800) 331-3510.
• *Alaska Atlas and Gazetteer,* published by DeLorme Mapping, P.O. Box 298, Freeport, ME 04032; (207) 865-4171.

For more information: Contact the BLM Glennallen District Office, P.O. Box 147, Glennallen, AK 99588; (907) 822-3217.

GULKANA RIVER

See letter O on map page 48

canoeing, fishing, kayaking, rafting, wildlife observation
This nationally designated Wild and Scenic River offers several outstanding trip options with excellent wildlife viewing. Beginning at the Denali Highway in the Tangle Lakes area, the route heads south for nine miles by paddle and portage through the Tangle Lakes Canoe Trail. The Middle Fork of the Gulkana flows out of Dickey Lake, and

while the first several miles are runnable, it is not recommended that you attempt them as they are extremely shallow and negotiating them is time consuming and difficult. Following the shallows, there are approximately three miles of swift, shallow and very rocky water that are not recommended for floating. Watch out for the rougher section between Swede Lake and Hungry Hollow Creek. The section ends by dropping steeply through a narrow rock canyon which requires careful and skillful lining. Most boaters prefer to begin their trip at Paxson Lake and float the main section of the Gulkana down to Sourdough Campground. That run is 50 miles and requires approximately three to four days of travel.

Once you're on the main Gulkana, you'll find that the river meanders, churning its way through sweepers and logjams in some sections and quiet floats in others.

There is one Class III to IV section named Canyon Rapids that should be run by experienced boaters only. There is a sign that marks a quarter-mile portage around the rapids if needed. Just after the portage, there is a trail on the left bank that leads to Canyon Lake, one mile away. Superb grayling fishing may be enjoyed here. From Canyon Rapids, the river drops in intensity to Class II for eight miles and then to Class I for the remainder of the trip.

Canoes, kayaks and rafts are ideal on this river, although crossing the nine miles of the Tangle Lakes Canoe Trail with rafts on the first day will be arduous at best. For a more remote journey, float the West Fork of the Gulkana which puts in at Lake Louise and continues through Susitna Lake and the Tyone River. The entire route travels through lake-dotted country that is ideal wildlife viewing habitat. There are a number of portages that can be difficult. The West Fork is one of the most remote and least-visited areas of the Gulkana watershed. The entire West Fork is a 110-mile adventure that takes approximately 8 to 10 days to complete. Canoes are recommended for this particular section.

Fish in season for rainbow trout, whitefish, Arctic grayling, red and king salmon, lake trout and burbot.

Wildlife viewing includes moose, brown and black bear, wolf, fox, caribou, muskrat, beaver, golden eagle, bald eagle, a variety of hawk and a multitude of waterfowl.

USGS topographic maps: Mount Hayes A-5; Gulkana B-3, B-4, C-4, D-4, D-5

Resources:

• *Alaska Atlas and Gazetteer*, published by DeLorme Mapping, P.O. Box 298, Freeport, ME 04032; (207) 865-4171.

For more information: Contact the BLM Glennallen District Office, P.O. Box 147, Glennallen, AK 99588; (907) 822-3217.

BLM Campgrounds

1. Salmon Lake Campground—Map A

Campsites, facilities: There are six sites, all with picnic tables and fire rings. There is **no water** available. The pit toilets are wheelchair-accessible. There is a 14-day stay limit.

Fee: There is no fee.

Who to contact: Kobuk District Office, 1150 University Avenue, Fairbanks, AK 99709; (907) 474-2330.

Location: In Kigluaik Mountains, at milepost 40 on the Nome-Taylor Highway.

Season: June to October, depending on snow.

2. Marion Creek Campground—Map B

Campsites, facilities: There are 27 sites, all with picnic tables and fire rings. Water is available. Pit toilets are available. There is a 14-day stay limit.

Fee: In the near future, the BLM will charge a fee, but the amount was not known at press time.

Who to contact: Arctic District Office, 1150 University Avenue, Fairbanks, AK 99709; (907) 474-2300.

Location: Approximately five miles north of Coldfoot on the Dalton Highway, located at milepost 180.

Season: June to early September.

3. Cripple Creek Campground—Map B

Campsites, facilities: There are 21 sites, six for tents only, all with fire rings and picnic tables. Water is available. Pit toilets are available. RVs over 20 feet are not allowed. No pets are allowed. There is a seven-day stay limit.

Fee: There is no fee.

Who to contact: Steese/White Mountain District Office, 1150 University Avenue, Fairbanks, AK 99709; (907) 474-2350.

Location: Northeast of Fairbanks near milepost 60.5 on the Steese Highway. The elevation is approximately 700 feet.

Season: June to November.

4. Eagle Campground—Map B

Campsites, facilities: There are 16 sites, all with picnic tables and fire rings. There is a spring water supply available. Pit toilets are available. There is a 10-day stay limit.

Fee: There is no fee.

Who to contact: Steese/White Mountain District Office, 1150 University Avenue, Fairbanks, AK 99709; (907) 474-2350.

Location: Near the town of Eagle, overlooking the historic U.S. Army Fort Egbert on the Yukon River, approximately one mile west of milepost 160.3 on the Taylor Highway. The campsite elevation is approximately 820 feet.

Season: May to September.

5. Walker Fork Campground—Map B

Campsites, facilities: There are 20 sites, all with picnic tables and fire rings. Pit toilets and water are available. There is a 10-day stay limit.

Fee: There is no fee.

Who to contact: Steese/White Mountain District Office, 1150 University Avenue, Fairbanks, AK 99709; (907) 474-2350.

Location: Approximately 14 miles north of Chicken, near milepost 82 on the Taylor Highway and on the banks of Fortymile National Wild and Scenic River.

Season: May 15 to September 30.

6. West Fork Campground—Map B

Campsites, facilities: There are 25 sites, all with picnic tables and fire rings. The pit toilets are wheelchair-accessible. There is **no water** available. There is a 10-day stay limit.

Fee: There is no fee.

Who to contact: Steese/White Mountain District Office, 1150 University Avenue, Fairbanks, AK 99709; (907) 474-2350.

Location: Approximately 19 miles south of Chicken, near milepost 49 on the Taylor Highway and on the banks of Fortymile National Wild and Scenic River.

Season: May 15 to September 30.

7. BRUSHKANA CAMPGROUND—MAP B

Campsites, facilities: There are 17 sites, all with tables and fire rings. Pit toilets are available. Water is available. You should bear-proof your campsite as grizzly frequent the area. There is a seven-day stay limit.

Fee: There is no fee.

Who to contact: Glennallen District Office, P.O. Box 147, Glennallen, AK 99588; (907) 822-3217.

Location: At milepost 104.3 on the Denali Highway, approximately 30 miles east of the town of Cantwell. The campsite elevation is approximately 2,600 feet.

Season: Officially, June to October depending on snowfall. You are allowed to camp here at any other time of the year, but the campground will be dry. Hunters often crowd the campground from mid-August to mid-September.

8. TANGLE LAKE WAYSIDE—MAP B

Campsites, facilities: There are 27 sites, all with tables and fire rings. Pit toilets and a boat ramp are available. Water is available. There is a seven-day stay limit.

Fee: There is no fee.

Who to contact: Glennallen District Office, P.O. Box 147, Glennallen, AK 99588; (907) 822-3217.

Location: Approximately 22 miles west of Paxson on the Denali Highway at milepost 21.5. The campsite elevation is approximately 3,000 feet.

Season: June to September, depending on snow.

9. TANGLE RIVER CAMPGROUND—MAP B

Campsites, facilities: There are seven sites, all with picnic tables and fire rings. Water is available. There is a boat ramp on the banks of the Tangle River. There is a seven-day stay limit.

Fee: There is no fee.

Who to contact: Glennallen District Office, P.O. Box 147, Glennallen, AK 99588; (907) 822-3217.

Location: Approximately 22 miles west of Paxson on the Denali Highway at milepost 21.5. The campsite elevation is approximately 3,000 feet.

Season: June to October, depending on snow.

10. PAXSON LAKE CAMPGROUND—MAP B

Campsites, facilities: There are 40 sites, all with picnic tables and fire rings. An RV dump station, water and wheelchair-accessible pit toilets are available. There is also a boat ramp and a wheelchair-accessible fishing pier. There is a seven-day stay limit.

Fee: There is $6 fee per night; pay on site.

Who to contact: Glennallen District Office, P.O. Box 147, Glennallen, AK 99588; (907) 822-3217.

Location: South of Paxson on the Richardson Highway near milepost 175.

Season: June to October.

11. SOURDOUGH CAMPGROUND—MAP B

Campsites, facilities: There are 42 sites, all with picnic tables and fire rings. There is water available. Pit toilets are available. There is also a boat ramp for access to the Gulkana River. There is a 14-day stay limit.

Fee: There is a $6 fee per night; pay on site.

Who to contact: Glennallen District Office, P.O. Box 147, Glennallen, AK 99588; (907) 822-3217.

Location: On the Gulkana River near the village of Sourdough, approximately 20 miles north of Gulkana off of the Richardson Highway. A very visible sign indicates the turnoff.

Season: Officially, May 15 to October 1, depending on snow. You are allowed to camp here off-season.

STATE INFORMATION OVERVIEW

ALASKA STATE OFFICE
222 West Seventh Avenue #13, Anchorage, AK 99513; (907) 271-5960

ANCHORAGE DISTRICT OFFICE
6881 Abbott Loop Road, Anchorage, AK 99507; (907) 267-1246

ARCTIC DISTRICT OFFICE
1150 University Avenue, Fairbanks, AK 99709; (907) 474-2300

GLENNALLEN DISTRICT OFFICE
P.O. Box 147, Glennallen, AK 99588; (907) 822-3217

KOBUK DISTRICT OFFICE
1150 University Avenue, Fairbanks, AK 99709; (907) 474-2330

Kotzebue Field Station, P.O. Box 1049, Kotzebue, AK 99752; (907) 442-3430

Nome Field Station, P.O. Box 952, Nome, AK 99762; (907) 443-2177

STEESE/WHITE MOUNTAIN DISTRICT OFFICE
1150 University Avenue, Fairbanks, AK 99709; (907) 474-2350

Steese National Conservation Area, 1150 University Avenue, Fairbanks, AK 99709; (907) 474-2352

White Mountains National Recreation Area, 1150 University Avenue, Fairbanks, AK 99709; (907) 474-2350

Tok Field Station, P.O. Box 309, Tok, AK 99780; (907) 883-5121

Fort Egbert/Eagle Historic District, P.O. Box 309, Tok, AK 99780; (907) 883-5121 (near Eagle—open seasonally)

ARIZONA

Maps—pp. 80, 82

(SEE MAP A)   **(SEE MAP B)**

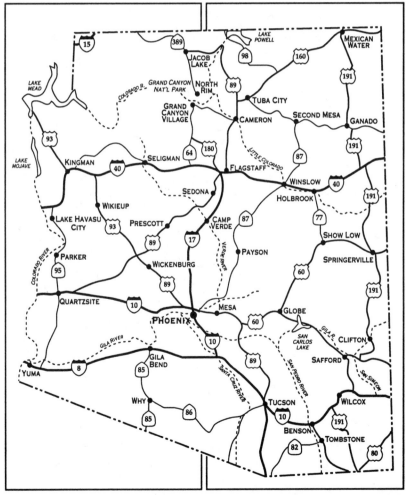

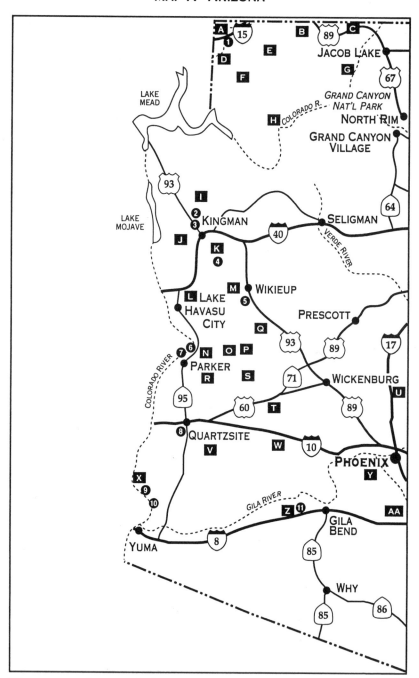

MAP REFERENCES

BLM CAMPGROUNDS

MAP B—ARIZONA

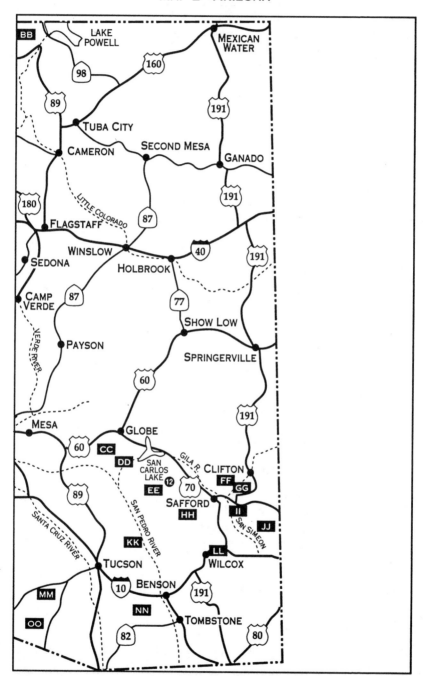

MAP REFERENCES

BLM CAMPGROUNDS

ARIZONA—MAP A

BEAVER DAM MOUNTAINS WILDERNESS AREA

See letter A on map page 80

backpacking, camping, hiking, wildlife observation

Located just north of Interstate 15, this wilderness area is wonderfully rugged and encompasses the alluvial plains and mountains of far northwestern Arizona and parts of Utah. Desert bighorn sheep, desert tortoise, numerous species of raptors and an endangered fish—the woundfin minnow—may be found here. There are no trails. All hiking and exploration is cross-country. Hikers must be extremely proficient at reading a map and compass. Of special note is the pretty Joshua tree forest in the lower elevations.

USGS topographic map: Littlefield

BLM surface map: Littlefield

For more information: Contact the BLM Shivwits Resource Area, 225 North Bluff Street, St. George, UT 84770; (801) 628-4491.

THE DUTCHMAN TRAIL FOR MOUNTAIN BIKES

See letter B on map page 80

cultural site, mountain biking

The Dutchman Trail winds its way through the engaging scenery of the Mojave Desert. The nine-mile loop trail is suitable for all levels of bikers with gradual slopes and generally a hard-pack surface of clay and gravel. The entire ride takes approximately two to three hours to enjoy. Since the trail surface is clay, it becomes somewhat sticky and not really conducive to biking when wet—can you say "bike hiking"?! The best seasons to enjoy the trail are fall, winter and spring. Summer is too blazing hot—melted lycra is not a pretty sight.

The trail is clearly delineated by bicycle trail markers. A great little side jaunt is a one-half mile pedal to the west to the Little Black Mountain Petroglyph Site. You must leave your bikes parked outside of the fenced area. This site is an outstanding showcase of ancient petroglyphs (rock carvings) created by Native Americans thousands of years ago. No permits are needed. This is a day-use only site—no overnight camping allowed.

Location: The trailhead is located southeast of St. George, Utah. Take Sunshine Trail Road approximately 10 miles to the parking area just south of the Arizona state line. The trail starts on the road heading west along the fence.

For more information: Contact the BLM Arizona Strip District Office, 390 North 3050 East, St. George, UT 84770; (801) 673-3545.

COTTONWOOD POINT WILDERNESS

See letter C on map page 80

backpacking, hiking, nature observation

Access is very difficult, but this convoluted plateau is worth a peek—check in with the BLM office for updated access information. It's located east of Colorado City on the Arizona/Utah border—consult the BLM office for directions. Many say that the rugged scenery is very much like a miniature Zion National Park. Indeed, the high cliffs and plateau, dissected by deep and narrow canyons with dense riparian vegetation, does remind one of Zion in some respects. Visit any time of year.

USGS topographic maps: Colorado City, Hildale, Moccasin

For more information: Contact the BLM Vermilion Resource Area, 225 North Bluff Street, St. George, UT 84770; (801) 628-4491.

VIRGIN RIVER CANYON RECREATION AREA

See letter D on map page 80

backpacking, camping, hiking, picnicking, wildlife observation

BLM insiders say that the Virgin River Gorge is one of the "most spectacular river canyons in the southwest, bar none." Located just off Interstate 15 and northeast of US 91, the Virgin River Gorge lies within the Virgin River Canyon Recreation Area, created in 1973. From the Virgin River Campground, you can access the Virgin River Interpretive Trail. This hike is one-quarter mile each way, and is an excellent way to get acquainted with the natural surroundings, geology and history of the Virgin River Gorge, as well as familiarize yourself with the area's native plant life. Signs along the way give the common names of plants native to the area. This trail is wheelchair accessible, but some assistance is required. Backpacking trips into the

Paiute Wilderness, south of the gorge, are also possible from here.

USGS topographic maps: Mountain Sheep Spring, Purgatory Canyon

For more information: Contact the BLM Shivwits Resource Area, 225 North Bluff Street, St. George, UT 84770; (801) 628-4491.

PAIUTE WILDERNESS

See letter E on map page 80

backpacking, camping, hiking, horseback riding, wildlife observation
Within this 55-square-mile wilderness, there is an immense variety of wildlife. Visitors typically see lizards, desert tortoise, chuckwallas, Gila monsters, chipmunks, blacktail jackrabbits, mountain lion and mule deer. The rugged nature of the area is its primary attraction, inviting challenge and solitude.

Activity Highlight: Backpacking
The Virgin Ridge Loop Trail is the best developed hike in the area with adequate trailhead parking. The eight-mile trail is very steep and rugged, requiring that hikers be in excellent physical condition and wearing very sturdy boots. A good working knowledge of a compass and topographic map-reading skills are essential. Carry at least two quarts of water in reserve; one gallon per person is best. The trail takes you up into a ponderosa forest on a ridge, more than a mile above the Mojave Desert to the west. The views are spectacular. Three miles from the trailhead, a second trail plunges down off the ridge through manzanita-covered slopes to Atkin Spring. With a short hike from Atkin Spring, visitors can wander among limestone cliffs and into a natural gateway to Sullivans Canyon. This canyon contains wild natural ecosystems ranging from the Mojave Desert to pinyon-juniper forests to ponderosa pine and Douglas fir stands.

Just north of the Paiute Wilderness, in the Virgin River Canyon Recreation Area and near the Virgin River Campground, is the Virgin River Interpretive Trail, which is an excellent way to acquaint yourself with the area's native plant life. (See the listing on page 85 of this chapter for more information.)

Location: In the northwestern corner of Arizona near the Utah and Nevada borders. The parking area and trailhead are near Cougar Spring. From St. George, Utah, take Quail Hill Road to Wolfhole Valley. From there, follow Black Rock Mountain Road to the junction with Elbow Canyon. Bear right on Elbow Canyon to Cougar

Spring. Undeveloped vehicle parking is located approximately one-half mile north of Cougar Spring at the trailhead.

Camping: There are no developed camping areas within the Paiute Wilderness, however the Virgin River Campground, located in the spectacular Virgin River Gorge, is a super base camp for both the Paiute Wilderness and the Beaver Dam Wilderness. To get there, drive 20 miles southwest of St. George, Utah or 16 miles north of Littlefield, Arizona on Interstate 15. The campground is located near the Cedar Pockets interchange. There is a fee charged for overnight camping. The campground is open year-round and facilities include 115 camping sites, flush toilets, drinking water, picnic areas and RV sites. No showers are available at this campground.

Season: Fall to spring is the best time of year to visit here.

USGS topographic maps: Littlefield, Mountain Sheep Spring

BLM surface map: Littlefield

Additional maps: A visitor map is available from the BLM Arizona Strip District Office.

Resources:
• *Arizona Traveler's Handbook,* by Bill Weir, published by Moon Publications, 722 Wall Street, Chico, CA 95928; (916) 345-5473.
• A brochure entitled "Paiute and Beaver Dam Mountains wilderness areas" is available from the BLM.

For more information: Contact the BLM Shivwits Resource Area, 225 North Bluff Street, St. George, UT 84770; (801) 628-4491; or the BLM Arizona Strip District Office, 390 North 3050 East, St. George, UT 84770; (801) 673-3545.

GRAND WASH CLIFFS WILDERNESS
See letter F on map page 80

backpacking, camping, hiking, horseback riding, wildlife observation
Located approximately 15 miles northeast of Grand Wash Bay on Lake Mead and 15 miles east of the Arizona/Nevada border, the 36,300-acre Grand Wash Cliffs Wilderness is relatively accessible by seasonal service roads. Check with the BLM office to determine the best access route at your time of visit. The cliffs are like giant 1,000-foot steps up to the Shivwits Plateau area. A number of picturesque canyons cut through the cliffs, providing interesting scrambling op-

portunities. Though no formal hiking trails exist, it is relatively easy to get to the top of the cliffs from the north. Bighorn sheep, Gila monsters, desert tortoise and the occasional mountain lion may be spotted in the area. Fall, winter and spring are the best times to visit.

USGS topographic maps: Cane Springs Southeast, St. George Canyon, Olaf Knolls, Last Chance Canyon, Grand Gulch Bench

For more information: Contact the BLM Shivwits Resource Area, 225 North Bluff Street, St. George, UT 84770; (801) 628-4491.

KANAB CREEK WILDERNESS
See letter G on map page 80

backpacking, canyoneering

Running south from the town of Fredonia, Kanab Creek crosses the Kaibab Indian Reservation, cuts deeper into the plateau as it crosses BLM lands, winds for about 10 miles through the bottom of a canyon in Kaibab National Forest and finally ends up dumping into the Colorado River in Grand Canyon National Park. While it is possible to backpack down Kanab Creek to the Grand Canyon—and then out via any number of alternate routes—the backpacking is very strenuous and should not be taken lightly. Fall is the best time to head out. Check with the BLM office for specific access and backpacking information.

USGS topographic maps: Heaton Knolls, Jumpup Canyon, Kanab Point

For more information: Contact the BLM Vermilion Resource Area, 225 North Bluff Street, St. George, UT 84770; (801) 628-4491.

MOUNT TRUMBULL WILDERNESS AND MOUNT LOGAN WILDERNESS
See letter H on map page 80

backpacking, camping, wildlife observation

With an elevation of 8,028 feet, Mount Trumbull is the highest point for miles around. Nearby Mount Logan (hard to find on maps) sits slightly lower at 7,966 feet. Virgin timber and ponderosa pine cover the upper reaches of Mount Trumbull. Slopes are steep and rocky, an ideal habitat for the pinyon and juniper that cling to them. In addition to the usual high-desert rodent population (mice, gophers, chipmunks, jackrabbits and such), the wilderness areas support porcupine, coyote, spotted skunk, mountain lion, bobcat and mule deer. On the west slope of Mount Logan, the Hells Hole, a giant rock amphitheater, provides a curious and colorful attraction.

Activity Highlight: Hiking

The Mount Trumbull Trail, 2.5 miles each way, is a good introduction to the area. To get to the trailhead, take the Toroweap Road (County Road 109) that branches off Highway 389, eight miles west of Fredonia. Follow the dirt road about 46 miles to County Road 5, which intersects it at a major fork. Bear right, heading west toward Mount Trumbull. After approximately six miles, you will reach an area known as Nixon Flat. A sign marks the trailhead. The trail ends atop the basalt cap about one mile from the summit, but don't attempt to access the summit unless you have strong map-reading and compass skills. Follow the northern edge of the basalt flow.

USGS topographic maps: Mount Trumbull Northwest, Mount Trumbull Northeast

BLM surface map: Mount Trumbull

Additional maps: A visitor map is available from the BLM Arizona Strip District Office.

For more information: Contact the BLM Vermilion Resource Area, 225 North Bluff, St. George, UT 84770; (801) 628-4491; or the BLM Arizona Strip District Office, 390 North 3050 East, St. George, UT 84770; (801) 673-3545.

MOUNT TIPTON WILDERNESS

See letter I on map page 80

backpacking, camping, hiking, mountain biking, rockhounding, wildlife observation

Part of the Cerbat Mountain Range, 7,148-foot Mount Tipton affords the visitor superb views of the surrounding peaks and ridges. It is located north of Kingman off US 93. Unpaved Big Wash Road is the main access into the Cerbat Range.

The BLM maintains the Packsaddle Campground and Windy Point Campground, which are open from May 1 to November 1; both sites serve as an excellent base from which to explore the wilderness. From Kingman, travel 23 miles northwest on Highway 93. Turn right on the BLM's dirt Chloride/Big Wash Road and drive nine miles to the Packsaddle Campground or 11 miles to the Windy Point Campground. There is no water, so bring your own. Facilities include seven tent sites (10 sites at Windy Point), vault toilets, fire grills and picnic areas. No fee is charged.

Mountain bikes are permitted on old mining roads and on trails outside of the designated wilderness area—use caution as off-highway vehicles use these trails, too.

There are hundreds of old mines in the area, which the BLM states are "ripe for exploration." As with any old site exploration, do it strictly at your own risk (there are extreme hazards possible when entering an old mine). The sites are protected—don't even think of removing artifacts.

Spectacular views of the nearby ridges may be enjoyed from the campgrounds. The shallow valleys and bowls and pinyon-laden slopes provide good habitat for kit fox, bobcat and mule deer. If you like to observe raptors, this is a good site for it. Numerous hawks and other raptors often play the thermals during the day.

USGS topographic maps: Dolan Springs, Mount Tipton, Mount Tipton 3 Southeast, Grasshopper Junction

For more information: Contact the BLM Kingman Resource Area, 2475 Beverly Avenue, Kingman, AZ 86401; (602) 757-3161.

BLACK MOUNTAINS

See letter J on map page 80

backpacking, camping, hiking, horseback riding, wildlife observation

This is a little-visited area, yet it is undeservedly ignored. It's located just west of Kingman and bordered by the Colorado River, Interstate 40 and US 93. Formed by volcanic flows, the mountains and canyons are rugged and steep, with seasonal springs that flow well into April during wet years. The best time to visit is between January and April. There are three wilderness areas within the Black Mountains: Mount Nutt, Warm Springs and Mount Wilson. Juniper, yucca, catclaw, creosote, and in riparian areas, willow, nettle (ouch!) and watercress are the most common plants. Besides the assortment of bats, reptiles and rodents, wildlife residents include coyote, gray fox, badger, spotted skunk, bobcat, bighorn sheep and mule deer. Camping is allowed anywhere. A number of unmaintained and unsigned roadways provide super access for informal base camps from which you can day-hike. There are no maintained trails. Travel is cross-country. Good map-reading skills are essential.

USGS topographic maps: Union Pass, Secret Pass, Oatman, Mount Nutt, Kingman Southwest, Boundary Cone, Warm Springs, Yucca Northwest, Warm Springs Southwest, Warm Springs Southeast, Yucca

For more information: Contact the BLM Kingman Resource Area, 2475 Beverly Avenue, Kingman, AZ 86401; (602) 757-3161.

WABAYUMA PEAK

See letter K on map page 80

backpacking, camping, hiking, horseback riding, mountain biking

Tucked into the Hualapai Mountains, approximately 30 miles southeast of Kingman and east of Interstate 40, lies Wabayuma Peak, a relatively large roadless area recovering from past abuse by cattle ranchers and mining interests. Many of the old road tracks are still evident, although they are growing over with vegetation. It can get a bit confusing in here, unless you are proficient with a compass and topographic map.

Wabayuma Peak is 7,601 feet high, making it appropriate for recreational use year-round, even when the temperatures in the lower elevations are downright hot and miserable. There are quite a number of springs, and most were used in the past for cattle. Be sure to purify all water. Despite the springs, it is recommended that you carry a day's supply of water with you at all times.

Hiking can be strenuous on the steep slopes of the peak and surrounding range. There are many roads in the Hualapai available for mountain biking, but no mountain biking is allowed in the Wabayuma Peak Wilderness Area—or in any other wilderness area, for that matter. Wildflowers are spectacular during the late spring and early summer.

The BLM recommends hiking the Wabayuma Peak Trail, which is three miles each way. The difficulty of the trail is rated as moderate. At times, the trail may become hard to follow—take your time.

Camping is available at Wild Cow Springs Campground, open from May 1 to November 1. A fee is charged for camping. To get there, take Hualapai Mountain Road out of Kingman. After passing through Hualapai Mountain County Park, turn right onto the dirt road marked with signs for Flag Mine Road and Wild Cow Springs—a high-clearance, four-wheel-drive vehicle is strongly suggested. Road conditions can become very hazardous when wet or icy. This road will also take you to the trailhead for Wabayuma Peak, 13.5 miles past the campground. Facilities at Wild Cow Springs include 22 tent or trailer sites, vault toilets, fire grills and picnic areas. No water is available, so you must bring your own. Summer temperatures have been known to dip into the 30s, so pack warmly.

USGS topographic map: Wabayuma Peak

BLM surface map: Valentine

For more information: Contact the BLM Kingman Resource Area, 2475 Beverly Avenue, Kingman, AZ 86401; (602) 757-3161.

CROSSMAN PEAK

See letter L on map page 80

backpacking, camping, hiking, horseback riding, off-highway-vehicle use

Approximately 10 miles northeast of Lake Havasu City, this area is best appreciated up close, because from a distance it looks barren and foreboding. Once within the area, however, you discover a number of hidden springs and a remarkable variety of desert plant life—all tucked within the numerous canyons and drainages.

USGS topographic map: Crossman Peak

For more information: Contact the BLM Havasu Resource Area, 3189 Sweetwater Avenue, Lake Havasu City, AZ 86406; (602) 855-8017.

BURRO CREEK

See letter M on map page 80

backpacking, birdwatching, camping, hiking, rockhounding, wildlife observation

Burro Creek is located near the town of Wikieup, off US 93 and approximately 60 miles northwest of Wickenburg. Fall, winter and spring are the best seasons to visit. The summer is too hot for outdoor recreation, although the occasional thunderstorm does offer a unique hiking opportunity and a cooling respite—if your timing is good.

The scenery is very dramatic, with vertical rock faces, spires, buttes, rugged canyons, springs and perennial streams. The numerous microhabitats created by the unique geography, coupled with the area's plant diversity and water, attract and support a wide variety of birds and wildlife. Beavers, raccoons, ringtails, gray foxes, a variety of skunks, javelinas, bobcats, mountain lions, mule deer and pronghorn antelope round out the wildlife population. You'll find all kinds of raptors, including bald eagles, osprey, kestrels, Cooper's and red-tailed hawks. With 150 reported species, birdwatching is reportedly superb.

Camping is available at Burro Creek Campground (a fee is charged). It's very scenic and features a desert garden. There are no formal trails. Hiking and backpacking are best along the canyons. Uplands are laced with several jeep tracks, but travel is challenging and navigational skills are a must. If you can't use a map and compass, stick to the canyons. Stream and spring water must be treated before drinking.

USGS topographic map: Kaiser Springs

Resources:
• Brochures entitled "Burro Creek Recreation Site" and "Burro Creek Desert Garden" are available from the BLM.

For more information: Contact the BLM Kingman Resource Area, 2475 Beverly Avenue, Kingman, AZ 86401; (602) 757-3161.

GIBRALTAR MOUNTAIN WILDERNESS

See letter N on map page 80

hiking, horseback riding, nature photography

The Gibraltar Mountain Wilderness is a gem for those seeking unique photography and sightseeing opportunities. Panoramas are constantly changing, leading the adventurous hiker or equestrian through an always varying landscape. The surrounding area has been heavily used by off-highway vehicles, but not enough to detract from the beauty of the site. Adjacent Buckskin Mountain State Park offers additional recreational opportunities.

This region is located about 10 miles northeast of Parker. Take Route 72 two miles south of Parker, turn east onto Shea Road and drive approximately five miles—the area is located to the north. Pack along plenty of water and far more than you think you'll need; store the extra in your car, just in case. Few trails exist within the region. Late fall, winter and early spring are the best times to visit. Summer temperatures can exceed 120°F.

USGS topographic maps: Cross Roads, Monkeys Head, Osborne Well, Black Peak, Bobs Well

For more information: Contact the BLM Havasu Resource Area, 3189 Sweetwater Avenue, Lake Havasu City, AZ 86406; (602) 855-8017.

BILL WILLIAMS RIVER/ SWANSEA WILDERNESS

See letter O on map page 80

backpacking, hiking, horseback riding

The Bill Williams River flows westward approximately 40 miles from Alamo Lake State Park through the Bill Williams River National Wildlife Refuge and into the Colorado River north of Parker Dam. The Swansea Wilderness lies about midway downstream and is bounded by private land. The area is accessible from the north and south by graded gravel roads that occasionally require a four-wheel-drive vehicle to negotiate. Inquire at the BLM office for advice on the best point of access and river flow information. While there are no designated hiking trails, you can meander along the river's edge. Side canyons may be explored and offer some interesting routes into the nearby mountains. One thing is for sure—you will probably have the area much to yourself as most visitors to the area bypass the surrounding BLM lands in favor of the Colorado River and Lake Havasu.

USGS topographic maps: Monkeys Head, Casteneda Hills Southwest, Centennial Wash, Planet, Swansea, Centennial

For more information: Contact the BLM Havasu Resource Area, 3189 Sweetwater Avenue, Lake Havasu City, AZ 86406; (602) 855-8017.

RAWHIDE MOUNTAINS WILDERNESS

See letter P on map page 80

backpacking, fishing, hiking, wildlife observation

Downstream of Alamo Lake and within the Rawhide Mountains Wilderness, the Bill Williams River meanders through a 600-foot-deep gorge. This canyon is formed by the relatively low-lying Rawhide Mountains Range to the north and the more dramatic Buckskin Mountains Range to the south. The gorge features perennial stream flows, colorful rock formations, and cottonwood/willow riparian vegetation. Hiking through the gorge is possible at low water flows, but will require several river crossings and an occasional swim—be prepared to get possibly cold and certainly wet. Pack along warm clothing. Call ahead for river flow information.

USGS topographic maps: Swansea, Reid Valley, Alamo Dam, Rawhide Wash, Artillery Peak

For more information: Contact the BLM Havasu Resource Area, 3189 Sweetwater Avenue, Lake Havasu City, AZ 86406; (602) 855-8017.

ARRASTRA MOUNTAIN WILDERNESS

See letter Q on map page 80

backpacking, hiking, wildlife observation

Located just south of Burro Creek and northeast of Alamo Lake, the Arrastra Mountain Wilderness Area is a vast acreage of rugged terrain, granite outcrops, volcanic hills, washes and serpentine canyons. The presence of vegetation and available water attracts a wide variety of birds, making the area an outstanding destination for birders. Washes make the best hiking routes, as do old jeep tracks, used to service now-abandoned mines. This region is truly outstanding for adventurous backpackers with expert map and compass skills who wish to spend several days in a wild and trailless area offering a high level of seclusion. The Santa Maria and Big Sandy rivers flow through the area seasonally. Access to this area requires a four-wheel-drive, high-clearance vehicle. The BLM requests that you inquire at their office for specific directions and current access conditions.

USGS topographic maps: Malpais Mesa Southwest, Arrastra Mountain Northeast, Artillery Peak, Palmerita Ranch, Arrastra Mountain Southeast, Arrastra Mountain, Thorn Peak (and others)

BLM surface map: Alamo Lake

For more information: Contact the BLM Lower Gila Resource Area, 2015 West Deer Valley Road, Phoenix, AZ 85027; (602) 780-8090.

CACTUS PLAIN WILDERNESS STUDY AREA/ EAST CACTUS PLAIN WILDERNESS

See letter R on map page 80

hiking, horseback riding, plant study

This is an immense, undulating area predominantly made up of sand dunes—some stable, some not, some linear, some crescent-shaped. It's like walking through snow. Sound is muffled, giving the visitor a feeling of complete and total isolation from the outside world. Hiking in the early morning or late afternoon as the sun is setting offers the most spectacular lighting. The ocotillo and cactus bloom is most impressive in April and May. A botanist friend tells me that the plants of primary interest in the area are woolly heads, Death Valley Mormon tea and sand flat milk vetch. Although extremely hard to spot, the elf owl also resides here, as does the flat-tailed horned lizard.

Divided by the Central Arizona Project (CAP) Canal, the area is located approximately 10 miles southeast of Parker. Southwest of the CAP Canal is the Cactus Plain Wilderness Study Area, accessible by either Swansea Road north of Bouse or Shea Road south of Parker; both roads exit off Highway 72. Northeast of the CAP is the East Cactus Plain Wilderness, which is also accessible by Swansea Road north of Bouse. No trails are maintained in the area. Pack along plenty of water—summer temperatures have been know to exceed 120°F.

USGS topographic maps: Powerline Well, Bobs Well, Bouse, Planet, Bouse Northwest, Bouse Hills West

For more information: Contact the BLM Havasu Resource Area, 3189 Sweetwater Avenue, Lake Havasu City, AZ 86406; (602) 855-8017.

HARCUVAR MOUNTAINS WILDERNESS

See letter S on map page 80

backpacking, camping, hiking, hunting

The Harcuvar Mountains provide spectacular views to the hiker willing to traverse the rugged 10-mile ridgeline of this BLM wilderness. This isolated mountain range provides habitat for abundant wildlife including mule deer, desert tortoise, mountain lion and various hawks. Several springs, seeps and an occasional waterfall may be enjoyed. Evidence of historic mining and ranching activities can be found in the various side canyons slicing into the ridgeline. The Harcuvar Mountains Wilderness is approximately 12 miles north of Wenden and is accessible via the Alamo Lake Road. Several dirt roads extend to the wilderness boundary from both the south and north sides of the range. The best time to visit this region is in late fall, winter and early spring as the summer temperatures can get rather extreme.

USGS topographic maps: Alamo Dam Southeast, Cunningham Pass, E.C.P. Peak, Webber Canyon

For more information: Contact the BLM Havasu Resource Area, 3189 Sweetwater Avenue, Lake Havasu City, AZ 86406; (602) 855-8017.

HARQUAHALA MOUNTAINS

See letter T on map page 80

backpacking, camping, hiking, historic site, horseback riding

There are few desert mountain ranges that can boast outstanding scenic splendor coupled with abundant water and lush, green campsites. The Harquahala Mountains Wilderness, whose Native American translation means, appropriately, "running water up high" is such a place. The range's namesake, Harquahala Peak (5,681 feet), is the highest point in southwestern Arizona. When the weather permits, it affords the visitor outstanding views of the surrounding desert and a number of distant mountain ranges. Table Top Mountain, over 100 miles to the southeast, and Chemehuevis, approximately 90 miles to the northwest, are two of the most prominent ranges in view. Harquahala's height is the predominant reason why the Smithsonian Institute built an observatory here in the 1920s, now a National Historic Site. There is also evidence of mining activity that may be found throughout the area—watch your step and use caution.

Activity Highlights: Backpacking and hiking

Although a legal, 10.5-mile, four-wheel-drive trail leads to Harquahala Peak , making driving to the top possible in good weather, hikers should try the more scenic and historic option up the north side of the mountain. The 5.4-mile (each way) Harquahala Mountain Pack Trail was constructed by the Smithsonian as a means of hauling supplies to the mountaintop for the observatory. Located entirely within the wilderness, the trail is now overgrown and obscure in places. It can be difficult to follow and is not signed or marked in any way, other than with a few rock cairns.

For the backpacker not so enamored with the idea of trekking on a trail, numerous opportunities exist for cross-country exploration, providing that your map and compass skills are strong. The area's high peaks, foothills, ridges and canyons are well suited for scrambling. The highest peaks and deepest, rockiest canyons exist on the western side of the range. The BLM reports that the range sports a large variety of vertebrates, more than most desert ranges, including the highest mule deer density in the western Arizona desert. A healthy bighorn sheep herd runs wild here as well. Brown's Canyon, a nine-mile-long canyon in the northeastern sector is home to desert tortoise.

Special note: Harquahala Peak lies on the border of the Harquahala Mountains Wilderness Area, as designated in the Arizona Desert Wilderness Act of 1990—no mechanized vehicles, including mountain bikes, are allowed into the wilderness. Thunderstorms on the peak are violent and dangerous. If stormy weather develops, leave the peak immediately. Watch where you place your hands and feet, as rattlesnakes inhabit the area.

Location: Approximately 15.5 miles west of Aguila and 40 miles west of Wickenburg. Take US 60 west from Aguila for 14 miles to the rest area on the south side of the highway. Turn south on the dirt road and follow it to the wilderness boundary—be sure to close the gate behind you. At the wilderness boundary, begin your hike on the old jeep trail, which you'll see from the parking area.

Season: November to April is the best time to visit, when perennial springs, seeps and the occasional seasonal waterfall may be enjoyed. Stay out of the range during the summer because temperatures can get hot enough to boil water on a rock.

USGS topographic maps: Harquahala Mountain, Socorro Peak, Webber Canyon, Gladden

BLM surface map: Salome

Resources:
• *Arizona Atlas & Gazetteer*, published by DeLorme Mapping, P.O. Box 298, Freeport, ME 04032; (207) 865-4171.

For more information: Contact the BLM Lower Gila Resource Area, 2015 West Deer Valley Road, Phoenix, AZ 85027; (602) 780-8090.

BLACK CANYON TRAIL

See letter U on map page 80

backpacking, hiking, horseback riding, wheelchair accessible

As this book goes to press, this trail is 13 miles in length each way. When the trail is completed (sometime in the next several years), it will be 62 miles long. It will provide an all-important link within the Arizona Trail System by effectively tying into the trail network within Prescott National Forest at the northern end. Talk about backpacking nirvana!

Lower elevations of this trail segment are wheelchair accessible. The entire trail has a historic origin—it has been used for livestock since the pioneer days. Located 35 miles north of Phoenix, take Highway 17 to the New River exit. Go west for approximately three miles. The trailhead is marked by a picnic area, ramadas and restrooms on the north side of the road. The best time to visit is between fall and spring. Hiking difficulty is rated as moderate, with elevations ranging from 1,500 to 4,500 feet.

USGS topographic maps: New River, Black Canyon City, Bumble Bee, Cleator

BLM surface maps: Phoenix North, Bradshaw Mountains

For more information: Contact the BLM Phoenix Resource Area, 2015 West Deer Valley Road, Phoenix, AZ 85027; (602) 780-8090.

NEW WATER MOUNTAINS

See letter V on map page 80

backpacking, camping, rockhounding

Located between Interstate 10 and the Kofa National Wildlife Refuge, this region of crags, spires, jagged ridges, steep smooth-walled canyons and big rock outcrops offers good backpacking and hiking opportunities. Nearly 20 miles worth of old vehicle byways make travel within the area easier. Vegetation is sparse. Pack all the water you will need; finding it in this area is next to impossible. Bighorn sheep and mule deer roam the mountains.

USGS topographic maps: Crystal Hill, New Water Mountains, New Water Well

For more information: Contact the BLM Yuma District Office, 3150 Winsor Avenue, Yuma, AZ 85365; (602) 726-6300.

EAGLETAIL MOUNTAINS

See letter W on map page 80

backpacking, camping, hiking, horseback riding, rock climbing

This area is truly spectacular because of the many arches, giant spires, monoliths and jagged ridges that rise above the surrounding flatlands. Courthouse Rock, a huge granite monolith just north of Eagle Peak, rises 1,274 feet toward the sky, making it an attractive hangout for rock climbers. Desert vegetation predominates and includes ocotillo, cholla, creosote, ironwood, saguaro, Mormon tea, barrel cactus and mesquite. With the heat-generated updrafts and a large population of desert rodents, expect to see numerous raptors as well as the great horned owl and coyote. Located south of Interstate 10 and west of Phoenix, the best access to the region is from the east via Harquahala Valley or Courthouse Rock roads. Summer temperatures are abominable—100°F is normal. Late fall, winter and early spring are the best times to visit.

USGS topographic maps: Lone Mountain, Little Horn Mountains Northeast, Eagletail Mountains West, Nott Busch Butte, Columbus Peak

For more information: Contact the BLM Yuma Resource Area, 3150 Winsor Avenue, Yuma, AZ 85365; (602) 726-6300.

SQUAW LAKE RECREATION SITE

See letter X on map page 80

boating, camping, canoeing, fishing, hiking, jetskiing, swimming

Located near Yuma, Arizona across the California border, this campground and recreation site is a popular destination for RVers and is open year-round. If it is solitude you seek, avoid this site. There is no wilderness value to be experienced here. However, if you want watersport recreation and a campground atmosphere, this is a good destination. Expect temperatures to be HOT. On average, over 100 days a year, they exceed the 100°F mark.

Fishing is for largemouth bass, bluegill, carp, flathead and channel catfish on nearby Squaw Lake. Campground facilities include 115 tent or RV sites, flush toilets, drinking water, fire grills, picnic areas, a beach area, a boat ramp and cold showers. A fee is charged for overnight camping.

One outstanding feature in this area, besides the Colorado River, is Betty's Kitchen, a half-mile interpretive trail that is a must-see if you are in the area, or even if you are just passing through. Hiking it takes only about 30 minutes—time well spent. To get there, take Highway 95 seven miles east from Yuma. Turn north on Avenue 7E and follow the road for nine miles until the paved road turns to gravel just past Laguna Dam. Turn left at the sign for Betty's Kitchen Wildlife and Interpretive Area on the right side of the road. The loop nature trail is maintained by the Betty's Kitchen Protective Association, (602) 627-2773, and is part of an old access road to the small cafe that the area is named after. There are outstanding birdwatching opportunities here. Be sure to pick up the Betty's Kitchen Interpretive Trail brochure for your self-guided walk. The best season to visit the trail is from September to May.

USGS topographic map: Laguna Dam

For more information: Contact the BLM Yuma Resource Area, 3150 Winsor Avenue, Yuma, AZ 85365; (602) 726-6300.

FRED J. WEILER GREEN BELT

See letter Y on map page 80

backpacking, birdwatching, camping, hiking

This area consists of a single, dense 100-mile strip of vegetation alongside the Gila River, stretching from just west of Phoenix to just above Date Palm. Although the river has limited flow year-round, numerous potholes in the sandy wash continue to hold water after the surface flow subsides, attracting many waterfowl and other wildlife. Dove and quail hunters frequent this area.

The strip is best accessed from Route 85 or Interstate 85. A few local access routes require the use of a four-wheel-drive vehicle. Pack plenty of water along—as much as you can carry or load in your vehicle. Spring, fall and winter are the best seasons to visit this area.

Arizona state law prohibits camping anywhere within 440 yards of a watering hole—this is to prevent wildlife from being driven away from one of their few life-sustaining watering places. Seasonal waterfowl include mallards, pintails, teals, redheads, canvasbacks and Canada geese. Songbirds include pyrrhuloxias, cardinals and a variety of finches, orioles, tanagers, woodpeckers and hummingbirds. Roadrunners and phainopeplas can also be seen in this area. Herons, egrets, yellowlegs and snipe also frequent the watering holes. Foxes, coyotes, raccoons, bobcats, mule deer and javelinas round out the "expect-to-see" wildlife listing.

Special note: This area has been experiencing current land ownership and access problems, as well as hazardous materials dumping (read drugs and associated paraphernalia). I would advise checking with the BLM before heading into this area. It is a super place to visit, but it is best to be on the safe side.

USGS topographic maps: Hassayampa, Arlington, Cotton Center, Cotton Center Northwest

BLM surface map: Phoenix South

For more information: Contact the BLM Phoenix Resource Area, 2015 West Deer Valley Road, Phoenix, AZ 85027; (602) 780-8090.

PAINTED ROCK PETROGLYPH CAMPGROUND / HISTORIC SITE

See letter Z on map page 80

hiking, historic site, rock climbing, rockhounding, camping

Located 120 miles southwest of Phoenix near the Gila River, the top of Painted Rock Mountain offers panoramic vistas of the Dendora Valley and Sentinel Plain stretching out below. The Gila River winds through this convoluted and rugged volcanic region. Ancient Indian rock drawings and carvings gave this site its name; visitors to the region will marvel at the extensive petroglyphs. There are no formal trails, but hiking through the open desert here is easy.

The campground is open year-round. No fee is charged. Facilities include 30 tent or RV sites, vault toilets, picnic areas, shade ramadas and fire grills. The Lake Campground, which previously offered RV facilities, has been closed indefinitely. To get here, take Highway 8 west from Gila Bend 20 miles to Painted Rock Road. Head north on Painted Rock and continue approximately 11 miles to the site.

For more information: Contact the BLM Lower Gila Resource Area, 2015 West Deer Valley Road, Phoenix, AZ 85027; (602) 780-8090.

ARIZONA

TABLE TOP MOUNTAIN WILDERNESS

See letter AA on map page 80

backpacking, hiking, horseback riding, hunting, wildlife observation
   If you happen to be in the Phoenix area, then Table Top is worth a visit. Primarily a day-hiking option, the views from the top are spectacular and the mountain itself is a well-recognized landmark. The top is unique in that it is a 40-acre plateau (hence the name) covered with desert grasses. The area around the mountain and the mountain itself is an important desert bighorn and desert tortoise habitat. Coyote and javelina round out the most-often-seen-wildlife category. The BLM offers a free map and trail brochure to the region There are over 34,000 acres of wilderness, creating ample opportunity for off-trail backpacking/hiking adventures. Access to the area is best with a high-clearance vehicle and a four-wheel-drive vehicle is strongly suggested. The BLM requests that you check with their office before heading out to determine current conditions and obtain specific access directions.

USGS topographic maps: Antelope Peak, Little Table Top, Vekol Mountains Northeast, Indian Bottle

For more information: Contact the BLM Lower Gila Resource Area, 2015 West Deer Valley Road, Phoenix, AZ 85027; (602) 780-8090.

ARIZONA—MAP B

PARIA CANYON /
VERMILION CLIFFS WILDERNESS

See letter BB on map page 82

backpacking, canyoneering, wildlife observation

Tom Wharton, outdoors editor for the *Salt Lake Tribune*, calls Paria Canyon one of the best backpacking locations in the West. Few who have traveled the trail dispute the claim—and you won't either, if it is desert and canyon hiking you prefer. The thoroughly wild and twisting canyon is part Eden, with its hanging gardens of ferns and orchids, and part sandstone sculpture, offering miles of colorful, swirling patterns in cliff walls; at times, they are so close together that they virtually block out the sky above. Ancient petroglyphs on the canyon walls are evidence that the Pueblo Indians used the canyon over 700 years ago for hunting and raising corn, beans and squash. In later years, when prospectors ventured into the surrounding terrain searching for gold and uranium, Paria Canyon remained virtually untouched. In 1984, following a recommendation by the BLM, the Arizona Wilderness Act designated Paria Canyon a protected wilderness area.

Activity Highlight: Hiking

Plan on four to six days to hike the 37 miles of the canyon in comfort. You should begin your hike at the Paria Canyon Information Station; this is where the closure of the canyon due to weather conditions is regulated. Be forewarned: The river can rush through the upper narrows at a depth of 40 feet during extreme weather. Your feet will be wet much of the time as you will probably be wading through ankle-deep, silty water. Wear boots that are comfortable even when wet. Pack plenty of sock changes or wear neoprene socks. If I'm expecting my feet to get and stay wet, I pack along old sneakers or sturdy all-terrain sandals to hike in if things get too soggy.

The backpack trip is considered moderately difficult—chiefly because of all the river crossings and loose terrain. While springs generally flow with sufficient frequency along the route, it is recommended that you carry containers that can hold at least one gallon of water per person, just in case. Check on current water conditions at the Paria Canyon Information Station or call the Kanab Resource Area office at (801) 644-2672. Water is usually available at the information station, but the water line has been known to stop working—you are advised to tank up at Kanab before heading to the trailhead. Due to possible chemical contamination from farms and ranches upstream, drinking directly from the river is not suggested.

By the way, there is quicksand along the route, but it is generally not more than knee deep and certainly not the variety made famous by Hollywood. A good hiking staff will allow you to probe the murky waters before stepping out into uncharted territory.

Location: Approximately 40 miles east of Kanab, Utah, near the Utah/Arizona border. From Page, follow US 89 west for 30 miles to the Paria Canyon Information Station near milepost 21. From Kanab, drive 40 miles east on US 89. The information station is located just off the south side of the highway. The White House Trailhead for Paria Canyon is two miles south of the station. You will need to plan on a car shuttle for this trip. Leave a second vehicle at Lees Ferry (a 145-mile trip from the trailhead) or arrange for your car to be shuttled. Page is your last stop for supplies and the traditional place to arrange for someone to shuttle your vehicle. Costs for a shuttle typically range from $55 and up if you use your car, and $150 and up if you use a driver's. There are numerous shuttle services offered at Marble Canyon.

Camping: There are two organized car campgrounds, one at either end of the trail: White House Campground at the beginning and Lees Ferry at the end. Keep in mind that Lees Ferry is a National Park Service campground where fees are charged for camping. Primitive camping is allowed anywhere along the trail itself, but no campfires are permitted within the canyon. Practice minimum-impact techniques within the canyon. No latrines are allowed within 100 feet of the river or campsite locations; always pack out your toilet paper.

Season: Spring, early summer and fall are the times to visit this area. Temperatures can become exceedingly hot during July and August. Flash floods, which are always a threat in the canyon, are most prevalent during the months of July through September. May and June are the busiest months, with the Easter holiday being notorious for "campsite competition derbies." Winter is the least crowded season, but also the chilliest—hikers frequently complain of cold feet.

Permits: Registration is required for traveling within the Paria Canyon. Recommended group size is three to four, although groups of up to 10 are permitted. Organized groups must contact the BLM Kanab office at (801) 644-2672 for permit information.

USGS topographic maps: Utah/Arizona: West Clark Bench, Bridger Point; Arizona: Wrather Arch, Water Pockets, Ferry Swale, Lees Ferry

BLM surface maps: Smokey Mountain, Glen Canyon Dam

Additional maps: For a district-wide visitor map, contact the BLM Arizona Strip District Office.

Resources:

• *Hiking the Southwest's Canyon Country,* by Sandra Hinchman, published by The Mountaineers, 1011 Southwest Klickitat Way, Suite 107, Seattle, WA 98134; (800) 553-4453.

• *Arizona Traveler's Handbook,* by Bill Weir, published by Moon Publications, 722 Wall Street, Chico, CA 95928; (916) 345-5473.

• A brochure entitled "The Hiker's Guide to Paria Canyon" is available from the BLM.

For more information: Contact the BLM Vermilion Resource Area, 225 North Bluff, St. George, UT 84770; (801) 628-4491; the BLM Kanab Resource Area, 320 North First East, Kanab, UT 84741; (801) 644-2672; or the BLM Arizona Strip District Office, 390 North 3050 East, St. George, UT 84770; (801) 673-3545.

WHITE CANYON WILDERNESS

See letter CC on map page 82

backpacking, camping, hiking, horseback riding, wildlife observation

Located just southeast of Superior, off Route 177 and south of Tonto National Forest, White Canyon's proximity to the national forest makes this site ideal for longer backpacking trips. There are no formal trails; all the hiking is cross-country or through the canyon itself. The sculptured rocky terrain holds pools of water, even after the stream has dried up. Seasonal rains create picturesque waterfalls that cascade from the canyon rim. White Canyon, part of the Mineral Mountain Range, is narrow in places, with walls that extend as high as 800 feet. An area known as the Rincon is a large rock amphitheater, spectacular in its enormity. Since water is often available here when it is scarce elsewhere, a wide variety of wildlife and birdlife is attracted to the canyon. Both black bears and mountain lions are known to frequent the region.

USGS topographic maps: Mineral Mountain, Tea Pot Mountain

BLM surface maps: Mesa, Globe

For more information: Contact the BLM Phoenix Resource Area, 2015 West Deer Valley Road, Phoenix, AZ 85027; (602) 780-8090.

NEEDLE'S EYE WILDERNESS

See letter DD on map page 82

backpacking, camping, hiking

The Needle's Eye Wilderness is formed where the Gila River Canyon slices through the Mescal Mountains, near Coolidge Dam and San Carlos Lake, adjacent to the San Carlos Indian Reservation. If you like your land rough and isolated, then this is the place. Access is strictly limited to four-wheel-drive vehicles and even then it's dicey! The San Carlos Indian Reservation is not open to the public, and you will be required to obtain a wilderness-access permit from the reservation before heading out. Call the BLM office for detailed access instructions. The Gila River Canyon is quite deep, very narrow, serpentine, and in most places, inaccessible from above.

Grapevine and Dick Spring are two side canyons worth a peek and also viable routes into the canyon itself. Once inside the canyon, it is river scrambling only—expect to get your feet wet. This river is NOT for boating. Fences, overhanging branches, widow makers and sweepers create hazards that are deadly at best—I don't even want to think about worst!

Visiting in the summer months is no fun, unless you enjoy feeling like an egg being pan-fried. Fall through spring is the best time of the year to visit. Along the canyon bottom, you will scramble through dense vegetation consisting of cottonwood, mesquite, sycamore, velvet ash, willow and salt cedar. Away from the canyon, the vegetation is more desert-like; you'll find barrel cactus, acacia, jojoba and saguaro. Raptors are the most frequently seen birds. Bald eagles nest here in the winter.

USGS topographic maps: El Capitan Mountain, Mescal Warm Spring, Coolidge Dam, Christmas

BLM surface map: Globe

For more information: Contact the BLM Phoenix District Office, 2015 West Deer Valley Road, Phoenix, AZ 85027; (602) 863-4464.

ARAVAIPA CANYON WILDERNESS

See letter EE on map page 82

backpacking, horseback riding, wildlife observation

This is the natural area that former U.S. Interior Secretary James Watt referred to as "a gem of the Southwestern desert." Journalists and outdoors writers also speak glowingly of the canyon as a unique, special and wonderful place. Colorful 1,000-foot walls make this area "one of the most scenic places in Arizona," according to the BLM. Fortunately, the BLM has taken steps to ensure that its pristine state is preserved by strictly limiting use.

Activity Highlight: Backpacking

The canyon is approximately 11 miles long. There are no marked trails, although history and use have established relatively clear routes. This is a wilderness area, so mountain bikes are prohibited! The hiking routes ford Aravaipa Creek numerous times, so it is essential that you have sturdy footgear that can get wet. Flash floods are always a possibility—stay alert and stay safe. All water must be treated prior to drinking. Hiking is considered easy. Elevations in the canyon bottom range from 2,600 feet to 3,100 feet.

Location: In the southeastern part of Arizona, approximately 45 miles west of Safford. To reach the west entrance, take Highway 177 south from Superior through Kearny, Hayden and Winkelman. At Winkelman, turn south on Highway 77 and continue for 11 miles to the Aravaipa Road. The turnoff is well marked. The last 12 miles are a combination of paved and gravel road suitable for all vehicles.

To reach the east entrance, drive approximately 13 miles northwest of Safford on US 70. Turn west on the Aravaipa-Klondyke Road and drive approximately 32 miles to the town of Klondyke. Aravaipa-Klondyke Road is graded dirt. From Klondyke, it's about 10 miles to Aravaipa and the trailhead. The road here crosses Aravaipa Creek several times and a high-clearance vehicle is recommended. Beyond Bear Canyon, a four-wheel-drive vehicle may be required, depending on the weather and current road conditions. Call the BLM for conditions before heading out.

Camping: Fourmile Canyon Campground is an excellent base camp for hiking excursions into the Aravaipa Canyon. From Safford, travel 13 miles northwest on US 70 to Aravaipa-Klondyke Road. Proceed 32 miles southwest to Klondyke; go left at Klondyke for one-quarter of a mile to the campground. There are 10 tent or RV sites. Flush toilets, fire grills, picnic tables and drinking water are all available. A $4-per-night fee is charged for each site. Within Aravaipa Canyon, overnight backpacking is allowed, providing you have a permit.

Season: Fall to spring is the best time to visit, although the canyon is open year-round.

Permits: Permits are required! No one can use this canyon without a permit, which allows a maximum stay of three days and two nights in the area. No more than 50 people are allowed within the canyon per day. A fee of $1.50 per person per day is required and may be paid at the self-service fee station at each trailhead. No pets are allowed. Group size is limited to a maximum of 10 people. Day-use horseback riding is allowed, but party size is limited to five horses. Reservations for permits may be made up to 13 weeks in advance of your planned entry date.

USGS topographic maps: Brandenburg Mountain, Booger Canyon

BLM surface map: Mammoth

Resources:
• A brochure entitled "Aravaipa Canyon Wilderness" is available from the BLM.

For more information: Contact the BLM Safford District Office, 711 14th Avenue, Safford, AZ 85546; (602) 428-4040.

BLACK HILLS BACK COUNTRY BYWAY

See letter FF on map page 82

backcountry driving, hiking, mountain biking, picnicking, rockhounding

The Black Hills Back Country Byway follows the historic road from Safford to Clifton. For 21 miles, the visitor will enjoy sweeping vistas, natural and cultural resources, and a variety of recreational opportunities. The byway passes a rockhounding area, cattle ranches, small and large mining operations, interpretive sites and historic sites, including a Civilian Conservation Corps camp. Towards the north end, the byway crosses the Gila River within the Gila Box Riparian National Conservation Area. There are picnic sites on each side of the river, which make for great places to stop for lunch or a brief repose with wine, crackers and cheese—now we're talking!

Activity Highlight: Backcountry driving

The byway provides an outstanding backcountry driving adventure. The road is unpaved, but accessible to high-clearance vehicles. Parts of the byway are narrow with steep drop-offs. The route is not recommended for those vehicles pulling a trailer or for vehicles exceeding 20 feet in length.

Activity Highlight: Mountain biking

This 20-mile route follows the historic road from Safford to Clifton, passing by active rockhounding and mining areas. The Gila and San Francisco river canyons, a historic Civilian Conservation Corps camp and a river picnic site can be enjoyed along the bike trail. The dirt road (also recognized as a National Back Country Byway) winds towards the foothills and mountains with sweeping views of the Gila Box Riparian National Conservation Area.

Location: Approximately 20 miles east of Safford, Arizona, and four miles south of Clifton. From Safford, drive 10 miles east on US 70 to US 191. Go north on US 191 to milepost 139, the southern end of the byway, or milepost 160, the northern end.

Season: Fall to spring is the best time to mountain bike here. Vehicles can travel the byway year-round. Summertime temperatures hovering around 100°F are common. Occasional winter snow is not unheard of, but it usually doesn't take too long to melt—forget about packing your skis. The bottom line: Be prepared for all weather for both yourself and your vehicle.

USGS topographic maps: Guthrie, Clifton, Gila Box, Tollgate Tank

BLM surface maps: Safford, Clifton

Resources:

• There is a free BLM brochure entitled "Black Hills Back Country Byway." There is also an audio log of the same name available for $10. Both may be obtained from the BLM office.

For more information: Contact the BLM Safford District Office, 711 14th Avenue, Safford, AZ 85546; (602) 428-4040.

GILA BOX RIPARIAN NATIONAL CONSERVATION AREA

See letter GG on map page 82

backpacking, camping, canoeing, fishing, hiking, horseback riding, mountain biking, rafting, wildlife observation

This area is very special, primarily because desert rivers are exceedingly rare. The visitor will wander through an oasis where Rocky Mountain bighorn sheep, mule deer, mountain lions, javelinas, numerous songbirds and raptors survive. The Gila River winds along a buff-colored canyon in which 1,000-foot slopes provide a striking contrast with the mesquite woodland on the riverbanks. Slopes are covered with creosote bush, ocotillo, prickly pear and desert grasses. Spires and notch canyons are but a few of the numerous geologic features along the canyon. There is a historic cabin located at Bonita Creek.

Activity Highlight: Hiking

While there are no established trails, one of the best ways to explore the area is by hiking cross-country through the canyon for 20 miles, along uneven terrain, over river cobbles and sandy beaches. There are several thigh-deep river fords. Elevation loss and gain are not noticeable. Hiking is only recommended when the river flow is at or below 250 cubic feet per second. The river is floatable at various other water flows, depending on the watercraft used. Sandy beaches make for excellent camping and the natural Gillard Hot Spring is available for soaking in at low water levels.

Location: In a desert river canyon 20 miles northeast of Safford. The best access is at the downstream end at Bonita Creek. Take Sanchez Road north at Solomon. Beyond Sanchez, follow the signs to Bonita Creek. You can also access the area at the upstream end at Old Safford Bridge Picnic Area. Take US 70 east to US 191. Follow US 191 to the north end of the Black Hills Back Country Byway. Follow the byway for four miles to Old Bridge. High-clearance vehicles are recommended for access to each end of the area.

Camping: Camping is allowed anywhere within the canyon.

Season: Fall to spring is the best time to visit. Summer temperatures can be extreme.

USGS topographic maps: Gila Box, Guthrie, Lone Star Mountain, Bonita Spring, San Jose

Activity Highlight: Safford-Morenci Trail

This hiking and horseback riding trail winds through the rugged canyons of the Gila and Turtle mountains. Native American cliff dwellings, remnants of early homesteads, incredible rock outcroppings and sweeping views of Bonita Creek in the Gila Box Riparian National Conservation Area may be enjoyed. The trail is maintained by volunteers and links the Gila Mountains, Bonita Creek, Turtle Mountain and Eagle Creek together. It is 15 miles each way. Streams and springs are scarce, but water normally can be found about halfway into Bonita Creek. Any water that is found must be purified. Elevations range from 3,700 to 6,000 feet. Hiking difficulty is considered moderate.

Location: Approximately 12 miles northeast of Safford. From Safford, take the San Juan Road northeast about eight miles. At the fork, bear left and head toward Walnut Springs and West Ranch. The trailhead is well signed. In wet weather, this road is considered impassable for two-wheel-drive vehicles.

USGS topographic maps: Lone Star Mountain, Bonita Spring, Copper Plate Gulch

BLM surface maps: Safford, Clifton

Resources:
• A brochure entitled "Safford-Morenci Trail" is available from the BLM.

For more information: Contact the BLM Safford District Office, 711 14th Avenue, Safford, AZ 85546; (602) 428-4040.

HOT WELL DUNES RECREATION AREA

See letter HH on map page 82

camping, hot springs, off-highway-vehicle use

The Hot Well Dunes Recreation Area is an off-highway-vehicle users' Mecca, with growling engines and huge dust-covered smiles the norm on crowded weekends. Approximately 1,700 acres of sand dune environment has been designated for off-highway-vehicle use. If you don't like off-highway vehicles, then stay the heck away. If you don't mind off-highway vehicles (and there is no reason you shouldn't), there is plenty of sand dune to explore without the fear of tire treads up your backside. The other attraction to the region is the warm-water artesian known as Hot Well, which produces in excess of 200 gallons of 106°F water per minute. Two hot tubs have been installed and are available for use by visitors.

There are five developed campsites and plenty of other space for undeveloped camping for those with tents and suitable vehicles—stays are limited to two weeks. Drinking water is not available, so pack in all that you will need. The nearest town of any size for supplies is Safford, approximately 32 miles to the northwest. Roads into and out of the area can be quite treacherous after a rain—be alert to changing weather conditions. Rattlesnakes are active during the warm months—it's not a problem as long as you watch where you step and where you grab.

There are three major access points to the dunes: Haekel Road—This road provides access from the Safford area. The turnoff to Haekel Road is south of the Inspection Station on US 70 and approximately seven miles east of Safford; Tanque Road—This road provides access from Highway 191. The turnoff from Highway 191 is near milepost 105; Fan Road—This road provides access from Bowie. In Bowie, turn north on Central Avenue and continue driving north until reaching Fan Road, approximately two miles away. Head east (right) on Fan Road for eight miles, then turn north (left) on Haekel Road and continue nine miles to the dune access.

For more information: Contact the BLM Safford District Office, 711 14th Avenue, Safford, AZ 85546; (602) 428-4040.

JAVELINA PEAK

See letter II on map page 82

backpacking, camping, hiking, horseback riding

This area is located southeast of Safford off US 70. Access is via Haekel Road. Javelina Peak lies among the Whitlock Mountain Range, tucked between the San Simon and Whitlock valleys. The mountains rise steeply from the valley floor. A small area of badlands and a sand dune area, located just south of the mountain range, are used heavily by off-highway vehicles and lie within the BLM region. Of great interest are the possible birdwatching opportunities during the drive along Haekel Road near the San Simon River. The river, which flows only after heavy rains, and a large number of ponds that exist in the area, attract a good population of waterfowl during the fall and winter season. Since traffic is typically light, birding is considered good for waterfowl, songbirds and raptors.

BLM surface map: Safford

For more information: Contact the BLM Safford District Office, 711 14th Avenue, Safford, AZ 85546; (602) 428-4040.

PELONCILLO MOUNTAINS

See letter JJ on map page 82

backpacking, camping, hiking, horseback riding

Like the Mescal Mountains, this area is rugged with a capital "R." Created from volcanic upheaval and eruptions, the Peloncillo Mountains feature a virtual maze of oak-lined canyons draining in every which way. There are enough private holdings in the area to make access difficult.

This area is located near the New Mexico and Arizona state borders, north of San Simon on Interstate 10 and south of Duncan on Route 75. Call the BLM prior to heading out to determine the best points of access. Fall through spring is the best time to visit.

USGS topographic maps: Arizona/New Mexico: Doubtful Canyon, Engine Mountain; Arizona: San Simon, Orange Butte

For more information: Contact the BLM Safford District Office, 711 14th Avenue, Safford, AZ 85546; (602) 428-4040.

REDFIELD CANYON WILDERNESS AREA

See letter KK on map page 82

backpacking, hiking, photography, wildlife observation

The 6,600-acre Redfield Canyon Wilderness is located approximately 32 miles north of Benson and offers a narrow, red-walled chasm suitable for hiking during the spring and fall. Tall, boulder-strewn cliffs are pocked with eroded caves and offer the visitor a smorgasbord of adventuring opportunities. Nature photographers will enjoy capturing the hidden cascades of the numerous side canyons, while the more casual wanders will find simple pleasure in splashing in the deep pools of the main canyon. Located in the eastern part of the wilderness is the impressive Galiuro Escarpment, an excellent example of the fault-block development of the Basin and Range Province. Other small canyons containing perennial streams may be discovered in the area by those willing to spend the time and energy seeking them out.

Location: To get to the Redfield Canyon Wilderness from Tucson, take Interstate 10 east to Benson and then north along Pomerene Road to Redington. At Redington, turn right beyond the bridge. You will need to obtain permission to cross State Trust lands and private lands at this point—inquire with the BLM office before heading out. A simpler option for last-minute trip planners is to take Interstate 10 to exit 340 at Willcox and drive approximately 32 miles to the Muleshoe Ranch. You will need to sign in at the Nature Conservancy registration area before continuing along Jackson Cabin Road, which is passable by high-clearance vehicles in good weather if you are careful, but is best traveled in a four-wheel-drive vehicle. There is limited parking at the wilderness boundary, beyond which no vehicles of any kind are allowed.

USGS topographic maps: The Mesas, Cherry Spring Peak

For more information: Contact the BLM Tucson Resource Area, 12661 East Broadway, Tucson, AZ 85748; (602) 722-4289.

DOS CABEZAS MOUNTAINS

See letter LL on map page 82

backpacking, camping, hiking, horseback riding, picnicking, wildlife observation

These mountains are located south of Interstate 10 and due east of Willcox in the southeastern corner of the state. A road south of the town of Bowie provides access into an area known as Happy Camp Canyon, where the BLM maintains a picnic area. The 11,700 acres of wilderness are predominantly roadless and worth exploring. There are three peaks over 7,000 feet within this area, as well as a number of pretty canyons. Howell Canyon, accessible from the picnic area, has vestiges of old road and housing foundations from turn-of-the-century mining operations. Government Peak, perhaps the most spectacular of all the area's peaks, stands at a proud 7,587 feet high, with boulders, rock outcrops, seasonal pools and waterfalls. Fall through spring is the best time to visit.

BLM surface maps: Willcox, Chiricahua Peak

For more information: Contact the BLM Safford District Office, 425 East Fourth Street, Safford, AZ 85546; (602) 428-4040.

COYOTE MOUNTAINS WILDERNESS

See letter MM on map page 82

backpacking, hiking, rockhounding, wildlife observation

Some consider this to be the little Yosemite of the Southwest, presumably because of the sheer cliffs and wide canyons. Although others see little resemblance to Yosemite, all agree that this area is highly scenic and only a fool wouldn't want to visit here. There are several miles of hiking trails within the mountain area, attracting hikers, artists, rock hounds, wildlife watchers and hunters from all over.

Located southwest of Tucson, south of Route 86 and east of Route 286, these mountains are in close proximity to the Baboquivari Range.

Special note: This mountain area has limited legal access at this time. To reach the mountains, you must cross private land on the east side of the wilderness, which requires landowners' permission. Visitors can also arrange for access and parking with the Tohono O'odham Reservation on its north and west sides, just off Route 86 west of Tucson.

For more information: Contact the BLM Tucson Resource Area, 12661 East Broadway, Tucson, AZ 85748; (602) 722-4289.

EMPIRE-CIENEGA RESOURCE CONSERVATION AREA

See letter NN on map page 82

birdwatching, camping, hiking, horseback riding, mountain biking, wildlife observation

Acquired by the BLM relatively recently (in 1988), the Empire and Cienega ranches together constitute a 45,000-acre wild area of rolling grasslands and woodlands. Tall lush grass, six feet high in some places, is the dominant feature of the region. Sitting at an elevation of 4,500 feet with 15 inches of annual rainfall, the high-desert basin setting supports some of the best examples of native grasslands in Arizona. In a state where most stream beds remain bone-dry throughout much of the year, the perennial flow of Cienega Creek makes it a highly valuable resource.

Giant cottonwoods hug the banks of the creek and are interspersed with willows and ash. Oak and juniper trees thrive on the hillsides. Birdwatching is considered quite good, with over 200 species of birds, identified by members of the Audubon Society and other volunteers, inhabiting the area. Camping is allowed anywhere.

The BLM's Empire Ranch headquarters and field station are 46 miles southeast of Tucson and 10 miles north of Sonoita. One entrance is seven miles north of Sonoita on the east side of Route 83, near mile marker 40. The other entrance is five miles east of Sonoita on the north side of Route 82, near mile marker 36.

BLM surface maps: Tucson, Fort Huachuca

For more information: Contact the BLM Tucson Resource Area, 12661 East Broadway, Tucson, AZ 85748; (602) 722-4289.

BABOQUIVARI PEAK WILDERNESS

See letter OO on map page 82

hiking, rock climbing

Baboquivari Peak Wilderness and the peak itself are well known to climbers as the only Grade 6 (multi-day) and Class 6 (requires aid) climb in all of Arizona. It's a massive granite monolith that rises to 7,734 feet, towering 1,000 feet above the surrounding Baboquivari Mountains and over 4,000 feet above the Altar Valley floor. It is possible to hike to the mountain crest, although it is a strenuous route.

This mountain area has limited legal access at this time. To reach the mountains from the east via Thomas Canyon, you must cross private land, which requires landowners' permission. While Thomas Canyon was previously owned by The Nature Conservancy, it was sold with a condition that an easement be provided to hikers visiting the BLM-managed Baboquivari Peak. But here's the problem: Currently, private lands hemming in the east side of the wilderness are not subject to the easement. Your other choice is to access the area via the west side and the Tohono O'odham Indian Reservation's developed and maintained Baboquivari Peak Park. The reservation charges for the use of the picnic/camping area at the base of the peak.

To get to the west-side access and the Baboquivari Peak Park headquarters, take Route 86 west from Tucson to Sells and then drive 19 miles south on Route 286 to the park entrance. Fall through spring is the best time to visit.

For more information: Contact the BLM Tucson Resource Area, 12661 East Broadway, Tucson, AZ 85748; (602) 722-4289.

BLM CAMPGROUNDS

1. VIRGIN RIVER CAMPGROUND—MAP A

Campsites, facilities: There are 115 sites, all with picnic tables and fire rings. Water and flush toilets are available. There is a 14-day stay limit.

Fee: There is a $5 fee per night; pay on site.

Who to contact: Shivwits Resource Area, 225 North Bluff Street, St. George, UT 84770; (801) 628-4491.

Location: In the Virgin River Gorge near the Paiute and Beaver Dam wilderness areas. From Littlefield, drive 16 miles north on Interstate 15 to the Cedar Pockets exit. The campground entrance is signed. The campground is set at 2,250 feet.

Season: All year.

2. PACKSADDLE CAMPGROUND—MAP A

Campsites, facilities: There are seven tent sites, all with grills and fire rings. Pit toilets are available. There is **no water**. There is a 14-day stay limit.

Fee: There is no fee.

Who to contact: Kingman Resource Area, 2475 Beverly Avenue, Kingman, AZ 86401; (602) 757-3161.

Location: In the Cerbat Mountains. Drive approximately 20 miles north on US 93 out of Kingman to Big Wash Road (BLM Road 15) near milepost 51. Turn right onto Big Wash Road and drive approximately nine miles to the campground. Low-clearance vehicles and travel trailers are not recommended on this road due to its steepness and tight switchbacks. The road may become impassable during periods of snowfall or prolonged rainfall. The campground sits at 5,700 feet.

Season: May to October, depending on the snow level. Night temperatures can dip below freezing, even in the summer.

3. WINDY POINT CAMPGROUND—MAP A

Campsites, facilities: There are seven campsites, all with picnic tables, fire rings and grills. Vault toilets are available. There is **no water**. There is a 14-day stay limit.

Fee: There is no fee.

Who to contact: Kingman Resource Area, 2475 Beverly Avenue, Kingman, AZ 86401; (602) 757-3161.

Location: From Kingman, drive 20 miles north on US 93 to Big Wash Road (BLM Road 15) near milepost 51 and turn right. Drive approximately 11 miles to the campground entrance. Low-clearance vehicles and travel trailers are not recommended on this road due to its steepness and tight switchbacks. The road may become impassable during periods of snowfall or prolonged rainfall. The campground sits at 5,700 feet.

Season: May to October, depending on snow.

4. WILD COW SPRING CAMPGROUND—MAP A

Campsites, facilities: There are 24 campsites, all with picnic tables, fire rings and grills. Vault toilets are available. There is **no water.** There is a 14-day stay limit. You must bring your own firewood.

Fee: There is a $4 fee per night; pay on site.

Who to contact: Kingman Resource Area, 2475 Beverly Avenue, Kingman, AZ 86401; (602) 757-3161.

Location: From Kingman, drive 14 miles south on Hualapai Mountain Road through Hualapai Mountain County Park into the small community of Pine Lake. Turn right at the Pine Lake Fire Station on an unpaved one-lane road. From here, it is approximately five miles to the campground entrance. High-clearance vehicles are strongly recommended from Pine Lake on. Travel trailers longer than 20 feet are not recommended beyond the fire station. The road may become impassable during periods of snowfall or prolonged rain. The campground sits at 6,200 feet.

Season: May to October, depending on snow. Temperatures can dip below freezing at night, even in the summer.

5. BURRO CREEK CAMPGROUND—MAP A

Campsites, facilities: There are 21 sites, all with picnic tables, grills, fire rings and sun ramadas. Flush toilets, water and an RV dump station are available. Some facilities are wheelchair accessible. There is a 14-day stay limit.

Fee: There is a $6 fee per night; pay on site.

Who to contact: Kingman Resource Area, 2475 Beverly Avenue, Kingman, AZ 86401; (602) 757-3161.

Location: On a beautiful creek with excellent swimming holes. From the town of Wikieup, drive approximately 14 miles south on US 93 to Burro Creek Road and turn right. Drive just over one mile to the campground entrance. The campground is set at 1,960 feet.

Season: All year. It's most crowded during the cool winter months.

6. CROSSROADS CAMPGROUND—MAP A

Campsites, facilities: There are eight sites, all with picnic tables and grills. Vault toilets are available. RVs up to 35 feet are allowed. There is a 14-day stay limit.

Fee: There is no fee.

Who to contact: Havasu Resource Area, 3189 Sweetwater Avenue, P.O. Box 685, Lake Havasu City, AZ 86406; (602) 855-8017.

Location: Beside the Colorado River near Empire Landing. From the town of Parker, cross over the California side of the river and drive north on Parker Dam Road for approximately eight miles to the campground entrance. The campground is set at 365 feet.

Season: All year. It gets very hot in the summer. During the year, the temperature rarely falls below 55°F.

7. EMPIRE LANDING CAMPGROUND—MAP A

Campsites, facilities: There are 76 sites, all with picnic tables and grills. Water, flush toilets, cold showers and an RV dump station are available. RVs up to 35 feet are allowed. There is a 14-day stay limit. This is a destination for boating, fishing, rockhounding and off-highway-vehicle use. There is a 14-day stay limit.

Fee: There is a $8 fee per night; pay on site.

Who to contact: Havasu Resource Area, 3189 Sweetwater Avenue, P.O. Box 685, Lake Havasu City, AZ 86406; (602) 855-8017.

Location: On the Colorado River. From Parker, head over to the California side of the Colorado River and drive north for approximately nine miles on Parker Dam Road. Empire Campground is located one mile past Crossroads Campground. The campground sits at 380 feet.

Season: All year.

8. LA POSA VISITOR AREA—MAP A

Campsites, facilities: There are 1,000 campsites. Water, vault toilets, pay phones and an RV dump station are available.

Fee: There is a $50 fee for an annual pass or a $10 fee per week; pay on site.

Who to contact: Yuma Resource Area, 3150 Winsor Avenue, Yuma, AZ 85365; (602) 726-6300.

Location: In the Sonoran Desert approximately one mile south of Quartzite on US 95. The campsites are located on both sides of the road.

Season: September to April. Out-of-season camping is allowed, but it's hot and there is no water off-season.

9. IMPERIAL DAM VISITOR AREA—MAP A

Campsites, facilities: This camp can provide up to 6,000 camping sites, all undesignated. Water, flush toilets, cold showers, pay phones and an RV dump station are available.

Fee: There is a $50 fee for an annual pass or a $10 fee per week; pay on site.

Who to contact: Yuma Resource Area, 3150 Winsor Avenue, Yuma, AZ 85365; (602) 726-6300.

Location: Near Imperial National Wildlife Refuge and Squaw Lake. From Yuma, drive 20 miles north on US 95 to Imperial Dam Road and turn left. Drive to Senator Wash Road and the campground entrance. The campground sits at 300 feet.

Season: September to April. Off-season camping is permitted, but no water is provided.

10. SQUAW LAKE CAMPGROUND—MAP A

Campsites, facilities: There are 73 sites, all with picnic tables and grills. One group site is available. Water, flush toilets, cold showers and a boat ramp are available. There is a 14-day stay limit.

Fee: There is a $4 fee per night; pay on site.

Who to contact: Yuma Resource Area, 3150 Winsor Avenue, Yuma, AZ 85365; (602) 726-6300.

Location: On the Colorado River. From Winterhaven, exit Interstate 8 onto County Road S-24. Drive 20 miles north to a paved road signed for Senator Wash and Squaw Lake. The campground entrance is signed. The campground sits at 200 feet.

Season: All year. Temperatures can be somewhat unbearable during the summer. Expect this campground to be crowded on holidays and most weekends.

11. PAINTED ROCK PETROGLYPH CAMPGROUND—MAP A

Campsites, facilities: There are 30 campsites, all with picnic tables, grills and sun shelters. Vault toilets are available. There is **no water**. There is a 14-day stay limit.

Fee: There is no fee.

Who to contact: Lower Gila Resource Area, 2015 West Deer Valley Road, Phoenix, AZ 85027; (602) 780-8090.

Location: Near the Gila River and Painted Rock. From Gila Bend, drive 20 miles west on Interstate 8 to Painted Rock Road. Drive north for approximately 11 miles to Rocky Point Road and follow it for approximately one-half mile to the campground entrance. The campground sits at 600 feet.

Season: All year.

12. FOURMILE CANYON CAMPGROUND—MAP B

Campsites, facilities: There are 10 sites, all with picnic tables and fire rings. Flush toilets and water are available. There is a 14-day stay limit.

Fee: There is a $4 fee per night; pay on site.

Who to contact: Safford District Office, 711 14th Avenue, Safford, AZ 85546; (602) 428-4040.

Location: On picturesque Aravaipa Creek. From the town of Pima, drive five miles west on US 70 to Aravaipa/Klondyke Road and turn left. Drive approximately 40 miles over an unpaved surface to Klondyke. Head left and drive approximately one-half mile to the campground entrance. The road to the campground can be impassable when wet. Four-wheel-drive vehicles are recommended.

Season: All year. Hunting season runs from September to October, so expect crowded conditions. It can get quite crowded with vacationers during December and January.

STATE INFORMATION OVERVIEW

ARIZONA STATE OFFICE
3707 North Seventh Street, P.O. Box 16563, Phoenix, AZ 85014; (602) 640-5501

ARIZONA STRIP DISTRICT OFFICE
390 North 3050 East, St. George, UT 84770; (801) 673-3545

Shivwits Resource Area, 225 North Bluff Street, St. George, UT 84770; (801) 628-4491

Vermilion Resource Area, 225 North Bluff Street, St. George, UT 84770; (801) 628-4491

PHOENIX DISTRICT OFFICE
2015 West Deer Valley Road, Phoenix, AZ 85027; (602) 780-8090

Kingman Resource Area, 2475 Beverly Avenue, Kingman, AZ 86401; (602) 757-3161

Lower Gila Resource Area, 2015 West Deer Valley Road, Phoenix, AZ 85027; (602) 780-8090

Phoenix Resource Area, 2015 West Deer Valley Road, Phoenix, AZ 85027; (602) 780-8090

SAFFORD DISTRICT OFFICE
711 14th Avenue, Safford, AZ 85546; (602) 428-4040

Gila Resource Area, 711 14th Avenue, Safford, AZ 85546; (602) 428-4040

San Simon Resource Area, 711 14th Avenue, Safford, AZ 85546; (602) 428-4040

Tucson Resource Area, 12661 East Broadway, Tucson, AZ 85748; (602) 722-4289

YUMA DISTRICT OFFICE
3150 Winsor Avenue, Yuma, AZ 85365; (602) 726-6300

Havasu Resource Area, 3189 Sweetwater Avenue, P.O. Box 685, Lake Havasu City, AZ 86406; (602) 855-8017

CALIFORNIA

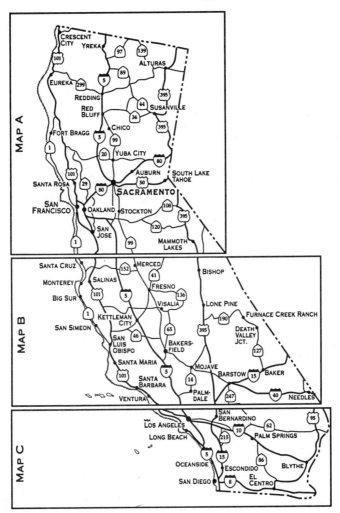

MAP A—CALIFORNIA

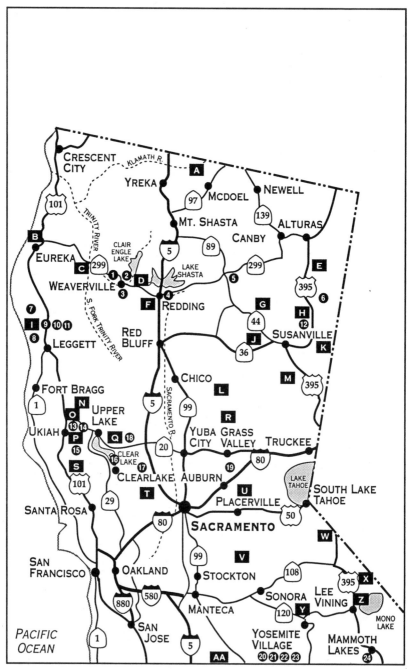

MAP REFERENCES

BLM CAMPGROUNDS

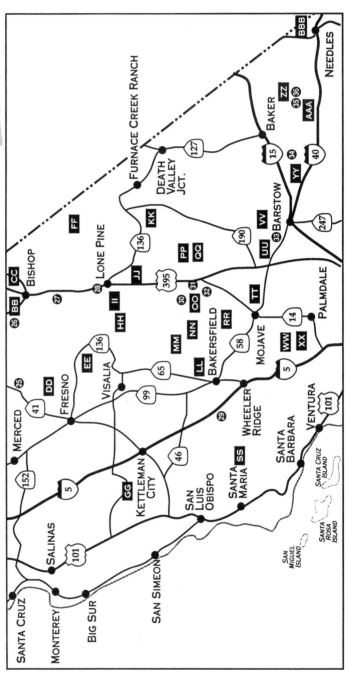

MAP B—CALIFORNIA

CALIFORNIA

MAP REFERENCES

BLM CAMPGROUNDS

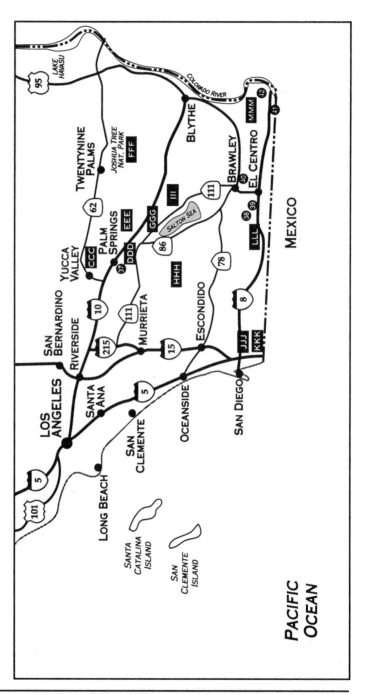

MAP C—CALIFORNIA

MAP REFERENCES

BLM CAMPGROUNDS

CALIFORNIA—MAP A

UPPER KLAMATH RIVER

See letter A on map page 126

backpacking, camping, canoeing, hiking, horseback riding, kayaking, mountain biking, rafting

Fishing and whitewater are the popular calling cards for this well-known river. California's second longest river, the Klamath provides excellent salmon and steelhead fishing in the winter and super trout angling (catch and release only) during the summer. Through Oregon, the Klamath rolls and roils along canyons green with pine, cedar, oak and juniper. Once across the border into California, the terrain flattens out into golden hills dotted with oak and littered with the remains of mines, ranches, mills and a historic 19th-century health spa. If you stretch your imagination, you can almost see a stagecoach rolling through the hillside off in the distance. Wildlife that inhabit the region include deer, falcon, black bear, osprey, blue heron and bald eagle.

Activity Highlight: Whitewater rafting

From just below the dam through Hell's Corner and Satan's Gate rapids, you'll find electrifying whitewater here. This is Class IV-plus water, with one gut-wrencher after another and little time to recover. Boaters must have previous rafting experience and be ready for this. From Rainbow Rock on down, the river subsides to a more relaxing series of Class II and III whitewater with periodic stretches of tranquil water. There are numerous commercial outfitters who run trips on the river.

Location: Along the California/Oregon border near Interstate 5. Take Interstate 5 north across the Oregon border to Highway 66, then head east approximately 43 miles to the John Boyle Powerhouse. A sign downstream marks the put-in point.

Camping: Camp anywhere along the river. Fire pans and porta-potties are required.

Season: To find out the best time to go, call the John Boyle Powerhouse at (800) 547-1501 for river flow information.

Permits: Permits are required and may be obtained from the BLM.

USGS topographic maps: Oregon: Parker Mountain; California: Hawkinsville, Iron Gate Reservoir, Copco

Resources:

• Call the California Outfitter Hotline at (800) 552-3635 for access to 45 California whitewater outfitters. You will receive a directory of licensed outfitters listing individual 800 numbers. The directory also offers basic information regarding what rivers are run and each outfitter's specialty: gourmet food, trips for singles, packages with mountain biking or hot-air ballooning, trips for families, women, men or disabled people, fishing trips, wilderness luxury trips and more.

• *Western Whitewater, From the Rockies to the Pacific*, by Jim Cassady, Bill Cross and Fryar Calhoun, published by North Fork Press, Berkeley, CA; (415) 424-1213.

For more information: Contact the BLM Redding Resource Area, 355 Hemsted Drive, Redding, CA 96002; (916) 224-2100.

SAMOA DUNES

See letter B on map page 126

hiking, horseback riding, mountain biking, off-highway-vehicle use

This 300-acre dunescape is worth a peek. It is a great place to kick back, fly a kite or let your toes play in the nearby surf. Scrounging for driftwood is a popular activity. Seagrasses and numerous species of wildflowers keep the dunes fairly stable and prevent rapid wind erosion. From US 101 in Eureka, follow the Samoa Bridge to Highway 255 and then go south to the end of Samoa Spit for dune access.

USGS topographic map: Eureka

For more information: Contact the BLM Arcata Resource Area, 1125 16th Street, Room 219, Arcata, CA 95521; (707) 822-7648.

TRINITY RIVER

See letter C on map page 126

backpacking, birdwatching, camping, canoeing, hiking, horseback riding, kayaking, mountain biking, whitewater rafting

The Trinity is ideal for a two-day canoe or raft trip through steep canyons and rustic meadows. This river offers a ringside seat for a glimpse into the surrounding region's Gold Rush legacy and spectacular views of the nearby and often snow-capped Trinity Alps. You'll encounter a wide variety of terrain along the way, from forests and canyons to flower-carpeted meadows. Wildlife includes black-tailed deer, otters, black bears, egrets, kingfishers and blue heron.

Activity Highlight: Whitewater rafting
The Trinity is an ideal river for the more adventurous to try paddling in inflatable kayaks. Rated at Class III, the river is dam-controlled and consequently has good paddling water throughout the summer. Along the way, boaters will enjoy visiting modern and historic mining operations. Gold panning is allowed along the river as long as you are not intruding on someone's claim. There are a number of commercial outfitters who run trips on the river.

Activity Highlight: Fishing
Fishing is excellent for steelhead, king and silver salmon, rainbow and brown trout.

Location: West of Redding, north of Highway 299 and east of Arcata. There are several access points along Highway 299. Put-ins are located at Bucktail Hole, Rush Creek, Steelbridge, Douglas City and North Fork. Take-outs are available all along the river south of the first put-in, Bucktail Hole.

Camping: You can camp anywhere along the river. Organized camping is available at the BLM's Trinity River campgrounds: 19 improved sites at Douglas City on Highway 199; 21 improved sites at Junction City on Highway 299; and eight improved sites east of Douglas City off Highway 299 and near the Steelbridge river access.

Season: The California Department of Water Resources provides water flow information for most California rivers. To determine the best time to go, call (916) 322-3327.

USGS topographic maps: Weaverville, Junction City, Dedrick, Helena, Del Loma

Resources:
• Call the California Outfitter Hotline at (800) 552-3635 for access to 45 California whitewater outfitters. You will receive a directory of licensed outfitters listing individual 800 numbers. The directory also offers basic information regarding what rivers are run and each outfitter's specialty: gourmet food, trips for singles, packages with mountain biking or hot air ballooning, trips for families, women, men or disabled people, fishing trips, wilderness luxury trips and more.

- *Western Whitewater, From the Rockies to the Pacific,* by Jim Cassady, Bill Cross and Fryar Calhoun, published by North Fork Press, Berkeley, CA; (415) 424-1213.

For more information: Contact the BLM Redding Resource Area, 355 Hemsted Drive, Redding, CA 96002; (916) 224-2100.

GENE CHAPPIE/SHASTA RECREATION AREA

See letter D on map page 126

backpacking, hiking, mountain biking, off-highway-vehicle use

Over 200 miles of fire roads and trails crisscross through this 50,000-acre site, making it a virtual treasure trove for mountain bikers and off-highway-vehicle users. From Interstate 5, exit at Shasta Dam. The road that crosses the dam leads to the recreation area.

USGS topographic map: Shasta Dam

For more information: Contact the BLM Redding Resource Area, 355 Hemsted Drive, Redding, CA 96002; (916) 224-2100.

BUCKHORN BACK COUNTRY BYWAY

See letter E on map page 126

mountain biking

Officially recognized as a Back Country Byway, suitable for two-wheel-drive, high-clearance vehicles, this route is also super for mountain biking. The 28-mile road passes alongside Buckhorn Canyon and through sagebrush country on the California/Nevada border. To reach the byway, head about 55 miles north of Susanville on US 395 to the town of Ravendale. Turn east on County Road 502 and continue four miles east, then four miles north (the road curves 90 degrees), and then another two miles east. Head straight approximately six miles east on Maar Road (County Road 526). Follow the road north half a mile. When it begins to climb a small hill, you have reached the Buckhorn Back Country Byway. Either do an out-and-back bike trip or arrange for a car shuttle. Early May to mid-June and from September through October are the most pleasant times to visit. Check with the BLM or Lassen County Roads at (916) 234-2014 for local road conditions before heading out.

USGS topographic maps: Buckhorn Canyon, Observation Peak, Buckhorn Lake, Dodge Reservoir

For more information: Contact the BLM Eagle Lake Resource Area, 705 Hall Street, Susanville, CA 96130; (916) 257-0456.

SACRAMENTO RIVER

See letter F on map page 126

boating, camping, canoeing, fishing, hiking, horseback riding, rafting, swimming

California's longest river attracts many visitors because of its easy access for swimming and boating. Canoes, rafts, kayaks and power boats all ply the tranquil waterways in seeming harmony. Shoreline fishing for salmon, steelhead and trout is fair to good. The best put-in for floaters and boaters is at the Redding Island Campground. From Redding, drive 15 miles south on Interstate 5 to Cottonwood. Turn east on Balls Ferry Road in Cottonwood and drive five miles to Adobe Road. Follow Adobe Road to the campground entrance and access to the Sacramento River.

BLM surface maps: Redding, Red Bluff

For more information: Contact the BLM Redding Resource Area, 355 Hemsted Drive, Redding, CA 96002; (916) 224-2100.

EAGLE LAKE

See letter G on map page 126

backpacking, boating, camping, canoeing, fishing, mountain biking, picnicking, wildlife observation

This 28,000-acre lake is great for every kind of water sport imaginable—in addition to a slew of shoreline activities. Eagle Lake is well known for game fish, including the Eagle Lake rainbow trout—unique to this lake. Wildlife is abundant and includes cormorants, terns, osprey, bald eagle, white pelican, cinnamon teal, egrets, muskrat and deer. From Susanville, drive north on Highway 139 for approximately 25 miles to Eagle Lake.

USGS topographic maps: Spalding Tract, Troxel Point, Gallatin Peak, Pikes Point

For more information: Contact the BLM Eagle Lake Resource Area, 705 Hall Street, Susanville, CA 96130; (916) 257-0456.

BISCAR WILDLIFE AREA

See letter H on map page 126

canoeing, wildlife observation

This area has a very small lake, tucked in an arid, high desert rimrock canyon. It is notable for its varied wildlife, including white pelican, osprey, muskrat, marsh wren, sage grouse, mule deer and pronghorn antelope. Located near the town of Litchfield. Drive approximately 20 miles north on US 395. Head west on Karlo Road for approximately six miles. Parking for the site is just across a set of railroad tracks.

USGS topographic map: Litchfield

For more information: Contact the BLM Eagle Lake Resource Area, 705 Hall Street, Susanville, CA 96130; (916) 257-0456.

KING RANGE NATIONAL CONSERVATION AREA

See letter I on map page 126

camping, backpacking, hiking, horseback riding, mountain biking, wildlife observation

For about 2,500 years, up until about 1,000 years ago, Sinkyone and Mattole Indians called these beaches and the surrounding area home. Shell mounds remain as evidence of their presence and are protected by federal legislation against being disturbed. The King Range rises abruptly from sea level to 4,087 feet, the summit of King Peak, in less than three miles. Steep streams cascade into the ocean and the eroding cliffs create huge rock slides and talus piles. Wildlife is abundant. Offshore, expect to see seals, sea lions and a variety of shorebirds playing in the kelp beds and tidal areas. In the Douglas fir- and chaparral-covered coastline, black-tailed deer and black bear make their homes. There are also several threatened species supported here, including the spotted owl and peregrine falcon.

Activity Highlights: Hiking and backpacking

The Lost Coast Trail is a beautiful 24-mile trek through one of the most pristine areas on the Pacific Coast. Bounded by the ocean and steep mountains and cliffs, the trail follows the beach most of the way, crossing numerous streams and grassy flats. Hiking the entire trail requires a shuttle, unless you're prepared for a 48-mile round-trip; allow for at least three days for the one-way trek. The terrain varies from fine-grained sand to large boulders. The walking is fairly level as it follows the beach most of the time. There are occasions when the trail wanders onto grassy flats above the beach and through Douglas fir, cypress, chemise, and possibly poison oak. Two areas, Sea Lion Gulch and Shipman Creek, will require the use of a tidetable as the trail is completely cut off by the incoming tide at times. Good camping areas may be found at Cooskie Creek, Spanish Flat and Shipman Creek. Driftwood is readily available for campfires, but a campfire permit must be obtained prior to the trip. Also, watch out for rattlesnakes when collecting wood!

The King Crest Trail offers an equally spectacular, but very different, alternative to the Lost Coast Trail. The 13-mile trail system is designated as a National Recreation Trail. Following the spine of the King Range, the trail traverses forested meadows and offers sweeping panoramas of miles of Pacific Coastal wilderness. Several spur trails connect the King Crest Trail to the Lost Coast Trail, offering a variety of loop-hike opportunities for the hardy backpacker. Water sources are limited up high, so pack along plenty.

Location: About 20 miles west of US 101 at Garberville, 70 miles south of Eureka in Northern California. The best route to travel when hiking the Lost Coast Trail is from north to south. Leave a car at one end to facilitate a shuttle, unless you're planning a round-trip excursion. The northern trailhead is located at Mattole Campground. The southern trailhead is located at Black Sands Beach near Shelter Cove. To reach the north trailhead from US 101, take the South Fork/Honeydew exit and drive to Lighthouse Road, just south of Petrolia. Follow Lighthouse Road west for five winding miles to Mattole Campground and the trailhead. Access is also possible via paved mountain roads from Ferndale, Humboldt Redwoods State Park and Redway. Try to schedule your visit away from summer holiday weekends to avoid crowds which occur at these times.

Camping: Camping is allowed anywhere within the wilderness area, unless otherwise posted. Four developed campgrounds are available, of which three accommodate tents and trailers, and one is intended for tents only.

Season: You can visit here year-round. This is typically the wettest region on the Pacific Coast, with an average of 100 inches of rainfall annually. Summer is typically cool and foggy along the coast, and warm to hot at the higher elevations inland.

Permits: Free campfire permits are required—obtain them from the BLM.

USGS topographic maps: Point Delgada, Cape Mendocino, Honeydew, Shelter Cove, Shubrick Peak, Bear Harbor, Briceland, Cooskie Creek, Petrolia, Buckeye Mountain

Resources: *The King Range National Conservation Area Recreation Guide* is available from the BLM.

For more information: Contact the BLM Arcata Resource Area, 1125 16th Street, Room 219, Arcata, CA 95521; (707) 822-7648.

BIZZ JOHNSON TRAIL

See letter J on map page 126

backpacking, hiking, horseback riding, mountain biking

The trail takes the traveler through several different ecological zones, beginning with ponderosa pine forests at 5,500 feet near Westwood and ending up in desert terrain at 4,400 feet near Susanville. Geology fans will enjoy the area because the Susan River establishes an approximate boundary between the southern reaches of the Cascade Mountains and the northern reaches of the Sierra Nevada. Sierra granite mingles magnificently with the igneous basalt cliffs and spires of agglomerate.

The historical significance of the trail is quite fascinating as well. From 1914 to 1956, the railroad was used to connect Westwood with Fernley, Nevada. A 1956 flood destroyed a bridge along the route; since the lumber company that had been using the rail line had closed, the bridge was never repaired and the rails were abandoned. In 1978, Southern Pacific received official permission to abandon the route. Recreational planners from the U.S. Forest Service and the BLM, with assistance from Congressman Harold T. "Bizz" Johnson, purchased the right-of-way and the trail was born.

Activity Highlights: Hiking and mountain biking

The Bizz Johnson Trail is an outstanding example of the success enjoyed by the Rails to Trails Conservancy. Extending from Mason Station to Susanville, the approximately 25-mile-long trail is ideal for horseback riding, mountain biking and backpacking. In snowy months, the trail can be used for cross-country skiing. The 18-mile segment along the Susan River from Westwood Junction to Susanville is considered the most scenic because of the adjacent river and canyon. The trail is at a gentle three-percent grade along the route. Take caution when crossing the planking on decked bridges and when proceeding through unlighted tunnels. There are trails that skirt the tunnels if you don't want to go inside. Fishing is also possible along the Susan River.

Location: In northeastern California at the town of Susanville. The trail is best accessed at Mason Station near Westwood, Highway 44 near Hog Flat Reservoir, Highway 36 near Devils Corral and Hobo Camp near Susanville. An ideal mountain bike ride (almost all downhill!) can be had by using a shuttle. Leave one car at Hobo Camp. From Susanville, drive west on Highway 36 to County Road A-21, just before Westwood. Turn right and drive three miles to County Road 101. Turn right again and drive one-half mile to the Mason Station Trailhead.

Camping: There is a seven-day limit to camping anywhere along the trail. No camping is allowed at the trailheads.

Season: You can visit year-round. The best times for hiking and biking are in the spring, summer and fall; there is good cross-country skiing in the winter.

Permits: Free campfire permits are required—obtain them from the BLM. Seasonal fire restrictions apply.

USGS topographic maps: Westwood East, Fredonyer Pass, Roop Mountain, Susanville

Additional maps: Obtain the Bizz Johnson Trail Map, published by the BLM and U.S. Forest Service, from the BLM. A map of Lassen National Forest is available from the U.S. Forest Service.

For more information: Contact the BLM Eagle Lake Resource Area, 705 Hall Street, Susanville, CA 96130; (916) 257-0456. This trail is jointly managed by the BLM and the U.S. Forest Service.

AMEDEE / SKEDADDLE MOUNTAINS

See letter K on map page 126

backpacking, camping, hiking

Rugged peaks, vertical cliffs and steep canyons are the geological recipe here. The higher elevations support scattered aspen groves. Patches of riparian vegetation and small meadows dot the canyon bottoms. There are numerous springs throughout the area, but all water must be treated. The BLM recommends visiting Wendel Canyon for its unique scenic value. Mule deer, pronghorn antelope and mountain lion call the ranges home.

From Susanville, drive east on US 395 for 18 miles, then head east on Wendel Road, which bounds the southwest edge of the range. Park off the road and head in.

USGS topographic maps: Spencer Creek, Wendel, Bull Flat, Little Mud Flat

For more information: Contact the BLM Susanville District Office, 705 Hall Street, Susanville, CA 96130; (916) 257-5381.

FORKS OF BUTTE CREEK

See letter L on map page 126

fishing, hiking, inner-tubing

Rugged canyons invite exploration while the waters of Butte Creek provide a cooling respite from the nearby Sacramento Valley heat. Fishing for pan-sized trout is good. Bring an inner tube and float sections of the creek. From Chico and Interstate 5, head east on Highway 32 for approximately 18 miles to Garland Road and turn right. Drive 2.8 miles to Doe Mill Road; turn left and drive 1.8 miles to Forks of Butte Creek. Watch for signs.

USGS topographic maps: Pulga, Paradise East, Kimshew Point, Stirling City

For more information: Contact the BLM Redding Resource Area, 355 Hemsted Drive, Redding, CA 96002; (916) 224-2100.

FORT SAGE LOOP

See letter M on map page 126

hiking, mountain biking, off-highway-vehicle use

This 18-mile trail is open to both mountain biking and all-terrain vehicles and provides an easy to moderate trek across sagebrush and tumbleweed country. It's a slice of the Old West. From US 395 south of Susanville, exit at Laver Crossing and follow the signs to the trail.

USGS topographic maps: Doyle, Calneva

For more information: Contact the BLM Eagle Lake Resource Area, 705 Hall Street, Susanville, CA 96130; (916) 257-0456.

SOUTH FORK EEL RIVER

See letter N on map page 126

canoeing, fishing, hiking, horseback riding, kayaking, mountain biking, whitewater rafting

A number of Class IV rapids within this river section help to keep the whitewater enthusiast grinning. For a directory of 45 licensed whitewater outfitters, call the California Outfitter Hotline at (800) 552-3635. The river runs along US 101 north of Laytonville. Put-in and take-out points are all along US 101.

USGS topographic maps: Tan Oak Park, Leggett, Lincoln Ridge

For more information: Contact the BLM Arcata Resource Area, 1125 16th Street, Room 219, Arcata, CA 95521; (707) 822-7648.

MIDDLE FORK EEL RIVER

See letter O on map page 126

camping, hiking, whitewater rafting, wildlife observation

This wild, rugged country of dense forests, lush meadows, rolling hills and steep-walled gorges makes for a thrilling river adventure. The area provides a truly unique opportunity to experience a remote wilderness in a river setting. For the first 26 miles or so, the Middle Fork of the Eel rolls steadily through a wide valley filled with firs and pines. Wildflowers are common, and at times they appear to carpet the entire open area. Resident wildlife includes deer, black bear, otter and coyote. The last four miles, the most difficult to paddle, channel into a narrow gorge where tributary streams create colorful waterfalls off both sides of the canyon.

Activity Highlight: Whitewater rafting

The river is rated Class IV overall with a blend of Class II to Class IV-plus along its length. It is recommended that paddlers tackle this 30-mile trip in three days, rather than two. The Middle Fork is entirely dependent on snowmelt and rainwater: A storm can raise the water level dramatically and change the character of the river. One challenging portage may be required during the final four miles of the run, where the most difficult whitewater is encountered. A few commercial outfitters run trips on the river.

Location: East of US 101 and north of Ukiah. From US 101, exit at Highway 162 to the U.S. Forest Service's Eel River Ranger Station.

Camping: Camping is allowed anywhere along the river. Fire pans and porta-potties are recommended.

Season: April 1 to May 31 is typically the whitewater season on the Eel, depending on water flow. River conditions are very variable so call before you go. The California Department of Water Resources provides water flow information for most California rivers. To determine the best time to go, call (916) 322-3327.

USGS topographic maps: Ukiah, Redwood Valley, Willits

Resources:
• Call the California Outfitter Hotline at (800) 552-3635 for access to 45 California whitewater outfitters. You will receive a directory of licensed outfitters listing individual 800 numbers. The directory also offers basic information regarding what rivers are run and each outfitter's specialty: gourmet food, trips for singles, packages with mountain biking or hot-air ballooning, trips for families, women, men or disabled people, fishing trips, wilderness luxury trips and more.
• *Western Whitewater, From the Rockies to the Pacific,* by Jim Cassady, Bill Cross and Fryar Calhoun, published by North Fork Press, Berkeley, CA; (415) 424-1213.

For more information: Contact the BLM Arcata Resource Area, 1125 16th Street, Room 219, Arcata, CA 95521; (707) 822-7648.

Cow Mountain

See letter P on map page 126

camping, backpacking, hiking, horseback riding, mountain biking, off-highway-vehicle use

The chaparral-covered slopes, peppered with pine and oak, are very steep and intertwined with miles of trails and fire roads—ideal for hiking, horseback riding and mountain biking. Off-road-vehicle use is restricted to South Cow Mountain. From US 101 at Ukiah, head east on Talmage Road, turn south on Eastside Road, then east on Mill Creek to Cow Mountain Access Road.

USGS topographic maps: Cow Mountain, Purdy's Garden, Lakeport

For more information: Contact the BLM Clear Lake Resource Area, 2550 North State Street, Ukiah, CA 95482; (707) 468-4000.

CACHE CREEK

See letter Q on map page 126

backpacking, camping, hiking, horseback riding, rafting (when the stream is flowing at high levels during spring runoff), wildflowers

In the Cache Creek area, valleys abound with spring wildflowers and streams that attract numerous types of wildlife. There is a seven-mile hiking trail that will take you into the heartland of this pastoral recreation area. Tule elk and bald eagle inhabit the area, but Cache Creek is well known for other species as well, including wild turkey, blue heron, belted kingfisher, river otter, golden eagle and black bear. To get there from Clear Lake Oaks, head east eight miles on Highway 20 to the site entrance.

USGS topographic maps: Lower Lake, Wilson Valley, Wilbur Springs, Glascock Mountain, Knoxville

For more information: Contact the BLM Clear Lake Resource Area, 2550 North State Street, Ukiah, CA 95482; (707) 468-4000.

SOUTH FORK YUBA RIVER

See letter R on map page 126

backpacking, camping, fishing, hiking, mountain biking, swimming, rafting

History, scenic beauty and whitewater combine to make this canyon river a thrilling and rewarding experience for all. The South Yuba Trail provides a 13.5-mile link between the trail systems of nearby Malakoff Diggins State Park and Tahoe National Forest. Within the South Yuba River Recreation Area, camping is restricted to designated sites in the South Fork Campground. The river is rated Class IV to V. From Nevada City, head 12 miles north on State Road 49, then turn right on Tyler Foote County Road.

USGS topographic maps: Washington, North Bloomfield

BLM surface maps: Truckee, Yuba City

For more information: Contact the BLM Folsom Resource Area, 63 Natoma Street, Folsom, CA 95630; (916) 985-4474.

LITTLE DARBY INTERPRETIVE TRAIL

See letter S on map page 126

hiking

The Little Darby is a super interpretive trail winding through a mini-preserve of virgin Douglas fir. From US 101 at Willetts, head east on Commercial Street to Hearst-Willetts Road. From there, follow the Berry Canyon Road to the Little Darby parking area.

USGS topographic map: Willits

For more information: Contact the BLM Clear Lake Resource Area, 2550 North State Street, Ukiah, CA 95482; (707) 468-4000.

KNOXVILLE OFF-HIGHWAY-VEHICLE AREA

See letter T on map page 126

hiking, off-highway-vehicle use, rare plant observation, rockhounding

Steep chaparral hills are ideal for off-road use, which this area sees a lot of. Still, it is a pleasant destination for others seeking a more sedentary way of life. At Lower Lake Road, where Highways 29 and 53 merge, take Morgan Valley Road. Go south to McLaughlin Mine. Follow the road past the tunnel to the Knoxville signs.

USGS topographic maps: Jericho Valley, Knoxville

For more information: Contact the BLM Clear Lake Resource Area, 2550 North State Street, Ukiah, CA 95482; (707) 468-4000.

AMERICAN RIVER—SOUTH FORK

See letter U on map page 126

backpacking, canoeing, hiking, horseback riding, kayaking, rafting

Encompassing the North, Middle and South forks of the American River, this region of popular whitewater runs slices right through the very heart and soul of the Mother Lode. Scenic canyons and oak woodlands surround the river, which offers rides ranging from the mildly tame on the South Fork to the wild and woolly on the Middle and North forks. Despite the crowds that gather on the South Fork on weekends, many visitors return again and again because of the scenic value. Unlike most Sierra rivers that carve through deep canyons, the South Fork of the American winds through golden foothills sprinkled with oaks and digger pines. Low rock walls of the final "canyon" section increase the whitewater excitement. Expect to see blue herons and golden eagles and, if you visit early enough in the spring, you will enjoy hills covered with California poppy, lilac, shooting star, lupine and more. The fishing isn't great, but expect to reel in the occasional trout. A historic site, Sutters Mill, sits along the river route, just upstream from Marshall Gold Discovery State Park. Sutters Mill was the site of the first significant California gold discovery.

Activity Highlight: Whitewater rafting

It's Class II-plus water in normal flows, increasing to Class III when the water flows above 2,500 cubic feet per second. The water level is dam-controlled at the Chili Bar Powerhouse, just upriver from the put-in site. The best time to raft is midweek. This is a very heavily used river due to its proximity to San Francisco, Sacramento and Lake Tahoe. While you can run the river from your private raft, it is recommended that you go with a commercial outfit since enough people are congesting the waterways already. Water is cold in the spring and wetsuits should be worn.

Location: Near Placerville off Highway 50. From Sacramento and Interstate 5, head east on Highway 50 to Placerville. To get to Chili Bar, head north from Placerville on Highway 49 to Highway 193. Turn right on Highway 193 and head three miles to the Chili Bar Bridge and put-in access.

Camping: There are several campgrounds around the Placerville and Coloma area. For updated and accurate campground information, see Tom Stienstra's book, *California Camping*, published by Foghorn Press, 555 DeHaro Street, San Francisco, CA 94107; (800) 364-4676.

Season: April through August or September is the whitewater season, depending on water flow. The California Department of Water Resources provides water flow information for most California rivers. To determine the best time to go, call (916) 322-3327.

Permits: Permits are required and may be obtained from the BLM.

USGS topographic maps: Coloma, Garden Valley, Pilot Hill, Auburn, Greenwood, Georgetown

BLM surface maps: Placerville, Sacramento, Truckee

Resources:
• Call the California Outfitter Hotline at (800) 552-3635 for access to 45 California whitewater outfitters. You will receive a directory of

licensed outfitters listing individual 800 numbers. The directory also offers basic information regarding what rivers are run and each outfitter's specialty: gourmet food, trips for singles, packages with mountain biking or hot-air ballooning, trips for families, women, men or disabled people, fishing trips, wilderness luxury trips and more.

• *Western Whitewater, From the Rockies to the Pacific,* by Jim Cassady, Bill Cross and Fryar Calhoun, published by North Fork Press, Berkeley, CA; (415) 424-1213.

For more information: Contact the BLM Folsom Resource Area, 63 Natoma Street, Folsom, CA 95630; (916) 985-4474.

MOKELUMNE RIVER

See letter V on map page 126

canoeing, inner-tubing, kayaking

A short three-mile jaunt past the Gold Rush towns of Jackson and Mokelumne Hill offers easy access and a few miles of whitewater ideal for the novice kayaker in training for more difficult runs. The river is rated Class I to II. Take Highway 49 to Jackson and then to Electra Road. The put-in is at the Electra Powerhouse.

USGS topographic maps: Jackson, Mokelumne Hill

BLM surface map: San Andreas

For more information: Contact the BLM Folsom Resource Area, 63 Natoma Street, Folsom, CA 95630; (916) 985-4474.

INDIAN VALLEY—WALKER RIDGE

See letter W on map page 126

camping, backpacking, hiking, horseback riding, mountain biking

This area includes two established hiking trails, two campgrounds and a network of primitive roads for exploring the diverse, mountainous area surrounding Indian Valley Reservoir. From Williams, head west on Highway 20 for approximately 14 miles. From Clearlake Oaks, drive east for approximately 14 miles. Turn north at the recreation sign indicating Indian Valley and the Walker Ridge Recreation Area.

USGS topographic maps: Hough Springs, Benmore Canyon, Leesville, Wilbur Springs

For more information: Contact the BLM Clear Lake Resource Area, 2550 North State Street, Ukiah, CA 95482; (707) 468-4000.

BODIE BOWL

See letter X on map page 126

cross-country skiing, hiking, mountain biking, off-highway-vehicle use

The ghost town of Bodie, a living example of a boomtown gone bust, is a California state park. The area surrounding the town is all BLM land and offers a tremendous opportunity to observe nature, photograph wildlife or natural scenery, or tour on a mountain bike. Quaking aspen in the drainages turn bright yellow and gold in fall. The adventurous explorer will revel in discovering the many hidden canyons, interior valleys and springs tucked in among the pinyon-covered hills.

From Bridgeport on US 395, head east on Aurora Canyon Road and then southeast on Bodie/Masonic Road. Mountain biking can be enjoyed on the several unpaved roads that enter the Bodie Hills through narrow canyons such as Aurora, Clearwater, Cottonwood and Bridgeport. You can enjoy views of Mono Lake and the Sierra from atop of some of the higher points.

USGS topographic maps: Bodie, Trench Canyon, Bridgeport, Aurora

BLM surface maps: Bridgeport, Excelsior Mountain

For more information: Contact the BLM Bishop Resource Area, 787 North Main, Suite P, Bishop, CA 93514; (619) 872-4881.

TUOLUMNE RIVER

See letter Y on map page 126

whitewater rafting

California's premier whitewater river is a slalom course of boulders of escalating intensity. Staircase rapids, chutes and pools by the score and the close proximity of Yosemite National Park help to create the ultimate wilderness river adventure—a journey that is both exhilarating and pristine. Fishing is available for trout. Wildflowers paint the hills during the spring; especially common are paintbrush, shooting star and lupine.

The river is rated Class IV to V. It is dam-controlled; water releases, although scheduled and easy to anticipate, drastically affect the quality of the run. In some cases, lack of water or too much water will make the river unrunnable. Wetsuits are needed until the summer months. Two-day trips are the norm. The only access to the river is at the put-in and take-out points.

Location: Near Yosemite National Park in the Sierra Nevada. Take Highway 49 south from Sonora to Highway 120. Head east on Highway 120 past Groveland about 7.5 miles (one-half mile past the turn for County Road J20). Turn left (north) and drive one mile. Turn right onto a dirt road and drive six miles to Lumsden Campground and the put-in point.

Camping: Camp only at designated sites.

Season: April through October is the time to run this river. The California Department of Water Resources provides water flow information for most California rivers. To find out the best time to go, call (916) 322-3327.

Permits: Permits are required and can be obtained from the BLM. There are numerous commercial outfitters who run trips on the river.

USGS topographic maps: Tuolumne, Standard Hull Creek

BLM surface map: Oakdale

Resources:

• Call the California Outfitter Hotline at (800) 552-3635 for access to 45 California whitewater outfitters. You will receive a directory of licensed outfitters listing individual 800 numbers. The directory also offers basic information regarding what rivers are run and each outfitter's specialty: gourmet food, trips for singles, packages with mountain biking or hot-air ballooning, trips for families, women, men or disabled people, fishing trips, wilderness luxury trips and more.

• *Western Whitewater, From the Rockies to the Pacific,* by Jim Cassady, Bill Cross and Fryar Calhoun, published by North Fork Press, Berkeley, CA; (415) 424-1213.

For more information: Contact the BLM Folsom Resource Area, 63 Natoma Street, Folsom, CA 95630; (916) 985-4474; or Stanislaus National Forest, Groveland Office, Highway 120, Star Route Road, Groveland, CA 95321; (209) 962-7825.

CONWAY SUMMIT

See letter Z on map page 126

camping, mountain biking

From the top of the summit, you can see for miles—truly an on-top-of-the-world feeling. Virginia Creek is super for trout fishing and the Virginia Creek Canyon provides an excellent opportunity for primitive camping. The summit is located between Bridgeport and Lee Vining. From US 395, head west on Virginia Lake Road to Conway Summit.

USGS topographic maps: Lundy, Dunberg Peak

BLM surface map: Bridgeport

For more information: Contact the BLM Bishop Resource Area, 787 North Main, Suite P, Bishop, CA 93514; (619) 872-4881.

MERCED RIVER

See letter AA on map page 126

backpacking, camping, fishing, hiking, horseback riding, kayaking, mountain biking, rafting

The Merced is a hard-charging and highly seasonal whitewater run. The river is rated Class III to IV. Fishing is good for trout in the Merced, and the dirt path along the riverbank are ideal for horseback riding and mountain biking, but let's face it—rafting's *the* thing to do here. To get there, take Highway 140 to Forest Bridge and then Forest Bridge Road to Incline Road. A put-in point at the intersection of Forest Bridge Road and Incline Road provides river access; other put-ins are available along Highway 140.

USGS topographic maps: Bear Valley, Buckhorn Peak, Feliciana Mountain, El Portal, Kinsley

BLM surface map: Merced River

For more information: Contact the BLM Folsom Resource Area, 63 Natoma Street, Folsom, CA 95630; (916) 985-4474.

CALIFORNIA—MAP B

CRATER MOUNTAIN

See letter BB on map page 128

hiking, mountain biking

You can have wonderful fun exploring the cinder cone, lava flows and tube caves from volcanic activity thousands of years ago. From US 395 in Big Pine, head west on Glacier Lodge Road. Drive approximately four miles and then turn left onto an unmarked dirt road to the left. Crater Mountain is visible to the south. Follow the dirt road to an unsigned but obvious parking site and hike to the mountain.

USGS topographic map: Fish Springs

BLM surface map: Bishop

For more information: Contact the BLM Bishop Resource Area, 787 North Main, Suite P, Bishop, CA 93514; (619) 872-4881.

FISH SLOUGH

See letter CC on map page 128

birdwatching, hiking, mountain biking, wildlife observation

Set between the White Mountains and the Sierra Nevada, this is a lush oasis standing in dramatic contrast to the surrounding stark volcanic tableland. Three natural springs flow from volcanic cliffs, creating a slough that has been turned into a cooperatively managed wildlife sanctuary overseen by the BLM, the California Department of Fish and Game and the Los Angeles Department of Water and Power. Two endangered fish species, the Owen's pupfish and the Owen's tui chub, may be viewed within the six acres of clear ponds. Other wildlife that can be seen include yellow-headed blackbird, prairie falcon, green-winged teal, black-crowned night heron and a multitude of shorebirds, songbirds and waterfowl.

From Bishop, take US 395 north to Highway 6. Go north for 1.5 miles and turn west on Five Bridges Road. Drive approximately 2.5 miles to Fish Slough Road, then turn right just after a sand and gravel plant. After approximately 6.5 miles, you will come to a fenced pond and Fish Slough.

USGS topographic maps: Mount Tom, Bishop, White Mountain Peak, Casa Diablo Mountain

BLM surface maps: Bishop, Benton Range

For more information: Contact the BLM Bishop Resource Area, 787 North Main, Suite P, Bishop, CA 93514; (619) 872-4881.

SAN JOAQUIN RIVER / SQUAW LEAP TRAILS

See letter DD on map page 128

backpacking, camping, hiking, horseback riding, mountain biking

The 2.5-mile BLM section of the 11-mile San Joaquin River Trail from Sierra National Forest to Millerton Lake State Recreation Area offers breathtaking views of the San Joaquin River Gorge. The Squaw Leap Trail is another developed trail with spectacular views of the San Joaquin River Gorge that reward the visitor to this region. Wildflowers will leave you wide-eyed in the spring. To get there, travel east from Fresno on Highway 168 to Prather and follow the signs to Auberry. Access is via Power House Road to Smalley Road. The trailheads are at the junction of Power House Road and Smalley Road.

USGS topographic map: Millerton Lake East

BLM surface map: Shaver Lake

For more information: Contact the BLM Folsom Resource Area, 63 Natoma Street, Folsom, CA 95630; (916) 985-4474.

CASE MOUNTAIN

See letter EE on map page 128

hiking, mountain biking, rare plant viewing, wildlife observation

Giant Sequoia grow in three separate small groves on public lands at Case Mountain. Several rare plant and animal species can be found within this rugged area of approximately 6,000 acres. A recent land exchange has provided public access from Skyline Drive to the Case Mountain area. Current public access is limited to hiking and mountain biking along the approximately eight-mile graded dirt road which gains nearly 4,000 feet from the gate to the summit. Whew, can you say "bike-hike"? From Three Rivers on Highway 198, head northeast for approximately four miles to Skyline Drive, then turn southeast (right) and continue to a locked gate located at the BLM boundary.

USGS topographic map: Case Mountain

BLM surface map: Three Rivers

For more information: Contact the BLM Caliente Resource Area, 3801 Pegasus Drive, Bakersfield, CA 93308-6837; (805) 391-6000.

EUREKA DUNES

See letter FF on map page 128

camping, hiking, photography

Climb California's highest sand dune at 700 feet, give or take a few inches. Race downhill to celebrate. Photographers thrill to the interplay of light and shadows among the dunes and playa. From Big Pine and US 395, drive east on Highway 168 for approximately 2.5 miles to a Y junction. Turn east and to the right on Death Valley Road, heading toward Saline Valley and Waucoba. In approximately 20.5 miles, you will reach another Y junction; head more or less straight (the other branch on the right heads to Saline Valley). After passing North Eureka Valley Road, keep a sharp eye out for South Eureka Valley Road in about one mile. Turn right and head south toward the dunes—it's a can't-miss-'em deal. Park along the road opposite the dunes and enjoy.

USGS topographic map: Last Chance Range

For more information: Contact the BLM Ridgecrest Resource Area, 300 South Richmond Road, Ridgecrest, CA 93555; (619) 384-5400.

COALINGA MINERAL SPRING

See letter GG on map page 128

hiking

If you are looking for solitude, then this is your spot. Few visit here, yet the hiking is marvelous and quiet along a two-mile trail to the mountain peak. From Coalinga, drive 20 miles west on Highway 198 to Coalinga Mineral Springs Road. Turn right (north) and drive four miles to the trailhead parking area at Coalinga Mineral Springs County Park.

USGS topographic map: Sherman Peak

BLM surface map: Coalinga

For more information: Contact the BLM Hollister Resource Area, 20 Hamilton Court, Hollister, CA 95023; (408) 637-8183.

NORTH FORK KAWEAH RIVER

See letter HH on map page 128

camping, fishing, hiking, swimming

The rustic ambience of this scenic section of the river offers excellent opportunities for fishing, swimming, sunbathing, hiking and primitive camping. Just before the town of Three Rivers on Highway 198 (heading toward Sequoia National Park), turn north onto North Fork Drive and drive for nine miles. There are three river access points—Paradise Site, Advance Site and Cherry Falls Site. Each is marked with a BLM sign and offers limited parking.

USGS topographic maps: Mount Kaweah, General Grant Grove

BLM surface maps: Three Rivers, Mount Whitney

For more information: Contact the BLM Caliente Resource Area, 3801 Pegasus Drive, Bakersfield, CA 93308-6837; (805) 391-6000.

ALABAMA HILLS

See letter II on map page 128

backpacking, camping, hiking, horseback riding, mountain biking

The Alabama Hills' weathered granite boulder piles and rounded terrain colored in old Southwestern hues have been used as a backdrop for countless Western classics. Remember Hopalong Cassidy? This is the pass where he rounded up all those bad guys. Now you can play here, too. Time your visit right and you can take in some film nostalgia during the annual Lone Pine Film Festival. The Alabama Hills are west of US 395 at Lone Pine.

USGS topographic map: Lone Pine

BLM surface map: Mount Whitney

For more information: Contact the BLM Bishop Resource Area, 787 North Main, Suite P, Bishop, CA 93514; (619) 872-4881.

DARWIN FALLS

See letter JJ on map page 128

backpacking, camping, hiking

Spring is the best time to visit the falls as this is when the canyon area is teeming with desert wildlife and migrating birds. There is much more to this area than just the falls, however. The Darwin Plateau rises 4,000 feet above the valley floor and is cut by deep chasms through volcanic rock faces. Spring-fed creeks within a number of these canyons create cool and moist oases from the desert which attract wildlife from all around. Located west of Death Valley National Monument. No permits are required. From Olancha on US 395, head 44 miles east on Route 190. Continue south on Darwin Canyon Road for 2.6 miles to a dirt road—follow the signs to the designated parking area.

USGS topographic map: Darwin

For more information: Contact the BLM Ridgecrest Resource Area, 300 South Richmond Road, Ridgecrest, CA 93555; (619) 384-5400.

PANAMINT MOUNTAINS AND VALLEY

See letter KK on map page 128

backpacking, camping, hiking

This is an expansive 210,000-acre area along the western boundary of Death Valley National Park, bisected by Route 190. A number of maintained roads provide decent access into the region and its four pristine wilderness study areas—Hunter Mountain, Panamint Dunes, Wildrose Canyon and Surprise Canyon. For the best mobility and access, as well as all-weather safety, a four-wheel-drive vehicle is highly recommended.

Hunter Mountain rises 7,454 feet above the valley floor. The road up and over its back is very hazardous in anything but sunny weather. Grapevine Canyon, which parallels the road, has an abundance of water from numerous springs originating high up on the slopes. Wildlife includes mule deer and bighorn sheep. The area is well regarded for birding opportunities.

Panamint Dunes are in a six-square-mile area of developed and developing sand dunes rising above a dry flat lakebed. Some of the dunes rise up to 250 feet above the valley floor. Vegetation varies from scrub in low-lying areas to pinyon pine and juniper in the higher and rockier reaches. Bighorn sheep and mule deer, along with chipmunk and golden eagle, are the main fare for wildlife viewing.

The Wildrose Canyon area is deeply cut by canyons from which gently sloping alluvial fans emerge out and onto the valley floor. Creosote bush and desert holly are the predominant vegetation.

Surprise Canyon is an area of outstanding scenic quality and has been designated an Area of Critical Environmental Concern. County-maintained Indian Ranch Road provides access into the area. Tele-scope Peak towers monarch over the area at 11,045 feet. The sur-rounding terrain is mostly rugged mountains and deeply cut canyons. There is a small badlands area to the northwest. The area has had a history of mining, which explains a number of roads that disappear into the mountainous terrain. Several of the canyons in the area sport flowing springs. Flower displays are seasonal and very colorful on the alluvial fans that extend out from many of the canyons.

USGS topographic maps: Harris Hill, Jackass Canyon, Wildrose Peak, Emigrant Pass, Maturango Peak Northeast, Panamint, Ballaraf, The Dunes

For more information: Contact the BLM California Desert District Office, 6221 Box Springs Boulevard, Riverside, CA 92507; (909) 697-5200.

OWENS PEAK WILDERNESS STUDY AREA

See letter LL on map page 128

backpacking, camping, hiking, horseback riding

Traveling through this area on the Pacific Crest Trail offers the visitor a delightful combination of rocky, steep slopes, rolling terrain, golden meadowlands and juniper, Joshua tree and pine forests. Views of the Domelands Wilderness Area and the Sierra Nevada can be en-joyed from a number of outstanding vista points.

Activity Highlights: Hiking and backpacking

Hiking here follows the Pacific Crest Trail. The hike begins just south of Walker Pass Campground and across Highway 178. Water sources along the route are infrequent, but adequate. Just be sure to carry at least one gallon per person as a reserve at all times. The hike terminates approximately 40 miles from Walker Pass in Rockhouse Basin, the boundary for the Domelands Wilderness Area. If you have the time, Rockhouse Basin is worth exploring. A number of streams cut through it, giving it a lush riparian environment that attracts wildlife. Only a campfire permit is required there. Bears are not a major problem near Owens Peak, but bear precautions should be the rule, not the exception.

Location: In the southernmost reaches of the Sierra Nevada, just east of Bakersfield and west of Death Valley. Take Highway 178 west from

Highway 14 (just west of [...] Walker Pass Trailhead Facility. You will need to a[...]wn shuttle or hike back. The most scenic porti[...] the upper 20 miles or so—I would recommend h[...]and-back hike at Chimney Creek Campgrou[...] Chimney Creek, go 2.5 miles north of Pears[...]95 and turn left on Nine Mile Canyon Road. (P[...]12 miles north of Inyokern.) Drive 11 miles up Nine [...] Road to just past the BLM Fire Station; bear left on [...]e Road. The campground is three miles from the fire station.

Camping: You can camp anywhere along the trail. Two maintained campgrounds, Walker Pass Trailhead Facility and Chimney Creek Campground, provide water, toilets, parking and fire grates.

Season: Travel is best from May to mid-November. Snow is possible in the higher elevations during the rest of the year. July and August may be uncomfortably hot in the lower elevations.

Permits: No permits are needed for backpacking. Campfire permits are required.

USGS topographic maps: Walker Pass, Owens Peak, Lamont Peak, White Dome, Rockhouse Basin

BLM surface maps: Isabella, Ridgecrest

Resources:
• *The Pacific Crest Trail, Vol. 1*, by Jeffrey Schaffer, published by Wilderness Press, 2440 Bancroft Way, Berkeley, CA 94704.
• A brochure entitled "Chimney Peak Recreation Area" is available from the BLM.

For more information: Contact the BLM Bakersfield District Office, 3801 Pegasus Drive, Bakersfield, CA 93308-6837; (805) 391-6000.

EL PASO MOUNTAINS

See letter MM on map page 128

backpacking, birdwatching, camping, hiking, wildlife observation

Twenty-two square miles of the El Paso Raptor Management Area are within this site, one of the principal breeding areas for golden eagle, prairie falcon and others. You can be virtually assured of blue-ribbon raptor watching. Last Chance Canyon runs through the region and has been given the BLM thumbs-up as a place of high scenic value. At times, the surrounding slopes of this badland-like area are a wildflower mosaic of color. It's located east of Route 14 and north of Red Rock-Randsburg-Garlock Road (it's just as tough to put on a sign as it is to say). Before heading out, contact the BLM office for detailed and specific directions and road condition information.

USGS topographic map: El Paso Peaks

For more information: Contact the BLM Ridgecrest Resource Area, 300 South Richmond Road, Ridgecrest, CA 93555; (619) 384-5400.

CHIMNEY PEAK RECREATION AREA

See letter NN on map page 128

backpacking, camping, fishing, hiking, horseback riding

Although this is officially called the Chimney Peak Recreation Area, it is bubbling Chimney Creek that is the prime attraction here. Set among the pinyon pines of the rugged Sierra Nevada foothills, the creek affords the avid angler an opportunity for good trout fishing. This area also serves as a hub of activity for backpackers, hikers and equestrians entering into the wilds via the Pacific Crest Trail. It adjoins the Domelands Wilderness Area, creating possibilities for semi-loop backpacking and horsepacking trips. Permits to enter the wilderness areas are required.

The area is near the Pacific Crest Trail in the Sierra Nevada. Drive north from Inyokern on US 395 for approximately 15 miles to County Road 152 (Nine Mile Canyon) and turn left. Drive another 13 miles, then veer left at the ranger station to the Chimney Peak Campground entrance, a good base for your explorations.

For more information: Contact the BLM Caliente Resource Area, 3801 Pegasus Drive, Bakersfield, CA 93308-6837; (805) 391-6000.

FOSSIL FALLS

See letter OO on map page 128

backpacking, camping, cultural site, hiking

Black lava, sculpted and polished during the Ice Age, creates a series of dry waterfalls here. Native Americans frequented this exceptional site because of the lavish formations created by volcanic activity—activity that provided materials for toolmaking. On your hike over the lava, you'll see rock rings—remnants of circular huts built by the Paiute Indians. The abundance of obsidian flakes in the area attest to the use of volcanic glass in making knives and other projectiles. Petroglyphs found here are thought to relate to hunting rituals. From Ridgecrest, drive approximately 45 miles north on US 395 to Cinder Cone Road. Turn right (east), then head south on unpaved Poleline Road to the signed and designated parking area.

USGS topographic map: Little Lake

For more information: Contact the BLM Ridgecrest Resource Area, 300 South Richmond Road, Ridgecrest, CA 93555; (619) 384-5400.

TRONA PINNACLES RECREATION LANDS
See letter PP on map page 128

backpacking, camping, hiking, horseback riding, mountain biking

If you are a Star Trek fan, you may recognize the pinnacles as the setting for the movie, *Star Trek V: The Final Frontier*. If not, you will find ultimate pleasure within this maze of monoliths jutting out of a dry lakebed. This is typical BLM land—wander wherever your feet will take you, but no further than you are willing to walk back. Trona Pinnacles is at Searles Lake, east of Highway 178 near Trona. From US 395 at Ridgecrest, take the Highway 178 exit heading east. Highway 178 begins as Ridgecrest Road and then turns into Trona Road. Turn right onto Pinnacles Road towards the Trona Pinnacles Recreation Lands. Exit left at the sign indicating Trona Pinnacles. Park in the designated area.

USGS topographic map: Searles Lake

For more information: Contact the BLM Ridgecrest Resource Area, 300 South Richmond Road, Ridgecrest, CA 93555; (619) 384-5400.

SPANGLER HILLS
See letter QQ on map page 128

backpacking, camping, hiking, horseback riding, mountain biking, off-highway-vehicle use

Although a fair number of off-highway vehicles frequent the area, there is plenty of room for hikers and mountain bikers to enjoy the recreational pleasures of this high-desert site. The best time to visit is in the spring when the area is sprinkled with color from seasonal wildflowers. At other times, the miles of rugged terrain that have been clearly carved up by off-roading amid the endless backdrop of creosote bush can get a little, shall we say, unappealing? Located south of Ridgecrest and east of US 395. From US 395 near Ridgecrest, exit on Highway 178. Turn south, (right) off Highway 178 on Randsburg Wash Road, then drive to Stephens Mine Road. Turn south (right) again. Numerous entrances head east and west off Stephens Mine Road—take your pick. There are no trails—it's free-form wandering.

USGS topographic maps: Spangler Hills East, Spangler Hills West

For more information: Contact the BLM Ridgecrest Resource Area, 300 South Richmond Road, Ridgecrest, CA 93555; (619) 384-5400.

KEYESVILLE

See letter RR on map page 128

camping, fishing, kayaking, mountain biking, rafting

Located near the town of Lake Isabella, this area can get a bit crowded at times. Still, it serves as a good base from which to enjoy whitewater activities on the nearby Kern River as well as fishing, camping and exploring old mine ruins.

USGS topographic maps: Lake Isabella, Miracle Hot Springs, Alta Sierra, Lake Isabella South

BLM surface map: Lake Isabella

For more information: Contact the BLM Caliente Resource Area, 3801 Pegasus Drive, Bakersfield, CA 93308-6837; (805) 391-6000.

CARRIZO PLAIN NATURAL AREA

See letter SS on map page 128

hiking, horseback riding, mountain biking, wildlife observation

This place was once referred to as the "next Serengeti Plain" by an enthusiastic BLM official during a press conference. Press conferences can inspire exaggeration, but not in this case. Carrizo Plain is indeed spectacular, partly because of its enormity—at 60 miles long, it is the largest wildlife preserve in the state. Nearly 5,000 sandhill cranes are known to winter here, attracted by a 3,000-acre alkali wetland. Surrounding grasslands are home to San Joaquin antelope squirrels, blunt-nosed lizards, San Joaquin kit fox, giant kangaroo rats, Western bluebirds, horned larks, tule elk and pronghorn antelope. There are also heavy concentrations of wintering birds of prey, including the short-eared owl, ferruginous hawk, Northern harrier and bald eagle. Hiking and mountain biking are recreational possibilities here.

Location: Near the towns of Maricopa and Taft in the San Joaquin Valley. From Buttonwillow on Interstate 5, take Highway 58 west for approximately 45 miles to Soda Lake Road. Turn south and drive approximately 14 miles to the signed entrance for the Guy L. Goodwin Education Center (Visitor Center).

Camping: Primitive camping within the area is allowed only at the KCL Camping Area and the Selby Parking Area, located on Soda Lake Road, south of the Guy L. Goodwin Education Center (Visitor Center). Water is not available, so you will need to bring all your supplies with you. The nearest towns offering basic services are Buttonwillow and Taft, approximately 50 minutes driving time to the east.

Season: You can visit here year-round, but winter is the best time to see migrating birds. Spring (April) is excellent for wildflowers. Summer can be very hot.

USGS topographic maps: McKittrick Summit, Painted Rock, Panorama Hills

BLM surface map: Taft

Resources:
• A brochure entitled "Carrizo Plain Natural Area" is available from the BLM.
• *California Wildlife Viewing Guide,* by Jeanne Clark, published by Falcon Press, P.O. Box 1718, Helena, MT 59624; (800) 582-2665.

For more information: Contact the BLM Caliente Resource Area, 3801 Pegasus Drive, Bakersfield, CA 93308-6837; (805) 391-6000; The Nature Conservancy, Carrizo Plain Natural Area, P.O. Box 3098, California Valley, CA 93453; or the California Department of Fish and Game, Region 3, P.O. Box 47, Yountville, CA 94599.

DESERT TORTOISE NATURAL AREA
See letter TT on map page 128

hiking, wildflowers, wildlife observation

Although this is a tortoise preserve, you will have to look hard to spot one—they are a bit shy and reclusive. The best time to view the threatened California state reptile is between early March and late May. If you spot one, keep your distance. Tortoises traumatize easily and human contact could lead to their death. Wildflowers are spectacular here during the spring with over 150 species in bloom. Check with the visitor center for guided tours during the spring. Summer is too hot to visit and viewing is poor anyway. From Highway 58 or Highway 14, take the California City exit to California City. Head through town, turning north on Randburg-Mojave Road. Drive 5.5 miles to the preserve's signed entrance.

USGS topographic map: California City North

For more information: Contact the BLM Ridgecrest Resource Area, 300 South Richmond Road, Ridgecrest, CA 93555; (619) 384-5400.

HARPER LAKE

See letter UU on map page 128

birdwatching, hiking, wildlife observation

Bring your binoculars. A number of short and unsigned trails crisscross the area, providing excellent access to an oasis of richly vegetated lakes and marshland in the middle of the Mojave Desert. This water attracts a wide variety of wildlife to the area, which is why it has been officially declared a Watchable Wildlife Viewing Area. Wading and songbirds can be seen year-round. You have a very high probability of viewing birds of prey, waterfowl and shorebirds from fall to spring. Keep a sharp eye out for the short-eared owls who live around the marshy area—nearly 300 have been officially reported and counted in one marsh. Wildflowers are super in the spring. There are no facilities nearby, so bring along plenty of water. Wear a wide-brimmed hat and sunscreen. The lake is northwest of Barstow. From Barstow, take Highway 58 west for approximately 25 miles to Harper Lake Road and turn north. The parking area and signed entrance to Harper Lake is located approximately five miles north on Harper Lake Road.

USGS topographic map: Lockhart

For more information: Contact the BLM Barstow Resource Area, 150 Coolwater Lane, Barstow, CA 92311; (619) 256-3591.

RAINBOW BASIN

See letter VV on map page 128

backpacking, camping, hiking, horseback riding, mountain biking, photography

Millions of years of geologic history are the primary drawing card here. Take a hike down Owl Canyon Wash or choose to drive or pedal your mountain bike on the short 1.5-mile loop trail through the basin. Geology enthusiasts will think that they have died and gone to rock heaven when they discover the wealth of rock formations that exist here. Don't forget your camera, either—the spectacular scenery demands to be photographed. From Barstow, take Camp Irwin Road north for five miles and then head west for five more miles on Fossil Beds Road. Turn right on a road signed for Rainbow Basin.

USGS topographic maps: Mud Hills, Lane Mountain

For more information: Contact the BLM Barstow Resource Area, 150 Coolwater Lane, Barstow, CA 92311; (619) 256-3591.

JAWBONE / DOVE SPRINGS

See letter WW on map page 128

backpacking, hiking, horseback riding, mountain biking, off-highway-vehicle use

Located in southern Kern County, this area offers the outdoor enthusiast an opportunity to enjoy just about every non-motorized and motorized recreational activity except water sports. Dramatic views with an equally dramatic blend of mountains, desert shrubs and flatlands provide a superb backdrop and a haven for an impressive inventory of mammals, reptiles and birds. From Highway 14 heading north from Mojave, head left (west) on Jawbone Road, just before the Garlock turnoff and Redroad Randsburg Road. Off-highway-vehicle use can be heavy at the head of the canyon areas. Vehicles are prohibited from entering the designated wilderness areas of the canyons, however.

USGS topographic maps: Freeman Junction, Cinco, Cross Mountain, Dove Spring, Pinyon Mountain

For more information: Contact the BLM Ridgecrest Resource Area, 300 South Richmond Road, Ridgecrest, CA 93555; (619) 384-5400.

RAND MOUNTAINS

See letter XX on map page 128

backpacking, camping, hiking, horseback riding, mountain biking, rockhounding, wildlife observation

Hikers, rockhounds, wildlife watchers and mountain bikers will enjoy the wide open spaces and dramatic ups and downs of existing roads that wind through this historic mining district. Head south on US 395 from Ridgecrest to the Redrock Randsburg Road and turn west. This road skirts the northern boundary of the Rand Mountains; numerous unsigned dirt roads head south and into the range. Munsey Road, which heads south of Redrock Randsburg Road, provides the most direct access to the range. From the cluster of small towns (if you can call them that) Randsburg, Johannesburg and Red Mountain, another road, Randsburg Mojave Road, heads west and skirts the southern boundary of the Rand Mountains. From here, a number of dirt roads lead into the range. Before heading out, contact the BLM office for detailed and specific directions and road condition information.

USGS topographic maps: Johannesburg, Saltdale Southeast

For more information: Contact the BLM Ridgecrest Resource Area, 300 South Richmond Road, Ridgecrest, CA 93555; (619) 384-5400.

AFTON CANYON

See letter YY on map page 128

backpacking, camping, hiking, horseback riding, mountain biking

Explore canyons, nooks and crannies wandered in past centuries by Native Americans, Spanish missionaries and mountain men. Wagon trains once stopped here to rest and water beside the Mojave River, which still flows most of the year. The sheer walls of this multicolored mini-Grand Canyon tower above the river. There are four short trails that will guide you past the multicolored cliffs and through the nooks and crannies of this magical region—all beginning at Afton Campground.

The canyon is northeast of Barstow. From Barstow, drive 33 miles east on Interstate 15 to the Afton turnoff. Follow the dirt road southwest for three miles to Afton Campground. The trailheads branch off from the campground. Day-use permits are not required.

USGS topographic maps: Dunn, Manix, Hidden Valley West

For more information: Contact the BLM Barstow Resource Area, 150 Coolwater Lane, Barstow, CA 92311; (619) 256-3591.

MOJAVE NATIONAL PRESERVE AREA
See letter ZZ on map page 128

backpacking, camping, hiking, historic sites, horseback riding, mountain biking, wildflowers, wildlife observation

The sawtooth mountains, salt-encrusted playas, weird yet wonderful Joshua trees, dramatic rock spires and flat-topped mesas of this region were the inspiration behind many of novelist Zane Grey's Western writings. Up until 1995, this was known as the East Mojave National Scenic Area. The California Desert Protection Act helped it become a national preserve, changing its name and boundaries. The BLM still plays a role in the region, but as this book went to press it was unclear which areas it would manage in the future. The highlights of the areas that the BLM managed in the past are as follows:

Activity Highlights: Hiking and backpacking

Excellent backpacking and hiking opportunities abound, from the rounded granite of Cima Dome to pinyon- and juniper-laden Caruthers Canyon and the booming Kelso Dunes.

Cima Dome: A four-mile round-trip trek over a primitive trail leads to the summit of Cima Dome. The 70-square-mile, gently rounded granite dome is reported to be the most symmetrical of its type anywhere in the nation. A weird and magical Joshua tree forest carpets the area and provides a home for a variety of desert wildlife. The cinder cones you see off in the distance are part of the Cinder Cones National Natural Landmark, noted for petroglyph-covered basalts and other geologic features.

From Barstow, drive 89 miles north on Interstate 15 to Cima Road. Turn right (south) and then drive 11 miles on Cima Road to the signs indicating the trailhead.

USGS topographic map: Cima Dome

Mid Hills to Hole-In-The-Wall Trail: This is the Old West at its best. The high-desert area with its dramatic volcanic formations punctuated by twisty stands of juniper is authentic cowboy country. Pungent sage perfumes this eight-mile point-to-point treadway over rolling hills—perfect for hikers, mountain bikers and horses. If you feel someone watching you, it's probably a desert bighorn sheep, wondering about your progress as he stands guard on a faraway ledge. We suggest that you begin your journey at Mid Hills Campground, spend the night at Hole-In-The-Wall, and then retrace yours steps the next day. Sure, you could go out and back in one day, but why rush your opportunity to soak up all this grandeur?

From Interstate 40 near Essex, take the Essex Road exit and drive 16 miles northwest on Essex Road to Black Canyon Road. Turn north on Black Canyon and drive 19 miles, following the signs to the campground.

USGS topographic maps: Fountain Peak, Van Winkle Spring, Mid Hills

Caruthers Canyon: Take a trek into a rock pine island amid a sea of desert. From the parking area, continue hiking up the now-abandoned mining road heading into a historic gold mining region. Old shafts still exist in the area. The BLM does not prohibit access to the shafts, but common sense would indicate that to explore these abandoned mines is dangerous and foolhardy—unless you are looking for a knock on the head from a rock fall. The pinyon pine and juniper woodland is a pleasure to hike through. Wander where you will—set up camp if you wish, as long as you have brought along plenty of water—and retrace your steps down the road to your car when ready. Fall through spring is the best time to visit. Summer is too hot!

From Barstow, drive approximately 120 miles east on Interstate 40 to Mount Springs Road and turn north. Drive to the town of Goffs and tank up with gas, water, and any other supplies you might need—it's your last stop. From Goffs, head north for approximately 25.5 miles on Ivanpah Road to New York Mountains Road (the turnoff is identified by OX Cattle Ranch buildings located at the intersection). Set your odometer to zero at the intersection. Head left (west) on New York Mountains Road and drive 5.6 miles to an unsigned junction with a dirt road heading north to Caruthers Canyon. Drive north for two miles on this dirt road to a wooded area and park—it has become somewhat of an informal campground here, so try not to park in obvious camping spots.

USGS topographic map: Ivanpah

Kelso Dunes: Trek or schlep up to the top of one of America's tallest sand dunes. Due to the shifting nature of sand and dunes, there is no official trail other than the first one-quarter mile or so to get you heading in the right direction. Head up the dunes on a route of your own choosing—we would recommend not heading straight up, unless you have bionic legs and lungs. Wildflowers are super on the way up in spring, sprinkling the lower dune sands with yellow, white and pink. Once at the top, stand quietly and take in the view and, if you are lucky, the vibrations emanating from the sonorous dunes. By way of explanation, the dunes are not actually singing, but vibrating as sand slides down the steep slopes—it's a deep sound that is almost felt more than heard. The trip down is outstanding, with somersaults optional.

From Interstate 40, head north on Kelbaker Road to a signed dirt road indicating Kelso Dunes to the left. Turn left and drive carefully along this sometimes rough road for approximately three miles to a designated BLM parking area for Kelso Dunes. The trailhead begins just up the dirt road from the parking area.

USGS topographic map: Kelso

General USGS topographic maps for East Mojave National Scenic Area: Granite Spring, Cow Cove, Cima Dome, Cima Hayden, Marl Mountain, Indian Spring, Old Dad Mountain, Kelso

Resources:

• The Southwest Natural and Cultural Heritage Association (SNCHA) publishes a series of 22 *Desert Access Guides* to the California desert regions. Each is available for $4 from SNCHA, Desert Information Center, 831 Barstow Road, Barstow, CA 92311; (619) 256-8313.

For more information: Contact the BLM California Desert District Office, 6221 Box Springs Boulevard, Riverside, CA 92507; (909) 697-5217; or the California State Parks at (805) 942-0662.

PROVIDENCE MOUNTAINS STATE RECREATION AREA

See letter AAA on map page 128

backpacking, camping, hiking, horseback riding, spelunking

The Providence Mountains extend northeast for about 20 miles from Granite Pass, just south of Kelso. Limestone cliffs and caverns add variety to the rhyolite crags and peaks and the broad *bajadas*. If you are a Zane Grey fan, you may recognize the large flat-topped

Wildhorse Mesa as the setting for his book of the same name—
Wildhorse Mesa. There are plenty of opportunities for hiking away
from it all and discovering a peaceful sense of isolation. Within the
designated state park boundaries, the primary attraction is the
Mitchell Caverns Natural Preserve. Reserved tours of the cavern are a
must; call (805) 942-0662. The recreation area is north of Interstate
40 near Essex. From Interstate 40, take the Essex Road exit and drive
17 miles northwest on Essex Road into the park.

USGS topographic maps: Fountain Peak, Van Winkle Spring

For more information: Contact the BLM California Desert District
Office, 6221 Box Springs Boulevard, Riverside, CA 92507; (909)
697-5200; or California State Parks; (805) 942-0662.

FORT PIUTE HISTORIC SITE

See letter BBB on map page 128

hiking, historic site, horseback riding

Though a four-wheel-drive vehicle is required for access, a visit
here is worth the effort. The mile-long oasis of Piute Creek has enjoyed a checkered history as one of the Mojave's most important
watering spots since prehistoric times. Nomadic Native Americans
camped here, as did the U.S. military who created a desert outpost.
Not only can you see the ruins of the fort, but you'll also have a
chance to view ancient Native American petroglyphs. The area is located on the California/Nevada border, west of US 95, east of Lanfair
Road and approximately 12 miles north of Needles. Access is via local
roads—ask at the BLM office for specific directions.

USGS topographic maps: Needles Northwest, Needles Southwest

For more information: Contact the BLM Needles Resource Area,
101 West Spikes Road, Needles, CA 92363; (619) 326-3896.

CALIFORNIA—MAP C

BIG MORONGO PRESERVE

See letter CCC on map page 130

birdwatching, hiking, picnicking, wheelchair access, wildlife observation

This desert oasis features deep canyons with a clear-running stream through lush desert riparian woodland. A developed trail system leads the visitor under a canopy of cottonwood and willow trees, which create a haven for raccoons, ringtails, bobcats and over 230 species of resident and migrant birds. There is a wheelchair-accessible boardwalk which leads out and over the springs. A number of other trails branching off from the boardwalk and parking area offer three-tenths to one-mile loops. In sharp contrast to the green canyon bottom are the surrounding desert slopes which rise to rocky 3,000-foot ridgetops inhabited by desert bighorn sheep. The region is interesting botanically because two desert vegetation zones, the Mojave and Sonoran, merge here. Birdwatchers flock to Big Morongo during both fall and spring migrations to spot unexpected avian travelers that find their way into this unique meeting place of coast and desert along the Pacific migratory flyway.

The preserve is closed on Monday and Tuesday. To get there from just northwest of Palm Springs on Interstate 10, drive Highway 62 north to Morongo Valley. Turn right (east) on Covington Park and follow the road north for a short distance to the signed entrance and parking area.

USGS topographic map: Morongo Valley

For more information: Contact the BLM Palm Springs-South Coast Resource Area, 63-500 Garnet Avenue, P.O. Box 2000, North Palm Springs, CA 92258; (619) 251-4800.

MECCA HILLS RECREATION AREA
See letter DDD on map page 130

backpacking, camping, hiking, horseback riding, mountain biking

Picturesque badlands, hidden palm oases, colorful box canyons, ridgetops with views south to the Salton Sea and west to the Santa Rosa Mountains offer excellent opportunities for adventurous exploration (cross the San Andreas Fault), hiking and photography. The Sheephole and Hidden Springs Oasis Trail offers a 2.5-mile hiking trail to a palm tree oasis. Ladder Canyon features approximately four miles of trail through narrow-walled canyons and up to scenic vistas. There are many other opportunities and informal trails for the willing and skilled adventurer.

The Mecca Hills are north of the Salton Sea, south of Interstate 10. From Palm Springs, head east on Interstate 10, past Cactus City and then to Cottonwood Springs Road/Box Canyon Road exit. Turn south on Box Canyon Road. In approximately 10 miles, you enter the Mecca Hills Recreation Area. Look for a BLM sign indicating the trailhead for Sheephole and Hidden Springs Oasis on the left. Further on down look for another BLM sign indicating Ladder Canyon on the right. Parking is available at each trailhead.

USGS topographic maps: Thermal Canyon, Mortmar, Cottonwood Basin

For more information: Contact the BLM Palm Springs-South Coast Resource Area, 63-500 Garnet Avenue, P.O. Box 2000, North Palm Springs, CA 92258; (619) 251-4800.

COACHELLA VALLEY PRESERVE
See letter EEE on map page 130

backpacking, birdwatching, hiking, horseback riding, wildlife observation

This 1,000 palm oasis is a joint BLM-Nature Conservancy preserve established to protect the endangered Coachella Valley fringe-toed lizard. Crystal-clear springs shaded by greenery attract a wide variety of wildlife and birds. The stunning 13,000-acre palm oasis was used once as the backdrop for Cecil B. DeMille's classic movie, *King of Kings*. Start by touring the self-guided nature trail. The more ambitious can head out on other signed trails leading past blow-sand dunes, through desert washes, and to overlooks which afford views all the way to the Salton Sea. Stay very alert on the Sand Dune Trail and you may even be lucky enough to see the tiny sand swimmer doing its laps.

From Palm Springs, take Interstate 10 east 10 miles to the Ramon Road exit. Drive east to Thousand Palms Canyon Drive. Turn north and drive two miles to the signed entrance to the preserve.

USGS topographic maps: Cathedral City, Myoma

For more information: Contact the BLM Palm Springs-South Coast Resource Area, 63-500 Garnet Avenue, P.O. Box 2000, North Palm Springs, CA 92258; (619) 251-4800.

JOSHUA TREE NATIONAL PARK AREA

See letter FFF on map page 130

hiking, backpacking, wildlife observation, rock climbing, horseback riding

Up until 1995, the BLM had jurisdiction over a wide range of territory surrounding Joshua Tree National Monument. Thanks to the California Desert Protection Act, the national monument has become a national park, which has caused boundaries throughout the region to be redefined. As this book went to press, the definitions of who was managing what areas were still fuzzy. Either way, it is still a spectacular area that is sure to convince even the most cynical outdoorsperson that desert terrain is far from boring or monotonous. Wildflower displays in the spring border on the spectacular. To reach the park, take Highway 62 from Interstate 10 to Twentynine Palms—the entrance to the visitor center is signed. Be sure to visit the following areas, which the BLM managed before the redesignation (and may continue to have a hand in managing):

Sheephole-Cadiz Recreation Areas: Vast desert valleys bounded by steep granite mountains make up this region of high wilderness that lies to the northeast of the monument. There is a spring in the Sheephole Mountains that provides sufficient water to support a small herd of desert bighorn sheep.

Eagle Mountains: The Eagle Mountains are rugged and highly complex, with jumbled boulder piles, numerous small canyons, steep slopes, washes and areas of thick vegetation. There are a number of fan palm oases in the region.

USGS topographic maps: New Dale, Clarks Pass, Cadiz Valley Southeast, Cadiz Valley Southwest, Coxcomb Mountains, East of Victory Pass, Victory Pass Buzzard Spring, Conejo Well, San Bernardino Wash, Placer Canyon, Pinto Wells, Hayfield

Resources:
• The best existing map of the region is still the Joshua Tree National Monument map with backcountry and hiking information, published by Trails Illustrated, P.O. Box 3610, Evergreen, CO 80439; (800) 962-1643. They plan to publish a map of the new national park once the chips settle.
• The Southwest Natural and Cultural Heritage Association (SNCHA) publishes a series of 22 *Desert Access Guides* to the California desert regions. Each is available for $4 from SNCHA, Desert Information Center, 831 Barstow Road, Barstow, CA 92311; (619) 256-8313.

For more information: Contact the BLM Palm Springs-South Coast Resource Area, 63-500 Garnet Avenue, P.O. Box 2000, North Palm Springs, CA 92258; (619) 251-4800; or Joshua Tree National Park, 74485 National Park Drive, Twentynine Palms, CA 92277-3597; (619) 367-7511.

CORN SPRINGS

See letter GGG on map page 130

camping, cultural site, hiking, wildlife observation

Set in a deep canyon among the fabled Chuckwalla Mountains, this site produces a wealth of botanical pleasures from groves of native fan palms to lush clumps of cattail. The water in the canyon attracts an impressive array of wildlife including screech owls, Western pipistrelle bats, Gambel's quail and cactus wrens. Tennis shoes will carry you nicely over this half-mile, well-maintained, self-guided interpretive trail. Signs along the trail highlight the canyon's ecology, wildlife and Native American art thousands of years old. The campground has 14 developed sites and two wheelchair-accessible toilets. Campground hosts are at the campground from November to April. A $4 per-site, per-night fee is collected. Stay away from here in the summer—too damn hot!

Corn Springs is east of the Salton Sea in the Chuckwalla Mountains. From Palm Springs, drive east on Interstate 10 to the Desert Center and Highway 177 turnoff. Continue for approximately 12 miles on Interstate 10 to Chuckwalla Road and turn right (south). Drive on Chuckwalla to Corn Springs Road, turn right again, and drive approximately eight miles west to the trailhead.

USGS topographic map: Corn Spring

For more information: Contact the BLM Palm Springs-South Coast Resource Area, 63-500 Garnet Avenue, P.O. Box 2000, North Palm Springs, CA 92258; (619) 251-4800.

SANTA ROSA NATIONAL SCENIC AREA

See letter HHH on map page 130

backpacking, birdwatching, hiking, historic site, horseback riding, mountain biking

Jolting skyward 7,000 feet in a spectacularly abrupt fashion from the surrounding Coachella Valley, the Santa Rosa Mountains offer the adventurer a playground landscape that varies from desert shrubbery to hidden palm canyons to conifer-capped peaks. This rugged desert wilderness of boulder-strewn mountains and twisted, eroded canyons is, at times, desolate in appearance. There are few places in Southern California where you can truly feel as if you have gotten away from it all, and this is one of them. America's largest remaining population of Peninsular bighorn sheep roam the rocky crags. Golden eagles, red-tailed hawks and other raptors soar overhead. Coyote, mule deer and bobcat, as well as two herds of wild horses, romp among the canyon and desert floors.

Activity Highlights: Hiking and backpacking

Few roads cross the Santa Rosa Mountains, but the range is accessible using a number of foot or horseback trails. Notable trails are the Cactus Springs Trail, the Coyote Creek Trail, the Palms to Pines Trail, the Palm Canyon Trail, the Horsethief Canyon Trail, the Martinez Mountain Indian Trail, the Rabbit Peak Trail and the Mirage Trail. Many of these and other existing trails connect a network of aboriginal and wildlife trails that have existed for eons. Two of the best, Palm Canyon and Horsethief Canyon, are detailed below.

Horsethief Canyon Trail: Legend has it that horse thieves used to ply their trade quite actively in these parts, rustling horses from down south, herding them into Horsethief Canyon for a brand change, and then herding them again to San Bernardino to sell. According to the ranger who shared the story, the rustlers had quite a scam going, because they would steal the horses again, repeat the rebranding process and sell them to the folks down south. As you drop into the canyon on this trek, perhaps you will feel, as we did, that the ghosts of horse rustlers past were still stirring up the dust on the canyon floor with renegade hooves—isn't imagination wonderful?

Hike east from the trailhead to Fire Road 7S01, south for one-quarter of a mile, and then left on the first road—note a sign indicating Cactus Spring (assuming it remains in place, which—with the way vandals are removing signs, according to one BLM official—is a 50-50 proposition) which means you are on the right track. As further verification you are heading the right way, you will soon pass the ruins of an old Dolomite Mine. Within one-half mile, you will come to a sign-in register at the wilderness boundary. Beyond the boundary, the trail winds and wends its way down to Horsethief Creek and, just beyond and across the creek, Horsethief Camp. Set up camp here and enjoy the surroundings. Walk up and down Horsethief Canyon among the cottonwoods and let your imagination run wild—my friend's and mine did. Retrace your steps back to the car whenever you're ready.

From Highway 111 in Palm Desert, drive approximately 16 miles up Highway 74 to the Pinyon Flat Campground. Opposite the campground entrance is Pinyon Flat Transfer Station Road which you will follow for approximately three-quarters of a mile. Directly before the Transfer Station (a rubbish dump) turn left onto a rough jeep trail and follow it for several hundred yards to the road's end and trailhead parking. The best time to hike in here is between October and early May. No permits are required, although you do have to sign in and out at the register located at the Santa Rosa National Scenic Area boundary.

USGS topographic maps: Toro Peak, Martinez Mountain

Palm Canyon Trail: According to the Bureau of Land Management, Palm Springs and the surrounding canyons are home to the largest concentration of palm trees in the United States—Florida, move over. For its display of palms, Palm Canyon is the area's crown jewel, with thousands of palms dotting a lush canyon made more pleasant by the presence of a meandering stream. From the trading post, hike down into Palm Canyon on the Palm Canyon Trail to a small but pretty grotto that is the ideal turnaround point.

An entry fee of $3.50 per person is charged to enter Agua Caliente

Tribal Lands. From Interstate 10, exit on Highway 111 (Palm Canyon Drive) and drive to downtown Palm Springs. In Palm Springs, the highway forks and you will continue straight, now on South Palm Canyon Drive. Follow the signs indicating "Indian Canyons." At the Agua Caliente Indians tollgate, pay the entrance fee and drive on to a parking area just beyond the gate at a trading post, at the head of Palm Canyon. Remember that the reservation is open from 8:30 a.m. to 5:00 p.m. daily and you must be off the reservation at closing.

USGS topographic map: Palm View Peak.

Location: North of the Anza Borrego Desert and south of Interstate 10. To get into the Santa Rosa National Scenic Area, you will need a road map. From Interstate 8 out of San Diego, head north on Highway 79 and then east on Highway 74. From Interstate 10, head south through Palm Springs on Highway 111 and then south on Highway 74.

Camping: There are a few campgrounds in the area. Once inside the boundaries of the Santa Rosa National Scenic Area, camping is allowed anywhere. Water is scarce. Be sure to carry all that you will need.

Season: November through April is the best time to visit.

General USGS topographic maps for the Santa Rosa National Scenic Area: Clark Lake Northeast, Fonts Point, Rabbit Peak, Seventeen Palms

Resources: *The Guide to Hiking, Biking and Equestrian Trails of the Coachella Valley*, published by the City of Rancho Mirage, is available through the BLM.

For more information: Contact the BLM Palm Springs-South Coast Resource Area, 63-500 Garnet Avenue, P.O. Box 2000, North Palm Springs, CA 92258; (619) 251-4800.

DAS PALMAS PRESERVE

See letter III on map page 130

hiking, wildlife observation

This is yet another joint BLM-Nature Conservancy Preserve—an island of biological diversity protecting the endangered pupfish and Yuma clapper rail. Hot in the summer, but worth a peek if you are passing through on Interstate 10—it's a mini-oasis. The preserve is just east of the Salton Sea. From the town of Indio, drive south on

Highway 111 approximately 25 miles to Parkside Drive. Turn left here and drive one mile to a right turn onto Desertaire Drive. The paved road will end, but keep driving on a dirt road for three miles to the signed preserve.

USGS topographic map: Ococopia Canyon

For more information: Contact the BLM Palm Springs-South Coast Resource Area, P.O. Box 2000, North Palm Springs, CA 92258; (619) 251-4800.

VALLEY OF THE MOON

See letter JJJ on map page 130

camping, hiking, rock climbing

From the parking area, hike up the jeep road, ignoring two intersections with roads branching first left and then right. Descend quickly toward a small mountain peak (the site of a now-abandoned amethyst mine) and continue hiking straight, ignoring side trails that lead to campsites among the rocks. Turn left just before the main road heads uphill to the mine and skirt the base of the mountain before dropping into the Valley of the Moon. Marvel at the giant granite outcrops laced with numerous cracks and fissures—they almost seem to be begging to be climbed, but don't try it without climbing experience and the correct gear. Late afternoon and sunset are especially beautiful here. Head back the way you came whenever you're ready.

From Interstate 8 east of San Diego, exit at In-Ko-Pah Road and drive approximately two-tenths of a mile south along the frontage road, also known as Old Highway 80, and turn left onto an unmarked dirt road. Drive approximately three-quarters of a mile up the road to a large turnout suitable for parking. Unless you are driving a four-wheel-drive vehicle, this is where your hike begins. Four-wheel-drive vehicles can actually head almost all the way to the Valley of the Moon and park near the primitive camping sites along the way.

USGS topographic map: In-Ko-Pah Gorge

BLM surface map: El Centro

For more information: Contact the BLM El Centro Resource Area, 1661 South Fourth Street, El Centro, CA 92243; (619) 337-4400.

OTAY MOUNTAIN

See letter KKK on map page 130

hiking, historical site

This spot is not particularly inspiring, except for the walk through a wonderful grove of cypress. The views from the top of Otay Mountain are good, assuming you can overlook the clutter of electronic gear on top. Follow the road for approximately seven miles each way, up and back, to your vehicle. Along the way you will pass remnants of the fortifications erected to repel the predicted Japanese attack in War World II.

From Interstate 805, south from San Diego, head east on the Otay Freeway which becomes Otay Mesa Road. Stay on Otay Mesa Road to Alta Road and turn left (north). Drive for approximately one mile on Alta Road to an unmarked road on the right just past the entrance to the Donovan State Prison and before some farm buildings. Park off the road.

USGS topographic map: Otay Mountain

For more information: Contact the BLM Palm Springs-South Coast Resource Area, P.O. Box 2000, North Palm Springs, CA 92258; (619) 251-4800.

MCCAIN VALLEY CONSERVATION AREA

See letter LLL on map page 130

backpacking, camping, hiking, horseback riding, off-highway-vehicle use

The BLM refers to this site as "an ideal family retreat year-round" because it is often uncrowded. Tucked into the In-Ko-Pah Mountains, part of the coastal range, it forms a rocky garden playground for bighorn sheep. A pair of BLM-managed campgrounds, Lark Canyon and Cottonwood, shaded by oak trees and cooled by the 3,500-foot elevation, offer a generally pleasing alternative to the searing heat of the surrounding desert during the summer months.

Activity Highlights: Hiking and backpacking

The Pepperwood Trail begins at Cottonwood Campground and heads north on an old jeep road. Ignore routes shunting off to the right and left along the way and stay on the main tread, which will begin descending into Pepperwood Canyon. The spicy aroma of pepperwood trees will begin to waft through the air. If you are lucky, the seasonal waterfall may be flowing. No matter what time of year you visit, the nearby spring is always running. The trail peters out after the spring, so if you are not feeling too adventurous, retrace your steps. If your navigational skills are up to snuff, however, you can continue out to Canebreak or attempt to head east to Sombrero Summit.

Location: South of Anza Borrego State Park. From Interstate 8, approximately 70 miles east of San Diego, take the Highway 94 exit and drive approximately one-half mile south to Old Highway 80. Turn left (east) and drive two miles to McCain Valley Road (it's a well-maintained dirt road) and then drive approximately 12 miles to Cottonwood Campground.

USGS topographic maps: Sombrero Peak, Agua Caliente Springs, Live Oak Springs

For more information: Contact the BLM El Centro Resource Area, 1661 South Fourth Street, El Centro, CA 92243; (619) 337-4400.

IMPERIAL SAND DUNES

See letter MMM on map page 130

camping, hiking, off-highway-vehicle use

The dunes of what some call "America's Sahara" rise 300 feet into the sky and stretch for nearly 40 miles along the eastern edge of Imperial Valley and near the ancient shoreline of Lake Cahuilla. Highway 78 bisects the area. South of the highway is known as one of the state's ultimate off-highway-vehicle playgrounds—a place to stay away from unless you enjoy listening to the incessant growling and whining of engines. North of the highway, however, you can find some peace, as the area is closed to vehicles and open to hiking and other less aggressive forms of recreation.

USGS topographic maps: Glamis, Glamis Northwest, Glamis Southeast, Glamis Southwest, Ogilby, Hedges, Cactus, Clyde, Acolita, Amos, Mammoth Wash, Tortuga

For more information: Contact the BLM El Centro Resource Area, 1661 South Fourth Street, El Centro, CA 92243; (619) 337-4400.

BLM CAMPGROUNDS

1. JUNCTION CITY CAMPGROUND—MAP A

Campsites, facilities: There are 26 sites, all with picnic tables and fire grills. Water and vault toilets are available. RVs up to 30 feet are allowed. There is a 14-day stay limit.

Fee: There is a $7 fee per night; pay on site.

Who to contact: Redding Resource Area, 355 Hemsted Drive, Redding, CA 96002; (916) 224-2100.

Location: On the Trinity River. From Junction City, drive 1.5 miles west on Highway 299 to the campground entrance.

Season: All year.

2. STEELBRIDGE CAMPGROUND—MAP A

Campsites, facilities: There are eight sites, all with picnic tables and fire rings. There is **no water**. Pit toilets are available. RVs up to 30 feet are allowed. There is a 14-day stay limit.

Fee: There is no fee.

Who to contact: Redding Resource Area, 355 Hemsted Drive, Redding, CA 96002; (916) 224-2100.

Location: On the Trinity River. From Weaverville, drive 6.3 miles east on Highway 299, passing through Douglas City to Steel Bridge Road on the left. Turn onto Steel Bridge Road and drive approximately four miles to the campground entrance. The campground sits at 2,000 feet.

Season: All year. Steelhead fishing is reported to be good from October to December.

3. DOUGLAS CITY CAMPGROUND—MAP A

Campsites, facilities: There are 19 sites, all with picnic tables and fire rings. Water and vault toilets are available. RVs up to 30 feet are allowed. There is a 14-day stay limit.

Fee: There is a $8 fee per night; pay on site.

Who to contact: Redding Resource Area, 355 Hemsted Drive, Redding, CA 96002; (916) 224-2100.

Location: On the Trinity River. From Weaverville, drive four miles east on Highway 299 to Steiner Flat Road. The campground entrance is a half mile down Steiner Flat Road. The campground sits at 2,000 feet.

Season: All year. The best fishing is from mid-August to December.

4. REDDING ISLAND CAMPGROUND—MAP A

Campsites, facilities: There are eight sites, all with picnic tables and fire rings. Vault toilets and water are available. The facilities are wheelchair accessible. There is a 14-day stay limit.

Fee: There is a $5 fee per night; pay on site.

Who to contact: Redding Resource Area, 355 Hemsted Drive, Redding, CA 96002; (916) 224-2100.

Location: On the Sacramento River. From Redding, drive 15 miles south on Interstate 5 to Cottonwood. Turn east on Balls Ferry Road in Cottonwood and drive five miles to Adobe Road. Follow Adobe Road to the campground entrance.

Season: All year.

5. PIT RIVER CAMPGROUND—MAP A

Campsites, facilities: There are 10 sites, all with picnic tables and fire rings. There is **no water**. Vault toilets are available. There is a 14-day stay limit.

Fee: There is no fee.

Who to contact: Alturas Resource Area, 608 West 12th Street, Alturas, CA 96101; (916) 233-4666.

Location: Near the Pit River. From Fall River Mills, drive 3.5 miles west on Highway 299 to Pit River Powerhouse Road (a dirt road) and turn south, following it along the river to the campground entrance.

Season: All year.

6. RAMHORN SPRINGS CAMPGROUND—MAP A

Campsites, facilities: There are 12 sites, all with picnic tables and fire rings. Vault toilets are available. There is **no water**. RVs up to 28 feet long are allowed. Horse corrals are available. There is a 14-day stay limit.

Fee: There is a $6 fee per night; pay on site.

Who to contact: Eagle Lake Resource Area, 705 Hall Street, Susanville, CA 96130; (916) 257-0456.

Location: From Susanville, drive north for 50 miles on US 395 to Post Camp Road and turn right (east), driving two miles to the campground entrance. The campground sits at 5,500 feet.

Season: All year, but typically crowded during hunting season.

7. MOUTH OF MATTOLE CAMPGROUND—MAP A

Campsites, facilities: There are five tent sites, all with picnic tables, fire grills and fire rings. Water and pit toilets are available. There is a 14-day stay limit. The campground may be closed in severe weather.

Fee: There is a $5 fee per night; pay on site.

Who to contact: Arcata Resource Area, 1125 16th Street, Room 219, Arcata, CA 95521; (707) 822-7648.

Location: On the Pacific Ocean at the Mattole River's mouth. From US 101 and the South Fork/Honeydew turnoff, drive to just south of Petrolia, take Lighthouse Road west five winding miles to the site. Large vehicles and trailers are not advised. The campground sits at 10 feet.

Season: All year. Severe weather may close the campground.

8. HORSE MOUNTAIN CAMPGROUND—MAP A

Campsites, facilities: There are nine sites for tents or RVs up to 20 feet long with picnic tables and fire rings. Water and vault toilets are available. There is a 14-day stay limit.

Fee: There is a $5 fee per night; pay on site.

Who to contact: Arcata Resource Area, 1125 16th Street, Room 219, Arcata, CA 95521; (707) 822-7648.

Location: In the King Mountains. From Redway on US 101, drive 17.5 miles west on Shelter Cove Road to Kings Peak Road. Turn north and drive another six miles to the campground entrance. The campground sits at 2,000 feet.

Season: All year.

9. WAILAKI CAMPGROUND—MAP A

Campsites, facilities: There are 12 sites, all with picnic tables and fire rings. Water and vault toilets are available. The entire campground is wheelchair accessible. RVs up to 20 feet are allowed. There is a 14-day stay limit.

Fee: There is a $8 fee per night; pay on site.

Who to contact: Arcata Resource Area, 1125 16th Street, Room 219, Arcata, CA 95521; (707) 822-7648.

Location: In the King Mountains. From Redway on US 101, drive approximately 17 miles on Shelter Cove Road to Chemise Mountain Road and turn left. Drive 2.5 miles to the campground entrance. The campground sits at 1,840 feet.

Season: All year.

10. NADELOS CAMPGROUND—MAP A

Campsites, facilities: There are 11 tent sites, all with picnic tables and fire rings. Water and vault toilets are available. The entire campground is wheelchair accessible. There is a 14-day stay limit.

Fee: There is an $8 fee per night; pay on site.

Who to contact: Arcata Resource Area, 1125 16th Street, Room 219, Arcata, CA 95521; (707) 822-7648.

Location: In the King Mountains. From Redway on US 101, drive approximately 17 miles on Shelter Cove Road to Chemise Mountain Road. Turn left and drive two miles to the campground entrance. The campground sits at 1,840 feet.

Season: All year.

11. TOLKAN CAMPGROUND—MAP A

Campsites, facilities: There are nine sites, all with picnic tables and fire rings. Water and pit toilets are available. The entire campground is wheelchair accessible. RVs up to 20 feet are allowed. There is a 14-day stay limit.

Fee: There is a $8 fee per night; pay on site.

Who to contact: Arcata Resource Area, 1125 16th Street, Room 219, Arcata, CA 95521; (707) 822-7648.

Location: In the King Range. From Redway on US 101, drive 17.5 miles west on Shelter Cover Road to Kings Peak Road. Turn north and drive 3.5 miles to the campground. The campground sits at 1,840 feet.

Season: All year.

12. NORTH EAGLE LAKE CAMPGROUND—MAP A

Campsites, facilities: There are 20 sites, all with picnic tables and fire rings. Water, vault toilets, a boat launch and an RV dump station are available. There is a 14-day stay limit.

Fee: There is a $6 per night; pay on site.

Who to contact: Eagle Lake Resource Area, 705 Hall Street, Susanville, CA 96130; (916) 257-0456.

Location: From Susanville, drive north for 29 miles on Highway 139 to County Road A1. Turn left (west) and drive a half mile to the campground entrance. The campground sits at 5,100 feet.

Season: Mid-May to mid-November.

13. MAYACMAS CAMPGROUND—MAP A

Campsites, facilities: There are nine tent sites, all with picnic tables and fire rings. Vault toilets are available. There is **no water**. There is a 14-day stay limit.

Fee: There is no fee.

Who to contact: Clear Lake Resource Area, 2550 North State Street, Ukiah, CA 95482; (707) 468-4000.

Location: Near the Russian River. From Ukiah, drive 1.5 miles east on Talmadge Road to Eastside Road and turn right. Drive three-tenths of a mile to a left turn onto Mill Creek Road and continue 2.5 miles on Mill Creek to Mendo Rock Road. Turn left again and drive seven miles to the campground entrance. The campground sits at 2,500 feet.

Season: All year.

14. RED MOUNTAIN CAMPGROUND—MAP A

Campsites, facilities: There are eight sites, all with picnic tables and fire rings. Water and vault toilets are available. There is a 14-day stay limit.

Fee: There is no fee.

Who to contact: Clear Lake Resource Area, 2550 North State Street, Ukiah, CA 95482; (707) 468-4000.

Location: Near Ukiah. From US 101 in Ukiah, drive east on Talmage Road for 1.5 miles to Eastside Road. Turn right and drive three-tenths of a mile to Mill Creek Road and turn left. Drive nine miles on Mill Creek to the campground entrance.

Season: All year.

15. SHELDON CREEK CAMPGROUND—MAP A

Campsites, facilities: There are six sites, all with picnic tables and fire rings. Water and pit toilets are available. There is a 14-day stay limit.

Fee: There is no fee.

Who to contact: Clear Lake Resource Area, 2550 North State Street, Ukiah, CA 95482; (707) 468-4000.

Location: From Hopland, drive three miles east on Highway 175 to

Old Toll Road and turn right. Drive eight miles to the campground entrance. The campground sits at 2,500 feet.

Season: All year.

16. Blue Oak Campground—Map A

Campsites, facilities: There are five sites, all with picnic tables and fire rings. Water and pit toilets are available. There is a 14-day stay limit.

Fee: There is no fee.

Who to contact: Clear Lake Resource Area, 2550 North State Street, Ukiah, CA 95482; (707) 468-4000.

Location: From Williams and Interstate 5, drive 21 miles west on Highway 20 to Walker Ridge Road, then follow signs seven miles to the campground entrance.

Season: All year.

17. Lower Hunting Creek Campground—Map A

Campsites, facilities: There are five sites, all with picnic tables, fire rings and shade shelters. Vault toilets are available. There is **no water.** There is a 14-day stay limit.

Fee: There is no fee.

Who to contact: Clear Lake Resource Area, 2550 North State Street, Ukiah, CA 95482; (707) 468-4000.

Location: Near Clearlake. From Lower Lake and Highway 29, head southeast on Morgan Valley Road for approximately 15 miles. Turn south onto Devilhead Road and drive two miles to the campground entrance.

Season: All year.

18. Wintun Campground—Map A

Campsites, facilities: There is one site with a picnic table and a fire ring. Water is available.

Fee: There is no fee.

Who to contact: Clear Lake Resource Area, 2550 North State Street, Ukiah, CA 95482; (707) 468-4000.

Location: Near Indian Valley Reservoir. From Williams, drive 21 miles west on Highway 20 to Walker Ridge Road, then seven miles on Walker Ridge to the campground entrance.

Season: All year.

19. SOUTH YUBA CAMPGROUND—MAP A

Campsites, facilities: There are 17 sites, all with picnic tables and fire rings. Water and vault toilets are available. RVs up to 30 feet are allowed. There is a 14-day limit.

Fee: There is a $3 per-night fee. Pay on site.

Who to contact: Folsom Resource Area, 63 Natoma Street, Folsom, CA 95630; (916) 985-4474.

Location: Near the Yuba River. From Nevada City, drive eight miles north on Highway 49 to Tyler Foote Crossing Road and drive to Grizzly Hills Road. Turn right onto Grizzly Hills Road and drive to North Bloomfield Road, turn left and drive to the campground entrance. The campground sits at 2,600 feet.

Season: March to October.

20. MCCABE FLAT CAMPGROUND—MAP A

Campsites, facilities: There are seven sites, all with picnic tables and fire rings. Pit toilets are available. There is **no water**.

Fee: There is no fee.

Who to contact: Folsom Resource Area, 63 Natoma Street, Folsom, CA 95630; (916) 985-4474.

Location: On the Merced River, near Yosemite National Park. From Mariposa, drive on Highway 140 to Briceburg, then follow the river access road to McCabe Flat Campground.

Season: All year.

21. RAILROAD FLAT CAMPGROUND—MAP A

Campsites, facilities: There are eight sites, all with picnic tables and fire rings. There is **no water**. Pit toilets are available. There is a 14-day stay limit.

Fee: There is no fee.

Who to contact: Folsom Resource Area, 63 Natoma Street, Folsom, CA 95630; (916) 985-4474.

Location: Near Yosemite, on the Merced River. From Mariposa, drive on Highway 140 to Briceburg and then follow the river access road to Railroad Flat Campground.

Season: All year.

22. UPPER WILLOW CAMPGROUND—MAP A

Campsites, facilities: There is one site with a picnic table and a fire ring. There is **no water** or pit toilets. There is a 14-day stay limit.

Fee: There is no fee.

Who to contact: Folsom Resource Area, 63 Natoma Street, Folsom, CA 95630; (916) 985-4474.

Location: Near Yosemite, on the Merced River. From Mariposa, drive on Highway 140 to Briceburg, then follow the river access road to Upper Willow Campground.

Season: All year.

23. WILLOW PLACER CAMPGROUND—MAP A

Campsites, facilities: There are five sites, all with picnic tables and fire rings. There is **no water**. Pit toilets are available. There is a 14-day stay limit.

Fee: There is no fee.

Who to contact: Folsom Resource Area, 63 Natoma Street, Folsom, CA 95630; (916) 985-4474.

Location: Near Yosemite, on the Merced River. From Mariposa, drive on Highway 140 to Briceburg. Follow the river access road to Willow Placer Campground.

Season: All year.

24. CROWLEY LAKE CAMPGROUND—MAP A

Campsites, facilities: There are 11 sites (five for tents only), all with picnic tables and fire rings. Water and flush toilets are available. RVs up to 22 feet long are allowed.

Fee: There is a $6 fee per night; pay on site.

Who to contact: Bishop Resource Area, 787 North Main, Suite E, Bishop, CA 93514; (619) 872-4881.

Location: In Rock Creek Canyon. From Mammoth Lakes and the Highway 203/US 395 junction, drive approximately 15 miles south on US 395 to Toms Place. Turn right (south) on Rock Creek Road and drive four miles to the campground entrance. The campground sits at 7,000 feet.

Season: April to September.

25. SQUAW LEAP CAMPGROUND—MAP B

Campsites, facilities: There are five sites (plus two designated group site areas), all with picnic tables and fire rings. All sites are walk-in only. There is **no water**. No trash facilities are provided, so pack out all that you pack in. Vault toilets and horse hitching posts are available. There is a 14-day stay limit.

Fee: There is no fee.

Who to contact: Folsom Resource Area, 63 Natoma Street, Folsom, CA 95630; (916) 985-4474.

Location: On the San Joaquin River. From Highway 99 in Madera, drive 19 miles east on Highway 145 to County Road 206. Turn right and drive to Friant. From Friant, drive 19 miles northeast on Millerton/Auberry Road to Auberry. From Auberry, drive two miles north on Powerhouse Road and turn left at the Squaw Leap Management Area sign at Smalley Road. Drive four miles to the campground entrance.

Season: All year.

26. HORTON CREEK CAMPGROUND—MAP B

Campsites, facilities: There are 52 sites, all with picnic tables and fire rings. Pit toilets are available. There is **no water**. No trash facilities are provided so you must pack out all you pack in. There is a 14-day stay limit.

Fee: There is a $6 fee per night; pay on site.

Who to contact: Bishop Resource Area, 787 North Main, Suite E, Bishop, CA 93514; (619) 872-4881.

Location: From Bishop, drive approximately five miles north on US 395 to Round Valley Road and turn left, driving another four miles to the campground entrance. The campground sits at 5,000 feet.

Season: April to October.

27. GOODALE CREEK CAMPGROUND—MAP B

Campsites, facilities: There are 62 sites, all with picnic tables and fire rings. Pit toilets are available. There is **no water**. No trash facilities are provided so you pack out what you pack in. There is a 14-day stay limit.

Fee: There is no fee.

Who to contact: Bishop Resource Area, 787 North Main, Suite E, Bishop, CA 93514; (619) 872-4881.

Location: From Big Pine, drive south approximately 16 miles on US 395 to Aberdeen Road. Turn right and drive west on Aberdeen Road for approximately two miles to the campground entrance. The campground sits at 4,100 feet.

Season: April to October.

28. Tuttle Creek Campground—Map B

Campsites, facilities: There are 84 sites, all with picnic tables and fire rings. Pit toilets are available. There is **no water**. No trash facilities are provided, so pack out all that you pack in. There is a 14-day stay limit.

Fee: There is no fee.

Who to contact: Bishop Resource Area, 787 North Main, Suite E, Bishop, CA 93514; (619) 872-4881.

Location: Near Mount Whitney. From Lone Pine, drive west on Whitney Portal Road for 3.5 miles to Horseshoe Meadow Road (County Road 15S01) and drive 1.5 miles to Tuttle Creek Road. Drive on Tuttle Creek Road to the campground entrance. The campground sits at 5,100 feet.

Season: May to October.

29. Carrizo Plains Campground—Map B

Campsites, facilities: This campground offers primitive camping with scattered sites. Portable toilets are available. There is **no water**. No trash facilities are provided, so pack out what you bring in. There is a 14-day stay limit.

Fee: There is no fee.

Who to contact: Caliente Resource Area, 3801 Pegasus Drive, Bakersfield, CA 93308-6837; (805) 391-6000.

Location: In the Carrizo Plain Natural Area. From Maricopa, drive on Highway 166 southwest to Soda Lake Road. Drive north on Soda Lake Road for approximately 17 miles to the KCL Camping Area and then drive 25 miles to the Selby Road turnoff and the campground entrance. The campground sits at 800 feet. There are plans for a developed site at Selby.

Season: All year.

30. LONG VALLEY CAMPGROUND—MAP B

Campsites, facilities: There are 11 sites, all with picnic tables and fire rings. Pit toilets are available. There is **no water**. No trash facilities are provided, so pack out all that you pack in. There is a 14-day stay limit.

Fee: There is no fee.

Who to contact: Caliente Resource Area, 3801 Pegasus Drive, Bakersfield, CA 93308-6837; (805) 391-6000.

Location: Near the Domeland Wilderness Area and the South Fork of the Kern River. From Pearsonville, drive north for approximately two miles on US 395 to Nine Mile Canyon Road. Turn left and drive approximately 11 miles to the BLM ranger station. Bear left at the ranger station and drive 14 more miles to the campground entrance. The campground sits at 5,200 feet.

Season: All year.

31. CHIMNEY CREEK CAMPGROUND—MAP B

Campsites, facilities: There are 36 sites, all with picnic tables and fire rings. Water and pit toilets are available. No trash facilities are provided, so pack out all that you bring in. There is a 14-day stay limit.

Fee: There is no fee.

Who to contact: Caliente Resource Area, 3801 Pegasus Drive, Bakersfield, CA 93308-6837; (805) 391-6000.

Location: Near the Pacific Crest Trail in the Sierra Nevada. Drive north from Inyokern on US 395 for approximately 15 miles to County Road 152 (Nine Mile Canyon) and turn left. Drive another 13 miles, heading left at the ranger station to the campground entrance. The campground is set at 5,700 feet.

Season: All year.

32. WALKER PASS CAMPGROUND—MAP B

Campsites, facilities: There are nine walk-in sites for tents only, all with picnic tables and fire rings. There are two tent/RV sites, both with limited parking. Water and pit toilets are available. No trash facilities are provided, so pack out all that you bring in. There is a 14-day stay limit.

Fee: There is no fee.

Who to contact: Caliente Resource Area, 3801 Pegasus Drive, Bakersfield, CA 93308-6837; (805) 391-6000.

Location: On the Pacific Crest Trail; this is intended as a campground for the trail. From Onyx, drive east on Highway 178 for 14 miles to the campground entrance. The campground sits at 5,200 feet.

Season: All year.

33. OWL CANYON CAMPGROUND—MAP B

Campsites, facilities: There are 31 sites, all with picnic tables and fire rings. Vault toilets are available. There is limited water—bring your own. There is a 14-day stay limit.

Fee: There is a $4 fee per night; pay on site.

Who to contact: Barstow Resource Area, 150 Coolwater Lane, Barstow, CA 92311; (619) 256-3591.

Location: From Barstow and Highway 58, drive north for six miles on Camp Irwin Road to Fossil Beds Road. Turn left (west) and drive two miles to the campground entrance. The campground sits at 2,600 feet.

Season: All year. The winter months are the most pleasant.

34. AFTON CANYON CAMPGROUND—MAP B

Campsites, facilities: There are 22 sites, all with picnic tables, grills, fire pits and sun shelters. Water and pit toilets are available.

Fee: There is a $6 fee per night; pay on site.

Who to contact: Barstow Resource Area, 150 Coolwater Lane, Barstow, CA 92311; (619) 256-3591.

Location: Near the Mojave River. From Barstow, drive east on Interstate 15 for approximately 37 miles to Afton Road. Drive south on Afton Road for four miles to the campground and Afton Canyon. The campground is set at 2,500 feet.

Season: All year. Winter season weekends are the most crowded. Summers can be extremely hot.

35. HOLE-IN-THE-WALL CAMPGROUND—MAP B

Campsites, facilities: There are 39 sites, all with picnic tables, fire rings and grills. Water and pit toilets are available. An RV dump station is available. There is a 14-day stay limit.

Fee: There is a $6 fee per night; pay on site.

Who to contact: Needles Resource Area, 101 West Spikes Road, Needles, CA 92363; (619) 326-3896.

Location: From Needles, drive west on Interstate 40 for approxi-

mately 41 miles to the Essex exit. Turn right and drive for approximately 10 miles to Black Canyon Road. Drive north for another 10 miles on Black Canyon Road to the campground. The campground sits at 4,200 feet.
Season: All year.

36. MID-HILLS CAMPGROUND—MAP B

Campsites, facilities: There are 26 sites, all with picnic tables, fire grills and fire rings. Water and pit toilets are available. There is a 14-day stay limit.
Fee: There is a $6 fee per night; pay on site.
Who to contact: Needles Resource Area, 101 West Spikes Road, Needles, CA 92363; (619) 326-3896.
Location: From Needles, drive west on Interstate 40 for approximately 40 miles to the Essex exit, then head right (north) for 10 miles to Black Canyon Road. Drive 20 miles north on mostly paved surface to Wild Horse Canyon Road, then drive two miles on unpaved surface to the campground entrance. The campground sits at 5,600 feet.
Season: All year.

37. CORN SPRINGS CAMPGROUND—MAP C

Campsites, facilities: There are 10 sites, all with picnic tables and fire rings and one group site. Water and pit toilets are available.
Fee: There is a $4 fee per night; pay on site.
Who to contact: Palm Springs-South Coast Resource Area, 63-500 Garnet Avenue, P.O. Box 2000, North Palm Springs, CA 92258; (619) 251-4800.
Location: Drive east from Indio on Interstate 10 and exit at Corn Springs Road. The campground entrance is signed.
Season: All year.

38. COTTONWOOD CAMPGROUND—MAP C

Campsites, facilities: There are 25 sites, all with picnic tables and fire rings. Water and pit toilets are available.
Fee: There is a $6 fee per night; pay on site.
Who to contact: El Centro Resource Area, 1661 South Fourth Street, El Centro, CA 92243; (619) 337-4400.
Location: From San Diego, drive 70 miles east on Interstate 8 to the Boulevard exit, then drive two miles east on Old Highway 80 to

McCain Valley Road. Head northwest for seven miles on McCain Valley Road to Lark Canyon Campground and then drive another six miles to the Cottonwood Campground entrance. The campground is set at 3,500 feet.

Season: All year.

39. LARK CANYON CAMPGROUND—MAP C

Campsites, facilities: There are 20 sites, all with picnic tables and fire rings. Water and pit toilets are available.

Fee: There is a $6 fee per night; pay on site.

Who to contact: El Centro Resource Area, 1661 South Fourth Street, El Centro, CA 92243; (619) 337-4400.

Location: From San Diego, drive 70 miles east on Interstate 8 to the Boulevard exit, then two miles east on Old Highway 80 to McCain Valley Road. Head northwest for seven miles on McCain Valley Road to Lark Canyon Campground. The campground is located at 3,500 feet.

Season: All year.

40. GECKO CAMPGROUND—MAP C

Campsites, facilities: There are 120 undesignated sites. Vault toilets and an RV dump station are available. There is **no water**.

Fee: There is no fee.

Who to contact: El Centro Resource Area, 1661 South Fourth Street, El Centro, CA 92243; (619) 337-4400.

Location: From Brawley, drive 27 miles east on Highway 78 and take the Gecko Road exit. Drive to the campground entrance.

Season: All year.

41. MIDWAY CAMPGROUND—MAP C

Campsites, facilities: There are 120 sites, all with picnic tables and fire rings. There is **no water**. Pit toilets and an RV dump station are available.

Fee: There is no fee.

Who to contact: El Centro Resource Area, 1661 South Fourth Street, El Centro, CA 92243; (619) 337-4400.

Location: From Interstate 8, exit at Sand Hills. Drive south to Gray's Well Road and then head west to the campground entrance.

Season: All year.

42. ROADRUNNER CAMPGROUND—MAP C

Campsites, facilities: There are 120 dispersed sites, all with picnic tables and fire rings. There is **no water**. Pit toilets are available.

Fee: There is no fee.

Who to contact: El Centro Resource Area, 1661 South Fourth Street, El Centro, CA 92243; (619) 337-4400.

Location: In Imperial Sand Dunes. From Interstate 8, exit at Highway 86 and drive north to Highway 78, then drive 20 miles to Gecko Road. Turn onto Gecko and drive three miles to the campground entrance.

Season: All year.

STATE INFORMATION OVERVIEW

CALIFORNIA STATE OFFICE
2800 Cottage Way, E-2841, Sacramento, CA 95825; (916) 978-4754

BAKERSFIELD DISTRICT OFFICE
3801 Pegasus Drive, Bakersfield, CA 93308-6837; (805) 391-6000

Bishop Resource Area, 787 North Main, Suite P, Bishop, CA 93514; (619) 872-4881

Caliente Resource Area, 3801 Pegasus Drive, Bakersfield, CA 93308-6837; (805) 391-6000

Folsom Resource Area, 63 Natoma Street, Folsom, CA 95630; (916) 985-4474

Hollister Resource Area, 20 Hamilton Court, Hollister, CA 95023; (408) 637-8183

UKIAH DISTRICT OFFICE
2550 North State Street, Ukiah, CA 95482; (707) 468-4000

Arcata Resource Area, 1125 16th Street, Room 219, Arcata, CA 95521; (707) 822-7648

Clear Lake Resource Area, 2550 North State Street, Ukiah, CA 95482; (707) 468-4000

Redding Resource Area, 355 Hemsted Drive, Redding, CA 96002; (916) 224-2100

SUSANVILLE DISTRICT OFFICE
705 Hall Street, Susanville, CA 96130; (916) 257-5381

Alturas Resource Area, 608 West 12th Street, Alturas, CA 96101; (916) 233-4666

Eagle Lake Resource Area, 705 Hall Street, Susanville, CA 96130; (916) 257-0456

Surprise Resource Area, 602 Cressler Street, Cedarville, CA 96104; (916) 279-6101

CALIFORNIA DESERT DISTRICT OFFICE

6221 Box Springs Boulevard, Riverside, CA 92507; (909) 697-5200

Barstow Resource Area, 150 Coolwater Lane, Barstow, CA 92311; (619) 256-3591

El Centro Resource Area, 1661 South Fourth Street, El Centro, CA 92243; (619) 337-4400

Needles Resource Area, 101 West Spikes Road, Needles, CA 92363; (619) 326-3896

Palm Springs-South Coast Resource Area, 63-500 Garnet Avenue, P.O. Box 2000, North Palm Springs, CA 92258; (619) 251-4800

Ridgecrest Resource Area, 300 South Richmond Road, Ridgecrest, CA 93555; (619) 384-5400

COLORADO

(SEE MAP A)　　　　　(SEE MAP B)

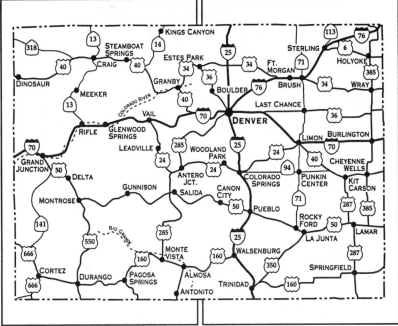

MAP A—COLORADO

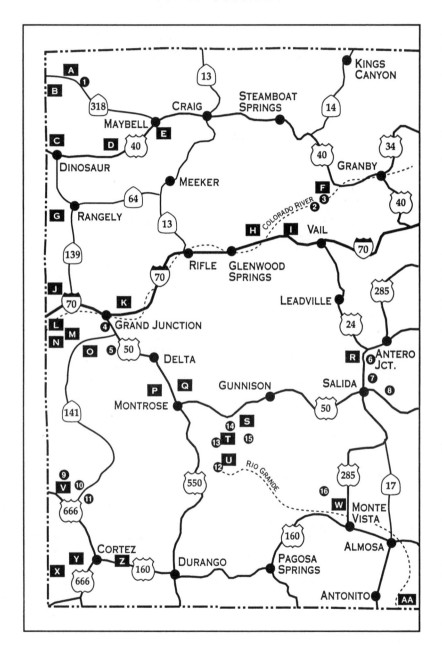

MAP REFERENCES

A. Irish Canyon —p. 202
B. Diamond Breaks Wilderness Study Area—p. 203
C. Bull Canyon, Willow Creek and Skull Creek Wilderness Study Area —p. 204
D. Cross Mountain Wilderness Study Area —p. 205
E. Little Yampa Canyon —p. 206
F. Upper Colorado River —p. 207
G. Rangely Loop Trail —p. 207
H. Deep Creek —p. 208
I. Eagle River —p. 208
J. Rabbit Valley Research Natural Area —p. 209
K. Little Book Cliffs Wild Horse Area —p. 209
L. Ruby Canyon —p. 211
M. Kokopelli's Trail —p. 211
N. Black Ridge Canyons Wilderness Study Area —p. 213
O. Dominguez Canyon Wilderness Study Area—p. 214
P. Tabeguache Mountain Bike Trail —p. 215
Q. Gunnison Gorge —p. 217
R. Colorado Midland Bike Trail—p. 219
S. Powderhorn Wilderness Area —p. 220
T. Alpine Loop Back Country Byway—p. 221
U. Alpine Gulch Trail—p. 222
V. Dolores River Canyon —p. 223
W. Penitente Canyon —p. 225
X. Cross Canyon Wilderness Study Area—p. 226
Y. Sand Canyon—p. 227
Z. Anasazi Heritage Center and Special Recreation Area —p. 228
AA. Rio Grande River —p. 228

BLM CAMPGROUNDS

1. Irish Canyon Campground—p. 233
2. Radium Campground—p. 233
3. Pumphouse Campground—p. 233
4. Mud Springs Campground—p. 234
5. Big Dominguez Campground—p. 234
6. Ruby Mountain Recreation Site—p. 235
7. Hecla Junction Recreation Site—p. 235
8. Rincon Recreation Site—p. 236
9. Bradfield Campground—p. 236
10. Dolores Canyon Overlook Campground—p. 237
11. Mountain Sheep Point Campground—p. 237
12. Mill Creek Campground—p. 237
13. The Gate Campground—p. 238
14. Red Bridge Campground—p. 238
15. Cebolla Creek Campground—p. 238
16. Penitente Campground—p. 239

MAP B—COLORADO

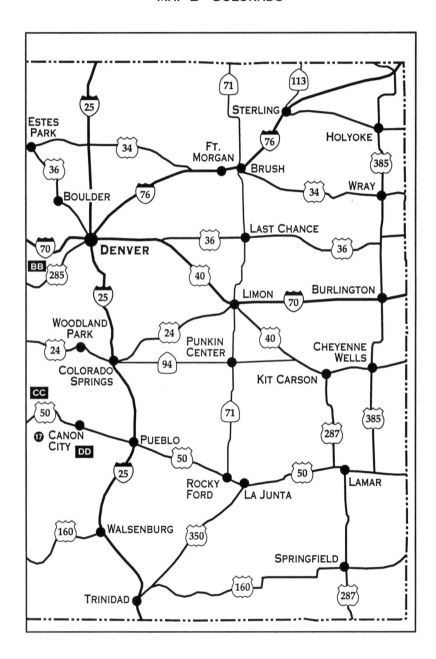

MAP REFERENCES

BLM CAMPGROUNDS

COLORADO—MAP A

IRISH CANYON

See letter A on map page 198

archaeological sites, backpacking, camping, hiking, mountain biking, wildlife observation

This scenic area is remote and receives few visitors. Twelve of the 22 geological formations found in the eastern Uinta Mountains are present here. Although there are no developed or maintained trails, hiking and mountain biking opportunities are excellent. Several miles of primitive dirt roads in the area provide challenges to the mountain biker in this colorful, semi-arid region. Hikers will find cross-country routes up to Limestone Ridge to the west with expansive views of the region. There are also opportunities to explore the colorful badlands of Vermillion Creek to the east. A small campground in the canyon has three campsites; a picnic site with ancient rock art is located at the south end of Irish Canyon. Water is scarce—snowmelt is often the only available natural source. Pack in all the water you will need. The best time to visit is from fall to spring. Summer is often hot and dry. October and November is big game hunting season, so wearing blazing orange from head to toe is a must. Personally, I would just stay out of the area during that time, unless you are hunting. Wildlife is abundant and includes mule deer, antelope, elk, mountain lion, coyote, fox, golden eagle, bald eagle, vulture and prairie falcon. Camping is allowed anywhere. Since the area is easily impacted, you must use backpacking stoves instead of fires. To get there, take State Route 318 north from US 40 at Maybell. Drive approximately 41 miles to Moffat County Road 10N, turn north and continue for four miles to Irish Canyon.

USGS topographic maps: Irish Canyon, Big Joe Basin

For more information: Contact the BLM Little Snake Resource Area, 1280 Industrial Avenue, Craig, CO 81625; (303) 824-4441.

DIAMOND BREAKS WILDERNESS STUDY AREA

See letter B on map page 198

backpacking, camping, cultural site, hiking, wildlife observation

Although Diamond Breaks gets its name from the "breaks" or canyons carved into Diamond Mountain by numerous creeks and drainages, the "diamonds" for which area is named come from an entirely different source—a con game played with, you guessed it, diamonds. Legend has it that a con artist in the late 1800s scattered diamonds all over the mountaintop in an effort to separate unsuspecting Eastern investors from their money in a "get rich quick" diamond mining scheme. Of course, there was no diamond cache and the shyster took the money and ran, leaving bewildered Easterners scrambling all over the barren terrain of Diamond Mountain.

Once you set foot in Diamond Breaks, however, the mythical diamonds will be the furthest things from your mind. From the ridges and peaks of the breaks, you will be dazzled with spectacular and panoramic views of the Green River Plain, the mighty Canyon of Lodore and its gates through which numerous rafters pass each year, the snow-capped peaks of the distant Uintas, the Zirkel Range and Cold Springs Mountain. Currently, 36,248 acres of Diamond Breaks have been recommended by the BLM for wilderness designation.

With a pack on your back, it is possible to wander for days, although keep in mind that the dissected terrain is extremely rugged and semi-arid. Your cross-country navigational skills must be strong and you should always carry plenty of water. The craggy terrain, rising dramatically from the sagebrush-covered plain of Browns Park, is broken frequently by draws and stands of aspen. Pinyon and juniper cover many ridges, and a stately grove of gnarled ponderosa pine clinging to the southern reaches—often growing right out of the rock itself. Both spring and fall offer rich contrasts of color literally bursting forth from the draws and canyons, with golden aspen in fall and a rainbow of colors from a wildflower explosion in spring.

Keep your eyes peeled for archaeological finds (look but don't touch!) as granaries, petroglyphs and large amount of lithic scatter have been documented within the region. There are even rumors that wickiups are tucked in among the rocks. Wildlife is abundant within the region. Mule deer, black bear, elk and even the elusive mountain lion call Diamond Breaks home. Pronghorn prance in the lower reaches around Browns Park.

The best hiking access is to be had from the Swinging Bridge Camping Area, just of Moffat County Road 83. First-time initiates should stick to the abandoned jeep trails until you get the lay of the land. A good bet is to follow the jeep trail that skirts the Green River's edge and leads to the western boundary of the Gates of Lodore. Along the way, another jeep trail branches off to the right and up Chokecherry Draw. Don't miss exploring this canyon; it leads to a long-deserted homestead whose crumbling foundations, running springs and rose bushes and fruit trees gone wild offer a lush retreat in the middle of a desert forest.

Special note: Camping is allowed anywhere within Diamond Breaks. Archaeological resources are protected under federal law. If you find a Native American site, report it to the BLM; do not attempt to explore it or otherwise do anything that might inflict permanent damage. If you see signs of vandalism, report them to the BLM or local authorities. Off-road vehicles are prohibited.

Location: On the northwestern Colorado/Utah state line, south of Highway 318 and adjacent to Dinosaur National Monument and Browns Park National Wildlife Refuge. From Vernal, Utah, follow the Diamond Breaks signs along Crouse Canyon Road (it turns into Moffat County Road 83 in Colorado). Crouse Canyon Road intersects with Highway 191 a few blocks north of the Vernal town center.

USGS topographic maps: Canyon of Lodore North, Hoy Mountain, Lodore School, Swallow Canyon

Resources:
• *Colorado Atlas and Gazetteer*, published by DeLorme Mapping, P.O. Box 298, Freeport, ME 04032; (207) 865-4171.

For more information: Contact the BLM Little Snake Resource Area, 1280 Industrial Avenue, Craig, CO 81625; (303) 824-4441; or the Craig Visitors Information Center, 360 East Victory Way, Craig, CO 81625; (303) 824-3046.

BULL CANYON, WILLOW CREEK AND SKULL CREEK WILDERNESS STUDY AREA

See letter C on map page 198

camping, hiking, wildlife observation

nyons await exploring, offering visitors a collage
ions. Views from high up are super and

wildlife viewing opportunities are good. While spring and fall are the best seasons to visit, they are not without their individual challenges—cedar gnats in the spring (wear plenty of insect repellent) and hunters in the fall (wear plenty of blazing orange and do nothing to imitate a deer). The area is perhaps best suited for hiking. Although backpacking is possible, rough terrain will create some difficulties. There are no maintained trails in this region. Water is scarce, so pack in all that you will need. Private property is interspersed throughout the region. Respect signed closures and stay off private land. Cattle is run in parts of this region—leave cattle gates as you find them.

To get to Bull Canyon, drive approximately one mile east from Dinosaur on US 40 to the Dinosaur National Monument turnoff. Drive 3.5 miles up Harper's Corner Road to Plug Hat Rock Picnic Area and overlook, or continue on for three miles to the Escalante Overlook/Parking Area.

USGS topographic maps: Plug Hat Rock, Snake John Reef

BLM surface map: Rangely

For more information: Contact the BLM White River Resource Area, 73455 Highway 64, P.O. Box 928, Meeker, CO 81641; (303) 878-3601.

CROSS MOUNTAIN WILDERNESS STUDY AREA

See letter D on map page 198

backpacking, camping, fishing, hiking, wildlife observation

Although there are no developed trails within this area, Cross Mountain offers the willing explorer super opportunities to wander through the plateau country of the easternmost extension of the Uinta Mountains. Views into the 1,000-foot-deep Cross Mountain Canyon are breathtaking. Day hikes to the south rim of Cross Mountain Canyon are popular. Multi-day backpack trips on the north end of the mountain offer solitude and beauty. The steep side canyons on the east and west provide rugged access routes to the top. From the broad summit of Cross Mountain, you can easily hike north or south to the canyon rim. Hiking along the Yampa River in the canyon itself is difficult, requiring rock scrambling and canyoneering skills, and is best attempted only at low water periods in late summer or fall. This area has been recommended for wilderness designation.

There are a number of archaeological sites within the area and the visitor will enjoy observing the numerous raptors that at times seem to own the sky. Wildflowers are spectacular in late spring and early summer. Bighorn sheep, elk, deer, antelope, mountain lion and coyote all frequent this area, although the mountain lion will likely see you more often than you will see it. Water is scarce so carry all that you will need. Rattlesnakes are abundant—stay alert!

The best access is via the National Park Service parking area at the mouth of Cross Mountain Canyon. To get there, take US 40 to Deerlodge Park Road, approximately 16 miles west of Maybell. Drive along Deerlodge, skirting the west side of Cross Mountain to the parking area. The best access to the south rim of the canyon is by hiking along the first drainage south of the parking area. The best times to visit are in late spring and in fall. Summer can be uncomfortably hot and dry and winter can be bitingly cold.

USGS topographic maps: Lone Mountain, Cross Mountain Canyon, Twelve-Mile Mesa, Peck Mesa

BLM surface maps: Canyon of Lodore, Rangely

Resources:
• The BLM publishes a free trail map and guide. Obtain it from the Little Snake Resource Area office.

For more information: Contact the BLM Little Snake Resource Area, 1280 Industrial Avenue, Craig, CO 81625; (303) 824-4441.

LITTLE YAMPA CANYON
See letter E on map page 198

backpacking, canoeing, fishing, hiking, mountain biking, rafting, wildlife observation

This 37-mile segment of the Yampa River is a super flat-water canoeing river. The river offers excellent spring float trips and an outstanding opportunity for viewing a wide variety of wildlife. Parts of the Yampa Valley Mountain Bike Trail have been completed and other sections are still being developed—contact the local BLM office for up-to-date information.

USGS topographic maps: Craig, Round Bottom, Horse Gulch, Juniper Hot Springs, Juniper Mountain, Maybell, Sunbeam, Peck Mesa, Cross Mountain Canyon, Twelve-Mile Mesa

BLM surface maps: Meeker, Canyon of Lodore, Rangely

Resources:
• *Western Whitewater, From the Rockies to the Pacific,* by Jim Cassady, Bill Cross and Fryar Calhoun, published by North Fork Press, Berkeley, CA; (415) 424-1213.

For more information: Contact the BLM Little Snake Resource Area, 1280 Industrial Avenue, Craig, CO 81625; (303) 824-4441.

UPPER COLORADO RIVER
See letter F on map page 198

canoeing, fishing, hiking, horseback riding, kayaking, mountain biking, rafting, wildlife observation

This 50-mile segment of the Colorado River offers Class II to III whitewater recreation for boaters. It lies within two hours of the major population centers of Colorado and consequently receives heavy use. Located near the town of Kremmling, the Pumphouse Recreation Site/Campground is the major put-in spot, although there are many others along the river.

USGS topographic maps: Kremmling, Radium, McCoy, State Bridge, Blue Hill, Burns North, Burns South, Dotsero

BLM surface map: Vail

For more information: Contact the BLM Kremmling Resource Area, 1116 Park Avenue, P.O. Box 68, Kremmling, CO 80459; (303) 724-3437; or the BLM Glenwood Springs Resource Area, 50629 Highways 6 and 24, P.O. Box 1009, Glenwood Springs, CO 81602; (303) 945-2341.

RANGELY LOOP TRAIL
See letter G on map page 198

archaeological sites, camping, mountain biking, wildlife observation

Located in the remote backcountry south of Rangely, Colorado, this 177-mile trail traverses changing landscapes of harsh desert, stark buttes, high ridges, mountains and cool forests. There is a variety of climates, country and spectacular vistas to be enjoyed along the entire route. The best times to bike here are spring and fall. Gnats can be a problem in spring. While there are natural springs along the way, it is suggested that you pack all the water you will need. Camping is permitted anywhere on BLM lands. There are numerous access points that will allow you to complete all or part of the entire route. The Rangely Loop Trail (detailed on the BLM surface maps listed below) may be most easily accessed from the towns of Dinosaur, Elk Springs and Rangely. Contact the BLM directly for trail conditions and specific access information.

USGS topographic maps: Rangely, Water Canyon, Banta Ridge, Texas Creek, Dragon, Davis Canyon, East Evacuation Creek, Baxter Pass, Douglas Pass, Calf Canyon, Brushy Point, Razorback Ridge, Black Cabin Gulch, Sagebrush Hill, Calamity Ridge, Gillam Draw

BLM surface maps: Rangely, Douglas Pass

For more information: Contact the BLM White River Resource Area, 73455 Highway 64, P.O. Box 928, Meeker, CO 81641; (303) 878-3601.

DEEP CREEK

See letter H on map page 198

camping, fishing, hiking, hunting, spelunking, wildlife observation

Deep Creek is a relatively small area, 2,380 acres, but well regarded for its scenic, deep-walled limestone and sandstone canyon carved over 2,000 feet into the side of the White River Plateau. There are a number of limestone caves for spelunking adventures. Fishing is primarily for trout.

For more information: Contact the BLM Glenwood Springs Resource Area, 50629 Highways 6 and 24, P.O. Box 1009, Glenwood Springs, CO 81602; (303) 945-2341.

EAGLE RIVER

See letter I on map page 198

canoeing, fishing, hiking, rafting, wildlife observation

Located just south of Interstate 70 at the town of Wolcott, the Eagle River flows through colorful canyons of red, yellow and pale brown sandstone dotted with pinyon, juniper and cottonwood. This Class IV whitewater rafting trip is approximately eight miles long and takes three to four hours. The BLM point of access is in Wolcott. Much of the river runs through private land; trespassing on the riverbank is prohibited. Put-in is at Wolcott Campground, about two miles outside of town off Interstate 70. Take-out is on public land once again at Eagle City Park.

Resources: *Western Whitewater, From the Rockies to the Pacific,* by Jim Cassady, Bill Cross and Fryar Calhoun, published by North Fork Press, Berkeley, CA; (415) 424-1213.

USGS topographic maps: Edwards, Wolcott, Eagle

For more information: Contact the BLM Glenwood Springs Resource Area, 50629 Highways 6 and 24, P.O. Box 1009, Glenwood Springs, CO 81602; (303) 945-2341.

RABBIT VALLEY RESEARCH NATURAL AREA

See letter J on map page 198

fossils, hiking

Often referred to as the "Trail Through Time," this interpretive trail is a unique opportunity for a family to enjoy a close-up view of an area that has been excavated for dinosaur fossils since 1982. There are numerous other field sites nearby that are well worth visiting if you are interested in the Jurassic Age. From Grand Junction, drive west on Interstate 70 for approximately 30 miles to the Rabbit Valley exit (exit 2). Turn right (north) and park in the designated parking area. Walk north on the dirt road to the signed trailhead. Brochures, which are available at the trailhead, will help guide you along.

For more information: Contact the BLM Grand Junction Resource Area, 2815 H Road, Grand Junction, CO 81501; (303) 244-3000; or the Museum of Western Colorado, P.O. Box, 20000-5020, Grand Junction, CO 81502; (303) 243-DINO. (What else did you expect?)

LITTLE BOOK CLIFFS WILD HORSE AREA

See letter K on map page 198

backpacking, camping, hiking, wildlife observation

A great area to hike and explore, this region offers views of spectacular canyons, fascinating and intricate rock formations, colorful desert flora and an opportunity to spot and observe wild horses. The wild-horse area encompasses 30,261 acres of rugged canyons and plateaus with elevations varying from 5,000 to 7,421 feet. Other wildlife that inhabits the region includes bobcats, mountain lions, mule deer, elk, coyotes and bald eagles.

Activity Highlight: Hiking

Coal Canyon is perhaps the best access route into the area. From the trail, there are an almost infinite number of opportunities to explore side canyons. Although the Coal Canyon Trail itself is nine miles each way, many more miles may be added by venturing off onto side and alternate routes. Navigation is not too difficult once you are off the route, but adequate map and compass skills are essential.

Canyons can become quickly choked with water, mud, rocks and logs during a flash flood. Always be ready to head for high ground if there is rain. Clouds filling the upland areas are a sure sign that flash floods could occur at any moment. There are a number of 1,000-foot-deep canyons that intersect the plateau area. The 1,500-foot escarpment known as the Book Cliffs creates a spectacular geological contrast extending up into Utah. Wild horses frequent the area, and if you keep alert, you stand a good chance of spotting one or more before they spot you—and gallop off.

The gates into Coal Canyon are closed to vehicles from December 1 through May 31 during the foaling season. The best opportunity to view wild horses on foot will be near the Coal Canyon Trailhead, in the North Soda area and around Indian Park. Remember to keep a respectful distance.

Location: Ten miles northeast of Grand Junction. From Grand Junction, take Interstate 70 east to the Cameo exit. Drive alongside the highway on the paved road, cross the Colorado River and pass the electrical generating plant. Follow the dirt road that takes you over an irrigation ditch and continues up into the canyon. The road will become progressively narrower and rougher, but it should be okay for most vehicles. However, four-wheel-drive vehicles are recommended from this point on if the road is wet and muddy. From the power plant, it is only about 1.5 miles to the main canyon. After heavy rainstorms, roads can become so slick that they are impassable, even with chains on your tires.

Camping: Camp anywhere within the area. Flash floods are always a hazard, so do not camp anywhere near a streambed or on a narrow canyon floor.

Season: Spring and fall are the best times to visit this area. However, certain areas are closed seasonally. Be sure to contact the BLM before heading out to determine what is open and what is not.

USGS topographic maps: Cameo, Round Mountain

Resources:
• While the USGS topographic maps for this region provide a general overview, it is recommended that you contact the BLM for more detailed trip-planning information for the region you intend to visit.
• *Hiker's Guide to Colorado*, by Caryn and Peter Boddie, published by Falcon Press, P.O. Box 1718, Helena, MT 59624; (800) 582-2665.

For more information: Contact the BLM Grand Junction Resource Area, 2815 H Road, Grand Junction, CO 81506; (303) 244-3000.

RUBY CANYON

See letter L on map page 198

canoeing, hiking, kayaking, rafting, wildlife observation
The beautiful Ruby Canyon of the Lower Colorado River provides excellent flat-water trips for canoeists, rafters and kayakers. In fact, the 25-mile stretch from the Loma Boat Launch, just below Grand Junction, to the Westwater Ranger Station take-out in Utah offers some of the best flat-water canoeing in the state. Along the way, you will gain access to seven spectacular canyons within the Black Ridge Canyons Wilderness Study Area. This region contains the largest concentration of natural sandstone arches in Colorado. Adventurous and experienced rafters and kayakers can make this the first leg of a journey into Utah's famed Westwater Canyon—but you must be an experienced boater and you must have a permit once past the Westwater Ranger Station! Be prepared for stiff upstream winds which can slow travel time considerably.

USGS topographic maps: Mack, Ruby Canyon, Bitter Creek Well, Westwater Southwest

For more information: Contact the BLM Grand Junction Resource Area, 2815 H Road, Grand Junction, CO 81506; (303) 244-3000.

KOKOPELLI'S TRAIL

See letter M on map page 198

backpacking, hiking, mountain biking
Kokopelli's Trail meanders its way through desert sandstone canyons and sagebrush prairies that parallel the Colorado River from just west of Grand Junction, Colorado to Moab, Utah. This 140-mile mountain biking trail offers a remote and scenic adventure with an

interesting combination of easy and very challenging trail segments. As with the Tabeguache Trail, this trail's existence is a direct result of the hard work and cooperative effort put forth by the BLM, the U.S. Forest Service, the Colorado Plateau Mountain Bike Trail Association and numerous volunteers. It is because of the COPMOBA's effort in developing this trail that I include it within this chapter on Colorado, even though the majority of the ride lies within the state of Utah.

Activity Highlight: Mountain biking

The trail begins at the Loma Boat Launch near Grand Junction, Colorado, and winds for 140 miles through sandstone and shale canyons and some forest until it reaches Moab, Utah. The entire route is well marked with brown fiberglass posts every half mile and at all junctions. If the route is wet, some sections may be impassable. If you plan on having a support vehicle, it is possible (but very difficult) for a high-clearance, four-wheel-drive vehicle to travel all but the single-track sections of the route.

Most of the trail is routed through remote BLM land. A good working knowledge of map and compass reading is a requisite. Water is not readily available along the route. The few water-resupply points that exist are spread far apart. Be sure to carry all the water that you will need with you for each day—one gallon per person minimum. Get in the habit of topping off at all available water sources. All water must be treated before drinking. Campfires are okay with the use of a fire pan. All charcoal must be packed out.

Location: The trail begins approximately 15 miles west of Grand Junction and follows the Colorado River all the way to Moab, Utah. To get to the Loma Boat Launch near Grand Junction, Colorado, take the Loma exit (exit 15) off Interstate 70, cross over the Interstate to the south and go left on the gravel road for three-tenths of a mile. The trail begins at the parking lot for the Loma Boat Launch.

Camping: Camp anywhere along the trail in designated camping areas or on public land. Stay off of private property. Camping is restricted in Utah along the Colorado River.

Season: March through May and September through November are the best times to ride the trail. Summer is possible, but it can get too hot to handle in the lower elevations.

Permits: No permits are necessary in Colorado, but camping permits are required along the Colorado River in Utah.

USGS topographic maps: Colorado: Mack, Ruby Canyon; Colorado/ Utah: Bitter Creek Well, Westwater; Utah: Agate, Big Triangle, Cisco Northeast, Dewey, Blue Chief Mesa, Fisher Valley, Mount Waas, Warner Lake, Rill Creek, Moab Southeast

BLM surface maps: Grand Junction, Westwater, Moab

Resources:
• Colorado Plateau Mountain Bike Trail Association (COPMOBA), P.O. Box 4602, Grand Junction, CO 81502; (303) 241-9561.
• *Mountain Bike Adventures in the Four Corners Region,* by Michael McCoy, published by The Mountaineers, Seattle, WA.

For more information: Contact the BLM Grand Junction Resource Area, 2815 H Road, Grand Junction, CO 81506; (303) 244-3000; or the BLM Grand Resource Area, P.O. Box M, Sand Flats Road, Moab, UT 84532; (801) 259-8193.

BLACK RIDGE CANYONS WILDERNESS STUDY AREA

See letter N on map page 198

backpacking, camping, hiking, mountain biking, wildlife observation

Located near Colorado National Monument, the Black Ridge Canyons Wilderness Study Area offers an opportunity for visitors to explore varied and spectacular desert canyon country. Rattlesnake Canyon in particular is known for its geological faults and numerous arches. Wildlife is abundant and includes desert bighorn sheep, deer, black bear, mountain lion and many species of raptor, including the golden eagle. The best seasons to visit are spring and fall. For an excellent introduction to the area, hike the Pollock Canyon Trail, which is not only the most accessible of all the trails in the region, but also the only trail that will guide you through the second largest concentration of natural arches in the world. (Mountain biking may be enjoyed on many of the jeep roads that exist outside of the Wilderness Study Area, but no mountain biking is allowed within the wilderness area.)

To reach the trailhead, drive west from Grand Junction on Interstate 70 to the Fruita exit. Bear south on Highway 340 towards Colorado National Monument. Just after crossing the Colorado River, turn right on King's View Road. At the fork in the road, bear left and follow the signs for Pollock Canyon. After approximately three miles, the road dips into the Flume Creek gully, just before reaching the Colorado River. Turn left on the road here and follow it three-tenths of a mile to the trailhead.

USGS topographic map: Mack

Resources: *Western Whitewater, From the Rockies to the Pacific,* by Jim Cassady, Bill Cross and Fryar Calhoun, published by North Fork Press, Berkeley, CA; (415) 424-1213.

For more information: Contact the BLM Grand Junction Resource Area, 2815 H Road, Grand Junction, CO 81506; (303) 244-3000.

DOMINGUEZ CANYON WILDERNESS STUDY AREA

See letter O on map page 198

backpacking, camping, canoeing, hiking, wildlife observation

Although there are few formal trails and travel within this area is moderate to strenuously difficult, this area of pristine wilderness canyons is not to be missed. Dominguez Canyon is the largest BLM Wilderness Study Area in Colorado. You must allow at least several days for playful exploration. There is great ecological variety here, from deserts to forests, arid playas to inner canyons filled with verdant pools and waterfalls, and canyon rock formations made of sandstone and Precambrian gneiss. Wildlife is also abundant and visible to those who keep a watchful eye out.

Activity Highlights: Hiking and backpacking

It is possible to put together a long, 11-mile backpacking trip across the length of Big Dominguez Canyon, but that requires a car shuttle between the Cactus Park Trailhead and Dominguez Campground. Water is available in the canyon bottom, but for traveling out of the canyon area, pack all the water you will need. Insect repellent is a must. In addition, there is at least one old mine shaft and possibly more in the area. Stay away from them—they are very hazardous.

Activity Highlight: Canoeing

With open canyon scenery and flat water, this section of the Gunnison River is very popular. The quiet, meandering river offers Class I and II boating alongside small ranches and apple orchards—creating a peaceful pastoral scene for relaxing and getting away from it all.

Location: Approximately 20 miles south of Grand Junction. Perhaps the best access to the area is via the Cactus Park Trailhead. Drive approximately nine miles south of Grand Junction on US 50 to Highway 141. Head 9.5 miles west to a sign for Cactus Park. Turn left and keep left at all forks in the road—this will keep you on the east side of Cactus Park. After approximately four miles, turn right at a junction and sign indicating "Dominguez Canyon Trail." After three-tenths of a mile, turn left again at what should be another signed road for Dominguez Canyon Trail. Once you come to the wilderness study area boundary, you will need to leave your vehicle, unless you have four-wheel-drive. The last two miles to the "official" trailhead can be mighty rough.

Camping: There is one organized campground, Dominguez Campground. Camping is allowed anywhere within the wilderness study area. To get to the Dominguez Campground, take Highway 141 west past Cactus Park Road to Divide Road. Turn left on Divide Road and drive approximately eight miles to another left on Dominguez Conservation Area Road. It's another six miles to the campground.

Season: Spring and fall are the best times to visit.

USGS topographic maps: Dominguez, Escalante Forks, Good Point, Jacks Canyon, Keith Creek, Triangle Mesa

BLM surface map: Delta

USFS map: Uncompahgre National Forest

Resources: *Hiker's Guide to Colorado*, by Caryn and Peter Boddie, published by Falcon Press, P.O. Box 1718, Helena, MT 59624; (800) 582-2665.

For more information: Contact the BLM Grand Junction Resource Area, 2815 H Road, Grand Junction, CO 81506; (303) 244-3000.

TABEGUACHE MOUNTAIN BIKE TRAIL

See letter P on map page 198

backpacking, hiking, mountain biking

The Tabeguache Mountain Bike Trail winds through both public and private land for 142 miles, connecting Montrose and Grand Junction. The trail winds through the Uncompahgre Plateau, where traces of man's presence dates back over 10,000 years. More recently, the plateau has seen cattle grazing, sheep herding, mining and lumber ventures, and evidence of these past and present uses dot the landscape. It is essential that modern and historic resources remain undisturbed—tread lightly and leave everything as you found it.

This magnificent mountain bike trail, one of the finest in the United States, is a result of a combined effort involving the BLM, the U.S. Forest Service and dozens of volunteers, all coordinated by the Colorado Plateau Mountain Bike Trail Association (COPMOBA). Their goal is to create a network of trails that will allow mountain bikers to travel off-road from Aspen, Colorado, to the Grand Canyon. If you are interested in helping out or want to learn more, contact COPMOBA at (303) 241-9561.

Activity Highlight: Mountain biking

The Tabeguache Trail begins in Shavano Valley, eight miles west of Montrose. The trail winds and weaves its way through canyons, mesas and highlands of the Uncompahgre Plateau, ending in "No Thoroughfare Canyon," a few miles west of Grand Junction. The entire route is well marked with brown fiberglass posts every half-mile and at all junctions. If the route is wet, some sections may be impassable. If you plan on having a support vehicle, it is possible (but very difficult) for a high-clearance, four-wheel-drive vehicle to travel all but the single-track sections of the route. Most of the trail is routed through remote and virtually unused BLM and U.S. Forest Service land. A good working knowledge of map and compass reading is required. Water is available along the route, although not abundant—look for drainages and established campgrounds. All water must be treated before drinking. Campfires are allowed with the use of a fire pan. All charcoal must be packed out.

Location: The Tabeguache Trail runs between Grand Junction and Montrose, west of Highway 50 and south of Interstate 70. To reach the Montrose Trailhead, drive six miles west of Montrose on Spring Creek Road. Turn right at 58.75 Road and continue for approximately two miles to Kiowa Road. Turn left on Kiowa Road and cross the valley to the Shavano Valley Road. The Tabeguache Trail begins as a jeep road near the north end of the Shavano Valley Road. To reach the Grand Junction Trailhead, drive west on Grand Junction Avenue to Highway 340. Turn left on Monument Road. Continue to the signed trailhead for the Tabeguache Trail.

Camping: Camping is allowed anywhere along the trail in designated camping areas or on public land. Stay off private property.

Season: May through October is the best time to ride the entire trail. Lower elevation sections may be pedaled all year as snow doesn't affect them. Bikers are warned, however, that September and October are prime hunting seasons. If you choose to pedal the route (and I recommend heartily that you don't!), you must wear blazing orange or other brightly-colored clothing.

USGS topographic maps: Hoovers Corner, Davis Point, Ute, Starvation Point, Windy Point, Keith Creek, Casto Reservoir, Triangle Mesa, Island Mesa, Dry Creek Basin, Antone Spring, Moore Mesa, Kelso Point, Snipe Mountain, Uncompahgre Butte, Jacks Canyon, Whitewater, Grand Junction

BLM surface maps: Grand Junction, Delta, Nulca

USFS maps: Uncompahgre National Forest

Resources:
• Colorado Plateau Mountain Bike Trail Association (COPMOBA), P.O. Box 4602, Grand Junction, CO 81502; (303) 241-9561.
• The Tabeguache Trail Map and Trail Log can be obtained from the BLM, the U.S. Forest Service or COPMOBA.

For more information: Contact the BLM Grand Junction Resource Area, 2815 H Road, Grand Junction, CO 81506; (303) 244-3000; or the BLM Uncompahgre Resource Area, 2505 South Townsend Avenue, Montrose, CO 81401; (303) 249-6047.

GUNNISON GORGE

See letter Q on map page 198

backpacking, camping, fishing, hiking, horseback riding, kayaking, rafting

Ute Park, and in particular the Ute Trail, provide a spectacular introduction to the world-famous Black Canyon of the Gunnison, which lies just upstream from this area. Listed as a gold-medal trout stream, and by all accounts a gold-medal whitewater river for kayakers, this area has been proposed for Wild and Scenic River, Wilderness and National Conservation Area status. Sandstone and shale are the predominant geological formations. Numerous faults and sequences of sedimentary rock strata (love that Geology 101 college class) are visible and quite stunning.

Activity Highlight: Hiking

The Ute Trail is known as the traditional route the Ute Indians used to ford the Gunnison River. Only 4.5 miles each way, the trail is an easy and enjoyable introduction to the canyon area. The Ute Trail is open to both horse and foot traffic. Fishing along the river is superb. The trailhead is a great spot for picnicking, with picnic tables that afford beautiful views both to the west, across the Uncompahgre Valley, and to the east, the Gunnison Gorge. Garçon—table for two, please.

There are three other trails within the canyon that are used primarily to access the river: The Bobcat Trail (one mile long), the Duncan Trail (one mile long) and the Chukar Trail (just over one mile long), which is preferred by rafters because it is less steep.

Activity Highlight: Whitewater rafting

One of the most remote river experiences in Colorado can be enjoyed by rafting or kayaking the Gunnison Gorge Wilderness Study Area. Access to the river is by horseback or foot only, via one of four steep trails in the area. The Chukar Trail, approximately two miles downstream from the Black Canyon, serves as the primary access for rafting and kayaking. The scenery in the gorge and the abundant wildlife are major attractions. Rapids range from Class II to Class IV. The trip is 14 miles long and can be made in one or two days.

Location: Ten miles northeast of Montrose. To get to the Ute Trailhead from Delta, take US 50 south for eight miles (give or take one-quarter of a mile or so) to a paved county road, Carnation. Head east to Carnation's end as it forms a "T" at County Road 62. Turn left and head northeast through the badlands until the road ends at Peach Valley Road. Turn left and drive four-tenths of a mile, keeping a vigilant eye out for a sign indicating the Ute Trail to the right. From there, the next 2.5 miles are recommended only for four-wheel-drive vehicles. If you have one, drive to the trailhead. If you don't, park your car and walk—otherwise you will be picking up bits and pieces of your car all the way back to the nearest road.

Camping: There are three established campsites at Ute Park especially for river runners. Backpackers and fishermen may want to explore less crowded accommodations away from the river's edge or up further into the canyon. Camping is allowed anywhere, but minimum-impact camping rules dictate no camping within 200 feet of the river. Along the canyon itself, there are limited camping opportunities for those who are boating. Porta-potties must be used by all boaters and fire pans are required.

Season: Spring through fall is the best time to visit.

Permits: No permits are necessary, but all hikers must register at the trailheads.

USGS topographic maps: Black Ridge, Red Rock Canyon, Lazear

BLM surface maps: Paonia, Gunnison Gorge River

Resources:

• *Hiker's Guide to Colorado,* by Caryn and Peter Boddie, published by Falcon Press, P.O. Box 1718, Helena, MT 59624; (800) 582-2665.

• *Western Whitewater, From the Rockies to the Pacific,* by Jim Cassady, Bill Cross and Fryar Calhoun, published by North Fork Press, Berkeley, CA; (415) 424-1213.

For more information: Contact the BLM Uncompahgre Resource Area, 2505 South Townsend Avenue, Montrose, CO 81401; (303) 249-6047.

COLORADO MIDLAND BIKE TRAIL

See letter R on map page 198

mountain biking

The Colorado Midland railway was originally completed in 1866 and consisted of over 338 miles of track. This mountain bike trail follows 16 miles of that route at elevations between 7,400 and 9,400 feet. From the town of Buena Vista, the trail winds through lands scattered with pinyon and juniper trees. As the trail gains in elevation, aspen and spruce trees dominate the landscape. The Collegiate Peaks can be seen from many places along the trail. Portions of the trail traverse county roads where motorized traffic may be encountered, but much of the trail lies on the original grade of the Midland Railroad where motorized travel is prohibited. Four major trailheads serve the Midland Bike Trail: Buena Vista River Park, Midland Hills, Shields Gulch and Chubb Park. The trail officially begins at Buena Vista. From Highway 50 in Buena Vista, turn east at East Main Street. Go 1.5 miles to the town's River Park. The trail begins at the park and is well signed. To get to the other trailheads, contact the BLM for detailed directions.

USGS topographic maps: Buena Vista East, Marmot Peak, Antero Reservoir

BLM surface map: Gunnison

For more information: Contact the BLM Royal Gorge Resource Area, 3170 East Main Street, P.O. Box 2200, Canon City, CO 81215-2200; (303) 275-0631.

POWDERHORN WILDERNESS AREA

See letter S on map page 198

backpacking, fishing, hiking, wildlife observation

You can't help but sense the vastness of this area as you trek upon its plateaus. These undulating plains are commonly recognized as the largest continuous sweep of alpine tundra in the Lower 48. Despite the expansive alpine beauty, sculpted escarpments and jewellike lakes, few travel this backcountry region. This is surprising. You would think that any place offering abundant water, dense forests, open grasslands and lots of wildlife would be overrun with visitors. Actually, the majority of the thousands who visit this region annually are local Coloradans. Enjoy spectacular views of the San Juan, Elk and Sawatch mountain ranges from atop of the 12,000-foot Calf Creek Plateau. Beaver are numerous, and one can also expect to see elk, mule deer and marmot. Mountain lion, black bear, bighorn sheep and bobcat also frequent the area, but are not often seen.

Activity Highlight: Hiking

Allow yourself three days to thoroughly enjoy a backpacking trip in this region. Be sure to self-register at the trailhead before entering the trail. Set off from the Indian Creek Trailhead, which will afford you a wide variety of options. Trout fishing can be enjoyed in three lakes, Powderhorn, Devils and Hidden, as well as in the area's nearly 28 miles of perennial streams. Most of the trails in this area follow streams. From Powderhorn Lakes and Devils Lake, a system of trails interconnect with U.S. Forest Service trails to the south and offer a virtual smorgasbord of possible loops. Most visitors currently use the Powderhorn Lakes Trail; if you are seeking solitude, you will want to branch out onto the other trails networking the region.

Temperatures can range from minus 50°F in the winter to 90°F in the summer. Plan for frost and snow at any time of the year. Thunderstorms are common and often occur daily in the summer months.

Expect strong winds when traveling above timberline—at or above 11,000 feet. If you head up onto Cannibal Plateau, take a moment to contemplate the fate of Alfred Packer's five expedition companions in 1874. Apparently, he dined upon them to stay alive while stranded at the western edge of the plateau, thereby becoming notorious as a cannibal. To be safe, I suggest packing along an extra meal or two if you are traveling with someone else. The BLM and the U.S. Forest Service jointly administer this area.

Location: Five miles northeast of Lake City and 25 miles southwest of Gunnison in the southwest quadrangle of Colorado. Take Highway 149 south from Highway 50. Approximately three miles past the Cebolla Creek Road intersection and a settlement named Powderhorn, turn left onto a dirt road and continue 10 miles to the Indian Creek Trailhead. All trails that lead into the western half of the Powderhorn Wilderness Area begin here.

Camping: You can camp at the Powderhorn Lakes and 10 Mile Springs trailheads. Primitive camping is allowed anywhere within the wilderness area.

Season: Mid-June to mid-October is the best time to travel here.

USGS topographic maps: Cannibal Plateau, Mineral Mountain, Powderhorn Lakes, Rudolph Hill

Resources:
• *Colorado BLM Wildlands*, by Mark Pearson and John Fielder, published by Westcliffe Publishers, 2650 South Zuni Street, Englewood, CO 80110.
• The BLM publishes a free trail information guide. Obtain it from the BLM Gunnison office.

For more information: Contact the BLM Gunnison Resource Area, 216 North Colorado, Gunnison, CO 81230; (303) 641-0471.

ALPINE LOOP BACK COUNTRY BYWAY

See letter T on map page 198

birdwatching, cross-country skiing, fishing, hiking, mountain biking, off-highway-vehicle use, snowmobiling, wildlife observation

The Alpine Loop is designated as a National Back Country Byway. A 63-mile circuit of mostly dirt roads used heavily by four-wheel-drive enthusiasts, the route is a high-altitude experience, climbing through two 12,000-foot passes, Cinnamon and Engineer. It's an endurance test for even the savviest rider. Much of the pedal will offer excellent views of the high-alpine tundra and spectacular scenery of the rugged San Juan Mountains. Wildlife viewing is for ptarmigan, marmots, pikas, elk, deer, blue grouse, goshawks, Clark's nutcrackers and more. Rivers and streams along the byway attract fishermen in search of rainbow, brook and cutthroat trout. Numerous hiking trails may be accessed from the Alpine Loop including routes that lead up to the summit of peaks over 14,000 feet. History buffs will enjoy viewing the many structures, mines and ghost towns remaining from the late 1800s. Wildflowers along the route are outstanding. The best viewing time is from late July to early August—pack along a camera. Nearby Lake City offers nearly 80 miles of groomed trail for cross-country skiing enthusiasts near the byway in the winter months. Snowmobiling is popular, too.

Location: This route links the historic mining towns of Lake City, Ouray and Silverton. It begins in Lake City, heading west from State Route 149, located south of Gunnison and US 50. The byway is signed the entire way.

For more information: Contact the BLM Gunnison Resource Area, 216 North Colorado, Gunnison, CO 81401; (303) 641-0471; or the BLM San Juan Resource Area, Federal Building, 701 Camino Del Rio, Durango, CO 81301; (303) 247-4082.

ALPINE GULCH TRAIL

See letter U on map page 198

backpacking, camping, historic site, wildlife observation

Alpine Gulch Trail begins at 9,000 feet and travels approximately six miles up to Grassy Mountain Saddle at an elevation of 12,480 feet. The trail is moderately difficult with some steep sections. It follows a narrow canyon with steep cliffs up onto narrow ridges and eventually into a large alpine meadow. This trail is used very lightly, even though the views of the San Juan Mountain Range are spectacular. There is also the option of hooking up with the Williams Creek Trail for a one-way shuttle-supported trip beginning at Henson Creek Road and ending up at the Williams Creek Campground near Lake San Cristobal. Remnants of historic cabins from turn-of-the-century mining claims and herds of deer and elk add a special flavor to this area.

The trail runs through the Gunnison Resource Area of southwestern Colorado. From Lake City, head two miles west on Henson Creek Road to the Alpine Gulch Trailhead. Parking is available at a wide pull-out on the north side of Henson Creek Road.

Camping: Camping is allowed anywhere within the area. Williams Creek Campground is located at the Williams Creek Trailhead. Restrooms and drinking water are available. A camping fee is charged.

Season: The best time to visit this area is from late June to mid October.

USGS topographic maps: Lake City, Lake San Cristobal

BLM surface maps: Silverton, Montrose

Resources: Obtain free, detailed trail information from the BLM.

For more information: Contact the BLM Gunnison Resource Area, 216 North Colorado, Gunnison, CO 81410; (303) 641-0471.

DOLORES RIVER CANYON

See letter V on map page 198

backpacking, camping, canoeing, hiking, kayaking, mountain biking, picnicking, rafting, swimming, wildlife observation

The 104-mile stretch of the Dolores River guides boaters and adventurers through one of Colorado's most remote river environments. Wildlife-viewing opportunities include the peregrine falcon, bighorn sheep, turkey, hawk, eagle and river otter. There are numerous opportunities for mountain biking, swimming and picnicking along the Dolores River Canyon Trail.

Activity Highlight: Mountain biking

A 26-mile mountain biking trail follows alongside the Dolores River in a very scenic high-desert route. Self-register at the trailhead before heading out. The trail is rated as intermediate for the first 11 miles and challenging for the remaining 15. It is marked with bicycle-emblem signposts and follows an abandoned jeep trail. Turn around at the 11-mile marker if you are not using the shuttle option. The remaining 15 miles are not as exciting or inspiring as the first stretch, although hard-core mountain bikers may delight in the pedal. Most people just enjoy the first 11 miles and then turn around. Five river crossings must be made; these crossings are considered unsafe if the river is running above 200 cubic feet per second. Call the BLM San Juan Resource Area Hotline at (303) 882-7600 for river-flow information.

Activity Highlight: River running

The Upper Dolores River is rated Class II to Class IV. From Bradfield Bridge to Slick Rock, the trip is 45 miles long and takes two to three days. From Slick Rock to Bedrock, the trip is 58 miles and also takes two to three days. The Slick Rock access site is privately owned and a fee is charged. See the owners at the Chuck Wagon Café, about one-quarter of a mile west of the Slick Rock Bridge, to obtain permission and pay the access fee. Fire pans and porta-potties are required for all boaters. The whitewater is fun. Even the names reflect the energy—how does the "Snaggletooth Rapid" grab you? There is a river hotline during rafting season (from May to June); for information, phone (303) 882-7600.

Location: In southwestern Colorado, northwest of Cortez in the San Juan Resource Area. To get to the mountain bike trail, drive north on US 666 for 34 miles. Turn right just southeast of Dove Creek at a large brown sign that says "Public Lands Access, Dolores River Canyon and Overlook." Follow the signs to Dolores Canyon's river access and park at the area near the pump station. A shuttle is necessary if you want to ride the entire 26-mile route. For a shuttle, leave a vehicle at the Chuck Wagon Café, one-quarter mile west of Slick Rock Bridge. You will need to ask the owners for permission and pay a parking fee. Take US 666 past Dove Creek. Head north on Highway 141 to the Nicholas Wash sign, four miles past Slick Rock and Dolores River Bridge. Road 13R is a half mile past the Nicholas Wash sign on the right. River access is at Bradfield Bridge near the town of Cahone, at the Dove Creek pump station, Slick Rock (it's private and a fee is charged), and at Big Gypsum Valley downriver from Slick Rock and Bedrock Bridge (access is a half mile upstream from the bridge).

Camping: Camping is allowed anywhere except on private land. Fires are allowed anywhere, but only if you pack in your own firewood. No campfire permit is necessary. Fire pans are required.

Season: The mountain biking season is from September to mid-October and in early June. In a normal rainfall year, the river crossings preclude safe mountain biking in the canyon. The river-running season is from May through June. In wet years, it runs from mid-April through early July.

Permits: No trail-use permits are necessary. Camping permits are required at the Bradfield Campground. Boaters are required to register at all put-ins, although no permits are required at this time.

USGS topographic maps: Secret Canyon, Joe Davis Hill, Hamm Canyon, Dolores Canyon, The Glade, Horse Range Mesa, Anderson Mesa, Paradox

Resources: *Western Whitewater, From the Rockies to the Pacific,* by Jim Cassady, Bill Cross and Fryar Calhoun, published by North Fork Press, Berkeley, CA; (415) 424-1213.

For more information: Contact the BLM San Juan Resource Area, Federal Building, 701 Camino Del Rio, Durango, CO 81301; (303) 247-4082.

PENITENTE CANYON

See letter W on map page 198

camping, fishing, hiking, mountain biking, rock climbing

Located approximately 22 miles northwest of the town of Monte Vista in the San Luis Valley, Penitente Canyon offers 2,500 acres of world-class rock climbing on outstanding quality limestone cliffs. Over 300 climbing routes have been identified and bolted. A climbing guide of this area is available at state retail outlets. Trout fishing is also good if you get tired of climbing. Cast your line into La Garita Creek. Other interesting features of the area include the fall chokecherry crop (very tasty) and the historic wagon tracks that have been deeply carved into the limestone bedrock by old logging and mining activity.

From the town of Del Norte on State Route 160, head north on State Route 112 toward the town of Center. Drive approximately four miles and turn off to the north onto County Road 38A. Drive past Elephant Rocks and look for a sign indicating Penitente Canyon and its access road leading to the west. Drive about one mile to the climbing area. Parking is along the road.

For more information: Contact the BLM San Luis Resource Area, 1921 State Street, Alamosa, CO 81101; (719) 589-4975.

CROSS CANYON WILDERNESS STUDY AREA

See letter X on map page 198

archaeological site, backpacking, hiking

Cross Canyon offers hikers the very unique opportunity of walking back through time among the small Anasazi Indian cliff dwellings and pueblo ruins of the 12th and 13th centuries. Much of the hiking follows a scenic route along a cottonwood- and willow-laden riparian area at the base of Cross Canyon, which cuts through the surrounding plateau country. Trails disappear quickly and good topographic map-reading and orienteering skills are mandatory. Water is available from Cross Creek, which runs year-round. Wildflowers are spectacular during the late spring and early summer—unfortunately, this is just the season you want to avoid, because of the obnoxious cedar gnats. The best times to visit are early spring, late summer and early fall. The area is accessible in winter, depending on weather conditions.

The best trailhead access is reachable only by high-clearance or four-wheel-drive vehicles. From Pleasant View, turn west on Pleasant Valley Road, near the radio tower. Look for the sign directing you to Lowry Ruin. Drive for 5.5 miles to an intersection and turn left toward Hovenweep. After approximately 24 miles, bear right at a sign directing you towards Cross Canyon. It is seven rough miles from here to the trailhead. Park at the Wilderness Study Area boundary.

Camping is allowed within the area, but not at archaeological or historical sites. Fires can be built if the fire rings are dismantled. I would heartily recommend going without a fire and using only a camping stove. Water is available from Cross Creek, but it must be treated. While the BLM encourages visitation, much of the policing of the area is left up to each of us individually. Report any and all signs of vandalism to the BLM. "Look but don't touch" is the rule. Take pictures and memories; leave only footprints.

USGS topographic maps: Ruin Point, Papoose Canyon, Ruin Canyon, Champagne Spring

BLM surface maps: Bluff, Cortez, Dove Creek

For more information: Contact the BLM San Juan Resource Area, Federal Building, 701 Camino Del Rio, Durango, CO 81301; (303) 247-4082.

SAND CANYON

See letter Y on map page 198

archaeological sites, backpacking, hiking, mountain biking, wildlife observation

Sand Canyon is an excellent area for exploring sandstone canyons and slick rock with numerous hidden Anasazi Indian cliff dwellings. Good views from high up also may be enjoyed. There are excellent opportunities to observe wildlife, including cottontail rabbit, coyote and deer. Raptors are abundant in the skies above.

Activity Highlight: Archaeological excavation

The Crow Canyon Archaeological Center performs excavation, in conjunction with the BLM, and offers programs that allow for public participation in the excavation process. If you are interested, contact the Crow Canyon Archaeological Center, 23390 County Road K, Cortez, CO 81321; (303) 565-8975.

Activity Highlight: Mountain biking

The Sand Canyon Pueblo to McElmo Canyon Mountain Bike Trail is marked with a bicycle-emblem sign and offers super views and an opportunity to visit ruin sites. The route is a dirt and gravel jeep route and is best traveled from east to west—a total of 16.2 miles one way, requiring approximately five hours to pedal. Only advanced mountain bikers should attempt riding west to east. To get to the trailhead, drive north on US 666 from Cortez for 5.3 miles and turn left on Road P. Drive 4.5 miles and turn left again onto Road 18. Drive five miles , then turn right at Road T. At 6.4 miles, turn left to mile 7.1, Road N, and bear right. Drive 9.5 miles and look for a BLM sign on the left that marks the Sand Canyon Pueblo.

Location: To get to Sand Canyon, head south from Cortez on US 666 for 2.5 miles to McElmo Canyon Road. Watch for signs indicating the airport and Hovenweep National Monument. Turn right and after 12 miles the road turns to dirt and crosses McElmo Creek. After approximately one-half mile, you will come to a parking area for the Sand and East Rock Canyon. Access to the BLM site is on the right.

USGS topographic maps: Battle Rock, Woods Canyon, Negro Canyon, Bowdish Canyon

BLM surface map: Cortez

Resources:
• Obtain the guidebook with maps entitled *Colorado Mountain Biking Adventures* from the BLM.

For more information: Contact the BLM San Juan Resource Area, Federal Building, 701 Camino Del Rio, Durango, CO 81301; (303) 247-4082.

ANASAZI HERITAGE CENTER AND SPECIAL RECREATION AREA

See letter Z on map page 198

archaeological sites, camping, hiking, mountain biking, rockhounding, wildlife observation

This 156,000-acre area near the town of Dolores has been set aside to "maintain its rich cultural and natural resource diversity for a variety of land uses while allowing visitors to explore the area largely on their own," according to the BLM mandate. Although archaeological artifacts and ruins abound throughout the large area, you'll learn a great deal more about the Anasazi culture from the outstanding interpretive exhibits, educational programs and outreach efforts of the Anasazi Heritage Center museum and visitor center. This striking facility receives over 40,000 visits annually. The center also serves as a regional research laboratory for continuing archaeological investigations in the Four Corners region of Colorado, New Mexico, Arizona and Utah. From the town of Cortez and US 160, head north on State Route 145 toward McPhee Reservoir. Turn left (west) at State Route 184 and drive approximately one mile to the signed entrance to the Anasazi Heritage Center.

For more information: Contact the BLM San Juan Resource Area, Federal Building, 701 Camino Del Rio, Durango, CO 81301; (303) 247-4082; or the Anasazi Heritage Center, 27501 Highway 184, Dolores, CO 81323; (303) 882-4811.

RIO GRANDE RIVER

See letter AA on map page 198

backpacking, canoeing, hiking, rafting, wildlife observation

The Colorado section of the Rio Grande River, located in south-central Colorado, offers easy floating opportunities for rafters and canoeists. Thirty miles long, the river flows through sagebrush and pinyon pine tucked in among low-lying rock formations. Deer, elk, beaver, muskrat, golden eagle and a variety of falcons may be seen. The Sangre de Cristo Range provides a spectacular and scenic backdrop to the solitude of the float. A word of caution: Before you become too engrossed in the tranquility, keep in mind that once across the border into New Mexico, the Rio Grande becomes quite turbulent and almost unrunnable. Only experienced rafters and kayakers should venture beyond the Colorado border. The Colorado section usually takes about two days to float. Put-in is at La Sauses Bridge, 10 miles east, 8.5 miles north and one-half mile east again from Manassa, off Highway 142. Take-out is at Lobatos Bridge, 15 miles east of Antonito on Country Road G.

USGS topographic maps: Misito Reservoir, Kiowa Hill, Ski Valley Ranch

For more information: Contact the BLM San Luis Resource Area, 1921 State Street, Alamosa, CO 81101; (719) 589-4975.

COLORADO—MAP B

GEORGETOWN BIGHORN VIEWING SITE

See letter BB on map page 200

wildlife observation

Jointly managed by the city of Georgetown, the BLM and the Colorado Division of Wildlife, this developed interpretive site overlooks an area that is the habitat for bighorn sheep nearly every month of the year. The best viewing is in fall, winter and spring. A viewing tower offers excellent opportunities to spot bighorn. Located near the town of Georgetown and Interstate 70.

For more information: Contact the BLM Royal Gorge Resource Area, 3170 East Main Street, P.O. Box 2200, Canon City, CO 81215-2200; (719) 275-0631.

ARKANSAS HEADWATERS RECREATION AREA

See letter CC on map page 200

camping, canoeing, fishing, kayaking, picnicking, rafting, rockhounding, wildlife observation

This outstanding whitewater river, located near Canon City, lies within a two- to three-hour drive of over two million Colorado residents—is it any wonder it gets so much use? Still, the 150-mile segment offers challenging whitewater recreation for anyone who loves to kayak, raft or whitewater canoe through rapids rated up to Class V. The river is extremely scenic and trout fishing is quite good. Put-ins and take-outs are spread out all along Highways 24, 285 and 50 near Granite, Railroad Bridge, Buena Vista, Fishermans Bridge, Ruby Mountain, Hecla Junction, Big Bend, Salida, Vallie Bridge, Pinnacle Rock, Parkdale and Canon City.

USGS topographic maps: Leadville South, Granite, South Peak, Buena Vista West, Howard, Cotopaxi, Royal Gorge, Harvard Lakes, Buena Vista East, Nathrop, Salida West, Salida East, Wellsville, Coaldale, Arkansas Mountain, Echo, McIntyre Hills, Canon City, Florence, Pierce Gulch, Hobson, Swallows

Resources: *Western Whitewater, from the Rockies to the Pacific,* by Jim Cassady, Bill Cross and Fryar Calhoun, published by North Fork Press, Berkeley, CA; (415) 424-1213.

For more information: Contact the BLM Royal Gorge Resource Area, 3170 East Main Street, P.O. Box 2200, Canon City, CO 81215-2200; (303) 275-0631; or the Arkansas Headwaters Recreation Area, 307 West Sackett Avenue, P.O. Box 126, Salida, CO 81201; (719) 539-7289.

THE GOLD BELT TOUR
NATIONAL BACK COUNTRY BYWAY
See letter DD on map page 200

fossils, hiking, mountain biking, off-road touring, rock climbing

Three unsurfaced roads—Phantom Canyon, Shelf and High Park roads—link the towns of Canon City, Cripple Creek, Victor and Florence. This scenic byway traverses some of Colorado's most interesting and historic mining and cattle country. During most of the year, all three routes may be traveled by standard two-wheel-drive vehicles. However, slow speeds and extra caution are advised on narrow, winding routes of Shelf and Phantom Canyon roads. High Park Road is the easiest to navigate. The byway accesses the Shelf Road Rock Climbing Area (guide and route map available from the BLM), as well as the Garden Park Dinosaur Fossil Area. The byway also provides trailhead access to the Beaver Creek Wilderness Area—but we have not included Beaver Creek in this guide as it is becoming overused and heavily impacted.

Activity Highlight: Rock climbing

At the Shelf Road Rock Climbing Area, climbers come from all over the world to scale these limestone walls. The climbs are short, but very difficult with limited handholds and many overhangs. Several backroads near the climbing area also provide interesting hiking and mountain biking opportunities for those not so vertically inclined.

Activity Highlight: Dinosaur fossil viewing

Othniel Lucas, a Garden Park school teacher, discovered massive bones in these badlands in 1876. The subsequent excavations led to the discoveries of such well-known dinosaurs as diplodocus, stegosaurus and allosaurus. A slide show and tour of this area is conducted each Saturday evening from mid-May to September. Contact the Canon City Chamber of Commerce at (719) 275-2331 for details.

Location: The Gold Belt Tour is located along the Front Range in southern Colorado, just one hour from Colorado Springs or Pueblo or two hours from Denver. Perhaps the best place to begin the tour, as there are several, is from the town of Florence, southeast of Canon City and near the junction of state routes 115, 160 and 67. The entire route is signed and easy to follow.

For more information: Contact the BLM Royal Gorge Resource Area, 3170 East Main Street, P.O. Box 2200, Canon City, CO 81215-2200; (303) 275-0631.

BLM CAMPGROUNDS

1. IRISH CANYON CAMPGROUND—MAP A

Campsites, facilities: There are three sites, all with picnic tables and fire rings. There is **no water**. Vault toilets are wheelchair accessible. No trash facilities are provided, so pack out all that you bring in. RVs up to 30 feet are allowed. There is a 14-day stay limit.
Fee: There is no fee.
Who to contact: Little Snake Resource Area, 1280 Industrial Avenue, Craig, CO 81625; (303) 824-4441.
Location: From US 40 in Maybell, drive northwest n Highway 318 for approximately 45 miles to County Road 10. Turn right and drive on a gravel surface for eight miles to the campground entrance. The campground is set at 6,000 feet.
Season: All year.

2. RADIUM CAMPGROUND—MAP A

Campsites, facilities: There are four sites, all with picnic tables, grills and fire rings. Vault toilets are wheelchair accessible. Boat-launch access is available. There is **no water**. No trash facilities are provided, so pack out all that you bring in. RVs up to 30 feet are allowed. There is a 14-day stay limit.
Fee: In the future, a fee between $5 to $7 per night will be collected on site, but the figure was not determined at press time.
Who to contact: Kremmling Resource Area, 1116 Park Avenue, P.O. Box 68, Kremmling, CO 80459; (303) 724-3437.
Location: On the Upper Colorado River. From Kremmling, drive south for two miles along Highway 9. Turn west on the gravel Trough Road (County Road 1) and drive 25 miles, passing Inspiration Point and the Pumphouse turnoff, to reach the campground. The campground is set at 7,000 feet.
Season: May to September.

3. PUMPHOUSE CAMPGROUND—MAP A

Campsites, facilities: There are 14 sites, all with picnic tables, grills, and fire rings. Vault toilets are wheelchair accessible. Water is available. There are no trash facilities, so pack out all that you bring in. Boat-launch access is available. RVs up to 30 feet are allowed. There is a 14-day stay limit.

Fee: In the future, a fee between $5 to $7 per night will be collected on site, but the figure was not determined at press time.

Who to contact: Kremmling Resource Area, 1116 Park Avenue, P.O. Box 68, Kremmling, CO 80459; (303) 724-3437.

Location: On the Upper Colorado River. From Kremmling, drive south for two miles along Highway 9. Turn west on the gravel Trough Road (County 1) and drive 14 miles, passing Inspiration Point, to a right turn on an access road signed for Pumphouse. The access road is 1.5 miles long. The campground is set at 7,000 feet.

Season: May to September.

4. MUD SPRINGS CAMPGROUND—MAP A

Campsites, facilities: There are 15 sites, all with picnic tables, grills and fire rings. Pit toilets and water are available. No trash facilities are provided, so pack out all that you bring in. RVs up to 30 feet are allowed. There is a 14-day stay limit.

Fee: There is no fee.

Who to contact: Grand Junction Resource Area, 50629 Highways 6 and 24, P.O. Box 1009, Glenwood Springs, CO 81602; (303) 945-2341.

Location: In Glade Park, set among aspens. From Grand Junction, drive along Monument Road into the Colorado National Monument. Turn east on East Glade Park Road. Turn left onto 16.5 Road and drive for six miles to the campground entrance. The campground is set at 8,000 feet.

Season: May to October.

5. BIG DOMINGUEZ CAMPGROUND—MAP A

Campsites, facilities: There are four sites, all with picnic tables and fire rings. Pit toilets are available. There is **no water**. No trash facilities are provided, so pack out all that you bring in. There is a 14-day stay limit.

Fee: There is no fee.

Who to contact: Grand Junction Resource Area, 50629 Highways 6 and 24, P.O. Box 1009, Glenwood Springs, CO 81602; (303) 945-2341.

Location: Near the Tabeguache Trail. From Grand Junction, drive southwest on US 6 to US 50, then continue southwest on Highway

141—a total distance of approximately 20 miles. At Divide Road, turn left and travel four miles to the Dominguez sign. Turn left again and drive another four miles to the campground. The eight miles from Highway 141 are unpaved and may become impassable when wet. A four-wheel-drive vehicle is recommended. The campground is set at 7,500 feet.

Season: May to October.

6. RUBY MOUNTAIN RECREATION SITE—MAP A

Campsites, facilities: There are six sites, all with picnic tables, fire rings and grills. Vault toilets are wheelchair accessible. A boat ramp is available. There is **no water.** No trash facilities are provided, so pack out all that you bring in. RVs up to 30 feet are allowed. A wheelchair-accessible campsite is planned for construction in 1995, but it may not be available until 1996—call for information. There is a 14-day stay limit.

Fee: There is a one-day $1 fee per person, plus $6 per vehicle per site (up to six people); pay on site.

Who to contact: Arkansas Headwaters Recreation Area, 307 West Sackett Avenue, P.O. Box 126, Salida, CO 81201; (719) 539-7289.

Location: Within the Arkansas Headwaters Recreation Area. From Buena Vista, drive south on US 285 for approximately seven miles to Fisherman's Bridge. Turn left on County Road 301, across the Arkansas River, and follow the signs for three miles to the campground. The campground is set at 7,600 feet.

Season: All year.

7. HECLA JUNCTION RECREATION SITE—MAP A

Campsites, facilities: There are 18 sites on-river with picnic tables and fire rings with grills. One campsite is wheelchair accessible. Vault toilets and changing rooms are wheelchair accessible. A boat ramp is available. There is **no water.** No trash facilities are provided, so pack out all that you bring in. RVs up to 30 feet are allowed. There is a 14-day stay limit.

Fee: There is a one-day $1 fee per person, plus $2 per vehicle per site (up to six people); pay on site.

Who to contact: Arkansas Headwaters Recreation Area, 307 West Sackett Avenue, P.O. Box 126, Salida, CO 81201; (719) 539-7289.

Location: Within the Arkansas Headwaters Recreation Area. From

Salida, drive north on Highway 291 to the junction with US 285. Turn right (north) and drive approximately one-half mile. Turn right (east) onto County Road 194 and drive 2.5 miles to the campground. The campground is set at 7,500 feet.

Season: All year.

8. RINCON RECREATION SITE—MAP A

Campsites, facilities: There are 20 sites, all with picnic tables, grills and fire rings. One campsite, scheduled to open on Memorial Day, 1995, will be fully wheelchair accessible. Vault toilets and changing rooms are wheelchair accessible. A boat ramp is available. There is **no water**. No trash facilities are provided, so pack out all that you bring in. RVs up to 30 feet are allowed. There is a 14-day stay limit.

Fee: There is a one-day $1 fee per person, plus $6 per vehicle per site (up to six people); pay on site.

Who to contact: Arkansas Headwaters Recreation Area, 307 West Sackett Avenue, P.O. Box 126, Salida, CO 81201; (719) 539-7289.

Location: Within the Arkansas Headwaters Recreation Area. From Salida, drive southeast on US 50 for nine miles to the campground entrance. From Howard, drive three miles northwest on US 50 to the campground entrance. The campground is set at 6,800 feet.

Season: All year.

9. BRADFIELD CAMPGROUND—MAP A

Campsites, facilities: There are 22 sites, all with picnic tables and fire grills. Vault toilets, water and boating access to the Dolores River are available. No trash facilities are provided, so pack out all that you bring in. RVs up to 30 feet are allowed. There is a 14-day stay limit.

Fee: There is a $6 fee per night; pay on site.

Who to contact: San Juan Resource Area, Federal Building, 701 Camino Del Rio, Durango, CO 81301; (303) 247-4082.

Location: From Cahone and US 666, head east at the north end of town on the forest access road for five miles to the Dolores River. At the river, follow the signs to the campground. The campground is set at 6,400 feet.

Season: April to October.

10. DOLORES CANYON OVERLOOK CAMPGROUND—MAP A

Campsites, facilities: There are six sites, all with picnic tables and fire rings. Vault and composting toilets are available. There is **no water**. There is a 14-day stay limit.

Fee: There is no fee.

Who to contact: San Juan Resource Area, Federal Building, 701 Camino Del Rio, Durango, CO 81301; (303) 247-4082.

Location: Overlooking the Dolores River. From Dove Creek and US 666, drive east on County Road J for approximately eight miles. Turn left (north) at the campground sign and drive another 3.5 miles to the site. The campground is set at 8,000 feet.

Season: May to October.

11. MOUNTAIN SHEEP POINT CAMPGROUND—MAP A

Campsites, facilities: There are three sites, all with picnic tables and grills. Composting toilets are available. There is **no water**. No trash facilities are provided, so pack out all that you bring in. RVs up to 30 feet are allowed. There is a 14-day stay limit.

Fee: There is no fee.

Who to contact: San Juan Resource Area, Federal Building, 701 Camino Del Rio, Durango, CO 81301; (303) 247-4082.

Location: In the Dolores River Canyon. From US 666 and the east side of Dove Creek, follow the signs along the Dolores River access road for five miles to the river and then along the river to the campground. Roads are narrow and can become difficult to drive on when wet. The campground is set at 6,100 feet.

Season: April to October. Expect crowds on July 4.

12. MILL CREEK CAMPGROUND—MAP A

Campsites, facilities: There are 22 sites, all with picnic tables and grills. Vault toilets and water are available. RVs up to 35 feet are allowed. There is a 14-day stay limit.

Fee: There is a $5 fee per day; pay on site.

Who to contact: Gunnison Resource Area, 216 North Colorado, Gunnison, CO 81230; (303) 641-0471.

Location: In the San Juan Mountains near the Gunnison River. From Lake City, drive south for three miles on Highway 149. Turn right onto the county road paralleling the Lake Fork of the Gunnison River. Turn left after 11 miles at the sign for the campground. The campground is set at 9,500 feet.

Season: June to September. Dry camping is allowed off-season.

13. The Gate Campground—Map A

Campsites, facilities: There are eight sites, all with picnic tables and fire rings. Vault toilets are available. There is **no water**. No trash facilities are provided, so pack out all that you bring in. RVs up to 30 feet are allowed. There is a 14-day stay limit.

Fee: There is no fee.

Who to contact: Gunnison Resource Area, 216 North Colorado, Gunnison, CO 81230; (303) 641-0471.

Location: On the banks of the Lake Fork of Gunnison River. From Lake City, drive approximately 16 miles north on Highway 149 to the campground entrance. The campground is set at 8,400 feet.

Season: May to October.

14. Red Bridge Campground—Map A

Campsites, facilities: There are seven sites, all with picnic tables, grills and fire rings. A vault toilet is available. There is **no water**. No trash facilities are provided, so pack out all that you bring in. RVs up to 30 feet are allowed. There is a 14-day stay limit.

Fee: There is no fee.

Who to contact: Gunnison Resource Area, 216 North Colorado, Gunnison, CO 81230; (303) 641-0471.

Location: Near the Lake Fork of the Gunnison River. From Lake City, drive north on Highway 149 for approximately 20 miles. Turn right onto Gateview Road (County Road 25) and drive two miles to the campground. The campground is set at 7,800 feet.

Season: May to October.

15. Cebolla Creek Campground—Map A

Campsites, facilities: There are three sites, all with picnic tables and fire grills. A vault toilet is available. There is **no water**. No trash facilities are provided, so pack out all that you bring in. There is a 14-day stay limit.

Fee: There is no fee.

Who to contact: Gunnison Resource Area, 216 North Colorado, Gunnison, CO 81230; (303) 641-0471.

Location: Near Gunnison. From US 50, turn south on Highway 149 and drive approximately 15 miles toward Lake City. Turn south on County Road 27 along Cebolla Creek and drive eight miles. Turn right to the area signed Cebolla Campground. The campground is set at 9,500 feet.

Season: June to October.

16. PENITENTE CAMPGROUND—MAP A

Campsites, facilities: There are 10 sites, all with picnic tables and fire rings. Pit toilets are available. There is **no water**. No trash facilities are provided, so pack out all that you bring in. There is a 14-day stay limit.

Fee: There is no fee.

Who to contact: San Luis Resource Area, 1921 State Street, Alamosa, CO 81101; (719) 589-4975.

Location: From the town of Del Norte and Highway 160, drive north on Highway 112 for approximately 2.5 miles to Pipeline Road (County Road 33). Stay on County Road 33—it turns into County Road 38-A and then County Road 38—to the town of La Garita. Turn left onto County Road 41-G and drive approximately three miles to the campground entrance. The campground is set at 7,800 feet.

Season: All year.

17. FIVE POINTS RECREATION SITE—MAP B

Campsites, facilities: There are 20 sites off-river, all with picnic tables, fire rings and grills. One campsite, scheduled to open by Memorial Day, 1995, will be fully wheelchair accessible. Vault toilets are wheelchair accessible. There is **no water**. No trash facilities are provided, so pack out all that you bring in. RVs up to 30 feet are allowed. There is a 14-day stay limit.

Fee: There is a one-day, $1 fee per person, plus $2 per vehicle per site (up to six people); pay on site.

Who to contact: Arkansas Headwaters Recreation Area, 307 West Sackett Avenue, P.O. Box 126, Salida, CO 81201; (719) 539-7289.

Location: Within the Arkansas Headwaters Recreation Area. From Canon City, drive west on US 50 for 18 miles, passing the junction with Highway 9 and Parkdale along the way. The campground lies on the south side of the highway near the Arkansas River. The campground is set at 6,000 feet.

STATE INFORMATION OVERVIEW

COLORADO STATE OFFICE
2850 Youngfield Street, Lakewood, CO 80215; (303) 239-3600

GRAND JUNCTION DISTRICT OFFICE
2815 H Road, Grand Junction, CO 81506; (303) 244-3000

Glenwood Springs Resource Area, 50629 Highways 6 and 24, P.O. Box 1009, Glenwood Springs, CO 81602; (303) 945-2341

Grand Junction Resource Area, 50629 Highways 6 and 24, P.O. Box 1009, Glenwood Springs, CO 81602; (303) 945-2341

CANON CITY DISTRICT OFFICE
3170 East Main Street, P.O. Box 2200, Canon City, CO 81212; (719) 275-0631

Royal Gorge Resource Area, 3170 East Main Street, P.O. Box 2200, Canon City, CO 81215-2200; (719) 275-0631

San Luis Resource Area, 1921 State Street, Alamosa, CO 81101; (719) 589-4975

MONTROSE DISTRICT OFFICE
2465 South Townsend Avenue, Montrose, CO 81401; (303) 249-7791

Gunnison Resource Area, 216 North Colorado, Gunnison, CO 81230; (303) 641-0471

San Juan Resource Area, Federal Building, 701 Camino Del Rio, Durango, CO 81301; (303) 247-4082

Uncompahgre Resource Area, 2505 South Townsend Avenue, Montrose, CO 81401; (303) 249-6047

CRAIG DISTRICT OFFICE
455 Emerson Street, Craig, CO 81625-1129; (303) 824-8261

Kremmling Resource Area, 1116 Park Avenue, P.O. Box 68, Kremmling, CO 80459; (303) 724-3437

Little Snake Resource Area, 1280 Industrial Avenue, Craig, CO 81625; (303) 824-4441

White River Resource Area, 73544 Highway 64, P.O. Box 928, Meeker, CO 81641; (303) 878-3601

IDAHO

Maps—pp. 244, 246
Idaho Map A Locations—pp. 248-253
Idaho Map B Locations—pp. 254-273
Information Resources—pp. 286-287

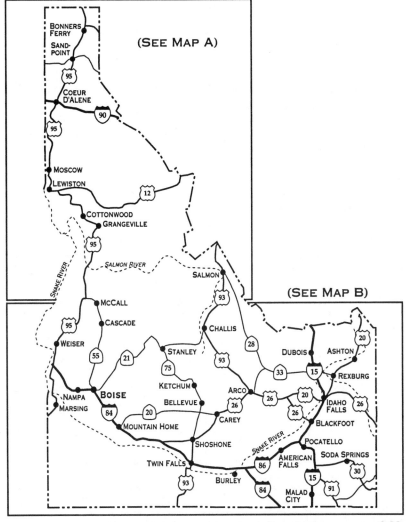

MAP A—IDAHO

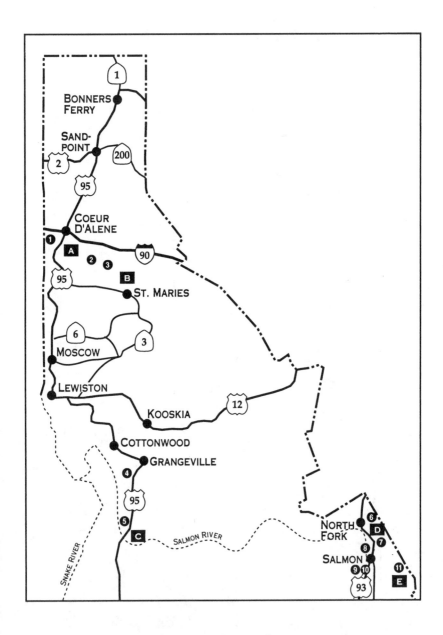

MAP REFERENCES

A. Wolf Lodge Bay —p. 248
B. Grandmother Mountain—p. 248
C. Lower Salmon River —p. 250
D. Freeman Peak / Freeman Creek —p. 252
E. Lewis and Clark Back Country Byway—p. 252

BLM CAMPGROUNDS

1. Killarney Lake Campground—p. 274
2. Tingley Springs Campground—p. 274
3. Huckleberry Campground—p. 274
4. Hammer Creek Campground—p. 275
5. Slate Creek Campground—p. 275
6. Smokey Clubs Campground—p. 275
7. McFarland Campground—p. 276
8. Tower Rock Campground—p. 276
9. Williams Lake Campground—p. 276
10. Shoup Bridge Campground—p. 277
11. Agency Creek Campground—p. 277

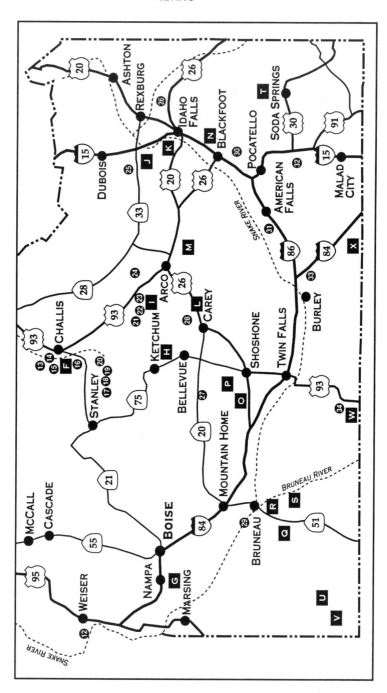

IDAHO—MAP B

MAP REFERENCES

BLM CAMPGROUNDS

IDAHO—MAP A

WOLF LODGE BAY

See letter A on map page 244

boating, hiking, picnicking, wildlife observation

Wolf Lodge is an area that attracts numerous migratory bald eagles when Lake Coeur d'Alene's kokanee salmon spawn and die in November. The Mineral Ridge National Recreation Trail, a wonderful interpretive trail, includes a 2.7-mile loop as part of its 3.3 total miles and offers excellent opportunities to view bald eagles as well as a wealth of other wildlife. The area is a super birding spot for song birds at other times of the year.

From Coeur d'Alene, take Interstate 90 east for seven miles; exit at Wolf Lodge Bay. Continue driving around the bay by crossing the bridge over Wolf Lodge Creek at the Highway 97 junction. Established turnouts are excellent wildlife-viewing locations. Obtain both the "Bald Eagles of Wolf Lodge Bay" and "Mineral Ridge Trail Guide" brochures from the BLM.

For more information: Contact the BLM Coeur d'Alene District Office, 1808 North Third Street, Coeur d'Alene, ID 83814; (208) 769-5000.

GRANDMOTHER MOUNTAIN

See letter B on map page 244

backpacking, camping, cross-country skiing, fishing, hiking, horseback riding, huckleberry picking, mountain biking, snowmobiling, wildlife observation

Grandmother Mountain Roadless Area, managed by both the BLM and the U.S. Forest Service, is an oasis of mountains and trees amid a region that has suffered from a past of extensive clear-cutting and development. Marble Creek, which runs through the area, was logged in the early 1920s using horses, steam donkeys and a series of splash dams. Remnants of the old logging camps, logging machinery and logging flumes and chutes remain visible today, offering a fascinating peek into a not-so-distant era of our nation's history. Well known to local elk and deer hunters, the high elevation lakes and meandering trails prove attractive to an increasing number of visitors during the summer months each year. A proliferation of huckleberry bushes also pulls in the visitors, as well as a concentration of black bears—all vying for their share of the tasty berry.

There are a number of notable trails within the 45-mile Marble Creek Trail System. A relatively easy and scenic 15-mile loop trip through BLM and the adjacent Panhandle National Forest can be put together by connecting the Delaney Creek Trail, Marble Divide Trail, Gold Center-Marble Creek Trail and the Marble Creek Trail. Sections of all four trails plus a few miles of the Lookout Mountain Trail (26.7 miles total) have been designated as National Recreation Trails. Plan to hike for two to three days so that you will have adequate time to explore and enjoy the rocky crags, subalpine meadows, high mountain lakes and forested canyon that is heavily populated with wildlife. Pack a fishing rod since cutthroat trout are known to swim the cold waters of Marble Creek. When planning your trip, keep in mind that in July the meadows are full of beargrass in bloom (a memorable explosion of color) and that the huckleberries typically ripen from mid-August to early September—a tasty fact that every bear within a hundred miles has memorized!

Location: Approximately 40 miles northwest of Moscow and 20 miles east of Clarkia. Don't even think about heading there without a detailed map and explicit, up-to-date directions from the BLM or the U.S. Forest Service—get directions with your map in front of you. Roughly, the trail systems can be accessed via BLM/USFS trailheads on Freezeout Saddle Road 301 and also from the USFS Road 321 at Marble Creek.

Season: The best time to visit is from July to mid-October. Bear precautions are a must. Winter offers excellent cross-country ski touring opportunities. Much of the area is covered with snow from November to late May or early June.

USGS topographic maps: Grandmother Mountain, Widow Mountain

Resources:
• Two brochures, "Freezeout Mountain Snowmobile Trail and Hiking" and "Horse/Pack Saddle Marble Creek Trail System" are available from either the BLM or the U.S. Forest Service.
• *Idaho Atlas and Gazetteer*, published by DeLorme Mapping, P.O. Box 298, Freeport, ME 04032; (207) 865-4171.

For more information: Contact the Bureau of Land Management, Coeur d'Alene District, 1808 North Third Street, Coeur d'Alene, ID 83814; (208) 769-5000; or the Avery Ranger District, Panhandle National Forest, Star Route Box 1, Avery, ID 83802; (208) 245-4517.

LOWER SALMON RIVER
See letter C on map page 244

camping, canoeing, fishing, kayaking, rafting

This high-desert river flows through land and canyon terrain that is both varied and spectacular. The river flows through four major canyons—Green, Cougar, Snowhole and Blue Canyon—which is where most of the Class III to IV whitewater occurs. Between the canyons the river calms to a tranquil float along rolling grassy slopes and smaller rock outcroppings. Since winter in the canyon is relatively mild when compared to the surrounding plains and hills, this is an important wintering ground for mule deer, white-tailed deer, elk, bear and mountain lion. River otter, coyote, chukar and golden eagle also frequent the canyon year-round. Fishing is considered good for rainbow trout, smallmouth bass and steelhead trout. There are numerous cultural sites throughout the river route, but many are becoming severely impacted and damaged beyond repair. Leave all artifacts where they lie and do not climb on or around old stone wall structures.

Activity Highlight: River running

Put-in is at Hammer Creek on the Salmon River and take-out is at Grande Ronde on the Snake River—total mileage is 73 river miles. The average trip takes four to five days. Shorter trips are possible by taking out at Pine Bar, 12 river miles from Hammer Creek. The take-out at Grande Ronde is managed by the BLM, which charges no fee—what a concept. There is also a privately operated take-out at Beamers Heller Bar. They also charge no fee. The maximum group size on the river is 30 people.

Location: North of Boise and alongside US 95. From Boise, head north on US 95. Exit at the turnoff for Hammer Creek and the put-in. A shuttle will need to be arranged for the full river trip and the drive is approximately 125 miles. Shuttle services are available in the towns of White Bird (near Hammer Creek) and Cottonwood. Information regarding shuttles and maps may be obtained from the Cottonwood BLM office.

Camping: There are numerous large sandy beaches suitable for camping. The Whitehouse Bar/Snowhole Canyon Area can get congested—avoid it if possible. Smaller groups are asked to leave obviously large camping areas for larger groups and to seek out smaller sites. The BLM no longer maintains campgrounds along the river, allowing them to revert to undeveloped status. Look for several undeveloped sites scattered along the river.

Season: March and April are perhaps the most colorful months to visit, when spring green-up is in full swing. Wildflowers and fruit trees are in full bloom. Water is also at its highest, creating increased river hazards in several of the more significant rapids. The river can essentially be floated all year, with each season offering unique perspectives on the area; however, it is considered unrunnable during the peak of spring runoff for approximately six weeks around June. July through October is the most popular time and most crowded. Daily river flow information may be obtained by calling (208) 962-3245. During fall, and in the hunting and fishing seasons, powerboats are prevalent on the lower reaches of the Salmon and especially on the Snake.

Permits: Permits are required on the Salmon River for all private outfitters leading overnight trips below Hammer Creek. Permits are available at Hammer Creek and Pine Bar launch sites and the BLM office in Cottonwood. The permits also allow for entry onto the Snake River.

Maps: "Lower Salmon River Guide," published by the BLM, is waterproof and available for $2 from the BLM Cottonwood Office.

Resources:

• A *River Runners Guide to Idaho*, published by the Idaho Department of Parks and Recreation and the BLM.

• *Western Whitewater, From the Rockies to the Pacific,* by Jim Cassady, Bill Cross and Fryar Calhoun, published by North Fork Press, Berkeley, CA; (415) 424-1213.

For more information: Contact the BLM Cottonwood Resource Area, Route 3, Box 181, Cottonwood, ID 83522; (208) 962-3246.

FREEMAN PEAK / FREEMAN CREEK

See letter D on map page 244

backpacking, climbing, fishing, hiking, historic gold and silver mine, mountain biking

Beginning on BLM land and ending in U.S. Forest Service territory, an old mining road leads up from the lower valley to the Continental Divide, offering spectacular views into Montana. The ruins of the Ore Cash Mine as well as snowfields, surrounding mountain peaks (often snow-covered) and nearby lakes make this an attractive destination or jumping-off point for longer journeys. Although the mine shafts are open and clearly evident, you would be foolish to attempt any spelunking adventures. Entering old mines is highly dangerous! Stay away and stay out of old mines.

Drive approximately five miles north from Salmon on US 93 to the town of Carmen. Head right on a paved road leading to Carmen Creek. After approximately six miles, the road turns to gravel and you will turn right onto the signed Freeman Creek Road. Drive 2.5 miles to the junction of Freeman Creek and Kirtley Creek roads. Head left at the fork toward Freeman Peak. It is advised that you park within the first mile after the junction and begin hiking or biking your way to the top. Although the road is presently legal for all vehicles, travel is highly hazardous. The U.S. Forest Service is contemplating closure of its section near the top and the mine.

USGS topographic maps: Badger Springs Gulch, Homer Youngs Peak

For more information: Contact the BLM Salmon District Office, P.O. Box 430, Salmon, ID 83467; (208) 756-5400; or the North Fork Ranger District, Salmon National Forest, P.O. Box 780, North Fork, ID 83466; (208) 867-2382.

LEWIS AND CLARK BACK COUNTRY BYWAY

See letter E on map page 244

auto touring, historical sites, snowmobiling, wildlife observation

The Lewis and Clark Back Country Byway and Adventure Road near Salmon offers those with a bent to get off the beaten path in their vehicle an opportunity to visit the area where Captain Lewis unfurled Old Glory for the first time west of the Continental Divide and claimed the Pacific Northwest for the United States. Cooperatively managed by the BLM and the U.S. Forest Service, this 38-mile loop road winds through the Bitterroot Range to the Continental Divide at Lemhi Pass—that point over which the Lewis and Clark expedition struggled to finally taste the waters of the great Columbia River. A side road along the route leads to an expedition campsite that is still much the same as when visited by the explorers. Signs along the byway also interpret the history of mining, the Red Rock Stage, range activities, wolves and more. The Lewis and Clark Back Country Byway is accessed off Highway 28, approximately 20 miles south of Salmon at Tendoy. Take the Tendoy intersection east and follow the signs. The road is a single lane with occasional pullouts for passing. It is gravel surfaced and may be driven in a normal passenger car. The road is usually closed to vehicles due to snowpack from November to June. In the winter, the byway is groomed for snowmobile access.

For more information: Contact the BLM Salmon District Office, P.O. Box 430, Salmon, ID 83467; (208) 756-5400; or the Leadore Ranger District, U.S. Forest Service, P.O. Box 180, Leadore, ID 83464; (208) 768-2371.

IDAHO—MAP B

UPPER SALMON RIVER / CHALLIS AREA

See letter F on map page 246

backpacking, camping, canoeing, fishing, hiking, kayaking, rafting, wildlife observation

The recreation destination in the Challis area is the Upper Salmon River, with 100 or so river miles managed by the BLM. The BLM maintains seven campgrounds and approximately 15 river access points along the Salmon River Scenic Byway, State Highways 9 and 75. There are many sections suitable for open canoes, rated at Class II. Check with the BLM for specific river information, which varies depending on water flow. Hiking or backpacking in the area can be enjoyed along the many primitive roads and jeep tracks. Fishing in the area's creeks and lakes is good—primarily for trout. The BLM Salmon office has a detailed map showing roads, river access points and camping areas.

USGS topographic maps: Bald Mountain, Bayhorse, Bradbury Flat, Challis, Allison Creek, Goldbug Ridge, Salmon, Bird Creek, North Fork, Hat Creek

Resources:

• *Western Whitewater, From the Rockies to the Pacific*, by Jim Cassady, Bill Cross and Fryar Calhoun, published by North Fork Press, Berkeley, CA; (415) 424-1213.

For more information: Contact the BLM Challis Resource Area, P.O. Box 430, Salmon, ID 83467; (208) 756-5400.

SNAKE RIVER BIRDS OF PREY NATIONAL CONSERVATION AREA

See letter G on map page 246

archaeological study, camping, canoeing, fishing, hiking, mountain biking, wildlife observation, wildlife photography

This area was established in 1980 to protect a unique environment in southwestern Idaho that supports one of the world's densest populations of nesting birds of prey. Within this region, falcons, eagles, hawks, owls and vultures play out the rhythms of life, but not within the usual confines of a zoo. In 1993, President Clinton signed a law designating the region as the Snake River Birds of Prey National Conservation Area. The birds are not on display here. Public facilities are few and very primitive within the area where the nesting birds concentrate. This is nature in all its raw and rough splendor—it's there if you are willing to spend some time to look closely.

With a good spotting scope or binoculars, you can expect to view the following, if your eyes and luck are good: prairie falcon, American kestrel, peregrine falcon, golden eagle, red-tailed hawk, ferruginous hawk, Swainson's hawk, rough-legged hawk, bald eagle, northern harrier, northern goshawk, Cooper's hawk, sharp-shinned hawk, osprey, great horned owl, long-eared owl, short-eared owl, western screech owl, common barn-owl, burrowing owl, turkey vulture and common raven.

Activity Highlights: Canoeing and floating

Canoeing and rafting are good ways to visit the area. Floating from Grand View to Swan Falls Dam or Walter's Ferry is the most popular trip; it requires one overnight. There are a number of outfitters who guide commercial trips—the BLM can provide a listing of permitted outfitters if you desire their service. For information on river levels, contact the Idaho Power Company at (800) 422-3143.

Activity Highlight: Hiking

Many miles of roads and trails are available for use. A popular trail runs along the north side of the Snake River from Swan Falls Dam to Celebration Park. This 10-mile stretch offers good wildlife viewing, fine scenery and easy access to the Snake River and it passes interesting old homesteads and cultural sites. Hiking is allowed anywhere within the area; however, you are not allowed to climb on cliff walls or otherwise do anything that might disturb nesting raptors. A 300mm high-speed telephoto lens is a minimum requirement for adequate photography, if that is your interest in this area.

Activity Highlight: Raptor watching

The World Center for Birds of Prey is the headquarters of the Peregrine Fund, a nonprofit organization dedicated to raptor conservation. The Velma Morrison Interpretive Center at the World Center is a must see! Through multimedia exhibits and interactive displays as well as live bird presentations, visitors are afforded a rare and unique opportunity to learn about birds of prey. The center is open Tuesday through Sunday 9 a.m. to 5 p.m. in summer, and in winter (November to February) from 10 a.m. to 4 p.m. To get to the World Center, take exit 50 south off Interstate 84. Follow the signs to South Cole Road. Continue south on South Cole Road for approximately six miles and up the hill to the World Center. To contact the interpretive center, phone (208) 362-8687.

Location: This area covers 483,000 acres in southwestern Idaho, south of Interstate 84 near Kuna. From Boise and Interstate 84, take Highway 69 (exit 44) south for eight miles to the town of Kuna. Continue south on Swan Falls Road, following signs for the Snake River Birds of Prey Area. The area officially begins five miles south of Kuna. At mile 15 there is a signed parking area and a short trail for canyon and raptor viewing.

Camping: Camping is allowed anywhere within the area except near nesting areas. Pack out everything that you pack in. Please use stoves only, no fires. Cove Recreation Site, on C.J. Strike Reservoir, is the BLM's only improved public camping facility within the National Conservation Area. It has drinking water, fire rings, picnic tables and a boat ramp.

Season: Mid-March through June is the best time to view birds of prey. During this period, the birds are courting, nesting, laying eggs and raising young. By July, most raptors have left the area, with prey becoming very scarce and summer temperatures beginning to reach the scorch and burn level. Canoeing and fishing are popular through October.

Permits: No permits are needed for hiking or camping in the area. Boaters must register before heading out on the Snake River.

USGS topographic maps: There are many maps for this area. Once you have determined the exact area that you wish to visit, contact the USGS and request maps.

BLM surface map: Murphy

Resources:

• *Snake River Birds of Prey National Conservation Area Visitor's Guide*, produced by the BLM, Idaho Travel Council and Kuna Futures, Inc.
• *Snake River Birds of Prey*, published by the BLM, Idaho Power Company and Idaho Department of Fish and Game.
• The Idaho Outfitter and Guides Association is an excellent source of information regarding outfitters who run raft trips down the Snake

that are geared toward raptor observation. Phone (208) 342-1438.

For more information: Contact the BLM Boise District Office, 3948 Development Avenue, Boise, ID 83705; (208) 384-3300; the Canyon County Parks and Waterways Celebration Park, (208) 495-2745; Lake Lowell, (208) 467-3989; or the Idaho Department of Fish and Game for fishing and hunting regulations at (208) 465-8465. For visitor services outside of the National Conservation Area, contact the Idaho Department of Commerce at (800) VISIT-ID.

SAWTOOTH MOUNTAINS / QUIGLEY CANYON

See letter H on map page 246

hiking, horseback riding, mountain biking

Wildflowers sprinkle the meadows and mountains during June. The Cove Creek area features a lush mixture of aspen, Douglas fir and sagebrush.

Activity Highlight: Mountain biking

The BLM reports that currently this mountain biking trail is not signed and there may be some questions regarding a crossing of private land with legal access undetermined. Contact the BLM before heading out. Part of the trail also crosses U.S. Forest Service lands. Traveling the Quigley Canyon Trail, you go along a dirt road for approximately four miles, climbing gradually. Cross Big Witch Creek and, ignoring the road branching right, continue straight for one-half mile. The road soon turns to trail and winds up a ridge, over the summit and past several beaver ponds. Bear right at the intersection with a two-track jeep trail. After approximately three-quarters of a mile, the jeep trail merges with Quigley/Baugh Creek Road. Follow this road over Quigley Summit, downhill to Hailey and take the bike path north to East Fork Road and the return trip to the parking area.

Location: Quigley Canyon is a 26-mile round-trip bike trail located in the Sawtooth Mountains, approximately five miles south of Ketchum on Highway 75. Drive south from Ketchum for five miles on Highway 75. Turn left (east) on East Fork Road. Drive seven miles to Cove Creek Road and park.

Camping: Camping is not recommended along the trail. There are nearby primitive campgrounds on East Fork Road and Trail Creek Road. Contact the BLM or the U.S. Forest Service for information.

Season: The best time to visit this area is in the spring. The trail usually opens about two weeks earlier than rides to the north. Rains tend to make the trail extremely muddy, however, during which time the trail should be avoided.

USGS topographic maps: Hailey, Sun Valley, Hyndman Peak, Baugh Creek Southwest

BLM surface map: Sun Valley Quadrangle

Resources:

• *Bike Routes in the Sawtooths*, a joint effort of the BLM, the U.S. Forest Service and local businesses, is available for $9.50 from the Ketchum Ranger Station, P.O. Box 2356, Sun Valley Road, Ketchum, ID 83340; (208) 622-5371.

For more information: BLM Shoshone District Office, P.O. Box 2B, Shoshone, ID 83352; (208) 886-2206.

APPENDICITIS HILL

See letter I on map page 246

backpacking, caving, hiking, horseback riding, mountain biking, wildlife observation

This area is suitable for weekend backpacking, mountain biking and day hiking. Head into the upper reaches of the region as the lower area is quite heavily used by cattle. Ridges and peaks up to 8,500 feet in elevation are cut by picturesque canyons. Aspen, willow and Douglas fir are the primary trees. Hunters use this area heavily in the fall looking for elk, mule deer, chukar partridge and sage grouse.

Location: From the town of Arco, head northwest eight miles on US 93 to Moore. Drive approximately one mile west on local roads.

USGS topographic maps: There are many for this area. Once you have determined the exact area you wish to visit, contact the U.S. Geological Survey and request maps.

For more information: Contact the BLM Idaho Falls District Office, 940 Lincoln Road, Idaho Falls, ID 83401; (208) 524-7500.

BIRCH CREEK VALLEY

See letter J on map page 246

backpacking, camping, cross-country skiing, fishing, hiking

The valley itself rests at about a 7,000-foot elevation, nestled between the Beaverhead Mountains to the northeast and the Lemhi Range on the southwest. Incidentally, the Lemhi Range, at over 70 miles long is the longest mountain range in Idaho that is uncrossed by any public access road. Birch Creek itself is a blue-ribbon trout stream.

Location: From Interstate 15 north of Idaho Falls, drive west on State Road 33 to Mud Lake and then 20 miles northwest on State Road 28 to the BLM's John Day Campground.

USGS topographic maps: There are many maps for this area. Once you have determined the exact area you wish to visit, contact the U.S. Geological Survey and request maps.

BLM surface map: Circular Butte

For more information: Contact the BLM Idaho Falls District Office, 940 Lincoln Road, Idaho Falls, ID 83401; (208) 524-7500.

HELLS HALF ACRE

See letter K on map page 246

hiking, volcano tubes

If you haven't gotten enough of the convoluted volcanic terrain offered in the Great Rift, here's more, and it is every bit as interesting. It's fascinating to actually view the anatomy of a volcano flow, even a 4,100-year-old volcano flow. See a source vent, a shield cone, various volcanic caves, tunnels and kipukas. Different than the extremely rough and jagged "a'a" formation of the Great Rift, this volcanic formation is more twisted, rope-like and billowing—and makes for much easier wandering.

Spring and fall are the peak times to visit, as the temperatures are most comfortable. I would recommend beginning your visit at the BLM's two paved interpretive trails and heading out from there to explore the wilder environs. To get to the trailheads, drive approximately 15 miles south of Idaho Falls on Interstate 15 to a signed parking area located at the rest stops on either side of the Interstate.

USGS topographic maps: There are many maps for this area. Once you have determined the exact area you wish to visit, contact the

U.S. Geological Survey and request maps.

BLM surface map: Blackfoot

For more information: Contact the BLM Idaho Falls District Office, 940 Lincoln Road, Idaho Falls, ID 83401; (208) 524-7500.

THE GREAT RIFT AND SNAKE RIVER PLAIN

See letter L on map page 246

archaeological sites, backpacking, camping, hiking, volcano tubes, wildlife observation

Lying adjacent to the Craters of the Moon National Monument, the Great Rift is every bit its equal in bizarre, twisted, convoluted craters and unusually formed lunar-like landscape. Lava cave tubes abound, creating a unique habitat for nesting birds and other wildlife. June wildflower blooms can be spectacular, depending on the water situation. Cross-country skiing is excellent in the winter. The few visitors who are fascinated by this remarkable area are often drawn to the kipukas—vegetated islands of older lava ranging in size from one acre to several thousand acres, each creating their own unique habitat. Junipers, some as old as 750 years, have found a tenuous hold in the small crevices.

Activity Highlight: Traveling the Great Rift

Here are some words of wisdom:

• *Roads:* Traveling by vehicle along the unimproved dirt roads is slow and difficult. Sharp lava rocks should be traversed with care to avoid puncturing a tire. In many places, wind and water erosion have caused ruts and holes in the road. The desert is remote, but expect to encounter oncoming vehicles. After a rain, roads can be slippery. Some parts of the southern edge of the Wapi Flow require a four-wheel-drive vehicle to negotiate sand. High-clearance vehicles are needed to travel on the primitive jeep trails.

• *Orienteering:* The Snake River Plain surrounding the Great Rift is covered by a vast network of roads. Look for landmarks like buttes, wells, survey markers and lava fingers extending into the desert to help locate your position on a map. Big Southern Butte is the most prominent landmark in the area. Orienteering for hikers can be difficult. The high iron content in the volcanic rocks distorts compass readings. The buttes in the area will be your best direction indicators. Park your vehicle on a high knoll so you can find it easily upon return.

• *Temperature:* During the summer season, temperatures often exceed 100°F. The black lava absorbs the sun's rays and intensifies the heat. Shade is not readily available since few trees exist on the flow, but shelter may be found in a lava crack, tube or behind a ridge. Light-colored clothing, a hat, sunglasses and sunscreen protect against the sun. Temperatures can be surprisingly cold at night, so carry warm clothing.

• *Water:* Since safe drinking water is a scarce commodity in the desert, it is essential that you bring your own. Hikers should carry at least one gallon per day per person to replace the tremendous amount of body fluid lost through perspiration. On rare occasions, pools or ice may be found within the lava flow, but these are most likely contaminated and must be treated. Although several wells are located on the desert for livestock use, the water may not be safe to drink.

• *Fire:* The desert is susceptible to wildfires. The exhaust system on a car can start a fire while parked or idling in grassy and vegetated areas. Vegetation entwined on the exhaust system can also ignite. Use caution and be fire-conscious. A shovel and fire extinguisher are invaluable equipment.

• *Terrain:* Hiking across the lava is a unique experience. Lava rock is extremely sharp, glassy and fragmented, and can be precariously loose, especially in the jagged "a'a" formation. Open cracks, lava tubes and caves are particularly hazardous. A sturdy pair of hiking boots provides the best foot protection. Before you start your hike, tell someone where you are going and when you will return. Carry a first-aid kit.

• *Snakes:* Rattlesnakes are a natural part of the Snake River Plain. If left alone, they are harmless, but when aggravated or surprised, they may strike. Snakes are found in desert areas and occasionally on the lavas. Yield the right-of-way to snakes.

• *Ticks:* Ticks live on the sagebrush and other vegetation in this area. Periodically check for this insect on your clothing and skin.

• *Archaeological sites:* Since much of the Great Rift is virtually unexplored, you may discover remnants from past cultures. Please leave them undisturbed and report your find to the BLM. Protective measures will be taken so that all may enjoy this resource. Remember, there are substantial penalties for the removal, defacement or destruction of archaeological sites for artifacts.

Location: South of Craters of the Moon National Monument. From Arco, take Interstate 93 southwest for approximately 18 miles past the

Craters of the Moon. The Arco-Minidoka Road parallels the
. section and then cuts into the middle of it. State Road 20
also provides access.

Camping: Camping is permitted anywhere within the Great Rift.

Season: The peak fair-weather seasons for outdoor activities such as
hiking, climbing and camping are from mid-April through mid-June
and from September through mid-October. The winter season invites
cross-country skiers to tour and explore the Craters of the Moon National Monument.

Maps: Obtain *A Guide to the Great Rift and Snake River Plain* from the
BLM. It contains a complete and extensive listing of all topographic
maps needed to travel throughout the region—a very long list.

For more information: Contact the BLM Idaho Falls District Office,
940 Lincoln Road, Idaho Falls, ID 83401; (208)524-7500; the BLM
Shoshone District Office, (208) 886-2206; or the BLM Burley District
Office, (208) 678-5514.

BIG SOUTHERN BUTTE

See letter M on map page 246

camping, hang gliding, hiking

Once a landmark for pioneers, this 7,550-foot-high butte is now a
National Natural Landmark, towering majestically above the surrounding Snake River plain. With swirling winds, this is a popular
year-round launching spot for highly experienced hang gliders and a
great spot to picnic and watch the man-made birds soar. From Atomic
City off US 26, head west 15 miles to the butte, which is shown on
most road maps.

For more information: Contact the BLM Idaho Falls District Office,
940 Lincoln Road, Idaho Falls, ID 83401; (208) 524-7500.

BLACKFOOT RIVER

See letter N on map page 246

camping, canoeing, fishing, hiking, wildlife observation

Little known and consequently lightly visited, the Blackfoot River
lies below the Blackfoot Reservoir, a popular water sport and recreation destination. The BLM maintains a campground, Dike Lake, at
the south end of the reservoir. Although the river canyon is quite

wide below the dam, it narrows the farther down you go.

Approximately 12 miles of the river are suitable for boating, rated Class II from the dam to the BLM Cutthroat Trout Campground. From the campground down to a take-out at Trail Creek, the river varies from Class II to Class IV. After Trail Creek, the river begins to boil and becomes unsuitable for boating, with rapids rated conservatively from Class V to Class VI.

The best time to visit is May to November. Wildlife observation opportunities are superb; it is rather like a miniature version of the Snake River Birds of Prey Area.

Location: From Blackfoot, take US 91 north about seven miles and turn right onto Wolverine Road. Head east for about 10 miles to Wolverine Creek. Turn right and cross the creek onto Cedar Creek Road. Follow this road for the next 10 miles as it parallels the river canyon's rim. This road will turn into Blackfoot River Road after several miles. Continue to Trail Creek Road, turning right onto it and crossing the river. Within the next six miles you will pass Morgans Bridge and Paradise Road on the left. Trail Creek will turn into Lincoln Creek Road and within the six-mile section you will pass Graves Creek, Cutthroat Trout and Sagehen campgrounds. This road will take you all the way to the reservoir.

USGS topographic maps: There are many maps for this area. Once you have determined the exact area you wish to visit, contact the U.S. Geological Survey and request maps.

BLM surface maps: Soda Springs, Pocatello, Blackfoot

For more information: Contact the BLM Idaho Falls District Office, 940 Lincoln Road, Idaho Falls, ID 83401; (208) 524-7500.

GOODING CITY OF ROCKS

See letter O on map page 246

backpacking, hiking, volcanic rock formations, wildflowers, wildlife observation

Hiking this area gives you a unique perspective into what the public rangelands of the West must have been like before cattle roamed the land. The canyon sections, highlighted by weird rock formations, tiny meadows and small creeks, have not been grazed by cattle, allowing for plants not normally seen to grow. Wildlife, too, is more abundant, including elk and black bear. A word of caution: Navigation can be quite tricky in here owing to the myriad of look-alike hoodoos. Your orientation skills and map-reading talents must be sharp.

Two recommended hikes in the Gooding City of Rocks are Fourmile Creek and Coyote Creek. Burnt Willow Canyon, several miles south of the City of Rocks and certainly more accessible in wet weather, is ideal for a two-day backpack outing. In early spring (May and June) water is available in several of the canyons in the region from spring runoff. Treat the water before drinking. Camping is allowed anywhere within the area.

Turn off Highway 20 several miles east of Fairfield onto Highway 46 south. Turn right after 14 miles onto a dirt road with BLM signs reading "Fir Grove 7, Coyote Springs 8, City of Rocks 9." After several miles, turn left onto a poor quality dirt road and find a suitable parking spot—this is the trailhead for Burnt Willow Canyon. To reach Gooding City of Rocks, drive several more miles to a signed junction indicating the City of Rocks. Use caution on the dirt roads; if they are wet they quickly become impassable. Four-wheel-drive vehicles won't even help you when it's wet—try walking on the stuff if you don't believe me.

Special note: This area is receiving a tremendous amount of impact. Please choose your visit time to avoid crowded weekends and holidays, pick up all trash whether or not it is yours, and travel using minimum-impact techniques.

USGS topographic maps: Fir Grove Mountain, McKinney Butte, McHan Reservoir, Thorn Creek Southwest

For more information: Contact the BLM Shoshone District Office 77, 400 West F Street, P.O. Box 2-B, Shoshone, ID 83352; (208) 886-2206.

THORN CREEK RESERVOIR

See letter P on map page 246

camping, fishing, hiking

This site has the advantage of close proximity to the Gooding City of Rocks. It also offers excellent trout fishing and is quiet and very scenic owing to the surrounding lava outcrops. Don't expect to see many people here as it is out of the way and primarily enjoyed by locals—they shouldn't mind your out-of-town presence if you are mind your manners.

Drive north on State Road 46 from Gooding. At approximately 20 miles and just past the turnoff for Gooding City of Rocks, head right on a dirt road—it's very slippery when wet so a four-wheel-drive vehicle is recommended. It's approximately four miles to the reservoir. Camping is primitive.

BLM surface map: Fairfield

For more information: Contact the BLM Shoshone District Office 77, 400 West F Street, P.O. Box 2-B, Shoshone, ID 83352; (208) 886-2206.

JARBIDGE RIVER
See letter Q on map page 246

backpacking, camping, fishing, hiking, kayaking, rafting

Before even considering this rugged canyon, head to the Bruneau River first; its access is easier, as is the passage. However, once you have the Bruneau under your belt and if you are eager for more, then this is it—a 31-mile-long canyon trek or float from the Nevada border to the confluence with the Bruneau. If you are hiking the canyon, plan on doing so after June, when the runoff has subsided and the river level is low enough to hike and/or float sections safely with minimum swimming and water hazard. Rock scrambling and creative poison ivy avoidance are the norm.

Floating is good from April to June with water appropriate for small rafts and kayaks. Boaters must register before heading out. Rapids are Class III and IV with numerous log jams and one portage. There are several outfitters who run trips on this river—check with the BLM for a current listing of permitted commercial outfits. Wildlife that may be spotted include bighorn sheep, mule deer, otter, golden eagle and chukar. Fishing is for trout.

Resources:
• *A River Runners Guide to Idaho*, published by the Idaho Department of Parks and Recreation and the BLM.
• *Bruneau-Jarbidge River Boating Guide*, published by the BLM Boise District.
• *Western Whitewater, From the Rockies to the Pacific*, by Jim Cassady, Bill Cross and Fryar Calhoun, published by North Fork Press, Berkeley, CA; (415) 424-1213.

For more information: Contact the BLM Boise District Office, 3948 Development Avenue, Boise, ID 83705; (208) 384-3300.

JACKS CREEK

See letter R on map page 246

backpacking, camping, fishing, hiking, horseback riding, wildlife observation

This area consists of absolutely spectacular canyons offering more than 50 miles of rugged, sheer-walled meandering adventure for the hiker or backpacker. Big Jacks Creek offers the best hiking, especially in and around Parker Trail. Fishing is adequate, but primarily limited to the mouth of the canyon. Mule deer, pronghorn antelope, beaver, sage grouse, chukar and golden eagles may all be seen. Spring, summer and fall are good times to visit.

Take State Road 51, just south of Bruneau to the Wickahoney-Battle Creek Road. This is one point of access, perhaps the best; it places you near the east side of Big Jacks Creek.

USGS topographic maps: There are many for this area. Once you have determined the exact area you wish to visit, contact the U.S. Geological Survey and request maps.

BLM surface maps: Sheep Creek, Glenns Ferry

For more information: Contact the BLM Boise District Office, 3948 Development Avenue, Boise, ID 83705; (208) 384-3300.

BRUNEAU RIVER CANYON

See letter S on map page 246

backpacking, camping, canoeing, fishing, hiking, kayaking, rafting, rockhounding, wildlife observation

Hot springs, a stunning riparian environment and mysterious canyons invite the visitor. Towering hoodoo spires highlight the magnificent geological displays. Expect to see river otter and a variety of waterfowl. The canyon cuts deeply through a high desert plateau, as deep as 800 feet in some places. Its narrowness, closing to only 30 feet wide occasionally and never exceeding 400 to 500 yards, adds to the feeling of drama within the canyon bottom.

Activity Highlight: Hiking

There is no designated trail—the stream along the canyon floor is the route. Watch out for thick infestations of poison ivy—sometimes so thick that it steers you into the river itself. Rattlesnakes are also prevalent, but shouldn't pose a problem unless you walk with your eyes closed and put your hands and feet into places where you can't see. Anticipate lots of rock scrambling. Some hikers bring along small inner tubes to float their gear in during deep-water crossings and sections requiring brief swims. The hiking season officially begins after spring runoff when the river flows are reduced—typically July to November.

Activity Highlights: Rafting and kayaking

Boaters must be able to run sustained sections of Class IV and V whitewater. The BLM recommends that the West Fork of the Bruneau be run only by expert kayakers, due to the demanding nature of the rapids and strenuous portages. Most people run a Jarbidge-Bruneau combination starting near Murphy Hot Springs. Throughout the river, anticipate challenging rapids and numerous portages. At flows of 1,000 cubic feet per second, the route is rocky; at 2,000 cubic feet per second, the river is a foaming, raging torrent of water. At levels much higher than 2,000 cubic feet per second, floating logs and flood debris add to the danger and challenge of running the river. There are several outfitters who run trips on this river—check with the BLM for a current listing of permitted commercial outfits.

Location: The Bruneau River runs from the Jarbidge Mountains in northeastern Nevada to the Snake River, 50 miles southwest of Boise, Idaho. From Boise, drive 45 miles east on Interstate 84 to Highway 51, then go south to Bruneau (20 miles). Take the Bruneau-Three Creeks Road south to the trailhead. This is a grueling 52-mile gravel road, the last 12 miles requiring dry weather and four-wheel drive. Not only is this a challenging river to run, but it's a bear of an access problem. But it's more than worth the effort to visit. Besides, since you have to earn your pleasure, you can bet the hordes of curios tourists will stay away.

Camping: Camp anywhere along the river's edge.

Season: The season for backpacking is from late June to early October, depending on the water flow. The season for boating is April 1 to June 15 with the usual high water peak by May 15.

Permits: No permits are required for backpacking. Registration is required for all boaters.

Maps: Obtain the "Bruneau-Jarbidge River Guide" brochure, available at the BLM Boise District Office.

Resources:
- *A River Runners Guide to Idaho*, published by the Idaho Department of Parks and Recreation and the BLM.
- *Western Whitewater, From the Rockies to the Pacific*, by Jim Cassady, Bill Cross and Fryar Calhoun, published by North Fork Press, Berkeley, CA; (415) 424-1213.

For more information: Contact the BLM Boise District Office, 3948 Development Avenue, Boise, ID 83705; (208) 384-3300.

FORMATION SPRINGS PRESERVE
See letter T on map page 246

caving, hiking, wildlife observation

A joint partnership between the BLM and The Nature Conservancy preserves this area of crystal-clear pools, wetlands and the Formation Cave—20 feet tall at the entrance and over 1,000 feet long. The spring water that feeds the pools and creek has been determined to be over 13,000 years old—eat your heart out Vichy Springs! The preserve supports a wildlife population that includes elk, mule deer and raptors. Spring, summer and fall are the best times to visit.

Location: From Soda Springs, take Highway 34 north for two miles, turn right onto Forest Road 124 and go one mile to the signed preserve on your left.

USGS topographic maps: There are many maps for this area. Once you have determined the exact area you wish to visit, contact the U.S. Geological Survey and request maps.

BLM surface map: Soda Springs

For more information: Contact The Nature Conservancy at (208) 726-3007.

OWYHEE UPLANDS NATIONAL BACK COUNTRY BYWAY
See letter U on map page 246

auto touring, mountain biking, wildlife observation

Beginning from Jordan Valley, Oregon, the 103-mile byway passes through lush irrigated hay meadows that follow the winding course of Jordan Creek. The road soon climbs through rolling desert uplands with views of Nevada's Santa Rosa Mountains on the southern horizon. The road reaches the rimrock of the North Fork Owyhee River Canyon, then descends into the river gorge. Tall rock pinnacles rise from the river's shoreline. A quiet BLM campground is nestled in the canyon at North Fork Crossing. Moving eastward, gnarled juniper woodlands dominate the landscape. Some of these trees are over 500 years old. Spring wildflowers are especially beautiful here, dotted among the grass and sagebrush. As the byway climbs, the sagebrush disappears and stands of mountain mahogany take their places, dotting the landscape among the grassy swales. The byway soon descends northward through steep-slope Poison Creek drainage. The creek is lined with willow, aspen and poplar. A BLM picnic area is located at Poison Creek Spring. The byway passes through a very dry, salt-desert landscape before reaching its end at Grand View, Idaho.

The byway may be reached from the west through Jordan Valley, Oregon and from the east via Highway 78 near Grand View, Idaho. If you are staying in Boise, the round-trip is approximately 250 miles and takes a full day. No services are located along the byway so be sure to pack along food, water and a spare tire and gas up and check your vehicle before heading out. The byway is suitable for all vehicles on its graveled surface. Snow may block the route from October to early May.

For more information: Contact the BLM Boise District Office, 3948 Development Avenue, Boise, ID 83705; (208) 384-3300.

OWYHEE CANYONLANDS

See letter V on map page 246

backpacking, camping, canoeing, fishing, hiking, horseback riding, kayaking, mountain biking, rafting

Although access to it is challenging, this 450,000-acre region is picturesque, dramatic, wild, isolated and well worth visiting. River runners and hunters are the predominant users, and there are not too many of them. The narrow canyons that cut into the plateau range from several hundred to one thousand feet deep—often with sheer walls from rimrock to river bottom. Mountain lion, bobcat, river otter, pronghorn antelope and bighorn sheep reside within the Owyhee canyon system.

Activity Highlights: Hiking and backpacking

There are no established routes. Hiking consists of either wandering along the canyon edges or along the canyon floors. The North Fork of the Owyhee is perhaps the most accessible area—a gravel road leads to the canyon—and is of particular interest and special beauty during spring wildflower season. Within the canyons themselves, hiking can be tedious and difficult, often requiring frequent rock and talus scrambles and at times river wading or swimming. Only experienced backpackers and those with knowledge and skills in canyoneering should venture into the canyon bottoms. Hiking is much easier on the mile-high desert plateau.

Water is not easily found on the plateau although some springs and hidden swimming holes do exist. Check with the BLM office for specific locations and advice as to potability (all water must be filtered and/or treated to guard against Giardia). Always carry adequate reserves just in case—one gallon per person per day is advised.

Activity Highlight: Boating

The Upper Owyhee consists of three forks: East, South and North. Both the East and South forks are boatable in rafts, kayaks and canoes. The river is rated Class II through IV with several very arduous portages on the East Fork before its confluence with the South. The BLM lists the North Fork as a river for "world class" expert kayakers only! Enough said.

The Middle Owyhee is a mixture of Class III through Class V+ rapids that are challenging for most boaters. Small 12- to 15-foot rafts and kayaks are recommended. The rapids feature long boulder gardens, some steep drops and several heavy hydraulics. Some portaging is required.

The Lower Owyhee offers Class II through Class IV rapids that any level of boater in all variety of craft—raft, canoe, kayak or drift boat—will find enjoyable. This is the most popular section of the river and is considered ideal for family groups and parties with inexperienced boaters. No party should attempt the river without several members being qualified intermediate boaters capable of navigating Class III and Class IV whitewater safely. The river is somewhat forgiving in that it is of the "pool and drop" variety, meaning that rapids are usually short, followed by calm pool sections where you can recover. The actual access to the river is located on private property. Please respect the rights of the property owner and tread carefully upon their land.

Location: In the high-desert region of southwestern Idaho, southwest of Grand View and Highway 78 and southeast of Jordan Valley,

Oregon, and US 95. The area is predominantly roadless—hence its attraction. The dirt roads that do exist can become impassable at any time. In fact, one river runner I talked to said that he considers the Owyhee to be a Class II river float with Class V access. The official *River Runners Guide to Idaho*, published by the BLM and the Idaho Parks and Recreation Department, states that "spring rains are common and the dirt tracks can quickly turn into an impassable quagmire of gumbo." Before visiting, check with the BLM office in Boise to determine which access route would be most appropriate during the time of your visit. Four-wheel drive is recommended for any route that is not gravel! The best access is via the Owyhee Uplands National Back Country Byway, a 103-mile gravel road, suitable for high-clearance vehicles, stretching from Grand View on Highway 78 to Jordan Valley in Oregon and US 95. There are numerous pullouts appropriate for overnight camping and embarking on short or extended backpacking explorations.

Camping: Camp anywhere within the canyon proper or on the plateau—campsites are evident and frequent. Select sites already established if you have the choice. A primitive campground, the Owyhee North Fork Recreation Site, is maintained by the BLM off the Back Country Byway—nestled in the bottom of the North Fork of the Owyhee Canyon.

Season: For hiking, May and June or September and October are best. July and August are hot and dry. May and early June are best for wildflowers. For boating, the best time is during the spring runoff from March through late May. River levels can fluctuate severely with cold or warm spells and periods of heavy rain. Call the River Forecast Center at (503) 249-0666 for current gauge readings.

Permits: No permits are needed for backpacking. Boaters, however, must register prior to embarking on any of the Owyhee River forks and tributaries. (Obtain boat registration information from the BLM Boise District Office.)

BLM surface maps: Riddle (South Fork, East Fork), Triangle (North Fork)

Resources:
• *The Owyhee River Boating Guide*, available through the Boise District BLM office.
• *Western Whitewater, From the Rockies to the Pacific,* by Jim Cassady,

Bill Cross and Fryar Calhoun, published by North Fork Press, Berkeley, CA; (415) 424-1213.

For more information: Contact the BLM Boise District Office, 3948 Development Avenue, Boise, ID 83705; (208) 384-3300.

SALMON FALLS CREEK AND RESERVOIR

See letter W on map page 246

camping, canoeing, fishing, hiking, horseback riding, swimming

This area is a fun place, known chiefly to locals, to come and recreate with the entire family. When the reservoir is full (and that's not too often as it gets drained down heavily), it holds 34,000 acre-feet of water. The area upstream of the dam is very scenic and offers opportunities for canoeing, hiking and camping in the spring. The canyons have sheer walls and broad bottoms with willow groves and grassy meadows. Downstream from the dam, the willow-lined canyon area offers opportunities for hiking, backpacking and fishing. Fishing is quite popular in the reservoir, even drawing a contingent of ice anglers in the winter. Fishing is for walleye, perch, salmon and trout. There is a BLM campground, Lud Drexler Park, near the dam.

BLM surface maps: Twin Falls, Rogerson

For more information: Contact the BLM Burley District Office, Route 3, Box 1, Burley, ID 83318; (208) 678-5514.

SILENT CITY OF ROCKS NATIONAL RESERVE

See letter X on map page 246

hiking, picnicking, rock climbing

These fantastic granite monoliths in pillars, knobs, cliffs, pinnacles and hoodoos create a wonderful playground for hikers and rock climbers. Once nearly trashed by irreverent vandals and off-road activity, this area was established as a National Reserve in 1988, thanks mainly to the efforts of local residents. It is also noteworthy as the only known area in the state supporting pinyon pine.

Activity Highlight: Rock climbing

Rocks with names such as Bath Rock, the Arrow and Turtle Rock are all popular and excellent climbing destinations. A number of outdoor programs use the area for climbing instruction.

Location: Approximately 45 miles directly southeast of Burley. From

Interstate 84, head south to the town of Malta. At Malta, take Highway 77 toward the mountains and then head south at Conner Junction to the hamlet of Almo. At Almo, take a gravel road for approximately one mile south and turn right onto yet another gravel road. Drive approximately four miles, past the ruins of a stone house to another junction and another gravel road. Here, head left to the Twin Sisters. Stay to the right and you will find any number of parking, picnicking and camping areas among the rocks.

Camping: Camp at designated sites among the rocks. There are vault toilets and one well for potable water.

Season: April through September is the best time to visit. Spring brings range wildflowers in colorful display soon after the snow melts. Summer can be very hot at times—almost too uncomfortable for climbing. Fall shows aspen trees in golden splendor.

USGS topographic maps: Almo, Cache Creek

For more information: Contact the BLM Burley District Office, Route 3, Box 1, Burley, ID 83318; (208) 678-5514; or the City of Rocks National Reserve, P.O. Box 169, Almo, ID 83312; (208) 824-5519.

BLM CAMPGROUNDS

1. KILLARNEY LAKE CAMPGROUND—MAP A

Campsites, facilities: There are 12 sites, all with picnic tables and fire rings. Pit toilets, water and a boat ramp are available. There is a 14-day stay limit.

Fee: There is no fee.

Who to contact: Coeur d'Alene District Office, 1808 North Third Street, Coeur d'Alene, ID 83814; (208) 769-5000.

Location: From Rose Lake, just south of Interstate 90 and west of Coeur d'Alene, drive southwest on Highway 3 for five miles to Killarney Lake Road and turn right; drive four more miles to the campground. The campground sits at 2,200 feet.

Season: All year.

2. TINGLEY SPRINGS CAMPGROUND—MAP A

Campsites, facilities: There are two sites, both with picnic tables and fire rings. Water is available. There are no pit toilets. No trash facilities are provided so pack out all that you bring in. There is a 14-day stay limit.

Fee: There is no fee.

Who to contact: Coeur d'Alene District Office, 1808 North Third Street, Coeur d'Alene, ID 83814; (208) 769-5000.

Location: From Cataldo, drive south for 15 miles on the Latour Creek Road. Turn right into the Tingley Springs Campground at the sign.

Season: All year.

3. HUCKLEBERRY CAMPGROUND—MAP A

Campsites, facilities: There are 23 sites, all with picnic tables and fire rings. Pit toilets, water and an RV dump station are available. There is a 14-day stay limit.

Fee: There is a $4 fee per night; pay on site.

Who to contact: Coeur d'Alene District Office, 1808 North Third Street, Coeur d'Alene, ID 83814; (208) 769-5000.

Location: From Calder, drive south across the St. Joe River and turn left on St. Joe River Road (County 350). Drive approximately four miles to the campground. The campground sits at 2,240 feet.

Season: April to November. Expect crowds on summer weekends.

4. HAMMER CREEK CAMPGROUND—MAP A

Campsites, facilities: There are eight sites, all with picnic tables, grills and fire rings. Pit toilets, water, a boat launch and an RV dump station are available. RVs up to 24 feet are allowed. There is a 14-day stay limit.

Fee: There is a $4 fee per night; pay on site.

Who to contact: Coeur d'Alene District Office, 1808 North Third Street, Coeur d'Alene, ID 83814; (208) 769-5000.

Location: On the Salmon River. From White Bird, drive 1.5 miles south on Highway 95 and then head north on a paved road with some gravel sections that is signed for the Salmon River/Hammer Creek Campground. The campground sits at 1,500 feet.

Season: All year.

5. SLATE CREEK CAMPGROUND—MAP A

Campsites, facilities: There are five sites, all with picnic tables, grills and fire rings. Pit toilets, water, pay phone and a boat launch are available. RVs up to 21 feet are allowed. There is a 14-day stay limit.

Fee: There is a $4 fee per night; pay on site.

Who to contact: Coeur d'Alene District Office, 1808 North Third Street, Coeur d'Alene, ID 83814; (208) 769-5000.

Location: On the Salmon River. From White Bird, drive nine miles south on Highway 95. The campground sits at 1,500 feet.

Season: All year.

6. SMOKEY CLUBS CAMPGROUND—MAP A

Campsites, facilities: There are eight sites, all with picnic tables and fire rings. Pit toilets and a boat ramp are available. There is **no water.** No trash facilities are provided, so pack out all that you bring in. There is a 14-day stay limit.

Fee: There is no fee.

Who to contact: Salmon District Office, P.O. Box 430, Salmon, ID 83467; (208) 756-5400.

Location: Near the Lemhi River. From Leadore, drive four miles north on Highway 29 (Railroad Canyon Road) toward Bannock Pass and the campground entrance. The campground sits at 5,000 feet.

Season: All year. Expect crowds in the fall during hunting season.

7. McFarland Campground—Map A

Campsites, facilities: There are 10 sites, all with picnic tables and fire rings. Pit toilets and water are available. No trash facilities are provided, so pack out all that you bring in. There is a 14-day stay limit.

Fee: There is no fee.

Who to contact: Salmon District Office, P.O. Box 430, Salmon, ID 83467; (208) 756-5400.

Location: Alongside the Lemhi River. From Leadore, drive north on Highway 28 for approximately 13 miles to the campground entrance.

Season: All year.

8. Tower Rock Campground—Map A

Campsites, facilities: There are six sites, all with picnic tables and grills. Pit toilets are available. There is **no water**. No trash facilities are provided, so pack out all that you bring in. There is a 14-day stay limit.

Fee: There is no fee.

Who to contact: Salmon District Office, P.O. Box 430, Salmon, ID 83467; (208) 756-5400.

Location: This is a historic Lewis and Clark expedition campsite along the Salmon River. From Salmon, drive north on US 93 for 11 miles to the campground entrance. The campground sits at 4,000 feet.

Season: All year.

9. Williams Lake Campground—Map A

Campsites, facilities: There are 11 sites, all with picnic tables and fire rings. Pit toilets are available. There is **no water**. No trash facilities are provided, so pack out all that you bring in. There is a 14-day stay limit.

Fee: There is no fee.

Who to contact: Salmon District Office, P.O. Box 430, Salmon, ID 83467; (208) 756-5400.

Location: Near the Thunder Mountain Historic Trail. From Salmon, drive south on US 93 for five miles to Forest Service 28, signed for Williams Lake. Turn right and drive to the campground entrance. The campground sits at 5,500 feet.

Season: All year.

10. SHOUP BRIDGE CAMPGROUND—MAP A

Campsites, facilities: There are six sites, all with picnic tables and fire rings. Pit toilets and a boat ramp are available. There is **no water**. There is a 14-day stay limit.

Fee: There is no fee.

Who to contact: Salmon District Office, P.O. Box 430, Salmon, ID 83467; (208) 756-5400.

Location: On the Salmon River. From Salmon, drive south on US 93 for five miles to the campground entrance. The campground sits at 4,000 feet.

Season: All year.

11. AGENCY CREEK CAMPGROUND—MAP A

Campsites, facilities: There are four sites, all with picnic tables and fire rings. Pit toilets are available. There is **no water**. No trash facilities are provided, so pack out all you bring in. There is a 14-day stay limit.

Fee: There is no fee.

Who to contact: Salmon District Office, P.O. Box 430, Salmon, ID 83467; (208) 756-5400.

Location: Near the Continental Divide. From Tendoy, drive east on Lemhi Pass Road for approximately six miles to the campground entrance. The campground is located at 5,000 feet.

Season: All year.

12. STECK CAMPGROUND—MAP B

Campsites, facilities: There are 38 sites, all with picnic tables and fire rings. Some of the pit toilets are wheelchair accessible. Water is available. RVs up to 25 feet are allowed. There is a 14-day stay limit.

Fee: There is a $5 fee per night; pay on site.

Who to contact: Boise District Office, 3948 Development Avenue, Boise, ID 83705; (208) 384-3300.

Location: From Weiser, drive 22 miles west on Olds Ferry Road to the campground entrance.

Season: April to October.

13. COTTONWOOD CAMPGROUND—MAP B

Campsites, facilities: There are six sites, all with picnic tables and fire rings. Pit toilets are available. There is **no water**. No trash facilities are provided, so pack out all you bring in. There is a 14-day stay limit.

Fee: There is no fee.

Who to contact: Salmon District Office, P.O. Box 430, Salmon, ID 83467; (208) 756-5400.

Location: On the banks of the Salmon River. From Challis, drive north on US 93 for approximately 16 miles to the campground entrance. From Ellis, drive south for approximately two miles on US 93. The campground sits at 5,000 feet.

Season: All year.

14. SPRING GULCH CAMPGROUND—MAP B

Campsites, facilities: There are 10 sites, all with picnic tables and fire rings. Water and pit toilets are available. RVs up to 30 feet are allowed. There is a 14-day stay limit.

Fee: There is a $5 fee per night; pay on site.

Who to contact: Salmon District Office, P.O. Box 430, Salmon, ID 83467; (208) 756-5400.

Location: From Challis, drive 10 miles north on US 93 to the campground entrance.

Season: May to November.

15. MORGAN CREEK CAMPGROUND—MAP B

Campsites, facilities: There are five sites, all with picnic tables and fire rings. Pit toilets are available. There is **no water**. No trash facilities are provided, so pack out all that you bring in. There is a 14-day stay limit.

Fee: There is no fee.

Who to contact: Salmon District Office, P.O. Box 430, Salmon, ID 83467; (208) 756-5400.

Location: From Challis, drive north on US 93 for approximately seven miles to Morgan Creek Road. Turn left and drive four miles to the campground entrance. The campground sits at 6,200 feet.

Season: All year.

16. BAYHORSE CAMPGROUND—MAP B

Campsites, facilities: There are 11 sites, all with picnic tables and fire rings. Pit toilets are wheelchair accessible. Water is available. RVs up to 28 feet are allowed. There is a 14-day stay limit.
Fee: There is a $5 fee per night; pay on site.
Who to contact: Salmon District Office, P.O. Box 430, Salmon, ID 83467; (208) 756-5400.
Location: Along the Salmon River. From Challis, drive eight miles south on Highway 75 to the campground entrance.
Season: May to October.

17. HERD LAKE CAMPGROUND—MAP B

Campsites, facilities: There are three sites, all with picnic tables and fire rings. Pit toilets are available. There is **no water**. No trash facilities are provided, so pack out all you bring in. There is a 14-day stay limit.
Fee: There is no fee.
Who to contact: Salmon District Office, P.O. Box 430, Salmon, ID 83467; (208) 756-5400.
Location: From Clayton, drive east on Highway 75 for approximately five miles to East Fork Road. Turn right and drive to Herd Lake Road. Head southeast on Herd Lake Road for approximately 10 miles to the campground.
Season: All year.

18. LITTLE BOULDER CREEK CAMPGROUND—MAP B

Campsites, facilities: There are three sites, all with picnic tables and fire rings. Pit toilets are available. There is **no water**. No trash facilities are provided, so pack out all you bring in. There is a 14-day stay limit.
Fee: There is no fee.
Who to contact: Salmon District Office, P.O. Box 430, Salmon, ID 83467; (208) 756-5400.
Location: From Clayton, drive east on Highway 75 for approximately five miles to East Fork Road. Turn right and drive 20 miles to the campground entrance.
Season: All year.

19. EAST FORK CAMPGROUND—MAP B

Campsites, facilities: There are 14 sites, all with picnic tables and fire rings. Pit toilets and water are available. RVs up to 25 feet are allowed. There is a 14-day stay limit.

Fee: There is a $4 fee per night; pay on site.

Who to contact: Salmon District Office, P.O. Box 430, Salmon, ID 83467; (208) 756-5400.

Location: From Challis, drive 18 miles southwest on Highway 95 to the campground entrance.

Season: June to October.

20. DEADMAN HOLE—MAP B

Campsites, facilities: There are 11 sites, all with picnic tables and fire rings. Water and pit toilets are available. No trash facilities are provided, so pack out all you bring in. There is a 14-day stay limit.

Fee: There is no fee.

Who to contact: Salmon District Office, P.O. Box 430, Salmon, ID 83467; (208) 756-5400.

Location: On the banks of the Salmon River. From Clayton, drive north on Highway 75 for approximately 10 miles, passing East Fork Campground, to the campground entrance. The campground sits at 5,000 feet.

Season: All year.

21. GARDEN CREEK—MAP B

Campsites, facilities: There are three sites, all with picnic tables and fire rings. There is **no water**. Pit toilets are available. No trash facilities are provided, so pack out all you bring in. There is a 14-day stay limit.

Fee: There is no fee.

Who to contact: Salmon District Office, P.O. Box 430, Salmon, ID 83467; (208) 756-5400.

Location: In an aspen grove next to the Big Lost River. From Mackay, drive northwest on U.S. 93 for 15 miles to Trail Creek Road. Turn left (southwest) and drive approximately 10 miles to the campground entrance. The campground sits at 6,300 feet.

Season: All year.

22. DEEP CREEK—MAP B

Campsites, facilities: There are two sites, both with picnic tables and fire rings. There is **no water**. Pit toilets are available. No trash facilities are provided, so pack out all you bring in. There is a 14-day stay limit.

Fee: There is no fee.

Who to contact: Salmon District Office, P.O. Box 430, Salmon, ID 83467; (208) 756-5400.

Location: At the confluence of the East and North forks of Big Lost River. From Mackay, drive northwest on US 93 for 15 miles to Trail Creek Road. Turn left (southwest) and drive approximately 19 miles to the campground entrance. The campground sits at 6,300 feet.

Season: All year.

23. MACKAY RESERVOIR CAMPGROUND—MAP B

Campsites, facilities: There are 59 sites, all with picnic tables, fire rings and grills. Pit toilets, water, an RV dump station and a boat ramp are available. There is a 14-day stay limit.

Fee: There is a $5 fee per night; pay on site.

Who to contact: Salmon District Office, P.O. Box 430, Salmon, ID 83467; (208) 756-5400.

Location: From Mackay, drive northwest on US 93 for five miles to the campground entrance and Mackay Reservoir.

Season: All year.

24. SUMMIT CREEK CAMPGROUND—MAP B

Campsites, facilities: There are nine sites, all with picnic tables and fire rings. Pit toilets and a boat ramp are available. There is **no water**. No trash facilities are provided, so pack out all that you bring in. There is a 14-day stay limit.

Fee: There is no fee.

Who to contact: Salmon District Office, P.O. Box 430, Salmon, ID 83467; (208) 756-5400.

Location: In Pahsimeroi Valley across from Barney Hot Springs. From Howe, drive northwest on Pahsimeroi Road for 41 miles to the campground entrance.

Season: All year.

25. JOHN DAY CAMPGROUND—MAP B

Campsites, facilities: There are 16 sites, all with picnic tables and fire rings. Pit toilets are available. There is **no water**. No trash facilities are provided, so pack out all you bring in. There is a 14-day stay limit.

Fee: There is a $4 fee per night; pay on site.

Who to contact: Idaho Falls District Office, 940 Lincoln Road, Idaho Falls, ID 83401; (208) 524-7500.

Location: From Mud Lake, west of Interstate 15, drive 20 miles northwest on Highway 28 to the campground entrance on the left side of the highway.

Season: May to October.

26. KELLY'S ISLAND CAMPGROUND—MAP B

Campsites, facilities: There are 20 sites, all with picnic tables and fire rings. Pit toilets and water are available. RVs up to 22 feet are allowed. There is a 14-day stay limit.

Fee: There is a $4 fee per night; pay on site.

Who to contact: Idaho Falls District Office, 940 Lincoln Road, Idaho Falls, ID 83401; (208) 524-7500.

Location: From Idaho Falls, drive 23 miles northeast on US 26 to the campground entrance.

Season: May to October.

27. MOONSTONE CAMPGROUND—MAP B

Campsites, facilities: There are two sites, both with picnic tables and grills. Pit toilets are available. There is **no water**. No trash facilities are provided, so pack out all that you bring in.

Fee: There is no fee.

Who to contact: Shoshone District Office, 400 West F Street, P.O. Box 2-B, Shoshone, ID 83352; (208) 886-2206.

Location: Eighteen miles east of Fairfield on Highway 20. Turn south at the sign to the campground entrance.

Season: All year.

28. FISH CREEK RESERVOIR CAMPGROUND—MAP B

Campsites, facilities: There are several undesignated sites, all with picnic tables and fire rings. Pit toilets and a boat ramp are available. There is **no water**. No trash facilities are provided, so pack out all you bring in. There is a 14-day stay limit.

Fee: There is no fee.

Who to contact: Shoshone District Office, 400 West F Street, P.O. Box 2-B, Shoshone, ID 83352; (208) 886-2206.

Location: On Fish Creek Reservoir. From Carey, drive east on U.S. 93 for six miles to a gravel county road signed for Fish Creek Reservoir and turn left. Drive five miles to the campground. The campground sits at 5,300 feet.

Season: April to November.

29. COVE CAMPGROUND—MAP B

Campsites, facilities: There are 26 sites, all with picnic tables and fire rings. Pit toilets and water are available. RVs up to 25 feet are allowed. There is a 14-day stay limit.

Fee: There is a $5 fee per night; pay on site.

Who to contact: Boise District Office, 3948 Development Avenue, Boise, ID 83705; (208) 384-3300.

Location: From Bruneau, drive two miles west on Highway 51 to Highway 78. Turn north (right) and drive five miles on Highway 78 to the campground entrance.

Season: April to October.

30. DIKE LAKE CAMPGROUND—MAP B

Campsites, facilities: There are 46 sites, all with picnic tables, grills and fire rings. Pit toilets and water are available. There is a 14-day stay limit.

Fee: There is no fee.

Who to contact: Idaho Falls District Office, 940 Lincoln Road, Idaho Falls, ID 83401; (208) 524-7500.

Location: At the southeast end of Blackfoot Reservoir. From Soda Springs, drive 11 miles north on Highway 34 to the Blackfoot Reservoir and the campground entrance.

Season: May to October.

31. PIPELINE CAMPGROUND—MAP B

Campsites, facilities: There are five sites, all with picnic tables and fire rings. Pit toilets and a boat ramp are available. There is **no water.** No trash facilities are provided, so pack out all that you bring in. There is a 14-day stay limit.

Fee: There is no fee.

Who to contact: Burley District Office, Route 3, Box 1, Burley, ID 83318; (208) 678-5514.

Location: Along the shore of the Snake River. From American Falls, drive on Interstate 86 to the Rockland Exit, then drive two miles west to the campground entrance. The campground sits at 4,700 feet.

Season: March to October.

32. HAWKINS CAMPGROUND—MAP B

Campsites, facilities: There are seven sites, all with picnic tables, grill, and fire rings. The pit toilets are wheelchair accessible. There is **no water**. No trash facilities are provided, so pack out all you bring in. There is a 14-day stay limit.

Fee: There is no fee.

Who to contact: Burley District Office, Route 3, Box 1, Burley, ID 83318; (208) 678-5514.

Location: On Hawkins Reservoir. From Arimo, drive south on Interstate 15 for five miles and exit at Downey. Drive 10 miles west on county road signed for the reservoir. The campground sits at 5,142 feet.

Season: April to December, expect crowds on Memorial Day.

33. MCCLENDON SPRING CAMPGROUND—MAP B

Campsites, facilities: There are two sites, both with picnic tables and fire rings. There is **no water**. No trash facilities are provided, so pack out all that you bring in. There is a 14-day stay limit.

Fee: There is no fee.

Who to contact: Burley District Office, Route 3, Box 1, Burley, ID 83318; (208) 678-5514.

Location: Five miles northwest of Malta, Idaho. Drive west on Highway 77 for approximately two miles and turn north at an unmarked junction. Drive several miles to the campground entrance.

Season: All year.

34. LUD DREXLER PARK CAMPGROUND—MAP B

Campsites, facilities: There are 20 sites (some with sun shades), all with picnic tables and fire rings. The pit toilets are wheelchair accessible. Water, an RV dump station and a boat ramp are available. There is a 14-day stay limit.

Fee: There is a $4 fee per night; pay on site.

Who to contact: Burley District Office, Route 3, Box 1, Burley, ID 83318; (208) 678-5514.

Location: From Rogerson, drive eight miles west on Jarbidge County Road to Salmon Falls Dam and the campground. The campground sits at 5,000 feet.

Season: All year. Holidays are generally crowded.

STATE INFORMATION OVERVIEW

IDAHO STATE OFFICE
3380 Americana Terrace, Boise, ID 83706; (208) 384-3000

BOISE DISTRICT OFFICE
3948 Development Avenue, Boise, ID 83705; (208) 384-3300

Bruneau Resource Area, 3948 Development Avenue, Boise, ID 83705; (208) 384-3300

Cascade Resource Area, 3948 Development Avenue, Boise, ID 83705; (208) 384-3300

Jarbidge Resource Area, 2620 Kimberly Road, Twin Falls, ID 83301; (208) 384-3300

Owyhee Resource Area, 3948 Development Avenue, Boise, ID 83705; (208) 384-3300

BURLEY DISTRICT OFFICE
Route 3, Box 1, Burley, ID 83318; (208) 678-5514

Deep Creek Resource Area, 138 South Main, Malad City, ID 83252; (208) 766-4766

Snake River Resource Area, Route 3, Box 1, Burley, ID 83318; (208) 678-5514

SHOSHONE DISTRICT OFFICE
400 West F Street, P.O. Box 2-B, Shoshone, ID 83352; (208) 886-2206

Bennett Hills Resource Area, 400 West F Street, P.O. Box 2-B, Shoshone, ID 83352; (208) 886-2206

Monument Resource Area, 400 West F Street, P.O. Box 2-B, Shoshone, ID 83352; (208) 886-2206

COEUR D'ALENE DISTRICT OFFICE
1808 North Third Street, Coeur d'Alene, ID 83814; (208) 769-5000

Cottonwood Resource Area, Route 3, Box 181, Cottonwood, ID 83522; (208) 962-3246

Emerald Empire Resource Area, 1808 North Third Street, Coeur d'Alene, ID 83814; (208) 769-5000

IDAHO FALLS DISTRICT OFFICE
940 Lincoln Road, Idaho Falls, ID 83401; (208) 524-7500

Big Butte Resource Area, 940 Lincoln Road, Idaho Falls, ID 83401; (208) 524-7500

Medicine Lodge Resource Area, 940 Lincoln Road, Idaho Falls, ID 83401; (208) 524-7500

Pocatello Resource Area, 1111 North Eighth Avenue, Pocatello, ID 83201-5789; (208) 236-6860

SALMON DISTRICT OFFICE
P.O. Box 430, Salmon, ID 83467; (208) 756-5400

Challis Resource Area, P.O. Box 430, Salmon, ID 83467; (208) 756-5400

Lemhi Resource Area, P.O. Box 430, Salmon, ID 83467; (208) 756-5400

CHAPTER SEVEN

MONTANA

Maps—pp. 290, 292
Montana Map A Locations—pp. 294-306
Montana Map B Locations—pp. 307-311
Information Resources—pp. 318-319

(SEE MAP A)   **(SEE MAP B)**

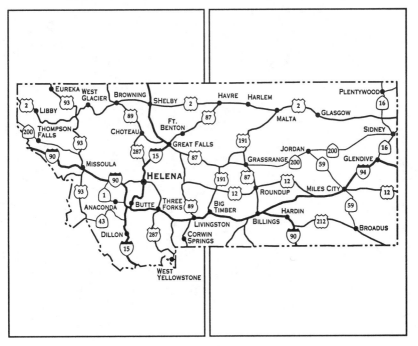

MAP A—MONTANA

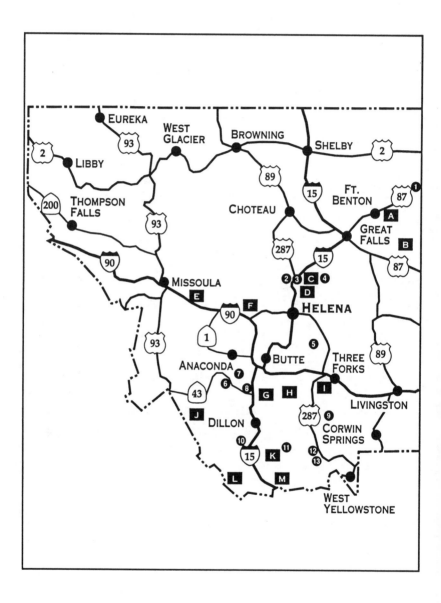

Map References

BLM Campgrounds

Map B—Montana

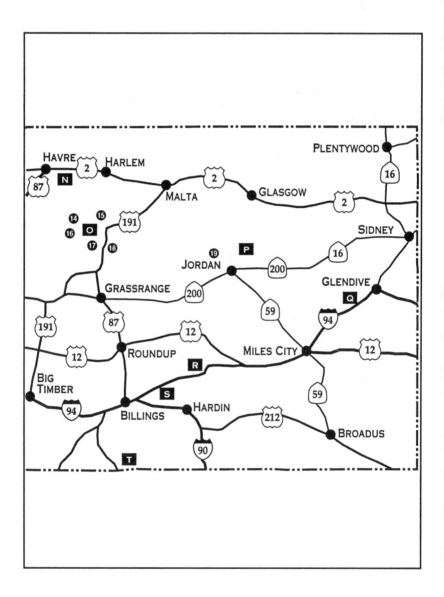

MAP REFERENCES

BLM CAMPGROUNDS

MONTANA—MAP A

UPPER MISSOURI NATIONAL WILD AND SCENIC RIVER FROM FORT BENTON

See letter A on map page 290

boating, camping, canoeing, hiking, wildlife observation

Designated a Wild and Scenic River in 1976, this 149-mile segment is the only portion of the mighty Missouri River to be protected and preserved in its natural and free-flowing state. It is also the premier segment of the Lewis and Clark National Historic Trail. You will enjoy scenic vistas that remain much as they were when first described by Lewis and Clark during their 1805-1806 expedition.

Following the expedition, the river became the major waterway route west toward the Rocky Mountains until the coming of the railroads in the late 1800s. At the riverside trading posts of Forts Lewis, Benton, McKenzie and Piegan, the fur trade flourished for a short time. Steamboats brought gold seekers and supplies as far as Fort Benton. LaBarge Rock, Hole-In-The-Wall, Dark Butte, Citadel Rock, all landmarks along the scenic White Rock section of the river recall the period of western expansion. Frame and log dwellings, left behind by homesteaders who found the valley and environment too harsh, remain for visitors to view and get a feeling for the dreams that might have been.

Activity Highlights: Canoeing and boating

Most boating trips are launched from either Fort Benton, Coal Banks Landing or Judith Landing. Floaters desiring a one-day outing often float between Fort Benton and Loma. Depending on the speed of travel, the float time between Coal Banks Landing, and Judith Landing, and Judith Landing and Fred Robinson Bridge, takes three days. When on shore, you should be aware that rattlesnakes do frequent the area. This is not a hazard if you watch where you place your feet and hands. Beware of the low-hanging cables at each of the ferry crossings.

Location: From Fort Benton on US 87 eastward to the US 191 bridge crossing at Charles M. Russell National Wildlife Refuge. See the designated put-in and take-out points listed below in tandem with the campgrounds. You can gain access to these areas via local and county roads. Check with the BLM prior to heading out to determine the best access routes and road conditions.

Camping: Camping is allowed anywhere along the river banks, however the BLM recommends that you camp only in designated sites. A great deal of private land bounds the river and if you choose to venture on to it, you are the landowner's guest—act like one. If you are asked to leave, that is the landowner's right. Camping is formally available at the following sites:
- Fort Benton, put-in and take-out point
- Loma Bridge, put-in and take-out point
- Coal Banks Landing, put-in and take-out point
- Judith Landing, put-in and take-out point
- Stafford Ferry, put-in and take-out point
- Woodhawk Creek, put-in and take-out point
- James Kipp Recreation Area, put-in and take-out point
- Little Sandy, Eagle Creek, Hole-In-The-Wall, Dark Butte, Slaughter River, Cow Island, Evans Bend

Season: The season runs from the weekend before Memorial Day (May) to the weekend following Labor Day (September).

Permits: No permits are necessary, but you are required to register for safety and management purposes.

Maps: *The Complete Floaters Guide,* including waterproofed maps 1, 2, 3 and 4, is available for $8 from the BLM.

Resources:
- *Western Whitewater, From the Rockies to the Pacific,* by Jim Cassady, Bill Cross and Fryar Calhoun, published by North Fork Press, Berkeley, CA; (415) 424-1213.
- BLM brochure: "Highlights of the Upper Missouri National Wild and Scenic River and Lewis and Clark National Historic Trail"
- BLM brochure: "Some Hazards on the Upper Missouri National Wild and Scenic River"

For more information: Contact the BLM Judith Resource Area, 80 Airport Road, P.O. Box 1160, Lewistown, MT 59457; (406) 538-7461.

SQUARE BUTTE

See letter B on map page 290

camping, hiking, wildlife observation

It may be small, only 1,947 acres, but don't think that the 5,703-foot-high Square Butte, jutting 2,400 feet above the surrounding plains, goes unnoticed—it doesn't. Even Lewis and Clark couldn't help but marvel at its size, making note of Square Butte as a significant landmark during their epic 1805 journey west. The Butte received its official name from the Stevens Intercontinental Railway Search Expedition in 1853. Centuries before, there is evidence that Square Butte was used for ceremonial purposes and vision quests by Native Americans. Tipi rings and lithic scatters around the base (protected by federal law) and a number of documented vision quest sites atop the butte are all that remain as reminders of the butte's early visitors.

Though it is technically and geologically known as a laccolith, an intrusive bubble of magma that has penetrated layers of the earth's crust, the butte's scientific moniker doesn't even begin to hint at its stunning beauty. Jutting out of the surrounding golden plain, the flat-topped butte, with its soaring buttresses, spires and pinnacles—dramatic evidence of the powers of erosion—is a compelling and imposing sight.

From the summit, it is possible to see the Highwood Mountains eight miles to the west, the Bears Paw and Little Rocky Mountains 80 miles to the northeast, the Little Belt Mountains to the south and the Big Snowy Mountains 50 miles to the southeast.

On the summit itself, it is interesting to note the vegetation, which has never been grazed by livestock—a tangible and natural museum characteristic of the historic vegetation that existed in the surrounding plains before grazing occurred. Wildlife on the butte includes golden eagle, great horned owl, prairie falcon, mule deer, elk and one of the few Rocky Mountain goat populations found east of the Rockies.

Special note: Square Butte has been designated as an Outstanding Natural Area, is a Wilderness Study Area and a National Natural Landmark. It is also a Montana Watchable Wildlife Area. Private landowner generosity ensures access to the site—respect the owner's privacy. This is a small site and while camping is allowed, the sites are limited and easily impacted. Practice minimum-impact camping and use camping stoves, not fires.

Location: South of Fort Benton and approximately 90 miles east of Great Falls. You literally can't miss it. Towering 2,400 feet above the surrounding prairie, it is possible to drive by it only if you are blind or asleep. The area is accessed across private property with permission from the landowner, please respect the arrangement. There is a registration box located on the approach to the landowner's house. Please register and stop at the house to obtain access permission. If the landowner is not home, register and proceed. Keep in mind that the landowner may have special restrictions during hunting season.

Drive to the town of Square Butte on State Route 80, south of Fort Benton and east of Great Falls.

USGS topographic maps: Pownal, Jiggs Flat

For more information: Contact the Bureau of Land Management, Judith Resource Area, Airport Road, Lewistown, MT 59457; (406) 538-7461.

HOLTER LAKE RECREATION AREA

See letter C on map page 290

boating, camping, fishing, hiking, horseback riding, swimming

Holter Lake is really nothing more than an expansive section of the Missouri River caused by Holter Dam. Numerous agencies and private ownership make up the management of the area. The BLM oversees three campgrounds along Holter Lake near Holter Dam at the northeast end of the "lake" and a much larger region, Sleeping Giant Wilderness Study Area, along the west edge of the lake.

Gates of the Mountains Wilderness, part of the Helena National Forest, lies along the southeast side of the recreation area. The terrain immediately around the lake is hilly to mountainous, semi-arid and features a number of rocky outcrops and timbered areas. Wildlife around the lake will likely include black bear, porcupine, cottontail, mule deer, whitetail deer, elk, bighorn sheep and Rocky Mountain goat. Birdwatching is considered very good. Fishing is for trout and salmon.

Spring, summer and fall are the best times to visit. To reach Holter Lake from Interstate 15 between the cities of Great Falls and Helena, take the Wolf Creek exit. Head east across the bridge and then south to the signed area.

USGS topographic maps: Beartooth Mountain, Sheep Creek Mountain

For more information: Contact the BLM Headwaters Resource Area, 106 North Parkmont, P.O. Box 3388, Butte, MT 59702; (406) 494-5059.

SLEEPING GIANT WILDERNESS STUDY AREA

See letter D on map page 290

camping, cross-country skiing, fishing, hiking, horseback riding, mountain biking, snowshoeing, wildlife observation

Access to this site is available via boat along Holter Lake. To gain access by vehicle, take the Interstate 15 frontage road and then go three miles along the improved gravel Wood Siding Gulch Road, which terminates at a proposed trailhead west of Sheep Creek. From the trailhead, opportunities for mountain biking abound over numerous established roads and trails throughout the 6,000 acres surrounding the Wilderness Study Area. Within the 10,000-acre Wilderness Study Area, hiking opportunities along the scenic ridgelines can be enjoyed eastward to the Missouri River and the Sleeping Giant profile at Beartooth Mountain. No established trails exist, but orienting yourself and finding a route is not too difficult. Views from on top of the ridgelines are outstanding. Wildlife includes mountain goats, bighorn sheep, elk, mule deer, red-tailed hawk, osprey, golden eagle and bald eagle. Rock spires in the area attract the more adventurous. Spring, summer and fall are the best times to visit.

USGS topographic maps: Beartooth Mountain, Sheep Creek Mountain

For more information: Contact the BLM Headwaters Resource Area, 106 North Parkmont, P.O. Box 3388, Butte, MT 59702; (406) 494-5059.

GARNET RECREATION TRAIL SYSTEM / GARNET GHOST TOWN

See letter E on map page 290

backpacking, camping, cross-country skiing, hiking, mountain biking, snowmobiling, wildlife observation

Garnet bustled and prospered as a gold-mining town from 1895 to 1911. Although it experienced a slight revival after the Great Depression, it was completely abandoned and left for the ghosts in 1950. Much of the area is filled with old mining shafts. It is also an area that has suffered from logging, and some activity is still going on in the vicinity.

Beginning and ending in the historic ghost town of Garnet, this trail system is primarily made up of roads, some well maintained, some not. According to the area recreation specialist, Chuck Hollenbaugh, a mountain biker may see between three to four vehicles during a two-day ride. The trail system is well used in the winter as a signed and well-maintained cross-country ski and snowmobile recreation area. Trails wind through open slopes and timber and skirt heavily-mined areas. Elevations range up to 7,000 feet. There are excellent vistas of the Blackfoot Valley, Mission Mountains, the Bob Marshall Wilderness and the Pintlar Range.

Activity Highlights: Mountain biking and backpacking

The recommended loop begins in Garnet. Parking is good, but let the volunteer on duty know that you are leaving your car if you are planning an overnight stay. There are numerous streams and springs in the area, but all water must be treated. From Garnet, head out on the Summit Cabin Trail, 4.2 miles to Elk Creek Summit. Continue straight for about a mile on the Keno Creek/Pearl Ridge Loop to the Top O'Deep Trail. Follow Top O'Deep around to rejoin with Keno Creek/Pearl Ridge after 3.5 miles. Go right on Keno Creek/Pearl Ridge for 1.7 miles to the intersection with Kennedy Creek Trail. Head straight, now on Kennedy Creek, for 7.1 miles until the road rejoins Keno Creek. Turn right on Keno Creek riding about half a mile to another junction. Bear left, staying on Keno Creek and pedal one mile to Elk Creek Junction. At Elk Creek, head right on the Range Road Trail and pedal 2.6 miles back to the town of Garnet.

Activity Highlight: Cross-country skiing

The Garnet National Winter Recreation Trail system is the hub for winter recreation in the Garnet Range east of Missoula. Cross-country skiing, snowshoeing and snowmobiling lure fun-hogs from all over the U.S. The main trail from Greenough to Garnet is groomed on a regular basis for both cross-country skiing and snowmobiling. Trails immediately around the ghost town are groomed on a regular basis. Outlying trails and lower elevation portions are groomed infrequently, if at all.

Location: In the Garnet Range east of Missoula. From Interstate 90, take either the Drummond or Bearmouth exit. Follow old US 10 to Bear Gulch Road, midway between the two exits. Follow Bear Gulch to the historic ghost town of Garnet.

Camping: Camping is allowed anywhere within the resource area. No camping is allowed in the immediate vicinity of Garnet Ghost Town.

Season: Heavy snow is typical from mid-September to late May in the higher elevations, and from November to late March in the lower elevations. Hunting season is a time when vehicular use dramatically increases and mountain bikers probably will not want to be on the roads. The general hunting season is from October 21 to December 1.

Permits: Check to see if a campfire permit is necessary. Normally no fire permit is required, however in times of high fire danger, permits must be carried.

USGS topographic maps: Greenough, Bata Mountain, Chamberlain Mountain, Union Peak, Elevation Mountain and Wild Horse Parks. Ask for Garnet Winter Recreation Trails map from the BLM Garnet Resource Area.

For more information: Contact the BLM Garnet Resource Area, 3255 Fort Missoula Road, Missoula, MT 59801; (406) 329-3914.

HOODOO MOUNTAINS

See letter F on map page 290

backpacking, camping, cross-country skiing, fishing, hiking, rock climbing, wildlife observation

Like the Garnet Recreation Trail System, the Hoodoos lie within the Garnet Range, which stretches from the town of Avon and US 12, just west of Helena, north along Route 141 to Nevada Lake. The best access to the range is via a primitive road from Nevada Lake. The BLM thought highly enough of this mountain region to designate it as a Wilderness Study Area. Tucked in among dense Douglas fir and lodgepole pine forests are grassy meadows, wet bogs, rocky outcroppings and fishable streams. Wildlife includes black bear, porcupine, elk, whitetail deer, porcupine and blacktail deer. Fishing is chiefly for cutthroat trout, although due to the size of the creeks, expect fish to be small and hardly abundant.

USGS topographic map: Helmville

For more information: Contact the BLM Butte District Office, 106 North Parkmont, P.O. Box 3388, Butte, MT 59702; (406) 494-5059.

HUMBUG SPIRES WILDERNESS STUDY AREA

See letter G on map page 290

backpacking, camping, cross-country skiing, fishing, hiking, rock climbing, wildlife observation

There are 9,000-plus publicly-owned acres of dense forests, meadows and canyons at the edge of the Big Hole River Valley between the Highland and Pioneer ranges. Moose Creek is the major tributary stream, tumbling through a narrow, boulder-filled canyon. There are numerous pools, beaver ponds and waterfalls. The steepest of the waterfalls create a natural barrier between trout in the lower reaches of the creek and native cutthroat in its upper environs. There are several rare and endangered plants in the canyon including Idaho sedge, Kelsey's milk-vetch and Rock Mountain douglasia. Weathering and erosion account for the unique spires for which the Humbug area is named. The size and number of these spires are unequaled in the Northwest. Excellent rock climbing opportunities exist on many of the spires, some that have yet to be climbed.

Activity Highlights: Hiking and backpacking

The developed trail is a short two-mile route heading northeast from the parking area through old-growth Douglas fir and then up over a small ridge to the northeast fork of Moose Creek. From here, the opportunities for the adventurous backpacker are numerous. Utilizing game trails extending in all directions, it is possible to access the many rock spires, some 200 to 600 feet high, that are located throughout the northern section of the area. Terrain is heavily timbered and hikers traveling off the established trail must be adept at using a topographic map and compass. Adequate drinking water should be carried at all times.

Location: Approximately 25 miles south of Butte along the west slopes of the Highland Mountains. To get to Humbug Spires, turn off Interstate 15 at the Moose Creek interchange and head east for about three miles on an improved gravel road. Parking is available at the trailhead.

Camping: Camping is allowed anywhere in the Humbug Spires.

Season: The season runs from June to late September. You may encounter light snow in late spring and early fall.

Permits: No permit is necessary. Campfires may be prohibited due to fire danger in dry season, so call the BLM office for an update.

USGS topographic maps: Melrose, Tucker Creek, Mount Humbug, Wickiup Creek

Resources:

• For brief, descriptive information and pictures of this and other Montana wild areas, get a copy of *Montana Wildlands*, by Bill Cunningham, published by Montana Magazine/American Geographic Publishing.

For more information: Contact the BLM Headwaters Resource Area, 106 North Parkmont, P.O. Box 3388, Butte, MT 59702; (406) 494-5059.

AXOLOTL LAKES

See letter H on map page 290

camping, cross-country skiing, fishing, hiking, horseback riding, wildlife observation

Southeast of Virginia City and State Route 287, follow a county road approximately four miles to the edge of the site. The BLM refers to this region as an "outstanding natural area," and well it should. Adjoining the north end of the Gravelly Range with elevations up to 10,500 feet, the Axolotl Lakes is a picturesque land of numerous small lakes (lakettes really), grasslands, meadows and forests—including aspen. Lightly visited, this area is a must-see opportunity. Wildlife observation will likely include elk, mule deer, moose, golden eagle and red-tailed hawk. Fishing is considered quite good in some of the larger lakes, most notably Axolotl and Blue, for cutthroat and rainbow trout.

USGS topographic maps: Varneg, Cirque Lake, Eightmile Creek, Virginia City

For more information: Contact the BLM Butte District Office, 106 North Parkmont, P.O. Box 3388, Butte, MT 59702; (406) 494-5059.

BEAR TRAP CANYON
WILDERNESS STUDY AREA

See letter I on map page 290

backpacking, camping, canoeing, cross-country skiing, fishing, hiking, kayaking, whitewater rafting, wildlife observation

Bear Trap Canyon was carved by the Madison River as it flowed west from Yellowstone National Park through the Madison Range. Its 1,500-foot walls provide a scenic backdrop for a wide range of recreational activities, from backpacking to whitewater rafting to trout fishing. Sections of the east side of the canyon abut with the Gallatin and Beaverhead national forests. North-facing slopes of the canyon are forested with Douglas fir, juniper and aspen. Sagebrush dots the south-facing slopes.

Activity Highlights: Hiking and backpacking

Bear Trap Canyon National Recreation Trail is nine miles long. Ticks can be a problem during the spring and summer months. Take the time to perform a tick check daily. Bear-proof camping precautions are necessary, as black bear frequent the canyon and a periodic visit from a grizzly is not unusual.

Activity Highlight: Whitewater rafting

The BLM maintains a list of licensed outfitters who run trips through the canyon.

Location: This wilderness is in the southwest corner of Montana, approximately 30 miles west of Bozeman. From Bozeman, travel approximately 30 miles west on State Highway 84 to the Bear Trap Canyon Trailhead at the north end of the canyon. Those interested in running the canyon by whitewater kayak or raft will put in at the south end, near the Montana Power Company powerhouse, located 10 miles north of the town of Ennis via local roads.

Camping: Red Mountain Campground, managed by the BLM, is located near the Bear Trap Canyon Trailhead. Primitive camping is allowed anywhere within the wilderness area for backpackers. River runners are prohibited from camping within the wilderness area.

Season: The season runs from early May to late September. The canyon is most heavily traveled during July and August. Winter is a super time for exploring the trail via cross-country skis, but expect harsh temperatures and heavy snows.

USGS topographic maps: Beartrap Creek, Norris, Ennis Lake

Resources:

• *The Sierra Club Guide to the Natural Areas of Idaho, Montana and Wyoming,* by John and Jane Perry, published by Sierra Club, 730 Polk Street, San Francisco, CA 94109; (415) 923-5600.

• *Western Whitewater, From the Rockies to the Pacific,* by Jim Cassady, Bill Cross and Fryar Calhoun, published by North Fork Press, Berkeley, CA; (415) 424-1213.

• *The Hiker's Guide to Montana,* by Bill Schneider, published by Falcon Press, P.O. Box 1718, Helena, MT 59624; (800) 582-2665.

• Obtain either the "Bear Trap Canyon Wilderness" folder with map or the "Bear Trap Canyon Floater's Guide" folder with map from the BLM.

For more information: Contact the BLM Butte District Office, 106 North Parkmont, Butte, MT 59702; (406) 683-2337.

BIG HOLE RIVER

See letter J on map page 290

camping, canoeing, fishing, hiking, horseback riding, swimming

This is primarily a water-based recreation destination with both primitive and developed camping allowed. Two campgrounds with boat ramps are located on the Big Hole River, the Dickie Bridge and East Bank campgrounds. From the Wise River on Highway 43, drive north for approximately seven miles to the Dickie Bridge entrance; drive west on Highway 43 from the Wise River for eight miles to East Bank.

For more information: Contact the BLM Headwaters Resource Area, 106 North Parkmont, P.O. Box 3388, Butte, MT 59702; (406) 494-5059.

RUBY MOUNTAINS

See letter K on map page 290

backpacking, camping, cross-country skiing, hiking, horseback riding, rock climbing, wildlife observation

Getting into the mountains can be a bit of a challenge as access is limited by private land surrounding the range. This necessitates that you check in with the BLM prior to your visit to determine the best route of access. Don't let that deter you, however. This mountainous area is spectacular! Steep and carved with deep canyons, the slopes are carpeted with lodgepole pine, Douglas fir, Engelmann spruce and limber pine. Rock walls, small caves, meadows with colorful wild-flower displays and small aspen groves add to the charm and splendor of the region. Wildlife includes elk, mule deer, black bear, grouse and porcupine.

USGS topographic maps: Mount Humbug, Tucker Creek

For more information: Contact the BLM Dillon Resource Area, 1005 Selway Drive, P.O. Box 1048, Dillon, MT 59725; (406) 683-2337.

BIG SHEEP CREEK

See letter L on map page 290

backpacking, camping, fishing, hiking, mountain biking, wildlife observation

Running through the middle of an area separating parts of the Beaverhead National Forest/Bitterroot Mountain Range, the Continental Divide and the Tendoy Mountains, is Big Sheep Creek Back Country Byway. Now, I know this is a book dealing with non-motorized recreation, but the beauty of this 50-mile route is that it provides super access to a world of adventure alongside the road. Although the route is traveled by vehicles, traffic is not heavy enough to deter from the pleasure of pedaling the route. Primitive camping is allowed anywhere along the route on BLM land, and a maintained primitive campground is located at Deadman Gulch. Among the wild-life that frequent the area are elk, mule deer, pronghorn antelope, moose and a variety of hawks, eagles and owls. Spring, summer and fall are all good times to visit.

Special note: This area is under appeal as a Back Country Byway. Contact the BLM to find out if it's open and for directions before heading out.

USGS topographic maps: Dell, Dixon Mountain, Deer Canyon, Graphite Mountain, Island Butte

For more information: Contact the BLM Dillon Resource Area, 1005 Selway Drive, P.O. Box 1048, Dillon, MT 59725; (406) 683-2337.

CENTENNIAL MOUNTAINS

See letter M on map page 290

backpacking, camping, canoeing, cross-country skiing, fishing, hiking, horseback riding, snowmobiling, wildlife observation

With the Continental Divide running along its crest, the Centennial Mountain Range is an imposing and often snow-capped wall that straddles the Montana/Idaho border, just east of Monida and Interstate 15. Designated a Wilderness Study Area, elevations range from 6,500 feet to just over 9,000 feet. Much of the region is forested with Douglas fir and lodgepole pine. The Continental Divide Trail runs through the Centennial Mountains, traversing 25 miles of BLM land, a section of the Targhee National Forest and the U.S. Sheep Experiment Station managed by the Agricultural Research Station. June through September is the best time to travel the trail. Bugs can be bothersome—pack plenty of insect repellent.

The trailhead may be best accessed at Red Rock Pass on the graveled Red Rock Pass Road from Highway 20, south of Henry's Lake in Idaho. The trailhead lies at the western end of the Continental Divide Trail segment at Long Creek in Idaho (managed by the Dubois Ranger District) and crosses Interstate 15 south of Monida Pass. Fishing in Blair Lake adjacent to the Continental Divide is considered good. A primitive campground exists a few mile east of Lakeview, Montana on the Centennial Road. One final note of caution: Although the access points are passable with a two-wheel-drive vehicle in good weather, wet conditions mandate four-wheel drive.

USGS topographic maps: Winslow Creek, Big Table Mountain, Corral Creek, Monida

For more information: Contact the BLM Dillon Resource Area, 1005 Selway Drive, P.O. Box 1048, Dillon, MT 59725; (406) 683-2337.

MONTANA—MAP B

NEZ PERCE NATIONAL HISTORIC TRAIL

See letter N on map page 292

hiking, historic site

Dedicated in 1986 as a National Historic Trail, this is the 1,170-mile trail that the Nez Perce Indians followed from Wallowa Lake, Oregon to Bears Paw Battlefield near Chinook, Montana. This trek must go down in history as one of the most remarkable odysseys of a persecuted people in recent times. Long friends of the white man, the Nez Perce found that a treaty guaranteeing them land in 1855 meant nothing in the face of gold fever. During subsequent renegotiations attempting to force the Nez Perce to cede some of the land to the whites, the tribe became split, some agreeing to renegotiation and others walking out of the talks. Those that left became known as the "non-treaty" Nez Perce and, after several unfortunate events, they were forced to flee in the face of U.S. Army reprisal. The flight began on June 15, 1877, and ended on October 5, 1877. Many abandoned segments of the trail can be located today, but most are overgrown by vegetation, or altered by floods, power lines or other man-made structures. The BLM manages a historic site along the Upper Missouri National Wild and Scenic River near Cow Island Landing. For specific directions to this and other sites, contact the BLM.

For more information: Contact the BLM Lewistown District Office, 80 Airport Road, P.O. Box 1160, Lewistown, MT 59457; (406) 538-7461; or the BLM Butte District Office, 106 North Parkmont, P.O. Box 3388, Butte, MT 59702; (406) 494-5059.

LITTLE ROCKY MOUNTAINS RECREATION AREA

See letter O on map page 292

camping, fishing, hiking, horseback riding, mountain biking, wildlife observation

Best known for providing shelter and refuge to assorted outlaws and whiskey traders including the likes of Butch Cassidy, Kid Curry and the Sundance Kid, the Little Rocky Mountains, surrounded by grassy plains and broken by the Missouri River, is now best regarded for its basement cargo of precious metals. Pegasus Gold Company runs an open-pit gold mine within the boundaries of the range. The BLM maintains a recreation area that offers hiking, camping, wildlife viewing, mountain biking and day exploring opportunities.

From Malta, drive about 47 miles southwest on Highway 191 to a BLM sign indicating the town of Zortman and the Camp Creek Campground. Access the Little Rocky Mountains from the campground.

For more information: Contact the BLM Phillips Resource Area, HC 65 Box 5000, Malta, MT 59538; (406) 654-1240.

Hell Creek Recreation Area

See letter P on map page 292

boating, camping, fishing/ice-fishing, wildlife observation

Managed by the BLM, Montana Fish, Wildlife and Parks, the Corps of Engineers and the U.S. Fish and Wildlife Service, the campground here provides access to Fort Peck Lake on the Missouri River. The area has a courtesy dock, boat ramp, some sheltered camp/picnic sites, one group picnic shelter and drinking water. The season is from Memorial Day weekend through the end of September. A marina on site provides boating and fishing supplies and boat gas, and has private boat slips and cabins for rent. Fort Peck Lake provides excellent fishing opportunities for walleye, northern pike, smallmouth bass, lake trout and, at certain times of the year, salmon. Winter ice-fishing is also reported to be quite good. Those wishing to view wildlife will find easy access to the Charles M. Russell National Wildlife Refuge all along the lake by boat. From the north end of Jordan, Montana, drive onto the graveled county road and head north for approximately 26 miles to the signed recreation area site.

For more information: Contact the BLM Big Dry Resource Area, Miles City Plaza, Miles City, MT 59301; (406) 232-7000.

TERRY BADLANDS
WILDERNESS STUDY AREA

See letter Q on map page 292

camping, hiking, mountain biking, rockhounding

These badlands are located four miles northwest of the town of Terry across the Yellowstone River. To get there from Interstate 94, exit at Terry, head north on County Road 253 for approximately 1.5 miles and then head five miles west on an access road. This will put you at a signed overlook to the region. From here, numerous cattle paths crisscross through the rugged topography of sandstone bridges, spires, mesas and buttes. Visitors will find fossils, petrified wood and interesting rocks. Major portions of the Terry Badlands have been designated as Wilderness Study Areas. During wet weather, routes within and around Terry Badlands become impassable. The Calypso Trail is a semi-improved trail that runs through the Terry Badlands. The trail is approximately eight miles in length and is ideally suited for mountain bikes. It can also be traveled by two-wheel-drive vehicles when conditions are ideal, but most folks don't want to drive the road.

USGS topographic maps: Terry, Calypso

For more information: Contact the BLM Big Dry Resource Area, Miles City Plaza, Miles City, MT 59301; (406) 232-7000.

HOWERY ISLAND RECREATION AREA

See letter R on map page 292

fishing, hiking, wildlife observation

Managed jointly by the Montana Department of Fish, Wildlife and Parks, Max Howery and the BLM, Howery Island is one of only four known active bald eagle nesting sites in southeastern Montana. Occasionally subjected to flooding as evidenced by dry channels, logjams and gravel deposits, the island lies six miles west of Hysham off Highway 311 and is located on the Yellowstone River. To get there, take Interstate 94 to Hysham, then follow Secondary Highway 311 west for 6.9 miles to the Myers Bridge fishing access site turnoff. Park near the fishing access site. There is a self-guided nature trail for wildlife viewing. Bring your binoculars, because birdwatching on the island is tremendous with red-tailed hawks, bald eagles, great horned owls, redheaded woodpeckers, great blue herons, warblers, turkeys and wood ducks most common. Wildlife includes deer, red fox and beaver.

USGS topographic maps: Myers, Eldering Ranch

For more information: Contact the BLM Powder River Resource Area, Miles City Plaza, Miles City, MT 59301; (406) 232-7000.

POMPEY'S PILLAR NATIONAL HISTORIC LANDMARK

See letter S on map page 292

hiking, historic site, picnicking, wildlife viewing

Pompey's Pillar is located just off Interstate 94 approximately 28 miles east of Billings. This 200-foot sandstone outcropping is the only site on the Lewis and Clark Trail where visible evidence of the Lewis and Clark Expedition may be viewed by the public. Captain William Clark and his command arrived at the Pillar on July 25, 1806. Clark climbed the rock and carved his name and date in the sandstone face. In his journal, Clark wrote, "I marked my name and the day of the month and year." The historic signature remains today. A boardwalk leads past the signature. A visitor information center at the site is open daily from Memorial Day weekend through September. Interpretive tours are available.

For more information: Contact the BLM Billings Resource Area, 810 East Main Street, Billings, MT 59105; (406) 657-6262.

PRYOR MOUNTAIN NATIONAL WILD HORSE RANGE

See letter T on map page 292

camping, cross-country skiing, hiking, horseback riding, mountain biking, spelunking, wildlife observation

Designated in 1968 as a reserve for the protection and management of wild horses, this region sees light use by visitors year-round. Portions of this region have been designated as Wilderness Study Areas. Numerous caves attract spelunkers, although the most popular one, Mystery Cave, is gated and may be accessed only with a guide or by permit because of the great harm human impact might cause. In addition to the 120 or so wild horses that occupy the range, native wildlife includes mule deer, bighorn sheep, black bear and ring-necked pheasant. The terrain is a variety of open and rolling grasslands, steep-walled canyons and grassy mesas. Access is limited to four-wheel-drive vehicles, due to the rugged nature of the interior access road. From Lovell, Wyoming, head north on Bad Pass Highway (37). Just before entering the Bighorn Canyon National Recreation Area, turn left on Crooked Creek Road.

USGS topographic maps: Red Pryor Mountain, East Pryor Mountain, Mystery Cave

For more information: Contact the BLM Billings Resource Area, 810 East Main Street, Billings, MT 59105; (406) 657-6262.

BLM Campgrounds

1. Coal Banks Landing Campground—Map A

Campsites, facilities: There are 10 sites (five are for tents only), all with picnic tables and fire rings. Pit toilets are available. There is **no water**. There is a 14-day stay limit.

Fee: There is no fee.

Who to contact: Judith Resource Area, 80 Airport Road, P.O. Box 1160, Lewistown, MT 59457; (406) 538-7461.

Location: From Big Sandy, drive 13 miles southwest on Highway 87 to a county road accessing the river and the campground.

Season: May to September.

2. Log Gulch Campground—Map A

Campsites, facilities: There are 90 sites, all with picnic tables and fire rings. Pit toilets, a boat ramp and water are available. There is a 14-day stay limit.

Fee: There is a $6 fee per night; pay on site. There is a $2 day-use fee.

Who to contact: Headwaters Resource Area, 106 North Parkmont, P.O. Box 3388, Butte, MT 59702; (406) 494-5059.

Location: From Helena, drive north on Interstate 15 to exit 226. Drive three miles east of Wolf Creek on a paved access road to a gravel road on the east side of the Missouri River, then drive eight miles to Log Gulch. Follow the campground signs.

Season: All year.

3. Departure Point Campground—Map A

Campsites, facilities: There are 10 sites, all with picnic tables and grills. Pit toilets are available. There is **no water**. There is a 14-day stay limit.

Fee: There is a $6 fee per night; pay on site. There is a $2 day-use fee.

Who to contact: Headwaters Resource Area, 106 North Parkmont, P.O. Box 3388, Butte, MT 59702; (406) 494-5059.

Location: From Wolf Creek, drive three miles east on a paved road, and then 8.4 miles on a gravel road on the east side of the Missouri River. Follow the signs for the campground.

Season: All year.

4. HOLTER LAKE CAMPGROUND—MAP A

Campsites, facilities: There are 50 sites, all with picnic tables and fire rings. Water, pit toilets and a boat ramp are available. There is a 14-day stay limit.

Fee: There is a $6 fee per night; pay on site. There is a $2 day-use fee.

Who to contact: Headwaters Resource Area, 106 North Parkmont, P.O. Box 3388, Butte, MT 59702; (406) 494-5059.

Location: On Holter Lake. From Wolf Creek, drive two miles north on Recreation Road. Turn right on a county road and drive three miles to the campground entrance.

Season: May to October.

5. TOSTON CAMPGROUND—MAP A

Campsites, facilities: There are seven sites, all with picnic tables and fire rings. Pit toilets and a boat ramp are available. There is **no water**. No trash facilities are provided, so pack out all you bring in. There is a 14-day stay limit.

Fee: There is no fee.

Who to contact: Headwaters Resource Area, 106 North Parkmont, P.O. Box 3388, Butte, MT 59702; (406) 494-5059.

Location: On the Toston Reservoir. From Toston, drive south on Highway 287 for two miles to the gravel access road to Toston Reservoir and Dam. Turn left and drive five miles to the campground entrance. The campground is set at 3,800 feet.

Season: All year.

6. EAST BANK CAMPGROUND—MAP A

Campsites, facilities: There are five sites, all with picnic tables and fire rings. Pit toilets and a boat ramp are available. There is **no water**. No trash facilities are provided, so pack out all that you bring in. There is a 14-day stay limit.

Fee: There is no fee.

Who to contact: Headwaters Resource Area, 106 North Parkmont, P.O. Box 3388, Butte, MT 59702; (406) 494-5059.

Location: Adjacent to Big Hole River. From Wise River and Highway 43, drive west for eight miles to the campground entrance. The campground is set at 5,700 feet.

Season: All year.

7. DICKIE BRIDGE CAMPGROUND—MAP A

Campsites, facilities: There are eight sites, all with picnic tables and grills. Pit toilets and a boat ramp are available. No trash facilities are provided, so pack out all that you bring in. There is **no water**. There is a 14-day stay limit.

Fee: There is no fee.

Who to contact: Headwaters Resource Area, 106 North Parkmont, P.O. Box 3388, Butte, MT 59702; (406) 494-5059.

Location: Located across from the Big Hole River. From Wise River on Highway 43, drive north for approximately seven miles to the campground entrance. The campground is set at 5,714 feet.

Season: All year.

8. DIVIDE BRIDGE CAMPGROUND—MAP A

Campsites, facilities: There are 35 sites (10 are for tents only), all with picnic tables and fire rings. Water, pit toilets and a boat ramp are available. No trash facilities are provided, so pack out all that you bring in. There is a 14-day stay limit.

Fee: There is no fee.

Who to contact: Headwaters Resource Area, 106 North Parkmont, P.O. Box 3388, Butte, MT 59702; (406) 494-5059.

Location: From Divide on Highway 43, drive west for approximately one mile to the campground entrance. The campground is set at 5,400 feet.

Season: All year. Expect crowds on Memorial Day weekend.

9. RED MOUNTAIN CAMPGROUND—MAP A

Campsites, facilities: There are 11 sites, all with picnic tables and fire rings. Pit toilets and water are available. No trash facilities are provided, so pack out all you bring in. There is a 14-day stay limit.

Fee: There is no fee.

Who to contact: Dillon Resource Area, 1005 Selway Drive, P.O. Box 1048, Dillon, MT 59725; (406) 683-2337.

Location: Near the Madison River. From Norris, drive east on Route 289 for eight miles to the campground entrance. The campground is set at 4,450 feet.

Season: All year.

10. DEADMAN GULCH CAMPGROUND—MAP A

Campsites, facilities: There are many undesignated sites for RV camping. A pit toilet is available. There is **no water**. There is a 14-day stay limit.
Fee: There is no fee.
Who to contact: Dillon Resource Area, 1005 Selway Drive, P.O. Box 1048, Dillon, MT 59725; (406) 683-2337.
Location: Fifty-five miles south of Dillon on Interstate 15. Turn west at the Dell exit and drive to the campground entrance.
Season: All year.

11. RUBY RESERVOIR CAMPGROUND—MAP A

Campsites, facilities: There are 10 sites, all with picnic tables. Pit toilets are available. There is **no water**. No trash facilities are provided, so pack out all you bring in. There is a 14-day stay limit.
Fee: There is no fee.
Who to contact: Dillon Resource Area, 1005 Selway Drive, P.O. Box 1048, Dillon, MT 59725; (406) 683-2337.
Location: Drive nine miles south of Alder on a paved road signed for Ruby Reservoir. The campground is located east of Ruby Reservoir.
Season: All year.

12. SOUTH MADISON CAMPGROUND—MAP A

Campsites, facilities: There are 11 sites, all with picnic tables, grills and fire rings. Water, pit toilets and a boat ramp are available. No trash facilities are provided, so pack out all you bring in. There is a 14-day stay limit.
Fee: There is a $5 fee per night; pay on site.
Who to contact: Dillon Resource Area, 1005 Selway Drive, P.O. Box 1048, Dillon, MT 59725; (406) 683-2337.
Location: Along the Madison River. From Ennis, drive south on Highway 287 for 26 miles to the South Madison Recreation Area sign and turn right. Drive for one mile to the campground entrance. The campground is set at 5,600 feet.
Season: All year.

13. WEST MADISON CAMPGROUND—MAP A

Campsites, facilities: There are 22 sites, all with picnic tables, grills and fire rings. Pit toilets and water are available. No trash facilities are provided, so pack out all you bring in. There is a 14-day stay limit.

Fee: There is a $5 fee per night; pay on site.

Who to contact: Dillon Resource Area, 1005 Selway Drive, P.O. Box 1048, Dillon, MT 59725; (406) 683-2337.

Location: Near the Madison River. From Ennis, drive south on Highway 287 for 17 miles to the Madison Campground sign and turn right, driving three miles south on a county road to the campground entrance. The campground is set at 5,500 feet.

Season: All year.

14. MONTANA GULCH CAMPGROUND—MAP B

Campsites, facilities: There are five sites, all with picnic tables and fire rings. Pit toilets are available. There is **no water**. There is a 14-day stay limit.

Fee: There is no fee.

Who to contact: Phillips Resource Area, HC 65 Box 5000, Malta, MT 59538; (406) 654-1240.

Location: From Landusky, drive northwest for one-half mile on a county road to the campground entrance.

Season: May to November.

15. CAMP CREEK CAMPGROUND—MAP B

Campsites, facilities: There are 21 sites, all with picnic tables and fire rings. Pit toilets and water are available. There is a 14-day stay limit.

Fee: There is a $5 fee per night; pay on site.

Who to contact: Phillips Resource Area, HC 65 Box 5000, Malta, MT 59538; (406) 654-1240.

Location: From Zortman in the Little Rocky Mountains, 47 miles south of Malta on Highway 191, drive one mile east on an unmarked county road.

Season: All year.

16. JUDITH CAMPGROUND—MAP B

Campsites, facilities: There are five sites, all with picnic tables and fire rings. Pit toilets and water are available. There is a 14-day stay limit.

Fee: There is no fee.

Who to contact: Judith Resource Area, 80 Airport Road, P.O. Box 1160, Lewistown, MT 59457; (406) 538-7461.

Location: On the Missouri River. Drive 26 miles northwest of Winifred on Highway 236 to the campground entrance.
Season: May to October.

17. WOODHAWK CAMPGROUND—MAP B

Campsites, facilities: There are five sites (two are for tents only), all with picnic tables. There is **no water**. There is a 14-day stay limit.
Fee: There is no fee.
Who to contact: Judith Resource Area, 80 Airport Road, P.O. Box 1160, Lewistown, MT 59457; (406) 538-7461.
Location: Drive 40 miles east of Winifred along the Missouri Breaks Back Country Byway.
Season: All year.

18. JAMES KIPP RECREATION AREA—MAP B

Campsites, facilities: There are 28 sites, all with picnic tables and fire rings. Pit toilets, water and a boat ramp are available. There is a 14-day stay limit.
Fee: There is a $5 fee per night; pay on site.
Who to contact: Judith Resource Area, 80 Airport Road, P.O. Box 1160, Lewistown, MT 59457; (406) 538-7461.
Location: On the Missouri River in the Charles Russell National Wildlife Refuge. Drive 65 miles northeast of Lewistown to where US 191 intersects with the Missouri River at the Fred Robinson Bridge.
Season: All year.

19. HELL CREEK CAMPGROUND—MAP B

Campsites, facilities: There are 40 sites, all with picnic tables and fire rings. Water, pit toilets, a courtesy dock and a boat ramp are available. There is a 14-day stay limit.
Fee: There is a $6 fee per night, pay on site.
Who to contact: Big Dry Resource Area, Miles City Plaza, Miles City, MT 59301; (406) 232-7000.
Location: Located adjacent to Fort Peck Lake on the Missouri River. From the north end of Jordan at milepost 213 along Highway 200, drive north on a gravelled county road for 26 miles to the campground entrance.
Season: Memorial Day weekend to September.

STATE INFORMATION OVERVIEW

MONTANA STATE OFFICE
Granite Tower, 222 North 32nd Street, P.O. Box 36800, Billings, MT 59107; (406) 255-2885

BUTTE DISTRICT OFFICE
106 North Parkmont, P.O. Box 3388, Butte, MT 59702; (406) 494-5059

Dillon Resource Area, 1005 Selway Drive, P.O. Box 1048, Dillon, MT 59725; (406) 683-2337

Garnet Resource Area, 3255 Fort Missoula Road, Missoula, MT 59801; (406) 329-3914

Headwaters Resource Area, 106 North Parkmont, P.O. Box 3388, Butte, MT 59702; (406) 494-5059

LEWISTOWN DISTRICT OFFICE
80 Airport Road, P.O. Box 1160, Lewistown, MT 59457; (406) 538-7461

Great Falls Resource Area, 812 14th Street North, Great Falls, MT 59401; (406)727-0503

Havre Resource Area, West Second Street, P.O. Drawer 911, Havre, MT 59501; (406) 265-5891

Judith Resource Area, 80 Airport Road, P.O. Box 1160, Lewistown, MT 59457; (406) 538-7461

Phillips Resource Area, HC 65 Box 5000, Malta, MT 59538; (406) 654-1240.

Valley Resource Area, Route 1—4775, Glasgow, MT 59230; (406) 228-4316

MILES CITY DISTRICT OFFICE
Gary Owen Road, P.O. Box 940, Miles City, MT 59301; (406) 232-4331

Big Dry Resource Area and Powder River Resource Area, Miles City Plaza, Miles City, MT 59301; (406) 232-7000

Billings Resource Area, 810 East Main Street, Billings, MT 59105; (406) 657-6262

NEVADA

(SEE MAP A)

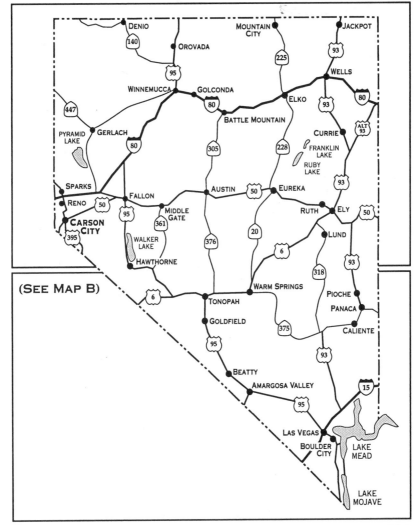

(SEE MAP B)

ANGEL LAKE

MAP A—NEVADA

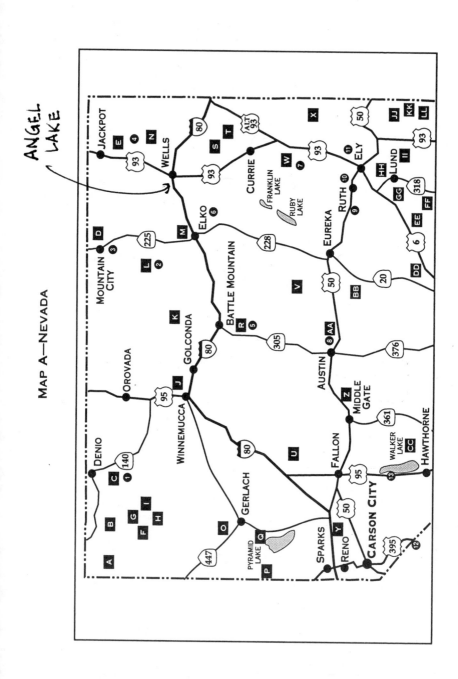

MAP REFERENCES

A. High Rock Canyon —p. 326
B. Mahogany Creek / Lahontan
   Cutthroat Trout Natural Area —
   p. 328
C. Pine Forest Range —p. 328
D. Owyhee River Canyon —p. 330
E. Salmon Falls Creek —p. 332
F. Black Rock Desert —p. 333
G. Black Rock Range—p. 334
H. Jackson Mountains —p. 334
I. Calico Mountains —p. 335
J. North Fork Little Humboldt
   River—p. 336
K. Rock Creek Canyon —p. 336
L. Little Humboldt River —p. 337
M. North Fork Humboldt River—
   p. 337
N. California Trail Back Country
   Byway—p. 337
O. Buffalo Hills—p. 338
P. Twin Peaks —p. 339
Q. Fox Range —p. 339
R. Mill Creek Recreation Area—
   p. 340

S. Spruce Mountain —p. 340
T. Goshute Mountains —p. 341
U. Stillwater Range —p. 342
V. Roberts Creek Mountains —p. 343
W. Goshute Canyon and Goshute
   Canyon Natural Area —p. 343
X. Blue Mass Scenic Area —p. 344
Y. Clan Alpine Mountains —p. 345
Z. Desatoya Mountains —p. 347
AA. Hickison Petroglyph —p. 348
BB. Antelope Range —p. 348
CC. Walker Lake —p. 349
DD. Railroad Valley Wildlife
   Management Area —p. 349
EE. Kawich Range —p. 350
FF. Lunar Crater Volcanic Field—
   p. 350
GG. Grant Range —p. 351
HH. South Egan Range —p. 351
II. Mount Grafton —p. 352
JJ. Gleason Canyon & the Charcoal
   Kilns—p. 352
KK. Ely Elk Viewing Area —p. 353
LL. Fortification Range —p. 353

BLM CAMPGROUNDS

1. Pine Forest Recreation Area—p. 369
2. Wilson Reservoir Recreation Area—p. 369
3. North Wildhorse Campground—p. 369
4. Tabor Creek Campground—p. 370
5. Mill Creek Recreation Area—p. 370
6. Zunino Reservoir Campground—p. 370
7. Goshute Creek Campground—p. 371
8. Hickison Petroglyphs Recreation Area—p. 371
9. Illipah Reservoir Campground—p. 371
10. Garnet Hill Campground—p. 372
11. Cleve Creek—p. 372
12. Indian Creek Campground—p. 372
13. Sportsman's Beach Campground—p. 373

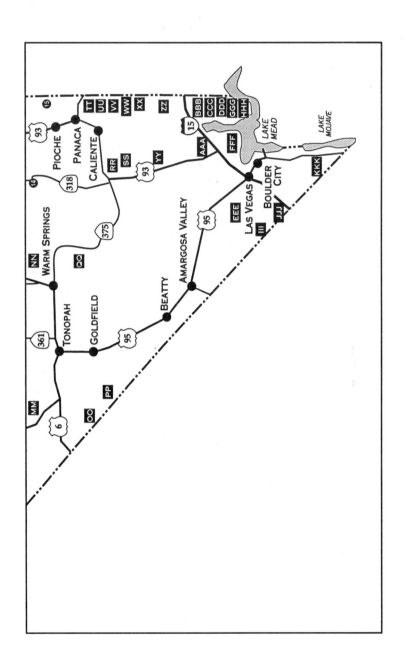

MAP B—NEVADA

MAP REFERENCES

BLM CAMPGROUNDS

NEVADA—MAP A

Always inquire locally for current road conditions before heading out on unimproved roads. Nevada secondary and dirt roads can become impassable and even hazardous when wet. For this reason, many area locations given in this chapter are not specific, requiring you to ask for additional directions.

HIGH ROCK CANYON

See letter A on map page 322

camping, hiking, backpacking, wildlife observation

The area from High Rock Canyon to Cottonwood Canyon is considered one of the most historically important desert canyon routes in the West. First documented by John C. Fremont during his 1843-1844 expedition to Oregon and California, and then subsequently used by settlers and wagon parties as an alternate route to the established Oregon Trail, the canyon became known as the Applegate Trail. During 1849, it is estimated that nearly half of the '49ers (no, not the football team) used this route to get to the gold fields of California, thinking it was the shortest way there. Troubles with Native Americans and the realization that this route was in fact longer than alternate routes, reduced the use somewhat. However, from 1851, when gold was discovered in the Siskiyou Mountains of Northern California, up until modern railroads and roads provided alternative routes in the late 1800s, the Applegate Trail through High Rock Canyon remained the primary path into and out of southern Oregon.

Activity Highlights: Hiking and backpacking

The High Rock Canyon Trail has been recognized by the BLM as an area of historical importance and is now designated as an Area of Critical Environmental Concern. A Cooperative Management Agreement has been signed by the BLM, the Friends of High Rock Canyon and the Desert Trail Association for the "express purpose of protecting the cultural and natural values of the canyon." Beginning at High Rock Lake, the trail meanders in a northwest direction along sandy washes and through sagebrush, rice grass, juniper, willow and greasewood. The geological formations are spectacular, as centuries of wind and rain have carved basaltic rock and volcanic ash into awesome canyons. Deer, antelope, rabbits, sage grouse and an unusually large population of raptors frequent the area. The High Rock Canyon Trail section ends at Cottonwood Canyon in the Sheldon National Wildlife Refuge.

Location: Approximately 160 miles due north of Reno and 100 miles south of Oregon; just east of the California/Oregon borders. Take Interstate 80 east from Reno to Wadsworth. Go north on State Highway 447 to Gerlach. Bear right on the county road just past Gerlach, north to Leadville and Vya. After approximately 60 miles, bear right on the road to High Rock Lake (the BLM sign designates this turnoff). It's approximately 15 miles to High Rock Lake. Park near the signed gate for the High Rock Canyon Area of Critical Environmental Concern.

Camping: There is designated camping in this area. The first good water stop is an area called Steven's Camp—17 miles from the parking area. Carry plenty of water.

Season: The best time to travel through the High Rock Canyon area is during the spring and fall. Fires, pets and radios are prohibited on the trail. Water is unreliable and hikers are advised to carry all that they will need. Water, if found, should be treated before drinking. The canyon is closed from mid-February to April 1 for raptor nesting season. It is open the rest of the year. The best times to backpack are in May and from September to November. Summer is uncomfortably hot. Temperatures can be extreme at any time so be prepared.

USGS topographic maps: High Rock Lake, Mahogany Mountain, Yellow Hills West, Yellow Hills East, Badger Mountain Southeast

Resources:
• *High Rock Canyon Hiking Guide*, published by the Desert Trail Association, P.O. Box 589, Burns, OR 97720.

For more information: Contact the BLM Susanville District Office, P.O. Box 1090, Susanville, CA 96130; (916) 257-5385.

MAHOGANY CREEK / LAHONTAN CUTTHROAT TROUT NATURAL AREA

See letter B on map page 322

birdwatching, hiking, wildlife observation

Mahogany Creek is a spawning habitat for the endangered Lahontan cutthroat trout. Fishing of any kind is not allowed! Spawning occurs from April through May. Birdwatching is superb in the area as it is both a migration corridor and a habitat for a variety of songbirds.

Two points of access are feasible with a high-clearance vehicle. From Winnemucca, head to Denio Junction on Route 140/291. Turn west at Denio Junction and travel 12 miles. Turn left on Gridley Lake Road and drive approximately 19 miles to the Little Idaho Canyon Road. Turn right and drive approximately 14 miles to the Summit Lake Indian Reservation. Bear left and drive about two miles to the Lahontan Cutthroat Trout Natural Area.

From Fernley in the south, head to Gerlach on Route 34. Continue past Gerlach for 15 miles to the Soldier Meadows Ranch Road. Turn right and travel about 56 miles to the ranch and then another 13 miles to the Summit Lake Indian Reservation. Turn right past the north end of the lake and drive about three miles to the Lahontan Cutthroat Trout Natural Area.

USGS topographic maps: Idaho Canyon Spring, New York Peak

For more information: Contact the BLM Winnemucca District Office, 705 East Fourth Street, Winnemucca, NV 89445; (702) 623-1500.

PINE FOREST RANGE

See letter C on map page 322

backpacking, camping, fishing, hiking, horseback riding, mountain biking, wildlife observation

The outstanding scenic quality of this region is worth the effort required to get there—you get cathedral-like peaks, high-mountain meadows, a clear subalpine lake, steep topography, colorful aspen groves and abundant water. Many of the high points in the area yield panoramic vistas that extend into nearby California and Oregon.

Always inquire locally for current road conditions before heading out on unimproved roads. Nevada secondary and dirt roads can become impassable and even hazardous when wet.

Activity Highlight: Hiking

Because access is moderately difficult—on 15 miles of rough road—day use is very light. Most visitors are overnight campers seeking fishing, backpacking, hunting, wildlife watching or other recreational pursuits. There is an obvious trail that leads from Onion Reservoir to Blue Lakes, a popular overnight destination for trout fishing. But many more opportunities for backpacking explorations exist for the experienced and moderately adventurous backpacker. Duffer Peak at 9,400 feet is the highest mountain in the Pine Range. It lies several cross-country miles south of Blue Lakes. Water is moderately plentiful, but hikers are cautioned to carry adequate reserves.

Activity Highlight: Mountain biking

Mountain-biking opportunities exist on the four-wheel-drive roads that are open outside of the vehicle-closure boundary. You can make an approximately 15-mile loop by putting together Alder Creek Road, Sand Basin Road, Cove Camp Road and Alta Creek Road. A connecting trail from Rodeo Flat over to Cove Camp Road makes the loop possible.

Location: Approximately 70 miles north of Winnemucca and Interstate 80 in the northwestern corner of the state. From Winnemucca, drive 30 miles north on US 95 and then 52 miles west on Highway 140. Turn left onto Alta Creek Road, just south of the highway maintenance station. It is a dirt road and only suitable for high-clearance vehicles. Four-wheel-drive vehicles are recommended. The trailhead for Blue Lakes and Duffer Peak is at the Onion Valley Reservoir, approximately 15 miles from Highway 140. Mountain bikers must camp outside of the vehicle closure area at Onion Valley or at another appropriate site.

Camping: Onion Valley Reservoir has designated primitive camping sites and porta-potties. Primitive camping is allowed anywhere else in the region. One word of caution: Nevada state law prohibits camping within 300 feet of watering holes that are used by livestock.

Season: While summer temperatures may climb into the 90s during the day, the nights are usually quite chilly. The best time to visit this area is from May to September. Snow in the winter closes the roads, but the more adventurous may find enjoyment in exploring the area on cross-country skis—check at the BLM office for the snow report.

USGS topographic maps: Railroad Point, Denio, Idaho Canyon, Duffer Peak

Resources:
• *The Hiker's Guide to Nevada,* by Bruce Grubbs, published by Falcon Press, P.O. Box 1718, Helena, MT 59624.

For more information: Contact the BLM Winnemucca District Office, 705 East Fourth Street, Winnemucca, NV 89445; (702) 623-1500.

OWYHEE RIVER CANYON

See letter D on map page 322

backpacking, camping, canoeing, hiking, fishing, kayaking, rafting

Although gaining access to it is challenging, this 450,000-acre region (much of it lying to the north in Idaho and known as the Owyhee Canyonlands) is picturesque, dramatic, wild, isolated and well worth your time. River runners and hunters are the predominant users, and there are not too many of those. The narrow canyons that cut into the plateau range anywhere from several hundred to 1,000 feet deep—often with sheer walls from rimrock to river bottom. Mountain lion, bobcat, river otter, pronghorn antelope and bighorn sheep reside within the Owyhee Canyon system.

Activity Highlight: Hiking

There are no established hiking routes here. Hiking trips entail either wandering along the canyon edges or along the canyon floors—following the game trails when available. Within the canyons themselves, hiking can be tedious at best, often requiring frequent rock and talus scrambles, and at times, river wading or swimming. Only experienced backpackers and those with knowledge and skills in canyoneering should venture into the canyon bottoms. Hiking is much easier on the mile-high desert plateau. Although some springs and hidden swimming holes do exist, water is not easily found on the plateau. Check with the BLM office for specific locations and potability information (all water must be filtered and/or treated to guard against Giardia). Always carry adequate reserves just in case—one gallon per person per day is advised.

Activity Highlight: Boating

Upper Owyhee: This river consists of three forks, the East (Idaho), South (Nevada into Idaho) and North (Idaho) Fork. Both the East and South forks are floatable in rafts, kayaks and canoes. The river is rated Class II through IV, with several very arduous portages on the East Fork before its confluence with the South. The South Fork is quite scenic with Class I to II water. The BLM lists the North Fork as a river for "world class" expert kayakers only! Enough said. If you continue on after the Nevada/Idaho section, the following is what to expect in Idaho:

Middle Owyhee: The Middle Owyhee is a mixture of Class III through Class V+ rapids that are challenging for most boaters. Small 12- to 15-foot rafts and kayaks are recommended. The rapids feature long boulder gardens, some steep drops and several heavy hydraulics. Some portaging is required.

Lower Owyhee: The Lower Owyhee offers Class II through Class IV rapids that any level of boater in all variety of crafts—raft, canoe, kayak or drift boat—will find enjoyable. This is the most popular section of the river and is considered ideal for family groups and parties with inexperienced boaters. No party should attempt the river unless several members are qualified intermediate boaters capable of safely navigating Class III and Class IV whitewater. The river is somewhat forgiving because it is of the "pool and drop" variety, meaning that rapids are usually short followed by calm, pool sections giving you time to recover.

Location: The northeastern high-desert region is north of Interstate 80, west of Highway 225 and the town of Owyhee. Also, the vast region includes the high-desert region of southwestern Idaho—southwest of Grand View and Highway 78 and southeast of Jordan Valley, Oregon and US 95. This area is predominantly roadless—hence its attraction. The dirt roads that do exist can become impassable at any time. In fact, one river runner I talked to said that he considered much of the Owyhee a Class II river float with Class V access. The official River Runners Guide to Idaho, published by the BLM and the Idaho Parks and Recreation states that "spring rains are common and the dirt tracks can quickly turn into an impassable quagmire of gumbo." The same is true for the Nevada portion of the Owyhee. Before visiting, check with the BLM office in Elko to determine which access route would be most appropriate during the time of your visit. Four-wheel-drive vehicles are recommended for any non-gravel route! Reach the best non-gravel access in Nevada 28 miles west of the town of Owyhee, on local and unimproved roads—river put-in is at Petan Ranch. The best access in Idaho is via the Owyhee Uplands National

Back Country Byway, a 101-mile gravel road, suitable for high-clearance vehicles. This road stretches from Grand View, on Idaho State Highway 78, to Jordan Valley in Oregon on US 95. There are numerous take-outs appropriate for overnight camping and embarking on short or extended backpacking explorations.

Camping: Camping is permitted anywhere within the canyon proper or on the plateau. Campsites are evident and frequent—select sites that are already established if you have the choice.

Season: The best hiking is in May and June or in September and October. July and August are hot and dry. May and early June are the best times for wildflowers. The best boating is during the spring runoff from March through June. River levels can fluctuate severely with cold or warm spells and periods of heavy rain. Call the River Forecast Center in Oregon at (503) 249-0666 for current gauge readings.

Permits: No permits are necessary for backpacking. Boaters, however, must register prior to embarking on any of the Owyhee River forks and tributaries.

BLM surface maps: Riddle (South Fork and East Fork), Triangle (North Fork), Bull Run Mountains (South Fork)

Resources:
• *Owyhee River Boating Guide* is available through the Elko, Vale, or Boise District BLM offices.
• *Western Whitewater, From the Rockies to the Pacific,* by Jim Cassady, Bill Cross and Fryar Calhoun, published by North Fork Press, Berkeley, CA; (415) 424-1213.

For more information: Contact the BLM Elko District Office, P.O. Box 831, 3900 East Idaho Street, Elko, NV 89803; (702) 753-0200.

SALMON FALLS CREEK
See letter E on map page 322

backpacking, camping, canoeing, hiking, fishing, kayaking, rafting
Salmon Falls Creek is located approximately two miles south of the town of Jackpot and just west of US 93. Boating is possible along a very quiet Class I section of the creek near the Nevada/Idaho border. Just past the border boundary, the stream dumps into the Salmon Creek Reservoir. The creek's winding route has cut a narrow, steep, relatively shallow canyon through a badlands topography. There isn't

much vegetation in the area, other than within the canyon. The fishing here is for rainbow and brown trout. There is a rest area near the town of Jackpot along US 93 which is suitable as a put-in for the river float to the reservoir. You will need to portage around the fish barrier downstream. Camping spots along the canyon are available, though limited and at times, creative. It's a pleasant destination year-round.

USGS topographic map: Jackpot

For more information: Contact the BLM Elko District Office, P.O. Box 831, 3900 East Idaho Street, Elko, NV 89803; (702) 753-0200.

BLACK ROCK DESERT

See letter F on map page 322

auto touring, camping, hiking, mountain biking, rockhounding

The Black Rock Desert is located roughly north of State Roads 48 and 49, between the towns of Gerlach and Winnemucca. If you look as far as you can in every direction, all you will see is bare, white playa surrounded by distant mountain ranges. If you gaze at the Black Rock Desert from above, you will see that it is shaped roughly like a giant Y. The western arm extends up to Soldier Meadows, has low shrub vegetation, and is bordered on the west by the Calico Range. The eastern arm is bordered by the Jackson Mountains and follows the water course of the Quinn River. The main body of the Y is all playa. This area is the remains of the ancient Lake Lahontan, a Pleistocene-age lake that formed other valley bottoms in northwestern Nevada. Would you believe that in some places, the silt underfoot is nearly a mile deep?

This barren area is appropriate for hiking, rockhounding, mountain biking and four-wheel-drive explorations—but only in the cooler months. Locals and those familiar with this vast desert, drive the playa during dry months. They either follow a historic route that links Gerlach and Winnemucca or venture freely into the interior. If you don't know the playa, don't wander into its vastness alone—strangers to the area have died from exposure once their vehicles became inextricably stuck. When the playa is wet, it becomes a quagmire of monumental proportions, impassable even on foot in many places.

USGS topographic maps: Highrock Canyon, Gerlach, Jackson Mountains, Eugene Mountain

For more information: Contact the BLM Winnemucca District Office, 705 East Fourth Street, Winnemucca, NV 89445; (702) 623-1500.

BLACK ROCK RANGE

See letter G on map page 322

backpacking, camping, hiking, horseback riding

The Black Rock Range divides the two arms of the Black Rock Desert and is accessed by Soldier Meadows Ranch Road (County Road HU 217) from Gerlach or from State Route 140 to the north. Backpacking, hiking and camping are good here, but be prepared for difficult access and a very rugged trip. The southern sections of the range feature deep drainages and rugged, rocky outcroppings. Several springs, some of them hot, may be found here. The northern sections of the range include the Lahontan Cutthroat Trout Natural Area at Mahogany Creek and areas of higher elevations cut with aspen and at times deep drainages. I suggest backpacking in the Big Mountain area. Camping is considered best here. Camping is also good at Colman Creek and Mid Meadows Creek. Spring and fall are the best times to visit.

USGS topographic maps: Pidgeon Spring, Clapper Creek, Big Mountain, Paiute Meadows, Burnt Springs, Red Mountain, Summit Lake, Idaho Canyon Spring, New York Peak

For more information: Contact the BLM Winnemucca District Office, 705 East Fourth Street, Winnemucca, NV 89445; (702) 623-1500.

JACKSON MOUNTAINS

See letter H on map page 322

backpacking, camping, hiking, horseback riding

The Jackson Mountains are located just east of the Black Rock Desert. You can reach this area via county roads south of Highway 140 or from Gerlach and Highway 447 to Sulphur. The road from Highway 140 heads south to the historic site of Sulphur, running along the western edge of the range. The road north from Sulphur to Route 140, runs along the western boundary of the region. Unlike in many other desert ranges in Nevada, water is relatively easy to find and this proves attractive to a wide variety of wildlife. King Lear Peak, at 8,910 feet, is the highest peak in the range. Much of the range sits above 5,000 feet. Towards the north, the deep canyons of Deer Creek, Mary Sloan, Happy Creek and Jackson Creek feature perennial streams and lush vegetation. The ridges and slopes are covered with juniper, snowberry, gooseberry and dogwood. Due to the rugged nature of the northern area, it is better to base-camp and day-hike in this area. In the south, you will find King Lear, McGill Canyon and other spectacular peaks lining the hike-able ridgeline. The backpacking is good, but be prepared for rugged hiking. Spring and fall are the best times to visit; summer can get pretty toasty.

USGS topographic maps: Hobo Canyon, King Lear Peak, Parrot Peak, Deer Creek Peak

For more information: Contact the BLM Winnemucca District Office, 705 East Fourth Street, Winnemucca, NV 89445; (702) 623-1500.

CALICO MOUNTAINS
See letter I on map page 322

camping, hiking, horseback riding, rockhounding, wildlife observation
The western border of the western arm of the Black Rock Desert is an outstanding location for rockhounding for jasper, fire opal, agate and petrified wood. County Road 217 (Soldier Meadows Road) along the eastern base of the range offers fair to good access. The road to High Rock Lake offers poor to fair access. Your best bet is to inquire at the BLM Winnemucca office or locally in the town of Gerlach. Wildlife observation is limited, as is the water. Pronghorn, mule deer, chukar, sage grouse and quail can be seen in this area. Donnelly Creek provides the best opportunity for wildlife viewing and water. Water is scarce everywhere else so pack all that you will need. The camping is best along Donnelly Creek and near the few springs that may be found around the Donnelly Peak area. The best hiking is around High Rock Lake, Fly Canyon, Donnelly Creek and Box Canyon.

USGS topographic maps: High Rock Lake, Mud Meadows, McConnel Canyon, Wagner Spring, Donnelly Peak, Division Peak Gerlach, High Rock Canyon

For more information: Contact the BLM Winnemucca District Office, 705 East Fourth Street, Winnemucca, NV 89445; (702) 623-1500.

NORTH FORK LITTLE HUMBOLDT RIVER

See letter J on map page 322

backpacking, camping, hiking, horseback riding, wildlife observation

Originating in the Humboldt National Forest, the North Fork of the Little Humboldt River flows southeast and then southwest, merging with the South Fork approximately 20 miles east of the town of Paradise Valley. You can reach this river via BLM Road 2003, also called Little Owyhee Road. The river gorge is the major feature within this region, and is also the best place for hiking, camping and wandering. Within the 14-mile-long canyon, you will find steep, colorful walls interrupted with numerous spires, cliffs, small caves and narrow side canyons. The wildlife is abundant and includes pronghorn antelope, mule deer, beaver, muskrat, mink, coyote, raccoon, bobcat and bats. Birds are also abundant—so bring your binoculars for sure! Great blue heron, turkey vulture, red-tailed hawk, sage grouse, great horned owl, belted kingfisher, a variety of swallows, northern oriole and a variety of wrens can be viewed here. Hiking and backpacking are best in the gorge. Camping is also good in the gorge.

USGS topographic maps: Little Poverty, Willow Point, Gumboot Lake

For more information: Contact the BLM Winnemucca District Office, 705 East Fourth Street, Winnemucca, NV 89445; (702) 623-1500.

ROCK CREEK CANYON

See letter K on map page 322

hiking

From the town of Battle Mountain, drive 23 miles north on Izzenhood Road and then eight miles east on local roads—ask at the BLM for specific directions. It's a small area, but the riparian environment of the eight-mile-long canyon is interesting and quite attractive. Spring, summer and fall are the times to visit.

USGS topographic maps: Squaw Valley Ranch, Rock Creek Canyon

For more information: Contact the BLM Elko District Office, P.O. Box 831, 3900 East Idaho Street, Elko, NV 89803; (702) 753-0200.

LITTLE HUMBOLDT RIVER

See letter L on map page 322

backpacking, camping, fishing, hiking, wildlife observation

The Little Humboldt River is located approximately 60 miles northwest of Elko, near the ghost town of Midas, west of Willow Creek Reservoir. The canyon that the Little Humboldt River flows through is super for hiking and backpacking. The wildlife includes wild horses and the endangered Lahontan cutthroat trout. Water is readily available. Game trails and old cattle trails make the best hiking routes; no formal hiking trail exists. You will need a four-wheel-drive vehicle for access to this area. Spring, summer and fall are good times to visit.

USGS topographic maps: Rodear Flat, Haystack Peak, Oregon Canyon, Snowstorm Mountain

For more information: Contact the BLM Elko District Office, P.O. Box 831, 3900 East Idaho Street, Elko, NV 89803; (702) 753-0200.

NORTH FORK HUMBOLDT RIVER

See letter M on map page 322

fishing, hiking

This is a relatively small area located approximately 35 miles north of Elko and east of Route 225. Much of the river runs through private land after it leaves the Humboldt National Forest, but a short section of approximately 12 miles is on BLM land. The BLM area runs through Devil's Gap and past Cottonwood Creek. The terrain is rolling and is well suited to day hiking, but forget about backpacking. Spring, summer and fall are the times to visit.

USGS topographic maps: Mahala Creek East, Tule Valley

For more information: Contact the BLM Elko District Office, P.O. Box 831, 3900 East Idaho Street, Elko, NV 89803; (702) 753-0200.

CALIFORNIA TRAIL BACK COUNTRY BYWAY

See letter N on map page 322

cultural/historic site, hiking, mountain biking, off-highway vehicles

The California Trail Back Country Byway is located in the northeastern corner of the state and follows the historic California Trail from the Goose Creek area in the extreme northeast corner of Elko

County to Thousand Springs, 26 miles north of Wells. The California Trail is included in the National Historic Trails System and provides the visitor with a close approximation of what westward bound emigrants on the trail encountered. Points of interest are identified along the trail by trail markers established by the Oregon/California Trails Association. Access to the trail is possible from two roads, the Thousand Springs access road (Elko County Road 765), 26 miles north of Wells off US 93 and the Delaplain access road (Elko County Road 761) one mile south of Jackpot also off US 93. Travelers along the road should be prepared for no services and little if any traffic—if you get into trouble you need to be able to get yourself out and not rely on encountering help. The road surface is gravel and dirt and is passable by low-clearance two-wheel-drive vehicles, however summer rainstorms, not uncommon in this region, can make the northern section of this trail impassable—a regular tire-swallowing quagmire.

BLM maps: Maps of the California Trail Back Country Byway and accompanying brochures are available at the District Office or at the Burger Bar, at the corner of Main and Humbolt avenues in Wells, Nevada.

USGS topographic map: Jackpot

For more information: Contact the BLM Elko District Office, P.O. Box 831, 3900 East Idaho Street, Elko, NV 89803; (702) 752-0200.

BUFFALO HILLS

See letter O on map page 322

backpacking, camping, hiking, horseback riding

The Buffalo Hills are bounded on the east by Route 447 and lie approximately 15 miles northwest of Gerlach. Since the area is so easily accessible, it is well suited for recreational uses. Water is readily available from many of the more than 50 springs (some on private land) and three major streams (Buffalo, Jones and Frog). The BLM stresses that due to water contamination from animals, a water filter or some other form of water treatment must be used before drinking. From the air, it is easy to see that the area is one giant plateau with deep canyons radiating out to the surrounding desert like spokes from a wheel. The canyons provide the best access from the desert floor up to the top of the plateau. Wildlife includes pronghorn antelope, deer, mountain lion, sage grouse and chukar. Visit in spring and fall.

USGS topographic maps: Squaw Valley, Poodle Mountain, Hillside Spring, Cruther Canyon, Wall Spring, Horse Canyon

For more information: Contact the BLM Winnemucca District Office, 705 East Fourth Street, Winnemucca, NV 89445; (702) 623-1500.

TWIN PEAKS

See letter P on map page 322

camping, hiking

This area lies immediately west of Buffalo Hills and is bounded by the Home Springs/Painter Flat Road to the north, and Sand Pass-Gerlach Road or Buffalo Meadow Road to the southeast. You can reach Twin Peaks from the town of Gerlach and from west of Route 447. Twin Peaks, the area's namesake, sits at 6,605 feet, watching over the surrounding range with elevations roughly around 4,000 feet. Shinn Creek and Smoke Creek provide perennial water to the region. The best hiking and exploring is found within Willow Creek Canyon, Buffalo Creek Canyon and Chimney Rock Creek Canyon. Willow and aspen may be found in some of the drainages.

USGS topographic maps: Buffalo Creek, Mixie Flat, Smoke Creek Ranch, Salt Marsh

For more information: Contact the BLM Susanville District Office, P.O. Box 1090, Susanville, CA 96130; (916) 257-5385.

FOX RANGE

See letter Q on map page 322

backpacking, camping, hiking, horseback riding, wildlife observation

The Fox Range is located southwest of Gerlach and north of the Pyramid Lake Indian Reservation. Access to this area is via a maintenance road, several local roads leading from Gerlach, or a power line road along the northeastern boundary. Water is very scarce; perennial streams run in Rodeo Creek on the east side of the range and in Wild Horse Canyon in the southwest of the range (please respect the private land in the canyon area). The southern part of the range is the best area for backpacking, especially along the ridge to Pah-Rum Peak, Poogh Canyon and in the other narrow and colorful canyons that carve through this area.

USGS topographic maps: Pah-Rum Peak, Fox Canyon, Smith Canyon

For more information: Contact the BLM Winnemucca District Office, 705 East Fourth Street, Winnemucca, NV 89445; (702) 623-1500.

MILL CREEK RECREATION AREA
See letter R on map page 322

camping, fishing, hiking

This area features a BLM-maintained campground with 10 tent sites and three RV sites. A canopy of tall cottonwood trees provides a shady spot for camping and fishing. No potable water is available on site. Restrooms are wheelchair accessible. The quiet campground is located on the site of the historic 1930s Civilian Conservation Corps (CCC) camp. A few structures still remain and may be visited—look but do not touch or attempt to collect.

From Battle Mountain, drive 23 miles south on Highway 305 to a signed gravel entrance road and turn left, driving four miles to the recreation area.

For more information: Contact the BLM Battle Mountain District, P.O. Box 1420, Battle Mountain, NV 89820; (702) 635-4000.

SPRUCE MOUNTAIN
See letter S on map page 322

hiking, photography, wildlife observation

Spruce Mountain and Spruce Mountain Ridge lie on the eastern side of US 93, approximately 35 miles southeast of Wells. There are two main access points to the area from US 93: The Tobar-Independence Valley access road, seven miles south of Wells, and the Spruce Mountain access road 40 miles south of Wells. Access is available to low-clearance vehicles from Spruce Mountain access road, however high-clearance four-wheel-drive vehicles are recommended from the top of Spruce Mountain Ridge to the Tobar-Independence Valley access road. Vegetation on Spruce Mountain is primarily Pinon pine and Utah juniper in the foothills with scattered sagebrush and bunch grasses to mountain mahogany, white fir, Ponderosa pine and bristlecone pine at the upper elevations. A bald eagle wintering roost, superb views of the East Humbolt and Ruby Mountain ranges and a birds-eye vantage point from which to view the Basin and Range topography unique to the Great Basin area are prime attractions and reason enough to spend some time exploring here. The old mining town of Sprucemont is located at the base of Spruce Mountain on the west side. The remnants of the Black Forest mining area are found on the east side of the mountain, but you will need four-wheel drive to get there. Visit any time of year.

USGS topographic map: Spruce Mountain

For more information: Contact the BLM Elko District Office, P.O. Box 831, 3900 East Idaho Street, Elko, NV 89803; (702) 753-0200.

GOSHUTE MOUNTAINS
See letter T on map page 322

backpacking, camping, hiking, horseback riding, wildlife observation

The Goshute Mountains contain the 69,770-acre Goshute Peak Wilderness Study Area (WSA). WSAs are areas currently under review by Congress for potential designation as wilderness areas. While traveling, camping and hiking in the WSA, be aware that vehicle travel is restricted to designated roads; off-highway vehicles and mountain bikes are restricted to roads and jeep trails. The mountain range itself runs northwest and southeast. Elevations extend from 6,000 feet along the foothills to 9,609-foot Goshute Peak, the highest point in the range. Numerous canyons cut through picturesque limestone cliffs in the region. Pinyon pine and Utah juniper cling to the foothills while mountain mahogany, limber pine, white fir and bristlecone pine dot the ridges and slopes in the upper elevations. High-clearance vehicles are recommended for travel throughout the area. It is critical to remember that while two-wheel-drive vehicles can access the region in dry weather, a sudden storm may render the roads and trails almost impassable—a problem only if you are stuck within the range with no hope of getting out until the route you wish to travel dries.

Activity Highlight: Wildlife observation

Located within the Goshute Mountains is the Goshute Raptor Project/Watchable Wildlife Viewing Area. A lookout site in a small limestone outcrop, at approximately 9,000 feet, may be reached providing you have a high-clearance vehicle. Raptors fly along the Goshute Range, taking advantage of the uplift created by the mountains and avoiding the Bonneville Salt Flats to the east in Utah. This area is considered the best migration lookout in the western United States. It is possible to observe over 200 raptors in a single day—days with over 1,000 sightings are not uncommon either. Primary sightings include the sharp-shinned hawk, Cooper's hawk, northern goshawk, red-tailed hawk, American kestrel, golden eagle, turkey vulture and northern harrier. If you are interested, it is possible to participate in counting or banding studies as well.

Location: From Wendover, drive south on US Alternate 93 for approximately 24 miles to the Old Ferguson Highway Maintenance Station. Turn right and drive by the station on a dirt road for about two miles to a "T" junction. Turn right and go about one mile on the main road. Bear left at the top of the hill, proceeding up the rocky jeep road into Christmas Tree Canyon. The trail to the top of the ridge is about a two-mile hike, considered moderately strenuous with 1,600 feet of elevation gain.

Season: Raptor migration begins in mid-August and continues into November.

USGS topographic maps: Goshute Peak, Lion Spring, Morgan Pass

For more information: Contact the BLM Elko District Office, P.O. Box 831, 3900 East Idaho Street, Elko, NV 89803; (702) 753-0200; or Hawk Watch International, P.O. Box 660, Salt Lake City, Utah 84110; (801) 524-8512.

STILLWATER RANGE

See letter U on map page 322

backpacking, camping, hiking, horseback riding

To reach this area from Frenchman, take US 50 east to Highway 121 and head north. Just west of Dixie Valley, take Dixie Hot Springs Road west to the canyons of Hare, Mississippi and White Rock. Water is not readily available; there are few springs and streams. Backpacking is best along the ridgeline, but remember to pack all the water you will need for your journey. Since there is periodic mine and oil/gas exploration (some of the range lies within gas and oil leases), check with the BLM for current and suggested best routes to avoid areas of development. Spring and fall are the best times to visit; summer can be hot.

USGS topographic maps: Table Mountain, Job Peak, Cox Canyon, IXL Canyon, Fondaway Canyon, Dixie Hot Spring, Dixie Hot Spring Northwest, Logan Peak

For more information: Contact the BLM Carson City District, 1535 Hot Springs Road, Suite 300, Carson City, NV 89706; (702) 885-6000.

ROBERTS CREEK MOUNTAINS

See letter V on map page 322

camping, hiking, horseback riding

These mountains are located 11 miles west of Eureka on US 50, and 20 miles north via local roads past Roberts Creek Ranch and up Roberts Creek. The peaks of this range are very rugged and broken. Roberts Creek Mountain sits at 10,133 feet, the highest point in the range. Hanson Creek features a nice waterfall and there are a number of small ponds and intermittent streams that water the rest of the area. It is quite scenic. A four-wheel-drive or a high-clearance, two-wheel-drive vehicle is required for access. It's a pleasant destination year-round.

USGS topographic maps: Cooper Peak, Roberts Creek Mountain

Resources: *Hiking the Great Basin*, by John Hart, published by Sierra Club Books, San Francisco, CA.

For more information: Contact the BLM Battle Mountain District, P.O. Box 1420, Battle Mountain, NV 89820; (702) 635-4000.

GOSHUTE CANYON AND GOSHUTE CANYON NATURAL AREA

See letter W on map page 322

backpacking, camping, cross-country skiing, fishing, hiking, horseback riding, rock climbing, spelunking, wildlife observation

This is an outstanding area for hikers, backpackers, spelunkers and other recreational users who revel in scenery. Be prepared, however, for rugged terrain. Don't miss the Goshute Canyon Natural Area; it is narrow near the road leading from Cherry Creek and widens as it heads west, opening into the Goshute Basin. The Goshute Basin is a large amphitheater rimmed by tall mountains and it serves as the headwaters for Goshute Creek. The entire canyon is wonderful to hike and camp in; it has limestone crags, cool springs (always treat water before drinking), aspen groves and pristine meadows.

Spelunkers head to the area to enjoy the 1,500 feet of limestone passages of Goshute Cave. Rare limestone formations may be viewed from within the cave. However, you must be experienced before venturing into any cave and know how to minimize the impact of your explorations. Human damage to a cave is virtually irreparable! It ruins future experiences for everyone. The wildlife here includes the great horned owl, golden eagle, Cooper's hawk, mule deer, mountain lion, yellow-bellied marmot and bobcat.

From Ely, head north on US 93 for approximately 45 miles to State Route 489. Drive west on Route 489 for another nine miles. From here, a local road will take you in a northeasterly direction for 11 miles to Goshute Creek. There are a number of spur roads that lead you off the local route as they head into the surrounding canyons. Recreation is excellent here year-round.

USGS topographic maps: Cherry Creek Station, Goshute Creek

For more information: Contact the BLM Ely District Office, 702 North Industrial Way, Box 33500, Ely, NV 89408; (702) 289-4865.

BLUE MASS SCENIC AREA

See letter X on map page 322

camping, hiking

The mountains here are not spectacular, but they are scenic. Blue Mass Creek flows through a winding canyon and can be easily accessed by an unimproved road running through the canyon. Hoodoo rocks weathered into all sorts of interesting shapes are the most memorable feature of this area, and they provide an interesting foreground to the backdrop of pinyon pine and aspen that dot the slopes. Drive 36 miles north of Ely on US 93. Approximately one-half mile beyond milepost 92, there is a Pony Express historical stop—turn right off the Highway here. Set your odometer to zero. Follow the excellent graded road for eleven miles to a junction marked by BLM signs. Fork right onto the road toward Tippett. Stay on the route through a number of junctions, heading towards Tippett at each junction. At mile 32.1, just past the abandoned ranch of Tippett, turn right toward Antelope Valley and into the Kern Mountains. At mile 46.8 head right onto the road leading into Blue Mass Canyon—a narrow and somewhat rough route, but easily navigable by two-wheel-drive vehicles if you drive cautiously. At mile 50.3 you will arrive at the heart of the scenic rock formations. Park and enjoy the area.

USGS topographic maps: Tippett, Tippett Canyon, Blue Mass Canyon, Grass Valley Wash, Skinner Canyon

BLM surface map: Kern Mountains

For more information: Contact the BLM Ely District Office, 702 North Industrial Way, Box 33500, Ely, NV 89408; (702) 289-4865.

CLAN ALPINE MOUNTAINS

See letter Y on map page 322

backpacking, camping, cross-country skiing, fishing, hiking, horseback riding, snowshoeing, wildlife observation

Tired of backcountry crowds muddling your hiking pleasure? Then head for the 196,000 roadless acres of the Clan Alpine Mountains. The BLM has recommended that 68,458 acres of this vast tract be designated as wilderness. With a high point of 9,966 feet at Mount Augusta, this canyon-dissected range towers nearly 6,500 feet above Dixie Valley to the west. The Clan Alpine Mountains are highly scenic, with a number of canyons sporting perennial streams and springs. Rock formations are colorful and abundant. Views from the ridge tops extend to the Sierra crest—100 miles westward. Aspen line several of the canyons, and mountain mahogany (rare in this part of Nevada) and pinon/juniper forests dot the slopes. The wildlife here includes the sage grouse, golden eagle, prairie falcon, mule deer and the mountain lion. Trout have been introduced here, but don't hold your breath waiting for them to bite—the fish remain scarce. Wild horses, majestic to watch, roam the mountain ranges. Still, the challenge of casting a line in a fishable stream—a rarity in this part of Nevada—is worth the added ounces of packing a fly rod along. Unfortunately, the lack of human presence and relative solitude may be interrupted periodically, as the Navy is in the process of increasing air operations over and around a number of Wilderness Study Areas—including the Clan Alpines. The Navy estimates that it may generate as many as three sonic booms a day. Fortunately, these audible intrusions are brief, although most annoying!

Activity Highlights: Backpacking and cross-country skiing

There are no trails within the Clan Alpines, but for the adventurous backpacker, this shouldn't pose a problem. Although some of the lower canyons are choked with vegetation, abundant game trails offer relatively easy passage to the upper ridgelines. The Clan Alpine's main ridge line is over 30 miles long. Near Mount Augusta, there are approximately eight miles of ridgeline high enough to catch enough snow during the winter months to provide for excellent backcountry ski-touring and snowshoeing opportunities. Although water is available in many of the canyons, there is no guarantee of its presence so carry all that you will need (one gallon per person per day). Game trails and old, unmaintained roads make good foot and horse routes.

Location: Due east of Reno and north of US 50 along Highway 121. From Reno, head east on Interstate 80, bearing right at Fernley on US 50. Follow US 50 approximately 50 miles to Route 121; turn left (north) on Route 121. Follow Route 121 north to the Dixie Valley turnoff, go right, then on into to Dixie Valley, just south of Humboldt Salt Marsh. There are a number of roads that branch off State Route 121 near milepost 24 that lead into the Clan Alpine Range. Services are few and far between—top off the tanks at every opportunity. Access from the east is also possible, call the BLM for directions.

Camping: Camping is allowed anywhere, but the lack of guaranteed potable water means you should carry all that you need—one gallon per person per day. The BLM advises that even with all the recent snow and rains, Nevada is still officially in a drought—running water is not guaranteed. Several unimproved roads in Deep Canyon, Horse Creek, Cow Canyon (on the west side) and Bench Creek, Cherry Creek and War Canyon (on the east side) provide vehicle access into the range and are suitable areas to set up a base-camp for day-hiking enjoyment.

Season: This area is available for year-round use. Access to winter recreation sites is difficult at best, and requires a four-wheel-drive vehicle. Inquire at the BLM office for updated access information. Summer months can be uncomfortably hot in the lower elevations, but should be tolerable once above 7,000 feet.

Permits: No permits are necessary.

USGS topographic maps: Wonder Mountain, Mount Augusta, Byers Creek, Shoshone Meadows, Cow Canyon, Clan Alpine Ranch, Tungsten Mountain, Camp Creek Canyon

For more information: Contact the BLM Carson City District, 1535 Hot Springs Road, Suite 300, Carson City, NV 89706; (702) 885-6000.

DESATOYA MOUNTAINS

See letter Z on map page 322

backpacking, camping, cross-country skiing, hiking, horseback riding, wildlife observation

This is an extremely scenic range with outstanding windswept views to the east of the Toiyabe Range, to the northwest of the Clan Alpine Range, and on clear days to the far west of the Sierra Nevada. Standing tall above the surrounding desert with a high point of 9,973 feet at Desatoya Peak, the range is sharply dissected by canyons—many of them narrow, rocky and featuring perennial streams. Big Den Canyon is the most noteworthy, well known for its 30-foot waterfall and colorful rock spires. Aspen, willow and wild rose line many of the canyon bottoms. Pinyon pine and juniper dot the slopes at the lower elevations. The wildflowers are super during the spring. According to the BLM, this is one of the best mountain ranges in northwestern Nevada for adventuring because of the scenery, accessibility and availability of water.

Activity Highlights: Hiking and backpacking

There are no formal hiking trails here. Follow the ridgeline or seek out game trails along the canyons that drop down from the ridge. Desatoya Peak, at 9,973 feet, lies north of the Carroll Summit Pass access point. Follow the ridgeline to get there.

Activity Highlight: Cross-country ski touring

Ski touring is quite good along the ridgeline above 7,500 feet, from December to March. Access can be challenging in the winter. Be prepared for very strong winds. Avalanche safety and rescue skills are a must for venturing into the backcountry.

Location: Roughly 112 miles east of Reno at Eastgate on Highway 722. From Reno, head east on Interstate 80. Turn right (south) on US 50 at Fernley towards Fallon. Follow US 50 to its intersection with State Highway 722 to Eastgate. Access to the Desatoya Mountains is possible from various points off Highway 722, which cuts the range into roughly equal parts, north and south. The best access to this area is at the Carroll Summit pass, elevation 7,452 feet.

Camping: Camping is permitted anywhere within this area.

Season: This area is available for year-round use. Access to winter recreation sites is difficult at best and requires a four-wheel-drive vehicle. Inquire at the BLM office for updated access information. Summer months can be uncomfortably hot in the lower elevations, but should be tolerable once above 7,000 feet.

USGS topographic maps: Buffalo Summit, Desatoya Peak, Carroll Summit, Cold Springs, Basque Summit

For more information: Contact the BLM Carson City District, 1535 Hot Springs Road, Suite 300, Carson City, NV 89706; (702) 885-6000.

HICKISON PETROGLYPH

See letter AA on map page 322

archaeological site, camping, hiking

The BLM maintains a campground here, which serves as a good base from which to take day hikes into the surrounding open country as well as enjoy historic examples of Native American petroglyphs. There is a six-tenths-of-a-mile interpretive walking trail around the petroglyphs. An interpretive brochure is available on site. This area is located 24 miles east of the town of Austin on US 50, just east of Hickison Summit. Look for the signed entrance road on the north side. The campground is dry (although the BLM plans to develop potable water here; call to find out if it has been done), so you will need to bring in all the water for your stay. The campground has twenty camping sites available for tents or RVs, although there are no hookups or a dump station available on site. Restrooms are wheelchair accessible. The nearest town for supplies is Austin. Spring, summer and fall are good times to visit.

USGS topographic maps: Hickison Summit, Cape Horn

For more information: Contact the BLM Battle Mountain District, P.O. Box 1420, Battle Mountain, NV 89820; (702) 635-4000.

ANTELOPE RANGE

See letter BB on map page 322

backpacking, camping, hiking, horseback riding

If you are looking for wilderness with untrammeled and pristine meadows, dense aspen groves, perennial streams and abundant wildlife, this is it. You can hike for miles without seeing any sign of human intrusion. Ninemile Peak sits as ruler of the range at 10,014 feet. You can expect snow in the higher elevations during the winter months. It is appropriate that the BLM has recommended this region for Wilderness Designation. From the town of Eureka, head west on US 50 for approximately 16 miles. Turn south on secondary State Route 82 and drive for approximately 23 miles. Then head east for about five miles on a local road to the northern boundary of the area and an intersection with another local road forming the western boundary.

USGS topographic maps: Segura Ranch, Fish Springs Northeast, Snowball Ranch, Ninemile Peak, Cockalorum Spring

BLM surface map: Summit Mountain

For more information: Contact the BLM Battle Mountain District, P.O. Box 1420, Battle Mountain, NV 89820; (702) 635-4000.

WALKER LAKE

See letter CC on map page 322

boating, camping, canoeing, fishing, hiking

Walker Lake is located southeast of Reno and just north of Hawthorne alongside US 95. It is a very scenic destination for the entire family at any time of the year, but summer here redefines the word hot. Regal Mount Grant towers above the lake to the southwest at 11,239 feet. Hiking in the wooded canyons all around the area is very pleasant. The BLM maintains one campground, Sportsman's Beach. This does not preclude you from setting up an informal camp elsewhere around the lake, however. Miles of sandy beaches make the lake a great recreational destination.

USGS topographic maps: Reese River Canyon, Gillis Canyon, Copper Canyon, Walker Lake, Mount Grant, Hawthorne West

For more information: Contact the BLM Carson City District, 1535 Hot Springs Road, Suite 300, Carson City, NV 89706; (702) 885-7800.

RAILROAD VALLEY WILDLIFE MANAGEMENT AREA

See letter DD on map page 322

fishing, wildlife observation

This area can be accessed via US 6 northeast of Tonopah, about halfway to Ely. There are four separate areas that provide suitable habitats for migratory and nesting waterfowl, non-game birds, mammals and fish. You cannot see the site from the highway, so it is somewhat of a surprise to head off on the dirt road and suddenly come upon a wetland full of tall reeds. March through June and early fall are the best times to visit. A four-wheel-drive vehicle is recommended for the safest access.

USGS topographic maps: Blue Eagle Springs Southwest, Blue Eagle Springs, Blue Eagle Springs Northeast, Meteorite Crater

For more information: Contact the BLM Battle Mountain District, P.O. Box 1420, Battle Mountain, NV 89820; (702) 635-4000.

KAWICH RANGE

See letter EE on map page 322

backpacking, camping, hiking

Although this area is near the Bombing and Gunnery Range, it is a nice respite for those seeking solitude among the mountains. The Kawich Range offers high-basin lakes and canyon streams. Longstreet's Canyon is noteworthy for its diverse vegetation. Trails do exist but they are indistinct and unmarked. Kawich Peak is the high point, sitting at 9,404 feet. Located south of the town of Warm Springs and US 6, Kawich Range is accessed by local and unimproved roads. A four-wheel-drive or high-clearance vehicle is recommended. It's a good destination any time of year.

USGS topographic maps: Kawich Peak, Bellehelen, Stinking Spring, Kawich Peak Northeast

For more information: Contact the BLM Battle Mountain District, Tonopah Resource Area, P.O. Box 911, Tonopah, NV 89049; (702) 482-7800.

LUNAR CRATER VOLCANIC FIELD

See letter FF on map page 322

camping, hiking, wildlife observation

This is a very large, colorful region, especially in years of good water, because the water helps to create a virtual carpet of wildflowers in some areas. The region is considered so scenic that the BLM has nominated it for consideration as a future Back Country Byway. Brochures are available at the Battle Mountain BLM office. NASA considered this area to be so lunar-like that early astronauts visited here.

Lunar Crater, a National Natural Landmark, measuring 430 feet deep and 3,800 feet in diameter, is located approximately seven miles south of US 6. The region can be accessed from US 6, and lies approximately 30 miles northeast of Warm Springs, just past Sandy Summit. You can visit any time of year, but summers get toasty.

USGS topographic map: Lunar Crater

For more information: Contact the BLM Battle Mountain District, Tonopah Resource Area, P.O. Box 911, Tonopah, NV 89049; (702) 482-7800.

GRANT RANGE

See letter GG on map page 322

camping, backpacking, hiking, horseback riding

Located south of the town of Currant on US 6, the Grant Range sits just east of the unpaved road connecting Currant and Nyala. It also features high mountains cut with deep and narrow canyons that wind through the region. You will find white fir and bristlecone pine on Blue Eagle Mountain. It is a good destination at any time of year.

USGS topographic maps: Blue Eagle Mountain, Heath Canyon, Currant

For more information: Contact the BLM Battle Mountain District, P.O. Box 1420, Battle Mountain, NV 89820; (702) 635-4000.

SOUTH EGAN RANGE

See letter HH on map page 322

backpacking, camping, hiking, horseback riding, rock climbing, spelunking

The South Egan Range is located south of Ely and east of Route 318, extending from the town of Lund south for approximately 35 miles. Although there is an abundance of streams and springs, there is also an abundance of cattle—so you must treat all the water thoroughly before drinking. This limestone mountain range is rugged and beautiful with dense groves of aspen, white fir, ponderosa pine and even bristlecone pine. Angel Cave and other caves in the area attract many spelunkers. The cliffs are quite climbable and attract a number of climbers every year. Visit in spring, summer or fall.

USGS topographic maps: Sawmill Canyon, Brown Knoll, Haggerty Spring, Parker Station, Shingle Pass, Shingle Pass Southeast, Cave Valley Well

For more information: Contact the BLM Ely District Office, 702 North Industrial Way, Box 33500, Ely, NV 89408; (702) 289-4865.

MOUNT GRAFTON

See letter II on map page 322

backpacking, camping, fishing, hiking, horseback riding, wildlife observation

This is an outstanding scenic area whose centerpiece is Mount Grafton, at 10,993 feet. Much of the ridge in the immediate vicinity of Mount Grafton lies above 10,000 feet, creating wonderful opportunities for enjoying spectacular views. In addition to the subalpine vegetation at the peak, the surrounding rocky crags sport stands of white fir and bristlecone pine. Just north of the mountain, in the North Creek Scenic Area, is a steep canyon with crystal water flowing down its course. The perennial creek provides water (purify before drinking) and decent trout fishing. Patterson Pass, just east of US 93 on a local road, provides the best southern access to the mountain area. The pass lies approximately seven miles south (as the crow flies) of Mount Grafton. Spring, summer and fall are the times to visit.

USGS topographic maps: Mount Grafton, Parker Station, Bullwhack Summit, Cattle Camp Spring

For more information: Contact the BLM Ely District Office, 702 North Industrial Way, Box 33500, Ely, NV 89408; (702) 289-4865.

GLEASON CANYON & THE CHARCOAL KILNS

See letter JJ on map page 322

backpacking, camping, horseback riding, wildlife observation

This little-known area east of Panaca is accessible from Highway 319. Turn north on a graded dirt road at the Panaca Summit. The BLM has restored two large charcoal kilns that were used in the late 19th and early 20th centuries to produce charcoal that was used by the mining industry in Pioche. The canyon is just to the east of the kilns and may be accessed via a dirt road on the west or south sides. The narrow canyon has created an unusual microenvironment for ponderosa pine and aspen. The surrounding hills are pinyon-juniper. If you are lucky, you may catch a glimpse of a bobcat as it slinks away, deer bounding through the trees, or the graceful flight of an eagle overhead. Visit any time of year.

USGS topographic map: Panaca Summit

BLM surface map: Caliente

For more information: Contact the BLM Las Vegas District Office, 4765 Vegas Drive, Las Vegas, NV 89107; (702) 647-5000; or the BLM Caliente Resource Area, P.O. Box 237, US 93, Caliente, NV 89008; (702) 635-4000.

ELY ELK VIEWING AREA

See letter KK on map page 322

wildlife observation

Located in the Egan Resource Area, south of Ely along Highway 93, the Ely Elk Viewing Area provides visitors an excellent opportunity to observe up to several hundred elk. The elk in this area are very tolerant of visitors providing you stay in your vehicle and drive slowly along the area dirt roads. The elk are generally found on the east side of the highway. Peak viewing times are October and early November, before elk-hunting season begins in mid-November, and in early spring during March and April. Bald eagles winter in the area. Golden eagles, pronghorn antelope and mule deer may also be seen here.

USGS topographic maps: Comins Lake, Ward Charcoal Ovens, Connors Pass

For more information: Contact the BLM Egan Resource Area, 702 North Industrial Way, Box 33500, Ely, NV 89408; (702) 289-4865.

FORTIFICATION RANGE

See letter LL on map page 322

camping, hiking, wildlife observation

Although the range itself is not all that remarkable, one canyon, Cottonwood Canyon, is worth the visit alone. The canyon is remarkable, stunning and exceptional. I leave it to you to agree or disagree. The head of the Cottonwood Canyon forms a natural amphitheater of towering and jagged rock formations, colored white, pink and mauve. The range is located west of Highway 93 and south of Highway 50—

contact the BLM for specific directions.

USGS topographic maps: The Gouge Eye, Indian Spring Knolls

For more information: Contact the BLM Ely District Office, 702 North Industrial Way, Box 33500, Ely, NV 89408; (702) 289-4865.

NEVADA—MAP B

GABBS VALLEY RANGE

See letter MM on map page 324

backpacking, camping, hiking, horseback riding, wildlife observation

US 361 bisects this range, from just south of the town of Gabbs to just north of the town of Luning. The range is quite scenic, with two notable canyons: Lost Canyon and Red Rock Canyon. Both offer water and pleasant camping. Access to this area is via unmaintained roads that run east and west from US 361. Visit any time of year. Wildlife, though not abundant, includes mule deer, wild horse, bobcat and golden eagle.

USGS topographic maps: Mount Ferguson, Gabbs Mountain, Luning, Winwan Flat

For more information: Contact the BLM Carson City District, 1535 Hot Springs Road, Suite 300, Carson City, NV 89706; (702) 885-7800.

MOREY PEAK

See letter NN on map page 324

camping, hiking

Morey Peak, at 10,246 feet, sits as the monarch of this tiny range. Sixmile Canyon extends to the south and features a number of springs and nice meadow vegetation. The region is quite scenic and untrammeled by man. The best access is via local roads that extend north from US 6, approximately 20 miles northeast of the town of Warm Springs and just south of Sandy Summit. A four-wheel-drive or high-clearance vehicle is recommended for access. For a detailed description, refer to John Hart's book, listed below. Visit in spring, summer or fall.

USGS topographic maps: Morey Peak, Hobble Canyon, Moores Station, Moores Station Southwest

Resources: *Hiking the Great Basin*, by John Hart, published by Sierra Club Books, San Francisco, CA.

For more information: Contact the BLM Battle Mountain District, Tonopah Resource Area, P.O. Box 911, Tonopah, NV 89049; (702) 482-7800.

FISH LAKE VALLEY

See letter OO on map page 324

wildlife observation

For birdwatching enthusiasts, Fish Lake Valley is a very exciting area to visit during the spring migration (May to early June) and fall migration (mid-September through late October). This is one area where "off-course" migratory birds may be seen—if you are lucky or persistent. Most strays are warblers, especially Eastern wood warblers. Other recorded sightings include the Philadelphia vireo, brown thrasher, rose-breasted grosbeak, little blue heron and upland sandpiper. The usual western migrants can be observed here in large numbers. Four-wheel-drive or high-clearance vehicles are required for access. From Tonopah, drive west on Highway 6/95 to Coaldale where the highways split. Continue driving west on Highway 6 for six miles, then turn left onto a dirt road signed for the town of Dyer and Fish Lake Valley and continue into the valley.

USGS topographic maps: Dyer, Chiatovica Ranch

For more information: Contact the BLM Battle Mountain District, Tonopah Resource Area, P.O. Box 911, Tonopah, NV 89049; (702) 482-7800.

QUEER MOUNTAINS

See letter PP on map page 324

backpacking, camping, hiking, horseback riding

This area has no outstanding features, but it makes a good stopping-off point and place to unroll your sleeping bag if you are headed somewhere else. The mountains in this range are rugged and will be of interest to geologists (amateur and otherwise) for their many geological features. Since it is also adjacent to Death Valley National Park, it is a good area to romp around if you need some time to stretch your legs. There is no water to be found; bring all that you will need. Route 267 bisects this range. A four-wheel-drive or high-clearance vehicle is required to access this area.

USGS topographic maps: Bonnie Claire Lake, Bonnie Claire, Bonnie Claire Southwest, Bonnie Claire Southeast, Gold Mountain

For more information: Contact the BLM Battle Mountain District, Tonopah Resource Area, P.O. Box 911, Tonopah, NV 89049; (702) 482-7800.

SOUTH REVEILLE RANGE
See letter QQ on map page 324

backpacking, camping, hiking, horseback riding, wildlife observation
The South Reveille Range lies west of Highway 375 and south of Warm Springs. The proximity to the Bombing and Gunnery Range does not significantly detract from the scenery, which includes steep-sided mountains and narrow canyons. The wildlife is abundant. A four-wheel-drive or high-clearance vehicle is required to access the area. Winter, spring and fall are good times to visit, but summer is too hot.

USGS topographic maps: Reveille Peak, Reveille Peak Southeast, Reveille Peak Northwest, Freds Well, Reveille Southeast

For more information: Contact the BLM Battle Mountain District, Tonopah Resource Area, P.O. Box 911, Tonopah, NV 89049; (702) 482-7800.

SOUTH PAHROC RANGE
See letter RR on map page 324

backpacking, camping, hiking, horseback riding
Canyons, washes, cliffs and interesting boulder fields are the main fare here. Though not exceedingly spectacular, the area is scenic enough to warrant a visit. Access is quite easy via local roads. US 93, west of Caliente, passes right over Pahroc Summit and through the middle of the range. Winter, spring and fall are good times to visit, but summer is too hot.

USGS topographic maps: Hiko Southeast, Alamo Northeast

For more information: Contact the BLM Las Vegas District Office, 4765 Vegas Drive, Las Vegas, NV 89107; (702) 647-5000.

Rainbow Canyon

See letter SS on map page 324

backpacking, camping, horseback riding, wildlife observation

This is a perfect destination for the really adventurous soul. Head into a canyon region that extends nearly 20 miles south from the town of Caliente. While the route into the canyon is paved for the first miles, there are numerous opportunities to explore by four-wheel drive or foot the many side canyons that twist and snake off from the main canyon. Tall cottonwood trees line the perennial stream that carves its way along the canyon floor and the beaver ponds along the way are evidence that beaver still call the canyon home. Recommended sidetrips are to Ella Mountain or Chokecherry Mountain. Once the paved route ends, the really hardy with a good vehicle will want to continue on down the canyon for approximately 30 miles on rough dirt roads toward Glendale.

USGS topographic maps: Farrier, Rox Northeast, Vigo, Vigo Northeast, Elgin, Elgin Northeast, Caliente, Carp, Lyman Crossing, Leith

BLM surface maps: Caliente, Clover Mountains

For more information: Contact the BLM Las Vegas District Office, 4765 Vegas Drive, Las Vegas, NV 89107; (702) 647-5000.

Condor Canyon

See letter TT on map page 324

backpacking, hiking, horseback riding, mountain biking, wildlife observation

The route through this canyon follows an old railroad line that once ran from Caliente to Pioche through Condor Canyon and Bullionville. The canyon is deep and narrow with a perennial stream running through it and at certain points the old trestles from the railroad line offer the only way to cross to the other side. At one point, a waterfall plunges into an inviting and deep pool suitable for cooling off on a hot afternoon. Remains of old mining operations are still visible within the canyon. Condor Canyon is located north of Panaca and southeast of Pioche—the BLM requests that you call for specific access information before heading out. It's a good destination any time of year.

USGS topographic maps: Panaca, Condor Canyon, Indian Cove, Caliente, Rose Valley, Pioche

BLM surface map: Caliente

For more information: Contact the BLM Las Vegas District Office, 4765 Vegas Drive, Las Vegas, NV 89107; (702) 647-5000; or the BLM Caliente Resource Area, P.O. Box 237, US 93, Caliente, NV 89008; (702) 726-8100.

PARSNIP PEAK

See letter UU on map page 324

backpacking, camping, hiking, horseback riding, wildlife observation

This area's chief attraction is its remoteness, which virtually guarantees solitude and isolation. There are a number of ridges in the area, all cut by deep canyons. Ponderosa pine and aspen dot the slopes, and springs may be found within this region. Parsnip Peak, the area's namesake, sits at a moderate 8,942 feet, but the unique and colorful volcanic ash rock formations that surround the peak more than make up for its lack of altitude. It is located south of Great Basin National Park and northeast of the town Pioche and US 93. Eagle Valley Road provides distant access, but to get into the range you have to hoof it. It will take you two to three hours of hard hiking just to get to the area.

USGS topographic maps: Parsnip Peak, Buckwash Well, Eagle Valley Reservoir, Pierson Summit

For more information: Contact the BLM Ely District Office, 702 North Industrial Way, Box 33500, Ely, NV 89408; (702) 289-4865.

PINE CANYON RESERVOIR

See letter VV on map page 324

camping, horseback riding, picnicking, wildlife observation

Located at the foothills of the scenic Clover Mountains, this reservoir was constructed by the Army Corps of Engineers as a flood control mechanism, although it sits practically empty much of the time. There is no developed water and, unlike at Mathews Canyon, there are few springs—pack along all the water you will need! Covered picnic tables (for both individual and group use), fire rings, trash receptacles, and permanent outhouses are available. Located approximately 15 miles southeast of Caliente. Take the Clover Canyon Road east out of Caliente for 3.5 miles to the Barnes Canyon Railroad Crossing. From here, head southeast (right) on Barnes Canyon Road for approximately 10 miles to "Five Points"—a very confusing intersection where five roads converge. Watch carefully for the signs leading to Pine Canyon Reservoir and follow them so you won't get led astray on the short three-mile jaunt to Pine Canyon. The dirt roads in the area are suitable for high-clearance vehicles from late spring through early fall—rains can turn the route into a muddy nightmare.

USGS topographic map: Fife Mountain

BLM surface maps: Nevada/Utah: Clover Mountains

For more information: Contact the BLM Caliente Resource Area, P.O. Box 237, US 93, Caliente, NV 89008; (702) 726-8100.

Clover Mountains

See letter WW on map page 324

backpacking, camping, hiking, horseback riding, wildlife observation

This is a rugged land of deep, serpentine canyons, jagged peaks, steep cliffs, colorful rocks and abundant water. Cattle roam the area, so you will have to be careful selecting and treating drinking water. Located roughly 100 miles northeast of Las Vegas, this area can be accessed by Route 317 south of Caliente and US 93. The road between Elgin and Carp is dirt and is frequently washed out. Four-wheel-drive vehicles are highly recommended for any travel in this region. Check with BLM before heading out to ascertain road conditions. Visit any time of year.

USGS topographic maps: Ella Mountain, Fife Mountain, Bunker Peak, Jacks Mountain, Garden Springs, Leith

For more information: Contact the BLM Las Vegas District Office, 4765 Vegas Drive, Las Vegas, NV 89107; (702) 647-5000.

Mathews Canyon Reservoir

See letter XX on map page 324

camping, horseback riding, picnicking, wildlife observation

The reservoir is located at the foothills of the scenic Clover Mountains, and although it was constructed by the Army Corps of

Engineers as a flood control mechanism, it usually sits empty. Still, despite the fact that there is no developed water available, numerous springs dot the terrain. Covered picnic tables (individual and group use), fire rings, trash receptacles and permanent outhouses are available. The reservoir is located approximately 20 miles southeast of Caliente. Take US 93 north for five miles to Beaver Dam Road. Beaver Dam is a dirt road that is suitable for most vehicles from late spring through early fall—heavy rains may make passage tenuous at best however. Drive southeast on Beaver Dam for approximately 18 miles to the historic ranching settlement of Barclay. From here look for the Mathews Canyon Reservoir signs and follow them for an additional 2.5 miles to the picnic area.

USGS topographic maps: Acoma, Bunker Peak

BLM surface maps: Nevada/Utah: Clover Mountains

For more information: Contact the BLM Caliente Resource Area, P.O. Box 237, US 93, Caliente, NV 89008; (702) 726-8100.

Ash Springs

See letter YY on map page 324

wildlife observation

Ash Springs, a significant, crystal-clear, spring-fed pool is located just east of Route 93 in the town of Ash Springs. The southern end of the pool nearest the highway is privately owned. The source and the back side of the pool are public. Besides being a good area for observing songbirds, the water is a protected habitat for the endangered White River spring fish. The site has a picnic table and a barbecue grill, and there is a developed bathing pool where visitors may soak year-round in warm water.

USGS topographic map: Ash Springs

BLM surface map: Pahranagat Range

For more information: Contact the BLM Caliente Resource Area, P.O. Box 237, US 93, Caliente, NV 89008; (702) 726-8100.

MEADOW VALLEY RANGE AND MORMON MOUNTAINS

See letter ZZ on map page 324

backpacking, camping, hiking, horseback riding, spelunking

Driving south from Caliente and US 93 on Route 317 will take you right into the middle of the Meadow Valley Range. To the south and east lie the Mormon Mountains, which protect several limestone caverns that are of interest to spelunkers. The area is rugged and predominantly dry, but strangely attractive because of its vastness. It is interesting to note that the Mormon Mountains derive their name from the old Spanish Trail/Mormon Road that passed through here. Spring and fall are the times to visit; summer is too hot and dry.

USGS topographic maps: Vigo Northwest, Vigo Northeast, Sunflower Mountain, Vigo, Carp, Toquop Gap, Wildcat Wash Northeast, Rox, Rox Northeast, Moapa Peak Northwest, Davidson Peak

For more information: Contact the BLM Las Vegas District Office, 4765 Vegas Drive, Las Vegas, NV 89107; (702) 647-5000.

ARROW CANYON

See letter AAA on map page 324

hiking, rock climbing, wildlife observation

Arrow Canyon is a remarkable canyon that is cut 300 feet deep with sheer cliffs running on both sides for several miles. The main part of the canyon is less than 50 feet wide and is dotted with petroglyphs. A rock dam, constructed by the Civilian Conservation Corps in the early part of this century, blocks vehicular travel through part of the canyon. Access is possible from Moapa Valley on an old jeep road which extends almost halfway up the canyon. The final mile or so of canyon travel can only be made on foot. Any time of year is good to visit.

USGS topographic maps: Arrow Canyon, Arrow Canyon NE, Arrow Canyon NW, Arrow Canyon SE

BLM surface map: Lake Mead

For more information: Contact the BLM Las Vegas District Office, 4765 Vegas Drive, Las Vegas, NV 89107; (702) 647-5000.

VIRGIN PEAK

See letter BBB on map page 324

backpacking, camping, horseback riding, mountain biking, wildlife observation

The Virgin Mountains and Virgin Peak are located a few miles south of Mesquite, Nevada. The remnant forest that crowns the peak has been established as a BLM Research Natural Area. There are numerous hiking trails and four-wheel-drive roads on the north side of the mountain. The easiest access to the 8,087-foot-high Virgin Peak is up Cabin Canyon or Nickel Creek Canyon. Small streams course through these canyons virtually year-round. A well-maintained dirt road begins in Mesquite and takes you up the *bajada* to the foot of the mountain. The remainder of the trip is steep and rocky. Many of the trails on the mountain are only accessible by mountain bike or on foot. In the upper reaches of Cabin Canyon, you will discover a number of historic cabins and other remnants of mining in the early part of the 20th century. Look and photograph but do not touch and never ever collect are the rules to follow in this historically sensitive area. For those few rugged enough to make the trek to the summit, you will be rewarded with an outstanding view of southern Nevada, northern Arizona, the Grand Wash Cliffs, Lake Mead and the mouth of the Grand Canyon. Other nearby attractions are the Gold Butte Back Country Byway (see below), Devil's Throat (see page 366), Cedar Basin, Lake Mead and the north rim of the Grand Canyon.

USGS topographic maps: Overton Northeast, Overton Southeast, Riverside, Hen Spring, Whitney Pocket, Virgin Peak, Devil's Throat, St. Thomas Gap

BLM surface maps: Lake Mead, Las Vegas

For more information: Contact the BLM Las Vegas District Office, 4765 Vegas Drive, Las Vegas, NV 89107; (702) 647-5000.

GOLD BUTTE BACK COUNTRY BYWAY

See letter CCC on map page 324

auto touring, backpacking, camping, horseback riding, mountain biking, wildlife observation

The Gold Butte Back Country Byway is one of several outstanding opportunities to explore the back roads of Nevada within the surrounding region. Located east of Las Vegas, on the east side of Lake Mead National Recreation Area, the byway begins near Mesquite, Nevada and loops through a Joshua tree forest and some of the most scenic and wild parts of the Mojave Desert. There are numerous possibilities for sidetrips including Devil's Throat (see page 366 in this chapter), Devil's Cove on Lake Mead, Virgin Peak (see page 362 in this chapter) and other highly scenic areas adjacent to the byway. The first portion of the byway, to Whitney Pockets, is paved, while the remainder of the byway is well-graded dirt road all the way to the historic Gold Butte site. A short portion of the trail is recommended for four-wheel-drive vehicles only.

USGS topographic maps: Flat Top Mesa, Riverside, Mesquite, Hen Spring, Whitney Pockets, Virgin Peak, Devil's Throat, St. Thomas Gap, Gold Butte, Azure Ridge, Jumbo Peak

BLM surface map: Overton, Lake Mead

For more information: Contact the BLM Las Vegas District Office, 4765 Vegas Drive, Las Vegas, NV 89107; (702) 647-5000.

BITTER SPRINGS TRAIL BACK COUNTRY BYWAY

See letter DDD on map page 324

camping, mountain biking, hiking, backpacking, horseback riding, wildlife observation, rock climbing

The Bitter Springs Byway is an approximately 36-mile route of discovery for a unique natural area and is suitable for travel by high-clearance, four-wheel-drive vehicles, dirt bikes, off-highway vehicles, mountain bikes, horses and foot traffic. Visitors will marvel at the dramatic contrast of colors between the bright red sandstone and the dark gray limestone, which formed during the Paleozoic (225 million years ago) and Mesozoic (26 million years ago) eras. There is ample opportunity to explore rock shelters and discover the art of prehistoric people preserved in petroglyphs, pottery, tools and the remains of their hunting weapons. (Look but don't touch and never ever collect are the rules when exploring this region.) This region is also well recognized for its healthy populations of bighorn sheep and wild horses. You'll also find colorful displays of plant life, such as the luster of the creosote bush, the bright pink spines of the barrel cactus, the golden yellows and deep reds of the hedgehog cactus and the teddy-bear-fuzzy appearance (as long as you don't touch) of the cholla cactus.

Bitter Springs Back Country Byway may be reached to traveling north from Las Vegas approximately 45 miles on Interstate 15. Exit at the Valley of Fire turnoff. Turn right and travel approximately 3.5 miles east to the entrance of the Bitter Springs Trailhead. Alternately, you can access the byway from North Shore Road in the Lake Mead National Recreation Area. Travel north on North Shore Road toward Echo Bay. Exit to your left at Echo Wash just before crossing the bridge. Visit any time of year.

USGS topographic maps: Piute Point, Muddy Peak, Bitter Spring, Echo Bay, Valley of Fire

BLM surface map: Lake Mead

For more information: Contact the BLM Las Vegas District Office, 4765 Vegas Drive, Las Vegas, NV 89107; (702) 647-5000.

RED ROCK CANYON
NATIONAL CONSERVATION AREA
See letter EEE on map page 324

backpacking, camping, hiking, horseback riding, mountain biking, rock climbing

The predominant geological feature in Red Rock Canyon, and a feature that attracts rock climbers from all over, is a spectacular 3,000-foot sandstone escarpment extending for much of the region's length. Named for the bright red colors of the stone, this canyon region contains over 40 springs, as well as many natural catch basins known as tanks. It is this presence of water, more prevalent than anywhere in the surrounding desert region, that supports a rich and concentrated plant and animal population. Joshua trees are predominant on the canyon floor. As the elevation rises, pinyon pine and juniper trees take over.

Activity Highlight: Hiking
There are many trails suitable for day hiking and a number of longer routes that are good choices for overnight backpacking. The BLM publishes a brochure, "Red Rock Canyon National Conservation Area Hiking," which lists and briefly describes 15 routes.

Activity Highlight: Mountain biking
There are a number of suitable mountain-bike routes that provide

good views of the surrounding terrain. The most notable trail is the Scenic Loop Ride, suggested by the BLM. You will share these roads with other vehicles, so watch your speed and control.

Activity Highlight: Wildlife observation

Wild horses and burros are popular attractions in the canyon—these were brought to the Great Basin area by early explorers. Over 100 species of birds have been identified in the area. The cooler canyons of Pine Creek and First Creek echo with the calls of canyon wrens. Keep an eye out for the occasional roadrunner streaking across the trails and roads. The desert tortoise, native to this area and listed as a threatened species, is most commonly seen after a summer rain or during cool spring days. The tortoise hibernates from October to March. Desert bighorn can be seen in the White Rock Spring area and the Willow Spring picnic area. Mating season occurs in late summer, with the reverberations of vigorous head-butting echoing up the canyon walls.

Location: Approximately 15 miles west of Las Vegas. From Las Vegas, head west on Route 159 (West Charleston Boulevard) to the visitor center. From Interstate 15, head west on Route 160, and then west again on State Route 159.

Camping: Primitive camping is allowed, but only in certain areas. You must register for overnight camping. Check with the BLM.

Season: The best season for this area is the spring. Summers can be uncomfortably hot.

Permits: No permits are necessary for day use. Registration is required for overnight use.

USGS topographic maps: La Madre Mountain, La Madre Spring, Blue Diamond

BLM surface map: Las Vegas

Resources:
• *The Hiker's Guide to Nevada,* by Bruce Grubbs, published by Falcon Press, P.O. Box 1718, Helena, MT 59624; (800) 582-2665.

For more information: Contact the BLM Red Rock Canyon National Conservation Area, 4765 Vegas Drive, Las Vegas, NV 89107; (702) 647-5000.

MUDDY MOUNTAINS

See letter FFF on map page 324

backpacking, camping, hiking, rockhounding, wildlife observation

Lying along the edge of Lake Mead National Recreation Area and just south of Valley of Fire State Park, the Muddy Mountains offer super hiking opportunities among colorful and at times, jagged sandstone formations. Opportunities to observe bighorn sheep are excellent here. The best time to visit is between September and May. Summer is too darn hot! The following are ideal destinations for hiking in the area: Hidden Valley, Color Rock Quarry, Wild Sheep Valley, Muddy Peak and Anniversary Narrows. Rock hounders will enjoy hunting for jasper, agate, amethyst and opal. The area is southeast of Interstate 15, south of Valley of Fire State Park. Numerous informal roads provide access—contact the BLM for specific directions.

USGS topographic maps: Dry Lake Southeast, Muddy Peak, Bitter Spring, Government Wash, Caliente Bay

For more information: Contact the BLM Las Vegas District Office, 4765 Vegas Drive, Las Vegas, NV 89107; (702) 647-5000.

DEVIL'S THROAT

See letter GGG on map page 324

backcountry touring, four-wheel-drive exploration, mountain biking

More than 90 feet across and currently almost 140 feet deep, Devil's Throat is a rare sink hole alongside the Gold Butte Back Country Byway—and it continues to grow deeper and deeper. It is not known what is causing the sink hole, although it has been hypothesized that there may be a larger cavity underground or water is slowly dissolving the gypsum underneath. The byway begins at the town of Riverside, Nevada. Simply follow the well-marked signs to the byway and Devil's Throat. The area is well worth setting up a tent nearby and spending several days exploring. Visit any time of year.

USGS topographic map: Devil's Throat

BLM surface maps: Overton, Lake Mead

For more information: Contact the BLM Las Vegas District Office, 4765 Vegas Drive, Las Vegas, NV 89107; (702) 647-5000.

ANNIVERSARY NARROWS

See letter HHH on map page 324

backpacking, hiking, rockhounding, wildlife observation

Accessed from the North Shore Road in the Lake Mead National Recreation Area east of Las Vegas, Calville Wash has cut through multicolored sandstone to create a deep, narrow, twisting canyon called Anniversary Narrows. The canyon provides excellent access to the badlands formations to the north and to Muddy Peak. At the entrance to Anniversary Narrows are the remnants of the historic mining operations at the Anniversary Mine. The area is also a popular year-round destination among rock collectors because of the agate fields near the canyon.

USGS topographic maps: Nevada/Arizona: Calville Bay

BLM surface map: Lake Mead

For more information: Contact the BLM Las Vegas District Office, 4765 Vegas Drive, Las Vegas, NV 89107; (702) 647-5000.

BIG DUNE

See letter III on map page 324

camping, off-highway-vehicle use

Big Dune sits as a solitary dune system right in the middle of the Amargosa Desert—the dunes are approximately one-half mile wide and one mile long. The main dune towers nearly 350 feet high. Currently the BLM manages this area for unrestricted off-highway-vehicle use, which is a hoot if that is your interest. If you are seeking quiet and solitude, however, you would do best to look elsewhere. Big Dune is located approximately two hours northwest of Las Vegas on US 95 between Lathrop Wells and Beatty. Take the Armagosa Farms Road south from US 95 and turn west on a signed dirt road leading to the dunes. You can visit any time of year, but summers are hot.

USGS topographic map: Big Dune

For more information: Contact the BLM Las Vegas District Office, 4765 Vegas Drive, Las Vegas, NV 89107; (702) 647-5000.

COTTONWOOD CANYON

See letter JJJ on map page 324

horseback riding, mountain biking, wildlife observation

Cottonwood Valley is located directly at the south end of the Red Rock Canyon National Conservation Area and has become very popular with mountain bikers and equestrians for good reason—more than 30 miles of trails for horseback riders and mountain bikers already exist and the BLM is in the process of developing a wider trail network and management plan for the area. Access to the canyon and the trails is signed, just off of Highway 160.

USGS topographic maps: Mountain Pass, Potosi, Blue Diamond, Cottonwood Pass

BLM surface map: Las Vegas

For more information: Contact the BLM Red Rock Canyon National Conservation Area, 4765 Vegas Drive, Las Vegas, NV 89107; (702) 647-5000.

KEYHOLE CANYON

See letter KKK on map page 324

cultural site, rock climbing

Keyhole Canyon is a small recreation area to the south of Boulder City, Nevada and west of Nelson. The canyon is becoming popular as a year-round climbing destination because of the hard granite cliffs that are inviting to those with sticky soled shoes, chalk bags and climbing rope. Many fine examples of petroglyphs and pictographs may be viewed in the canyon as well. There are no facilities and the area is designated as day-use only. To get to Keyhole Canyon, travel south of Las Vegas on Highway 95 for five miles to Highway 165, turn left and then take the first powerline road south of Highway 165 on the road to Nelson.

USGS topographic map: Keyhole Canyon

BLM surface map: Boulder City

For more information: Contact the BLM Las Vegas District Office, 4765 Vegas Drive, Las Vegas, NV 89107; (702) 647-5000.

BLM CAMPGROUNDS

1. PINE FOREST RECREATION AREA—MAP A

Campsites, facilities: There is primitive camping at three sites within the recreation area: Blue Lakes, Onion Reservoir and Knott Creek Reservoir. Vault toilets are available. There is **no water**. No trash facilities are provided, so pack out all you bring in. There is a 14-day stay limit.

Fee: There is no fee.

Who to contact: Winnemucca District Office, 705 East Fourth Street, Winnemucca, NV 89445; (702) 623-1500.

Location: Drive approximately 75 miles northwest of Winnemucca on Highway 140 to the recreation area. The campgrounds are set at 7,900 feet.

Season: June to October.

2. WILSON RESERVOIR RECREATION AREA—MAP A

Campsites, facilities: There are 15 sites, all with picnic tables and fire rings. Water, pit toilets, an RV dump station and a boat ramp are available. RVs up to 30 feet are allowed. There is a 14-day stay limit.

Fee: There is a $3 fee per night. There is a $1 day-use/boat-launching fee. Pay on site.

Who to contact: Elko District Office, P.O. Box 831, 3900 East Idaho Street, Elko, NV 89803; (702) 753-0200.

Location: From Elko, drive north for 27 miles on Highway 225. Turn left onto Highway 226 and drive 40 miles, watching for Wilson Reservoir signs. The last 16 miles of the road may be impassable if wet. The campground is set at 5,300 feet.

Season: April to September.

3. NORTH WILDHORSE CAMPGROUND—MAP A

Campsites, facilities: There are 18 sites, all with picnic tables, fire rings and grills. Water and pit toilets are available. RVs up to 20 feet are allowed. There is a 14-day stay limit.

Fee: There is a $3 fee per night; pay on site.

Who to contact: Elko District Office, P.O. Box 831, 3900 East Idaho Street, Elko, NV 89803; (702) 753-0200.

Location: On the north shore of Wildhorse Reservoir. From Elko, drive 70 miles north on Highway 225 to the campground entrance. The campground is set at 6,200 feet.

Season: Memorial Day to November.

4. TABOR CREEK CAMPGROUND—MAP A

Campsites, facilities: There are 10 sites, all with picnic tables and fire rings. There is **no water**. No trash facilities are provided, so pack out all you bring in. There is a 14-day stay limit.

Fee: There is no fee.

Who to contact: Elko District Office, P.O. Box 831, 3900 East Idaho Street, Elko, NV 89803; (702) 753-0200.

Location: In the Snake Mountain foothills. From Wells, drive 12 miles north on US 93 to a gravel road and exit, driving 10 miles to the campground entrance. The road can become impassable when wet. The campground is set at 6,300 feet.

Season: May to November. Expect crowds during hunting season.

5. MILL CREEK RECREATION AREA—MAP A

Campsites, facilities: There are 10 sites (three are for tents only), all with picnic tables, fire rings and grills. Pit toilets are available. There is **no water**. There is a 14-day stay limit.

Fee: There is no fee.

Who to contact: Battle Mountain District Office, P.O. Box 1420, 50 Bastian Road, Battle Mountain, NV 89820; (702) 635-4000.

Location: From Battle Mountain, drive 23 miles south on Highway 305 to a signed gravel entrance road and turn left, driving four miles to the campground entrance. The campground is set at 4,500 feet.

Season: All year.

6. ZUNINO RESERVOIR CAMPGROUND—MAP A

Campsites, facilities: There are two tent-only sites, both with picnic tables and grills. Undesignated-site, primitive camping is allowed. Pit toilets are available. There is **no water**. There is a 14-day stay limit.

Fee: There is no fee.

Who to contact: Elko District Office, P.O. Box 831, 3900 East Idaho Street, Elko, NV 89803; (702) 753-0200.

Location: From Elko, drive east for seven miles on Highway 227. Turn right onto Highway 228 and drive 23 miles to the campground entrance. The campground is set at 5,600 feet.

Season: All year. The reservoir is dry from midsummer on.

7. GOSHUTE CREEK CAMPGROUND—MAP A

Campsites, facilities: There are two sites, both with picnic tables and fire rings. There is **no water.** Firewood is supplied intermittently. RVs up to 20 feet are allowed. There is a 14-day stay limit.

Fee: There is no fee.

Who to contact: Ely District Office, McGill Highway near Airport, HC Box 33, Box 150, Ely, NV 89301-9408; (702) 289-4865.

Location: From Ely, drive 45.1 miles north on US 93 to milepost 98.56 and turn west onto Highway 489, driving 6.9 miles to a right turn on a graded county road. Drive 10.7 miles on the county road to a road signed for Goshute Canyon and turn west, driving 1.5 miles to the mouth of the canyon and the campground. The campground is set at 6,230 feet.

Season: All year.

8. HICKISON PETROGLYPHS RECREATION AREA—MAP A

Campsites, facilities: There are 21 sites (five are for tents only), all with picnic tables, grills and fire rings. Pit toilets are available. There is **no water.** There is a 14-day stay limit.

Fee: There is no fee.

Who to contact: Battle Mountain District Office, P.O. Box 1420, 50 Bastian Road, Battle Mountain, NV 89820; (702) 635-4000.

Location: From Austin, drive 24 miles east on US 50 to a signed gravel entrance road and turn left, driving eight-tenths of a mile to the campground entrance. The campground is set at 6,500 feet.

Season: All year. Expect it to be very hot in the summer. Heavy snows are possible in the winter months.

9. ILLIPAH RESERVOIR CAMPGROUND—MAP A

Campsites, facilities: There are 17 sites, all with picnic tables and fire rings. Pit toilets are wheelchair accessible. Firewood is supplied intermittently. There is **no water.** There is a 14-day stay limit.

Fee: There is no fee.

Who to contact: Ely District Office, McGill Highway near Airport, HC Box 33, Box 150, Ely, NV 89301-9408; (702) 289-4865.

Location: From Ely, drive west on US 50 for 37.1 miles to the signed

gravel entrance road for the reservoir. Turn west and drive one-tenth of a mile to a junction and then head south for 1.3 miles to the campground entrance. The campground is set at 6,840 feet.
Season: All year.

10. GARNET HILL CAMPGROUND—MAP A

Campsites, facilities: There are two tent-only sites, both with picnic tables and fire rings. There is **no water**. There is a 14-day stay limit.
Fee: There is no fee.
Who to contact: Ely District Office, McGill Highway near Airport, HC Box 33, Box 150, Ely, NV 89301-9408; (702) 289-4865.
Location: From Ely, drive approximately 6.4 miles west on US 50 and turn east on a graded road, driving 1.7 miles to a road junction. Take the right fork and drive south and then west 1.4 miles to the parking area near Garnet Hill and the campground. The campground is set at 7,280 feet.
Season: All year.

11. CLEVE CREEK—MAP A

Campsites, facilities: There are 12 sites, all with picnic tables and fire rings. Pit toilets are wheelchair accessible. There is **no water**. RVs up to 24 feet are allowed. There is a 14-day stay limit.
Fee: There is no fee.
Who to contact: Ely District Office, McGill Highway near Airport, HC Box 33, Box 150, Ely, NV 89301-9408; (702) 289-4865.
Location: In the Schell Creek Mountain Range. From Major's Place near the junction of Highway 893 and US 6/50, southeast of Ely, drive approximately 12.2 miles north on Highway 893. Turn left on an unsigned graded road to the campground. The campground is set at 6,200 feet.
Season: All year.

12. INDIAN CREEK CAMPGROUND—MAP A

Campsites, facilities: There are 29 sites (10 are for tents only), all with picnic tables and fire rings. A group site is available by reservation only. Water, pit toilets and a boat launch are available.
Fee: There is a $8 per-night fee for drive-in sites. There is a $6 per-night fee for tent sites. Pay on site. Group camping for 40 or more is available by reservation at $12 per night.
Who to contact: Carson City District Office, 1535 Hot Springs Road,

Suite 300, Carson City, NV 89706; (702) 885-6000.

Location: Inside California near the California/Nevada state line. Head south from Carson City on US 395 to Highway 88 and turn right. Cross the California state line and drive to Woodfords and the junction of highways 88 and 89. Turn south (left) onto Highway 89 toward Markleeville. Drive to the campground turnoff on the left, signed for the Indian Creek Reservoir Recreation Area.

Season: May to November.

13. Sportsman's Beach Campground—Map A

Campsites, facilities: There are 17 sites, all with picnic tables and fire rings. Pit toilets and a boat ramp are available. There is **no water**. There is a 14-day stay limit.

Fee: There is no fee.

Who to contact: Carson City District Office, 1535 Hot Springs Road, Suite 300, Carson City, NV 89706; (702) 885-6000.

Location: On the west shore of Walker Reservoir. From Hawthorne, drive north for 16 miles on US 95 to the campground entrance. The campground is set at 4,500 feet.

Season: All year.

14. Gap Mountain Campground—Map B

Campsites, facilities: There are six sites, all with picnic tables and fire rings. Pit toilets are wheelchair accessible. There is **no water**. RVs up to 24 feet are allowed. There is a 14-day stay limit.

Fee: There is no fee.

Who to contact: Ely District Office, McGill Highway near Airport, HC Box 33, Box 150, Ely, NV 89301-9408; (702) 289-4865.

Location: Southwest of Ely. Drive south on Nevada 318 to Nye and milepost 11.9. Turn right on an access road to the south for the Kirch Wildlife Area. The campground is set at 5,200 feet.

Season: All year.

15. Meadow Valley Campground—Map B

Campsites, facilities: There are six tent-only sites, all with picnic tables and fire rings. Pit toilets are available. There is **no water**. Firewood is supplied intermittently. There is a 14-day stay limit.

Fee: There is no fee.

Who to contact: Ely District Office, McGill Highway near Airport, HC Box 33, Box 150, Ely, NV 89301-9408; (702) 289-4865.

Location: From Ely, drive 26.4 miles southeast on US 6/50 to US 93 and head south for 80.8 miles to Highway 322. Turn east on Highway 322 and drive 17 miles to the campground entrance, located west of the road and eight-tenths of a mile south of the Spring Valley State Park entrance sign. The campground is set at 5,740 feet.
Season: All year.

STATE INFORMATION OVERVIEW

NEVADA STATE OFFICE
850 Harvard Way, P.O. Box 12000, Reno, NV 89520-0006; (702) 785-6586

BATTLE MOUNTAIN DISTRICT OFFICE
P.O. Box 1420, Battle Mountain, NV 89820; (702) 635-4000

CARSON CITY DISTRICT OFFICE
1535 Hot Springs Road, Suite 300, Carson City, NV 89706; (702) 885-6000

ELKO DISTRICT OFFICE
P.O. Box 831, 3900 East Idaho Street, Elko, NV 89803; (702) 753-0200

ELY DISTRICT OFFICE
McGill Highway near Airport, HC Box 33, Box 150, Ely, NV 89301-9408; (702) 289-4865

Egan Resource Area, 702 North Industrial Way, Box 33500, Ely, NV 89408; (702) 289-4865

LAS VEGAS DISTRICT OFFICE
4765 Vegas Drive, Las Vegas, NV 89107; (702) 647-5000

Caliente Resource Area, P.O. Box 237, US 93, Caliente, NV 89008; (702) 726-8100

Red Rock Canyon National Conservation Area, 4765 Vegas Drive, Las Vegas, NV 89107; (702) 647-5000

WINNEMUCCA DISTRICT OFFICE
705 East Fourth Street, Winnemucca, NV 89445; (702) 623-1500

NEW MEXICO

Maps—pp. 378, 380
New Mexico Map A Locations—pp. 382-403
New Mexico Map B Locations—pp. 403-408
Information Resources—pp. 417-418

(SEE MAP A)   **(SEE MAP B)**

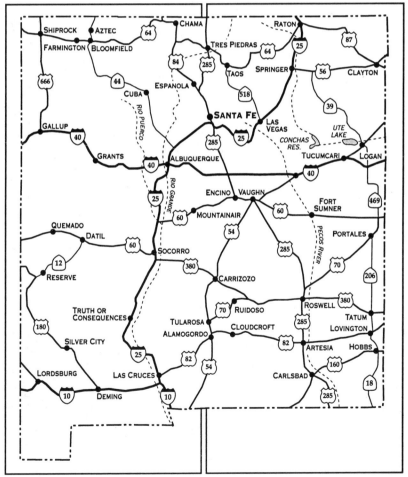

MAP A—NEW MEXICO

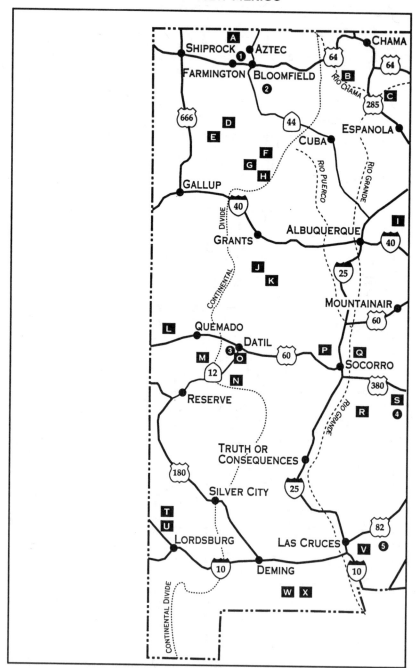

MAP REFERENCES

BLM CAMPGROUNDS

MAP B—NEW MEXICO

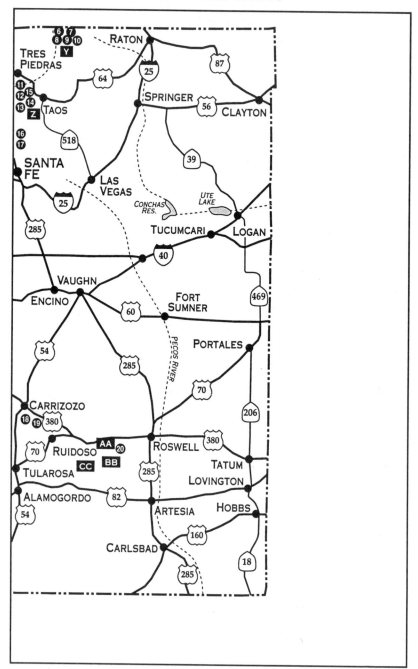

MAP REFERENCES

BLM CAMPGROUNDS

NEW MEXICO—MAP A

THE CONTINENTAL DIVIDE
NATIONAL SCENIC TRAIL

See Map A on page 378

backpacking

The Continental Divide Trail runs roughly along the lower ridge that stretches northeast to southwest through the western half of the state. Expect blistering temperatures in the south from May to September and snow on the higher reaches in the north from November through February. The route is not marked at all on BLM land except within Socorro Resource Area, which has posts marked with an emblem only—no developed treadway (see page 394 for more details). No permits are needed. There are no designated campsites. Permission to cross Native American land is required. Contact the Jicarilla Apache Tribe, Tourism Director, P.O. Box 507, Dulce, NM 87528, and the Ramah Navajo Tribe, Ramah, NM 87321. Other landowners may require permission to cross their land as well, so it is critical that you obtain information and maps from the BLM detailing the approximate trail route and land ownership information.

Maps: The following BLM surface maps will provide initial planning assistance by showing land ownership, major topographical features, major roads and trails, cities and towns: Chama, Chaco Canyon, Abiquiu, Chaco Mesa, Zuni, Fence Lake, Quemado, Tularosa Mountains, San Mateo Mountain, Truth or Consequences, Silver City, Lordsburg and Animas.

For more information: Contact the BLM New Mexico State Office, 1474 Rodeo Road, P.O. Box 27115, Santa Fe, NM 87505; (505) 438-7400.

SIMON CANYON

See letter A on map page 378

backpacking, camping, fishing, hiking

From just below the Navajo Dam to the San Juan River lies easily accessible Simon Canyon. This area is recovering nicely from illegal off-highway-vehicle activity, which occurred frequently in the past.

This is a super site when no one is around. Side canyons are pretty and worth exploring. If you visit during the week or in the off-season, you will likely have the canyon area to yourself. The area is used predominantly by fishermen working the quality waters of the San Juan. Archaeological sites lie within the region, although most have been thoroughly vandalized.

To get there, from US 550 at the town of Aztec, head approximately 23 miles east on Route 173. At the signed exit, a three-mile unpaved access road leads to the site and the Cottonwood Campground, run by the state parks. Tent camping only is allowed at Simon. RVs are required to stay at Cottonwood.

USGS topographic maps: Archuleta, Anastacio Spring

For more information: Contact the BLM Farmington District Office, 1235 La Plata Highway, Farmington, NM 87401; (505) 599-8900.

RIO CHAMA WILD AND SCENIC RIVER

See letter B on map page 378

backpacking, camping, canoeing, fishing, hiking, rafting, wildlife observation

Although the upland area is rather unspectacular (unless you are particularly attracted to open grazing range), the meandering canyon through which the Rio Chama Wild and Scenic River flows is stunning with its colors and unique rock formations. The "gorge" begins at El Vado Reservoir, flowing for the first 10 miles through BLM-managed lands, including a wilderness study area. The next 20 miles wind through Chama River Canyon Wilderness of the Santa Fe National Forest. The final seven miles, which include the majority of rapids, flow past Christ in the Desert Monastery before dumping into Abiquiu Reservoir.

To access the canyon from Tierra Amarilla, head approximately two miles south on US 112 and then west on BLM Road 1023. There are a number of branch roads, suitable for four-wheel-drive, high-clearance vehicles, which access the canyon from the east side. Do not head out before checking with the BLM office in Taos to determine road conditions. The river is usually floatable from April to early June and from mid-July to late August with Class I to Class III water. Permits are required for the upper sections of the river, although no permits are yet required for the lower seven miles.

Fishing is considered good for rainbow and brown trout. Hiking and backpacking are good throughout the canyon. Wildlife of the region includes mule deer, elk, mountain lion, bobcat, beaver and raccoon. Coopers Ranch, the official put-in, provides the launching facilities as well as informal camping. There is a per-person charge for launching and a per-vehicle charge for parking overnight. They also offer a vehicle shuttle service to the take-out at Big Eddy. Contact Coopers Ranch at (505) 588-7354.

Maps: The BLM Carson District and Santa Fe National Forest, in conjunction with the U.S. Army Corps of Engineers, publish a map and brochure entitled "Rio Chama: A Wild and Scenic River."

Resources:

• *Western Whitewater, From the Rockies to the Pacific,* by Jim Cassady, Bill Cross and Fryar Calhoun, published by North Fork Press, Berkeley, CA; (415) 424-1213.

For more information: Contact the BLM Taos Resource Area, 224 Cruz Alta Road, Taos, NM 87571; (505) 758-8851.

SANTA CRUZ LAKE

See letter C on map page 378

boating, camping, canoeing, fishing, hiking

This is a good family destination for water recreation. Santa Cruz Lake is an irrigation lake. Access is decent; a paved road leads to the boat launch ramp maintained by the BLM. From US 84/285, approximately 20 miles north of Santa Fe, bear right on Route 503. Travel nine miles to reach the Overlook Campground turnoff, and an additional four miles to Route 596. Make a left turn to reach Northlake Campground. Several trails provide access on foot to most of the lakeshore and the banks of the creek that feeds the lake. There is also an easy trail from the Overlook Campground leading to the south shore. Scenery in this badlands area is spectacular. For a campground-style getaway with a boat and fishing pole, this is the place. Couple that with the fact that BLM officials say this is one of their most beautiful recreation areas and you have all the elements necessary for a fun, family escape. Fishing is for rainbow and brown trout. Summer temperatures range from 54°F to 82°F and winter temperatures from 15°F to 45°F. Historic sites and artifacts are located within the region—please help to protect the resources.

BLM surface maps: The BLM publishes a map/brochure entitled "Santa Cruz Lake."

For more information: Contact the BLM Taos Resource Area, 224 Cruz Alta Road, Taos, NM 87571; (505) 758-8851.

DE-NA-ZIN WILDERNESS

See letter D on map page 378

backpacking, hiking, horseback riding

Designated as wilderness, the De-Na-Zin has no formal trails or any designated entrance to speak of. It's just there, spread out for wandering among the wind-carved bluffs, badlands, mesas and striking color variations which are accented at sunset. Although there isn't much plant life, save for the small areas of rolling grassland and pockets of pinyon pine and juniper, there is an interesting animal population, which includes desert cottontails, prairie dogs, coyotes and badgers. Expect to find petrified wood and numerous fossils within the boundaries, although collecting is strictly prohibited by federal law. You can pick up and look, just don't pocket and carry.

Activity Highlight: Hiking and backpacking

There is no set hiking trail. Travel is by map and compass, leaving the visitor free to wander and explore the twisted and magical topography. You must be proficient with a map and compass to safely and easily navigate your way through the region.

Location: The De-Na-Zin Wilderness is 170 miles northwest of Albuquerque, near the "four corners" region where New Mexico meets Utah, Arizona and Colorado. From Bloomfield, drive approximately 30 miles south on Route 44 to El Huerfano Trading Post and then continue 11 miles southwest on County Road 7500 to the parking area. The road is generally good, although it can become slippery when wet. This usually occurs in the early spring and late summer.

Camping: Camping is allowed anywhere within the wilderness area. The BLM is considering prohibiting camping in the commonly visited day-use areas. Minimum-impact camping techniques help encourage you to stay away from these areas, regardless. Bring all the water you will need as there is none available in the wilderness.

Season: The best times to visit are in late winter, spring and fall. Summer will cook your brains for sure.

Permits: No permits are necessary. Campfires are not permitted anywhere. Parts of this region are closed seasonally by the BLM to protect nesting raptors. Check with the office for closure information.

USGS topographic maps: Alamo Mesa West, Alamo Mesa East, Huerfano Trading Post Southwest

BLM surface maps: Chaco Canyon, Toadlena

For more information: Contact the BLM Farmington District Office, 1235 La Plata Highway, Farmington, NM 87401; (505) 599-8900.

BISTI WILDERNESS
See letter E on map page 378

backpacking, hiking, horseback riding

The 3,946-acre Bisti Wilderness is very remote and stark. The weathered sandstone of the region makes spectacular formations known as hoodoos. Once heavily populated by diverse primitive forms of animal life living in swamps and forests, the area is now desolate badlands. This world of bizarre rock formations and prehistoric remains, sometimes referred to as an eerie moonscape, is a wilderness monument to a primeval wonderland. Very little wildlife inhabits this region. An occasional lizard, snake, tarantula or scorpion may be seen scuttling along among petrified wood remains. Even ferruginous hawks or golden eagles may be observed riding the thermals overhead. For the most part, silence and solitude reign supreme.

Activity Highlights: Hiking and backpacking

There is no set hiking trail. Travel is by map and compass, leaving the visitor free to wander and explore the twisted and magical topography. You must be proficient with a map and compass to safely and easily navigate your way through the region.

Location: Located 170 miles northwest of Albuquerque, near the "four corners" region where New Mexico meets Utah, Arizona and Colorado. From Albuquerque, take Interstate 40 to Highway 371. Take Highway 371 north to Crown Point. From Crown Point, continue north another 45 miles until you see signs for the turnoff for Bisti Wilderness, approximately 37 miles south of Farmington. Turn east and follow this gravel road for two miles to an undeveloped parking area and the trailhead—actually just an opening in the barbed wire fence.

Camping: Camping is allowed anywhere within the wilderness area at the present time. The BLM is considering prohibiting camping in the commonly visited day-use areas. Minimum-impact camping techniques help encourage you to stay away from these areas, regardless. Bring all the water you will need as there is none available in the wilderness.

Season: The best time to visit this area is in late winter, spring and fall. Summer is brutally hot.

Permits: No permits are necessary. Campfires are not permitted anywhere. Parts of this region are closed seasonally by the BLM to protect nesting raptors. Check with the office for closure information.

USGS topographic maps: Bisti Trading Post, Alamo Mesa West, Tanner Lake

BLM surface map: Toadlena

Resources: *The Hiker's Guide to New Mexico*, by Laurence Parent, published by Falcon Press, P.O. Box 1718, Helena, MT 59624; (800) 582-2665.

For more information: Contact the BLM Farmington District Office, 1235 La Plata Highway, Farmington, NM 87401; (505) 599-8900.

CABEZON WILDERNESS STUDY AREA

See letter F on map page 378

backpacking, camping, hiking, horseback riding, mountain biking, rock climbing, wildlife observation

Views from the mesas and rolling hills are superb and the entire region is richly dotted with historical, archaeological and geological features. You will need to carry all your water as there are no guaranteed water sources within the region. Camping is allowed anywhere, but minimum-impact camping techniques are essential. Gravel and dirt roads network a large portion of this region and are suitable (outside the Wilderness Study Area) for four-wheel-drive access, mountain biking and car-camping base camps. Once again, even if base-camping, practice minimum-impact camping techniques.

Cabezon Peak is a 7,775-foot-high volcanic plug. There is a primitive trail along the south side of the peak that takes two and a half to four hours to climb. A visitor's register at the summit indicates that hikers from as far away as Europe come to experience this climb, which is appropriate for both beginning and intermediate hikers. The south face of the plug features a popular rock-climbing route.

Wildlife is abundant and includes badgers, bobcats, coyotes, porcupine, chipmunks, prairie dogs and numerous and varied rodents. Birds and raptors are also abundant here which feed upon the population of rodents. Route 279, approximately 20 miles north of San Ysidro, off Route 44, travels through the village of San Luis to the northwestern boundary of Cabezon Wilderness Study Area, near the privately-owned ghost town of Cabezon. Be sure to top off your gas tank at San Ysidro before heading out.

USGS topographic map: Cabezon Peak

Resources:

• The BLM publishes an informal booklet entitled *Rio Puerco Mountain Bike Routes* and a brochure entitled "Cabezon."

For more information: Contact the BLM Rio Puerco Resource Area, 435 Montano Road, Northeast, Albuquerque, NM 87107; (505) 761-8700.

IGNACIO CHAVEZ/CHAMISA WILDERNESS STUDY AREA

See letter G on map page 378

backpacking, camping, hiking, horseback riding, mountain biking, wildlife observation

This is a lightly visited area with a variety of terrain and scenic canyons. It is through the Ignacio Chavez/Chamisa Area across the level terrain of the mesas that the proposed Continental Divide National Scenic Trail will cross. Views from the mesas and rolling hills are superb and the entire region is richly dotted with historical, cultural and geological features. You will need to carry all your water as there are no guaranteed water sources within the region. Camping is allowed anywhere. BLM Road 1103 is opened on a seasonal basis for vehicle access. All other roads are closed to vehicle traffic within the wilderness study areas. Wildlife is abundant and includes badger, bobcat, coyote, porcupine, chipmunks, prairie dogs and numerous and varied rodents. Birds are also abundant as are raptors, which feed upon the populations of rodents. Route 279, located approximately 20 miles north of San Ysidro off Route 44, travels through the village of San Luis and turns into County Road 25, following the northern border of

Ignacio Chavez/Chamisa Area. Be sure to top off your gas tank at 乚
Ysidro before heading out. BLM 1103 is a seasonal road that runs to
the top of the mesa and over to Forest Service Road 239A. Fall and
spring are the best times to visit.

USGS topographic maps: Mesa Cortada, Cerro Parido, Guadalupe

For more information: Contact the BLM Rio Puerco Resource Area,
435 Montano Road, Northeast, Albuquerque, NM 87107; (505)
761-8700.

OJITO WILDERNESS STUDY AREA

See letter H on map page 378

backpacking, camping, hiking, rock climbing, wildlife observation

To get to Ojito, drive Route 44 south from San Ysidro for two
miles. A maintained dirt road heads west to Ojito, seven miles away.
The Ojito area is made up of steep, rocky terrain interspersed with
steep canyons and pockets of badlands topography. Roads outside of
the wilderness study area are suitable for mountain biking and four-
wheel-drive-vehicle-based camping. This site lies just south of the
Cabezon boundary and offers super views of the imposing volcanic
plug known as Cabezon Peak. Visit in fall and spring; it gets pretty hot
here in summer.

USGS topographic maps: Ojito Spring, San Ysidro, Sky Village
Northeast, Sky Village Northwest

Resources:
• The BLM publishes a brochure entitled "Ojito."

For more information: Contact the BLM Rio Puerco Resource Area,
435 Montano Road, Northeast, Albuquerque, NM 87107; (505)
761-8700.

TENT ROCKS AREA OF CRITICAL ENVIRONMENTAL CONCERN

See letter I on map page 378

hiking, mountain biking (only off Forest Service Road 266)

The BLM told me "the brochure doesn't even begin to describe
the remarkable beauty of this place." Upon further checking, I was
frankly amazed that even though Tent Rocks is so close to both Santa
Fe and Albuquerque, it receives only moderate visitation—not that

I'm complaining. It is sometimes used as a movie location because of its unique rock formations and badlands topography. Most unique are the tent-shaped rocks (which look like huge tepees at 40 to 90 feet high) for which the area is named. Climbing is not allowed on any of the tent formations due to their fragile nature. They were formed by erosion and are in a constant state of erosion—one day this site will no longer be here. A two-mile National Recreation Trail was designated here in 1993. A kiosk providing hiking details is located at the parking area. This best way to get here is to drive approximately three miles via Forest Service Road 266, just off Route 22 near the Cochiti Pueblo. The turnoff from Route 22 is marked by a colorful water tower.

USGS topographic map: Canada

USFS map: Santa Fe National Forest

Resources:

• The BLM publishes an informal booklet entitled *Mountain Bike Excursions in Tent Rocks* and a map/brochure entitled "Tent Rocks."

For more information: Contact the BLM Rio Puerco Resource Area, 435 Montano Road, Northeast, Albuquerque, NM 87107; (505) 761-8700.

EL MALPAIS NATIONAL CONSERVATION AREA

See letter J on map page 378

backpacking, camping, hiking, historical sites, mountain biking

Travelers speak of a ghostly silence within the El Malpais National Conservation Area, a silence occasionally broken by a rush of wind or the growl of a passing vehicle. While Native Americans made use of the area, early Spanish and American explorers disdained the rugged terrain, referring to it as El Malpais—the badlands. Indeed, the area is forbidding, with a dramatic landscape created from numerous cinder and spatter cones, ice caves, pressure ridges and some of the longest lava tubes on the continent. High sandstone bluffs add a remarkable contrast to the lava flows, with winds leaving balancing stones and creative sculptures that rival anything seen in the world's best art galleries.

The lava crevices harbor an amazing amount of vegetation including grasses, cacti, aspen and more. Naturalists at the visitor center say that lava fields create a kind of microclimate which is more moist than the surrounding terrain. In some of the island-like depressions

(Hole-In-The-Wall, described below, is the biggest), windblown debris has collected, allowing trees such as the pinyon pine, juniper, ponderosa pine and Douglas fir to take root. This area demands a light touch, however, as archaeological sites continue to be vandalized, trees cut are for firewood, and signed vehicle closures are often ignored. Every impact eventually leads to the destruction of an irreplaceable resource that is valuable to us all.

Activity Highlights: Hiking and backpacking

Numerous backpacking and exploring opportunities present themselves within the 40,000-acre wilderness of the West Malpais Wilderness. Hiking is very rugged—hiking for one mile on lava is equivalent to several miles on regular terrain. For those who are not experienced in desert-type backpacking, setting up a base camp near your vehicle and spending the time day-hiking is recommended. Hiking is generally easiest on the jeep roads, which are closed to all vehicle traffic in the wilderness, making them ideal for foot traffic. There is no water to be had within the National Conservation Area or National Monument, so you must carry all you need—one gallon per person per day is the minimum recommended amount. The north plains of the area are primarily grasslands interspersed with juniper trees. Six thousand acres of this wilderness, named Hole-In-The-Wall, forms a peninsula that juts out northeast into the National Monument; many more exploration possibilities exist there. Hole-In-The-Wall is an island of older lava flow blanketed with ponderosa pine. Gloves, long sleeves and long pants are recommended for hiking here, as are sturdy leather boots. Lava can be very unforgiving on the skin as it is sharp and brittle. Lava tubes may be explored at your own risk as long as you have three sources of light, a helmet and protective clothing.

Activity Highlight: Mountain biking

Brazo Canyon features several remote and forested canyons that demand exploration. Although four-wheel-drive vehicles are allowed, the route is traveled lightly enough that mountain biking becomes an attractive alternative. Carry a copious amount of water—two quarts just won't cut it. Be sure to pack extra parts and plenty of patching material. Mountain bikes are not allowed in the nearby wilderness areas; respect the closures.

Location: Approximately 10 miles south of Grants, New Mexico and south of Interstate 40 in the northwestern quadrant of the state. From

Grants, drive south on Highway 117 to the eastern boundary of this area. Highway 117 cuts through the eastern edge of the region and is very scenic. High-clearance vehicles are required on all the dirt county roads for access into the wilderness areas—anything less and you are liable to leave body parts behind (the car's, not yours). Without a high-clearance vehicle, stick to Highway 53 or Highway 117. Limited pull-outs for overnight parking are available along the highways. Do not leave your vehicle in the two places marked with signs prohibiting overnight stays.

Camping: Several commercial camping sites do exist. Primitive camping is allowed throughout the BLM conservation and wilderness areas. Water is not available anywhere within the wilderness areas—pack plenty.

Season: Spring and fall are the best seasons to visit this area. Summer can be exceedingly hot. Winter brings periodic snowfalls and freezing temperatures.

Permits: A permit is required. Campfires are prohibited at times— check with the ranger. The gathering of firewood is prohibited, so you must bring your own.

Maps: *The El Malpais Recreation Guide Map* is published by the BLM and distributed through the visitor center. Topographic maps needed for your particular venture may be purchased at the El Malpais Ranger Station.

Resources:

• *New Mexico Mountain Bike Guide,* published by Big Ring Press, P.O. Box 8266, Albuquerque, NM 87198.

For more information: Contact the BLM Grants Field Station, 620 East Santa Fe, Grants, NM 87020; (505) 285-5041; or El Malpais Information Center, 620 East Santa Fe Avenue, Grants, NM 87020; (505) 285-5406.

CEBOLLA WILDERNESS

See letter K on map page 378

backpacking, camping, hiking, horseback riding, wildlife observation

Lying adjacent to El Malpais (although officially it is still part of the El Malpais National Conservation Area), just east of Route 117, is an area of scenic sandstone bluffs, canyons, mesas and draws that provide easier access than the challenging and forbidding volcanic terrain of El Malpais. There are primitive roads in Cebolla Canyon, Sand Canyon, and Armijo Canyon that are suitable for foot or horse. Pack all the water you will need because there is none naturally available within this region. A notable feature within Cebolla is La Ventana, one of the largest natural arches in New Mexico. There is a signed parking area just off Route 117, approximately 17 to 18 miles south of Interstate 40. Be careful that you do not travel within the adjacent Acoma Indian Reservation or disturb archaeological sites that they consider very sacred. Visit any time of year, but expect summers to be hot.

USGS topographic maps: Arrosa Ranch, Bonine Canyon, Cebollita Peak, Laguna Honda, Los Pilares, North Pasture, Sand Canyon

For more information: Contact the BLM Rio Puerco Resource Area, 435 Montano Road, Northeast, Albuquerque, NM 87107; (505) 761-8700; or the El Malpais Information Center, 620 East Santa Fe Avenue, Grants, NM 87020; (505) 285-5406.

EAGLE PEAK WILDERNESS STUDY AREA

See letter L on map page 378

camping, hiking, wildlife observation

This is a generally arid and barren area that offers pleasant enough desert hiking through various volcanic landforms, sandstone mesas and canyons, and rolling hills. There are even a few small cinder cones. The largest cone, Cerro Pomo, shelters Zuni Salt Lake—a historic source of salt for Native American tribes and a ground of spiritual importance that is neutral for all tribes. Flash-flooding is possible in this area during the rainy season of July through September—watch out for serious thunderstorms. From Quemado on US 60, drive northwest on unpaved Route 32 to the town of Salt Lake. Head south on County Road A007 to Eagle Peak.

USGS topographic maps: Zuni Salt Lake, Blaines Lake, Tejana Mesa, Lake Armijo, Tejana Mesa Southwest, Armstrong Canyon

For more information: Contact the BLM Socorro Resource Area, 198 Neel Avenue, Northwest, Socorro, NM 87801; (505) 835-0412.

HORSE MOUNTAIN WILDERNESS STUDY AREA

See letter M on map page 378

camping, hiking, horseback riding, wildlife observation

This is a fine destination for a view or peak-bagging hike, as the mountain's 9,490-foot elevation practically towers above the Plains of San Agustine below. When the weather is clear, you can see for up to 100 miles in all directions. The routes up are steep, but for the sure-footed, the going is relatively easy. There are a number of undeveloped trails that date back to logging days. They have since grown over, but they offer sure footing. This is a perfect place to set up a weekend base-camp from which to explore the peak and surrounding area. From the town of Datil off US 60, head southwest for 26 miles on Route 12 to Horse Springs. At Horse Springs, head north for approximately four miles on an unpaved county road. Then drive east on a very primitive access road nearly one mile to the boundary of the site. Summer temperatures are warm to hot in the day and cooler at night. Winter temperatures hover around the freezing mark.

USGS topographic maps: Wallace Mesa, Log Canyon, Horse Mountain West, Horse Mountain East

For more information: Contact the BLM Socorro Resource Area, 198 Neel Avenue, Northwest, Socorro, NM 87801; (505) 835-0412.

THE CONTINENTAL DIVIDE NATIONAL SCENIC TRAIL

See letter N on map page 378

archaeological sites, backpacking, hiking, horseback riding

This 34-mile section of the Continental Divide National Scenic Trail (CDNST) is the only marked and signed section across BLM land in New Mexico. Some national forests in New Mexico also have portions of the trail developed. The route across BLM land, however, is mostly primitive with little visible treadway and marked only by rock cairns and posts sporting a CDNST emblem.

The trail meanders east to west through over 68,000 acres of rolling grasslands and rugged forested mountains. This general area and trail corridor, administered by the BLM, is bordered roughly on three sides by the Gila National Forest—to the south, east and west.

With no perennial streams or running water, this remote, relatively unknown and inaccessible area sees limited use (less than 50 hikers per year). The majority of visitors to this region are those few who are attempting the entire trail or hunters on a quest for the pronghorn antelope, elk or mule deer that call the region home. Despite—or perhaps because of—the limited publicity, the region offers superb opportunities for enjoying solitude and excellent scenery.

Traveling along the cross-country trail, the hiker or horseback rider will traverse a stunning variety of terrain, from rolling, grass-covered hills to broken escarpments and scenic canyons. The vast expanse of smooth, rolling hills, which extend to the east and south of Pelona Mountain (elevation 9,212 feet and one of the highest peaks in the area), create a dramatic landscape—especially at sunset. The pastel browns, greens and yellows of the hills are backdropped by dark mountains and extend as far as the eye can see with few human structures evident, save an occasional fence, dirt road or windmill.

Numerous vantage points exist along the pine-forested ridges and offer spectacular vistas. One escarpment, along the western edge of the Continental Divide Wilderness Study Area overlooks the Plains of San Agustine and a large slice of west-central New Mexico.

July through September is perhaps the best time of year to travel this trail segment; although temperature extremes can vary wildly, daytime temperatures average in the mid-80s, dropping to an average temperature in the 40s at night. Much of the region's precipitation falls during this time period. Frequent and intense, though brief thunderstorms underscore the need for carrying raingear. Even though the rain is falling, water sources are not guaranteed. Pack all the water you will need.

Special note: A number of archaeologically significant sites, both documented and undocumented, exist within and around the trail corridor. Please respect these sites and leave them untouched. Heavy visitation of an archeological site can severely damage it—through what the BLM calls "innocent vandalism." All archaeological sites and artifacts are protected by federal law. Although the trail itself does not pass across any private land in this sector, it does meander near private boundaries. Private land may not be traveled on without express permission—respect owners' privacy.

Location: In Catron Country, south of the Plains of San Agustine and approximately 29 miles as the crow flies south of the town of Datil, New Mexico. The BLM section of the CDNST is best accessed from Highway 12 via County Roads B019 and C016. It is strongly suggested that you check with the BLM prior to visiting to obtain up-to-date access information and directions.

USGS topographical maps: Fullerton, Paddy's Hole, Mohonera Canyon, Rael Canyon, O Bar O Canyon, Indian Peaks West, Pelona Mountain

For more information: Contact the BLM Socorro Resource Area, 198 Neel Avenue, Northwest, Socorro, NM 87801; (505) 835-0412.

DATIL WELL
See letter O on map page 378

camping, hiking

What was once a well along the historic Magdalena Stock Driveway livestock trail is now the site of a BLM-maintained campground. A three-mile nature and hiking trail winds through pinyon pine and juniper woodlands to viewpoints that overlook the Plains of San Agustine. The BLM publishes a leaflet about the area. It is located just off US 60, approximately one mile northwest of the town of Datil. A $5 overnight fee is charged.

USGS topographic map: Datil

For more information: Contact the BLM Socorro Resource Area, 198 Neel Avenue, Northwest, Socorro, NM 87801; (505) 835-0412.

SIERRA LADRONES WILDERNESS STUDY AREA
See letter P on map page 378

backpacking, camping, fossil seeking, hiking, horseback riding, rock climbing, rockhounding, wildlife observation

Sitting in the car at Interstate 25 near Bernardo and looking west, it is not hard to imagine the ruggedness that the Sierra Ladrones embody—the jagged escarpments of the range virtually dominate the horizon. Ladron Peak, at 9,176 feet, is forbidding in its size, with the peak towering nearly 4,000 feet above the base. Rock climbers come here to enjoy the technically difficult rock faces. Fall through spring is the best time to visit—summer is too damn hot! The Sevilleta National Wildlife Refuge lies on the east side of the range and is closed to the public. Pinyon pine and juniper dominate the slopes, with some aspen and Douglas fir sneaking into the mix among the canyons. Wildlife is abundant and includes coyote, bobcat, badger, cottontail, jackrabbit, gray fox, and a number of bats. Bighorn sheep were recently released into the area and can be seen if you have a sharp eye. To get to the area, head west on County Road 67 from Interstate 25 at Bernardo.

USGS topographic maps: Ladron Peak, Riley, Carbon Springs, Silver Creek

For more information: Contact the BLM Socorro Resource Area, 198 Neel Avenue, Northwest, Socorro, NM 87801; (505) 835-0412.

SIERRA DE LAS CANAS WILDERNESS STUDY AREA; PRESILLA WILDERNESS STUDY AREA

See letter Q on map page 378

camping, hiking, horseback riding, rock climbing, wildlife observation

Both units are located east of the Rio Grande at the town of Socorro. Cross the bridge from US 85 at Escondido and continue driving east on BLM-maintained Quebradas Road—it's rough but okay in a high-clearance vehicle. Popular with locals from Socorro, the area is used primarily for hiking, rock climbing, camping, horseback riding and rock hounding. Within Presilla lies the Tinajas Natural Area of Critical Environmental Concern. Sierra De Las Canas is further away from Socorro and sees only light visitation. Rugged and multicolored rock escarpments, narrow canyons, sharp ridges, and broad mesas make up the topography of this region. There are also many good opportunities for sightseeing and outdoor photography during rainstorms, which create beautiful rainbows. Visit any time of year, but expect temperatures to be hot in summer.

USGS topographic maps: Sierra De Las Canas: Loma De Las Canas, Bustos Well, Canon Agua Bueno, San Antonio; Presilla: Loma De Las Canas

For more information: Contact the BLM Socorro Resource Area, 198 Neel Avenue, Northwest, Socorro, NM 87801; (505) 835-0412.

JORNADA DEL MUERTO WILDERNESS STUDY AREA

See letter R on map page 378

geological sightseeing, hiking

Where else can you hike within a missile range, I ask you? Imagine moseying along and then being evacuated for a test firing—don't laugh. It could happen, since this site is entirely within the safety net imposed by the White Sands Missile Range. But that's not why this place is called the Journey of Death. Rather, it is because of the harsh and forbidding volcanic terrain of tubes and ridges—many silted in by blowing sand and clay. El Camino Real Trail is in the same geographic area dating back to the Spanish explorers who journeyed through this area. The area is located south of San Antonio and US 380 off County Roads 2268 and 2322. It is a good year-round destination, but summers get hot here.

USGS topographic maps: Harriet Ranch, Fuller Ranch

For more information: Contact the BLM Socorro Resource Area, 198 Neel Avenue, Northwest, Socorro, NM 87801; (505) 835-0412.

VALLEY OF FIRES RECREATION AREA

See letter S on map page 378

camping, caving, hiking, picnicking, wildlife observation

Formerly Valley of Fires State Park, the Valley of Fires site is an outstanding area to view and hike over one of the youngest flows of lava in the United States. The lava spewed from volcanic vents at the northern end of the flow between 1,500 and 2,000 years ago. The lava flow covers over 125 square miles and is approximately five miles wide and forty-four miles long. A visitor center is located at the recreation area, which also houses a sales outlet for the Southwest Natural and Cultural Heritage Association. There is a one-mile-loop interpretive trail through the lava where the hiker can view native plants that are unique to the area. More experienced hikers will want to venture out and across the lava on unmarked routes to view the bubbles, crevasses, and different flow features. A 20-site campground is located in the recreation area. It has electricity and water hook-ups, a dump station, a group picnic shelter, water, flush-type restrooms and pull-through camping spaces. Camping is allowed only in designated sites; it costs

$7 per vehicle, plus $4 if electricity is desired. A $5-per-vehic
use fee is collected if you are not camping. The Valley of Fires Recreation Area is located adjacent to US 380, approximately four miles
west of Carrizozo. The recreation area is open all year, although most
visitation occurs between March and November. The BLM publishes
a free brochure to the area.

USGS topographic maps: Carrizozo, Chihuahua Ranch, Little Black
Peak

BLM surface maps: Carrizozo, Oscura Mountains

For more information: Contact the Valley of Fires Recreation Area,
P.O. Box 871, Carrizozo, NM 88301; (505) 648-2241.

GILA RIVER: LOWER BOX

See letter T on map page 378

backpacking, camping, canoeing, hiking, kayaking, wildlife observation

This tranquil and relatively shallow section of the Gila River
flows through a highly scenic and lightly visited area just south of the
Gila National Forest. Large rock outcroppings and a partly steep-
walled canyon with numerous side canyons provide ample opportunity
for exploring on foot. Hoodoos and columns add an almost magical
nature to the area. Camping is allowed anywhere within the area.
Water levels are low and the river is best floated in March or immediately following a rainy period. The water flow is rated Class I throughout the river. Access to the canyon and the river is best from the Red
Rock Bridge on Route 464 north of Lordsburg. There are a number of
local roads offering access to other points along the canyon, but it is
best to ask locals regarding these put-in spots.

USGS topographic maps: Canador Peak, Nichols Canyon

Resources:

• *Western Whitewater, From the Rockies to the Pacific,* by Jim Cassady,
Bill Cross and Fryar Calhoun, published by North Fork Press, Berkeley, CA; (415) 424-1213.

For more information: Contact the BLM Las Cruces District Office,
1800 Marquess Street, Las Cruces, NM 88005; (505) 525-4300.

GUADALUPE CANYON
OUTSTANDING NATURAL AREA

See letter U on map page 378

backpacking, hiking, wildlife observation

Well known to avid birders for the excellent birdwatching opportunities to be found here, the Guadalupe Canyon is a remote and special destination for anyone who enjoys solitude and shallow canyonland geography. Since the area borders on the wilderness study area of the Coronado National Forest, extended backpacking trips are possible. There is a stream that flows periodically through the canyon, usually during the late summer and early fall when the thunderstorms are frequent. Over 159 species of birds have been sighted and recorded within the canyon—many at their most northerly point of migration. Camping is allowed anywhere, but for safety's sake, camp only on high ground because flash-flooding is a real hazard. There is a trail that leads to Bunk Robinson Peak within the Peloncillo Mountains of the Coronado National Forest.

The canyon area is surrounded by private lands and there is no legal public access. Private landowners will allow access if you ask permission. Directions to the area are quite complicated—before heading out, contact the BLM for directions and the names of those whose land you must cross. This makes a good destination at any time of year.

USGS topographic maps: Guadalupe Spring, Guadalupe Canyon

USFS map: Coronado National Forest

For more information: Contact the BLM Las Cruces District Office, 1800 Marquess Street, Las Cruces, NM 88005; (505) 525-4300.

ORGAN MOUNTAINS

See letter V on map page 378

camping, backpacking, hiking, horseback riding, mountain biking, rock climbing, wildlife observation

There is a tremendous diversity of life within the arid environment of the Organ Mountains. In the lower elevations, you will find creosote bush and mesquite, which give way to juniper and oak as the elevation increases. In the highest reaches of the mountains, enclaves of ponderosa pine, juniper and mountain mahogany may be found. There are also many species of birds, mammals and reptiles to be seen.

Most common are quail, rabbits, deer, tree lizards and rattlesnakes. The geology is severe, looking rather like a dried-up Swiss Alps.

Activity Highlight: Mountain biking

The Baylor Pass National Recreation Trail is one of the few trails in these BLM holdings that is limited to hiking, horseback riding and mountain biking. No vehicles are allowed. Total riding distance is six miles each way. Beginning at Aguirre Springs Campground, with elevation of approximately 5,540 feet, the trail winds and climbs to a height of 6,340 feet. From there, the trail descends rapidly to an elevation of 4,865 feet and intersects with Baylor Canyon Road. The Baylor Pass National Recreation Trail is an out-and-back proposition.

Activity Highlight: Rock climbing

The "needles" (splinter-like rock towers) and a rock formation known as Sugarloaf attract climbers from all over.

Activity Highlight: Hiking

There are a number of trails that wind through the region including the Baylor Pass Trail described above. The Pine Tree Trail is for hiking only and is a loop trail requiring approximately three hours to walk and covering 4.5 miles. It begins and ends in the Aguirre Springs Campground.

Location: In the Organ Mountains, 3.5 miles east of Organ and just south of US 70. Drive 25 miles northeast from Las Cruces on US 70. Follow the signs to the Organ Mountains.

Camping: Camping is available at the Aguirre Springs Campground—it's crowded, but it's the only game in town. There is a seven-day camping limit. The only drinking water available in the recreation area is located at the A. B. Cox Visitor Center just off Baylor Canyon Road.

Season: The best time to visit this area is from fall to spring. Summers can be uncomfortably hot.

USGS topographic maps: Organ Peak, Organ New Mexico

BLM surface map: Las Cruces

Additional maps: Recreation maps for the Organ and Franklin Mountains are available from the BLM Mimbres office.

For more information: Contact the BLM Mimbres Resource Area, 1800 Marquess Street, Las Cruces, NM 88005; (505) 525-4300.

FLORIDA MOUNTAINS

See letter W on map page 378

backpacking, camping, hiking, rockhounding, wildlife observation

Rising up out of the surrounding desert for nearly 3,000 feet, the Florida Mountains are the most noteworthy geological feature for miles. The topography is jagged and rugged, carved open with steep canyons—many with near-vertical walls. Four-wheel-drive roads skirt the entire range making access quite easy when the roads are dry. Numerous springs and small seeps dot the region creating mini-oases of riparian vegetation. The wildlife here includes mule deer, coyote, kit fox, ringtail, badger and Persian ibex—yep, you read it right. The Persian ibex were released here in the early '70s and have flourished. Rockhounding is a big draw to the area, chiefly because of the close proximity to Rock Hound State Park, which actually encourages rock hounding and tills the soil to help rock hounders unearth geodes, jasper, agate, rhyolite and more. The state park has a campground with approximately 30 sites that is open all year. This makes a good destination at any time of year.

From Demming, head east on Highway 549 for about six miles to a signed, paved road to Rock Hound State Park. From the turnoff to Spring Canyon, various county and ranch roads lead to the east and south, providing access into the Florida Mountains.

USGS topographic maps: Capitol Dome, South Peak, Florida Gap, Gym Peak

For more information: Contact the BLM Las Cruces District Office, 1800 Marquess Street, Las Cruces, NM 88005; (505) 525-4300.

WEST POTRILLO MOUNTAINS

See letter X on map page 378

auto touring, camping, hiking, rockhounding, wildlife observation

This area is volcanic and then some. Over 48 volcanic cones cluster in the area ranging from 1,000 to 3,000 feet in diameter. Indian Basin, a large depression in the southwestern part of the mountains, is rimmed with sand dunes and sometimes filled with water, giving ducks a temporary home. Aden Crater is a nearly circular crater with a one-quarter mile diameter that lies within the Aden Lava Flow. There is a four-wheel-drive-vehicle trail wandering through the area, which is used by many locals. Kilbourne Hole is approximately two miles south of Aden Lava Flow and has been designated a National Natural Landmark. Kilbourne is defined as a *maar*, a crater caused by a volcanic explosion of gas, not lava, and is more rare than cinder cones. Kilbourne is up to two miles across and 450 feet deep in places. Wildlife watchers will enjoy knowing that golden eagles, great-horned owls and bats nest among the formations. The abundance of rodents has made for a very healthy raptor population.

USGS topographic maps: POL Ranch, Potrillo Peak, Guzman's Lookout Mountain, Mount Riley, Mount Riley Southeast, Mount Aden Southwest, Aden Crater

For more information: Contact the BLM Las Cruces District Office, 1800 Marquess Street, Las Cruces, NM 88005; (505) 525-4300.

NEW MEXICO—MAP B

RIO GRANDE WILD AND SCENIC RIVER/ WILD RIVERS RECREATION AREA

See letter Y on map page 380

backpacking, camping, canoeing, fishing, hiking, rafting, wildlife observation

The Rio Grande was one of the first rivers in the Lower 48 to achieve protected status under the Wild and Scenic Rivers Act. The protected area includes 48 river miles south of the Colorado border and also the lower four miles of the Red River tributary. The Rio Grande cuts an ever-deepening swath through the Taos Plateau, beginning at the Colorado border at a 200-foot depth and then slicing even deeper, ending up flowing nearly 880 feet below the Plateau, down at the confluence with the Red River. The gorge is a picture in stark contrast—dry and forbidding on top with sparse vegetation, yet lush and inviting along the river's edge with a riparian environment of cottonwood, ponderosa pine, willow, horsetail and the ever-present poison ivy. Transitional vegetation on the slopes and benches include oak, cactus, pinyon pine, juniper and various wildflowers. Expect to see numerous birds attracted by the water and all the available food, and expect also to view wildlife that includes mule deer, elk, coyote, beaver, muskrat, raccoon, porcupine, black bear, bobcat and mountain lion. The fishing for rainbow and German brown trout and northern pike is excellent.

Activity Highlights: Hiking and backpacking

Guided hikes and campfire talks are offered each weekend from Memorial Day through Labor Day. There are 12 miles of developed and maintained trails with trailheads located near each of the campgrounds—the system is made up of five separate trails, ranging from three-quarters to 1.25 miles in length connecting with a trail along the river. The trails system has been designated as part of the National Recreation Trails System. A new five-mile loop trail winds through the pinyon along the canyon rims.

Activity Highlight: Mountain biking

There are 10 miles of mountain biking trails.

Activity Highlight: Whitewater rafting

The Upper Box run begins at Lobatos Bridge in Colorado. Upper Box is closed to boating from March 1 to June 1 each year to protect wildlife. Since some downstream sections are unrunnable, boaters must obtain detailed portage and river information prior to putting in. Taos Box is the most popular run; it begins at the John Dunn Bridge Recreation Site. The river is rated Class I to Class IV within this section. The length of the Lower Box run is approximately 16 river miles. Take-out is at Taos Junction Bridge. Write to the BLM for a current listing of commercial river companies offering half-day to overnight trips on the Rio Grande or Rio Chama.

Location: Beginning approximately 50 miles north of Taos, near the Colorado/New Mexico border and ending 20 miles south of Taos near Pine, New Mexico. Three miles north of the town of Questa on Route 522, turn left on Route 378. Follow the signs which mark the access points and the visitor center.

Camping: Camping is allowed only in designated sites on the rim and along the river. There are five campgrounds along the rim with 47 individual sites and one group site available. Rim campground fees are $7 per site.

Season: The boating season lasts from May to July, depending on the water levels.

Permits: No permits are necessary for hiking or backpacking. All whitewater use requires a permit that is issued only if you can demonstrate adequate experience and proper equipment. Permits are available at the Art Zimmerman Visitor's Center or at the John Dunn Bridge.

USGS topographic maps: Guadalupe Mountain

BLM surface map: Wheeler Peak

Resources:
- *Western Whitewater, From the Rockies to the Pacific,* by Jim Cassady, Bill Cross and Fryar Calhoun, published by North Fork Press, Berkeley, CA; (415) 424-1213.
- The BLM publishes a brochure and map entitled "Rio Grande Wild and Scenic River."

For more information: Contact the BLM Taos Resource Area, 224 Cruz Alta Road, Taos, NM 87571; (505) 758-8851.

ORILLA VERDE RECREATION AREA

See letter Z on map page 380

camping, canoeing, fishing, flat-water rafting, hiking, picnicking

Formerly Rio Grande State Park, the Orilla Verde Recreation Site is a good family destination year-round for water recreation and hiking activities. Fishing is for rainbow and brown trout and northern pike. There are petroglyphs and artifacts remaining in the area—help to protect the resources by looking but not touching. There are a number of trails within the area that are suitable for exploring the side canyons. Camp in the designated campgrounds or primitive sites along the river. There are organized and guided nature hikes and interpretive programs scheduled from Memorial Day through Labor Day. It is north of Santa Fe—contact the BLM for specific directions.

USGS topographic maps: Carson, Taos Southwest

BLM surface map: Taos

For more information: Contact the BLM Taos Resource Area, 224 Cruz Alta Road, Taos, NM 87571; (505) 758-8851.

FORT STANTON RECREATION AREA

See letter AA on map page 380

backpacking, camping, cross-country skiing, fishing, hiking, horseback riding, mountain biking, picnicking, wildlife observation

Nestled in the foothills of the Capitan and Sierra Blanca Mountains, the Fort Stanton Recreation Area offers a unique blend of mountain streams, rolling hills, mesa tops and open bottomlands. The entire region is easily accessible from US 380, which passes through the north end of the area heading east from Capitan or west from Lincoln.

Activity Highlight: Mountain biking

The 17-mile Tlaloc Mountain Bike Trail offers the biker an opportunity to enjoy the rich diversity of the landscape from the vantage point of a bike seat. Elevation gains are moderate, with 1,000 feet of climbing over the first nine miles and 1,000 feet of descent over the next eight miles. To get to the trailhead, drive northwest on US 380 from Lincoln for approximately 5.6 miles to the signed entrance to the Fort Stanton Special Management Area. Turn left on the first dirt road, about a half mile from the entrance. Park at the Fort Stanton Cave and Campground parking area. The trailhead begins at the cave parking lot. Be sure to check the bulletin board for cautions and announcements regarding trail conditions.

Activity Highlights: Horseback riding and hiking

The Fort Stanton Horse Trails System is considered one of the best-kept secrets in New Mexico—whoops, now the word is out. The trails themselves lie within small canyons and ridges between the Sacramento and Capitan mountains. Views are stunning and the sunsets are, well, unbelievable. The trailhead, known as the Horse Trails Parking Lot is reached either by traveling west from Roswell, east from Carrizozo on US 380, or north from Ruidoso on Road 37 to US 380 at Capitan. From US 380, drive to the Fort Stanton Cutoff, State Road 214 and head south, driving nine-tenths of a mile to the signed trailhead. The Capitan Trail begins through the gate across the paved road. This is the easier of the two trails. It is 7.5 miles long, with a moderate elevation gain and loss. The Big Tank/East Well Trail begins at the southeast corner of the parking lot; it is 10 miles long, with an elevation gain and loss of 600 feet. It is steep and rocky in places. Water is available at East Well and Rio Bonito Creek. It is a good destination year-round, but summers get hot.

For more information: Contact the BLM Roswell Resource Area, Federal Building, Room 216, Fifth and Richardson streets, P.O. Drawer 1857, Roswell, NM 88202; (505) 624-1790.

FORT STANTON CAVE

See letter BB on map page 380

caving

The BLM manages more than 195 caves from the Roswell Resource Area Office. There are approximately five caves that are managed intensively and require permits to enter. The three most noteworthy caves are Crockett, Torgac and Fort Stanton. Fort Stanton and Torgac caves are National Natural Landmarks. Fort Stanton Cave is approximately 12 miles long, with large limestone and serpentine passages. Some of the passages are twisting and very narrow. The cave is well regarded for its rare formations of velvet as well as helictites, selenite needles and forms of gypsum. Caving requires skill, knowledge and care. If you have the proper equipment and expertise, and can prove it, the BLM will be happy to issue you a permit to enter this wild cave. Most explorable caves are gated and locked. Three listed endangered species of bats hibernate here in the winter. For that reason, the cave is closed from November 1 to April 15 each year. The BLM has cave maps and brochures for the asking.

For more information: Contact the BLM Roswell Resource Area, Federal Building, Room 216, Fifth and Richardson streets, P.O. Drawer 1857, Roswell, NM 88202; (505) 624-1790.

MESCALERO SANDS
OUTSTANDING NATURAL AREA

See letter CC on map page 380

hiking, wildlife observation

This 6,300-acre area contains the largest drifting sand dunes in southeastern New Mexico, traveling approximately one foot northeast every year—coming to a state near you in the next century? The buff-colored quart particle dunes tower up to 60-feet above the surrounding terrain. Plants such as shinnery oak, sand bluestem and yucca cling to the dunes, as does cottonwood. Beetles, kangaroo rats and the rare sand-dune sagebrush lizard, along with other mammals, birds, insects and reptiles, call Mescalero home. The lesser prairie chicken resides in the shinnery oak community. Spring, fall and winter are the best times to visit—summertime temperatures can reach a mind-warping 116°F—yeah, but it's a dry heat, hah! Be sure to bring plenty of drinking water and adequate sun and wind protection, no matter what season you visit. Head east from Roswell on US 380 and drive approximately 40 miles. Turn south at the signs located halfway between mileposts 193 and 194.

For more information: Contact the BLM Roswell Resource Area, Federal Building, Room 216, Fifth and Richardson streets, P.O. Drawer 1857, Roswell, NM 88202; (505) 624-1790.

CHOSA DRAW

caving

The BLM manages more than 150 caves from the Carlsbad Resource Area office. The caves are formed in three different rock types: limestone, gypsum and lava. Seventeen of the caves are gated and require permits for access. The rest are open for public use and enjoyment. The Chosa Draw has been designated an Area of Critical Environmental Concern because of the outstanding and complex system of gypsum caves—many tied together hydrologically by underwater passages. In fact, the second-longest gypsum cave in the U.S. is located in this region. More than 160 sinkholes and cave entrances provide for point sources of groundwater recharge. Some of the underwater river systems in the area support species of cave-adapted fish and freshwater shrimp.

Caving is a risky activity, and is potentially damaging to the environment if not done with care. For that reason, I have chosen not to print specific locations of caves within this region. If you are serious about wanting to explore the caves in the area and can prove your competence, the BLM will be more than happy to provide you with all the assistance possible.

For more information: Contact the BLM Carlsbad Resource Area, 630 East Greene, Carlsbad, NM 88220; (505) 234-5272.

BLM CAMPGROUNDS

1. SIMON CANYON CAMPGROUND—MAP A

Campsites, facilities: There are undesignated sites for tent camping only. Two picnic tables are available. No fires are permitted. There is **no water**. No trash facilities are provided, so pack out all you bring in.

Reservations, fees: There is no fee.

Who to contact: Farmington District Office, 1235 La Plata Highway, Farmington, NM 87401; (505) 599-8900.

Location: Along the San Juan River. To get there, from US 550 at the town of Aztec, head approximately 23 miles east on Route 173. A signed exit and three-mile unpaved access road leads to the site and the Cottonwood Campground, run by the New Mexico State Parks. Tent camping only is allowed at Simon. RVs are required to stay at Cottonwood. The campground is set at 5,700 feet.

Season: All year.

2. ANGEL PEAK CAMPGROUND—MAP A

Campsites, facilities: There are 10 sites, all with picnic tables, grills and fire rings. Pit toilets and sun shelters are available. There is **no water**. There is a 14-day stay limit.

Reservations, fees: There is no fee.

Who to contact: Farmington District Office, 1235 La Plata Highway, Farmington, NM 87401; (505) 599-8900.

Location: From Bloomfield, drive south for 15 miles on Highway 44. Turn left at the sign indicating the campground onto a gravel road and drive another five miles to the entrance. The campground is set at 6,000 feet.

Season: All year.

3. DATIL WELL CAMPGROUND—MAP A

Campsites, facilities: There are 22 sites, all with picnic tables, grills and fire rings. Several sun shelters, water, pit toilets and firewood are available. No wood cutting is allowed. There is a seven-day stay limit.

Reservations, fees: There is a $5 fee per night; pay on site.

Who to contact: Socorro Resource Area, 198 Neel Avenue, Northwest, Socorro, NM 87801; (505) 835-0412.

Location: One mile west of Datil. The campground may be accessed via Highway 12 or US 60. The campground is set at 7,000 feet.

Season: April to October.

4. VALLEY OF FIRES RECREATION AREA—MAP A

Campsites, facilities: There are 25 sites (five designated for tents only), all with picnic tables, grills and fire rings. Water, sun shelters, a pay phone, an RV dump station, flush toilets and a Visitor Contact Station complete with a bookstore are available. A campground host is on site. There is a 21-day stay limit.

Reservations, fees: There is a $7 fee for a developed site plus $4 if electricity is needed. A $5 fee is charged for primitive camping. All fees are per night and collected on site.

Who to contact: Valley of Fires Recreation Area, P.O. Box 871, Carrizozo, NM 88301; (505) 648-2241.

Location: The Valley of Fires Recreation Area is adjacent to US 380 approximately four miles west of Carrizozo. The campground is set at 6,300 feet.

Season: All year. The heaviest visitation occurs between March and November.

5. AGUIRRE SPRINGS CAMPGROUND—MAP A

Campsites, facilities: There are 53 sites, all with picnic tables, grills and fire rings. There is **no water**. Quiet hours are enforced. No firearms or fireworks are allowed. There is a seven-day stay limit.

Reservations, fees: There is a $3 fee.

Who to contact: Mimbres Resource Area, 1800 Marquess Street, Las Cruces, NM 88005; (505) 525-4300.

Location: From Organ, drive 3.5 miles east on US 70 to Aguirre Spring Road. Drive approximately five miles on Aguirre Spring Road to the campground entrance. The entrance gate closes at 6 p.m. in the winter and 8 p.m. in the summer. The campground is set at 5,500 feet.

Season: All year.

6. LA JUNTA CAMPGROUND—MAP B

Campsites, facilities: There are six sites, all with picnic tables and grills. Pit toilets and water are available. There is a 14-day stay limit.

Reservations, fees: There is a $7 fee per night for campsites along the river rim. Pay on site. Campsites along the river require a hike and cost $5 per night.

Who to contact: Taos Resource Area, 224 Cruz Alta Road, Taos, NM 87571; (505) 758-8851.

Location: In the Wild Rivers Recreation Area. Three miles north of the town of Questa on Route 522, turn left on Route 378. Follow the signs that mark the campground access points and the visitor center.

Season: All year.

7. LITTLE ARSENIC SPRING CAMPGROUND—MAP B

Campsites, facilities: There are four sites, all with picnic tables and grills. Pit toilets and water are available. There is a 14-day stay limit.

Reservations, fees: There is a $7 fee per night for campsites along the river rim. Pay on site. Campsites along the river require a hike and cost $5 per night.

Who to contact: Taos Resource Area, 224 Cruz Alta Road, Taos, NM 87571; (505) 758-8851.

Location: In the Wild Rivers Recreation Area. Three miles north of the town of Questa on Route 522, turn left on Route 378. Follow the signs that mark the campground access points and the visitor center.

Season: All year.

8. BIG ARSENIC SPRINGS CAMPGROUND—MAP B

Campsites, facilities: There are six sites, all with picnic tables and grills. Pit toilets and water are available. There is a 14-day stay limit.

Reservations, fees: There is a $7 fee per night for campsites along the river rim. Pay on site. Campsites along the river require a hike and are $5 per night.

Who to contact: Taos Resource Area, 224 Cruz Alta Road, Taos, NM 87571; (505) 758-8851.

Location: In the Wild Rivers Recreation Area. Three miles north of the town of Questa on Route 522, turn left on Route 378. Follow the signs that mark the campground access points and the visitor center.

Season: All year.

9. El Aguaje Campground—Map B

Campsites, facilities: There are six sites, all with picnic tables and grills. Pit toilets and water are available. There is a 14-day stay limit.

Reservations, fees: There is a $7 fee per night for campsites along the river rim. Pay on site. Campsites along the river require a hike and cost $5 per night.

Who to contact: Taos Resource Area, 224 Cruz Alta Road, Taos, NM 87571; (505) 758-8851.

Location: In the Wild Rivers Recreation Area. Three miles north of the town of Questa on Route 522, turn left on Route 378. Follow the signs that mark the campground access points and the visitor center.

Season: All year.

10. Montoso Campground—Map B

Campsites, facilities: There are two sites, both with picnic tables and grills. Pit toilets and water are available. There is a 14-day stay limit.

Reservations, fees: There is a $8 fee per night for campsites along the river rim. Pay on site. Campsites along the river require a hike and cost $5 per night.

Who to contact: Taos Resource Area, 224 Cruz Alta Road, Taos, NM 87571; (505) 758-8851.

Location: In the Wild Rivers Recreation Area. Three miles north of the town of Questa on Route 522, turn left on Route 378. Follow the signs that mark the campground access points and the visitor center.

Season: All year.

11. Taos Junction Campground—Map B

Campsites, facilities: There are four sites, all with shelters, picnic tables and grills. Flush toilets, water, a group shelter and campsite are available. There is a 14-day stay limit.

Reservations, fees: There is a $7 fee per night and a $3 day-use fee. Pay on site. The group shelter is available for $40 per night or $30 for day use only.

Who to contact: Taos Resource Area, 224 Cruz Alta Road, Taos, NM 87571; (505) 758-8851.

Location: Within the Orilla Verde Recreation Area along the Rio Grande. From Taos, head south for 12 miles on Highway 68 to Highway 570 and turn right (west). Once within the Orilla Verde Recreation Area, there are five available campgrounds situated along Highway 570 in the following order: Taos Junction Campground, Petaca Campground, Arroyo Hondo Campground, Orilla Verde Campground, Pilar Campground.

Season: All year.

12. PETACA CAMPGROUND—MAP B

Campsites, facilities: There are five sites, all with picnic tables, shelters and grills. Water and vault toilets are available. There is a 14-day stay limit.

Reservations, fees: There is a $7 fee per night and a $3 day-use fee. Pay on site.

Who to contact: Taos Resource Area, 224 Cruz Alta Road, Taos, NM 87571; (505) 758-8851.

Location: In the Orilla Verde Recreation Area along the Rio Grande. From Taos, head south for 12 miles on Highway 68 to Highway 570 and turn right (west). Once within the Orilla Verde Recreation Area, there are five available campgrounds situated along Highway 570 in the following order: Taos Junction Campground, Petaca Campground, Arroyo Hondo Campground, Orilla Verde Campground, Pilar Campground.

Season: All year.

13. ARROYO HONDO CAMPGROUND—MAP B

Campsites, facilities: There are five sites, all with picnic tables, grills and fire rings. A vault toilet is available. There is **no water**. There is a 14-day stay limit.

Reservations, fees: There is a $5 fee per night and a $3 day-use fee. Pay on site.

Who to contact: Taos Resource Area, 224 Cruz Alta Road, Taos, NM 87571; (505) 758-8851.

Location: Within the Orilla Verde Recreation Area along the Rio Grande. From Taos, head south for 12 miles on Highway 68 to Highway 570 and turn right (west). Once within the Orilla Verde Recreation Area, there are five available campgrounds situated along Highway 570 in the following order: Taos Junction Campground, Petaca Campground, Arroyo Hondo Campground, Orilla Verde Campground, Pilar Campground.

Season: All year.

14. ORILLA VERDE CAMPGROUND—MAP B

Campsites, facilities: There are 10 sites, all with picnic tables, grills and fire rings. Water, vault and flush toilets, several sun shelters, a group shelter and a pay phone are available. No firearms or fireworks are allowed. There is a 14-day stay limit.

Reservations, fees: There is a $7 fee per night and a $3 day-use fee. Pay on site. A group shelter is available for $40 per night and $30 for day use only.

Who to contact: Taos Resource Area, 224 Cruz Alta Road, Taos, NM 87571; (505) 758-8851.

Location: In the Orilla Verde Recreation Area along the Rio Grande. From Taos, head south for 12 miles on Highway 68 to Highway 570 and turn right (west). Once within the Orilla Verde Recreation Area, there are five available campgrounds situated along Highway 570 in the following order: Taos Junction Campground, Petaca Campground, Arroyo Hondo Campground, Orilla Verde Campground, Pilar Campground.

Season: All year.

15. PILAR CAMPGROUND—MAP B

Campsites, facilities: There are five sites, all with picnic tables, shelters, fire rings and grills. Water and a portable toilet are available. There is a 14-day stay limit.

Reservations, fees: There is a $7 fee per night and a $3 day-use fee. Pay on site.

Who to contact: Taos Resource Area, 224 Cruz Alta Road, Taos, NM 87571; (505) 758-8851.

Location: In the Orilla Verde Recreation Area along the Rio Grande. From Taos, head south for 12 miles on Highway 68 to Highway 570 and turn right (west). Once within the Orilla Verde Recreation Area, there are five available campgrounds situated along Highway 570 in the following order: Taos Junction Campground, Petaca Campground, Arroyo Hondo Campground, Orilla Verde Campground, Pilar Campground.

Season: All year.

16. OVERLOOK CAMPGROUND—MAP B

Campsites, facilities: There are five sites, all with picnic tables and grills. Pit toilets and water are available. There is a 14-day stay limit.

Reservations, fees: There is a $7 fee per night; pay on site.

Who to contact: Taos Resource Area, 224 Cruz Alta Road, Taos, NM 87571; (505) 758-8851.

Location: From Santa Fe, drive north on US 84/285 for approximately 20 miles and turn right onto Route 503. Drive nine miles to the campground entrance turnoff.

Season: All year.

17. NORTHLAKE CAMPGROUND—MAP B

Campsites, facilities: There are five sites, all with picnic tables and grills. Pit toilets, a boat ramp and water are available. There is a 14-day stay limit.

Reservations, fees: There is a $7 fee per night; pay on site.

Who to contact: Taos Resource Area, 224 Cruz Alta Road, Taos, NM 87571; (505) 758-8851.

Location: From Santa Fe, drive north on US 84/285 for approximately 20 miles and turn right onto Route 503. Drive 13 miles to Route 596 and turn right to get to the campground entrance.

Season: All year.

18. THREE RIVERS PETROGLYPH SITE CAMPGROUND—MAP B

Campsites, facilities: There are six sites, all with picnic tables, grills and fire rings. Water, pit toilets and sun shelters are available. No firearms or fireworks are allowed. There is a 14-day stay limit.

Reservations, fees: There is a $2 fee.

Who to contact: Caballo Resource Area, 1800 Marquess Street, Las Cruces, NM 88005; (505) 525-4300.

Location: From Tularosa, drive 17 miles north on US 54 to the town of Three Rivers. Head four miles east on County Road 830 to the petroglyph site entrance. The campground is set at 4,990 feet.

Season: All year.

19. RIO BONITO CAMPGROUND—MAP B

Campsites, facilities: There are five sites, all with picnic tables and fire rings. Pit toilets are available. There is **no water**. There is a 14-day stay limit.

Reservations, fees: There is no fee.

Who to contact: Roswell Resource Area, Federal Building, 2nd Floor, Fifth and Richardson streets, P.O. Box 1857, Roswell, NM 88202; (505) 624-1790.

Location: Drive west on US 380 from Lincoln for approximately six miles, turn south on Highway 214 to Fort Stanton. Continue west through the Fort Stanton grounds for approximately one mile to the signed access road leading to the campground. Follow the improved graveled road for three miles to the campground.

Season: All year.

20. FORT STANTON CAVE CAMPGROUND—MAP B

Campsites, facilities: The campsites are primitive and undesignated. Two sites have picnic tables and fire rings. A pit toilet is available. There is **no water**. No trash facilities are provided, so pack out all you bring in. There is a 14-day stay limit.

Reservations, fees: There is no fee.

Who to contact: Roswell Resource Area, Federal Building, 2nd Floor, Fifth and Richardson streets, P.O. Box 1857, Roswell, NM 88202; (505) 624-1790.

Location: Drive west on US 380 from Lincoln for approximately 5.6 miles to the signed entrance to the Fort Stanton Special Management Area. Turn left (south), cross a cattle guard and drive onto a dirt road. Drive about a half mile to the campground. Park at the Fort Stanton Cave parking area.

Season: All year.

STATE INFORMATION OVERVIEW

NEW MEXICO STATE OFFICE
1474 Rodeo Road, P.O. Box 27115, Santa Fe, NM 87505; (505) 438-7400

TULSA DISTRICT OFFICE
9522-H East 47th Place, Tulsa, OK 74145; (918) 581-6480

Oklahoma Resource Area, 221 North Service Road, Moore, OK 73160; (404) 794-9624

ROSWELL DISTRICT OFFICE
1717 West Second Street, Roswell, NM 88201; (505) 627-0272

Roswell Resource Area, Federal Building, Room 216, Fifth and Richardson streets, P.O. Drawer 1857, Roswell, NM 88202; (505) 624-1790

Carlsbad Resource Area, 630 East Greene, Carlsbad, NM 88220; (505) 234-5272

ALBUQUERQUE DISTRICT OFFICE
435 Montano Road, Northeast, Albuquerque, NM 87107; (505) 761-8700

Rio Puerco Resource Area, 435 Montano Road, Northeast, Albuquerque, NM 87107; (505) 761-8700

Grants Field Station, 620 East Santa Fe Avenue, Grants, NM 87020; (505) 758-8851

Taos Resource Area, 224 Cruz Alta Road, Taos, NM 87571; (505) 758-8851

FARMINGTON DISTRICT OFFICE
1235 La Plata Highway, Farmington, NM 87401; (505) 599-8900

LAS CRUCES DISTRICT OFFICE
1800 Marquess Street, Las Cruces, NM 88005; (505) 525-4300

Mimbres Resource Area, 1800 Marquess Street, Las Cruces, NM 88005; (505) 525-4300

Caballo Resource Area, 1800 Marquess Street, Las Cruces, NM 88005; (505) 525-4300

Socorro Resource Area, 198 Neel Avenue Northwest, Socorro, NM 87801; (505) 835-0412

CHAPTER TEN

OREGON

Maps—pp. 420, 422
Oregon Map A Locations—pp. 424-444
Oregon Map B Locations—pp. 444-453
Information Resources—p. 480

(SEE MAP A)   (SEE MAP B)

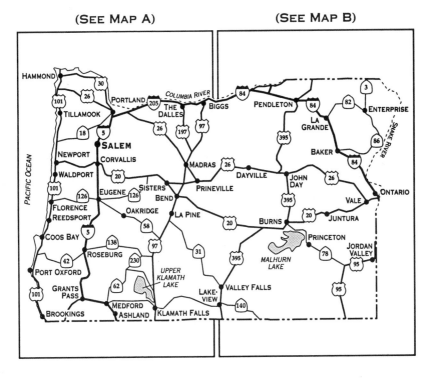

MAP A—OREGON

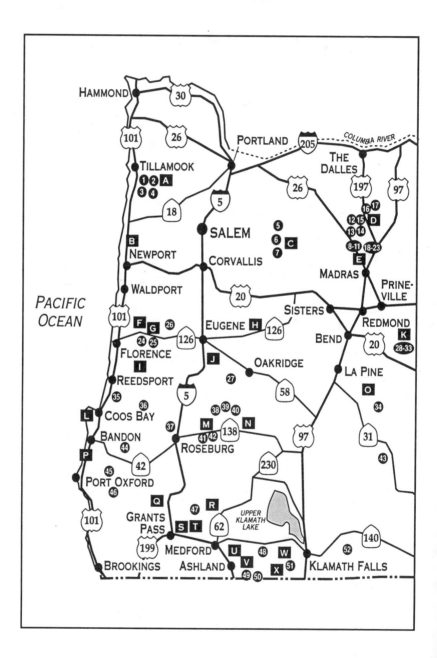

MAP REFERENCES

BLM CAMPGROUNDS

MAP B—OREGON

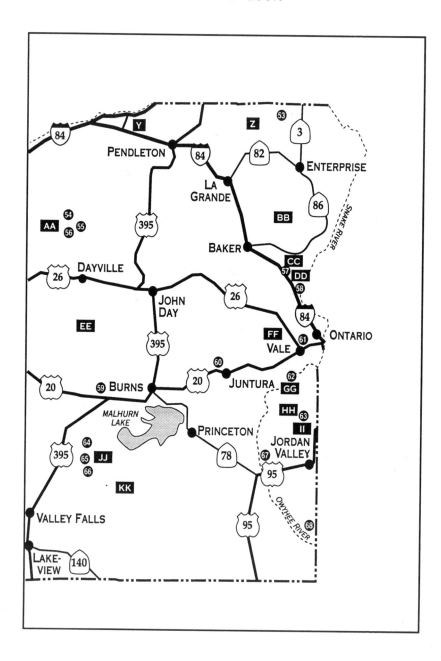

MAP REFERENCES

BLM CAMPGROUNDS

OREGON—MAP A

NESTUCCA RIVER

See letter A on map page 420

camping, hiking, inner-tubing, mountain biking, wildlife observation
The Nestucca River is a lush riparian system that supports nearly 200 species of wildlife and anadromous fish—chinook and coho salmon and steelhead trout. Bear Creek and Alder Creek are the best sites for wildlife viewing. The Nestucca River Road provides access to several recreation sites along the river and is designated as a National Back Country Byway, but be cautious of logging traffic on the road. Deer, elk, songbirds and bald eagles may be seen here. From Interstate 5, exit at Wilsonville and proceed west to Newberg. Follow Highway 240 west to Highway 47 at Yamhill and then continue south to Carlton. From Carlton, take Meadow Lake Road west for approximately 12 miles where it becomes the BLM's Nestucca River Road.

BLM surface map: Yamhill

For more information: Contact the BLM Salem District Office, 1717 Fabry Road Southeast, Salem, OR 97306; (503) 375-5646.

YAQUINA HEAD OUTSTANDING NATURAL AREA

See letter B on map page 420

hiking, tidepooling, wildlife observation
This coastal headland and offshore rocky area provides vital habitat for a variety of marine wildlife. Tidepool invertebrates such as hermit crabs, sea anemones, sea stars and sea urchins may be enjoyed year-round as are harbor seals. The BLM has created a barrier-free intertidal zone, some three acres in extent, which has been open to persons with disabilities and all other visitors since fall, 1994. Gray whales may be seen migrating at Christmas time and from March to May every year, and "resident" whales can often be seen just offshore during the summer. There is an historic lighthouse, built in 1872, that is maintained by the BLM and overlooks the Pacific Ocean. The BLM offered tours of the lighthouse since June, 1994. The site is located just north of Newport along US 101.

BLM surface map: Corvallis

For more information: Contact the BLM Yaquina Head Outstanding Natural Area, P.O. Box 936, Newport, OR 97365; (503) 375-2863.

TABLE ROCK WILDERNESS AREA

See letter C on map page 420

backpacking, camping , hiking, horseback riding, wildlife observation

Table Rock Wilderness Area is located in Clackamas County along the western foothills of the Cascade Range. Molalla, with a population of approximately 3,100, is the largest town near the wilderness; the town lies 19 miles to the northwest by road. The terrain is steep and rugged and is the largest block of undeveloped forest land in an otherwise heavily logged or developed area. The wilderness area is also the habitat for the northern spotted owl. Deer and elk use the area as a wintering range. There are 16 miles of developed trails within the wilderness area; from on top of the ridges, you can see Mount Rainier, Mount St. Helens, Mount Adams, Mount Hood, Mount Jefferson and the North, Middle and South Sisters.

Four trailheads provide access to many trails within the region: Old Bridge, Table Rock, Rooster Rock Road and Peachuck Lookout. From Molalla, just off Highway 211, drive to the eastern end of town and head right at the fork in the road. This places you on South Mathias Road. After three-tenths of a mile, the road curves and turns into South Feyrer Park Road. Drive 1.9 miles to a junction and turn right on South Dickey Prairie Road. Continue for 5.2 miles and cross the Molalla River, at which point the road changes names again—this time it's South Molalla Road. Drive 12.7 miles to the junction of Middle Fork and Copper Creek Roads and make a left on Middle Fork Road. Then drive 2.6 miles to the Table Rock Access Road. Turn right and head 6.6 more miles to the signed Table Rock trailhead.

USGS topographic map: Rooster Rock

BLM surface map: North Santiam River

Additional maps: A map of the Table Rock Wilderness is available from the BLM.

For more information: Contact the BLM Salem District Office, 1717 Fabry Road Southeast, Salem, OR 97306; (503) 375-5646.

DESCHUTES WILD AND SCENIC RIVER / SHERAR'S FALLS

See letter D on map page 420

camping, fishing, hiking, rafting, whitewater kayaking, wildlife observation

At Sherar's Falls, one can view Native Americans using traditional dip-netting methods for catching steelhead trout and chinook salmon. The heaviest fishing takes place from April to June for spring chinook and from August to October for fall chinook and steelhead. From Maupin, 30 miles south of Dalles on Highway 197, follow the Deschutes River Access Road (a National Back Country Byway) downstream along the river for eight miles to the falls. Continue down the road to find Beavertail and Macks Canyon campgrounds as well as river access to the Deschutes. You will enjoy the scenery of this river area as it follows a serpentine route carved deeply into the ancient lava flows of the Columbia River Plateau. Four small BLM campgrounds exist upriver from Maupin and eight more below Maupin—this is in addition to the larger sites at Beavertail and Macks Canyon.

BLM surface maps: Lower Deschutes River Map. Order this map from the BLM for $4.

Resources

• *Western Whitewater, From the Rockies to the Pacific*, by Jim Cassady, Bill Cross and Fryar Calhoun, published by North Fork Press, Berkeley, CA; (415) 424-1213.

For more information: Contact the BLM Prineville District Office, 185 East Fourth Street, P.O. Box 550, Prineville, OR 97754; (503) 447-4115.

MIDDLE DESCHUTES RIVER

See letter E on map page 420

backpacking, camping, fishing, hiking, wildlife observation

The Middle Deschutes River is located upriver from Lake Billy chinook and northwest of Redmond, Oregon. A 19-mile river segment from Odin Falls to the upper end of Lake Billy chinook has been designated a component of the National Wild and Scenic River system. Outstanding scenic, recreational, cultural, geological, wildlife and historic sites exist within the rugged, steep-walled basalt canyon. The canyon increases in depth as it proceeds northward. Three waterfalls and a wide variety of riparian vegetation enhance the qualities of this region. Fishing is excellent for rainbow and German brown trout, Dolly Varden and kokanee salmon. The region also harbors prehistoric sites, rock art, rock shelters and a historic river crossing.

The best access to the river is at Steelhead Falls, where a Civilian Conservation Corps trail still runs along the bank. There is also an informal camping area here that the BLM hopes to develop into a seven-site campground in late 1995. From Highway 97, north of Redmond, head left (west) on Lower Bridge Market; from Lower Bridge Road, head right onto an unsigned road following the signs toward Crooked River Ranch. Turn left on Chinook Drive at the T-intersection. Head left on Badger Road, which will turn into Blacktail Drive. At the T-intersection, take a right onto Quail Road and then turn left onto River Road. Follow River Road all the way to the trailhead and the parking area.

Map: The Central Oregon Public Lands Map is available from the BLM for $4.

For more information: Contact the BLM Prineville District Office, 185 East Fourth Street, P.O. Box 550, Prineville, OR 97754; (503) 447-4115.

LAKE CREEK FALLS

See letter F on map page 420

hiking, wildlife observation

This is an excellent spot to view chinook and coho salmon between November and December, and steelhead trout from February to March. The site features several waterfalls, two fish ladders, five concrete weirs and interpretive signs. From Eugene take Highway 36 east to Triangle Lake and park at the Blachly-Lane Campground. Follow the path along the highway to the fish ladder access point.

USGS topographic map: Triangle Lake

BLM surface map: Eugene

For more information: Contact the BLM Eugene District Office, 2890 Chad Drive, P.O. Box 10266, Eugene, OR 97440; (503) 683-6600.

WHITTAKER CREEK RECREATION SITE

See letter G on map page 420

camping, fishing, hiking, wildlife observation

Whittaker Creek offers good wildlife-viewing opportunities of migrating coho and chinook salmon in November and December, as well as deer, elk, and songbirds the rest of the year. The site has a 1.5-mile trail through old growth forest to a scenic view point. To reach the recreation area, take Highway 126 west from Eugene to Austa. Turn south on Siuslaw River Road (BLM Road 18-8-34). Drive 1.5 miles to BLM Road 18-8-21. Turn right and proceed to Whittaker Creek Recreation Site; follow trails to the creek.

USGS topographic map: Roman Nose Mountain

BLM surface map: Eugene

For more information: Contact the BLM Eugene District Office, 2890 Chad Drive, P.O. Box 10266, Eugene, OR 97440; (503) 683-6600.

McKENZIE RIVER

See letter H on map page 420

boating, camping, canoeing, hiking, wildlife observation

Wildlife is common year-round along this river area and may be viewed best from the river. Expect to see a variety of raptors, waterfowl, songbirds, beavers and deer. From Springfield, take Highway 126 east to the BLM-managed section of river between Vida and Blue River. Perhaps the most popular boating trip is from a put-in at Finn Rock Bridge to a take-out at the Dorris State Park. A BLM Watchable Wildlife site with interpretive sign is located at the Silver Creek Boat Launch off Highway 126.

USGS topographic map: Vida

BLM surface map: McKenzie River

For more information: Contact the BLM Eugene District Office, 2890 Chad Drive, P.O. Box 10266, Eugene, OR 97440; (503) 683-6600.

DEAN CREEK ELK VIEWING AREA

See letter I on map page 420

wildlife observation

Roosevelt elk commonly graze the meadows near Dean Creek, adjacent to Highway 38, three miles east of Reedsport. Throughout most of the year, the elk can be viewed at any time of the day, except in early spring when the female cows seek cover to give birth and raise calves. Large numbers of waterfowl will also be visible, including mallards, wood ducks, great blue heron and Canada geese, as well as osprey and bald eagle. A small outdoor interpretive center explains the local wildlife.

For more information: Contact the BLM Coos Bay District Office, 1300 Airport Lane, North Bend, OR 97459; (503) 756-0100.

ROW RIVER TRAIL

See letter J on map page 420

fishing, hiking, horseback riding, mountain biking, wildlife viewing

The Oregon Pacific and Eastern (OPE) railroad line was built to provide rail transport for timber products from the Culp Creek Mill to the city of Cottage Grove for further processing or shipment to other parts of the country. Unfortunately, or fortunately depending on your view, a number of events caused the owners to abandon the operation and leave the OPE railroad to fade into disuse.

It didn't take the BLM long to muster up support from other public and private agencies to create the rails-to-trails conversion. The actual trail will extend 14.1 miles between the covered bridge at Mosby Creek Road and the town of Culp Creek. Although the trail is intended for mountain bikers, equestrians and hikers, it will not be immediately available to all users until a number of railroad bridge crossings are surfaced. The current trail is diverted to nearby county road bridges for river crossings, but since these roads are lightly traveled, the BLM doesn't feel that this will detract from the beauty of the trail in any manner. Negotiations are in process to extend the trail an additional six miles to connect the route with the boundary of the Umpqua National Forest and an entirely different network of trail exploration opportunities.

The abandoned rail bed skirts the banks of the Row River to Dorena Reservoir, running along the shore for approximately six miles, and then rejoins the river following its banks once again until reaching the old Bohemia lumber mill in Culp Creek. Along the way, the trail crosses four bridges, which the BLM hopes to have surfaced by the end of the year.

In keeping with the National Trails Day mandate of "trails for all Americans" the Row River Trail is more than just a pathway or rails-to-trails conversion. The 14.1 miles offer ready access to nearby Dorena Reservoir for swimming, fishing and birdwatching, as well as being an ideal connecting route to the various Lane County parks and smaller communities that lie along the trail.

From the trail, it is also possible to connect a bike ride east into the Bryce Creek Recreation Area or head north to Mount June and the Lost Creek Back Country Byway which leads to the cities of Pleasant Hill and Eugene. Bikers also have an option of continuing through the Willamette National Forest into the town of Oakridge.

It is believed that the scenic and other virtues of the Row River Trail could easily attract 200,000 visitors a year to the area, revitalizing the local economy from extraction based to tourist based.

Location: Just south of Eugene and east of Interstate 5 near the community of Cottage Grove. The Row River Trail begins on the eastern outskirts of the city of Cottage Grove, south of the Mount View School and Cottage Grove Airport and at the intersection of Lang and Mosby Creek roads. An undeveloped parking area exists at this time although there are plans to create a formal parking area with room for up to 40 vehicles.

Camping: There are two campgrounds within reach of the trail. The one operated by the Army Corps of Engineers, Schwarz Park Campground, is just south of the trail on Dorena Reservoir. The other campground, Sharps Creek Campground, is managed by the BLM and is located approximately 2.5 miles south of the trail on the Sharps Creek Road Calapooya Divide Back Country Byway.

Season: Spring, summer and fall are the best times to explore the trail.

USGS topographic maps: Cottage Grove, Blue Mountain, Culp Creek, Dorena Lake

BLM surface map: Eugene

Additional maps: *Oregon Atlas and Gazetteer*, published by DeLorme Mapping, P.O. Box 298, Freeport, ME 04032; (207) 865-4171.

For more information: Contact the BLM Eugene District, 2890 Chad Drive, P.O. Box 10226, Eugene, OR 97440-2226; (503) 683-6121.

CROOKED RIVER

See letter K on map page 420

camping, fishing, hiking, wildlife observation

Crooked River is a designated Wild and Scenic River, and for good reason—it's beautiful. Many call this spectacular river canyon one of the best areas the BLM has to offer in Oregon. There is a BLM campground at Chimney Rock, 17 miles south of Prineville. There are also nine primitive campgrounds along the canyon and river. Highway 27 south from Prineville is designated a National Back Country Byway and provides access to much of the river canyon and camping areas.

On the other side of Prineville Reservoir, to the east and still on the Crooked River, is an excellent spot to view bald eagles and other birds of prey. The best time to view bald eagles is between February and March. From Prineville, drive one mile east on Highway 26 and then turn south onto the Paulina Highway. Drive for 25 miles to Post and then continue on the Paulina Highway along the Crooked River.

Maps: The Central Oregon Public Lands Map is available from the BLM for $4.

For more information: Contact the BLM Prineville District Office, 185 East Fourth Street, P.O. Box 550, Prineville, OR 97754; (503) 447-4115.

COOS BAY SHORELANDS

See letter L on map page 420

hiking, wildlife observation

The Coos Bay Shorelands are composed of the North Spit, a sand spit five miles long and up to one mile in width, and Coos Head, a rugged coastal headland with rocky cliffs more than 100 feet high. More than 270 bird species reside in or migrate through Coos Bay, Oregon's largest estuary. Unique birds here include the brown pelican, tufted puffins and peregrine falcons. Seals and California sea lions are also common in this area. The North Spit has the largest great blue heron rookery on Oregon's south coast. In early September, the annual Shorebird Festival is held by the Cape Arago Audubon Society, which offers guided trips. In addition, the North Spit includes active coastal sand dunes, forested upland habitat and freshwater wetlands adjacent to ocean and estuary environments. The confluence of habitats makes this area extraordinarily diverse. The North Spit may be reached from US 101. Take the turnoff to Horsefall Beach and Dune Access and then turn left on the Trans-Pacific Highway. Access beyond the highway, to the interior of the spit, is limited to foot traffic and all-terrain or four-wheel-drive vehicles because of the sand. A BLM boat ramp is available.

USGS topographic maps: Empire, North Bend, Charleston

For more information: Contact the BLM Coos Bay District Office, 1300 Airport Lane, North Bend, OR 97459; (503) 756-0100.

DEADLINE FALLS
See letter M on map page 420

hiking, mountain biking, fishing, wildlife observation

Located along the North Umpqua Trail on the Tioga segment, Deadline Falls offers a unique opportunity to view chinook and coho salmon and steelhead trout attempting to migrate up the falls. The best time to view this phenomenon is between May and September. To get there, from Roseburg head 23 miles east on Highway 138 to the Swiftwater Bridge. Immediately after crossing the bridge, park in the lot on the left. Follow the North Umpqua Trail approximately one-quarter mile to the spur trail leading to an observation point. (For more information on the North Umpqua Trail, see the listing below.)

For more information: Contact the BLM Roseburg District, 777 Northwest Garden Valley Boulevard, Roseburg, OR 97470; (503) 440-4930.

NORTH UMPQUA RIVER AND TRAIL
See letter N on map page 420

backpacking, camping, fishing, hiking, horseback riding, kayaking, mountain biking, wheelchair access, whitewater rafting, wildlife observation

Umpqua was the Native American name for the area around the Umpqua River. The name was adopted by European settlers as both the name of the river and of the Native Americans who fished and hunted in the area until the 1850s when white settlers began to push them out. The area is perhaps best known for winter and summer steelhead fishing, which brought novelist Zane Grey to the river for many years. For those interested in fishing, a wheelchair-accessible fishing platform is available year-round at the Swiftwater Recreation Site on the North Umpqua River.

Activity Highlight: Mountain biking

The entire trail consists of an 11-mile segment on BLM lands with 66 additional miles on U.S. Forest Service land. Mountain bikes are allowed on all but a three-mile segment of Boulder Creek Wilderness and an approximately 10-mile segment of the Mount Thielsen Wilderness. Riders report that the best mountain biking with minimum equestrian use is on the BLM section. The trail is close to the river, with excellent opportunities for views. The trail width is a minimum 36 inches wide, making it ideal for mountain biking, horseback riding and hiking. The trail condition is good, but riders should be alert for slides and loose rocks that may contribute pedaling hazards at any time. Bob Butte within the BLM section is a steep grade approximately one-half mile long.

Activity Highlight: Whitewater rafting

The river is rated Class III to IV and is considered good for families and first-timers as long as experienced boaters are along on the trip. A number of outfitters run commercial trips on the river. Check with the BLM for a list of licensed outfitters. This is the river many whitewater guides head to on their days off since the rapids are lively, the water clear and the canyon thickly forested.

Location: Near Roseburg, Oregon. Take Highway 138 to Swiftwater Bridge just one mile east of Idleyld Park. Parking is available on both sides of the river. There are restrooms and an information kiosk at the trailhead.

Camping: Campgrounds are available, but typically they are on the opposite side of the river and inaccessible to trail-users. Camping is allowed along the trail, but always set up camp away from meadows, shorelines and the trail.

Season: The best time for trail use is May through October. Be sure to check on weather conditions—the trail can sometimes be very muddy in the rainy season. Large numbers of trees often fall across the trail, which could make it very frustrating for a mountain biker who rides the trail prior to its annual maintenance—maintenance is usually in May. The boating season is from June to July. Also, it is a good idea to check on fire conditions with the BLM before heading out.

Permits: No permits are necessary for the trail. Permits are required for commercial boating.

USGS topographic maps: Sutherlin, Roseburg

Additional map: Umpqua National Forest Visitors Map

Resources

• *Western Whitewater, From the Rockies to the Pacific,* by Jim Cassady, Bill Cross and Fryar Calhoun, published by North Fork Press, Berkeley, CA; (415) 424-1213.

For more information: Contact the BLM Roseburg District, 777 Northwest Garden Valley Boulevard, Roseburg, OR 97470; (503) 440-4930. This area is jointly managed by the BLM and the U.S. Forest Service.

CHRISTMAS VALLEY

See letter O on map page 420

backpacking, camping, hiking, mountain biking, rockhounding, spelunking, wildlife observation

The Fort Rock Basin and Christmas Valley is an amazingly diverse region set right in the middle of central Oregon's dramatic volcanic features. There is a National Back Country Byway that winds through the region—in some places requiring a high-clearance vehicle for access. The route is suitable for mountain bikes, although you will want to watch for drivers who are more intent on the scenery than the road in front of them. The byway takes you through sagebrush, lava flows, cinder cones, sand dunes, alfalfa fields and a beautiful forested area. Primitive camping is allowed anywhere along the backcountry route, but please use only previously established sites. The region is located about 70 miles southeast of Bend; the byway loop begins at the Fort Rock turnoff on Highway 31, 18 miles north of Silver Lake. Visit in spring, summer or fall.

The following are some of the more significant natural features in the area:

• Derrik Cave is a unique lava tube cave over 440 yards long and, in places, over 30 feet high. The cave was used as a civil defense fallout shelter in the early 1950s and was stocked with provisions during that time.

• The Devil's Garden, Squaw Ridge and Four Craters lava beds are classified as Wilderness Study Areas with unique geological and botanical features to enjoy. Rugged boots and protective clothing are a must for hiking in this region.

• Crack-In-The-Ground is a large fracture in basalt which is 40 feet deep and nearly two miles long.

BLM surface map: Christmas Valley

For more information: Contact the BLM Lakeview District Office, 1000 Ninth Street South, P.O. Box 151, Lakeview, OR 97630; (503) 947-2177.

NEW RIVER

See letter P on map page 420

hiking, wildlife observation

New River is like none other purely because it is less than 100 years old. Beginning at the outlet creek from Floras Lake, New River flows north about nine miles, separated from the ocean by a single foredune, before emptying into the ocean. The landscape of shore pine, grasses and bare sand supports a rich population of wildlife, including migrating birds. An estuary, freshwater ponds, meadows and shrublands provide habitat diversity. Several are endangered including the snowy plover, peregrine falcon, bald eagle and Aleutian Canada goose. The best times for waterfowl-viewing are from April to May and from August to September. To get there from Bandon, drive 8.3 miles south on US 101, then turn west onto Croft Road. Drive 1.5 miles and enter a dirt one-lane tract. This road leads to the Storm Ranch. A site host is present to answer any questions.

For more information: Contact the BLM Coos Bay District Office, 1300 Airport Lane, North Bend, OR 97459; (503) 756-0100.

KING MOUNTAIN ROCK GARDEN AREA OF CRITICAL ENVIRONMENTAL CONCERN

See letter Q on map page 420

hiking

A short trail provides access to this day-use area. Several species of flowers and birds make their home (or at least their spring and summer home) here and make this a most enjoyable high-elevation hike.

Location: King Mountain Rock Garden ACEC is approximately seven miles east of the town of Wolf Creek off Interstate 5. From southbound Interstate 5 near the town of Wolf Creek, take the Speaker Road exit (exit 77); this exit runs you through the town of Wolf Creek, under the north interchange, and down the frontage road to Speaker Road. Drive about four miles on this paved road until you reach the gravel section where the road splits. This is the end of county maintenance. Take BLM Road 33-5-10. There will be several side roads off this main road; stay on 33-5-10 for approximately three miles past Burma Pond to the top of King Mountain. A developed parking area is located just below the King Mountain summit. The trail to the summit begins near the information board in the parking area.

Camping: Camping is prohibited to protect the sensitive plant species in the area.

Season: Late spring is the best time for viewing the wildflowers. Winter snows stay late on the mountain and can delay the spring bloom. Check with the BLM to be sure the roads are clear and the flowers are blooming. Bring warm clothes and a wind breaker along with your wildflower- and bird-identification books.

USGS topographical maps: Glendale Northeast, Wimer Northwest

Additional maps: BLM Medford District Transportation Map

Resources

• The "King Mountain Rock Garden ACEC" and "Medford District Bird Checklist" brochures are available from the BLM.

For more information: Contact the BLM Medford District Office, Glendale Resource Area, 3040 Biddle Road, Medford, OR 97504; (503) 770-2399.

FLOUNCE ROCK AREA OF CRITICAL ENVIRONMENTAL CONCERN

See letter R on map page 420

mountain biking, wildlife observation

From Stewart State Park at Lost Creek Reservoir, take Crater Lake Highway 62, drive northeast for 3.7 miles and turn left on Ulrich Road. Ulrich Road is an 8.6-mile tour along a volcanic ridge-top offering nice views and good wildlife-viewing possibilities. The wildlife here includes golden eagle, red-tailed hawk, black-backed woodpecker (you'll hear them well before you see them), deer, Roosevelt elk and mountain chickadees. Visit in spring, summer or fall.

USGS topographic map: Battle Falls Northeast

For more information: Contact the BLM Medford District Office, 3040 Biddle Road, Medford, OR 97504; (503) 770-2200.

HISTORIC KELSEY PACKTRAIL

See letter S on map page 420

hiking

One of the original trails in the Rogue Canyon, the Historic Kelsey Packtrail was reopened in 1990 for hiking use. The trail provides another opportunity for hikers who enjoy history as much as scenery.

Location: The Historic Kelsey Packtrail is accessed from approximately 14 miles down the Rogue River National Recreation Trail, adjacent to the wild section of the Rogue River. Another access point for the trail is from Marial, about a two-hour drive from the trailhead. The walk from this access point is about four miles back along the river. From the small town of Merlin, follow the Back Country Byway signs staying on the main road past the Rand Visitor Center to the Grave Creek Bridge, the second crossing of the Rogue River. At the bridge, a road on the left drops down to the river. This is the trailhead for the Rogue River National Recreation Trail. The Kelsey Historic Packtrail is approximately 14 miles down this hiking-only trail.

An alternate route to the trail can be taken by continuing past the Grave Creek Bridge turn-off up the Mount Reuben Road (BLM Road 34-8-1), the Grave Creek to Marial Back Country Byway. Stay on this road for about 14 miles, at which point it turns into BLM

Road 32-7-19.3, the Dutch Henry Road. Continue another mile, now on the Dutch Henry Road, to a left turn onto BLM Road 32-8-31, the Kelsey-Mule Road. Four miles farther is Ninemile Saddle. Continue to follow the Back Country Byway signs and turn onto BLM Road 32-9-14.2, the Marial Road. Stay on Marial Road for 12 miles to Marial and another access point to the Rogue River Trail. The Kelsey Historic Packtrail is located about four miles east.

Camping: No designated or maintained campsites are along the pack trail. Campsites are available at either end of the Rogue River National Recreation Trail.

Season: Spring is an especially good time to visit, as the wildflowers will be out and the weather will be cool. Summers can be quite hot—sometimes the mercury creeps as high as 105°F.

USGS topographic maps: Marial Northeast, Kelsey Peak

Additional maps: The BLM Medford District Transportation, Wild Rogue Wilderness Topographic Map is available from the Siskiyou National Forest at (503) 479-5301.

Resources
• "The Historic Kelsey Packtrail" brochure and *Rogue River Trail* guide are available from the BLM office.

For more information: Contact the BLM Medford District Office, 3040 Biddle Road, Medford, OR 97504; (503) 770-2200.

ROGUE RIVER CANYON

See letter T on map page 420

backpacking, camping, canoeing, hiking, kayaking, whitewater rafting, wildlife observation,

The backpacker is likely to see black-tailed deer, black bear, raccoon, mink, California ground squirrel and perhaps the ring-tailed cat in this canyon. Rattlesnakes may also be encountered and caution is advised. The Rogue River has a rich and diverse pioneer past and vestiges of these days may still be viewed on the river. Cabin ruins, artifacts (look, don't touch), abandoned mine shafts and bits and pieces of old mining equipment are evidence of the Rogue's historic heritage. The cabin at Whisky Creek is a Registered National Historic Landmark maintained by the BLM. A museum at Rogue River Ranch is on the National Register of Historic Places and is open to the public from May through October.

Activity Highlight: Whitewater rafting

Rafts and kayaks are ideal, and although the BLM doesn't recommend it, whitewater-canoe enthusiasts do run the river every year. Rapids are rated Class III+. This is considered an ideal river trip for families. Quite a number of river outfitters offer trips on this river. Contact the Rand Visitor Center at (503) 479-3735, for more information.

Activity Highlights: Hiking and backpacking

The Rogue River National Recreation Trail, between Grave Creek and Illahe, falls completely within the portion of the river protected by the Wild and Scenic Rivers Act of 1968. The first 24 miles of this trail, from Grave Creek to Marial, are administered by the BLM. The remaining 16 miles are administered by the Siskiyou National Forest Service. The BLM maintains a series of small campsites located at convenient points along the trail. Many of these sites have pit toilets. Once on forest service land, there is only one maintained site, but there are numerous areas suitable for camping. Fire pans are required within 400 feet of the Rogue River. Since the surrounding terrain is steep, the best campsites fall within this 400 feet. Backpackers should plan on carrying several sheets of heavy gauge aluminum foil with them to fashion into a fire pan. All ashes and remaining garbage must be packed out, not buried—use a triple layer of garbage bags for this purpose. The alternative is to use a backpacking stove.

If hiking this trail in the summer, be aware that the heat can be sweltering. It is recommended that you hike in reverse, from Illahe to Grave Creek, during this time so the afternoon sun is at your back. The 15-mile section of trail from Kelsey Creek to Grave Creek is the hilliest and least-sheltered section of the trail. Keep in mind that in some of the canyons, the white rock reflects the heat turning the area into a veritable oven—Mule Creek Canyon temperatures have been recorded in excess of 120°F. I recommend bear-bagging your food, as bears are becoming increasingly bold along the river.

Location: In southwestern Oregon, just west of Interstate 5 between Grants Pass and Gold Beach. From Interstate 5 north of Medford, take the exit 61 and follow the Merlin-Galice Road approximately 23 miles northwest to the Grave Creek boat landing. There is a car shuttle service at the Galice Resort and Store that will arrange to have your car at Foster Bar landing at a prearranged time. A fee is charged. Or you can call Rand Visitor Center from June 1 to September 15 at (503) 479-3735 to inquire about other shuttle options and to obtain river and trail information. If hiking, the trail is 40 miles long; plan on five days hiking time.

Camping: Camping is allowed anywhere within the Rogue River Wild and Scenic area. The BLM maintains camps in the area and in order to minimize impact in the land, they request that you use them.

Season: The hiking season is all year. The best seasons are spring and fall. The best boating times are from June 1 to September 15.

Permits: No permits are necessary for hiking. Permits are required for floating the section from Grave Creek to Foster Bar between May 15 and October 15. Commercial permits are required for floating any section of the river.

USGS topographic maps: Glendale, Galice, Marial, Agness

Additional maps: The Rogue River Recreation Guide and Rogue River Float Guide are available from the BLM Medford District

Resources:
• *Where the Trails Are*, by Bill Williams; published by Independent Publishing Company, Ashland, OR.
• *Western Whitewater, From the Rockies to the Pacific*, by Jim Cassady, Bill Cross and Fryar Calhoun, published by North Fork Press, Berkeley, CA; (415) 424-1213.

For more information: Contact the BLM Medford District Office, 3040 Biddle Road, Medford, OR 97504; (503) 770-2200.

PACIFIC CREST NATIONAL SCENIC TRAIL

See letter U on map page 420

backpacking, cross-country skiing, fishing, hiking

The Pacific Crest National Scenic Trail extends from Mexico to Canada, covering a distance of approximately 2,500 miles. Predominantly managed by the U.S. Forest Service in Oregon, a significant 42-mile section in southern Oregon is managed by the BLM. The trail begins in the south along the transition zone and runs between the Klamath River Basin and the Rogue River Basin. This portion of the trail could be divided into two excellent weekend hikes. Hyatt Lake, approximately the halfway point, has campgrounds and hot showers if you need them. Attractions along this segment of trail include Pilot Rock, Bean Cabin, Soda Mountain Wilderness Study Area, Little

Hyatt Lake, Hyatt Lake and several segments of the National Historic Applegate Trail.

Access to the trail is available at a number of public road crossings. The most common are the following.

• Interstate 5 at the Mount Ashland exit and east to the Callahans Restaurant parking lot

• Highway 66 at Greensprings Summit, 19 miles east of the Highway 66 exit off Interstate 5

• Little Hyatt Lake, three miles from Greensprings Summit on Little Hyatt Lake County Road

• Keno Road, from Interstate 5 at the Highway 66 exit, turning east to the Dead Indian Memorial County Road, then left 20 miles to the Keno Road and right five miles to the Keno Road Trailcrossing

USGS topographic maps: Hyatt, Ashland, Mount McLoughlin

BLM surface map: Medford District

For more information: Contact the BLM Medford District Office, 3040 Biddle Road, Medford, OR 97504; (503) 770-2200.

HYATT LAKE-HOWARD PRAIRIE LAKE SPECIAL RECREATION MANAGEMENT AREA

See letter V on map page 420

boating, camping, cross-country skiing, fishing, hiking, innertubing, mountain biking, snowmobiling, snowshoeing, wheelchair access, wildlife observation

In warm months, this is an excellent recreation spot for camping, mountain biking and hiking on the Pacific Crest Trail, with good opportunities for wildlife viewing. Bald eagles, osprey, Canada geese, cormorants, Caspian terns and numerous ducks, black-tailed deer, gray and Douglas squirrels, porcupines, coyotes and chipmunks are all common. Osprey and eagles are the most active between April and June when they are fishing and feeding their young. September is an excellent time for observing the many species of waterfowl who utilize Hyatt Lake during their annual migrations. To reach Hyatt Lake, take Interstate 5 to the Ashland exit and then proceed east on Highway 66 for 17.5 miles to the East Hyatt Lake access road. Turn north here and continue for approximately three miles and then turn left on Howard Prairie Road. Follow this road for one mile to the lake.

In winter, you'll find sports opportunities for general snow play on

Table Mountain, cross-country skiing on three groomed loop trails and snowmobile access on seasonally closed roads in the area. From Interstate 5 and the Highway 66 exit, head east and travel about one mile to the Dead Indian Memorial County Road. Turn left and travel 17 miles to the Buck Prairie parking lot for cross-country skiing enthusiasts. Access is also available from Interstate 5 at the Highway 66 exit, by turning east and traveling 20 miles to the Hyatt/Prairie Road. Turn left and travel three-tenths of a mile to the snowmobile parking area, 1.5 miles to the Camper's Cove cross-country skiing parking lot, or four miles to the winter play hill.

USGS topographic map: Hyatt Reservoir Northwest

For more information: Contact the BLM Medford District Office, 3040 Biddle Road, Medford, OR 97504; (503) 770-2200.

TABLE ROCKS

See letter W on map page 420

hiking, wildflower observation, wildlife observation

Not only is this a great place to hike and observe wildlife, it is also the place to see spectacular wildflowers between March and June. Stay on the trails though, because poison oak is everywhere. From Medford, take Interstate 5 north to Central Point. Take exit 32 and head east on Biddle Road, then continue north on Table Rock Road. Turn west on Wheeler Road to Lower Table Rock or turn east on Modoc Road to reach Upper Table Rock. The wildlife here includes red-tailed hawk, osprey, turkey vulture, acorn woodpecker, blue-grey gnatcatcher, western fence lizard, western rattlesnake and the California kangaroo rat.

Activity Highlight: Hiking

The Upper Table Rock Trail (1.25 miles) and Lower Table Rock Trail (1.75 miles) offer scenic panoramas of the Rogue Valley and Kelley Slough, vernal pools and over 75 species of blooming wildflowers from February to May. Drive north from Medford on Table Rock Road to Modoc Road. Turn right and continue one mile to the parking area on the northwest side of the road. Both trails have abundant poison oak growing alongside them, as well as ticks, rattlesnakes and high cliffs. There is no potable water along the trails, so bring all that you will need. Brochures are available for both trails, and guided interpretive hikes are offered on weekends during April and May.

USGS topographic map: Medford Northwest

For more information: Contact the BLM Medford District Office, 3040 Biddle Road, Medford, OR 97504; (503) 770-2200.

KLAMATH RIVER CANYON

See letter X on map page 420

backpacking, camping, hiking, kayaking, rafting, whitewater canoeing, wildlife observation

This steep-walled canyon stretches for 15 miles from the John C. Boyle Dam south to the California/Oregon border. The dramatic cliffs, rimrock and large pines offer a haven for raptors who nest and hunt in the canyon. Wildlife visible along the riverbanks include black-tailed deer, Roosevelt elk, black bear, rabbits, beaver and waterfowl. Camping and picnicking facilities are available at the Tosy Recreation Site beside the John C. Boyle Reservoir.

Activity Highlight: Whitewater rafting

Whitewater rafting here is for experts only, as it is rated at Class IV+. The rapids come one after another, in an almost out-of-control rush to get to the sea. Wet suits are recommended, not because the water is cold, but because if you get tossed and go for a swim, the wet suit will protect you from the sharp volcanic rock that lines the river bottom and canyon walls.

Location: Near Klamath Falls and Highway 66 in southern Oregon. Access into the canyon is possible in a high-clearance vehicle from the Oregon side via the John C. Boyle Dam Road or from the California side via the community of Copco.

Camping: Camping and picnicking facilities are available at Tosy Recreation Site beside the John C. Boyle Reservoir. Otherwise, primitive camping is allowed as long as you are on BLM designated lands. There are private land inholdings along the river. There are also a number of designated camping areas along the river.

Season: The best time to visit the canyon is between April and June, although the roads are usually passable until August. Whitewater seekers will want to run the river April through June—later depending on water levels.

Permits: Permits are required for boating on the river.

USGS topographic maps: Mule Hill, Chicken Hills

Resources

• *Western Whitewater, From the Rockies to the Pacific,* by Jim Cassady, Bill Cross and Fryar Calhoun, published by North Fork Press, Berkeley, CA; (415) 424-1213.

For more information: Contact the BLM Lakeview District Office, 1000 Ninth Street South, P.O. Box 151, Lakeview, OR 97630; (503) 947-2177.

OREGON—MAP B

POWER CITY WILDLIFE AREA

See letter Y on map page 422

hiking, wildlife observation

Bring along your binoculars to this small but picturesque Watchable Wildlife Site near the Washington/Oregon border. Trails lead around the ponds in the desert-bounded wetland. Winter is the best time to view waterfowl while spring and summer are best for songbirds. Groves of olive trees provide excellent songbird habitat. From Pendelton, head west on Interstate 84 to the Stanfield/Hermiston exit. Head north on US 395 through Stanfield and Hermiston. At the north end of Hermiston, there is a boat shop on the left side. Opposite the store and heading off to the right is Benzel Road, which leads to the Power City Wildlife Area. After one-quarter mile, you will come to a parking area for the Watchable Wildlife Site.

For more information: Contact the BLM Baker Resource Area, 1550 Dewey Street, Baker, OR 97814; (503) 523-1256.

GRANDE RONDE WILD AND SCENIC RIVER

See letter Z on map page 422

backpacking, camping, canoeing, fishing, hiking, kayaking, rafting, wildlife observation

The Grande Ronde river system, which includes part of the Wallowa River, is considered to be one of Oregon and Washington's most scenic rivers. A segment of the river, the Goosenecks, has been established as a National Natural Landmark. The river corridor is about 90 miles long with an overall rating of Class III; it is suitable for rafts, kayaks or canoes. Principle river access points are located in small communities in northeastern Oregon and southeastern Washington, such as Minam and Troy in Oregon and Bogan's Oasis and Heller's Bar in Washington. Spring, summer and fall are the best times to visit.

USGS topographic maps: Oregon: Minam, Tros; Washington: Mountain View, Lime Kiln Rapids

BLM surface maps: Washington/Oregon: Wallowa; Washington: Clarkston

For more information: Contact the BLM Vale District Office, 100 Oregon Street, Vale, OR 97918; (503) 473-3144; or the Baker Resource Area Office, 1550 Dewey, P.O. Box 987, Baker, OR 97814; (503) 523-1256.

JOHN DAY RIVER

See letter AA on map page 422

backpacking, camping, canoeing, hiking, kayaking, whitewater rafting

A trip on the lower John Day River will usually involve two to five days with weather ranging from the extremely hot to the extremely cold—talk about having to pack layers. The best time to run the John Day is March through June. Much of the river, downstream from Service Creek, located 15 miles southeast of the town of Fossil on Highway 19, is a leisurely waterway with several Class III rapids and one Class IV rapid to be negotiated. The river runs through semi-arid, high-desert country and is ideally suited to the novice as long as there are boaters with experience along in the group. You will enjoy floating by sheer cliffs and bluffs that are home to a variety of wildlife as well as by the area for historical and archaeological sites.

Maps: The Lower John Day River Public Lands Map is available from the BLM for $4.

Resources

• *Western Whitewater, From the Rockies to the Pacific,* by Jim Cassady, Bill Cross and Fryar Calhoun, published by North Fork Press, Berkeley, CA; (415) 424-1213.

For more information: Contact the BLM Prineville District Office, 185 East Fourth Street, P.O. Box 550, Prineville, OR 97754; (503) 447-4115.

POWDER WILD AND SCENIC RIVER

See letter BB on map page 422

camping, fishing, hiking, wildlife observation

Located 13 miles northeast of Baker and extending from the Thief Valley Reservoir to the Keating Valley (Highway 203), this river segment is 11.7 miles long and provides excellent raptor nesting and foraging habitat as well as bald eagle habitat and recreational possibilities. The spring and summer seasons are the best times to visit. From the town of Hermiston, head north on US 395 for approximately two miles to the signed Watchable Wildlife Site branching off the highway on a gravel road to the right (east). The parking area is located just off the highway.

For more information: Contact the BLM Vale District Office, 100 Oregon Street, Vale, OR 97918; (503) 473-3144; or the Baker Resource Area Office, 1550 Dewey, P.O. Box 987, Baker, OR 97814; (503) 523-1256.

SNAKE RIVER—MORMON BASIN BACK COUNTRY BYWAY

See letter CC on map page 422

auto touring, fishing, mountain biking, wildflowers, wildlife observation

Head north on Interstate 84 from the Farwell Bend Interchange for approximately 13 miles to the town of Dixie. The 130-mile-long byway is clearly signed and will provide you access to some of the spectacularly diverse landscapes of northeastern Oregon. Travel along winding river canyons, through aspen-lined meadows and basins filled with wildflowers in the spring. Don't forget your binoculars for wildlife viewing or a camera to capture the scenery. If you are so inclined, pack along your rod and reel because the fishing in the warm-water fisheries along the road is reportedly excellent, "one of the best in the West." Plan on four to five hours of driving time. The two-lane road is paved, with narrow gravel or dirt in places—RVs are discouraged. Roads are not plowed in the winter and are muddy or slippery when wet.

For more information: Contact the BLM Vale District Office, 100 Oregon Street, Vale, OR 97918; (503) 473-3144; or the Baker Resource Area Office, 1550 Dewey, P.O. Box 987, Baker, OR 97814; (503) 523-1256.

OREGON TRAIL—BIRCH CREEK TRAIL RUTS

See letter DD on map page 422

hiking, historic site

Located 1.5 miles west of the Farewell Bend Interchange of Interstate 84, the Birch Creek Trail Ruts provide an opportune moment to get out of your car, stretch your legs briefly, and view ruts of the Oregon National Historic Trail. The trail is only one-tenth of a mile along the ruts over rolling terrain. Access is via a signed, graded dirt road leading from the Farwell Bend Interchange. The road is not recommended for navigation in wet weather as it gets very slippery and muddy. The best time to visit is between April and October. The site is surrounded by private land—please stay on the trail and do not venture beyond the BLM site boundaries. If the area appeals to you, then I would recommend heading off on a nearby driving tour on the BLM Snake River-Mormon Basin Back Country Byway (see the listing on page 446).

For more information: Contact the BLM Vale District Office, 100 Oregon Street, Vale, OR 97918; (503) 473-3144; or the Baker Resource Area Office, 1550 Dewey, P.O. Box 987, Baker, OR 97814; (503) 523-1256.

SOUTH FORK OF THE JOHN DAY RIVER / MURDERERS CREEK

See letter EE on map page 422

camping, fishing, hiking, mountain biking, wildlife observation

Along the South Fork of the John Day River is the site known as Murderers Creek; an excellent area to view mule deer, Rocky Mountain elk, bighorn sheep and a variety of waterfowl and raptors. Four-wheel-drive or high-clearance vehicles are recommended as the road can be rough and rutted—even impassable in the winter. Mountain bikes are suitable on the route, just watch out for motorized vehicles. From Prineville, drive east on Highway 26 to Dayville and then south along the South Fork of the John Day River—this road is a National Back Country Byway. Camping is allowed anywhere along the river on public lands—do not camp on private land. To minimize impact, please use only sites that have already been established. This scenic canyon offers much in the way of views, solitude and quiet hiking opportunities.

Maps: The Upper John Day River Public Lands Map is available from the BLM for $4

For more information: Contact the BLM Prineville District Office, 185 East Fourth Street, P.O. Box 550, Prineville, OR 97754; (503) 447-4115.

OREGON TRAIL—KEENEY PASS

See letter FF on map page 422

hiking, historic site, wildlife viewing

Located six miles west of Vale on Lytle Boulevard, this site features a segment of parallel, deeply eroded Oregon Trail ruts and a rare opportunity to see the entire distance of a day's travel by the westward emigrants. The site consists of an open ramada with two of the sites, eight interpretive panels and a third of a mile of developed foot path with rest benches. Unless you hike very briskly, you won't be needing these benches to rest on. Scan the rolling hills around the trail to see if you can spot antelope. From Main Street in Vale, head south on Glen Street which will become Lytle after crossing the Malheur Bridge. The Keeney Pass site is signed and located within the Lytle Boulevard National Historic Register District along Lytle Boulevard—an area designated to protect the remaining trail ruts on public land in the area. This is a good year-round destination.

For more information: Contact the BLM Vale District Office, 100 Oregon Street, Vale, OR 97918; (503) 473-3144.

OWYHEE CANYONLANDS / OWYHEE RIVER CANYON

See letter GG on map page 422

backpacking, camping, canoeing, fishing, hiking, kayaking, rafting, wildlife observation

Although access is challenging, this 450,000-acre region (lying within Nevada, Idaho and Oregon) is picturesque, dramatic, wild, isolated and well worth your time. River runners and hunters are the predominant users, and there are not too many of those. The narrow canyons that cut into the plateau range anywhere from several hundred to one thousand feet deep—often with sheer walls from rimrock to river bottom. Access to this area is best from Three Forks, Rome, and the

Historic Birch Creek Ranch. Mountain lion, bobcat, river otter, mule deer and bighorn sheep reside within the Owyhee Canyon system.

Activity Highlight: Lower Owyhee Canyon Watchable Wildlife Site
Within the Oregon region, there is a 13-mile access road to Owyhee Dam and the Lower Owyhee River Canyon that provides an excellent introduction to the canyon habitats typical of eastern Oregon. Songbirds, raptors, waterfowl and upland birds are all readily visible from the road, especially where cottonwood and willows are well established along the river bottom. The access road is located west of Highway 201, 7.5 miles south of Nyssa, Oregon. From Owyhee Junction, follow the signs southwest to Lake Owyhee State Park. The wildlife-viewing route begins after nine miles. (See also the Owyhee River Canyon in the Nevada chapter on page 330.)

For more information: Contact the BLM Vale District Office, 100 Oregon Street, Vale, OR 97918; (503) 473-3144; or the BLM Boise District Office, 3948 Development Avenue, Boise, ID 83705; (208) 384-3300.

LESLIE GULCH

See letter HH on map page 422

backpacking, camping, fishing, hiking, wildlife observation
Leslie Gulch is, by most accounts, a highly scenic and even spectacular area. The well-graded road makes it accessible by car during the summer months. Not only are the rock formations, pinnacles and monoliths in the eight miles of Leslie Gulch spectacular, but each side canyon, Slocum Canyon, Timber Gulch, Juniper Gulch and several lesser side canyons, offer some of the most extraordinary and awe-inspiring formations to be seen anywhere in the United States. Leslie Gulch is within the north rim of the ancient Mahogany Mountain Caldera, with formations composed chiefly of deeply eroded volcanic ash and tufaceous material. Bighorn sheep, deer and chukar are readily seen as are a variety of raptors. Warm-water fishing in Lake Owyhee is excellent, but be aware that the Oregon State Health Department has issued a warning concerning the mercury content of fish taken from the reservoir. Due to the extremely fragile nature of this region, the BLM has implemented special management restrictions to protect the area's unique features. Please tread lightly and do not attempt to climb on any of the rock formations.

Activity Highlight: Hiking

Hiking is primarily along the dry washes of canyon floors, which make for quite easy walking.

Location: Good access is off US 95, approximately 25 miles on a well-graded gravel road. The signed exit is located approximately 18 miles north of Jordan Valley or 35 miles south of Ontario, Oregon. Eight miles south of Adrian, Oregon (or seven miles west of Homedale, Idaho), take the Highway 201 and follow the Leslie Gulch/Succor Creek National Back Country Byway signs on the graded Succor Creek Road. Or take the graded McBride Creek Road from US 95, south of Homedale, Idaho. You are advised that roads may become hazardous or impassable in wet or winter conditions. Towing large trailers is discouraged due to the steep, narrow and winding road that leads into the upper reaches of the Gulch. The best road conditions exist from mid-April to October, although the canyon is subject to flash-flooding at any time.

Camping: There is an established primitive campground near the lower end with tables and vault toilets. Water is available at a developed spring on a small parcel of private land at Dago Canyon. A boat ramp provides access to the southern portion of Owyhee Reservoir.

Season: The best time to visit this area is during the spring and fall. The summer can be brutally hot.

USGS topographic map: Rooster Comb

BLM surface map: Mahogany Mountains

For more information: Contact the BLM Vale District Office, 100 Oregon Street, Vale, OR 97918; (503) 473-3144.

SOLDIER CREEK LOOP

See letter II on map page 422

auto touring, hiking, mountain biking, wildlife observation

This route is primarily a graded, gravel access road that passes through some of the best pronghorn antelope and sage grouse areas in Oregon. The best viewing is from April to September. Driving is limited to high-clearance vehicles and only in dry weather. From Jordan Valley, follow the North Fork Owyhee Back Country Byway east into Idaho, then south to the Three Forks turnoff. The loop is completed by returning to Highway 95 on Soldier Creek Road.

For more information: Contact the BLM Vale District Office, 100 Oregon Street, Vale, OR 97918; (503) 473-3144.

STEENS MOUNTAIN

See letter JJ on map page 422

backpacking, camping, fishing, hiking, mountain biking, wildlife observation

Steens Mountain stands as a 9,773-foot-high reminder of the earth's power—a 30-mile-long fault-block mountain rising abruptly one mile above the Alvord Desert to the east. Glacial action has added to the visual drama by carving half-mile-deep trenches that have formed four immense U-shaped gorges and a number of hanging valleys. The Donner Und Blitzen National Scenic River cuts through the region and numerous streams, springs and lakes dot the landscape. Wildlife abounds, including the local speed demon, the pronghorn antelope. Elk, bighorn sheep and mule deer are also frequently spotted.

Activity Highlights: Hiking and backpacking

The best route on foot is via the Desert Trail, part of the Oregon State Recreational Trails System and a designated National Recreation Trail. This trail segment begins at Page Springs Campground. Hiking time for the entire trail through the Steens Mountain region is an estimated seven to eight days. Shorter loops and sections are possible. Water is plentiful throughout the Steens Mountain area, but hikers are advised to carry adequate reserves at all times. Water sources must be purified. Lightning and thunderstorms are common in July and August. Take appropriate precautions to prevent being caught exposed on the high ridges.

Activity Highlight: Fishing

Mann Lake is said to be one of the best-kept fishing secrets in Oregon. Well, the word's out now for sure. Mann Lake cutthroat trout, up to 20 inches, are taken regularly from the lake, which also provides for excellent ice-fishing in the winter. Special regulations are in effect for fishing this lake—contact the BLM for current rules and guidelines.

Location: Approximately 60 miles south of Burns, Oregon and US 395. If you are going to be based out of Page Springs Campground, a passenger car is suitable. Further travel along the Steens Mountain Loop Road currently requires a four-wheel-drive vehicle, and at times the road may be impassable due to muddy conditions and/or snow. The BLM has plans to begin upgrading the road from Page Springs Campground east up the mountain to East Rim Overlook. By 1996, the BLM hopes to have the entire road upgraded to provide for easy access for passenger vehicles. Check at the BLM Burns office for current road conditions before heading out. Hiking from Page Springs to the Alvord Desert requires a shuttle. Inquire at the BLM office about appropriate parking areas near Frog Spring—the termination point of the Steens Mountain section. To get to Page Springs from Burns, drive south for 62 miles on Highway 205. At Frenchglen, take the Steens Mountain Loop Road for approximately 2.5 miles to Page Springs Campground.

Camping: There are several formal BLM campgrounds with vault toilets and drinking water along the Steens Mountain Loop Road Back Country Byway, including Page Springs, Fish Lake and Jackman Park. A camping fee is charged. Another private campground, Camper Corral, has RV facilities, a phone and a store for last-minute munchies. Primitive camping is allowed anywhere along the Desert Trail. Campfires are discouraged—use a stove. Campsites should be set up at least 200 feet from the nearest spring or waterhole so animals can drink without fear. A new campground is currently being planned with construction expected to begin sometime in 1995 at the south limb of the Steens Loop Road near the entrance to Big Indian Gorge.

Season: The season runs from mid-June to mid-September. Fall colors are superb in late September, with Fish Lake being particularly beautiful. Spring wildflowers are often at their best in the high country from late June to early July.

Maps: The best maps for this area are published by the Desert Trail Association, P.O. Box 589, Burns, OR 97720. Ask for both the Steens Mountain to the Alvord Desert and Steens Mountain to Page Springs maps.

For more information: Contact the BLM Burns District, 12533 Highway 20 West, Hines, OR 97738; (503) 573-5241.

WARNER WETLANDS AREA OF CRITICAL ENVIRONMENTAL CONCERN

See letter KK on map page 422

canoeing, hiking, wildlife observation

A designated Area of Critical Environmental Concern, this special habitat of interconnected lakes, marshes and wet meadows called Warner Wetlands supports thousands of birds. There are over 400 miles of shoreline to walk on or canoe alongside. The best wildlife-viewing times are during the nesting season of April through July and the migration season from September through October. The area is a natural one, which goes through periodic wet and dry cycles that are important to its health. It is best to call the BLM prior to heading out to determine the conditions. To get there, travel north from the store (that's right, the only store) in the town of Plush, nine-tenths of a mile on Lake County Road 3-10. Turn east on County Road 3-12. Follow this paved road for five miles to the Warner Wetlands sign and interpretive area.

BLM surface maps: Adel, Bluejoint Lake

For more information: Contact the BLM Lakeview District Office, 1000 Ninth Street South, P.O. Box 151, Lakeview, OR 97630; (503) 947-2177.

BLM CAMPGROUNDS

1. ALDER GLEN CAMPGROUND—MAP A

Campsites, facilities: There are 11 sites, all with picnic tables and fire rings. Water and pit toilets are available. No trash facilities are provided, so pack out all that you bring in. RVs up to 30 feet are allowed. There is a 14-day stay limit.

Reservations, fees: There is no fee.

Who to contact: Salem District Office, 1717 Fabry Road Southeast, Salem, OR 97306; (503) 375-5646.

Location: Along the Nestucca River. From Carlton, drive west on Nestucca River Road (BLM Road 32) for approximately 22 miles to the campground entrance. The campground is set at 800 feet.

Season: All year.

2. FAN CREEK CAMPGROUND—MAP A

Campsites, facilities: There are 12 sites, all with picnic tables and fire rings. Water and pit toilets are available. RVs up to 30 feet are allowed. There is a 14-day stay limit.

Reservations, fees: There is a $6 fee per night; pay on site.

Who to contact: Salem District Office, 1717 Fabry Road Southeast, Salem, OR 97306; (503) 375-5646.

Location: Along the Nestucca River. From Carlton, drive west on Nestucca Road (BLM Road 3-6-13) for approximately 15 miles to the campground. The campground is set at 1,200 feet.

Season: April to November.

3. DOVRE CAMPGROUND—MAP A

Campsites, facilities: There are nine sites, all with picnic tables and fire rings. Water and pit toilets are available. No trash facilities are provided, so pack out all that you bring in. RVs up to 30 feet are allowed. There is a 14-day stay limit.

Reservations, fees: There is a $6 fee per night. Each additional vehicle costs $4 extra. Pay on site.

Who to contact: Salem District Office, 1717 Fabry Road Southeast, Salem, OR 97306; (503) 375-5646.

Location: Along the Nestucca River. From Carlton, drive west on

Nestucca Road (BLM Road 3-6-13) for approximately 13 miles to the campground. The campground is set at 1,500 feet.

Season: April to November.

4. ELK BEND CAMPGROUND / DAY-USE AREA—MAP A

Campsites, facilities: There are four sites, all with picnic tables and fire rings. Water and pit toilets are available. No trash facilities are provided, so pack out all that you bring in. There is a 14-day stay limit.

Reservations, fees: There is a $6 fee per night for one vehicle. Each additional vehicle costs $4 extra. Pay on site.

Who to contact: Salem District Office, 1717 Fabry Road Southeast, Salem, OR 97306; (503) 375-5646.

Location: Along the Nestucca River. From Carlton, drive west on Nestucca Road (BLM Road 3-6-13) for approximately 17 miles to the campground. The campground is set at 1,200 feet.

Season: April to November.

5. ELKHORN VALLEY CAMPGROUND—MAP A

Campsites, facilities: There are 23 sites, all with picnic tables and fire rings. Water and pit toilets are available. RVs up to 18 feet are allowed. There is a 14-day stay limit.

Reservations, fees: There is a $6 fee per night for one vehicle. Each additional vehicle costs $4 extra. Pay on site.

Who to contact: Salem District Office, 1717 Fabry Road Southeast, Salem, OR 97306; (503) 375-5646.

Location: Near the Little North Santiam River. From Salem, drive east on Highway 22 for 24 miles to Elkhorn Road/North Fork Road and then 10 miles northeast on Elkhorn to the campground entrance. The campground is set at 1,000 feet.

Season: May to September.

6. FISHERMAN'S BEND CAMPGROUND—MAP A

Campsites, facilities: There are 38 sites, all with picnic tables and fire rings. Flush toilets, showers and water are available. RVs up to 32 feet are allowed. There is a 10-day stay limit.

Reservations, fees: There is a $8 fee per tent site and $12 fee per trailer site. Each additional vehicle costs $4 extra. Pay on site.

Who to contact: Salem District Office, 1717 Fabry Road Southeast,

Salem, OR 97306; (503) 375-5646.

Location: From Salem, drive 32 miles east on Highway 22 to the campground entrance.

Season: May to September.

7. YELLOWBOTTOM CAMPGROUND—MAP A

Campsites, facilities: There are 21 sites, all with picnic tables and fire rings. Pit toilets and water are available. There is a 16-day stay limit.

Reservations, fees: There is a $6 fee per night. Each additional vehicle costs $4 extra. Pay on site.

Who to contact: Salem District Office, 1717 Fabry Road Southeast, Salem, OR 97306; (503) 375-5646.

Location: Near Green Peter Reservoir. From Sweet Home, drive northeast on Quartzville Road along the north side of Foster Reservoir for approximately 25 miles to the campground entrance. The campground is set at 1,500 feet.

Season: May to September.

8. GERT CANYON CAMPGROUND—MAP A

Campsites, facilities: There are four sites, all with picnic tables and fire rings. Water, pit toilets and a boat launch are available. RVs up to 30 feet are allowed. There is a 14-day stay limit.

Reservations, fees: There is a $3 fee per night for one vehicle. Each additional vehicle costs $1 extra. Pay on site.

Who to contact: Prineville District Office, 185 East Fourth Street, P.O. Box 550, Prineville, OR 97754; (503) 447-4115.

Location: In the Deschutes River Canyon. From the town of Maupin, just before the bridge and past the city park, turn left onto Lower Access Road and drive nine miles. Turn right at the stop sign and then left; you're still on Lower Access Road, but now it's a gravel surface. Signs leading to the site indicate Deschutes River Recreation Lands and Macks Canyon. Drive to the campground. The road dead-ends in 17 miles at Macks Canyon Campground. Other campgrounds along the canyon route are Oakbrook, Twin Springs, Jones Canyon, Beavertail, Macks Canyon and Rattlesnake. The campground is set at 500 feet.

Season: All year. No open fires are allowed from June 1 to October 15.

9. JONES CANYON CAMPGROUND—MAP A

Campsites, facilities: There are seven sites, all with picnic tables and fire rings. Water, pit toilets and a boat launch are available. RVs up to 30 feet are allowed. There is a 14-day stay limit.

Reservations, fees: There is a $3 fee per night for one vehicle. Each additional vehicle costs $1 extra. Pay on site.

Who to contact: Prineville District Office, 185 East Fourth Street, P.O. Box 550, Prineville, OR 97754; (503) 447-4115.

Location: In the Deschutes River Canyon. From the town of Maupin, just before the bridge and past the city park, turn left onto Lower Access Road and drive nine miles. Turn right at the stop sign and then left; you are still on Lower Access Road, but now it's a gravel surface. Signs leading to the site indicate Deschutes River Recreation Lands and Macks Canyon. Drive to the campground. The road dead-ends in 17 miles at Macks Canyon Campground. Other campgrounds along the canyon route are Oakbrook, Twin Springs, Beavertail, Gert Canyon, Macks Canyon and Rattlesnake. The campground is set at 500 feet.

Season: All year. No open fires are allowed from June 1 to October 15.

10. RATTLESNAKE CAMPGROUND—MAP A

Campsites, facilities: There are eight sites, all with picnic tables and fire rings. Water, pit toilets and a boat launch are available. RVs up to 30 feet are allowed. There is a 14-day stay limit.

Reservations, fees: There is a $3 fee per night for one vehicle. Each additional vehicle costs $1 extra. Pay on site.

Who to contact: Prineville District Office, 185 East Fourth Street, P.O. Box 550, Prineville, OR 97754; (503) 447-4115.

Location: In the Deschutes River Canyon. From the town of Maupin, just before the bridge and past the city park, turn left onto Lower Access Road and drive nine miles. Turn right at the stop sign and then left; you're still on Lower Access Road, but now it's a gravel surface. Signs leading to the site indicate Deschutes River Recreation Lands and Macks Canyon. Drive to the campground. The road dead-ends in 17 miles at Macks Canyon Campground. Other campgrounds along the canyon route are Oakbrook, Twin Springs, Jones Canyon, Gert Canyon, Macks Canyon and Beavertail. The campground is set at 500 feet.

Season: All year. No open fires are allowed from June 1 to October 15.

11. Oakbrook Campground—Map A

Campsites, facilities: There are three sites, all with picnic tables and fire rings. Water, pit toilets and a boat launch are available. RVs up to 30 feet are allowed. There is a 14-day stay limit.

Reservations, fees: There is a $3 fee per night for one vehicle. Each additional vehicle costs $1 extra. Pay on site.

Who to contact: Prineville District Office, 185 East Fourth Street, P.O. Box 550, Prineville, OR 97754; (503) 447-4115.

Location: In the Deschutes River Canyon. From the town of Maupin, just before the bridge and past the city park, turn left onto Lower Access Road and drive nine miles. Turn right at the stop sign and then left; you're still on Lower Access Road, but now it's a gravel surface. Signs leading to the site indicate Deschutes River Recreation Lands and Macks Canyon. Drive 17 miles to Macks Canyon Campground and road's end. Other campgrounds along the canyon route are Twin Springs, Jones Canyon, Gert Canyon, Beavertail, Macks Canyon and Rattlesnake. The campground is set at 500 feet.

Season: All year. No open fires are allowed from June 1 to October 15.

12. Devils Canyon Campground—Map A

Campsites, facilities: There are five sites, all with picnic tables. Pit toilets and a boat ramp are available. There is **no water**. No trash facilities are provided, so pack out all that you bring in. There is a 14-day stay limit.

Reservations, fees: There is a $3 fee per night for one vehicle. Each additional vehicle costs $1 extra. Pay on site.

Who to contact: Prineville District Office, 185 East Fourth Street, P.O. Box 550, Prineville, OR 97754; (503) 447-4115.

Location: In the Deschutes River Canyon. From US 197 driving north, enter the town of Maupin and head left onto Upper Access Road, a gravel surface route you will follow for approximately five miles to the campground entrance. Other campgrounds in the canyon that are accessed from this route are Wapinitia, Long Bend and Nena Creek. The campground is set at 980 feet.

Season: All year. No open fires are allowed from June 1 to October 15.

13. Nena Creek Campground—Map A

Campsites, facilities: There are three sites, all with picnic tables. Pit toilets and a boat ramp are available. There is **no water**. No trash facilities are provided, so pack out all that you bring in. There is a 14-day stay limit.

Reservations, fees: There is a $3 fee per night for one vehicle. Each additional vehicle costs $1 each. Pay on site.

Who to contact: Prineville District Office, 185 East Fourth Street, P.O. Box 550, Prineville, OR 97754; (503) 447-4115.

Location: In the Deschutes River Canyon. From US 197 driving north, enter the town of Maupin and head left onto Upper Access Road, a gravel surface route you will follow for approximately six miles to the campground entrance. Other campgrounds in the canyon that are accessed from this route include Wapinitia, Long Bend and Devils Canyon. The campground is set at 980 feet.

Season: All year. No open fires are allowed from June 1 to October 15.

14. WAPINITIA CAMPGROUND—MAP A

Campsites, facilities: There are five sites, all with picnic tables. Pit toilets and a boat ramp are available. There is **no water**. No trash facilities are provided, so pack out all that you bring in. There is a 14-day stay limit.

Reservations, fees: There is a $3 fee per night for one vehicle. Each additional vehicle costs $1 extra. Pay on site.

Who to contact: Prineville District Office, 185 East Fourth Street, P.O. Box 550, Prineville, OR 97754; (503) 447-4115.

Location: In the Deschutes River Canyon. From US 197 driving north, enter the town of Maupin and head left onto Upper Access Road, a gravel surface route you will follow for approximately three miles to the campground entrance. Other campgrounds in the canyon that are accessed from this route include Nena Creek, Long Bend and Devils Canyon. The campground is set at 980 feet.

Season: All year. No open fires are allowed from June 1 to October 15.

15. LONG BEND CAMPGROUND—MAP A

Campsites, facilities: There are eight sites, all with picnic tables. Pit toilets and a boat ramp are available. There is **no water**. No trash facilities are provided, so pack out all that you bring in. There is a 14-day stay limit.

Reservations, fees: There is a $3 fee per night for one vehicle. Each additional vehicle costs $1 extra. Pay on site.

Who to contact: Prineville District Office, 185 East Fourth Street, P.O. Box 550, Prineville, OR 97754; (503) 447-4115.

Location: In the Deschutes River Canyon. From US 197 driving north, enter the town of Maupin and head left onto Upper Access Road, a gravel surface route you will follow for approximately four miles to the campground entrance. Other campgrounds in the canyon that are accessed from this route are Wapinitia, Nena Creek and Devils Canyon. The campground is set at 980 feet.

Season: All year. No open fires are allowed from June 1 to October 15.

16. BEAVERTAIL CAMPGROUND—MAP A

Campsites, facilities: There are 18 sites, all with picnic tables and fire rings. Water, pit toilets and a boat launch are available. RVs up to 30 feet are allowed. There is a 14-day stay limit.

Reservations, fees: There is a $3 fee per night for one vehicle. Each additional vehicle costs $1 extra. Pay on site.

Who to contact: Prineville District Office, 185 East Fourth Street, P.O. Box 550, Prineville, OR 97754; (503) 447-4115.

Location: In the Deschutes River Canyon. From the town of Maupin, just before the bridge and past the city park, turn left onto Lower Access Road and drive nine miles. Turn right at the stop sign and then left; you're still on Lower Access Road, but now it is a gravel surface. Signs leading to the site indicate Deschutes River Recreation Lands and Macks Canyon. Drive to the campground. The road dead-ends in 17 miles at Macks Canyon Campground. Other campgrounds along the canyon route are Oakbrook, Twin Springs, Jones Canyon, Gert Canyon, Macks Canyon, and Rattlesnake. The campground is set at 500 feet.

Season: All year. No open fires are allowed from June 1 to October 15.

17. MACKS CANYON CAMPGROUND—MAP A

Campsites, facilities: There are 16 sites, all with picnic tables and fire rings. Water, pit toilets and a boat launch are available. RVs up to 30 feet are allowed. There is a 14-day stay limit.

Reservations, fees: There is a $3 fee per night for one vehicle. Each additional vehicle costs $1 extra. Pay on site.

Who to contact: Prineville District Office, 185 East Fourth Street, P.O. Box 550, Prineville, OR 97754; (503) 447-4115.

Location: In the Deschutes River Canyon. From the town of Maupin, just before the bridge and past the city park, turn left onto Lower Access Road and drive nine miles. Turn right at the stop sign and then left; you're still on Lower Access Road, but now it's a gravel surface. Signs leading to the site indicate Deschutes River Recreation Lands and Macks Canyon. Drive 17 miles to Macks Canyon Campground and road's end. Other campgrounds along the canyon route are Oakbrook, Twin Springs, Jones Canyon, Gert Canyon, Beavertail and Rattlesnake. The campground is set at 500 feet.

Season: All year. No open fires are allowed from June 1 to October 15.

18. TROUT CREEK CAMPGROUND—MAP A

Campsites, facilities: There are 20 sites, all with picnic tables and fire rings. There is **no water**. Pit toilets and a boat launch are available. RVs up to 30 feet are allowed. There is a 14-day stay limit.

Reservations, fees: There is a $3 fee per night for one vehicle. Each additional vehicle costs $1 extra. Pay on site.

Who to contact: Prineville District Office, 185 East Fourth Street, P.O. Box 550, Prineville, OR 97754; (503) 447-4115.

Location: In the Deschutes River Canyon. From the town of Madras, drive north on US 97 for approximately three miles to Cora Drive. Drive on Cora to Gateway and turn right toward the Deschutes River and onto Clemens Drive. The road is steep and can be slippery when wet. The campground is set at 1,300 feet.

Season: All year. No open fires are allowed from June 1 to October 15.

19. BLUE HOLE CAMPGROUND—MAP A

Campsites, facilities: There are five sites, all with picnic tables. Pit toilets are wheelchair accessible. There is **no water**. No trash facilities are provided, so pack out all that you bring in. There is a 14-day stay limit.

Reservations, fees: There is a $3 fee per night for one vehicle. Each additional vehicle costs $1 extra. Pay on site.

Who to contact: Prineville District Office, 185 East Fourth Street, P.O. Box 550, Prineville, OR 97754; (503) 447-4115.

Location: In the Deschutes River Canyon. From the town of Maupin, just before the bridge past the city park, turn left onto Lower Access Road. On the paved Lower Access Road you will pass campgrounds in this order: Blue Hole, Grey Eagle, Oak Springs, and then Oasis Flat. Blue Hole Campground is set at 800 feet.

Season: All year. No open fires are allowed from June 1 to October 15.

20. Oasis Flat Campground—Map A

Campsites, facilities: There are 15 sites, all with picnic tables. Pit toilets are available. There is **no water**. No trash facilities are provided, so pack out all that you bring in. There is a 14-day stay limit.

Reservations, fees: There is a $3 fee per night for one vehicle. Each additional vehicle costs $1 extra. Pay on site.

Who to contact: Prineville District Office, 185 East Fourth Street, P.O. Box 550, Prineville, OR 97754; (503) 447-4115.

Location: In the Deschutes River Canyon. From the town of Maupin, just before the bridge and past the city park, turn left onto Lower Access Road. On the paved Lower Access Road you will pass campgrounds in this order: Blue Hole, Grey Eagle, Oak Springs and then Oasis Flat. Oasis Flat Campground is set at 800 feet.

Season: All year. No open fires are allowed from June 1 to October 15.

21. Grey Eagle Campground—Map A

Campsites, facilities: There are five sites, all with picnic tables. Pit toilets are available. There is **no water**. No trash facilities are provided, so pack out all that you bring in. There is a 14-day stay limit.

Reservations, fees: There is a $3 fee per night for one vehicle. Each additional vehicle costs $1 extra. Pay on site.

Who to contact: Prineville District Office, 185 East Fourth Street, P.O. Box 550, Prineville, OR 97754; (503) 447-4115.

Location: In the Deschutes River Canyon. From the town of Maupin, just before the bridge and past the city park, turn left onto Lower Access Road. On the paved Lower Access Road, you will pass campgrounds in this order: Blue Hole, Grey Eagle, Oak Springs and Oasis Flat. Grey Eagle Campground is set at 800 feet.

Season: All year. No open fires are allowed from June 1 to October 15.

22. Oak Springs Campground—Map A

Campsites, facilities: There are nine sites, all with picnic tables. Pit toilets are available. There is **no water**. No trash facilities are provided, so pack out all that you bring in. There is a 14-day stay limit.

Reservations, fees: There is a $3 fee per night for one vehicle. Each additional vehicle costs $1 extra. Pay on site.

Who to contact: Prineville District Office, 185 East Fourth Street, P.O. Box 550, Prineville, OR 97754; (503) 447-4115.

Location: In the Deschutes River Canyon. From the town of Maupin, just before the bridge and past the city park, turn left onto Lower Access Road. On the paved Lower Access Road, you will pass campgrounds in this order: Blue Hole, Grey Eagle, Oak Springs and Oasis Flat. Oak Springs Campground is set at 800 feet elevation.

Season: All year. No open fires are allowed from June 1 to October 15.

23. SOUTH JUNCTION CAMPGROUND—MAP A

Campsites, facilities: There are 11 sites, all with picnic tables and fire rings. There is **no water**. Pit toilets and a boat launch are available. There is a 14-day stay limit.

Reservations, fees: There is a $3 fee per night for one vehicle. Each additional vehicle costs $1 extra. Pay on site.

Who to contact: Prineville District Office, 185 East Fourth Street, P.O. Box 550, Prineville, OR 97754; (503) 447-4115.

Location: In the Deschutes River Canyon. From the town of Madras, drive north on US 97 for approximately 29 miles to Shaniko and the junction of US 97 and US 197. Look for the sign indicating BLM Recreation Site and turn left onto the gravel access road. Drive to the campground entrance. The campground is set at 1,280 feet.

Season: All year. No open fires are allowed from June 1 to October 15.

24. CLAY CREEK CAMPGROUND—MAP A

Campsites, facilities: There are 20 sites, all with picnic tables, grills and fire rings. Water and chemical toilets are available. There is a 14-day stay limit.

Reservations, fees: There is a $5 fee per night; pay on site.

Who to contact: Eugene District Office, 2890 Chad Drive, P.O. Box 10266, Eugene, OR 97440; (503) 683-6600.

Location: At the confluence of Clay Creek and Siuslaw River. From Loran, drive 28 miles west on the narrow but paved Siuslaw River Road to the campground entrance. The campground is set at 1,400 feet.

Season: May to November.

25. WHITTAKER CREEK CAMPGROUND—MAP A

Campsites, facilities: There are 31 sites, all with picnic tables, grills and fire rings. Chemical toilets, water and a boat ramp are available. There is a 14-day stay limit.

Reservations, fees: There is a $5 fee per night; pay on site.

Who to contact: Eugene District Office, 2890 Chad Drive, P.O. Box 10266, Eugene, OR 97440; (503) 683-6600.

Location: Near the Siuslaw River. From Mapleton, drive 15 miles east on Highway 126 to Siuslaw River Road and then head south to the campground entrance. The campground is set at 1,300 feet.

Season: May to November.

26. ALSEA FALLS CAMPGROUND—MAP A

Campsites, facilities: There are 16 sites, all with picnic tables and fire rings. Water and pit toilets are available. There is a 14-day stay limit.

Reservations, fees: There is a $5 fee per night; pay on site.

Who to contact: Salem District Office, 1717 Fabry Road Southeast, Salem, OR 97306; (503) 375-5646.

Location: On the South Fork Alsea River in the Coast Range. From Alsea, drive southeast on South Fork Alsea Road for approximately seven miles to the campground entrance. The campground is set at 800 feet.

Season: May to October.

27. SHARPS CREEK CAMPGROUND—MAP A

Campsites, facilities: There are 10 sites, all with picnic tables and grills. Chemical toilets and water are available. RVs up to 25 feet are allowed. There is a 14-day stay limit.

Reservations, fees: There is a $5 fee per night; pay on site.

Who to contact: Eugene District Office, 2890 Chad Drive, P.O. Box 10266, Eugene, OR 97440; (503) 683-6600.

Location: From Culp Creek, drive 1.5 miles south on Sharps Creek Road to the campground entrance. The campground is set at 2,700 feet.

Season: May to November.

28. CHIMNEY ROCK CAMPGROUND—MAP A

Campsites, facilities: There are 16 sites, all with picnic tables. Pit toilets are available. There is **no water**. Quiet is enforced from 10 p.m. to 7 a.m. There is a 14-day stay limit.

Reservations, fees: There is a $3 fee per night for one vehicle. Each additional vehicle costs $1 extra. Pay on site.

Who to contact: Prineville District Office, 185 East Fourth Street, P.O. Box 550, Prineville, OR 97754; (503) 447-4115.

Location: In Crooked River Canyon. From Prineville, drive along

Highway 27, which parallels Crooked River, to access Chimney Rock Campground, Stillwater Campground, Lone Pine Campground, Lower Palisades Campground, Castle Rock Campground, Cobble Rock Campground, Post Pile Campground and Poison Butte Campground.

Season: All year.

29. POISON BUTTE CAMPGROUND—MAP A

Campsites, facilities: There are five sites, all with picnic tables. Pit toilets and water are available. Quiet is enforced from 10 p.m. to 7 a.m. There is a 14-day stay limit.

Reservations, fees: There is a $3 fee per night for one vehicle. Each additional vehicle costs $1 extra. Pay on site.

Who to contact: Prineville District Office, 185 East Fourth Street, P.O. Box 550, Prineville, OR 97754; (503) 447-4115.

Location: In Crooked River Canyon. From Prineville, drive along Highway 27, which parallels Crooked River, to access Chimney Rock Campground, Stillwater Campground, Lone Pine Campground, Lower Palisades Campground, Castle Rock Campground, Cobble Rock Campground, Post Pile Campground and Poison Butte Campground.

Season: All year.

30. CASTLE ROCK CAMPGROUND—MAP A

Campsites, facilities: There are five sites, all with picnic tables. Pit toilets and water are available. Quiet is enforced from 10 p.m. to 7 a.m. There is a 14-day stay limit.

Reservations, fees: There is a $3 fee per night for one vehicle. Each additional vehicle costs $1 extra. Pay on site.

Who to contact: Prineville District Office, 185 East Fourth Street, P.O. Box 550, Prineville, OR 97754; (503) 447-4115.

Location: In Crooked River Canyon. From Prineville, drive along Highway 27, which parallels Crooked River to access Chimney Rock Campground, Stillwater Campground, Lone Pine Campground, Lower Palisades Campground, Castle Rock Campground, Cobble Rock Campground, Post Pile Campground and Poison Butte Campground.

Season: All year.

31. POST PILE CAMPGROUND—MAP A

Campsites, facilities: There are seven sites, all with picnic tables. Pit toilets and water are available. Quiet is enforced from 10 p.m. to 7 a.m. There is a 14-day stay limit.

Reservations, fees: There is a $3 fee per night for one vehicle. Each additional vehicle costs $1 extra. Pay on site.

Who to contact: Prineville District Office, 185 East Fourth Street, P.O. Box 550, Prineville, OR 97754; (503) 447-4115.

Location: In Crooked River Canyon. From Prineville, drive along Highway 27, which parallels Crooked River, to access Chimney Rock Campground, Stillwater Campground, Lone Pine Campground, Lower Palisades Campground, Castle Rock Campground, Cobble Rock Campground, Post Pile Campground and Poison Butte Campground.

Season: All year.

32. COBBLE ROCK CAMPGROUND—MAP A

Campsites, facilities: There are six sites, all with picnic tables. Pit toilets and water are available. Quiet is enforced from 10 p.m. to 7 a.m. There is a 14-day stay limit.

Reservations, fees: There is a $3 fee per night for one vehicle. Each additional vehicle costs $1 extra. Pay on site.

Who to contact: Prineville District Office, 185 East Fourth Street, P.O. Box 550, Prineville, OR 97754; (503) 447-4115.

Location: In Crooked River Canyon. From Prineville, drive along Highway 27, which parallels Crooked River, to access Chimney Rock Campground, Stillwater Campground, Lone Pine Campground, Lower Palisades Campground, Castle Rock Campground, Cobble Rock Campground, Post Pile Campground and Poison Butte Campground.

Season: All year.

33. LOWER PALISADES CAMPGROUND—MAP A

Campsites, facilities: There are 12 sites, all with picnic tables. Pit toilets and water are available. Quiet is enforced from 10 p.m. to 7 a.m. There is a 14-day stay limit.

Reservations, fees: There is a $3 fee per night for one vehicle. Each additional vehicle costs $1 extra. Pay on site.

Who to contact: Prineville District Office, 185 East Fourth Street,

P.O. Box 550, Prineville, OR 97754; (503) 447-4115.

Location: In Crooked River Canyon. From Prineville, drive along Highway 27, which parallels Crooked River, to access Chimney Rock Campground, Stillwater Campground, Lone Pine Campground, Lower Palisades Campground, Castle Rock Campground, Cobble Rock Campground, Post Pile Campground and Poison Butte Campground.

Season: All year.

34. GREEN MOUNTAIN CAMPGROUND—MAP A

Campsites, facilities: The sites are undesignated and have picnic tables and fire rings. There are no other facilities, so come prepared.

Reservations, fees: There is no fee.

Who to contact: Lakeview Resource Area, 1000 Ninth Street South, P.O. Box 151, Lakeview, OR 97630; (503) 947-2177.

Location: Just below the Green Mountain summit. From Christmas Valley, drive on county and BLM roads for eight miles, following signs to the campground.

Season: All year. Snow can close the road.

35. SMITH RIVER FALLS CAMPGROUND—MAP A

Campsites, facilities: The sites are undesignated and have picnic tables and fire rings. Pit toilets are available. There is **no water**. There is a 14-day stay limit.

Reservations, fees: There is no fee.

Who to contact: Coos Bay District Office, 1300 Airport Lane, North Bend, OR 97459; (503) 756-0100.

Location: Along the Smith River. From Reedsport, drive north on US 101 across the Umpqua River and turn right onto Smith River Road (County Road 48) and drive 20 miles to the campground entrance.

Season: All year.

36. EAST SHORE CAMPGROUND—MAP A

Campsites, facilities: There are eight tent sites, all with picnic tables and fire rings. Pit toilets are available. There is **no water**. There is a 14-day stay limit.

Reservations, fees: There is a $5 fee per night; pay on site.

Who to contact: Coos Bay District Office, 1300 Airport Lane, North Bend, OR 97459; (503) 756-0100.

Location: On Loon Lake in Elliot State Forest. From Reedsport, drive 13 miles east on Highway 38 and then head south for seven miles on Ash Road to the campground entrance. The campground is set at 310 feet.

Season: All year.

37. TYEE CAMPGROUND—MAP A

Campsites, facilities: There are 15 sites, all with picnic tables and grills. Water, vault toilets and firewood are available. RVs up to 25 feet are allowed. There is a 14-day stay limit.

Reservations, fees: There is a $5 fee per night; pay on site.

Who to contact: Roseburg District Office, 777 Northwest Garden Valley Boulevard, Roseburg, OR 97470; (503) 440-4930.

Location: On the Umpqua River. From Roseburg and Interstate 5, drive north and take exit 136, heading west on Highway 138. Drive 12 miles to Bullock Bridge. Cross the bridge and turn right onto the County Road; drive another one-half mile to the campground entrance.

Season: May to October.

38. MILLPOND CAMPGROUND—MAP A

Campsites, facilities: There are 12 sites, all with picnic tables and grills. Vault and flush toilets and water are available. There is limited wheelchair accessibility.

Reservations, fees: There is a $6 fee per night; pay on site.

Who to contact: Roseburg District Office, 777 Northwest Garden Valley Boulevard, Roseburg, OR 97470; (503) 440-4930.

Location: From Roseburg and Interstate 5, drive east for 22 miles on Highway 138. Turn northeast (left) and drive six miles on Rock Creek Road to the campground entrance.

Season: May to October.

39. ROCK CREEK CAMPGROUND—MAP A

Campsites, facilities: The sites are undesignated and have picnic tables and grills. Water, a pit toilet and a raft launch are available. There is a 14-day stay limit.

Reservations, fees: There is no fee.

Who to contact: Roseburg District Office, 777 Northwest Garden Valley Boulevard, Roseburg, OR 97470; (503) 440-4930.

Location: From where US 95 crosses the Owyhee River, drive south eight-tenths of a mile to the campground entrance.

Season: All year.

40. SCARED MAN CAMPGROUND—MAP A

Campsites, facilities: There are nine sites, all with picnic tables and grills. Pit toilets and water are available. RVs from 21 to 40 feet are allowed. There is a 14-day stay limit.

Reservations, fees: There is no fee.

Who to contact: Roseburg District Office, 777 Northwest Garden Valley Boulevard, Roseburg, OR 97470; (503) 440-4930.

Location: From Glide, drive 40 miles east on Oregon 138 to Steamboat. Turn north (left) onto Steamboat Creek and drive one quarter of a mile to Canton Creek Road. Turn northwest onto Canton Creek Road and drive three miles to the campground entrance.

Season: May to October. Camping out of season is allowed, but no water or maintenance are provided.

41. CAVITT CREEK FALLS CAMPGROUND—MAP A

Campsites, facilities: There are eight sites, all with picnic tables and grills. Vault toilets and water are available. RVs from 21 to 38 feet are allowed. There is a 14-day stay limit.

Reservations, fees: There is a $5 fee per night; pay on site.

Who to contact: Roseburg District Office, 777 Northwest Garden Valley Boulevard, Roseburg, OR 97470; (503) 440-4930.

Location: From Roseburg and Interstate 5, drive east for 16.5 miles on Highway 138 to Glide. Turn southeast on Little River Road and drive seven miles to Cavitt Creek Road. Turn south and drive three miles to the campground entrance.

Season: May to October.

42. SUSAN CREEK CAMPGROUND—MAP A

Campsites, facilities: There are 31 sites, all with picnic tables and grills. Showers, flush toilets and water are available. RVs from 24 to 48 feet are allowed. The campground is wheelchair accessible. There is a 14-day stay limit.

Reservations, fees: There is an $8 fee per night; pay on site.

Who to contact: Roseburg District Office, 777 Northwest Garden Valley Boulevard, Roseburg, OR 97470; (503) 440-4930.

Location: On the North Umpqua River. From Roseburg and Interstate 5, drive east for 29 miles on Highway 138 to the campground entrance.

Season: May to October.

43. UNCAN RESERVOIR CAMPGROUND—MAP A

Campsites, facilities: There are five sites, all with picnic tables. Pit toilets and a boat ramp are available. There is **no water**. No trash facilities are provided, so pack out all that you bring in. There is a 14-day stay limit.

Reservations, fees: There is no fee.

Who to contact: Lakeview Resource Area, 1000 Ninth Street South, P.O. Box 151, Lakeview, OR 97630; (503) 947-2177.

Location: From Silver Lake, drive east for five miles on Highway 31. Turn right on County Road 4-14 and drive one mile to BLM Road 6197. Drive south on BLM Road 6197 for four miles to the campground entrance. The campground is set at 4,800 feet.

Season: All year. Severe weather may close it.

44. PARK CREEK CAMPGROUND—MAP A

Campsites, facilities: The sites are undesignated and have picnic tables, grills and fire rings. Pit toilets are available. There is **no water**. There is a 14-day stay limit.

Reservations, fees: There is no fee.

Who to contact: Coos Bay District Office, 1300 Airport Lane, North Bend, OR 97459; (503) 756-0100.

Location: From Coquille, drive 15 miles south on Coquille/Fairview Road for 15 miles to Fairview. Turn right onto Coos Bay Wagon Road and drive four miles. Turn left onto Middle Creek Access Road and drive 15 miles to Park Creek Access Road. Turn onto Park Creek and drive to the campground. The campground is set at 500 feet.

Season: All year.

45. SIXES RIVER CAMPGROUND—MAP A

Campsites, facilities: There are 20 sites, all with picnic tables and grills. Water is available, but the BLM recommends treating it as they don't test for purity. Pit toilets are available. RVs up to 24 feet are allowed. There is a 14-day stay limit.

Reservations, fees: There is no fee.

Who to contact: Coos Bay District Office, 1300 Airport Lane, North Bend, OR 97459; (503) 756-0100.

Location: From Sixes, drive east on Sixes River Road (County Road 184) for 11 miles. You are sharing the route with logging vehicles, so stay alert! Turn right at the sign indicating the campground entrance. The campground is set at 1280 feet.

Season: All year.

46. TUCKER FLAT CAMPGROUND—MAP A

Campsites, facilities: There are 10 sites, all with picnic tables and grills. Pit toilets are available. There is **no water**. RVs up to 20 feet are allowed. There is a 14-day stay limit.

Reservations, fees: There is no fee.

Who to contact: Medford District Office, 3040 Biddle Road, Medford, OR 97504; (503) 770-2200.

Location: On the Rogue River and near the Rogue River Trail. From Interstate 5, take exit 61 at Merlin and drive 20 miles west on Galice Road to Grave Creek Bridge. Turn left onto Grave Creek/Marial National Back Country Byway and drive approximately 33 miles to the campground. The BLM advises that more specific directions and road information are needed. Do not head to this camping area without first checking in with the Medford District Office. Under no circumstances should you attempt to travel to this campground without an adequate map to the area, also available from the Medford District Office. The campground is set at 1,000 feet.

Season: May to October.

47. ELDERBERRY FLAT CAMPGROUND—MAP A

Campsites, facilities: There are nine sites, all with picnic tables and fire rings. Pit toilets are available. There is **no water**. RVs up to 30 feet are allowed. There is a 14-day stay limit.

Reservations, fees: There is no fee.

Who to contact: Medford District Office, 3040 Biddle Road, Medford, OR 97504; (503) 770-2200.

Location: Along the West Fork of Evans Creek. From Interstate 5 at Rogue River, take exit 48 and drive north on Evans Creek Road for 20 miles to West Fork Evans Creek Road. Turn left and drive nine miles to the campground entrance. The campground is set at 1,500 feet.

Season: May to November.

48. SURVEYOR CAMPGROUND—MAP A

Campsites, facilities: There are five sites, all with picnic tables and fire rings. Pit toilets are wheelchair accessible. Water is available. There is a 14-day stay limit.

Reservations, fees: There is no fee.

Who to contact: Klamath Falls Resource Area, 2795 Anderson Avenue, Building 25, Klamath Falls, OR 97603; (503) 883-6916.

Location: From Klamath Falls, drive south for three miles on US 97 to Highway 66. Drive on Highway 66 west for 15 miles to Keno Access Road and drive 14 miles northwest on Keno to the campground entrance. The campground is set at 5,200 feet.

Season: May to October.

49. HYATT LAKE CAMPGROUND—MAP A

Campsites, facilities: There are 29 sites, all with picnic tables and grills. Water, walk-in tent sites, two full bathrooms with showers, a boat launch and fish-cleaning stations are available. There are no RY hookups. There is a 14-day stay limit.

Reservations, fees: There is a $10 fee per night; pay on site.

Who to contact: Medford District Office, 3040 Biddle Road, Medford, OR 97504; (503) 770-2200.

Location: From Ashland on Interstate 5, take exit 14 and drive east on Highway 66 for 20 miles to Hyatt Lake Road. Turn left and drive three miles to East Hyatt Lake Road. Turn right and drive approximately 300 yards to the campground entrance. The campground is set at 5,200 feet.

Season: May to November.

50. WILDCAT CAMPGROUND—MAP A

Campsites, facilities: There are 12 sites, all with picnic tables and grills. Water, two full bathrooms with showers, a boat launch, fish-cleaning stations and walk-in tent sites are available. There are no RV hookups available. There is a 14-day stay limit.

Reservations, fees: There is a $6 fee per night; pay on site.

Who to contact: Medford District Office, 3040 Biddle Road, Medford, OR 97504; (503) 770-2200.

Location: From Ashland on Interstate 5, take exit 14 and drive east on Highway 66 for 20 miles to Hyatt Lake Road. Turn left and drive three miles to East Hyatt Lake Road. Turn right and drive 1.5

miles past Hyatt Lake Campground to the campground entrance on the left. The campground is set at 5,200 feet.

Season: May to October.

51. TOPSY CAMPGROUND—MAP A

Campsites, facilities: There are 15 sites, all with picnic tables and fire rings. Pit toilets are wheelchair accessible. Water, a boat ramp, a boat dock and a gray-water dump are available. There is a 14-day stay limit.

Reservations, fees: There is a $4 fee per night.

Who to contact: Klamath Falls Resource Area, 2795 Anderson Avenue, Building 25, Klamath Falls, OR 97603; (503) 883-6916.

Location: On the John C. Boyle Reservoir and Upper Klamath River. From Klamath Falls, drive three miles south on US 97 to Highway 66 and turn right, driving 14.5 miles to the Klamath River. Turn left onto Topsy Road and drive one mile on dirt surface to the campground entrance. The campground is set at 4,200 feet.

Season: April to September.

52. GERBER RESERVOIR CAMPGROUND—MAP A

Campsites, facilities: There are 50 sites, all with picnic tables, grills and fire rings. Pit toilets, an RV dump station, a boat ramp, a boat dock and a fish cleaning station are available. RVs up to 30 feet are allowed. There is a 14-day stay limit.

Reservations, fees: There is a $5 fee per vehicle per night; pay on site.

Who to contact: Klamath Falls Resource Area, 2795 Anderson Avenue, Building 25, Klamath Falls, OR 97603; (503) 883-6916.

Location: From Bonanza, drive 11 miles east on Langell Valley Road to Gerber Road and turn left, driving another eight miles to the campground entrance. The campground is set at 4,700 feet.

Season: May to October.

53. MUD CREEK CAMPGROUND—MAP B

Campsites, facilities: The sites are undesignated and have picnic tables. Pit toilets and a boat ramp are available. There is **no water**. No trash facilities are provided, so pack out all that you bring in. There is a 14-day stay limit.

Reservations, fees: There is no fee.

Who to contact: Vale District Office, 100 Oregon Street, Vale, OR 97918; (503) 473-3144.

Location: From Troy, drive six miles south on a gravel access road along Mud Creek to the campground.

Season: All year.

54. BIG BEND CAMPGROUND—MAP B

Campsites, facilities: There are four sites, all with picnic tables and fire rings. Pit toilets and a boat ramp are available. There is **no water**. The campsites are wheelchair accessible. No trash facilities are available so pack out all you bring in. There is a 14-day stay limit.

Reservations, fees: There is no fee.

Who to contact: Prineville District Office, 185 East Fourth Street, P.O. Box 550, Prineville, OR 97754; (503) 447-4115.

Location: On the North Fork of the John Day River. From Kimberly, drive north on Highway 402 for approximately 2.5 miles to the campground entrance. The campground is set at 1,200 feet.

Season: All year.

55. MULE SHOE CAMPGROUND—MAP B

Campsites, facilities: There are nine sites (four designated tents-only), all with picnic tables, grills and fire rings. Pit toilets and a boat ramp are available. There is **no water**. No trash facilities are provided, so pack out all that you bring in. The campground is wheelchair accessible. There is a 14-day stay limit.

Reservations, fees: There is no fee.

Who to contact: Prineville District Office, 185 East Fourth Street, P.O. Box 550, Prineville, OR 97754; (503) 447-4115.

Location: Along John Day River. Drive east from Fossil or west from Spray on Highway 19. The campground entrance is located approximately two miles east of Service Creek Trading Post. The campground is set at 600 feet.

Season: All year.

56. LONE PINE CAMPGROUND—MAP B

Campsites, facilities: There are eight sites, all with picnic tables. Pit toilets and water are available. Quiet is enforced from 10 p.m. to 7 a.m. There is a 14-day stay limit.

Reservations, fees: There is a $3 fee per night for one vehicle. Each additional vehicle costs $1 extra. Pay on site.

Who to contact: Prineville District Office, 185 East Fourth Street, P.O. Box 550, Prineville, OR 97754; (503) 447-4115.

Location: In Crooked River Canyon. From Prineville, drive along Highway 27, which parallels Crooked River, to access Chimney Rock Campground, Stillwater Campground, Lone Pine Campground, Lower Palisades Campground, Castle Rock Campground, Cobble Rock Campground, Post Pile Campground and Poison Butte Campground.

Season: All year.

57. BASSER DIGGINS CAMPGROUND—MAP B

Campsites, facilities: The sites are undesignated and have picnic tables and fire rings. Pit toilets and water are available. There is a 14-day stay limit.

Reservations, fees: There is no fee.

Who to contact: Vale District Office, 100 Oregon Street, Vale, OR 97918; (503) 473-3144.

Location: From Durkee, drive nine miles south on Highway 84 and then turn onto a dirt road leading to Lookout Mountain and signed for Basser Diggins Campground. The campground is located at 6,000 feet.

Season: May to November.

58. SPRING CAMPGROUND—MAP B

Campsites, facilities: The sites are undesignated and have picnic tables, grills and fire rings. Pit toilets, a boat ramp and water are available. RVs up to 30 feet are allowed. There is a 14-day stay limit.

Reservations, fees: There is a $4 fee per night; pay on site.

Who to contact: Vale District Office, 100 Oregon Street, Vale, OR 97918; (503) 473-3144.

Location: On Brownlee Reservoir. From Huntington, drive five miles east on a paved access road (some gravel) toward Brownlee Reservoir and the campground entrance. The campground is set at 2,500 feet.

Season: All year.

59. CHICKAHOMINY CAMPGROUND—MAP B

Campsites, facilities: There are four picnic sites, all with picnic tables. Undesignated camping for RV vehicles is in the graveled parking lot. Two vault toilets, a boat ramp and a fish-cleaning station with water are available. There is a 14-day stay limit.

Reservations, fees: There is no fee.

Who to contact: Burns District Office, 21533 Highway 20 West, Hines, OR 97738; (503) 573-4400.

Location: From Burns, drive 34 miles west on US 20 to the campground entrance. The campground is set at 4,350 feet.

Season: All year.

60. CHUKAR PARK CAMPGROUND—MAP B

Campsites, facilities: The sites are undesignated and have picnic tables, grills and fire rings. Water and pit toilets are available. There is a 14-day stay limit.

Reservations, fees: There is a $4 fee per night; pay on site.

Who to contact: Vale District Office, 100 Oregon Street, Vale, OR 97918; (503) 473-3144.

Location: Near the Malheur River. From Juntura and US 20, drive approximately six miles north on a graded road, signed for the campground. The campground is set at 3,200 feet.

Season: May to October.

61. SNIVELY HOT SPRINGS CAMPGROUND—MAP B

Campsites, facilities: The sites are undesignated and have pit toilets. There is **no water**. There is a 14-day stay limit.

Reservations, fees: There is no fee.

Who to contact: Vale District Office, 100 Oregon Street, Vale, OR 97918; (503) 473-3144.

Location: On the Owyhee River near Snively Hot Springs. From Vale, drive south on Lytle Boulevard (marked as the Oregon Trail Route) for 16 miles to Cow Hollow Road. Follow the signs to Lake Owyhee for 10 miles.

Season: All year.

62. TWIN SPRINGS CAMPGROUND—MAP B

Campsites, facilities: There are six sites, all with picnic tables and fire rings. Water, pit toilets and a boat launch are available. RVs up to 30 feet are allowed. There is a 14-day stay limit.

Reservations, fees: There is a $3 fee per night for one vehicle. Each additional vehicle costs $1 extra. Pay on site.

Who to contact: Prineville District Office, 185 East Fourth Street, P.O. Box 550, Prineville, OR 97754; (503) 447-4115.

Location: In the Deschutes River Canyon. From the town of Maupin, just before the bridge and past the city park, turn left onto Lower Access Road and drive nine miles. Turn right at the stop sign and then left; you're still on Lower Access Road, but now it's a gravel surface. Signs leading to the site indicate Deschutes River Recreation Lands and Macks Canyon. Drive to the campground. The road dead-ends in 17 miles at Macks Canyon Campground. Other campgrounds along the canyon route are Oakbrook, Beavertail, Jones Canyon, Gert Canyon, Macks Canyon and Rattlesnake. The campground is set at 500 feet.

Season: All year. No open fires are allowed from June 1 to October 15.

63. SLOCUM CANYON CAMPGROUND—MAP B

Campsites, facilities: The sites are undesignated. Pit toilets and a boat ramp are available. There is **no water**. There is a 14-day stay limit.

Reservations, fees: There is no fee.

Who to contact: Vale District Office, 100 Oregon Street, Vale, OR 97918; (503) 473-3144.

Location: Beside the Owyhee Reservoir. Eight miles south of Adrian, Oregon (or seven miles west of Homedale, Idaho), take the Highway 201 and follow the Leslie Gulch/Succor Creek National Back Country Byway signs on the graded Succor Creek Road. Or take the graded McBride Creek Road from US 95, south of Homedale, Idaho. You are advised that roads may become hazardous or impassable in wet or winter conditions. Towing large trailers is discouraged due to the steep, narrow and winding road that leads into the upper reaches of the Gulch. The best road conditions exist from mid-April to October, although the canyon is subject to flash-flooding at any time.

Season: April to November.

64. PAGE SPRINGS CAMPGROUND—MAP B

Campsites, facilities: There are 30 sites, all with picnic tables, grills and fire rings. Water and pit toilets are available. RVs up to 24 feet are allowed. There is a 14-day stay limit.

Reservations, fees: There is a $4 fee per night per vehicle, pay on site.

Who to contact: Burns District Office, HC 74-12533, US 20 West, Hines, OR 97738; (503) 573-5241.

Location: In the Steens Mountain area on Blitzen River, bordering

Malheur Wildlife Refuge. Drive four miles southeast of Frenchglen on Steens Mountain Loop Road to the campground entrance. The campground is set at 4,100 feet.

Season: May to October.

65. FISH LAKE CAMPGROUND—MAP B

Campsites, facilities: There are 24 sites, all with picnic tables and grills. Water, pit toilets and firewood are available. There is a nearby boat-launch facility. RVs up to 24 feet are allowed. There is a 14-day stay limit.

Reservations, fees: There is a $4 fee per vehicle per night; pay on site.

Who to contact: Burns District Office, HC 74-12533, US 20 West, Hines, OR 97738; (503) 573-5241.

Location: Located in the Steens Mountain area. From Burns, head south on Highway 205 for 61 miles to Frenchglen and then drive east for 16 miles on Steens Mountain Road to the campground entrance. The campground is set at 7,900 feet.

Season: July to October, depending on snow.

66. JACKMAN PARK CAMPGROUND—MAP B

Campsites, facilities: There are six sites, all with picnic tables and grills. Water, a nearby boat launch, pit toilets and firewood are available. RVs up to 24 feet are allowed. There is a 14-day stay limit.

Reservations, fees: There is a $4 fee per vehicle per night; pay on site.

Who to contact: Burns District Office, HC 74-12533, US 20 West, Hines, OR 97738; (503) 573-5241.

Location: In the Steens Mountain area. From Burns, head south on Highway 205 for 61 miles to Frenchglen and then drive east for 20 miles on Steens Mountain Road to the campground entrance. The campground is set at 8,100 feet.

Season: July to October, depending on snow.

67. ROME CAMPGROUND—MAP B

Campsites, facilities: There are 18 sites, all with picnic tables and grills. Water and vault toilets are available. RVs from 24 to 67 feet are allowed. There is a 14-day stay limit.

Reservations, fees: There is a $5 fee per night; pay on site.

Who to contact: Vale District Office, 100 Oregon Street, Vale, OR 97918; (503) 473-3144.

Location: From Roseburg and Interstate 5, drive east for 22 miles on Highway 138. Turn northeast (left) on Rock Creek Road and drive 7.5 miles to the campground entrance.

Season: May to October.

68. THREE FORKS CAMPGROUND—MAP B

Campsites, facilities: The sites are undesignated and have picnic tables and fire rings. A pit toilet is available. There is **no water**. No trash facilities are provided, so pack out all that you bring in. There is a 14-day stay limit.

Reservations, fees: There is no fee.

Who to contact: Vale District Office, 100 Oregon Street, Vale, OR 97918; (503) 473-3144.

Location: At the confluence of the Main and North Fork Owyhee Rivers. From Jordan Valley, drive 13 miles south on US 95 to Three Forks Road and turn left. Drive 26 miles on a rough, sometimes steep, dirt road. Four-wheel-drive vehicles are recommended. The campground is set at 4,000 feet.

Season: May to November.

STATE INFORMATION OVERVIEW

OREGON STATE OFFICE
1300 Northeast 44th Avenue, P.O. Box 2965, Portland, OR 97208; (503) 280-7001

BURNS DISTRICT OFFICE
HC 74-12533, US 20 West, Hines, OR 97738; (503) 573-5241

ROSEBURG DISTRICT OFFICE
777 Northwest Garden Valley Boulevard, Roseburg, OR 97470; (503) 440-4930

COOS BAY DISTRICT OFFICE
1300 Airport Lane, North Bend, OR 97459; (503) 756-0100

EUGENE DISTRICT OFFICE
2890 Chad Drive, P.O. Box 10266, Eugene, OR 97440; (503) 683-6600

PRINEVILLE DISTRICT OFFICE
185 East Fourth Street, P.O. Box 550, Prineville, OR 97754; (503) 447-4115

LAKEVIEW DISTRICT OFFICE
1000 Ninth Street South, P.O. Box 151, Lakeview, OR 97630; (503) 947-2177

SALEM DISTRICT OFFICE
1717 Fabry Road Southeast, Salem, OR 97306; (503) 375-5646

MEDFORD DISTRICT OFFICE
3040 Biddle Road, Medford, OR 97504; (503) 770-2200

Klamath Falls Resource Area, 2795 Anderson Suite 25, Klamath Falls, OR 97601; (503) 883-6916

VALE DISTRICT OFFICE
100 Oregon Street, Vale, OR 97918; (503) 473-3144

Baker Resource Area Office, 1550 Dewey, P.O. Box 987, Baker City, OR 97814; (503) 523-1256

CHAPTER ELEVEN

UTAH

Maps—pp. 482, 484
Utah Map A Locations—pp. 486-495
Utah Map B Locations—pp. 496-517
Information Resources—pp. 531-532

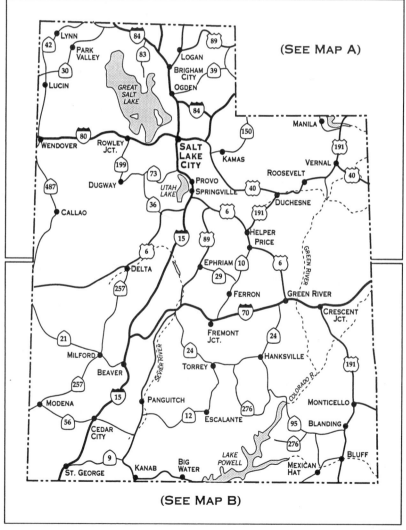

(SEE MAP A)

(SEE MAP B)

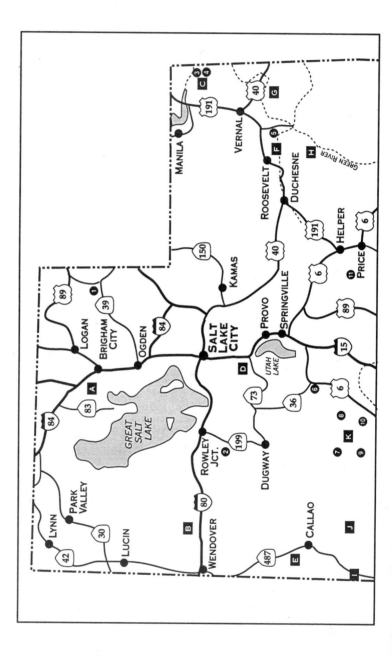

MAP A—UTAH

MAP REFERENCES

A. Transcontinental Railroad Back Country Byway—p. 486
B. Bonneville Salt Flats—p. 486
C. Browns Park —p. 487
D. Pony Express Trail Back Country Byway—p. 487
E. Deep Creek Mountains —p. 488
F. Pariette Wetlands —p. 489
G. White River—p. 489
H. Desolation Canyon / Gray Canyon —p. 491
I. Crystal Ball and Gandy Mountain Caves —p. 493
J. Swasey Mountain —p. 493
K. Little Sahara Recreation Area—p. 494

BLM CAMPGROUNDS

1. Birch Creek Campground—p. 520
2. Clover Spring Campground—p. 520
3. Bridge Hollow Campground—p. 521
4. Indian Crossing Campground—p. 521
5. Pelican Lake Campground—p. 521
6. Simpson's Springs Campground—p. 522
7. Oasis Campground—p. 522
8. Jericho Campground—p. 522
9. Sand Mountain Campground—p. 523
10. White Sands Campground—p. 523
11. Price Canyon Campground—p. 523

MAP B—UTAH

Map References

BLM Campgrounds

UTAH—MAP A

TRANSCONTINENTAL RAILROAD BACK COUNTRY BYWAY

See letter A on map page 482

cultural/historic site, mountain biking

Visitors may travel 90 miles on the original route of the nation's first transcontinental railroad. The Back Country Byway begins at Golden Spike National Historic Site, 32 miles west of Brigham City. The route follows the actual grade of the Central Pacific Railroad, which was completed in 1869. Many town sites and railroad sites are identified by interpretive signs. This trip is suitable for most high-clearance vehicles less than 20 feet long. The railroad grade is a narrow roadway with gravel or dirt surface, no shoulders and occasional ruts. Flats are not uncommon so carry at least one spare tire. Pack along plenty of water for both your vehicle and yourself. There are no developed campsites, services or water sources along the route. Camping is allowed on BLM lands along the way, but you must be careful not to disturb historic sites or drive in areas where off-highway vehicles are prohibited—even on mountain bikes.

For more information: Contact the BLM Bear River Resource Area, 2370 South 2300 West, Salt Lake City, UT 84119; (801) 977-4300.

BONNEVILLE SALT FLATS

See letter B on map page 482

historic/natural site

Stretching over 30,000 acres and so flat that you can actually see the curvature of the earth, the Bonneville Salt Flats are both a natural wonder and a world-famous destination because of the speed records that have been set here. It is a somewhat alien world here, so barren that life cannot exist upon its surface, yet so mystically beautiful that thousands are drawn to view it each year. Camping is prohibited on the Bonneville Salt Flats, but allowed on the surrounding public lands. Nearby Wendover has a number of private campgrounds if you desire them. You must stay on existing roads or areas designated for vehicles for your own safety. Despite the hard appearance of the crusty surface, much of the region is nothing more than a thin crust of salt over very gooey mud—the kind that swallows vehicles.

Be aware that in the summer the temperature can exceed 100°F and in the winter drop below 0°F. There are no facilities of any kind on the salt flats. Many points of entry are possible to area; it is north of Interstate 80 and six miles east of Wendover.

Resources:
• The BLM distributes a free brochure called "The Bonneville Salt Flats."

For more information: Contact the BLM Salt Lake District Office, 2370 South 2300 West, Salt Lake City, UT 84119; (801) 977-4300.

BROWNS PARK

See letter C on map page 482

camping, canoeing, fishing, hiking, rafting

Browns Park is an alluvial valley surrounded by high mountain plateaus and located in the northeastern corner of Utah. The focus of recreation in this region is fishing the Green River, a blue-ribbon fishery that attracts visitors from all over the world. The park is along the Colorado/Utah state line, south of Highway 318 and near Dinosaur National Monument and Browns Park National Wildlife Refuge. From Vernal, head northeast on Jones Hole Road, past Red Fleet State Park Road to Browns Park and the Green River. It makes a good destination any time of year.

For more information: Contact the BLM Vernal District Office, 170 South 500 East, Vernal, UT 84078; (801) 789-1362.

PONY EXPRESS TRAIL BACK COUNTRY BYWAY

See letter D on map page 482

birdwatching, camping, cultural/historic site, hiking, horseback riding, hunting, mountain biking, rockhounding

The Pony Express Trail Back Country Byway follows 133 miles of the original Pony Express Trail. The route, from Fairfield, Utah to the Nevada border, is a maintained dirt road. Along the byway, sites of 15 Pony Express Stations, each marked with rock monuments erected by the Civilian Conservation Corps (CCC), may be seen. A picnic area and Back Country Byway information kiosk is located on the trail just west of Faust Junction. The BLM maintains interpretive sites with wayside exhibits at Faust Station, Simpson Springs, Boyd Station and Canyon Station. Simpson Springs also includes a replica of the Pony Express Station, the ruins of a CCC camp from the 1930s and a developed campground with 14 sites at Simpson Springs. In addition to the historic interest, visitors will discover a wealth of recreational opportunities along the trail. Photographers will enjoy the picturesque vistas of the Great Basin mountain ranges. Hikers, mountain bikers and horseback riders can explore the numerous opportunities for side trips off the Pony Express Trail. Bird watchers and hunters will find easy access to the nearby Fish Springs National Wildlife Refuge, while rockhounds will enjoy picking their way through the Dugway Geode Beds. Keep your eyes peeled as you wander through this area and you may be rewarded with glimpses of another holdover from the Old West, wild horses. Horses of the Onaqui Mountain herd can be viewed sometimes north of the Pony Express Trail.

Maps: Ask for the free BLM Pony Express Trail National Back Country Byway brochure and map.

For more information: Contact the BLM Salt Lake District Office, 2370 South 2300 West, Salt Lake City, UT 84119; (801) 977-4300; or the BLM Richfield District Office, 150 East 900 North, Richfield, UT 84701; (801) 896-8221.

DEEP CREEK MOUNTAINS

See letter E on map page 482

backpacking, camping, cross-country skiing, fishing, hiking, wildlife observation

The Deep Creek Mountains are located approximately 140 miles southwest of Salt Lake City and 72 miles northwest of Delta. It is the only mountain range in the interior of Utah's Great Basin with an abundance of water. Six perennial streams on the eastern slopes of the range support populations of rainbow and cutthroat trout. Mule deer, bighorn sheep, mountain lion, antelope, grouse and chukar can all be seen. With 12,000-foot peaks, streams, lush vegetation and a rich wildlife population, the mountain can be a pristine wilderness escape. The BLM suggests that backcountry skiers have a working knowledge of avalanche safety before venturing out.

USGS topographic maps: Indian Farm Creek, Partoun, Trout Creek,

Trout Creek Southwest

BLM surface map: Fish Springs

For more information: Contact the BLM House Range Resource Area, P.O. Box 778, Fillmore, UT 84631; (801) 743-6811.

PARIETTE WETLANDS

See letter F on map page 482

hiking, wildlife observation

Pariette Wetlands is a relatively unique marsh in the middle of miles and miles of desert. Wet meadows, freshwater ponds and alkali bulrush shelter a wide variety of waterfowl, shorebirds and raptors. Take US 40 to Fort Duchesne and head south approximately five miles to the Myton Y-intersection. Turn south off the road to Myton onto a dirt road and drive another 16 miles across Leland Bench to Pariette Wash. Follow the signs to the overlook. Visit any time of year, but expect summers to be hot.

For more information: Contact the BLM Vernal District Office, 170 South 500 East, Vernal, UT 84078; (801) 789-1362.

WHITE RIVER

See letter G on map page 482

backpacking, hiking, whitewater boating, wildlife observation

You won't find this river canyon in any hiking guidebook, but don't think for a minute that it isn't worth a peek. White River is considered by the BLM to be one of Utah's best-kept secrets, seeing fewer than 500 canoeists and only a handful of backpackers each year.

Historically, trappers and traders walked the river's banks with regularity, exchanging goods with Native Americans until, fed up with unfair trading practices, the Uinta Ute Indians burned the region's trading post—Fort Kit Carson—to the ground. Gilsonite, a rare and solid hydrocarbon that forms in veins and is used for industrial purposes was mined at the river. The river served too, as a crossing to the Uinta Railway stage line. Wagon freighters and stage coach travelers headed south across the river to meet up with the narrow gauge railroad at Watson (now only a ghost town), 10 miles south on Evacuation Creek.

Today, the only travelers are recreationists. They seek pleasure in the cold, muddy waters born in the snowmelt and springs high in the mountains above Trapper Lake in western Colorado—100 miles away. Very little remains to remind a visitor of the White River's well-traveled past. The winding high-desert river cuts its way westward, carving the 800-foot-high, weathered-sandstone cliffs ever deeper. Along the river's banks, islands of cottonwoods cling tenuously to the shore above the rushing waters.

A closer look at the shale along the shoreline will reveal fossil beds, indicating that this area once lay under Lake Uinta, a vast body of water that extended north to the snow-capped peaks, 70 miles to the south, and 120 miles to the east and west. Fossils now lie exposed to the air and curious adventurers—an abundance of remains only overshadowed by nearby Dinosaur National Monument, which boasts the world's largest concentration and variety of fossil bones.

Taking the time to periodically clamber out of the river corridor and up on top of the sandstone walls will reward the hiker with glimpses of the snow capped Uinta Mountains to the north.

From September through March or early April are the best times to enjoy the river on foot, when it is usually flowing at 600cfs or below, allowing for stable, shallow river crossings. The first frosts typically hit in late September. During September and October, the river corridor turns into a wonderland of colors as the cottonwood leaves turn. Summer months are suitable for canoeing, but bring plenty of insect repellent to ward of the hordes of gnats, deer flies and mosquitoes. Water flows during May and June are typically fast and require intermediate to advanced paddling skills.

Whether you come to the river to experience its purity or its paucity of human sounds, or for the beauty of its sandstone buttes and the echoing cries of birds of prey, the White River is guaranteed to invite you back again and again—each time putting on a different face.

Location: In northeastern Utah, near the Colorado/Utah border and south of the town of Vernal and Dinosaur National Monument. The best place to begin canoeing or backpacking is at the Bonanza Highway Bridge on Highway 45, southeast of Vernal on Interstate 40. The turnoff for the launch and parking area is located approximately one-half mile north of the bridge. Watch carefully for the sign. The takeout, or vehicle shuttle parking area, is located 32 river miles downstream at Mountain Fuel Bridge. The shuttle between the two bridges goes approximately 20 miles on graded dirt roads. It is possible to extend the trip by beginning your trip at Cowboy Canyon, nine miles upriver from Bonanza Highway Bridge on a very rough four-wheel-drive road. Be extremely cautious when leaving a vehicle at the start or launch points during spring runoff. Daily flows can increase dramatically.

Special note: Minimum-impact camping techniques are requisite. Although campfires are allowed, use only driftwood and please build fires only in fire pans or on fire blankets.

Permits: No boating, hiking or camping permits are needed. A $2 overnight parking permit is required when parking on tribal property at the Mountain Fuel Bridge or 22 miles downriver near the confluence of the Green and White Rivers. Parking permits may be obtained from the Uintah and Ouray Tribal Fish and Game, P.O. Box 190, Fort Duchesne, UT 84026; (801) 722-5511.

USGS topographic maps: Southam Canyon, Asphalt Wash, Archy Bench, Red Wash

BLM surface maps: Vernal and Seep Ridge

Resources:
• *Utah Atlas and Gazetteer*, published by DeLorme Mapping, P.O. Box 298, Freeport, ME 04032; (207) 865-4171.

For more information: Contact the BLM Vernal District Office, 170 South 500 East, Vernal, Utah 84078; (801) 789-1362.

DESOLATION CANYON / GRAY CANYON

See letter H on map page 482

backpacking, camping, canoeing, hiking, kayaking, whitewater rafting, wildlife observation

Besides being the deepest canyons in Utah and rich in Fremont and Ute Indian cultural sites, the Desolation Canyon and the Gray Canyon are on the National Register of Historic Places. They earned this distinction because of explorer John Wesley Powell, who traveled the canyons in the late 1800s and named them. They remain on the National Register chiefly because visitors can still largely find the canyons in the same condition as when Powell viewed them. Other famous and infamous characters were also drawn here during the early 1800s. Trapper Denis Julian left his mark in the form of canyon graffiti in 1830, and Butch Cassidy and the Sundance Kid escaped the law within the mazes of canyons here.

The mighty Green River cuts through the Tavaputs Plateau creating the Desolation and the Gray canyons. Numerous side canyons beg to be hiked and reveal archaeological sites, abandoned homesteads and excellent camping among verdant cottonwoods and sandy beaches.

Activity Highlight: Whitewater rafting

The float time on this river is four to seven days. It is 75 miles from the put-in at Sand Wash Ranger Station to the first take-out point at Nefertiti Rapid, and 84 miles to the second take-out point at Swaseys Rapid at the end of Green River Daily. Of the 67 rapids you will encounter, most are Class II, but several are rated up to Class IV, depending on the water level.

For a list of authorized (permitted) operators running the Desolation, call the BLM at (801) 637-4584.

Location: Along the Green River, just north of the town of Green River. From Myton, drive 42 miles south of US 40 on a single-lane road to the Sand Wash Ranger Station.

Camping: Camping is allowed anywhere along the river on BLM land. Camping permits are required if camping within the Uintah and Ouray Indian Reservation between mile 88 and 26. For more information, contact the BLM. Minimum impact camping techniques are required and all solid waste must be packed out. Bagless river-runner's toilets are mandatory.

Season: The season runs from May through September.

Permits: Advanced reservations, permits and fees are necessary for all private and commercial river trips.

USGS topographic maps: Nutters Hole Southwest, Firewater Canyon Northwest, Flat Canyon Northeast, Butter Canyon, Gunnison Butte Southeast

BLM surface maps: Vernal, Seep Ridge, Price, Huntington, Westwater

Resources:
• *Western Whitewater, From the Rockies to the Pacific,* by Jim Cassady, Bill Cross and Fryar Calhoun, published by North Fork Press, Berkeley, CA; (415) 424-1213.

• The Canyonlands Natural History Association publishes a catalog and sells topographic maps as well as river guides and other information useful to visitors in this region. Call (801) 259-6003.

For more information: Contact the BLM Price River Resource Area, 900 North Seventh East, Price, UT 84501; (801) 637-4584.

CRYSTAL BALL AND GANDY MOUNTAIN CAVES

See letter I on map page 482

spelunking

Approximately 60 miles north of the Great Basin National Park along the Utah/Nevada border, the Gandy Mountains rise above the valley floor dramatically. This mountain range contains two caves, Crystal Ball and Gandy Mountain, both of which are attractive to spelunkers interested in exploring limestone solution caverns. Crystal Ball is noteworthy as it is one of the few caves in the world with unique deposits of dogtooth spar, Icelandic spar, helictites and other speleothems. Pleistocene mammal bones also have been excavated from within. Gandy Cave is smaller, but was once suggested as a national monument site. Unfortunately, the caves exist under a mining claim. The owner has been protecting the site, but could exercise claim rights and mine the area at any time, irreparably destroying the cave environment. BLM is working to ensure that it doesn't happen. If you wish to visit the caves, you must first check with the BLM office in Fillmore to obtain safety information and access directions.

For more information: Contact the BLM House Range Resource Area, P.O. Box 778, Fillmore, UT 84631; (801) 743-6811.

SWASEY MOUNTAIN

See letter J on map page 482

camping, fossils, hiking, horseback riding, rockhounding, spelunking

Swasey Mountain is a part of the House Range which consists of high distinct peaks, narrow twisting canyons and palisade cliffs to the west, descending into low washes and indistinct flat desert terrain to the east. There are wild horses, small caves and trilobite rockhounding areas within the range. A three-mile gravel road winds across a plateau to the Sinbad Overlook for a spectacular view of the Tule Valley. You can reach this area via local and county roads leading northwest from Highway 50/6, just south of Hinckley.

USGS topographic maps: Sand Pass, Swasey Peak Southeast, Swasey Peak Northwest, Swasey Peak Southwest, Swasey Peak, Whirlwind Valley Northwest, Whirlwind Valley Southwest, Marjum Pass

BLM surface maps: Tule Valley, Fish Springs

For more information: Contact the BLM House Range Resource Area, P.O. Box 778, Fillmore, UT 84631; (801) 743-6811.

LITTLE SAHARA RECREATION AREA

See letter K on map page 482

camping, hiking, off-highway-vehicle use, picnicking, wildlife observation

Little Sahara Recreation Area is located 120 miles south of Salt Lake City just off US 6. The area offers 60,000 acres of moving sand dunes, sagebrush flats and juniper hills. The varied terrain provides a haven not only for off-highway-vehicle enthusiasts, but also for those seeking natural wonders, camping and picnicking, and especially children who delight at the thought of hours of play in an oversized sandbox.

White Sands continues to be one of the most favored off-highway-vehicle spots, and it also offers a fenced-in area for the protection of those seeking non-motorized enjoyment. In addition to the challenges afforded the off-highway driver, Little Sahara presents an endless array of other recreational opportunities. Day hikes through the Rockwell Natural Area provide a glimpse of desert wildlife and plants unique to the region. The dunes themselves are a sunbather's paradise (just be sure to wear at least 30spf sunscreen and a hat), and for those who fancy themselves at a vast inland beach, sand castle building is in order. Photographers have been known to drive for hours to capture the interesting shadows and sand dune patterns.

Location: Approximately 27 miles west of Nephi and 35 miles north of Delta. From Santaquin on Interstate 15, drive southwest 38 miles, then turn right onto a paved county road (signed for the dunes) and drive another 4.5 miles. From Nephi, drive west on State Road 132 for 13 miles; then turn right onto a paved county road until it meets US 6. Continue driving west for another 4.5 miles.

Camping: Oasis Campground features four paved loops with 114 camping units and an adjacent trailer dump station. White Sands Campground features three graveled loops with 99 camping units. Both offer drinking water, restrooms, picnic tables and charcoal grills. Parking loops near Sand Mountain, with its 500-foot near-vertical face, offer camping opportunities for those who prefer undeveloped areas. Miles of desert solitude are also available throughout Little Sahara for campers who seek to get away from it all. Fires are allowed only in the grills or fire pits within the designated campgrounds.

Season: The area is open year-round, but the spring and fall have the most comfortable temperatures.

Permits: A day-use fee of $5 per vehicle is charged. Annual passes are available for $35.

Maps: BLM Recreation and Vehicle Guide to the House Range Resource Area

BLM surface map: Lynndyl

Resources:
• Free area brochures are available at the visitor center.

For more information: Contact the BLM House Range Resource Area, P.O. Box 778, Fillmore, UT 84631; (801) 743-6811.

UTAH—MAP B

Visitors to southeastern Utah can now get information about the region's parks, forests and recreation areas from the relatively new Monticello Interagency Information Center. The information center is the result of a partnership arrangement that includes San Juan County, the San Juan County Economic Development Board, the BLM, the U.S. Forest Service, the National Park Service and the Canyonlands Natural History Association. The facility is located in the San Juan County Courthouse. Winter hours, from October to April 15 are 9 a.m. to 5 p.m., Monday through Friday. From April 15 to September, the center is open seven days a week from 9 a.m. to 6 p.m. Call (801) 587-3235 for information.

CLEVELAND-LLOYD DINOSAUR QUARRY

See letter L on map page 484

dinosaur bones, hiking

Cleveland-Lloyd is a National Natural Landmark and one of the most productive dinosaur bone quarries in the world. Since 1931, scientists have removed more than 14,000 fossil bones, representing over 70 dinosaurs of 14 different species. The BLM operates a visitor center near the quarry, which features an assembled allosaurus skeleton and on-site interpretation by a naturalist. Other facilities at the quarry include the Rock Walk Nature Trail, a picnic area and drinking water. The quarry is usually open on weekends from Easter through Memorial Day, and seven days a week from Memorial Day through Labor Day. It is closed for the remainder of the year. To get there from Price, drive south on Highway 10 and follow the dinosaur signs to the quarry. Since the hours are somewhat variable, the BLM suggests calling ahead before beginning your drive to confirm that the quarry will be open when you arrive.

For more information: Contact the BLM Price River Resource Area, 900 North Seventh East, Price, UT 84501; (801) 637-4584.

SAN RAPHAEL SWELL RECREATION AREA

See letter M on map page 484

hiking, backpacking, mountain biking, camping, wildlife observation

The San Rafael Swell rises above the desert, west of the Green River, as a complex area of canyons, colorful rock formations and mesas. The recreation area includes approximately 876,000 acres of public land. The San Rafael Campground has been reconstructed and upgraded from primitive to a site with water and pit toilets, and, guess what? That means fees! Beginning in 1995, a fee will be collected, most likely $4 per campsite per night. The campground is located along the San Rafael River. The fall months are the best for visiting, as temperatures are cool and the gnats (voracious little buggers) have all but departed. There is a BLM brochure, "Recreation Guide to the San Rafael Swell," available. The region is located south of the town of Price and west of the Green River. The Wedge Overlook is worth visiting and is alongside the river.

USGS topographic maps: Hadden Holes, Horn Silver Gulch, Sids Mountain, Bottleneck Peak, Devils Hole, Drowned Hole Draw, Mexican Mountain, Spotted Wolf Canyon, Jessie's Twist

BLM surface maps: Huntington, San Rafael Desert

Resources:
• The Canyonlands Natural History Association publishes a catalog and sells topographic maps, guidebooks and other useful information. Call (801) 259-6003.

For more information: Contact the BLM Price River Resource Area, 900 North Seventh East, Price, UT 84501; (801) 637-4584.

LABYRINTH CANYON

See letter N on map page 484

camping, canoeing, hiking

Located along the Green River between the town of Green River and Canyonlands National Park, the Labyrinth Canyon Recreation Management Area encompasses 49,000 acres along the river for approximately 70 miles. Labyrinth Canyon is best suited to lazy floating through deep, multicolored canyons and enjoying hikes to Native American petroglyphs, historic inscriptions and natural features.

Activity Highlights: Canoeing and floating

It is 68 river miles from the launch point at Green River State Park in Green River City to the take-out at Mineral Bottom, and 123 miles to Spanish Bottom just below the confluence of the Green and Colorado rivers. There are no rapids along this section of the Green River, making it excellent for multi-day canoe trips. Visitors using rafts should plan in plenty of time to float as the river flows at a leisurely pace, especially during the summer and fall. Sandbars can, at times, present problems for rafts. Ruby Ranch, 20 miles below Green River State Park is an alternate access point. A fee is charged for parking and launching. Mineral Bottom is the last take-out point accessible by road before the rapids of Cataract Canyon. If you choose to continue your float and take-out at the confluence of the Green and Colorado rivers or just below at Spanish Bottom, you will need to make arrangements to have you and your boats taken back upriver by a jet boat. There is no road access to Spanish Bottom. Jet boat service is offered by two companies at this time: Tag-A-Long Expeditions, (801) 259-8946, or Tex's Riverways, (801) 259-5101. Both companies are based in Moab.

Activity Highlights: Hiking and backpacking

The hike to the top of the neck at Bowknot Bend offers expansive views of the river and its canyon setting.

Location: Just south of the city of Green River. Boaters can launch from either Green River State Park or from a private launching area downstream at Ruby Ranch. Mineral Bottom is the take-out point for some, and also a put-in point for trips running down to the confluence of the Green and Colorado rivers (Spanish Bottom) at Cataract Canyon. There are two outfitters that rent canoes and provide a jet boat pick-up service back to Moab from just below the confluence of the Colorado and Green rivers. These outfitters are Tag-A-Long Expeditions, (801) 259-8946 and Tex's Riverways, (801) 259-5101.

Camping: Camping is allowed anywhere in the canyon. Practice minimum-impact river camping.

Season: The season runs from April through September.

Permits: You must obtain a permit from the National Park Service to enter Stillwater Canyon. The BLM now requires registration at its launch areas and anticipates initiating a permit system for river use within Labyrinth Canyon within the year—call for current river status.

USGS topographic maps: Green River, Daly East, Horsebench, Green River Southeast, 10 Mile Point, Bowknot Bend, Mineral Canyon

BLM surface maps: San Raphael Desert, Moab

Resources:

• *Western Whitewater, From the Rockies to the Pacific,* by Jim Cassady, Bill Cross and Fryar Calhoun, published by North Fork Press, Berkeley, CA; (415) 424-1213.

• The Canyonlands Natural History Association publishes a catalog and sells topographic maps as well as river guides such as the *Canyonlands River Guide* and other useful information. Call (801) 259-6003.

For more information: Contact the BLM San Rafael Resource Area, 900 North Seventh East, Price, UT 84501; (801) 637-4584.

WESTWATER CANYON
WILDERNESS STUDY AREA
See letter O on map page 484

camping, hiking, mountain biking (outside the Wilderness Study Area), whitewater rafting, wildlife observation

Westwater Canyon, located within the Westwater Canyon Wilderness Study Area, is considered by many to be one of the nation's best overnight whitewater river trips. The combination of major rapids and a spectacular 17-mile-long canyon setting draws boaters from all over, but you must be experienced or go with a skilled outfitter. The river is nothing to be trifled with; it has killed seven people since 1982. A small seasonal waterfall is located on the Little Dolores River about 200 yards upstream from its confluence with the Colorado River. Several small arches are located near the Little Dolores River and one large arch is located just below Star Canyon along the skyline. You will see an old miner's cabin, the "outlaw cave" and some Native American sites within the canyon. These are protected by law, but more importantly, they should be respected as remnants of our cultural heritage—leave all you find for others to appreciate.

Activity Highlight: Whitewater rafting

The float time for this river is one or two days. This is a serious whitewater trip with 11 rapids rated up to Class IV, depending on the water level. For a list of authorized (permitted) operators running the Westwater, call the BLM at (801) 259-8193.

Activity Highlight: Mountain biking

A section of the Kokopelli's Trail runs just north of the West-water Canyon area (see the listing on page 501 in this chapter). Mountain biking is restricted to the plateau overlooking Westwater Canyon and areas outside the Wilderness Study Area.

Location: Northeast of Moab, the first canyon along the Colorado River within Utah. From Interstate 70 north of Moab and east of Green River, take the Westwater exit (exit 225).

Camping: Campsites are assigned at the ranger station at launch time. There are only 10 sites. Minimum-impact camping techniques are required and all solid waste must be packed out. Bagless river-runner's toilets are mandatory.

Season: The best time to visit is from April into October.

Permits: Permits are required and fees are charged for river use. No permits are necessary for hiking or primitive camping.

USGS topographic maps: Agate, Westwater, Cisco, Big Triangle, Marble Canyon

BLM surface map: Westwater

Resources:

• *Western Whitewater, From the Rockies to the Pacific,* by Jim Cassady, Bill Cross and Fryar Calhoun, published by North Fork Press, Berkeley, CA; (415) 424-1213.

• The Canyonlands Natural History Association publishes a catalog and sells topographic maps as well as river guides such as the *Canyonlands River Guide* and other useful information. Call (801) 259-6003.

For more information: Contact the BLM Grand Resource Area, P.O. Box 970, Moab, UT 84532; (801) 259-8193.

MOAB SLICKROCK BIKE TRAIL / NATIONAL RECREATION TRAIL

See letter P on map page 484

hiking, mountain biking

This 10-mile-long mountain bike and motorcycle loop trail follows a roller coaster route through a maze of sandstone domes and fins to overlooks of the Colorado River and Arches National Park. Additional connecting and spur trails are available for more skilled riders—test your metal on this loop before branching out on the connecting alternatives. Trailhead facilities include a parking area, restrooms and an information board. The fall is one of the best times to ride due to cooler temperatures and the absence of gnats. Expect the trail to be covered with snow during January and February. To reach the trailhead, drive 2.3 miles east on Sand Flats Road from its intersection with Mill Creek Drive in Moab. It is important to note that desert soils are delicate—stick to the route; do not create your own path. You will encounter pockets of sand, little gardens of cactus, juniper, grass and cryptogamic soil, which will be destroyed if you ride through them. Ride around! At Shrimp Rock, you may find a pool of water full of little creatures. Do not ride through or bathe in the pool or other potholes along the trail as you will destroy a delicate balance of life. This is one of the most popular destinations in the West for mountain bikers. You can expect mammoth crowds during the spring and fall. The BLM recommends utilizing the Moab Area Bike Trail Brochure for finding alternative, less traveled routes.

USGS topographic map: Moab

BLM surface map: Moab

For more information: Contact the BLM Grand Resource Area, P.O. Box 970, Moab, UT 84532; (801) 259-8193.

Kokopelli's Trail

See letter Q on map page 484

backpacking, camping, hiking, mountain biking, wildlife observation

Kokopelli's Trail connects Moab with Loma, Colorado. This rugged 140-mile mountain bike trail follows seldom-visited back roads and some newer single-track trail. The route traverses spectacular forest, canyon and desert country. You can ride the trail in day-long segments or as a multi-day adventure. Most of the trail can be accessed or ridden by high-clearance, four-wheel-drive support vehicles. There are a series of mini-camps along the route, constructed in 1990. The trailheads are located at the Moab Slickrock Bike Trail (see the previous listing) and the Loma Boat Ramp, just west of Fruita, Colorado. The higher elevations of this trail are impassable during the winter. (Also see the listing for Kokopelli's Trail in the Colorado chapter on page 211.)

For more information: Contact the BLM Grand Resource Area, P.O. Box 970, Moab, UT 84532; (801) 259-8193.

WAH WAH MOUNTAINS

See letter R on map page 484

backpacking, cross-country skiing, hiking, horseback riding, wildlife observation

Located 20 miles from the Utah/Nevada border, approximately 35 miles west of Beaver, Utah, the Wah Wah Mountain Range is one of the most remote and untouched areas in Utah's western desert region. The sense of vastness within the range is amplified by the broad valleys and often snow-capped peaks. Crystal Peak, visible from distances of 50 miles or more, is the most prominent peak of the range and draws picnickers from local areas. One unique feature of the range is a rare stand of bristlecone pine. Of additional note is the fact that this range is a critical year-round habitat for the golden eagle.

To get there from Interstate 15 at Beaver, drive 24 miles west on Route 21. Where the route passes through the San Francisco Mountains, at milepost 54, turn left on a gravel road. Drive approximately 2.5 miles and bear right, continuing southwest for approximately 13 miles to the interior of the Wah Wahs. Leave your car at the high point. There are no trails. Hiking is cross-country, so you must have strong navigational skills.

USGS topographic maps: Crystal Peak, Middle Mountain, Pine Valley Hardpan, Pine Valley Hardpan North, Grassy Cove, Wah Wah Cove, Wah Wah Summit

BLM surface map: Wah Wah Mountains North

Resources:
• *The Hiker's Guide to Utah*, by Dave Hall; published by Falcon Press, P.O. Box 1718, Helena, MT 59624; (800) 582-2665.

For more information: Contact the BLM Richfield District Office, 150 East 900 North, Richfield, UT 84701; (801) 896-8221.

HENRY MOUNTAINS

See letter S on map page 484

backpacking, camping, hiking, horseback riding, mountain biking, rock climbing, rockhounding, wildlife observation

The Henry Mountains, called the Unknown Mountains by the Powell Expedition, were the last range to be explored and named in the Lower 48 states. They have remained largely undeveloped and remote. In addition to historic gold-mining sites, the mountains are also home to some bison. The bison were transplanted into the Burr Desert below the mountains in 1941. Since then they have established themselves on the Henry Mountains and have become a popular attraction for both viewing and hunting.

This resource area contains spectacular geological structures and associated erosional features in the heart of the Colorado Plateau. Colorful canyons abound. Until the damming of Glen Canyon, the region was only accessible by a dirt road. Even today, there are few paved roads and services are very limited. Small towns provide the basic tourist facilities.

Activity Highlights: Hiking and backpacking

There are very few trails within the mountain range. Much of your travel will be cross-country. Good map and compass skills are requisite. Water is available, but it is suggested that you always carry ample supplies with you just in case.

Location: Just north of Glen Canyon National Recreation Area. Access to the Henry Mountains is off routes 276 and 24. The best starting point is in the town of Hanksville, where you can check in at the BLM office and inquire about current road conditions and the best access points for the area you wish to roam.

Camping: Three campgrounds are maintained in and around the Henry Mountains. McMillan Spring Campground, located on the west side of the Henry Mountains, is 8,400 feet and set in a Ponderosa pine forest. Excellent views of the Waterpocket Fold and high plateaus can be enjoyed from here. No camping fee is charged and this campground is open from May to November. The Starr Spring Campground is located on Mount Hillers, at 6,300 feet, and set in an oak grove. Views of the area surrounding Mount Hillers are spectacular. This campground is open from April through October. There is a camping fee charged. The third campground is Lonesome Beaver Campground, located in the Sawmill Basin at 8,000 feet. Open from May through October, this site is tucked in among spruce, fir and aspen. A hiking trail leads from the camp to nearby Mount Ellen, which reaches 11,506 feet. No camping fee is charged. Primitive camping is allowed anywhere within the Henry Mountains region.

Season: The best time to visit the upper elevations runs from April through October. Visitation is year-round in the lower reaches.

Permits: No permits are necessary.

Maps: The Henry Mountains and Surrounding Deserts General Recreation Map, available from the BLM in Hanksville.

Resources:

• *Back Country Byways*, by Stewart M. Green, published by Falcon Press, P.O. Box 1718, Helena, MT 59624; (800) 582-2665.

For more information: Contact the BLM Henry Mountains Resource Area, P.O. Box 99, Hanksville, UT 84734; (801) 542-3461.

CANYON RIMS RECREATION AREA

See letter T on map page 484

backpacking, camping, hiking, horseback riding, mountain biking, rock climbing, wildlife observation

The Canyon Rims region sprawls out along the eastern and southern boundaries of Canyonlands National Park and is located in both the Grand and San Juan BLM resource areas. Two developed viewpoints are accessible by vehicles: The Needles and Anticline overlooks offer excellent examples of the spectacular vistas that have made Canyon Country famous. The many canyons, mesas and pinnacles within the area offer outstanding settings for hiking, outdoor photography and rock climbing. Windwhistle and Hatch Point are two developed campsites within this region. A camping fee is charged for both. Water is available from mid-April through October. To get there from Monticello, drive north on Highway 191 for 17 miles to the Canyon Rims Recreation Area entrance road (Hatch Point area); from there, drive west on the paved BLM road. The southern region of this area is accessible from Utah Scenic Byway 211.

USGS topographic maps: Shafer Basin, Trough Springs Canyon, Kane Springs, Lockhart Basin, Eightmile Rock, LaSal Junction, North Six Shooter Peak, Harts Point North, Hatch Rock

BLM surface map: LaSal

Resources:

• The Canyonlands Natural History Association publishes a catalog and sells topographic maps, guidebooks and other useful information. Call (801) 259-6003.

For more information: Contact the BLM Grand Resource Area, P.O. Box 970, Moab, UT 84532; (801) 259-8193; or the BLM San Juan

Resource Area, 435 North Main, P.O. Box 7, Monticello, UT 84535; (801) 587-2141.

CALF CREEK RECREATION AREA

See letter U on map page 484

backpacking, camping, hiking, wildlife observation

This recreation area is located 15 miles east of Escalante on Scenic Byway 12. There are 14 camping units, with water; they are available on a first-come, first-served self-registration basis. A fee is charged. A free trail guide to the Lower Calf Creek Falls Nature Trail is available at the campground. If the BLM campground is full, seek out the Boulder Mountain Forest Service campground on Scenic Byway 12 or the Escalante State Park Campground two miles south of Escalante.

BLM surface maps: Smokey Mountain, Escalante

For more information: Contact the BLM Escalante Resource Area, P.O. Box 769, Escalante, UT 84726; (801) 826-4291.

ESCALANTE RESOURCE AREA

See letter V on map page 484

backpacking, camping, hiking, mountain biking, rock climbing

The Escalante, an outstanding example of Utah's slickrock and riparian canyon environments, consists of an unbelievably intricate network of canyons, plateaus, cliffs, sandstone arches, natural bridges, domes, water pockets, meandering streams, and more. The area is so difficult to navigate that it has proved a formidable barrier to vehicle traffic since the days of the horse and buggy. In fact, the Escalante River was not even bridged until 1935, crediting Boulder City as one of the last communities to gain automobile access. Over 60 mammals, 150 birds and 20 reptiles call the Escalante home. Some of the more common animals are mountain lion, mule deer, gray fox, coyote, deer mice, Ord's kangaroo rat, scrub jay, canyon wren and numerous hawks.

Activity Highlights: Hiking and backpacking

The Escalante Canyons continue to retain their reputation as one of the premier backpacking regions in the Southwest. Expect this area to be crowded throughout the spring, summer and fall. If you want to avoid the crowds, there are many routes you could take. The westside tributary canyons are accessible from trailheads on the Hole-In-The-

Rock Scenic Byway. The eastern canyons are accessible from trail-heads on the Burr Trail Road and Circle Cliffs. The main stem of the Escalante River Canyon is entered at the Highway 12 bridge or in Escalante. Death Hollow, another canyon, is accessible from the Hells Backbone Road.

Rain and water runoff can occur any time during the spring. It is vital that you contact the Escalante Resource Area office for current trail and road conditions. Fall is an excellent time to backpack in the Escalante River backcountry. Evenings are cool, water levels are low, and insects are less bothersome.

Calf Creek to Harris Wash is one of many hiking/backpacking trails available in this area. It is a moderately strenuous 26.4-mile one-way trip, offering an excellent three- to four-day backpacking opportunity. There is a ruin of a homestead settled in 1890 along the way, adding a historical flavor. The hiking season runs from late March through June and from early September through October. The route description is quite detailed and can be tricky in places. *Hiking the Escalante,* by Rudi Lambrechtse, provides a detailed six-page explanation of the route.

The parking area for this trail is approximately 15 miles east of Escalante on Highway 12, where the highway crosses the river. Park next to the BLM sign. The trail begins on the south side at the trail register. There is a designated river-access point on the north side—cross only at this point as both sides of the river are private property. After two river crossings, you will enter BLM property on the south side, surrounded by a fence. The maps needed for this trail include the BLM Escalante Resource Area Recreation Map and the USGS topographic maps for Calf Creek, King Bench and Red Breaks.

Activity Highlight: Mountain biking

The Wolverine Loop Route is one of many possible mountain-biking routes, and is approximately 34.2 miles. A two-day trip is recommended for easy cycling. The mountain-biking season runs from late fall to early spring. Mountain bikes are not allowed in any of the natural areas—please respect signs indicating closures. Abuse and misuse of closed trails has been a problem, and if it continues, more trails may be closed to mountain bikes. There is no guaranteed water along the route and mountain bikers are reminded to carry adequate supplies.

From the parking area, pedal 10.4 miles to Wolverine Petrified Wood Natural Area. Approximately 2.8 miles past this area, bear left where the route forks. After eight miles, the trail runs into Burr Road. Head left and pedal eight miles through White Canyon Flat. Remain on Burr Road through all intersections, keeping to the left. Once you are through White Canyon Flat, head east on Burr Trail Road for five more miles to get back the parking area. To get to the parking area from Boulder, take Burr Trail Road 19 miles to the Wolverine turnoff. Park at the designated area.

Helpful maps for this route include the BLM Escalante Resource Area Recreation Map and the USGS topographic maps for King Bench, Steep Creek Bench, Wagon Box Mesa and Moody Creek.

Location: North of the Arizona border, east of Bryce Canyon and west of Glen Canyon National Recreation Area. From Cedar City on Interstate 15, take Highway 14/148 east to Highway 89. Drive north on Highway 89 to Highway 12 and Bryce Canyon National Park. Stay on Highway 12 to Escalante.

Camping: Camping is allowed anywhere within the Escalante Resource Area. Fires are allowed, but using a fire is questionable because of its environmental impact.

Permits: Hiking in the Escalante Natural Area requires a permit. Permits can be obtained for free from the BLM office. Hiking in areas outside the Escalante Natural Area does not require a permit, but registration at the trailhead is requested for safety reasons.

Maps: Utah Map Series: Canyons of the Escalante, published by Trails Illustrated, P.O. Box 3610, Evergreen, CO 80439; (800) 962-1643.

Resources:
• *Hiking the Escalante*, by Rudi Lambrechtse, published by Wasatch Publishers, Salt Lake City, UT.
• *Hiking the Southwest's Canyon Country*, by Sandra Hinchman, published by The Mountaineers, Seattle, WA.

For more information: Contact the BLM Escalante Resource Area, P.O. Box 225, Escalante, UT 84726; (801) 826-4291.

DARK CANYON PRIMITIVE AREA
See letter W on map page 484

backpacking, camping, hiking, mountain biking (outside of the primitive area), wildlife observation

Dark Canyon runs from the Manti-La Sal National Forest down

to the desert environment along Lake Powell. This remote canyon system features outstanding backpacking opportunities. Mountain biking is good along four-wheel-drive roads outside the designated wilderness area managed by the U.S. Forest Service and the Dark Canyon Primitive Area administered by the BLM. Deep canyons, open valleys and sloping plateaus fill the menu here. Dark Canyon dazzles visitors with its 1,400-foot-high stair-stepped walls. Many canyons within this region feature this unique sandstone/limestone combination, which creates numerous benches from which rainwater runs off in spectacular waterfalls, forming picturesque "water curtains" and refreshing pools. From upper plateaus, excellent views of the nearby Henry Mountains and the Colorado River may be enjoyed. Wildlife includes black bear, bobcat, mountain lion, coyote, beaver, fox, mule deer and bighorn sheep.

Activity Highlights: Hiking and backpacking

Water is scarce in some areas, most notably Dark Canyon itself. You must be prepared to carry at least one gallon of water per person per day at all times. Many of the routes you will follow have no trail—just stay along the canyon floors. You must also be wary of flash floods at all times.

Location: Twenty-five miles west of Blanding and south of Canyonlands National Park. North of Highway 95, travel toward Natural Bridges National Monument. After about a mile on Natural Bridges Road, turn right and follow the graded road up Little Maverick Point and then over Bears Ears Pass. Approximately two miles north of Bears Ears, you will turn left at a junction. Two miles from the junction is a corral at the turnoff to Twin Springs and the head of Peavine Canyon. Park here.

Camping: Camping is allowed anywhere within the canyon area. Always camp above the high-water mark as flash flooding is a constant possibility.

Season: The best times to visit this area are from late spring to early summer and in the fall.

USGS topographic maps: Poison Canyon, Warren Canyon, Black Steer Canyon, Bowdie Canyon, Fable Valley

Additional maps: National Forests in Utah Map Series: *Trails of Manti-La Sal National Forest featuring Dark Canyon*, published by Trails Illustrated, P.O. Box 3610, Evergreen, CO 80439; (800) 962-1643.

Resources:
• The Canyonlands Natural History Association is currently in production creating a new Dark Canyon Trail Guide for the BLM and the USFS which is anticipated to be released in the summer of 1995. Call (801) 259-6003.
• *The Hiker's Guide to Utah,* by Dave Hall, published by Falcon Press, P.O. Box 1718, Helena, MT 59624; (800) 582-2665.

For more information: Contact the BLM San Juan Resource Area, 435 North Main, P.O. Box 7, Monticello, UT 84535; (801) 587-2141.

THREE KIVA PUEBLO

See letter X on map page 484

archaeological site
This ancient Native American ruin was once the scene of a small Anasazi settlement. The ruins have been stabilized by the BLM and are open for visits. The ruins are located in Montezuma Creek Canyon, east of Blanding, Utah. To get specific directions and a tour map, contact the BLM office. Visit any time of year.

For more information: Contact the BLM San Juan Resource Area, 435 North Main, P.O. Box 7, Monticello, UT 84535; (801) 587-2141.

DEEP CREEK WILDERNESS STUDY AREA

See letter Y on map page 484

camping, cross-country skiing, fishing, hiking, snowmobiling, wildlife observation
This area is only 9,000 acres, but it's packed! Deep Creek, Crystal Creek, Box Canyon, Volcano Knoll, Indian Trail, Kolob Creek and Giant Oak Tree sites offer ample opportunity for stream-based and primitive recreation activities. The difficulty will be finding a legal point of access since private lands block much of the area. At present, the only public access that remains consistently open is via the Box Canyon area. It is essential that you contact the BLM Dixie Resource Area Office before attempting to head out in order to avoid disturbing private landowners and creating problems that might affect gaining access rights in the future. The BLM reports that at times access has been denied from private lands to Deep Creek, Crystal Creek, Volcano Knoll, Indian Trail, Kolob Creek and Giant Oak Tree. It is also

important to remember that even if the private landowners grant access rights, Mother Nature may make the roads impassable with occasional summer thunderstorms.

USGS topographic maps: Kolob Reservoir, Cogswell Point, The Guardian Angels, Temple of Sinawava

BLM surface map: Kanab

For more information: Contact the BLM Dixie Resource Area, 225 North Bluff Street, St. George, UT 84770; (801) 673-4654.

GRAND GULCH PRIMITIVE AREA
See letter Z on map page 484

backpacking, camping, hiking, historic site, wildlife observation

It is within this twisting canyon maze that some of the most bewitching scenery and the largest concentrations of Anasazi ruins in all of southeastern Utah reside. Beginning at an elevation of 6,400 feet, Grand Gulch cuts a serpentine swath through Cedar Mesa, running southwest to the San Juan River, dropping a tortuous 2,700 feet in just 53 miles. Sheer cliffs, sharp pinnacles, Anasazi cliff dwellings, rock-art sites, natural bridges, and sandstone amphitheaters make up Grand Gulch and its many surrounding tributaries. Keep your eyes peeled for signs of mountain lion, black bear, bobcat, fox, mule deer, coyote, ringtail cat and skunk. Raptors frequently carve and slice their way through the blue sky above. Pinyon pine, juniper, cottonwood, willow, sagebrush and prickly pear cactus are the predominant species of vegetation.

The Anasazi have left a legacy that includes hundreds of cliff dwellings and thousands of pictographs and petroglyphs, and historical evidence has shown that their influence on the canyon dates back as far as 200 A.D. Take special care not to touch or climb on the ruins, as this kind of wear and tear can cause what the BLM refers to as "innocent vandalism." Souvenir hunting is also a major problem within the entire region. Please leave what you find in its place and report any suspicious activity to the BLM. Vandalism ruins the experience for everyone.

Activity Highlights: Hiking and backpacking

If you want to hike from Collins Spring to Kane Gulch Ranger Station, plan on five days to navigate the route. You will cover approximately 38 very arduous miles through the best this area has to offer. This particular section of the Grand Gulch Primitive Area offers the hiker a chance to not only cover more ground, but also to view more ruins and experience more solitude than anywhere else in the region. Careful navigation is required in some parts to prevent becoming confused and heading off-route down a side canyon. Expect tedious bushwhacking between mile 16 and 20 of the hike. Take a break at Step Canyon, around mile 18.5, where Anasazi sites abound. Spend enough time to locate Two Story Ruin, concealed by thick overgrowth to the right of the canyon. Springs provide the primary water source throughout the canyon, but they aren't always reliable. Check at the ranger station for current water conditions and always carry at least one gallon per person with you.

Location: Approximately 10 miles north of Mexican Hat and 25 miles west of Blanding in southeastern Utah. Travel south of Blanding on Highway 191 and turn west onto Highway 95. At the intersection with Highway 261, turn south on Highway 261. Drive approximately four miles to the Kane Gulch Ranger Station. A car shuttle must be taken between the Collins Spring trailhead and the Kane Gulch Ranger Station—it's 29 miles, including nine on dirt. Shuttle services are sometimes available. Inquire at the Monticello Interagency Information Center.

Camping: Primitive camping is allowed anywhere along the trail for those who are hiking. Stock use is allowed overnight only in Kane Gulch, Collins Canyon, Government Trail, Grand Gulch from Kane Gulch to Collins Canyon, Fish Creek Canyon from Comb Wash to the confluence with Owl Canyon, Mule Canyon south of Highway 95, Road Canyon, Johns Canyon, Lime Creek Canyon and Arch Canyon.

Season: Spring and autumn are the ideal times to travel in this region. Summer months are possible, but you will want to avoid the midday heat. Winter brings snow and ice, which can make travel on slick-rock sections extremely hazardous.

Permits: Permits are required for all travel within the Grand Gulch Primitive Area. Permits are $5; the money goes to enhance on-the-ground management of the region. Groups over 12 people are prohibited. All organized groups of eight or more and parties using stock animals are required to obtain a permit from the BLM Monticello office at least three weeks prior to their proposed use. No more than 10 pack animals per group are allowed. No pets are allowed. There is a ban on the use of rock climbing equipment to access archeological sites.

USGS topographic maps: Bears Ears, Cedar Mesa, Grand Gulch

Additional maps:

• The Canyonlands Natural History Association publishes a catalog and sells topographic maps as well as a new edition of the Grand Gulch brochure/topographic map produced by the BLM, and other useful information. Call (801) 259-6003.

• Utah Map Series: *Grand Gulch Plateau*, published by Trails Illustrated, P.O. Box 3610, Evergreen, CO 80439; (800) 962-1643.

Resources:

• *Hiking the Southwest's Canyon Country*, by Sandra Hinchman, published by The Mountaineers, 1011 Southwest Klickitat Way, Suite 107, Seattle, WA 98134; (800) 553-4453.

• *Utah Handbook*, by Bill Weir, published by Moon Publications, 722 Wall Street, Chico, CA 95928; (916) 345-5473.

• *The Hiker's Guide to Utah*, by Dave Hall, published by Falcon Press, P.O. Box 1718, Helena, MT 59624; (800) 582-2665.

For more information: Contact the BLM San Juan Resource Area, 435 North Main, P.O. Box 7, Monticello, UT 84535; (801) 587-2141.

BEAVER DAM MOUNTAIN

See letter AA on map page 484

hiking, whitewater rafting, wildlife observation

Managed as a habitat for bighorn sheep and desert tortoise, the Beaver Dam region is in the southwestern corner of Utah, along Interstate 15 as it winds through the spectacular Virgin River Gorge. Extreme faulting, folding and natural erosion from the river has resulted in a complex mix of steep craggy cliffs and buttes made up of colorful layers of sandstone and fossil-laden limestone. You can blaze your own hiking trail here or raft the Virgin River's rushing whitewater. Visit any time of year.

BLM surface map: St. George

For more information: Contact the BLM Dixie Resource Area Office, 225 North Bluff Street, St. George, UT 84220; (801) 673-4654.

Red Cliffs Recreation Site

See letter BB on map page 484

camping, hiking, horseback riding, wildlife observation

Set among wind-hewn sandstone cliffs with three trails for day hikes, Red Cliffs Recreation Site is accessible via the campground of the same name. North of St. George on Interstate 15 (4.5 miles southwest of Leeds), Red Cliffs Campground offers overnight camping on a self-registered, first-come, first-served basis. It makes an ideal base for touring the area, because it is centrally located between the Kolob Canyons and Zion Canyon areas of Zion National Park, Snow Canyon State Park and Pine Valley Mountain. Also in the vicinity are Quail Lake Recreation Area, the Sand Mountain dune-riding area, Cottonwood Canyon Wilderness Study Area, the Dinosaur Tracks paleontological site and Old Fort Pearce.

USGS topographic map: Harrisburg Junction

BLM surface map: St. George

For more information: Contact the BLM Dixie Resource Area, 225 North Bluff Street, St. George, UT 84770; (801) 673-4654.

Canaan Mountain

See letter CC on map page 484

backpacking, camping, hiking, horseback riding, wildlife observation

Along US 50, the spectacular Canaan Mountain plateau is made up of three closely connected sandstone terraces. The 54,000-acre plateau is considered part of the Grand Staircase unit of the Colorado Plateau. The escarpment towers majestically 2,000 feet above the highway. The top of the plateau is a panorama of rippling slickrock, sandstone pinnacles, cones, balanced boulders, fractures and scours interspersed with lush pockets of aspen and ponderosa pine—some say the terrain compares favorably with that found in nearby Zion. Within the Canaan Mountain Wilderness Study Area, points of high beauty and outstanding geological scenery are Water Canyon, Eagle Crags, Squirrel Canyon, Canaan Mountain and Broad Hollow Trails.

Access to the Canaan Mountain interior is via the two miles of constructed Eagle Crags Trail (out of Rockville), or via Water Canyon—which is very steep and difficult to find in places—and Squirrel Canyon (Hildale-Colorado City). To reach the Squirrel Canyon

Trailhead, from the town of Hurricane, drive southeast on Highway 59 for approximately 24 miles to the town of Hildale. At the northeastern end of town, drive north along a dirt road for 1.5 miles to a small parking lot and the trailhead. If you wish to leave a vehicle on the other side of the mountains, take Highway 9 to Rockville; at the eastern end of town, head south on the paved road and cross the Virgin River at the Rockville Bridge. After a short distance, the road will swing right, but you continue straight on a dirt road one-and-a-half miles to the trailhead parking area. Pack as much water as you think you will need because finding water can be a problem on Canaan Mountain. Also note that although there are trails leading toward the plateau, there are no maintained trails on the plateau itself. Your navigation skills must be exemplary!

USGS topographic maps: Springdale West, Springdale East, Smithsonian Butte, Hildale

BLM surface maps: St. George, Kanab

For more information: Contact the BLM Dixie Resource Area, 225 North Bluff Street, St. George, UT 84770; (801) 673-4654.

PARIA CANYON-VERMILION CLIFFS WILDERNESS

See letter DD on map page 484

backpacking, camping, hiking, wildlife observation

The 120,000-acre Paria Canyon-Vermilion Cliffs Wilderness was officially designated by Congress in 1984. Since then, the four-day backpacking trip in the Paria River Canyon and Buckskin Gulch to Lees Ferry, Arizona, has become one of the most popular backpacking excursions in the Southwest. Trailhead access is through the Paria Ranger Station (Highway 89) at White House Trailhead. Buckskin Gulch access is from the Wire Pass or Buckskin Trailheads. Water conditions in the Paria River are ankle-deep with several waist-deep crossings to be expected. Commercial car shuttles are available. You can obtain free hiking permits at the Paria Ranger Station or by calling (801) 644-2672, no more than 24 hours in advance. Flash flood information is available at the Kanab Resource Office or from the National Weather Service at (801) 524-5133. The length of the hike in Paria Canyon is 34 miles. The Buckskin Gulch section is 11 miles.

You can obtain *The Hiker's Guide to Paria* by mail or at the BLM Kanab office for $1. Group size is limited to 15—but I would recommend far less to ensure minimizing impacts on the canyon (even eight is too many). Another major attraction is the ghost town and old movie set contained within the wilderness area. (For location and other information, see the Paria Canyon listing in the Arizona chapter on page 104.)

For more information: Contact the BLM Kanab Resource Area Office, 318 North First Street, Kanab, Utah 84741; (801) 644-2672.

PARIA RIVER-HACKBERRY CANYON
See letter EE on map page 484

backpacking, camping, hiking

This backpacking area is upstream from the Paria Canyon Wilderness. It is a very colorful and scenic canyon area that offers many hiking routes. Although use is on the increase, visitation remains far below that in the Paria Canyon region. A good book, *Hiking and Exploring the Paria River* by Michael Kelsey, is available through the BLM Kanab office. For hiking routes in and specific directions to the Paria River and Hackberry Canyon, it is recommended that you consult with the BLM Kanab office. The roads to the canyon can be impassable with rain.

For more information: Contact the BLM Kanab Resource Area Office, 318 North First Street, Kanab, Utah 84741; (801) 644-2672.

GREAT WESTERN TRAIL
See letter FF on map page 484

backpacking, camping, cross-country skiing, hiking, horseback riding, mountain biking, snowmobiling

The Great Western Trail is a partnership effort involving several public land management agencies, thousands of volunteers, community leaders and business partners, all with the goal of linking a trail that runs all the way from Canada to Mexico. Much of the route, when complete, will become a corridor of existing trails and passageways designed to serve the interests of many recreational users. Approximately 90 percent of the Utah portion of the Great Western Trail utilizes existing roads and trails. It enters the state in the north near Beaver Dam Mountain in the Wasatch-Cache National Forest, and continues south through the Uinta, Manti-La Sal, Fishlake and Dixie national forests. The trail crosses BLM-administered land before exiting into Arizona. The entire trail will be signed with the Great Western Trail symbol.

For information about how you can participate as a volunteer to help build or maintain the trail, contact: Great Western Trail Association, P.O. Box 1428, Provo, UT 84602.

For more information: Contact the BLM Kanab Resource Area Office, 318 North First Street, Kanab, Utah 84741; (801) 644-2672.

SAN JUAN RIVER

See letter GG on map page 484

camping, canoeing (experts only), kayaking, whitewater rafting, wildlife observation

The BLM manages the San Juan River from Montezuma Creek for 104 miles downstream to Clay Hills Crossing. The lower 39 miles flow through Glen Canyon National Recreation Area and are jointly managed with the National Park Service. The Upper San Juan, between Sand Island near Bluff and Mexican Hat, is well known for the superb Native American rock art left by the Anasazi culture. Visitors may also want to hike around to view the ruins of Anasazi dwellings and the remains of a historic trading post. The Lower San Juan, below Mexican Hat, cuts through Cedar Mesa and has carved the deepest set of entrenched "goosenecks" in North America. There is also an excellent opportunity to hike into the lower reaches of Grand Gulch to view rarely seen Anasazi ruins. You must preregister your hike before heading out on the river if you intend to wander more than three miles from the river. For a list of BLM-authorized (permitted) operators running the San Juan, call the BLM office at (801) 587-2141.

Activity Highlight: Whitewater rafting

The Upper San Juan from the Sand Island Recreation Site to Mexican Hat offers one- to three-day float opportunities on rapids up to Class III. The Lower San Juan from the BLM boat ramp at Mexican Hat to the take-out at Clay Hills Crossing offers three- to five-day float opportunities on rapids up to Class III.

Location: The Upper San Juan begins approximately three miles west of Bluff; the Lower San Juan is located to the west of Mexican Hat.

Sand Island is near Bluff on US 163.

Camping: Camping is allowed anywhere along the river providing you have a permit from the Navajo Nation—contact the BLM for information. Practice minimum-impact river camping. There is a campground at Sand Island.

Season: The boating season runs from March through October. Although the flows in the later part of the summer and into the fall are quite low, commercial outfits still run the river then.

Permits: Permits are required ; there is a fee for river trips.

USGS topographic maps: Horse Bench West, Horse Bench East, Spring Canyon, Moonshine Wash, Green River Southeast

BLM surface maps: Bluff, Navajo Mountain

Resources:
• *Western Whitewater, From the Rockies to the Pacific*, by Jim Cassady, Bill Cross and Fryar Calhoun, published by North Fork Press, Berkeley, CA; (415) 424-1213.
• The Canyonlands Natural History Association publishes a catalog and sells topographic maps as well as river guides such as the *Canyonlands River Guide* and other useful information. Call (801) 259-6003.

For more information: Contact the BLM San Juan Resource Area, 435 North Main, P.O. Box 7, Monticello, UT 84535; (801) 587-2141.

SAND ISLAND RECREATION SITE

See letter HH on map page 484

camping, whitewater rafting

Sand Island is a small, tree-shaded campground nestled below a sandstone bluff adjacent to the San Juan River. Of special interest to visitors is the large Native American rock-art panel just a short stroll from the campground. The site is popular as a launch area for raft trips in the San Juan River. A fee is charged for camping. No drinking water is available at this site. To get there from Bluff, drive three miles west on Highway 191 and turn left at the entrance sign. The best times to visit are spring, summer and fall.

For more information: Contact the BLM San Juan Resource Area, 435 North Main, P.O. Box 7, Monticello, UT 84535; (801) 587-2141.

Canyon Country Minimum-Impact Practices
*(published courtesy of the Canyon Country Partnership's
Science Committee and the BLM)*

Each year, millions of visitors enjoy Canyon Country. The impact of so much recreational use is threatening the area's biological and cultural resources. You can help protect this fragile and beautiful land by following these five minimum-impact practices.

- **Tread lightly when traveling and leave no trace of your camping.**

Drive and ride only on roads and trails where such travel is allowed; hike only on established trails, on rock or in washes. Camp at designated sites or, where allowed, at previously used sites. Avoid placing tents on top of vegetation and use a camp stove instead of making a campfire. Unless signs indicate otherwise, leave gates open or closed as you find them.

Why it matters: much of this area is a desert where plants are sparse and grow very slowly. Shallow soils erode quickly when vegetation is removed or protective cryptobiotic soil crusts are destroyed. These crusts are a complex of slowly growing cyanobacteria, algae, mosses and lichens that bind the soil together, retain scarce water, and provide a usable source of nitrogen for desert plants. Your tracks do matter. Once a plant or soil crust are damaged, they may not recover in your lifetime. Wood is a scarce resource that provides wildlife habitat and contributes to nutrient cycling. Gates help to protect fragile resources.

- **Help keep Canyon Country clean.**

Pack out your trash and recycle it, clean up after less thoughtful visitors, and dispose of human waste properly.

Why it matters: Trash, human waste, and toilet paper are significant problems that can quickly become health hazards and eyesores. Food scraps and garbage can turn wildlife into problem animals. No one wants to walk or camp where someone has left trash and human waste.

- **Protect and conserve scarce desert water resources.**

Camp at least 300 feet away from isolated water sources to allow for wildlife access. Where possible, carry your own drinking water. Leave potholes undisturbed and wash well away from pools or springs.

Why it matters: Many desert animals, especially birds, depend on the plants around isolated water sources for food and habitat. Camping near water sources damages plants and prevents wildlife from approaching. Small quantities of pollutants can make springs and ponds unusable for wildlife. Body lotions and vehicle lubricants can remain in the water and harm aquatic life, which in egg or larval form may be invisible to the naked eye.

- **Allow space for wildlife.**

When encountering wildlife, maintain your distance and remain quiet. Teach children not to chase or pick up animals. Keep pets under control.

Why it matters: Canyon Country has great wildlife-viewing opportunities, including the chance to see desert bighorn sheep, deer, elk, peregrine falcon, bald eagle, river otter and a variety of small creatures. Harassing or approaching wild animals will cause them to flee, possibly causing injury and definitely using up the vital energy reserves they need for mating, raising young, winter survival and other activities.

- **Leave historic sites, Native American rock art, ruins and artifacts untouched for the future.**

Admire rock art from a distance and never touch it. Stay out of ruins, leave artifacts in place, and report violations.

Why it matters: Canyon Country has an abundance of archaeological and historic sites, including rock art, historic inscriptions, old mines, cowboy camps, and Indian cliff dwellings. The people who created this legacy are gone. Now, the physical remains of their occupation are disappearing at an alarming rate. Small actions can add up to major damage. Rock art can be damaged just by touching it. The oil from fingertips speeds erosion by chemically altering ancient painted pigments and the rock itself. Sitting or climbing on rock walls turns ruins into rubble. Walking across middens, the ancient trash heaps below ruins, can damage sites. Moving or taking artifacts destroys their scientific value.

- **Special rules:** In some areas, visitors must follow special rules designed to protect natural and cultural resource values. Ask at agency offices and visitor centers if any special rules apply to the area you plan to visit.

BLM CAMPGROUNDS

Special camping note: Camping is no longer allowed along the Colorado Riverway unless you are in a developed campground or at specially designated undeveloped sites. Undeveloped sites are identified by posts with a tent symbol. To camp at an undeveloped site, you must provide your own toilet system. This system needs to be washable and reusable like the systems now required and in use on river trips. The Moab District has informed me they will be creating more fee sites along the river in the future to meet visitor's needs in this popular destination.

1. BIRCH CREEK CAMPGROUND—MAP A

Campsites, facilities: There are four tent sites, all with picnic tables, fire rings and grills. Pit toilets are available. There is **no water**. There is a 14-day stay limit.

Fee: There is no fee.

Who to contact: Bear River Resource Area, 2370 South 2300 West, Salt Lake City, UT 84119; (801) 977-4300.

Location: From Woodruff, drive nine miles west on Highway 39 to the campground access road. Turn and drive one mile to the campground entrance. The campground is set at 7,500 feet.

Season: All year. Expect crowds on weekends. This area is thick with mosquitoes in the early summer.

2. CLOVER SPRING CAMPGROUND—MAP A

Campsites, facilities: There are 12 sites, all with picnic tables and grills. There is **no water**. Vault toilets are wheelchair accessible. There is one group site. RVs up to 24 feet are allowed. There is a 14-day stay limit.

Fee: There is no fee.

Who to contact: Salt Lake District Office, 2370 South 2300 West, Salt Lake City, UT 84119; (801) 977-4300.

Location: The campground entrance is off Highway 199, approximately five miles west of Clover and 50 miles west of Salt Lake City.

3. BRIDGE HOLLOW CAMPGROUND—MAP A

Campsites, facilities: There are 13 sites, all with picnic tables, grills and fire rings. Chemical toilets, water, a raft-launching ramp and a pay phone are available. There is a 14-day stay limit.

Fee: There is a $4 fee per night; pay on site.

Who to contact: Vernal District Office, 170 South 500 East, Vernal, UT 84078; (801) 789-1362.

Location: In Browns Park on the Green River. From Dutch John, drive north on US 191 to the Utah/Wyoming border. Turn right onto a dirt road and follow the signs for Browns Park to the campground entrance. The campground is set at 4,200 feet.

Season: May to September.

4. INDIAN CROSSING CAMPGROUND—MAP A

Campsites, facilities: There are 10 sites (six are for tents only), all with picnic tables, grills and fire rings. Water, chemical toilets and a raft-launching ramp are available. No trash facilities are provided, so pack out all that you bring in. There is a 14-day stay limit.

Fee: There is a $2 fee per night; pay on site.

Who to contact: Vernal District Office, 170 South 500 East, Vernal, UT 84078; (801) 789-1362.

Location: On the banks of the Green River in Browns Park. From Dutch John, drive north on US 191 to the Utah/Wyoming state line and turn right onto a dirt road. The road may become difficult to drive when wet. Follow the signs to Browns Park and the campground entrance. The campground is set at 4,200 feet.

Season: May to September.

5. PELICAN LAKE CAMPGROUND—MAP A

Campsites, facilities: There are 14 sites, all with picnic tables, grills and fire rings. Chemical toilets, a boat ramp and a boat dock are available. There is **no water**.

Fee: There is no fee.

Who to contact: Vernal District Office, 170 South 500 East, Vernal, UT 84078; (801) 789-1362.

Location: Along the south end of Pelican Lake. From Vernal, drive 15 miles west on US 40 to Highway 88 and turn left. Drive eight miles to the lake and the campground access road that leads around the west side to the south end. The campground is set at 4,800 feet.

Season: April to October.

6. SIMPSON'S SPRINGS CAMPGROUND—MAP A

Campsites, facilities: There are 14 sites, all with picnic tables, grills and fire rings. Pit toilets and water are available. There is a 14-day stay limit.

Fee: There is a $2 fee per night; pay on site.

Who to contact: Salt Lake District Office, 2370 South 2300 West, Salt Lake City, UT 84119; (801) 977-4300.

Location: Along the Pony Express Trail. From Tooele, drive 32 miles south on Highway 36 to Faust and then 20 miles west on a county road. Follow the Pony Express signs and signs for Simpson's Springs Campground.

Season: March to October.

7. OASIS CAMPGROUND—MAP A

Campsites, facilities: There are 84 sites, all with picnic tables and grills. An RV dump station, water and flush toilets are available. There is a 14-day stay limit.

Fee: There is a $5 fee per night; pay on site.

Who to contact: House Range Resource Area, P.O. Box 778, Fillmore, UT 84631; (801) 743-6811.

Location: In the Little Sahara Recreation Area. From Eureka, drive on US 6 south for approximately 19 miles to a BLM road and turn right. Follow the signs to the campground. The campground is set at 5,100 feet.

Season: All year. Expect crowds in the spring and fall. This area is heavily used by off-highway-vehicle enthusiasts.

8. JERICHO CAMPGROUND—MAP A

Campsites, facilities: There are 41 sites, all with picnic tables and grills. Sun shelters, water and flush toilets are available. There is a 14-day stay limit.

Fee: There is a $5 fee per night; pay on site.

Who to contact: House Range Resource Area, P.O. Box 778, Fillmore, UT 84631; (801) 743-6811.

Location: In the Little Sahara Recreation Area. From Eureka, drive on US 6 south for approximately 19 miles to a BLM road and turn right. Follow the signs to the campground. The campground is set at 5,900 feet.

Season: All year. Expect crowds in the spring and fall. This area is heavily used by off-highway-vehicle enthusiasts.

9. SAND MOUNTAIN CAMPGROUND—MAP A

Campsites, facilities: There are 300 sites, all with picnic tables and grills. Water and pit toilets are available. There is a 14-day stay limit.

Fee: There is a $5 fee per night; pay on site.

Who to contact: House Range Resource Area, P.O. Box 778, Fillmore, UT 84631; (801) 743-6811.

Location: In the Little Sahara Recreation Area. From Eureka, drive on US 6 south for approximately 19 miles to a BLM road and turn right. Follow the signs to the campground. The campground is set at 5,100 feet.

Season: All year. Expect crowds in the spring and fall. This area is used heavily by off-highway-vehicle enthusiasts.

10. WHITE SANDS CAMPGROUND—MAP A

Campsites, facilities: There are 99 sites, all with picnic tables and grills. Water and flush toilets are available. There is a 14-day stay limit.

Fee: There is a $5 fee per night; pay on site.

Who to contact: House Range Resource Area, P.O. Box 778, Fillmore, UT 84631; (801) 743-6811.

Location: In the Little Sahara Recreation Area. From Eureka, drive on US 6 south for approximately 19 miles to a BLM road and turn right. Follow the signs to the campground. The campground is set at 5,100 feet.

Season: All year. Expect crowds in the spring and fall. This area is heavily used by off-highway-vehicle enthusiasts.

11. PRICE CANYON CAMPGROUND—MAP A

Campsites, facilities: There are 18 sites, all with picnic tables, fire rings and grills. Pit toilets and water are available. There is a 14-day stay limit.

Fee: There is a $6 fee per night; pay on site.

Who to contact: San Rafael Resource Area, 900 North Seventh East, Price, UT 84501; (801) 637-4584.

Location: From Price, drive north on US 6 for 15 miles to a steep BLM road heading off to the left. Turn left onto the BLM road and drive three miles to the campground entrance. Snow can close the road. The campground is set at 8,000 feet.

Season: June to October.

12. SAN RAFAEL BRIDGE CAMPGROUND—MAP B

Campsites, facilities: There are eight sites, all with picnic tables, grills and fire rings. Pit toilets are available. There is **no water**. There is a 14-day stay limit.

Fee: There is a $5 fee per night; pay on site.

Who to contact: San Rafael Resource Area, 900 North Seventh East, Price, UT 84501; (801) 637-4584.

Location: From Cleveland, drive approximately 25 miles southeast on a dirt county road to the campground entrance.

Season: All year.

13. DEWEY BRIDGE CAMPGROUND—MAP B

Campsites, facilities: There are seven sites, all with picnic tables and grills. Pit toilets are available. There is **no water**. There is a 14-day stay limit.

Fee: There is a $5 fee per night; pay on site.

Who to contact: Moab District Office, 82 East Dogwood, P.O. Box 970, Moab, UT 84532; (801) 259-6111.

Location: On the Colorado Riverway. From Moab, drive north on US 191 to Highway 128. Turn right onto Highway 128 and drive northeast for 28.7 miles to the campground entrance. The campground is set at 4,000 feet.

Season: All year.

14. HITTLE BOTTOM CAMPGROUND—MAP B

Campsites, facilities: There are 10 sites, all with picnic tables, grills and fire rings. Pit toilets are available. There is **no water**. There is a 14-day stay limit.

Fee: There is a $5 fee per night; pay on site.

Who to contact: Moab District Office, 82 East Dogwood, P.O. Box 970, Moab, UT 84532; (801) 259-6111.

Location: On the Colorado Riverway. From Moab, drive north on US 191 to Highway 128. Turn right onto Highway 128 and drive northeast for 22.5 miles to the campground entrance. The campground is set at 4,000 feet.

Season: All year.

15. BIG BEND CAMPGROUND—MAP B

Campsites, facilities: There are 23 sites, all with picnic tables and grills. Pit toilets are available. There is **no water**. There is a 14-day stay limit.

Fee: There is a $5 fee per night; pay on site.

Who to contact: Moab District Office, 82 East Dogwood, P.O. Box 970, Moab, UT 84532; (801) 259-6111.

Location: On the bank of the Colorado River. From Moab, drive north on US 191 for two miles to Highway 128 and turn right, driving another six miles to the campground entrance. The campground is set at 5,100 feet.

Season: All year.

16. HAL CANYON CAMPGROUND—MAP B

Campsites, facilities: There are seven sites, all with picnic tables and grills. Pit toilets are available. There is **no water**. There is a 14-day stay limit.

Fee: There is a $5 fee per night; pay on site.

Who to contact: Moab District Office, 82 East Dogwood, P.O. Box 970, Moab, UT 84532; (801) 259-6111.

Location: On the Colorado Riverway. From Moab, drive north on US 191 to Highway 128. Turn right onto Highway 128 and drive northeast for 6.6 miles to the campground entrance. The campground is set at 4,000 feet.

Season: All year.

17. OAK GROVE CAMPGROUND—MAP B

Campsites, facilities: There are seven sites, all with picnic tables and grills. Pit toilets are available. There is **no water**. There is a 14-day stay limit.

Fee: There is a $5 fee per night; pay on site.

Who to contact: Moab District Office, 82 East Dogwood, P.O. Box 970, Moab, UT 84532; (801) 259-6111.

Location: On the Colorado Riverway. From Moab, drive north on US 191 to Highway 128. Turn right onto Highway 128 and drive northeast for 6.9 miles to the campground entrance. The campground is set at 4,000 feet.

Season: All year.

18. JAYCEE PARK CAMPGROUND—MAP B

Campsites, facilities: There are 11 sites, all with picnic tables and grills. Pit toilets are available. There is **no water**. There is a 14-day stay limit.

Fee: There is a $5 fee per night; pay on site.

Who to contact: Moab District Office, 82 East Dogwood, P.O. Box 970, Moab, UT 84532; (801) 259-6111.

Location: On the Colorado Riverway. From Moab, drive north on US 191 to Highway 279. Turn left onto Highway 279 and drive south for 4.2 miles to the campground entrance. The campground is set at 4,000 feet.

Season: All year.

19. ROCK CORRAL CAMPGROUND—MAP B

Campsites, facilities: There are three sites, all with picnic tables and fire rings. Pit toilets are available. There is **no water**. There is a 14-day stay limit.

Fee: There is no fee.

Who to contact: Cedar City District Office, 176 East D.L. Sargent Drive, Cedar City, UT 84720; (801) 865-3053.

Location: West of Interstate 15 and the city of Beaver. From Highway 21 at Milford, drive approximately one-quarter of a mile to a small sign indicating the turnoff to the campground, an unpaved county road. Drive approximately nine miles to the campground entrance, following campground signs all the way. The campground is set at 6,900 feet.

Season: May to October.

20. LONESOME BEAVER CAMPGROUND—MAP B

Campsites, facilities: There are five sites, all with picnic tables, grills and fire rings. Water and pit toilets are available. No trash facilities are provided, so pack out all that you bring in. There is a 14-day stay limit.

Fee: There is a $4 fee per night; pay on site.

Who to contact: Henry Mountains Resource Area, P.O. Box 99, Hanksville, UT 84734; (801) 542-3461.

Location: In the Henry Mountains, near the base of Mount Ellen. From Hanksville, drive 21.7 miles on a rough access road signed for the campground. High-clearance vehicles are recommended. The campground is set at 8,000 feet.

Season: May to October.

21. McMillian Spring Campground—Map B

Campsites, facilities: There are 10 sites, all with picnic tables, grills and fire rings. Water and pit toilets are available. There is a 14-day stay limit.

Fee: There is no fee.

Who to contact: Henry Mountains Resource Area, P.O. Box 99, Hanksville, UT 84734; (801) 542-3461.

Location: In the Henry Mountains. From Hanksville, drive west on Highway 24 for 28.5 miles and turn left onto rough Notom/Bullfrog Road. Drive 31.5 miles to the campground entrance. High-clearance vehicles are strongly recommended. The campground is set at 8,400 feet.

Season: May to November.

22. Starr Springs Campground—Map B

Campsites, facilities: There are 12 sites, all with picnic tables, grills and fire rings. Pit toilets and water are available. Large vehicles will find the site inaccessible. No trash facilities are provided, so pack out all that you bring in. There is a 14-day stay limit.

Fee: There is a $4 fee per night; pay on site.

Who to contact: Henry Mountains Resource Area, P.O. Box 99, Hanksville, UT 84734; (801) 542-3461.

Location: In the Henry Mountains. From Hanksville, drive south on Highway 95 for 26.5 miles to Highway 276 and head right or south. Drive on Highway 276 for 17.5 miles to Starr Spring Road and turn right onto a dirt surface for roughly another four miles to the campground. The campground is set at 6,300 feet.

Season: April to October.

23. Deer Creek Campground—Map B

Campsites, facilities: There are three sites, all with picnic tables and grills. Pit toilets are available. There is **no water**. There is a 14-day stay limit.

Fee: There is no fee.

Who to contact: Escalante Resource Area, P.O. Box 769, Escalante, UT 84726; (801) 826-4291.

Location: From Boulder, drive six miles southeast on the Burr Trail to the campground entrance.

Season: May to December.

24. CALF CREEK CAMPGROUND—MAP B

Campsites, facilities: There are 13 sites, all with picnic tables and grills. Pit toilets and water are available. There is a 14-day stay limit.

Fee: There is a $6 fee per night; pay on site.

Who to contact: Escalante Resource Area, P.O. Box 769, Escalante, UT 84726; (801) 826-4291.

Location: From Escalante, drive 15 miles east on Highway 54 to the campground entrance.

Season: May to December.

25. HATCH POINT CAMPGROUND—MAP B

Campsites, facilities: There are 10 sites, all with picnic tables, grills and fire rings. Pit toilets are available. There is **no water**. There is a 14-day stay limit.

Fee: There is a $6 fee per night; pay on site.

Who to contact: Moab District Office, 82 East Dogwood, P.O. Box 970, Moab, UT 84532; (801) 259-6111.

Location: From Monticello, drive north on US 191 for 22.5 miles to a BLM road and turn left; follow the signs and drive another 22.5 miles to the campground. The last 10 miles or so of the BLM road are unpaved and can become slippery when wet. Snow can close the road. The campground is set at 5,900 feet.

Season: April to October. Dry camping off-season is allowed if access is possible.

26. WIND WHISTLE CAMPGROUND—MAP B

Campsites, facilities: There are 19 sites, all with picnic tables and grills. Water and pit toilets are available. There is a 14-day stay limit.

Fee: There is a $6 per night; pay on site.

Who to contact: Moab District Office, 82 East Dogwood, P.O. Box 970, Moab, UT 84532; (801) 259-6111.

Location: In the Canyon Rims Recreation Area. From Monticello, drive north on US 191 for approximately 22.5 miles to a BLM road signed for the campground. Turn left (west) and drive six miles to the campground entrance. The campground is set at 6,000 feet.

Season: April to October

27. BAKER DAM CAMPGROUND—MAP B

Campsites, facilities: There are 10 sites, all with picnic tables and grills. Pit toilets are available. There is **no water**. There is a 14-day stay limit.

Fee: There is no fee.

Who to contact: Dixie Resource Area, 225 North Bluff Street, St. George, UT 84770; (801) 673-4654.

Location: Overlooking Baker Reservoir and the Santa Clara River. From St. George, drive 25 miles north on Highway 18 to the campground entrance. The campground is set at 5,000 feet.

Season: All year.

28. RED CLIFFS CAMPGROUND—MAP B

Campsites, facilities: There are 10 sites, all with picnic tables and grills. Water and a combination of pit and chemical toilets are available. There is a 14-day stay limit.

Fee: There is a $4 fee per night; pay on site.

Who to contact: Dixie Resource Area, 225 North Bluff Street, St. George, UT 84770; (801) 673-4654.

Location: In a gorgeous red-rock canyon near Zion National Park. From the Leeds exit off Interstate 15, approximately 15 miles north of St. George, follow the signs to the campground entrance. The campground is set at 3,600 feet.

Season: All year.

29. PONDEROSA GROVE CAMPGROUND—MAP B

Campsites, facilities: There are eight sites, all with picnic tables, grills and fire rings. Pit toilets are available. There is **no water**. RVs up to 22 feet are allowed. There is a 14-day stay limit.

Fee: There is no fee.

Who to contact: Kanab Resource Area Office, 318 North First Street, Kanab, Utah 84741; (801) 644-2672.

Location: Adjacent to Coral Pink Sand Dunes State Park. From Kanab, drive north on US 89 for approximately 7.5 miles to a gravel road on the left signed for Coral Pink Sand Dunes State Park. Turn left onto this road and drive approximately seven miles to the campground entrance. The campground is set at 6,380 feet.

Season: April to October.

30. WHITE HOUSE CAMPGROUND—MAP B

Campsites, facilities: There are three sites, all with picnic tables, grills and fire rings. Pit toilets are available. There is **no water**. RVs up to 23 feet are allowed. There is a 14-day stay limit.

Fee: There is no fee.

Who to contact: Kanab Resource Area Office, 318 North First Street, Kanab, Utah 84741; (801) 644-2672.

Location: On the banks of Paria River near the Paria Wilderness. From Kanab, drive east on US 89 for 40 miles to a gravel access road signed on the right for the campground. Turn right and drive two miles to the campground. Heavy rains may close the road as it is susceptible to flooding. The campground is set at 4,600 feet.

Season: All year.

31. SAND ISLAND CAMPGROUND—MAP B

Campsites, facilities: There are six sites, all with picnic tables and grills. Pit toilets and a boat ramp area available. There is **no water**. There is a 14-day stay limit.

Fee: There is a $5 fee per night; pay on site.

Who to contact: San Juan Resource Area, 435 North Main, P.O. Box 7, Monticello, UT 84535; (801) 587-2141.

Location: On the San Juan River. From Bluff, drive three miles west on US 163 to the campground entrance. The campground is set at 4,300 feet.

Season: All year.

STATE INFORMATION OVERVIEW

UTAH STATE OFFICE
P.O. Box 45155, Salt Lake City, UT 84145; (801) 539-4010

SALT LAKE DISTRICT OFFICE
2370 South 2300 West, Salt Lake City, UT 84119; (801) 977-4300

Pony Express Resource Area, 2370 South 2300 West, Salt Lake City, UT 84119; (801) 977-4300

Bear River Resource Area, 2370 South 2300 West, Salt Lake City, UT 84119; (801) 977-4300

CEDAR CITY DISTRICT OFFICE
176 East D.L. Sargent Drive, Cedar City, UT 84720; (801) 865-3053

Dixie Resource Area, 225 North Bluff Street, St. George, UT 84770; (801) 673-4654

Kanab Resource Area Office, 318 North First Street, Kanab, Utah 84741; (801) 644-2672.

Escalante Resource Area, P.O. Box 769, Escalante, UT 84726; (801) 826-4291

Beaver River Resource Area, 444 South Main, Suite C, Cedar City, UT 84720; (801) 586-2458

MOAB DISTRICT OFFICE
82 East Dogwood, P.O. Box 970, Moab, UT 84532; (801) 259-6111

Price River Resource Area, 900 North Seventh East, Price, UT 84501; (801) 637-4584

San Rafael Resource Area, 900 North Seventh East, Price, UT 84501; (801) 637-4584

Grand Resource Area, P.O. Box 970, Moab, UT 84532; (801) 259-8193

San Juan Resource Area, 435 North Main, P.O. Box 7, Monticello, UT 84535; (801) 587-2141

VERNAL DISTRICT OFFICE
170 South 500 East, Vernal, UT 84078; (801) 789-1362

RICHFIELD DISTRICT OFFICE
150 East 900 North, Richfield, UT 84701; (801) 896-8221

Sevier River Resource Area, 150 East 900 North, Suite F, Richfield, UT 84701; (801) 896-8221

Henry Mountains Resource Area, P.O. Box 99, Hanksville, UT 84734; (801) 542-3461

House Range Resource Area, P.O. Box 778, Fillmore, UT 84631; (801) 743-6811

Warm Springs Resource Area, P.O. Box 778, 84631; (801) 743-6811

CHAPTER TWELVE

WASHINGTON

Maps—pp. 534, 536
Washington Map A Locations—pp. 538-539
Washington Map B Locations—pp. 539-550
Information Resources—p. 554

(SEE MAP A)   **(SEE MAP B)**

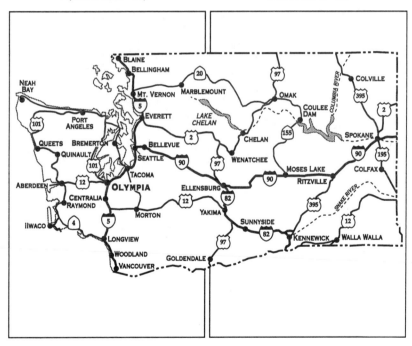

MAP A—WASHINGTON

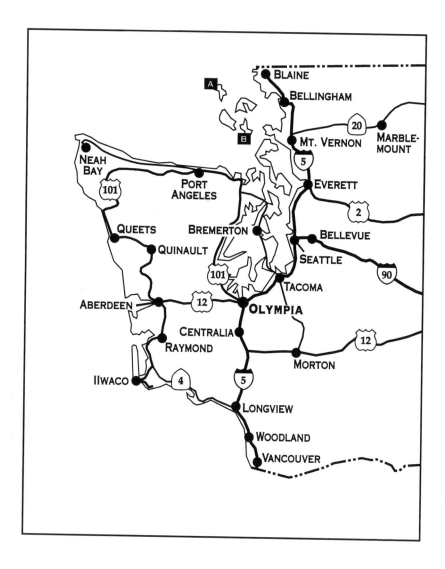

MAP REFERENCES

MAP B—WASHINGTON

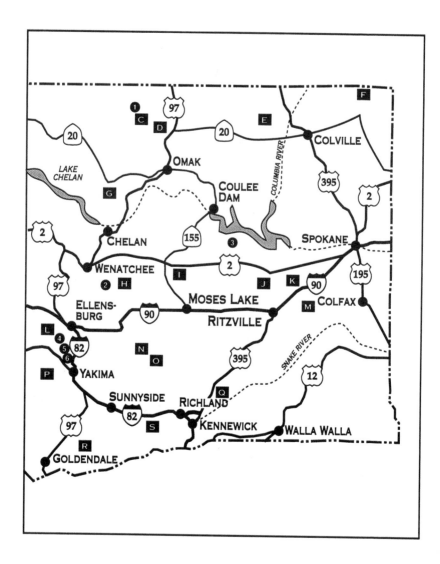

MAP REFERENCES

BLM CAMPGROUNDS

WASHINGTON—MAP A

TURN POINT, STUART ISLAND (SAN JUAN ISLANDS)

See letter A on map page 534

boating, hiking, photography, sea kayaking, wildlife observation

With a view toward Canada across the Boundary Pass, this old lighthouse station and surrounding area offer expansive scenery of forest and sea. It also provides an opportunity to view bald eagles, seabirds, deer and marine mammals, and to explore tidepools and coves along the coast. The old lighthouse, though not open to the public, is a historic landmark. It is accessible by charter or rental boat from Friday Harbor, a 1.5-mile hike from the boat dock at Prevost, or from Reid Harbor State Park on Stuart Island. Visit at any time of year.

USGS topographic map: Stuart Island

For more information: Contact the BLM Spokane District Office, 1103 North Fancher, Spokane, WA 99212; (509) 536-1200.

CHADWICK HILL, LOPEZ ISLAND (SAN JUAN ISLANDS)

See letter B on map page 534

hiking, mountain biking, wildlife observation

This forested headland on Lopez Island offers spectacular views of the Cascades to the east, Rosario Strait and the San Juan Islands. The "hill" has many diverse plant communities, and offers good wildflower viewing in the spring. Bald eagle and peregrine falcon frequent the cliffs and a marsh lies adjacent to the property to the south. Seabirds, sea lions and whales may often be viewed. From the ferry terminal on Lopez Island, go southeast on Mud Bay Road to Watmaugh Bay Road, then south 1.5 miles to the property boundary. Signs indicate private property in the area. Please stay off private land and respect the owners' rights. The cliffs on the south and east side of the hill drop sharply to the ocean—exercise extreme caution! Any time of year is good to visit, but expect winter to be rainy.

USGS topographic map: Lopez Pass

For more information: Contact the BLM Spokane District Office, 1103 North Fancher, Spokane, WA 99212; (509) 536-1200.

WASHINGTON—MAP B

CHOPAKA LAKE

See letter C on map page 536

boating, camping, canoeing, fishing, hiking, mountain biking, wildlife observation

Located 10 miles north of Loomis, Washington in northeast Okanogan County, Chopaka Lake offers spectacular views of the eastern Cascade slope and is the gateway to hiking in the Chopaka Mountain Wilderness Study Area. The two-mile ridge trail around Bowers Lake to the north is considered an excellent introduction to the region. Chopaka is rimmed by forest and meadow, and some limited camping is available at BLM and state sites. No vehicles are permitted past the Wilderness Study Area boundary. The boat launch on state land is not developed—only canoes and small boats are allowed. There is good fishing for rainbow trout. The mile-long waterway offers a chance for solitude and boat access to some remote hiking opportunities. Wildlife includes deer, waterfowl, bear and mountain goat in the Wilderness Study Area. To get to Chopaka, drive three miles north of Loomis and watch for a gravel road to the left, leading up the mountain. The lake is located in a basin above the main valley. The road junction may not be signed; inquire at the Loomis store. Spring, summer and fall are the best times to visit.

USGS topographic maps: Loomis, Nighthawk

BLM surface map: Oroville

For more information: Contact the BLM Spokane District Office, 1103 North Fancher, Spokane, WA 99212; (509) 536-1200.

SPLIT ROCK RECREATION SITE

See letter D on map page 536

birdwatching, boating, fishing, hiking, wildlife observation

To reach the Split Rock Recreation Site, drive five miles north of Loomis on the Loomis-Oroville Road. The best area for wildlife observation is on the southeast shore of Palmer Lake. Bring your binoculars because it is possible to see mountain goats on nearby Grandview Mountain—one mile to the northwest across from the southeast shore of Palmer Lake. Around the lake, expect to see a wide variety of shorebirds, waterfowl, grebes, loons and songbirds.

USGS topographic maps: Loomis, Nighthawk

For more information: Contact the BLM Spokane District Office, 1103 North Fancher, Spokane, WA 99212; (509) 536-1200.

KETTLE RIVER

See letter E on map page 536

camping, canoeing, fishing, rafting, wildlife observation

The Kettle River flows into northeast Washington from Canada and has secondary highway access along most of its length. Most of the river is ideally suited for canoeing, with very little whitewater. In the summer, small sand beaches dot the shoreline. Fishing is for rainbow and brown trout. Eagles, osprey, kingfisher and other birds populate the cottonwood groves; bighorn sheep can be seen on the canyon walls near the town of Curlew. There are both private and public access points to the river. Twenty miles north of Republic, on Highway 21, the river crosses at the town of Curlew. From there, the river road goes northwest (upriver) to Canada, and northeast (downriver). Inquire at the Curlew store for boating and fishing information.

USGS topographic maps: Vulcan Mountain, Curlew

BLM surface map: Republic

For more information: Contact the BLM Spokane District Office, 1103 North Fancher, Spokane, WA 99212; (509) 536-1200.

PEND OREILLE RIVER CANYON

See letter F on map page 536

boating, canoeing, fishing, rafting, wildlife observation

This remote stretch of river meanders through a steep-walled limestone canyon, bordered by U.S. Forest Service and BLM land. The wildlife here includes deer, elk, bighorn sheep, osprey, bald eagle and a variety of other birdlife. Fishing is for both cold- and warm-water species. The sheer canyon walls rise straight up from the river in many locations, and the effect is striking.

Activity Highlight: Hiking

Recreational hiking is possible from both shores where roads and trails come down to the river. Shorelines are steep and forested for the most part. The lake behind Boundary Dam is popular for boating, but is never crowded. Streams and waterfalls dot the canyon walls in a few locations. There is a boat-launch site at Boundary Dam and near Metaline Falls. The falls are visible at lower water levels, and must be floated with care due to currents, eddies and upwellings caused by underwater turbulence. The balance of the float is in flat, though moderate, currents.

Location: The Pend Oreille River Canyon runs north from the town of Metaline Falls to Boundary Dam on the Canadian border. Metaline Falls is located on Highway 31, 100 miles northeast of Spokane near the Canadian border. This highway parallels the Pend Oreille River for many miles.

Camping: Camping is allowed along the river on BLM lands only

Season: The boating season runs from May to October.

USGS topographic maps: Metaline Falls, Boundary Dam

BLM surface map: Colville

For more information: Contact the BLM Spokane District Office, 1103 North Fancher, Spokane, WA 99212; (509) 536-1200.

METHOW RIVER

See letter G on map page 536

fishing, rafting, wildflowers

The Methow (pronounced "Met-how"), located in Okanogan County, is a tributary of the Columbia River. It is a small river with some steep gradients and Class IV whitewater. Commercial rafting companies float the river in the spring and summer. Fishing is for resident rainbow trout and steelhead. Bald eagle, deer and other wildlife can be viewed along the river. The Methow is accessible via Highway 153 between Pateros and Twisp. There are public access points at various locations; check locally for the best access.

USGS topographic maps: Pateros, Methow, Twisp East, Twisp West

BLM surface maps: Twisp, Robinson Mountain

For more information: Contact the BLM Spokane District Office, 1103 North Fancher, Spokane, WA 99212; (509) 536-1200.

DOUGLAS CREEK

See letter H on map page 536

camping, fishing, hiking, mountain biking, wildlife observation

Douglas Creek is a desert canyon with steep basalt cliffs and a well-defined riparian corridor featuring a trout stream. Many varieties of songbirds and raptors may be enjoyed here. The wildlife includes deer, porcupine, coyote, beaver and more. An old railroad bed makes an excellent hiking trail. From Highway 28, 3.5 miles south of Rock Island Dam, turn northwest on Palisades Road to Douglas Creek Road. Drive north to the canyon. Douglas Creek Road traverses about half of the lower canyon, then becomes "H" Road and connects with US 2 near Waterville.

USGS topographic maps: Palisades, Altown, Douglas

BLM surface map: Wenatchee

For more information: Contact the BLM Spokane District Office, 1103 North Fancher, Spokane, WA 99212; (509) 536-1200.

WILSON CREEK CANYON

See letter I on map page 536

hiking, wildflowers, wildlife observation

A designated Watchable Wildlife/Wildflower Area, this little canyon is home to a number of songbirds, waterfowl and raptors—and features a well-developed riparian zone and a live desert stream. Deer, beaver, coyote and an occasional bobcat can be seen in the region. The canyon was used as an outlaw hideout during the late 1800s. The interpretive trail is located one-half mile south of the Lewis Bridge, and leads through a natural plant community to a canyon overlook. From the junction four miles west of Wilbur, drive south past the community of Govan to the end of the pavement (five miles), then continue west one mile to Lewis Bridge over Wilson Creek. The area lies downstream. Spring, summer and fall are the times to visit.

USGS topographic map: Almira Southeast

BLM surface map: Coulee Dam

For more information: Contact the BLM Spokane District Office, 1103 North Fancher, Spokane, WA 99212; (509) 536-1200.

LAKEVIEW RANCH / LAKEVIEW CREEK CANYON

See letter J on map page 536

camping, hiking, mountain biking, wildlife observation

One of the largest continuous parcels of native steppe habitat in the eastern Columbia Basin, this area offers excellent opportunities to observe and interpret the geology of the basin and to hike remote, scenic canyons. Wildlife includes raptors, upland birds, waterfowl, deer and other animals. This is one of the last strongholds for the sage grouse in Washington. A number of primitive trails are open to mountain bike and hiking use. The ranch is located off Highway 21, about six miles north of the town of Odessa. Maps are available from the BLM District Office and at the Odessa Community Visitor Center.

USGS topographic maps: Pacific Lake, Sullivan Lake

BLM surface map: Coulee Dam

For more information: Contact the BLM Spokane District Office, 1103 North Fancher, Spokane, WA 99212; (509) 536-1200.

GOOSE BUTTE

See letter K on map page 536

hiking, mountain biking, wildlife observation

A desert canyon with a seasonal stream, this region offers good off-season backcountry exploring opportunities. The basalt cliffs are home to nesting raptors and other songbirds and waterfowl are abundant in spring. Deer, grouse, owls, rabbits, coyote and other animals may be viewed occasionally. Six miles north of the Interstate 90 junction at the Tokio Weigh Station, access is via an old jeep trail which runs west off the Tokio-Harrington Highway (Hills Road). Motorized vehicles are not permitted beyond the gate, but parking is available near the Crab Creek Bridge. A BLM sign is on the cable gate, just north of the bridge. Adjacent private lands are marked—please respect landowners' privacy and stay off marked private lands.

USGS topographic maps: Harrington Southeast, Lamona

BLM surface map: Ritzville

For more information: Contact the BLM Spokane District Office, 1103 North Fancher, Spokane, WA 99212; (509) 536-1200.

YAKIMA RIVER CANYON

See letter L on map page 536

camping, canoeing, fishing, hiking, kayaking, rafting, wildlife observation

Along the canyon, it is possible to see bighorn sheep, songbirds of many varieties and numerous raptors. The best place for viewing bighorn is during the spring and winter, 1.5 to 2.5 miles north of Umtanum and across the river.

Powerboating, waterskiing, canoeing, picnicking, hiking, horseback riding, fishing and hunting are all popular activities in this area. The river is regarded as a blue ribbon trout stream. Trails for anglers and hikers run along the west bank.

Location: East of the Cascade Mountain Range between the cities of Ellensburg and Yakima. You can access the area off Highway 821, west of Interstate 82, between Ellensburg and Selah. The Yakima River Canyon Recreation Area extends for nearly 24 of the more than 30 river miles that separate the cities of Ellensburg and Yakima.

Camping: Three recreation sites with primitive campgrounds are along the route: Umtanum Creek, Squaw Creek and Roza. Each has restrooms and boat-launching facilities.

Season: This area is available for access year-round for wildlife observation and hiking. Boating is best during the warm spring and summer months—but these months are also the most crowded!

BLM surface map: Yakima

For more information: Contact the BLM Spokane District Office, 1103 North Fancher, Spokane, WA 99212; (509) 536-1200.

FISHTRAP LAKE AREA

See letter M on map page 536

birdwatching, boating, cross-country skiing, fishing, hiking, mountain biking, wildlife observation

Formerly private lands, the 8,000-acre Fishtrap Lake Area has just recently been opened to the public. Although there is a small store and marina located at the north end of Fishtrap Lake, the majority of the region remains wild and primitive, perfect for exploring on foot. As you wander through the flood-scoured basalt area formed during the ice-age over 10,000 years ago, you will find your imagination dazzled by odd-shaped basalt cliffs, caves and mazes of small canyons.

Activity Highlight: Hiking

There is no formal trail system, but old jeep roads, now overgrown with disuse, serve nicely as informal foot paths. Beginning at the headquarters, it is possible to link a number of roads and explore an eight-mile loop. Cross-country ambling is the preferred mode of travel, however, if you are comfortable enough with your navigation skills.

Activity Highlight: Fishing

Fishtrap Lake is over three miles long and lies tucked into a narrow, basalt canyon. Wandering around the lake rim and through the canyon bottom is a super way to spend an afternoon birdwatching, relaxing, or, if you are so inclined, fishing. Anglers should pack light tackle. Rumor has it that the best fishing is to be had at the south end of the lake, although this is one fishing "secret" that probably isn't too secret with the locals. For more fishing solitude, head to the lake during midweek.

Activity Highlight: Wildlife observation

If you tire of hanging out by the lake's edge, then head into the wilds and out among the wetlands, pothole ponds, cool ponderosa pine forests and open prairie vistas. Those with a sharp eye for wildlife will enjoy watching for deer, coyotes, eagles, and waterfowl. Elk may be viewed here as well, but only in the winter and early spring. The spring is an especially beautiful time to visit because the grassland is carpeted in lush green and sprinkled generously with spectacular displays of color from numerous varieties of wildflowers.

When the weather turns crisp and ice rims the streams and ponds, Fishtrap puts on another face that is equally attractive to the visitor. Following a fresh snowfall, with enough depth, it is possible to don skis and tour throughout Fishtrap Lake. Just because it's winter doesn't mean you can't fish. December to April, Hog Canyon Lake, a three-mile trek or ski from the park headquarters, is open to ice fishing...Brrrrr!

Special note: Because it is closed to all motorized vehicles, including snowmobiles, Fishtrap provides an excellent opportunity to cross-country ski in the winter. Excellent opportunities also exist to view waterfowl, song birds, deer, elk and other animals—pack your binoculars and camera.

Location: Approximately 30 miles west of Spokane. Take the Fishtrap exit off Interstate 90, thirty miles west of Spokane, and drive four miles south on the old county road to the area headquarters and parking area.

Permits: No permits are necessary for day use. Camping permits are required and may be obtained by mail from the district office. Open fires are not allowed at any time.

USGS topographic maps: Fishtrap Lake, Tyler

BLM surface map: Spokane

Resources:

• *Washington Atlas and Gazetteer*, published by DeLorme Mapping, P.O. Box 298, Freeport, ME 04032; (207) 865-4171.

For more information: Contact the BLM Spokane District Office, 1103 North Fancher, Spokane, WA 99212; (509) 536-1200.

COLUMBIA RIVER-HANFORD REACH

See letter N on map page 536

boating, canoeing, fishing, wildlife observation

This last free-flowing stretch of the Columbia River is located between Wanapum Dam and the city of Richland, Washington. There are a number of access points and boat-launch sites along the river. For canoeing or floating, the undeveloped launch at the Vernita Bridge is popular. Fishing is for steelhead and king salmon. Bald eagles concentrate along the river in the winter. Deer, coyotes, raptors and many shorebirds and waterfowl can also be viewed along the river. The BLM islands and the U.S. Fish and Wildlife Service refuge islands offer unique habitats to explore and are used by Canada geese for nesting sites in the spring. To reach the Vernita Bridge, drive north of Richland on Highway 240 for approximately 30 miles. The float down to Richland can be done in one or two days. Water levels fluctuate with releases from Wanapum Dam. Do not leave a boat unattended or untethered. Spring, summer and fall are the best times to visit.

USGS topographic maps: Wooded Island, Savage Island, Hanford, Locke Island, Coyote Rapids, Vernita Bridge

BLM surface maps: Richland, Priest Rapids

For more information: Contact the BLM Spokane District Office, 1103 North Fancher, Spokane, WA 99212; (509) 536-1200.

SADDLE MOUNTAIN

See letter O on map page 536

camping, hang gliding, hiking, mountain biking, off-highway-vehicle use, rockhounding

A steep escarpment, Saddle Mountain offers expansive vistas of the Columbia Basin, the Columbia River and the Crab Creek National Wildlife Refuge to the north. The sage-covered ridge is crisscrossed with primitive jeep roads and trails. The steep north slope is a good place to view raptors. The area is a popular rockhounding location, and is a good spot to see wildflowers in the spring. South of Interstate 90, drive 15 miles to Mattawa. Continue east of Mattawa one mile to "R" Road, and north into the western region. The eastern region is accessible through Wahluke Wildlife Area, 20 miles east of

Mattawa. Visit in spring, summer or fall.

USGS topographic maps: Beverly, Smyrna, Corfu

BLM surface map: Priest Rapids

For more information: Contact the BLM Spokane District Office, 1103 North Fancher, Spokane, WA 99212; (509) 536-1200.

COWICHE CREEK CANYON

See letter P on map page 536

hiking, wildlife observation

This small canyon is located just west of Yakima, along Cowiche Creek. There is an established hiking trail on an old railroad grade through the canyon. Old railroad bridges still cross the creek. Numerous species of birds can be viewed within the riparian habitat. The geology of the exposed basalt canyon is very interesting. Interpretive signs are located at each end of the canyon and trail guide brochures are available at the trailheads or from the BLM offices in Wenatchee or Spokane. The canyon makes an excellent half-day side trip, and the 3.2-mile walk is considered easy. To reach the lower trailhead, take 40th Avenue west out of Yakima. Turn left on Powerhouse Road. Another left on Cowiche Canyon Road leads you to the trailhead. Spring, summer and fall are the best times to visit.

USGS topographic maps: Wiley City, Yakima West, Naches

BLM surface map: Yakima

For more information: Contact the BLM Spokane District Office, 1103 North Fancher, Spokane, WA 99212; (509) 536-1200.

JUNIPER DUNES WILDERNESS

See letter Q on map page 536

hiking, wildflowers, wildlife observation

This "pocket wilderness" of 8,000 acres offers a unique combination of sand dunes and juniper trees that combine to make a special habitat area. The dunes were designated a Wilderness Area in 1984. Wildflowers are spectacular in the spring. The area is recognized as a critical nesting habitat for a number of raptor species. Many other birds may also be viewed here. From Pasco, drive northeast on the Kahlotus Highway. The wilderness area lies 1.5 miles north of the highway between mile 15 and mile 18. Currently, access is only available over private lands and permission is required. Call the BLM office in Spokane before entering for the latest access information.

USGS topographic maps: Levy Southeast, Levy Southwest

BLM surface map: Walla Walla

For more information: Contact the BLM Spokane District Office, 1103 North Fancher, Spokane, WA 99212; (509) 536-1200.

ROCK CREEK CANYON

See letter R on map page 536

backpacking, fishing, hiking, wildlife observation

This is a remote, narrow canyon running through a very wild and scenic area. Ponderosa pine and oak woodlands grow on the slopes, with the creek creating a well-defined riparian zone. Fishing is for resident rainbow trout, although Coho salmon and steelhead trout do spawn in the lower stream.

Activity Highlight: Backpacking

The lower canyon walls rise 1,000 feet above the creek and hiking into and out of the canyon may be strenuous. There are no established trails. Once down in the inner canyon, the explorer will find that the area is quite remote, scenic and peaceful. You must carry or treat all drinking water.

Location: Near Goldendale in Klickitat County. Few access points to this area exist. The best one is off US 97, eight miles north of Goldendale and two miles south of Brooks Memorial Park. Here, a forest access road leads east for 3.5 miles to the creek crossing. Park at the bridge and hike down the canyon. Other access points lead off the forest road further south, but parking is limited and you must cross private lands (although most of the canyon itself is either state or BLM lands, some private ownership does occur). Please respect private lands, which may or may not be marked.

Camping: There are good backpacking campsites along the creek.

Season: The best time to visit is from May to October.

USGS topographic maps: Status Pass, Goodnoe Hills

BLM surface map: Goldendale

For more information: Contact the BLM Spokane District Office, 1103 North Fancher, Spokane, WA 99212; (509) 536-1200.

BADGER SLOPE

See letter S on map page 536

hang gliding, hiking, wildlife observation

A north-facing escarpment overlooking the lower Yakima River Valley, Badger Slope offers expansive vistas, showy spring wildflowers and soaring raptors. Golden eagles, ferruginous and red-tailed hawks, prairie falcons and other birds may be enjoyed during the spring and summer—bring binoculars! The slope is covered with wildflowers in April and early May. The ridgeline can be hiked from east to west using the McBee Grade Road from Kiona Junction, off Interstate 12, eleven miles west of Richland. Drive to the top of the grade and hike west along the top of the slope. Keep a sharp eye out for rattlesnakes. Note that the wheat fields to the south are private lands and must be avoided.

USGS topographic maps: Webber Canyon, Whitstran Northeast

BLM surface map: Richland

For more information: Contact the BLM Spokane District Office, 1103 North Fancher, Spokane, WA 99212; (509) 536-1200.

BLM CAMPGROUNDS

1. CHOPAKA LAKE CAMPGROUND—MAP B

Campsites, facilities: There are six sites, all with picnic tables and fire rings. Pit toilets, water and boat ramp are available. No trash facilities are provided, so pack out all that you bring in. There is a 14-day stay limit.

Fee: There is no fee.

Who to contact: Wenatchee Resource Area Office, 915 North Walla Walla Avenue, Wenatchee, WA 98801; (509) 665-2100.

Location: West of US 97 on the western shore of Chopaka Lake. From Loomis, drive north on County Road 9425 for two miles and turn left onto Toats Coulee Road. Drive 1.5 miles and turn right onto a narrow, unmarked road. Drive 3.5 miles to a junction, stay left and drive 1.5 miles more to another junction. Head right and drive two miles to the lake and the campground.

Season: All year. Snow may close access to the site from December to February.

2. DOUGLAS CREEK CAMPGROUND—MAP B

Campsites, facilities: Primitive camping. There are no facilities available, so come prepared. No trash facilities are provided, so pack out all that you bring in. There is a 14-day stay limit.

Fee: There is no fee.

Who to contact: Wenatchee Resource Area Office, 915 Walla Walla Avenue, Wenatchee, WA 98801; (509) 665-2100.

Location: From east Wenatchee, drive 14 miles south on Highway 28. Turn east on Palisades Road; drive approximately 12 miles and turn north onto an unmarked road leading to Douglas Canyon. After crossing a creek, within 1.5 to two miles, you will have entered the designated camping area.

Season: All year.

3. LAKEVIEW CANYON CAMPGROUND—MAP B

Campsites, facilities: There are five sites, all with picnic tables and grills. A corral and pit toilets are available. There is **no water**. There is a 14-day stay limit.

Fee: There is no fee.

Who to contact: Spokane District Office, 1103 North Fancher, Spokane, WA 99212-1275; (509) 536-1200.

Location: From Odessa, drive north on Highway 21 for 2.5 miles and turn west onto Lakeview Ranch Road. Drive 4.5 miles to the campground entrance.

Season: All year.

4. UMTANUM CAMPGROUND—MAP B

Campsites, facilities: There are many undesignated sites for tents only. Pit toilets are available. There is **no water**. There is a foot bridge across the river. There is a seven-day stay limit.

Fee: There is no fee.

Who to contact: Wenatchee Resource Area Office, 915 Walla Walla Avenue, Wenatchee, WA 98801; (509) 665-2100.

Location: In the Yakima River Canyon. From Ellensburg, drive south on Highway 821 (Canyon Road) for approximately nine miles to the campground entrance on the right or west side of road.

Season: All year.

5. SQUAW CREEK CAMPGROUND—MAP B

Campsites, facilities: There are four sites, all with picnic tables and grills. Pit toilets are available. There is **no water**. There is a seven-day stay limit.

Fee: There is no fee.

Who to contact: Wenatchee Resource Area Office, 915 Walla Walla Avenue, Wenatchee, WA 98801; (509) 665-2100.

Location: In the Yakima River Canyon. From Ellensburg, drive south on Highway 821 (Canyon Road) for approximately 13 miles to the campground entrance on the right (west) side of the road.

Season: All year.

6. ROZA CAMPGROUND—MAP B

Campsites, facilities: In the Yakima River Canyon. There are seven sites, all with picnic tables and grills. Pit toilets and a boat launch are available. There is **no water**. There is a seven-day stay limit.

Fee: There is no fee.

Who to contact: Wenatchee Resource Area Office, 915 Walla Walla Avenue, Wenatchee, WA 98801; (509) 665-2100.

Location: In the Yakima River Canyon. From Ellensburg, drive south on Highway 821 (Canyon Road) for approximately 18 miles to the campground entrance on the right (west) side of the road.

Season: All year.

STATE INFORMATION OVERVIEW

SPOKANE DISTRICT OFFICE
East 4217 Main Avenue, Spokane, WA 99202; (509) 536-1200

Wenatchee Resource Area Office, 915 North Walla Walla Avenue, Wenatchee, WA 98801; (509) 665-2100

Chapter Thirteen

WYOMING

(SEE MAP A)   **(SEE MAP B)**

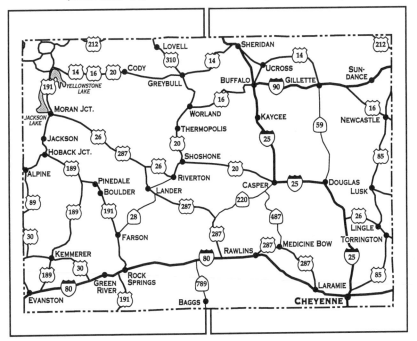

MAP A—WYOMING

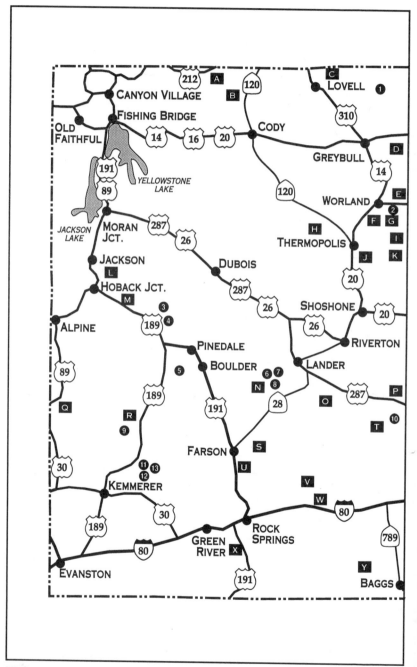

MAP REFERENCES

BLM CAMPGROUNDS

MAP B—WYOMING

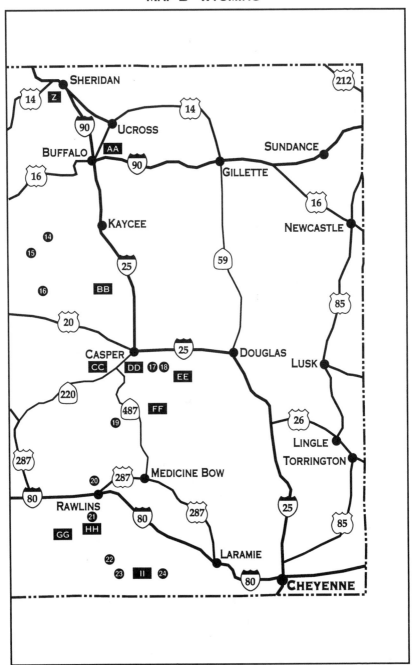

MAP REFERENCES

BLM CAMPGROUNDS

WYOMING—MAP A

CODY HISTORIC TRAILS STATE RECREATION MANAGEMENT AREA

See letter A on map page 556

hiking

The Cody Resource Area manages several significant historical trails in northwestern Wyoming, including the Nez Perce, the Bridger, the Bozeman and the Red Lodge to Meeteetse Stage Route. The Nez Perce Trail has been designated a National Historic Trail. This trail is the route that Chief Joseph and his tribe followed in 1877 during their attempt to escape to Canada rather than remain on their reservation. The Bridger Trail was used more heavily by stage coaches than the Bozeman Trail, because the Sioux focused their efforts on stopping travel along the Bozeman. The Red Lodge to Meeteetse Stage Route was an important freight route in the 1800s. It provided a vital link to the railroads, which did not enter the area until much later. Hiking is the best way to explore these trails. Access to all parts of the trails is limited. There are some conflicting accounts as to where the actual trails originally existed. For specific directions, inquire at the BLM Cody office. The best hiking is in spring, summer or fall.

For more information: Contact the BLM Cody Resource Area, 1002 Blackburn Avenue, P.O. Box 518, Cody, WY 82414; (307) 587-2216.

McCULLOUGH PEAKS

See letter B on map page 556

hiking, horseback riding

The McCullough Peaks region is a dramatic and scenic badlands area that is heavily eroded and very colorful. Wild horse, mule deer and pronghorn sheep live on the sparse vegetation. The golden eagle, prairie falcon, kestrel, red-tailed hawk and great horned owl rule the skies. A 25,000-acre Wilderness Study Area is also located within the region. The entrance is five miles east of Cody via local roads. Wet conditions may make these roads impassable—check with the Cody Resource Area office for road information and directions before heading out.

USGS topographic maps: Stone Barn Camp, Gilmore Hill, Ralston, Gilmore Hill Northwest

For more information: Contact the BLM Cody Resource Area, 1002 Blackburn Avenue, P.O. Box 518, Cody, WY 82414; (307) 587-2216.

PORCUPINE CREEK / DEVIL CANYON

See letter C on map page 556

backpacking, fishing, hiking, historic sites, mountain biking, wildlife observation

This area is located just northeast of the town of Lovell and Bighorn Lake, near the Montana/Wyoming border. Porcupine Creek flows for almost its entire length through the highly scenic Devil Canyon—characterized by massive limestone rock walls dropping steeply several hundred feet to the canyon floor. According to the BLM, "few canyons in the region have walls as high or as vertical, and few canyons are as undisturbed by the evidence of man." The canyon area is a critical wintering habitat for bighorn sheep and is also noteworthy for the large number of raptor nests. Segments of the canyon have open sites and rock shelters that are listed on the National Register of Historic Places. Native Americans have shown increased interest in the region due to its geographic relationship with the Medicine Wheel and Spirit Mountain. Access is limited and should be first approved by calling the BLM office in Cody to obtain up-to-date information. Visit in spring, summer or fall.

USGS topographic maps: Natural Trap Cave, Simmons Canyon, Mexican Hill

For more information: Contact the BLM Cody Resource Area, 1002 Blackburn Avenue, P.O. Box 518, Cody, WY 82414; (307) 587-2216.

WORLAND CAVES SPECIAL RECREATION MANAGEMENT AREA

See letter D on map page 556

hiking, spelunking

The Worland District contains at least 40 known caves throughout the Bighorn Basin of north central Wyoming. More caves are certain to be discovered with time. The best-known caves are Horsethief, Titan, Natural Trap, Spirit Mountain Cavern, Holey Sheep, Tres

Charros and the Great Expectation Cave system. The spelunking highlights are as follow:

• **Horsethief Cave:** Horsethief Cave includes approximately 15 miles of known passage, much of which has been mapped. Most of the cave is dry, but wet formations (stalactites, stalagmites and flowstones) are present in the cave. The cave itself displays extensive, diverse and beautiful cave formations. In fact, some formations represent some of the very best displays of mineralization found in any cold-climate cave in the U.S. Horsethief Cave is a "wild" cave, meaning no passage modifications have been undertaken and nothing has been added to or removed to decrease hazards or make the cave more accessible.

The 1.2-mile Horsethief Cave Underground National Recreation Trail is an unimproved primitive trail. Trail passageways vary in size from crawlways to rooms with thousands of square feet. Some sections of the trail require crawling and squeezing through constricted passageways—a daunting psychological task for some. Other portions of the trail are located in expansive rooms permitting individual exploration of the cave environment. The majority of the trail is dry and dusty and no attempts to improve or otherwise modify the trail are planned.

• **Natural Trap:** It is well known internationally for its paleontological resources, which include the remains of a North American lion, a woolly mammoth and a Pleistocene-era camel. Access requires an 80-foot free rappel.

Special note: At press time, this cave was closed to recreational use in order to protect the paleontological resources. The BLM will be re-evaluating this closure in the future.

• **Spirit Mountain Caverns:** The caverns were discovered by a local spelunker in 1904 and became a National Monument under an executive order signed by Teddy Roosevelt. It then became a commercial cave under a recreation and public purpose lease and finally reverted back to the BLM. Since the cave is easily accessible from the town of Cody, it sees a lot of novice cavers. A permit is required for entry and may be obtained from the BLM Cody Resource Area.

• **Holey Sheep Cave:** Discovered in 1988, the cave contains outstanding examples of rare minerals and unusual formations. For that reason, and because the cave has a very high radon danger, the BLM is understandably being very strict in limiting access to this area. The gate to the cave is only opened to those most experienced cavers with a distinct purpose to enter.

• **Tres Charros and Great Expectation:** Both of these caves are critically important as part of the water recharge network for the Madison Aquifer.

Location: Horsethief Cave is located on Little Mountain, approximately 25 miles east of Lovell. I am deferring to BLM's request to specifically avoid giving directions to any of the other caves in order to enforce visitor safety and protect fragile cave resources. If you are an experienced spelunker, contact the BLM for permit and location information.

Season: This area is open all year, depending on the snow level and access road conditions—check with the BLM prior to heading out.

Permits: Permits to enter Horsethief Cave and use its trail are available at no cost from the BLM in Cody. Use of the cave is controlled through a locked gate located immediately inside the cave entrance. It is restricted to two groups per day, with a maximum of eight per group. Pets are not allowed inside the cave. Group leaders must demonstrate extensive cave exploration experience or have previous experience traveling in Horsethief Cave.

The BLM will issue permits to all who want to visit other caves in the region, as long as they can demonstrate sufficient prior spelunking experience. In some cases, the BLM may be able to recommend a spelunking club that would be willing to "guide" novices through a cave if they show genuine interest.

For more information: Contact the BLM Worland District Office, 101 South 23rd Street, Worland, WY 82401; (307) 347-9871.

MEDICINE LODGE CANYON

See letter E on map page 556

backpacking, camping, fishing, hiking, horseback riding, wildlife observation

This 1,000-foot-deep canyon is spectacular and provides excellent access to the adjacent Bighorn National Forest. There is a streamside campground at the mouth of the canyon that is maintained by the Wyoming Recreation Commission. Medicine Lodge State Archaeological Site, which features many well-preserved petroglyphs, can also be accessed and enjoyed. The trail running through the canyon and up into the National Forest is named Dry Medicine Lodge Canyon and is the only maintained trail in the region. All other hiking is off-trail. Access into the Cloud Peak Wilderness makes this an attractive backpacking exploration area. Fishing is for rainbow, brown, brook, and cutthroat trout. Wildlife includes elk, deer, black bear, mountain lion and cottontail rabbit. Wild turkey and pheasant can also be seen. The area is closed from December 1 to June 1 to protect sensitive wintering wildlife.

To get there from Worland, take Highway 31 east toward the Bighorn Mountains and the town of Hyattville. One-half of a mile north of Hyattville you will end up on the Alkali/Cold Springs Road. The road turns to gravel and heads north, but you will stay on the paved Cold Springs Road for four miles to a sign indicating the Medicine Lodge Habitat Unit. From here continue approximately 1.5 miles on the gravel road to a parking area.

USGS topographic maps: Allen Draw, Hyatt Ranch

For more information: Contact the BLM Worland District Office, P.O. Box 119, 101 South 23rd Street, Worland, WY 82401; (307) 347-9871.

WEST SLOPE SPECIAL RECREATION MANAGEMENT AREA

See letter F on map page 556

backpacking, camping, fishing, hiking, snowmobiling, wildlife observation

Characterized by deep canyons that bisect the rolling and sometimes steep west slope of the Bighorn Mountains, the West Slope Special Recreation Management Area supports trout fisheries and a whole host of recreational opportunities. Five Springs Falls Campground, Middle Fork of the Powder River Campground and several hiking trails provide developed recreational opportunities. The West Slope area is adjacent to Big Horn National Forest. From Lovell, drive 23 miles east on US 14A to the area. It makes a good year-round destination.

For more information: Contact the BLM Worland District Office, 101 South 23rd Street, Worland, WY 82401; (307) 347-9871.

PAINT ROCK CANYON

See letter G on map page 556

backpacking, fishing, hiking, mountain biking, wildlife observation

A number of local stories have it that the name Paint Rock comes either from the individuals who found Native American pictographs on a nearby cliff or from the Native American's themselves who, it is rumored, used the multicolored clay found on the creek's banks for ceremonial and war paint.

However the area got its name, one thing is for certain—you will remember this area best for its massive limestone cliffs, towering above the pristine stream that snakes for over six miles along the canyon floor. Pack along a fishing rod because large trout are reported to ply the waters. Raptor and swallow activity is amazing, especially around sunset.

Activity Highlights: Hiking and backpacking

Hiking is easy and you may camp anywhere—except on the first 1.7 miles of the trail, which is owned by the Hyatt Ranch. From the parking area, stick to the road that skirts several large fields. Leave all gates as you find them—either open or closed. Just before entering the canyon, BLM land will be marked with a sign and a fence. The following six miles of trail—well, the trail actually disappears, but the hiking is so easy it might as well be a trail—lead the hiker up and into the canyon along a level and relatively smooth route. Hiking through the huge junipers with the rushing sound of the nearby creek is a magical experience. Just past the confluence of North and Middle Paint Rock creeks is the Big Horn National Forest boundary—you can easily and enjoyably extend your backpacking trip here, if you so desire. If you wish to access the Paint Rock Canyon year-round (other than Hyatt access from April through September), you may, but only via a BLM access requiring a high-clearance vehicle to get to the trailhead. Road conditions can change dramatically—check with the BLM before departing. The trail itself is named Lone Tree and winds through very fragile cryptobiotic soil. As Dave Baker of the BLM puts it, "please tiptoe through the crypto."

Special note: Public access to the canyon is allowed from April to September, but only through a special agreement with the owners of Hyatt Ranch, who allow visitors to hike across 1.7 miles of their land to enter the canyon. Respect their privacy and close all gates. April and May are the best times to visit the canyon area, as the summer air is hot and filled with deer flies and the grasses become very dry, turning your socks into a walking seed sampler. Native American archaeological artifacts exist throughout the region—please enjoy them but leave them untouched and where they lie.

Location: In the foothills west of Bighorn Mountains and just east of the town of Worland. Take Highway 31 east from Worland toward the Bighorn Mountains and the town of Hyattville. One-half mile north of town you will find be Alkali/Cold Springs Road. Alkali turns to gravel and heads north, but you will stay on paved Cold Springs Road to a fork, where the pavement ends. Bear right at the fork on Hyatt Lane to the signed parking area for Paint Rock.

USGS topographic maps: Hyatt Ranch, Allen Draw, Lake Solitude

BLM surface map: Worland

USFS map: Bighorn National Forest

Resources:

• *Wyoming Atlas and Gazetteer*, published by DeLorme Mapping, P.O. Box 298, Freeport, ME 04032; (207) 865-4171.

For more information: Contact the BLM Worland District, P.O. Box 119, 101 South 23rd Street, Worland, Wyoming 82401; (307) 347-9871.

BOBCAT DRAW

See letter H on map page 556

backpacking, hiking, wildlife observation

Wyoming is not famous for its badlands, and yet it probably should be. Bobcat Draw is an outstanding example of magical formations formed by the powers of erosion—arches, windows, hoodoos, mushrooms and more. Colors are spectacular. Wildlife is limited, due to lack of available water, but pronghorn sheep and wild horses may still be seen. Probably the best way to experience this region is to hike in a short way and set up a base camp from which to explore. Be sure to pack in all the water you will need as there is none available within Bobcat. This area is located west of Worland on Route 431. Inquire at the Worland District office for more detailed and up-to-date access information. Visit in spring, summer or fall.

USGS topographic map: Dead Indian Hill, Dutch Nick Northwest

For more information: Contact the BLM Worland District Office, P.O. Box 119, 101 South 23rd Street, Worland, WY 82401; (307) 347-9871.

HONEYCOMB AND OREGON BUTTES

See letter I on map page 556

backpacking, camping, hiking, horseback riding, rockhounding

This is an excellent example of badlands topography with stunning vertical relief. Buttes rise sharply above the low sagebrush hills and greasewood flats. The area features cliffs and caves and offers a good habitat for pronghorn, mule deer, elk, bobcat and coyote. Numerous wild horses also frequent the area. Although there are a few springs and a number of small reservoirs built for livestock, pack all the water that you will need, because the area is predominantly dry. Rockhounders will enjoy the opportunity to find agate, jade and petrified wood. From Atlantic City drive 10 miles south on Highway 28. Then turn south on Oregon Buttes Road (County Road 445) and drive for approximately eight miles.

USGS topographic maps: Five Fingers Butte, Circle Bar Lake, Bob Jack Well, Continental Peak, Dickie Springs, John Hay Reservoir, Frayer Gap, Pacific Springs

For more information: Contact the BLM Green River Resource Area, 1993 Dewar Drive, Rock Springs, WY 82901; (307) 362-6422.

BIG HORN RIVER SPECIAL RECREATION MANAGEMENT AREA

See letter J on map page 556

camping, fishing (including spear-gun fishing), float boating, wildlife observation

Located 15 miles north of Thermopolis, the Bighorn River meanders through a cottonwood riparian area, agricultural lands and badlands. An especially scenic segment of the river is where it dissects the Sheep Mountain Anticline and Little Sheep Mountain. The state of Wyoming classifies this segment of the river as a Class I fishery, which means it is a fishery of national prominence. Large rainbow and brown trout may be fished within this section. Consistent public access to the river is a problem in many areas, so it is critical that you check with the BLM before heading out. Visit in spring, summer or fall.

For more information: Contact the BLM Worland District Office, 101 South 23rd Street, Worland, WY 82401; (307) 347-9871; or the Cody Resource Area (for information on the region from Greybull to Yellowtail Reservoir), P.O. Box 518, 1002 Blackburn Avenue, Cody, WY 82414; (307) 587-2216.

NATURAL CORRALS
See letter K on map page 556

camping, hiking, volcano-tubing

Contrary to popular legend, Butch Cassidy didn't bury his loot here. But that's okay, because the ice caves amid the jumble of huge volcanic boulders are more than worth the time spent visiting here. Wear old clothing, long pants and sleeves because volcanic rock is very abrasive. From Interstate 80 and Point of Rocks, head north and then east about eight miles on County Road 4-15 to the Jim Bridger Power Station. After two miles, turn west toward Superior at the Superior cutoff road. After another 3.5 miles, bear right at the fork. From here on, four-wheel-drive vehicles are recommended. After 2.5 miles, a faint track to the left will take you into the site. Visit here any time of year.

BLM surface maps: Kinney Rim, Red Desert Basin

For more information: Contact the BLM Green River Resource Area, 1993 Dewar Drive, Rock Springs, WY 82901; (307) 362-6422.

WYOMING CONTINENTAL DIVIDE SNOWMOBILE TRAIL
See letter L on map page 556

cross-country skiing, snowmobiling, snowshoeing, winter wildlife observation

The Wyoming Continental Divide Snowmobile Trail extends from Lander to the boundaries of Grand Teton National Park, with over 250 miles of marked and groomed snowmobile trail. Much of it passes through BLM lands. A publication, *Wyoming Continental Divide Snowmobile Trail*, outlines information regarding the trail and includes a map of the entire trail network expanse. The publication is available from any Wyoming BLM office, the Wyoming Snowmobile Program, or communities along the trail. There are numerous other maintained "winter" trails throughout Wyoming. In fact, Wyoming has some of the most expansive and developed snowmobiling trails in the continental United States. Snowmobiling maps are available from the Wyoming Snowmobile Program, 2301 Central Avenue, Cheyenne, WY 82002; (307) 777-7550. Find out snow conditions around the state by calling (307) 777-6503.

For more information: Contact the BLM Wyoming State Office, 2515 Warren Avenue, P.O. Box 1828, Cheyenne, WY 82003; (307) 775-6BLM.

SCAB CREEK WILDERNESS STUDY AREA

See letter M on map page 556

backpacking, cross-country skiing, fishing, hiking, horseback riding, rock climbing, wildlife observation

Many visitors use this region as a doorstep to the nearby Bridger-Teton National Forest and Bridger Wilderness lake region. The National Outdoor Leadership School uses this area for winter activities. The terrain is characterized by steep and rocky granite outcrops, which have been cut and sculpted by glaciers and streams. Off-trail hiking is possible, but very difficult. Orienteering skills and strong map-reading skills are necessary. There is a 2.5-mile maintained trail that receives very heavy use by those heading to the U.S. Forest Service area boundary. The trailhead features a small campground without potable water, and holding pens for horses. The abundant wildlife in this area includes elk, moose, mule deer, black bear, bobcat, mountain lion, coyote, badger, snowshoe hare and wolverine. From Boulder and US 191, head east for seven miles on Route 353 and then north on County Road 23-122 and BLM Road 5423. The roads are dirt and require a high-clearance vehicle when dry, and a four-wheel-drive vehicle when wet.

USGS topographic maps: Scab Creek, Raid Lake

For more information: Contact the BLM Pinedale Resource Area, P.O. Box 768, Pinedale, WY 82941; (307) 367-4358.

SOUTH PASS HISTORIC MINING AREA
SPECIAL RECREATION MANAGEMENT AREA

See letter N on map page 556

fishing (limited), hiking, historic site, mountain biking

The state's most notable gold rush began here in the late 1860s. The mining area contains the small town of Atlantic City, the South Pass State Historic Site and the remains of Miner's Delight, another early center of gold-mining activity. Prospect pits and abandoned gold mines dot the area, and although some small claims continue to operate today, no large scale mining has taken place for years. Amateur geologists will enjoy viewing some of the oldest rocks on the continent, which lie exposed here. Mule deer, pronghorn antelope and moose make up the most commonly seen wildlife population. There are two developed campgrounds located near Atlantic City. For a brief hike, a quiet fishing trip or a peaceful pedal, follow the trail that leads from South Pass City along Willow Creek. This area is located near Highway 28, approximately 30 miles south of Lander.

USGS topographic map: Lander

BLM surface maps: Lander, South Pass

For more information: Contact the BLM Lander Resource Area, 125 Sunflower Street, Lander, WY 82520; (307) 332-7822.

SWEETWATER CANYON

See letter O on map page 556

backpacking, birdwatching, fishing, hiking, wildlife observation

This very wild canyon is a Wilderness Study Area with excellent opportunities for fishing. Solitude and quiet abound. Geological formations are spectacular and birdlife is abundant.

Activity Highlights: Hiking and backpacking

Game trails wander throughout the canyon. Discernible trails follow the river—eight to nine miles each way through the canyon. Ticks and deer flies are prevalent during the summer—take appropriate precautions. Hiking is very rugged and not for the faint of heart. The reward, however, is the thrill of hiking in a spectacular prairie canyon where few have tread.

Location: South of Lander and near the southeast reaches of the Wind River Range. From Atlantic City or Sweetwater Station, take the Hudson Atlantic City Road; the road is signed BLM Road 2302. There are a number of connecting trails, all heading south from BLM Road 2302, but not passable by two-wheel-drive vehicles. If you choose to hike to the canyon, park your vehicle off to the side of BLM Road 2302, anywhere that you are not obstructing traffic. There are places to leave four-wheel-drive vehicles near the canyon at the end of the access trails, but the canyon itself is closed to vehicular traffic. Wet conditions could make any of the roads impassable. Call the Lander Station first for detailed access- and road-condition information.

Camping: Camping is allowed anywhere within Sweetwater Canyon.

Season: The best time to visit is from July through September. Snow, high water or wet conditions can make access to the canyon area impossible—always check with the BLM Lander office before heading out.

USGS topographic maps: Lewiston Lakes, Radium Springs

BLM surface maps: Lander, South Pass

Resources:
• *Wyoming Atlas and Gazetteer*, published by DeLorme Mapping, Main Street, Freeport, ME 04032; (800) 227-1656.

For more information: Contact the BLM Lander Resource Area, P.O. Box 589, Lander, WY 82520; (307) 332-7822.

SWEETWATER ROCKS

See letter P on map page 556

backpacking, camping, hiking, rock climbing, rockhounding

Sweetwater Rocks is known around the U.S. as a super climbing spot, primarily because of its gigantic granite slabs, domes and spires. The terrain is rugged and mountainous—it is no wonder the National Outdoor Leadership School uses this area as a training site. Both Lankin Dome and McIntosh Peak are well-recognized climbing spots. If you are not going to be climbing, don't despair; the region is well suited for just scrambling around as well. In addition, the birding is excellent. However, access is challenging to say the least. Your best bet is to contact the BLM office for current access and road condition information before heading out. I recommend the following: From Jeffrey City, drive approximately seven miles east on US 287 and then head northeast on Agate Flat Road/BLM Road 2004, which runs along the western edge of the region.

USGS topographic map: Rattlesnake Hills

BLM surface maps: Bairoil, Rattlesnake Hills

For more information: Contact the BLM Rawlins District Office, P.O. Box 670, 1300 North Third Street, Rawlins, WY 82301; (307) 324-7171.

RAYMOND MOUNTAIN WILDERNESS STUDY AREA
See letter Q on map page 556

backpacking, birdwatching, camping, cross-country skiing, fishing, hiking, horseback riding, rock climbing

Most people who visit this area come for the fishing (Bonneville or Bear River cutthroat trout) or picnicking. For the hiker or backpacker, unless it is hunting season, the area will be largely unpopulated. Water is abundant, but must be purified. Numerous waterfowl are attracted to the area because of Huff Lake and area beaver ponds. Elk, moose and mule deer may be spotted in the region. Camping is allowed anywhere within the area. Raymond Mountain is located near the Wyoming/Idaho border between US 30 and US 89. I advise checking with the BLM for specific access information and road restrictions/conditions before heading out. Visit here any time of year.

USGS topographic maps: Salt Flat, Neugent Park, Big Park, Porcupine Creek, Marse

For more information: Contact the BLM Kemmerer Resource Area, 312 US 189 North, Kemmerer, WY 83101; (307) 877-3933.

LAKE MOUNTAIN WILDERNESS STUDY AREA
See letter R on map page 556

camping, cross-country skiing, hiking, horseback riding

This area has a mountainous terrain, with deep draws featuring aspen, Engelmann spruce and Douglas fir. Small meadows lush with wildflowers dot the landscape. Elevations range from 7,400 to 9,600 feet. Wildlife includes elk, deer, moose, black bear, beaver, pika and ruffed grouse. From La Barge, head south for one-and-a-half miles on US 189. Then turn west onto County Road 315. County Road 315 parallels La Barge Creek, and miles 12 to 18 represent the southwest boundary of Lake Mountain.

USGS topographic map: Lake Mountain

For more information: Contact the BLM Pinedale Resource Area, P.O. Box 768, Pinedale, WY 82941; (307) 367-4358.

CONTINENTAL DIVIDE NATIONAL SCENIC TRAIL SPECIAL RECREATION MANAGEMENT AREA

See letter S on map page 556

backpacking, camping, cross-country skiing, hiking

Although this route was officially designated as a National Scenic Trail by Congress in 1978, it is not officially marked yet. This is because of the unusually restrictive laws prohibiting access to private lands which checkerboard the entire route, most obviously in the BLM-managed section between South Pass City and Medicine Bow National Forest. Although many hikers choose different routes, the best route through this section to date is as follows: Follow the Sweetwater River from South Pass City to the lower end of Sweetwater Canyon and then head east/southeast along the flank of Crooks and Green mountains. From there, either head south along the high rims to Rawlins or go through the Ferris and Haystack mountains to Rawlins. Once at Rawlins, the route heads southwest along the Atlantic Rim to Miller and Middlewood Hills and then to Medicine Bow National Forest. Potable water is scarce and a backpacker must carry plenty of reserves. This route makes for good hiking year-round. Before crossing private land, you must secure the landowners' permission—check with the BLM for the best way to do this.

BLM surface maps: Rawlins, Bairoil, Baggs, South Pass

Resources:

• You may wish to obtain a copy of *The Guide to the Continental Trail, Volume 3: Wyoming*. This booklet, published by the Continental Divide Trail Society, provides descriptions of the trail, including distances, elevations and sources of water. Contact: The Continental Divide Trail Society, P.O. Box 30002, Bethesda, MD 20814.

For more information: Contact the BLM Rawlins District Office, P.O. Box 670, 1300 North Third Street, Rawlins, WY 82301; (307) 324-7171.

GREEN MOUNTAINS

See letter T on map page 556

camping, fishing, hiking, hunting, mountain biking

Cottonwood Campground is located here and there is a superb view to be enjoyed from on top of Wild Horse Overlook. This area has seen clear-cut timber harvests, mining exploration and the building of the roads that were necessary for all the vehicle traffic. Fortunately, the area seems to be recovering nicely. There are access roads from here that lead south to the Continental Divide. From Jeffrey City, drive six miles east on US 287 and then turn south onto Green Mountain Road.

USGS topographic maps: Split Rock Northwest, Sagebrush Park

BLM surface map: Bairoil

For more information: Contact the BLM Rawlins District Office, P.O. Box 670, 1300 North Third Street, Rawlins, WY 82301; (307) 324-7171.

OREGON / MORMON PIONEER / CALIFORNIA PONY EXPRESS NATIONAL HISTORIC TRAILS SPECIAL RECREATION MANAGEMENT AREA

See letter U on map page 556

auto touring, fishing, hiking, historic sites, horseback riding, hunting, mountain biking

Because of the South Pass across the Rocky Mountains, Wyoming is home to the major east-west immigrant trails. Over 500,000 hardy pioneers are believed to have made the trek, beginning in 1843 and ending in the late 1860s. The easiest way to visit remaining trail segments on public lands in Wyoming is by car. There is good access to pristine ruts and swales on about 350 miles of trails on public lands. There are designated loop tour/byway routes that require no landowner permission since they use county or state highways. In many cases, landowners willingly grant access to trail segments and related historic features on their properties—just ask first. The BLM has many maps, diary excerpts and other information on the trails, and they can help point the visitor to choice places where trails are in much the same condition as they were when the early wagon trains found them. Visit in spring, summer or fall.

For more information: Contact the BLM Wyoming State Office, 2515 Warren Avenue, P.O. Box 1828, Cheyenne, WY 82003; (307) 775-6BLM; or the Historic Trails Center, 1701 East E Street, Casper, WY 82601; (307) 261-7600.

SAND DUNES SPECIAL RECREATION MANAGEMENT AREA
See letter V on map page 556

camping, hiking, historic site

This area is at the very heart of the largest active dune field in North America, with the dunes up to 200 feet and under constant change and flux—blown eastward by constant westerly winds. Good skills with a map and compass are essential if you are to stay on course and enjoy the five to six miles of hiking it takes to fully appreciate the area. Believe it or not, there are pools of water at the base of many of these dunes, some crystal clear and as deep as seven to eight feet. Mule deer and the area's only herd of desert elk inhabit the sand dunes. The Ord kangaroo rat, coyote, red fox, bobcat and wild horse also call the moving sands home. The Boar's Tusk, a prominent volcanic plug shaped into a spire, is similar to Devil's Tower National Monument in northeastern Wyoming. Shoshone petroglyphs also can be found nearby. From Rock Springs, drive 10 miles north on US 191. Turn right on Tri-Territory Road/County Road 4-17. At the intersection with County Road 4-16, turn left and continue on County Road 4-16 approximately six miles to the site boundary on the right.

USGS topographic maps: Boar's Tusk, North Table Mountain, Tule Butte, Ox Yoke Springs, Essex Mountain

For more information: Contact the BLM Green River Resource Area, 1993 Dewer Drive, Rock Springs, WY 82901; (307) 362-6422.

RED DESERT
See letter W on map page 556

backpacking, camping, hiking, horseback riding, wildlife observation

The Red Desert is a vast, treeless area named for the brick-red soil that stretches as far as the eye can see in all directions. Light rainfall and oppressive summer temperatures make this a harsh place, yet it is worth a peek as it is the largest unfenced stretch of open land in the

Lower 48. In fact, some of the biggest herds of wild horses run free here, alongside herds of antelope. The Red Desert is located in the Great Divide Basin west of Rawlins and north of Interstate 80.

BLM surface map: Red Desert Basin

For more information: Contact the BLM Green River Resource Area, 1993 Dewar Drive, Rock Springs, WY 82901; (307) 362-6422.

GREEN RIVER

See letter X on map page 556

camping, canoeing, fishing, hiking, wildlife observation

South from Fontenelle Reservoir to the Flaming Gorge National Recreation Area, the Green River offers tranquil waters on which to float and fish—ideal for the entire family. The only developed camping along the way is Weeping Rock Campground, which has tables and a vault toilet, but no potable water. All water is obtained from the river and must be treated before drinking. The river route floats through the Seedskadee National Wildlife Refuge, which offers some of the finest birding opportunities in the state. Canoeists and rafters are likely to see moose, deer and antelope. From La Barge, drive south on US 189 for 24 miles to Highway 372 and turn left. Drive five miles to just below Fontenelle Reservoir Dam. Visit in spring, summer or fall.

For more information: Contact the BLM Rock Springs District Office, P.O. Box 1869, Rock Springs, WY 82901; (307) 382-5350.

ADOBE TOWN WILDERNESS STUDY AREA

See letter Y on map page 556

camping, hiking

Remote and rugged, this high-desert plateau embodies the dramatic nature of badlands. Buttes and escarpments have been carved by wind and water into colorful and often contorted formations. For some time, Congress has been debating whether to officially designate this area as a wilderness; in the meantime, the BLM has continued to manage it as a Wilderness Study Area. Water is not available, so pack all that you will need—keep in mind that the summer heat can be oppressive. Getting there is creative at best—almost as much of an adventure as you are likely to have once there. Contact the BLM office for specific, detailed directions. High-clearance, four-wheel-drive vehicles are required for driving on the BLM roads. However, rain will make the roads impassable—even with four-wheel drive.

USGS topographic maps: Kinney Spring, Prehistoric Rim, Monument Valley, Manual Gap, Barrel Springs Southwest, Upper Powder Spring, Cow Creek Reservoir, Salazar Butte, Powder Mountain

BLM surface maps: Kinney Rim, Baggs

For more information: Contact the BLM Rawlins District Office, P.O. Box 670, 1300 North Third Street, Rawlins, WY 82301; (307) 324-7171.

WYOMING—MAP B

TRAPPER CANYON

See letter Z on map page 558

backpacking, fishing, hiking, wildlife observation

Those who have braved the difficult terrain come away saying that Trapper Canyon is one of the most spectacular and scenic canyons on the west slope of the Bighorn Mountain Range. It is little wonder, as the dramatic cliffs, rock spires, massive outcroppings, clear and cascading stream, and the wide variety of vegetation and wildlife have earned this canyon BLM's "most scenic" rating. Even the Department of Fish and Game rates the stream "a fishery of regional importance" because of the presence of brown, rainbow and cutthroat trout. Vegetation in and around the stream includes currant, gooseberry, grapevine, chokecherry, cottonwood, and aspen—at times so dense that passage may be impeded. When the berries are in season, keep a lookout for black bears, which have sometimes been reported in the canyon. Those with a sharp eye for wildlife may spot bobcat, mountain lion, golden eagle, bald eagle and peregrine falcon. Several hundred deer and elk also use the canyon as a wintering ground. This entire canyon system has been recommended for wilderness designation by the BLM.

Activity Highlights: Hiking and backpacking

There is no developed trail system. Getting around is on game trails and by scrambling over rocks and loose talus slopes. The canyon is approximately 13 miles long with several side canyons, most of them hanging, and offers the adventurous and experienced back-packer ample opportunity to fully enjoy a pure wilderness setting.

Activity Highlight: Spelunking

Great Expectations Cave, recognized as the third deepest cave in the United States, lies within the boundaries of Trapper Canyon Wilderness Study Area. This cave is technically difficult and risky to enter—do not explore without a permit and plenty of experience, under any circumstances.

Location: West of Interstate 90 and southwest of the city of Sheridan, just south of the Montana border. Travel on the dirt access roads can be rough, muddy and challenging, four-wheel-drive vehicles are highly recommended. The point of access is five miles southeast of the town of Shell and State Road 14. Black Mountain Road provides access. There are private holdings along the road and bordering the canyon area—do not trespass without express permission from the owner. Before entering, check with the BLM regarding legal and approved access points to the canyon.

Camping: Primitive camping is allowed anywhere within Trapper Canyon.

Season: Although the canyon is passable year-round, snow frequently blocks the use of access roads between the months of December and April. The best time to visit is from May to October. Check with the BLM regarding current road conditions.

Permits: No permits are necessary for camping or backpacking. Seasonal campfire restrictions exist—check with the BLM office. Of special note is the entrance to the third deepest cave in the U.S., the Great Expectations Cave, which lies within the boundaries of Trapper Canyon. Permits for exploration are required—obtain them from the BLM. They are only issued to those who have demonstrated spelunking experience.

USGS topographic maps: White Sulphur Springs, Bush Butte, Spanish Point, Black Mountain

Resources:
• *The Sierra Club Guide to the Natural Areas of Idaho, Montana and Wyoming,* by John and Jane Perry; published by Sierra Club, 730 Polk Street, San Francisco, CA 94109.

• *Wyoming Atlas and Gazetteer*, published by DeLorme Mapping, Main Street, Freeport, ME 04032; (800) 227-1656.

For more information: Contact the BLM Worland District Office, 101 South 23rd Street, Worland, WY 82401; (307) 347-9871.

DRY CREEK PETRIFIED TREE ENVIRONMENTAL EDUCATION AREA

See letter AA on map page 558

geologic formations, hiking, wildlife observation

As you travel around a one-mile loop nature trail, you will go back 60 million years to a time when this area was a jungle-like region, with rivers that flowed north to a distant ocean. You will learn how the uplifting of the Big Horn Mountains helped to create the prairie ecosystem we see today. Visitors will also learn about early vegetation and the formation of coal, scoria, petrified trees, and other indicators of the past. From Buffalo, take Interstate 90 northeast for six miles to the Red Hills/Tipperary Road exit, then drive six miles north to the signed entrance. Visit in spring, summer or fall.

USGS topographic map: Buffalo Southeast

For more information: Contact the BLM Buffalo Resource Area, 189 North Cedar Street, Buffalo, WY 82834; (307) 684-5586.

MIDDLEFORK SPECIAL RECREATION MANAGEMENT AREA

See letter BB on map page 558

backpacking, camping, fishing, hiking, horseback riding, spelunking, wildlife observation

Made famous by the legends of Butch Cassidy and the Hole-In-The-Wall Gang, this area is remote and rugged. The Hole-In-The-Wall is actually a gap that provides a passable breach in the Red Wall, a 30-mile-long bright red sandstone cliff that rises 300 feet in some places and creates a physical barrier to passage. The other significant breach in the wall is created by the more visually stunning Middle Fork Canyon—carved by the eroding action of the Middle Fork of the Powder River. The west/east canyon runs up to 1,000 feet deep in some places and provides excellent opportunities for hiking, backpacking and fishing. Wildlife seen in the area include elk, bighorn sheep, mule deer, pronghorn, snowshoe hare, blue grouse and wild turkey. The best time to visit is between May and September. The summer can get quite warm, but it isn't too uncomfortable. From Kaycee, take Highway 192 off Interstate 25. Four-wheel-drive vehicles are recommended and it is essential that you contact the local Casper District BLM office for detailed road conditions and access information. Those interested in spelunking will want to inquire about Outlaw Cave.

USGS topographic map: Gordon Creek

For more information: Contact the BLM Buffalo Resource Area, 189 North Cedar Street, Buffalo, WY 82834; (307) 684-5586.

JACKSON CANYON

See letter CC on map page 558

wildlife observation

Located approximately five miles southwest of Casper on Route 220, Jackson Canyon serves as a roosting area for nearly 60 bald eagles from December through March. Although you cannot hike into the canyon (it is closed to public access to protect the eagles), the BLM and Audubon Society have collaborated to construct a birdwatching area at a signed area just off the road. There are plaques to help identify raptors.

For more information: Contact the BLM Worland District Office, P.O. Box 119, 101 South 23rd Street, Worland, WY 82401; (307) 347-9871.

GARDEN CREEK FALLS

See letter DD on map page 558

hiking

As long as you happen to be in the Casper area, a detour to the Garden Creek Falls is well worth the time and effort—especially in the spring when the falls truly resemble a cascade. Expect to find hordes of locals on weekends as this is a "hot" picnic and party spot. To get there from Interstate 25, turn south onto Highway 258/Wyoming Boulevard. Drive around the southern reaches of Casper for approximately 6.5 miles to a stoplight at the intersection with Highway 251 and Casper Mountain Road. Follow Highway 251 south and uphill to Highway 252. Turn right and drive for three-tenths of a mile, keeping a sharp eye out for a blue Rotary Park sign indicating a road heading left to the parking area for Garden Creek Falls.

USGS topographic map: Casper

BLM surface map: Casper

For more information: Contact the BLM Casper District Office, 1701 East E Street, Casper, WY 82601; (307) 261-7600.

MUDDY MOUNTAIN
SPECIAL RECREATION MANAGEMENT AREA

See letter EE on map page 558

backpacking, camping, cross-country skiing, hiking, snowmobiling, wildlife observation

Two campgrounds, a picnic area and good access make this an attractive recreational destination for anyone living in or visiting the Casper area. Cool in the summer and snowy in the winter, this region is a recreational playground. It is approximately 12 miles south of Casper on Highway 251. Muddy Mountain is closed from the first major snowfall until June 1 to protect an elk calving area from disturbance, as well as to protect against possible road and trail damage.

USGS topographic map: Crimson Dawn

For more information: Contact the BLM Casper District Office, 1701 East E Street, Casper, WY 82601; (307) 261-7600.

PATHFINDER RESERVOIR

See letter FF on map page 558

boating, camping, canoeing, fishing, hiking, swimming

Fishing and birdwatching are the most popular activities in this region. Camping is allowed anywhere outside the signed Pathfinder National Wildlife Refuge. Fishing is for brown, brook, and rainbow trout and walleye pike. The reservoir is located on the North Platte River and linked to the Alcova Reservoir downstream by the "miracle mile," more formally called Fremont Canyon. Miracle mile is so named because it is a trout fishery of outstanding quality. To get there from Casper, drive approximately 36 miles west on Highway 220 and then drive south on County Road 409 for eight miles.

For more information: Contact the BLM Casper District Office, 1701 East E Street, Casper, WY 82601; (307) 261-7600.

North Platte River Special Recreation Management Area

See letter GG on map page 558

birdwatching, camping, canoeing, fishing, float boating, hiking, wildlife observation

This area offers a quiet float along a tranquil river and excellent birding opportunities. The route is an historic one, previously used by Native Americans, explorers and trappers. The river meanders along both public and private lands. Red signs along the river mark the private lands; blue signs indicate public land and public access points. Waterfowl, shorebirds, great blue herons, bald eagles, grouse and numerous songbirds may be viewed. Wildlife includes mule deer, antelope, badger, beaver, muskrat and rabbit—but keep a sharp eye out as they are reclusive. BLM manages campgrounds at Bennett Peak, Corral Creek and the Dugway. In addition, the Wyoming Game and Fish Department maintains numerous public easements, which provide access to the river. This recreation area is located between the Medicine Bow National Forest and Seminoe Reservoir State Park.

Additional information: *The Upper North Platte River: A Fisherman's Guide and River Runner's Map/Guide*, Wyoming Game and Fish Department

BLM surface maps: Saratoga, Medicine Bow, Rawlins

For more information: Contact the BLM Casper District Office, 1701 East E Street, Casper, WY 82601; (307) 261-7600.

Ferris Mountains Wilderness Study Area

See letter HH on map page 558

backpacking, fishing, hiking, wildflowers, wildlife observation

This is a Wilderness Study Area beyond compare (no roads or even trails—it's all cross-country here). Public access is available at several locations along the north side of the mountains. Peaks range from 8,000 to 10,000 feet, cut with deep canyons, crystal clear streams, wildflowers galore and sweetly scented pine forests. Wildlife is abundant here.

Activity Highlights: Hiking and backpacking

This is not an area for the inexperienced backpacker or hiker. Solid orienteering and map-reading skills are requisite. No trails exist in this region and hiking is essentially cross-country. Park your car, pick an area that looks inviting and head out. Just remember that you must have the awareness and navigational skills necessary to find your way back to your vehicle again. Water is abundant and of good quality, although you must treat it prior to drinking.

Location: Approximately 45 miles north of Rawlins. The BLM currently recommends the following access, however it may change at any time so it is important that you contact the Rawlins district office to obtain current and accurate access information. From Rawlins, drive approximately 45 miles north on US 287, which will bring you to a blink-and-you'll-pass-right-through-it town named Muddy Gap, which is located at the intersection of US 287 and Highway 220. From here, the Ferris Mountains lie to the southeast. Proceed northeast approximately eight miles on Highway 220 and turn right onto Carbon County Road 499. Several BLM-maintained roads branch off Carbon County Road 499, leading to the Ferris Mountains. Rain and snow make the routes impassable. Four-wheel-drive vehicles are an absolute necessity on any of the BLM roads in this region. Rain turns BLM dirt routes into impassable quagmires until the sun dries them— not a problem unless you are in the Ferris Mountain Area trying to get out.

Camping: Camping is allowed anywhere within the BLM Ferris Mountains Wilderness Study Area—except on private land and boundary parcels. If you think that you may be on private land, even if it is not clearly signed, move on and don't camp. Please use low-impact camping techniques.

Season: The best time to visit is from May to November, depending on snow levels.

USGS topographic maps: Spanish Mine, Youngs Pass, Muddy Gap, Ferris

BLM surface map: Bairoil

Resources:
• *The Hiker's Guide to Wyoming,* by Bill Hunger, published by Falcon Press, P.O. Box 1718, Helena, MT 59624; (800) 582-2665.

• *Wyoming Atlas and Gazetteer*, published by DeLorme Mapping, Main Street, Freeport, ME 04032; (800) 227-1656.

For more information: Contact the BLM Rawlins District Office, P.O. Box 670, 1300 North Third Street, Rawlins, WY 82301; (307) 324-7171.

ENCAMPMENT RIVER

See letter II on map page 558

backpacking, camping, fishing, hiking, wildlife observation

More of a large stream than a river, the Encampment River area is an awesome combination of rugged, unpopulated canyon country, framed by a variety of woodland and riparian settings. The BLM section, a Wilderness Study Area, provides a fitting four-mile introduction to the 16-mile-long route—the remaining miles belong to the Medicine Bow National Forest. Brook, brown and native trout ply the waterways, offering the angler a super fishing opportunity. Spending any less than two days in this area is a mistake, as the rushing rapids, interspersed with tranquil waters, create an almost undeniable desire to kick up the feet and let time slip away amid a unique wilderness setting.

Activity Highlight: Hiking and backpacking

In order to best experience the Encampment River Trail, a car shuttle is required. The hike begins at the BLM-managed Encampment River Campground. The other vehicle must be left at Commissary Park on Forest Service Road 496, just off Forest Service Road 550 and Highway 70. Although the entire river is considered a blue ribbon trout stream, be aware that the first mile of the river, from the Encampment River Campground, has no public access (a notorious problem throughout the state of Wyoming). This doesn't matter because the remaining 15 miles offer good access and fishing. Very few people venture along the entire route—your gain, their loss. This is really a superb wilderness trek. The first few miles are lined with cottonwood amid scrub and sage hillsides. As the canyon quickly narrows, conifers and aspen dominate the terrain. Sections of the canyon narrow into a gorge and are quite rocky, turning the stream into a roaring and tumbling imitation of a powerful river.

Location: Approximately two miles south of the town of Encampment. To get to the Encampment River Campground and the Encampment River Trailhead, take Highway 70 for approximately two-tenths of a mile west of the town of Encampment. A BLM sign indicates the Encampment River Campground at BLM Road 3407—turn left on a dirt/gravel road and drive two miles. The road is not well graveled and is heavily rutted when wet. It has a steep grade in some places and a few tight turns that would be difficult in large motor homes.

Camping: In addition to the U.S. Forest Service Lakeview Campground near Commissary Park, there is also a BLM-managed Encampment River Campground, which serves as the trailhead for the Encampment River Trail. Primitive camping is allowed anywhere within the canyon, but keep in mind that the best sites are found within the first nine miles of the trail. Once into the narrow canyon, campsites become scarce and of poor quality. Please remember to use low-impact camping techniques.

Season: The best time to visit is from May to November, depending on snow levels. Ticks are prevalent once the snow melts away; conduct frequent tick checks.

USGS topographic maps: Encampment, Dudley Creek

BLM surface map: Saratoga

USFS map: Medicine Bow National Forest

Resources:
• *The Hiker's Guide to Wyoming,* by Bill Hunger, published by Falcon Press, P.O. Box 1718, Helena, MT 59624; (800) 582-2665.
• *Wyoming Atlas and Gazetteer*, published by DeLorme Mapping, Main Street, Freeport, ME 04032; (800) 227-1656.

For more information: Contact the BLM Rawlins District Office, 1300 North Third Street, P.O. Box 670, Rawlins, WY 82301; (307) 324-7171; or the Hayden Ranger District, Medicine Bow National Forest, 204 West Ninth Street, Encampment, WY 82325; (307) 327-5481.

BLM CAMPGROUNDS

1. FIVE SPRINGS FALLS CAMPGROUND—MAP A

Campsites, facilities: There are eight sites, all with picnic tables and fire rings. Water and vault toilets are available. There is a 14-day stay limit.

Reservations, fees: There is a $6 fee per night; pay on site.

Who to contact: Cody Resource Area, P.O Box 518, 1002 Blackburn Avenue, Cody, WY 82414; (307) 587-2216.

Location: Adjacent to Bighorn National Forest. From Lovell, drive 23 miles east on US 14A to the campground entrance road located on the north side of the highway. Drive approximately one mile on the access road to the campground.

Season: June to October.

2. CASTLE GARDEN SCENIC AREA CAMPGROUND—MAP A

Campsites, facilities: There are two sites, both with picnic tables, grills and fire rings. Pit toilets and water are available. No trash facilities are provided, so pack out all that you bring in. There is a 14-day stay limit.

Reservations, fees: There is no fee.

Who to contact: Worland District Office, P.O. Box 119, 101 South 23rd Street, Worland, WY 82401; (307) 347-9871.

Location: From Ten Sleep, drive approximately one mile west on US 16 to Castle Gardens Scenic Area access road. Follow the signs for approximately six miles on a dirt road to the campground entrance. The campground is set at 4,500 feet.

Season: May to November.

3. UPPER GREEN RIVER CAMPGROUND—MAP A

Campsites, facilities: There are 12 sites, all with picnic tables and fire rings. Pit toilets are available. There is **no water**. There is a 14-day stay limit.

Reservations, fees: There is no fee.

Who to contact: Pinedale Resource Area, P.O. Box 768, Pinedale, WY 82941; (307) 367-4358.

Location: Along the Green River. From Pinedale, drive northwest on

US 192 for 23 miles to the Green River. Turn right onto a gravel access road and drive north along the river for 10 miles. Campsites are scattered along the river bank.

Season: June to September.

4. WARREN BRIDGE CAMPGROUND—MAP A

Campsites, facilities: There are 17 sites, all with picnic tables and fire rings. Water and pit toilets are available. There is a 14-day stay limit.

Reservations, fees: There is a $5 fee per night; pay on site.

Who to contact: Pinedale Resource Area, P.O. Box 768, Pinedale, WY 82941; (307) 367-4358.

Location: Along the Green River. From Pinedale, drive northwest on US 192 for 23 miles to the Green River and the campground entrance.

Season: June to September.

5. NEW FORK CAMPGROUND—MAP A

Campsites, facilities: There are five sites, all with picnic tables and fire rings. Pit toilets and water are available. There is a 14-day stay limit.

Reservations, fees: There is no fee.

Who to contact: Rock Springs District Office, P.O. Box 1869, US 191 North, Rock Springs, WY 82901; (307) 382-5350.

Location: On the New Fork River. From Marbleton, drive north on US 189 for three-quarters of a mile to Highway 351 and turn right. Drive 10 miles to the New Fork River and the campground.

Season: All year.

6. ATLANTIC CITY CAMPGROUND—MAP A

Campsites, facilities: There are 18 sites, all with picnic tables, grills and fire rings. Vault toilets and water are available. The facilities are wheelchair accessible. There is a 14-day stay limit.

Reservations, fees: There is a $4 fee per night; pay on site.

Who to contact: Lander Resource Area, P.O. Box 589, 125 Sunflower Street, Lander, WY 82520; (307) 332-7822.

Location: Near the South Pass Historical District. From Lander, drive south on Highway 28 for approximately 25 miles to the Atlantic City turnoff. Turn left (east) and drive for approximately one mile on a gravel road to the campground entrance. The campground is set at 8,100 feet.

Season: June to October. The heaviest use occurs in September and October.

7. ATLANTIC GULCH CAMPGROUND—MAP A

Campsites, facilities: There are 21 sites, all with picnic tables, grills and fire rings. Pit toilets and water are available. There is a 14-day stay limit.

Reservations, fees: There is a $5 fee per night; pay on site.

Who to contact: Lander Resource Area, P.O. Box 589, 125 Sunflower Street, Lander, WY 82520; (307) 332-7822.

Location: Near the South Pass Historical District. From Lander, drive south on Highway 28 for approximately 17 miles to the Atlantic City turnoff. Turn left (east) and drive for approximately one-half mile on a gravel road to the campground entrance. The campground is set at 8,100 feet.

Season: June to November. The heaviest use occurs in September and October.

8. BIG ATLANTIC GULCH CAMPGROUND—MAP A

Campsites, facilities: There are eight sites, all with picnic tables, grills and fire rings. Vault toilets and water are available. There is a 14-day stay limit.

Reservations, fees: There is a $4 fee per night; pay on site.

Who to contact: Lander Resource Area, P.O. Box 589, 125 Sunflower Street, Lander, WY 82520; (307) 332-7822.

Location: Near the South Pass Historical District. From Lander, drive south on Highway 28 for approximately 25 miles. Turn left (east) on Atlantic City Road and drive for approximately one-half mile to BLM Road 2324 and turn left, driving another one-half mile to the campground entrance. The campground is set at 8,100 feet.

Season: June to October. Sometimes the camp will open in May depending on snow. The heaviest use occurs in September and October.

9. FONTENELLE CREEK CAMPGROUND—MAP A

Campsites, facilities: There are 72 sites, all with picnic tables and fire rings. Flush and pit toilets, water and boat ramps are available. There is a 14-day stay limit.

Reservations, fees: There is a $5 fee per night; pay on site.

Who to contact: Pinedale Resource Area, P.O. Box 768, Pinedale, WY 82941; (307) 367-4358.

Location: Near the Green River. From La Barge, drive south on US

189 for approximately 10 miles to the campground entrance.
Season: June to October.

10. COTTONWOOD CAMPGROUND—MAP A

Campsites, facilities: There are 21 sites, all with picnic tables, grills and fire rings. Vault toilets and water are available. There is a 14-day stay limit.

Reservations, fees: There is a $4 fee per night; pay on site.

Who to contact: Lander Resource Area, P.O. Box 589, 125 Sunflower Street, Lander, WY 82520; (307) 332-7822.

Location: From Jeffrey City, drive east on US 287 for six miles to BLM Road 2411 and turn south towards the Green Mountains. Drive 10 more miles to the campground entrance. The campground is set at 7,700 feet.

Season: June to October.

11. TAILRACE CAMPGROUND—MAP A

Campsites, facilities: There are three sites, all with picnic tables and fire rings. Pit toilets are available. There is **no water**. There is a 14-day stay limit.

Reservations, fees: There is no fee.

Who to contact: Kemmerer Resource Area, 312 US 189 North, Kemmerer, WY 83101; (307) 877-3933.

Location: From La Barge, drive south on US 189 for 24 miles to Highway 372 and turn left. Drive six miles to just below Fontenelle Reservoir Dam. Cross the dam and follow signs to the campground entrance.

Season: All year.

12. WEEPING ROCK CAMPGOUND—MAP A

Campsites, facilities: There are four sites, all with picnic tables and fire rings. Pit toilets are available. There is **no water**. There is a 14-day stay limit.

Reservations, fees: There is no fee.

Who to contact: Kemmerer Resource Area, 312 US 189 North, Kemmerer, WY 83101; (307) 877-3933.

Location: From La Barge, drive south on US 189 for 24 miles to Highway 372 and turn left. Drive five miles to just below Fontenelle Reservoir Dam.

Season: All year.

13. SLATE CREEK CAMPGROUND—MAP A

Campsites, facilities: There are 12 sites, all with picnic tables and fire rings. Water and pit toilets are available. RVs up to 22 feet are allowed. There is a 14-day stay limit.

Reservations, fees: There is no fee.

Who to contact: Kemmerer Resource Area, 312 US 189 North, Kemmerer, WY 83101; (307) 877-3933.

Location: From Darby, drive four miles south on US 93 to County Road 473. Drive 21.5 miles on County Road 473 to County Road 96. Drive two miles to the campground entrance.

Season: June to September.

14. OUTLAW CAVE CAMPGROUND—MAP B

Campsites, facilities: There are four tent sites, all with picnic tables and fire rings. Pit toilets are available. There is **no water**. There is a 14-day stay limit.

Reservations, fees: There is no fee.

Who to contact: Casper District Office, 1701 East E Street, Casper, WY 82601; (307) 261-7600.

Location: Overlooking the Middle Fork of the Powder River. From Kaycee, drive west on Highway 191 for one mile to Highway 190 and turn left. Drive approximately 17 miles and turn left towards Bar C Ranch. Drive 8.6 miles past Hole-In-The-Wall overlook to the campground entrance. The campground is set at 6,100 feet.

Season: May to November.

15. MIDDLE FORK CAMPGROUND—MAP B

Campsites, facilities: There are five sites, all with picnic tables, grills, and fire rings. Pit toilets are available. There is **no water**. No trash facilities are provided, so pack out all that you bring in. There is a 14-day stay limit.

Reservations, fees: There is no fee.

Who to contact: Worland District Office, P.O. Box 119, 101 South 23rd Street, Worland, WY 82401; (307) 347-9871.

Location: From Ten Sleep, drive 20 miles south on Highway 434 to Big Trails. Turn left onto Road 85 (Dry Farm Road), and drive approximately 13 miles to Hazelton Road. Turn right and drive approximately 17 miles to the campground entrance. The campground is set at 7,500 feet.

Season: June to October.

16. LODGEPOLE CAMPGROUND—MAP B

Campsites, facilities: There are three sites, all with picnic tables and fire rings. Pit toilets are available. There is **no water**. RVs up to 16 feet are allowed. There is a 14-day stay limit.

Reservations, fees: There is no fee.

Who to contact: Casper District Office, 1701 East E Street, Casper, WY 82601; (307) 261-7600.

Location: Along the South Big Horn/Red Wall Scenic Byway. From Arminto, drive north on Highway 109 for eight miles to the campground entrance. The road can be rough.

Season: All year.

17. MUDDY MOUNTAIN CAMPGROUND—MAP B

Campsites, facilities: There are 15 sites, all with picnic tables and fire rings. Pit toilets and water are available. There is a 14-day stay limit.

Reservations, fees: There is a $4 fee per night; pay on site.

Who to contact: Casper District Office, 1701 East E Street, Casper, WY 82601; (307) 261-7600.

Location: From Casper, drive south on Highway 251 for 15 miles to the campground entrance. The campground is set at 8,200 feet.

Season: All year.

18. RIM CAMPGROUND—MAP B

Campsites, facilities: There are 15 sites, all with picnic tables and fire rings. Pit toilets are available. There is **no water**. There is a 14-day stay limit.

Reservations, fees: There is a $4 fee per night; pay on site.

Who to contact: Casper District Office, 1701 East E Street, Casper, WY 82601; (307) 261-7600.

Location: From Casper, drive south on Highway 251 for 15 miles to the campground entrance. The campground is set at 8,200 feet.

Season: All year.

19. PRYOR FLAT CAMPGROUND—MAP B

Campsites, facilities: There are five sites, all with picnic tables and fire rings. Pit toilets are available. There is **no water**. There is a 14-day stay limit.

Reservations, fees: There is no fee.

Who to contact: Rawlins District Office, P.O. Box 670, 1300 North Third Street, Rawlins, WY 82301; (307) 324-7171.

Location: From Sinclair, drive north on County Road 351 to County Road 291 and turn right. Drive one mile to County Road 102 and turn left. Drive 12 miles to the campground entrance. The campground is set at 7,000 feet.

Season: May to November.

20. DUGWAY CAMPGROUND—MAP B

Campsites, facilities: There are seven sites, all with picnic tables and fire rings. Pit toilets are available. There is **no water**. There is a 14-day stay limit.

Reservations, fees: There is no fee.

Who to contact: Rawlins District Office, P.O. Box 670, 1300 North Third Street, Rawlins, WY 82301; (307) 324-7171.

Location: Located along the North Platte River. From Sinclair, drive north on County Road 351 for approximately eight miles to the campground entrance. The campground is set at 6,650 feet.

Season: All year.

21. TETON CAMPGROUND—MAP B

Campsites, facilities: There are five sites, all with picnic tables and fire rings. Pit toilets and a boat ramp are available. There is **no water**. No trash facilities are provided, so pack out all that you bring in. There is a 14-day stay limit.

Reservations, fees: There is no fee.

Who to contact: Rawlins District Office, P.O. Box 670, 1300 North Third Street, Rawlins, WY 82301; (307) 324-7171.

Location: From Rawlins, drive south on Highway 71 for 12 miles to BLM Road 3418 and turn left. Drive to the campground entrance on the west side of the reservoir. The campground is set at 7,000 feet.

Season: All year.

22. BENNETT PEAK CAMPGROUND—MAP B

Campsites, facilities: There are 12 sites, all with picnic tables and fire rings. Water, pit toilets and a boat ramp are available. There is a 14-day stay limit.

Reservations, fees: There is a $3 fee per night; pay on site.

Who to contact: Rawlins District Office, P.O. Box 670, 1300 North

Third Street, Rawlins, WY 82301; (307) 324-7171.

Location: Along the North Platte River. From Riverside, drive east on Highway 230 for approximately four miles to County Road 660 and turn left. Drive eight miles to BLM 3404 and turn left again. Drive approximately six miles to the campground entrance. The campground is set at 7,400 feet.

Season: June to November.

23. CORRAL CREEK CAMPGROUND—MAP B

Campsites, facilities: There are 12 sites, all with picnic tables and fire rings. Pit toilets and water are available. There is a 14-day stay limit.

Reservations, fees: There is a $3 fee per night; pay on site.

Who to contact: Rawlins District Office, P.O. Box 670, 1300 North Third Street, Rawlins, WY 82301; (307) 324-7171.

Location: Along the North Platte River. From Riverside, drive east on Highway 230 for approximately four miles to County Road 660 and turn left. Drive eight miles to BLM 3404 and turn left again. Drive approximately five miles to the campground entrance. The campground is set at 7,400 feet.

Season: June to November.

24. ENCAMPMENT RIVER CAMPGROUND—MAP B

Campsites, facilities: There are seven sites, all with picnic tables and fire rings. Pit toilets are available. There is **no water**. No trash facilities are provided, so pack out all that you bring in. There is a 14-day stay limit.

Reservations, fees: There is no fee.

Who to contact: Rawlins District Office, P.O. Box 670, 1300 North Third Street, Rawlins, WY 82301; (307) 324-7171.

Location: On the banks of the Encampment River, at the Encampment River Trailhead. From Encampment, drive west on Highway 70 for one mile to County Road 353 and turn left. Drive for one mile and turn left again on BLM 3407. Drive one more mile to the campground entrance. The campground is set at 7,400 feet.

Season: All year.

STATE INFORMATION OVERVIEW

WYOMING STATE OFFICE
2515 Warren Avenue, P.O. Box 1828, Cheyenne, WY 82003; (307) 775-6BLM

CASPER DISTRICT OFFICE
1701 East E Street, Casper, WY 82601; (307) 261-7600

Platte River Resource Area, 815 Connie Street, Mills, WY 82644; (307) 261-5191

Buffalo Resource Area, 189 North Cedar, Buffalo, WY 82834; (307) 684-5586

Newcastle Resource Area, 1501 Highway 16 Bypass, Newcastle, WY 82701; (307) 746-4453

RAWLINS DISTRICT OFFICE
P.O. Box 670, 1300 North Third Street, Rawlins, WY 82301; (307) 324-7171

Great Divide Resource Area, P.O. Box 670, 812 East Murray, Rawlins, WY 82301; (307) 324-4841

Lander Resource Area, P.O. Box 589, 125 Sunflower Street, Lander, WY 82520; (307) 332-7822

ROCK SPRINGS DISTRICT OFFICE
P.O. Box 1869, Highway 191 North, Rock Springs, WY 82901; (307) 382-5350

Green River Resource Area, 1993 Dewar Drive, Rock Springs, WY 82902; (307) 362-6422

Kemmerer Resource Area, 312 US 189 North, Kemmerer, WY 83101; (307) 877-3933

Pinedale Resource Area, P.O. Box 768, Pinedale, WY 82941; (307) 367-4358

WORLAND DISTRICT OFFICE
P.O. Box 119, 101 South 23rd Street, Worland, WY 82401; (307) 347-9871

Grass Creek Resource Area, P.O. Box 119, 101 South 23rd Street, Worland, WY 82401; (307) 347-9871

Washakie Resource Area, P.O. Box 119, 101 South 23rd Street, Worland, WY 82401; (307) 347-9871

Cody Resource Area, P.O. Box 518, 1002 Blackburn Avenue, Cody, WY 82414; (307) 587-2216

INDEX

RECREATIONAL ACTIVITIES BY STATE

The following listings show major outdoor recreational activities in BLM lands according to activity and state. See the corresponding page numbers for more information on each activity.

ARCHAEOLOGICAL/CULTURAL SITES

Alaska:	Tangle Lakes Archaeological District—p. 69
Arizona:	Dutchman Trail for Mountain Bikes—p. 84
California:	Fossil Falls—p. 158
	Corn Springs—p. 172
	Otay Mountain—p. 177
Colorado:	Irish Canyon—p. 202
	Diamond Breaks Wilderness Study Area—p. 203
	Rangely Loop Trail—p. 207
	Cross Canyon Wilderness Study Area—p. 226
	Sand Canyon—p. 227
	Anasazi Heritage Center/Special Recreation Area—p. 228
Idaho:	Lower Salmon River—p. 250
	Lewis and Clark Back Country Byway—p. 252
	Snake River Birds of Prey National Conservation Area—p. 254
	The Great Rift and Snake River Plain—p. 260
Montana:	Hickison Petroglyph—p. 348
New Mexico:	El Malpais National Conservation Area—p. 390
	Eagle Peak Wilderness Study Area—p. 393
Utah:	Desolation Canyon/Gray Canyon—p. 491
	Three Kiva Pueblo—p. 509
Wyoming:	Paint Rock Canyon—p. 565

CROSS-COUNTRY SKIING

Alaska:	Kigluaik Mountains—p. 52
	White Mountains National Recreation Area—p. 57
California:	Bizz Johnson Trail—p. 139
	Bodie Bowl—p. 148
Colorado:	Alpine Loop Back Country Byway—p. 221
Idaho:	Grandmother Mountain—p. 248
	Birch Creek Valley—p. 259
	Sleeping Giant Wilderness Area—p. 298
Montana:	Garnet Recreation Trail System—p. 298
	Hoodoo Mountains—p. 300
	Humbug Spires Wilderness Study Area—p. 301

KAYAKING/WHITEWATER RAFTING

ROCK CLIMBING

ROCKHOUNDING

WINTER RECREATION

SPELUNKING/CAVING

THE CALIFORNIA DESERT PROTECTION ACT

After years of haggling and promises made and broken, the United States Congress voted to protect a vast chunk of California desert by adding millions of acres to those already under federal management and administration. The California Desert Protection Act of 1994 adds over six million acres to the three million already protected, in an effort to preserve unique wildlife and flowers, ancient cultural sites, spectacular scenery and the last known dinosaur tracks in North America.

The following bullet outline will help you understand the changes as they affect you and your recreation in the region now known as the California Desert Conservation Area. The Act does the following:

- Designates 69 Bureau of Land Management and Forest Service wilderness areas, totaling 3,677,020 acres and divided as follows—3,571,520 acres administered by the BLM and 95,500 acres managed by the U.S. Forest Service.

- Establishes eight new wilderness areas that will be administered by the BLM, totaling 326,430 acres.

- Upgrades Death Valley from a National Monument to a National Park. Approximately 1.3 million acres of previously BLM-administered lands are transferred to Death Valley National Park's existing 2,067,627 acres.

- Designates 3,162,000 acres of Death Valley National Park as official wilderness.

- Upgrades Joshua Tree from a National Monument to a National Park. Approximately 234,000 acres of previously BLM-administered lands are transferred to Joshua Tree National Park's 559,000 acres.

- Designates 132,000 acres of Joshua Tree National Park as official wilderness.

- Designates the Mojave National Preserve with a total acreage of 1,419,800.

- Designates 695,000 acres in the Mojave National Preserve as official wilderness.

- Creates a 590-acre Dinosaur Trackway Area of Critical Environmental Concern.

- Transfers 20,500 acres from BLM administration to Red Rock Canyon State Park.

- Protects 6,000 acres in Bodie Bowl, adjacent to Bodie State Historic Park, from mining and mineral leasing.

While the Act looks good on paper, it represents a monumental task of administrative overhaul as the various agencies cooperatively gear up to assume control and establish interactive, though independent, operations. As the various stages of the Act are implemented, it will result in changes in management practices. This will mean changes for desert visitors as well as different approaches regarding the protection and use of natural and cultural resources.

The BLM has assured me that while they may not officially be administering an area anymore, they will do their best to provide accurate information about any land they used to administer, or they will direct any questions to the new administrating body. To help make the transition smoother, the Department of Interior has provided the following addresses which they suggest you contact with any questions regarding land use in the California Desert Conservation Area.

BUREAU OF LAND MANAGEMENT

California State Office, 2800 Cottage Way, Sacramento, CA 95825; (916) 978-4754.

California Desert District, 6221 Box Springs Boulevard, Riverside, CA 92507; (909) 697-5200.

Barstow Resource Area, 150 Coolwater Lane, Barstow, CA 92311; (619) 256-3591.

El Centro Resource Area, 1661 South Fourth Street, El Centro, CA 92243; (619) 353-1060.

Needles Resource Area, P.O. Box 888, 101 West Spikes Road, Needles, CA 92363; (619) 326-3896.

Palm Springs / South Coast Resource Area, P.O. Box 2000, 63-500 Garnet Avenue, North Palm Springs, CA 92258; (619) 251-0812.

Ridgecrest Resource Area, 300 South Richmond Road, Ridgecrest, CA 93555; (619) 375-7125.

Desert Information Center, 831 Barstow Road, Barstow, CA 92311; (619) 256-8313.

Bakersfield District Office, Caliente Resource Area, 3801 Pegasus Avenue, Bakersfield, CA 93308; (805) 391-6000.

Bishop Resource Area, 785 North Main Street, Suite E, Bishop, CA 93514; (619) 872-4881.

NATIONAL PARK SERVICE

Death Valley National Park, Death Valley, CA 92328; (619) 786-2331.

Joshua Tree National Park, 74485 National Monument Drive, Twentynine Palms, CA 92277; (619) 367-7511.

Western Region Information Center, Golden Gate National Recreation Area, Fort Mason, Building 201, San Francisco, CA 94123; (415) 556-0560.

Western Region Information Center, Santa Monica Mountains National Recreation Area, 30401 Agoura Road, Suite 100, Agoura Hills, CA 91301; (818) 597-9192.

ABOUT THE AUTHOR

Michael Hodgson is the senior editor for *Adventure West* magazine, contributing editor of *Backpacker Magazine*, a self-syndicated columnist for major western newspapers, and technical editor for *Outdoor Retailer* magazine.

Michael is the author of eight books on the outdoors, and was named California Outdoor Writer of the Year in 1993. He is a multiple first-place award winner with the Outdoor Writers Association of America, and was awarded a Maggie in 1993 for Best Technical Writing for western magazines.

About the National Parks and Conservation Association

The National Parks and Conservation Association (NPCA) is America's only private nonprofit citizen organization dedicated solely to protecting, preserving, and enhancing the U.S. National Park System. An association of "Citizens Protecting America's Parks," NPCA was founded in 1919, and has more than 450,000 members. Programs include:

- **National Park Advocacy:** NPCA works at the national, regional, and grassroots levels to address a wide variety of environmental and other issues affecting existing national parks, as well as working to expand the National Park System to protect the most significant of America's historic, cultural, and ecological areas.

- **Regional Advocacy:** To address regional park issues and encourage grassroots action on behalf of parks, NPCA staffs eight field offices in the Alaska, Heartland, Northeast, Northwest, Pacific, Rocky Mountain, Southeast, and Southwest regions.

- **Park Activist Network:** NPCA's Park Activist Network is made up of park activists and ParkWatchers. This grassroots program alerts members to severe threats facing the parks, immediately mobilizing them into action. Park activists write letters encouraging opinion leaders to protect our national parks. ParkWatchers provide NPCA's staff with critical information from all over the country about new and continued threats to specific parks.

- **Congressional Initiatives:** NPCA experts consult with members of Congress and representatives of various federal agencies on laws and regulations to protect and enhance the national parks. In addition, NPCA is often called upon to testify at congressional hearings and help formulate park protection legislation. NPCA also works to ensure protection of parklands at the local, state, and regional levels.

- **Publications:** NPCA publishes *National Parks*, an award-winning magazine covering the most important issues facing the national parks. The bimonthly magazine reaches more than 450,000 readers. NPCA also produces *The ParkWatcher*, a bimonthly newsletter on regional issues requiring grassroots citizen action.

- **March for Parks:** The nation's first and largest walk event for parks and open spaces, March for Parks is held each year in April in conjunction with Earth Day. With support from Foghorn Press, other national corporations and local businesses, more than 700 marches in all 50 states are planned by environmental and conservation associations, hiking and walking groups, schools, youth and service clubs, and individuals. These events raise money for park improvement, protection, and education projects benefiting local, state, regional, and national parks.